Deciphering the Maya Script

Deciphering the
Maya Script

David Humiston Kelley

University of Texas Press, Austin

This book has been published with the help of the following:

A grant from Cecil and Lenore March of St. Paul, Minnesota.

A grant from the Humanities Research Council of Canada, using funds provided by the Canada Council.

Preparation of the work was also assisted by a grant from the Roland Scott Hall Fund for Hieroglyphic Research of the Middle American Research Institute, Tulane University.

Grateful acknowledgment is made for permission to quote from the following:

El libro de los libros de Chilam Balam, translated by Alfredo Barrera Vásquez and Silvia Rendón, by permission of the publisher, Fondo de Cultura Económica, Mexico City.

"Materiales lingüísticos para el estudio de las relaciones internas y externas de la familia de idiomas mayanos," by Terrence S. Kaufman, in *Desarollo cultural de los mayas*, edited by Evon Z. Vogt and Alberto Ruz Lhuillier, by permission of the editors and the publishers, Universidad Nacional Autónoma de México, Mexico City.

Library of Congress Cataloging in Publication Data
Kelley, David H
    Deciphering the Maya script.

    Bibliography: p.
    Includes index.
    1. Mayas—Writing. 2. Mayas—Antiquities.
3. Mexico—Antiquities. 4. Central America—
Antiquities. I. Title.
F1435.3.P6K44   497'.4   75-17989
ISBN 0-292-71504-8

Contents

Illustrations

Preface

In this book I have attempted to present a summary of what is known about Maya writing, accompanied by critical analyses of the work of others and some account of my own work. In subjects about which more is known, assured knowledge is usually presented separately from new suggestions. In Mayan studies, at their present stage, what is acceptable is still largely a matter of debate. Hence, this must, of necessity, be a summary which is also the expression of a very personal viewpoint. In general, I have tried to present as adequately as possible the evidence on both sides of disputed questions. However, on most of these matters I have my own opinions, and one can never do full justice to arguments one finds unconvincing. If those who disagree with my interpretations find my presentation of their viewpoints and arguments inadequate, this inadequacy is not deliberate.

Chapter 9, dealing with phoneticism in the Maya script, is the most polemical. The subject is one which has aroused strong emotions in Mayanists since the 1890's, and it is one on which I hold an extreme position. Given these two factors, it would be foolish to hope to write an objective summary. The question is a vital one which could not be ignored, and I have tried to answer most of the arguments which have been made against the position I hold.

Chapter 11, dealing with places and people, contains more personal hypotheses than the other chapters. On most of the subjects, I have summarized and criticized published material, but in this chapter there is a considerable amount of previously unpublished surmise. Chapter 10 is a much fuller attempt to consider the grammatical structure of the script than has been published previously, but at a detailed level it depends largely on previously published interpretations. I am not conscious of any strong biases affecting my treatment of this material, and I have drawn heavily but critically from the previous work, especially that of J. Eric S. Thompson, Yurii V. Knorozov, and Thomas S. Barthel. The formal structural analysis of Chapter 13 is a tool for glyph studies which I have found extremely useful. I find that I see a great many things in a text presented in this way which remain obscure in conventional presentations of the material.

The plan to write a summary of what was then known about the decipherment of Maya writing took shape in 1957, and actual writing began in 1958. This has led to a rather complex relationship between the book and some of my articles. Chapter 9 is a revised, enlarged, and updated version of my article "Fonetismo en la escritura Maya" (Kelley 1962c), which was itself a rewritten version of my first draft for

Chapter 9. The introductory chapter is closely related in subject matter and conclusions to "A History of the Decipherment of Maya Script" (Kelley 1962*a*), which grew out of my attempts to ascertain what was reasonably well known and acceptable in previous work. "Glyphic Evidence for a Dynastic Sequence at Quirigua, Guatemala" (Kelley 1962*b*) was rewritten from a section of what is now Chapter 11. My paper with Heinrich Berlin on "The 819-day Count and Color-Direction Symbolism among the Classic Maya" (Berlin and Kelley 1961) derived, on my side, from material actually written for what is now Chapter 3, "Directions and Colors," the present chapter incorporating our joint results. Other articles are not as closely related to this book in any specific sense.

Writing of the text and preparation of plates and figures went on, in part, concurrently, but in some cases a figure was prepared for a section that was still not written, while in many other cases I made references to figures which were planned but had not been prepared. Since the sections were not written in consecutive order, figure numbers were only assigned after a preliminary draft of the entire book had been completed in June 1967. At that time, I discovered I had referred to over ninety figures, of which only about thirty were completed. Preparing the figures led to occasional minor discoveries which involved rewriting the text. There has also been some rewriting due to the many important articles which have appeared since the text was completed. However, in most cases I have incorporated only the most striking results from papers appearing later than 1966. I believe that the coverage is good for articles in the older literature and fair through the late 1950's, but it has been impossible to keep up with the spate of new literature which has appeared in the 1960's. To attain adequate coverage of that data might well have delayed the appearance of this book another two or three years.

I have tried to make the bibliographic citations as full as possible and, particularly, to include first names, which are of prime importance in seeking information in any card catalogue. I have been much less worried about place of publication, which is of almost no help in locating an article. After ten years, some references which seemed fully adequate when I made them now puzzle me, and I have not always been able to verify statements made without adequate documentation in earlier drafts. Moreover, the libraries of Texas Technological College, the University of Nebraska, and The University of Calgary have very different coverage on Maya matters. Successively using these different libraries, I have found myself unable to recheck matters to which I had had regular

access. For all these reasons, the bibliographic citation is occasionally inadequate. Also, where a good summary source is in existence, giving various views with previous references, I have often not attempted to incorporate the material from the previous references.

Some minor points of style should be mentioned. In general, I have used italics for the citation of basic sources, such as the *Dresden* codex. I have used single quotes to mark off meanings of Maya words, as given by dictionaries, or assumed meanings of Maya glyphs. I have preferred in-text citation of articles and books by author and date only, in accordance with normal anthropological usage; information which might have been footnoted has been incorporated in the text.

In preparing a book over a period of twelve years and in the training which leads up to the idea of the book, one piles up a tremendous number of obligations, which can be acknowledged only in a most inadequate way. Intellectual and personal obligations are intermingled, and friends who played no directly discernible role in helping with the book have sometimes affected my thinking at a more general level. The customary acknowledgments do not seem to me sufficient, and I want, here, to make a more blanket "thank you" to those who have encouraged me in scholarly pursuits and have aided me in thinking more clearly.

My primary obligation as a Mayanist is to my aunt, Alice Humiston, to whom this book would be dedicated if she were still alive. At Christmas 1939 she gave me a copy of Ann Axtell Morris's *Digging in Yucatan.* The excitement which the book engendered still lingers and has determined much of the pattern of my life. Alice was a friend of a niece of Sylvanus G. Morley in Los Angeles, and that great Mayanist sent some postcards of material from Chichen Itza to me, via his niece: a small act for which I am still profoundly grateful.

While the desire to study the Mayas persisted, the mechanics of becoming a Mayanist seemed difficult. It was Alfred M. Tozzer who encouraged me to come to Harvard, before that seemed possible, and who let me take his famed graduate courses on the Mexicans and the Mayas while I was still an undergraduate. It was Tozzer who instilled in me a respect (albeit rather grudging) for bibliography and Tozzer who led me to appreciate, much more wholeheartedly, that scholarship is cumulative and that one needs to know the work of previous scholars. Personally and intellectually, Tozzer has been a basic influence in the writing of this book.

While my most important intellectual debts are usually acknowledged as fully as possible in the text, a few would not be entirely apparent. Linton Satterthwaite has worked chiefly on problems which are quite different from most of those dealt with in the text, and his name appears infrequently. Nonetheless, extensive correspondence with him has been of great help in formulating my ideas. Tania Proskouriakoff has gone over first drafts of many of my articles, insisting on clarity both of expression and of presentation, pointing out dubious assumptions and use of doubtful data, and generally improving the articles immeasurably. It is my hope that some of what I have learned from her will be apparent in the following pages.

Yurii Knorozov did much to restimulate and redirect my interest in the decipherment of Maya. His concepts of how problems should be approached and his ideas of what constitutes evidence are closely similar to my own. Our lengthy conversations in Copenhagen in 1956 were an important prelude to the present book. He gave me difficult-to-obtain copies of his earlier articles and sent me a copy of his important Russian magnum opus on the decipherment of the Maya script, now partly available in English.

I have also profited greatly from the work of Eric Thompson, Knorozov's bitterest opponent. My frequent disagreements with Thompson's opinions in no way detract from my respect for his imaginative capabilities nor from my gratitude for the stream of reprints I have received from him and his accessibility in giving information and advice.

A helpful attitude has been typical of my colleagues in Mayan studies. Thomas Barthel and Dieter Dütting have both sent manuscripts and reprints, as has Jacinto Quirarte. Heinrich Berlin's helpful articles and letters always contain some interesting new idea or information. Ed Shook sent me a good photo of the early Kaminaljuyu altar text (Fig. 114), which aided in making some corrections of the published drawings of it. Leonardo Manrique Castañeda helped me in getting good photos of those Yaxchilan Structure 12 lintels that had not previously been published in drawings. V. A. Ustinov very kindly sent me copies of the catalog of Maya glyphs which he published with E. V. Evreinov and Y. G. Kosarev and likewise sent copies of their transcriptions of the *Madrid* and *Dresden* codices. Terrence S. Kaufman has been of great help in allowing the complete incorporation of his reconstructions of ancestral Maya vocabulary. Alberto Ruz Lhuillier not only has sent me many useful publications but also has supplied spare copies of the drawing of the remarkable Palenque tablet which he discovered (Figs. 99 and 100). The drawing was done by Agustín Villogra. I must thank Linton

Satterthwaite, Annemarie Seuffert, and the University Museum of the University of Pennsylvania for drawings of the remarkable "bones texts" done from the originals by Annemarie Seuffert for the University Museum (Figs. 80 and 81). Michael D. Coe and Elizabeth P. Benson have granted permission for the reproduction of the Palenque tablet now in the Dumbarton Oaks collection (Fig. 20), and Coe has supplied a substantial number of helpful suggestions. Giles Healey sent me books on long-term loan and has been otherwise very helpful. Richard E. W. Adams has been obliging indeed in sending drawings and photographs of unpublished material, particularly from pottery inscriptions. E. Wyllys Andrews has given me publications and helpful data, published and unpublished. I must thank William R. Coe and the University Museum for the excellent drawing of Tikal, Stela 31, utilized in preparing Plate 6 and Figure 109.

Pat Allgood, of Lubbock, Texas, was responsible for the drawing of many of the earlier figures, on which she did an excellent and impressive job. In Lincoln, the majority of the drawings I had done were prepared by Marcia Laging Cummings, to whom I am deeply grateful for the time and effort she put in. Minor portions of plates were drawn by Don Blakeslee, Knut Fladmark, and David Keenlyside. I appreciate their willingness to undertake a task for which I am not myself suited and was delighted to have adequate drawings of glyphs to fill in gaps in various figures. It is no disparagement of any of these helpful artists to say that I wish their skill could have been accompanied by my own familiarity with the glyphs. It is a very difficult matter to attempt to point out to someone else a just barely visible dot or line in a not very good photo of a badly eroded monument, and one cannot expect others to see it in precisely the way that it appears to one who has had a great deal of practice in looking at such material. As all students of the glyphs must, I have drawn heavily on the drawings of the codices by Carlos A. Villacorta and on the magnificent drawings of glyphic texts by Miss Annie Hunter, prepared for the Maudslay volumes. While many of these were redrawn, others were copied photographically. I must also thank Grayson Meade for photographic help in preparing some of the figures. John F. Phinney did a great deal of the basic work in compiling the bibliography for me, an arduous task for which I am very grateful. I also wish to thank Peter Mathews of Calgary, who prepared the map and drew several glyphs which were added in the final stages of preparation of the manuscript.

I owe an important debt to Texas Technological College for a research grant in the summer of 1961 and for another which relieved me half-time from my teaching duties during the spring of 1962. I am equally obligated to the University of Nebraska for a research grant for the summer of 1965 and to the American Philosophical Society for Grant 676 from the Johnson Fund for research and writing done during the summer of 1966. I must also thank the Seminario de Cultura Maya and the Mexican government for inviting me to participate in the extremely rewarding First International Congress for the Decipherment of the Maya Writing in Mexico City in December 1966 and in an intermediate work session in Mérida in June 1968.

Additional problems in getting the manuscript ready for publication have been met by more help. The necessity for setting the figures in type prior to submitting them to the press meant that a great deal of money and effort were needed. Through the good offices of Robert Wauchope, a grant was obtained from the Roland Scott Hall Fund for Hieroglyphic Research of the Middle American Research Institute of Tulane University, which paid for this very expensive task. The actual typesetting was done by the Foothills Printers, of Calgary, and Larry Frantz, of that organization, was very helpful. I must thank the Department of Archaeology of the University of Calgary for assigning Robert Steinhauser to me as a Special Graduate Assistant and Steinhauser himself for his aid in setting the type on the figures. I must also thank the Department of Archaeology for supporting a final retyping of the manuscript by the Stenographic Services Department of the University of Calgary, under the direction of Mrs. E. L. Wittig.

The actual typing and proofreading were patiently and efficiently done by Evelyn Moorhouse and Donna Limpert. I must also thank Joe Stewart for helping me with proofreading.

During the preparation of the manuscript and the plates, I received considerable encouragement and support from Bruce Nicoll of the University of Nebraska Press. At that time, he hoped that it would be possible for Nebraska to publish the manuscript, but when the magnitude of the expenses involved became apparent, the University of Nebraska Press decided in June 1971 that it would be impossible to publish it.

The Humanities Research Council of Canada agreed to help support the publication of the book, and the University of Texas Press decided to publish it, if it was financially possible. Dr. Richard E. W. Adams, now Dean of the College of Humanities and Social Sciences of the University of Texas at San Antonio, urged the book's merits on Mr. and Mrs. Cecil March, of St. Paul, Minnesota, who very kindly supplied enough additional money to make it possible for the University of Texas Press to publish the book. My gratitude is great to all the many people who have assisted in so many different ways.

My wife, Jane, pointed out to me that the text should always be able to stand on its own as a comprehensible statement without the accompanying figures and that summaries are a vital necessity of this type of writing. For these major suggestions, which have strongly affected the book, and for the host of smaller ways, cumulatively even more important, in which she has helped me, I am deeply grateful.

Abbreviations Used

Ach.:	the Achi Maya language
Agc.:	the Aguacatecan Maya language
Alt.:	altar
Balak.:	Balakbal
C:	consonant, either in the sense of *any consonant* or in the sense of *an unknown consonant*
Cak.:	the Cakchiquel Maya language
CEEM:	Comisión para el Estudio de la Escritura Maya
Chc.:	the Chicomuceltec Maya language
Chu.:	the Chuh Maya language
Chl.:	the Cholan Maya language
Chn.:	the Chontal Maya language
Chr.:	the Chorti Maya language
C.I.:	Chichen Itza
Col.:	column
Cop.:	Copan
CR:	calendar round
D:	*Dresden* codex; generally followed by a number, indicating the page of the codex to which reference is made, sometimes with a letter indicating a division of the page (e.g., D50a indicates the top division of *Dresden* page 50)
DN:	Distance Number
DNIG:	Distance Number Introducing Glyph
E.:	east
EG:	Emblem Glyph
EKU:	the Evreinov, Kosarev, and Ustinov catalog of Maya glyphs; followed by the catalog number of a particular glyph
Fej.-May.:	*Fejervary-Mayer* codex
G:	god; prefixed to a series of letters or numbers to indicate particular deities by their characteristics (see Chapter 4)
Gl.:	glyph
H.:	the Huaxtec Maya language
HS:	hieroglyphic stairway
IG:	Introducing Glyph (same as ISIG)
Inaug.:	inaugural date

IS:	Initial Series
ISIG:	Initial Series Introducing Glyph
Ixil.:	the Ixil Maya language
Jac.:	the Jacaltecan Maya language
K:	the Knorozov catalog of Maya glyphs; followed by the catalog number of a particular glyph
Kan.:	the Kanhobal Maya language
Kek.:	the Kekchi Maya language
L:	lintel
Lac.:	the Lacandon Maya language
LC:	long count
M:	*Madrid* codex; generally followed by a number, indicating the page of the codex to which reference is made, sometimes with a letter indicating a division of the page (e.g., M20a indicates the top division of *Madrid* page 20)
ME:	Maya Era
Mop.:	the Mopan Maya language
MT:	miscellaneous texts
Mot.:	the Motocintlecan Maya language
MZ:	the Mixean-Zoquean language
N.:	north
Nar.:	Naranjo
P:	*Paris* codex; generally followed by a number, indicating the page of the codex to which reference is made
P1, P2:	variant forms of the Palenque Emblem Glyph
Pal.:	Palenque
Pch.:	the Pokomchi Maya language
Pl.:	Plate
PM:	proto-Mayan
P.N.:	Piedras Negras
Pok.:	the Pokomam Maya language
Q.:	the Quiche Maya language
Q:	in reconstructed Maya words, means it is not known whether the sound was *kw or *q
Quir.:	Quirigua

S.:	south
St.:	stela; normally designated by the name of the site where found and an accompanying number or letter
Struc.:	structure
T:	the Thompson catalog of Maya glyphs; followed by the catalog number of a particular glyph
Tab.:	tablet
TC:	Temple of the Cross at Palenque
Tem.:	Temple
TFC:	Temple of the Foliated Cross at Palenque
Thr.:	throne
TI:	Temple of Inscriptions at Palenque
Tik.:	Tikal
Toj.:	the Tojolabal Maya language
TS:	the miscalled Temple of the Sun at Palenque
Tzel.:	the Tzeltal Maya language
Tzo.:	the Tzotzil Maya language
Uaxac.:	Uaxactun
V:	vowel, either in the sense of *any vowel* or in the sense of *an unknown vowel*
X:	in reconstructed Maya words, indicates /h/ or /vocalic quantity/ or both
Xcal.:	Xcalumkin
Y1, Y2:	variant forms of the Yaxchilan Emblem Glyph
Yax.:	Yaxchilan
Yuc.:	the Yucatec Maya language
Z:	the Zimmerman catalog of Maya hieroglyphs; followed by the catalog number of a particular glyph
Zut.:	the Zutuhil Maya language

Notes on Symbols

A boldface **x** is used to indicate an unknown element in transcriptions of glyphs.

A transcription followed by a question mark in parentheses (?) indicates that the reading is doubtful or uncertain.

Brackets are used in transcriptions to indicate information which is not demonstrably present, because of erosion or destruction of glyphs, but which can be assumed to have existed, on the basis of the other information given. Parentheses indicate optional or alternative readings, parenthetical remarks, etc.

Deciphering the Maya Script

Introduction to the Script

From Veracruz, Mexico, throughout Chiapas and the Yucatan peninsula, through all of British Honduras and much of Guatemala, the aboriginal inhabitants speak a series of related languages called Mayan. The exact relationships of these languages are still in doubt, but Table 2 shows the major subdivisions of the Mayan family.

There are numerous monumental inscriptions in the territories now occupied by Cholan and Yucatecan groups. Similar inscriptions have also been discovered on rare occasions in the territory of some of the other groups. The hieroglyphs found in these inscriptions correspond to a considerable degree to some given by Bishop Diego de Landa, in the sixteenth century, as the form of writing of the Yucatec Mayas whom he knew, and they agree still more closely with the writing found in the three surviving codices, or native books. These are now known as the *Dresden, Paris,* and *Madrid* codices. The publication of Landa's writings by Charles E. Brasseur de Bourbourg in 1864 was the first step towards the decipherment of this script, which has been recognized as a Mayan script by all scholars working on the material since that time. Since then, a great deal of information has been accumulated and many studies of special features of the Maya script have been made, but summaries have been few. In 1885, Daniel Garrison Brinton published *A primer of Maya hieroglyphs,* which critically summarized all available information and gave new analyses.

In 1915, Sylvanus G. Morley published *An introduction to the study of the Maya hieroglyphs,* a work which advanced our knowledge of the calendrical glyphs but did not even give the data on such well-known glyphs as those of many of the animals. In 1950, J. Eric S. Thompson, the leading scholar working in the United States in the American tradition of the study of the Mayan hieroglyphs, published his *Maya hieroglyphic writing: Introduction.* This work presented much of the available knowledge and introduced many new readings of great importance but again largely ignored the animal glyphs and some others not directly pertinent to the calendar. In 1956, Günter Zimmermann published in Germany an annotated index to the glyphs in the codices. At the time, this catalog was a major advance in organizing our understanding of the glyphs, but Zimmermann deliberately avoided many problems of interpretation. In 1962, Eric Thompson published a very important *Catalog of Maya hieroglyphs,* including all the glyphs in the inscriptions as well as the codices. Although this work contained important new suggestions for the decipherment of particular glyphs, it omitted mention of most previous decipherments, even when generally accepted. The Thompson catalog numbers have been used in most of the discussions of particular glyphs in this book. The following year, Yurii V. Knorozov produced a compendium detailing his system of decipherment of phonetic glyphs and giving very extensive references to previous decipherments. These are the only works which may in any sense claim to be replacements of Brinton, and even Knorozov's work was written prior to the establishment of the historical content of many of the inscriptions.

While there has been a continuing growth of knowledge of the glyphs and a constant, if slow, accumulation of certain decipherments, the nature of the script as a whole has remained open to dispute. One group of scholars, starting with Brasseur de Bourbourg, has maintained that the script is primarily phonetic. Léon de Rosny, one of the earliest scholars of this group, recognized a number of glyphs which have become generally accepted. Cyrus Thomas, operating on generally similar premises, made some brilliant analyses of specific groups of glyphs. He was also the first to establish mathematically the order in which the glyphs are to be read, by pointing out the existence of sequential clauses in inscriptions at Palenque (Thomas 1882, p. 200). I believe that he had a clearer view of the nature of the script than any other man of his period. However, both de Rosny and Thomas vitiated much of their work by attempting to go beyond the really solid evidence which they had, and Thomas (1904) eventually repudiated the "phonetic key" which at one time he thought he had established. In the 1930's, Benjamin Lee Whorf, a great scholar of American Indian linguistics, especially of the Uto-Aztecan languages, made several studies of phoneticism in the Maya script, some of which are still unpublished. Whorf's brilliance was completely negated by his unfamiliarity with the work previously done, and not one of his original readings has been accepted by any other scholar in the field to my knowledge. In Whorf's translation of a single sentence, which forms the conclusion of a forty-page paper, Thompson has pointed out that five glyphic elements are misidentified (three of them having been given by Landa, on whose material Whorf professedly based his study) and one element is ignored. No attempt is made to translate the rest of the sentence, which is said to be the name of the goddess represented in a picture below. Actually, only the second glyph block is the name of the goddess. Such work fully warranted Thompson's scathing criticism of it and was far inferior to Thomas's work forty years earlier. The emphasis on phoneticism was revived in 1952 by

Yurii Knorozov of the Leningrad Institute. Knorozov grasped something which had eluded all previous investigators: the importance of the inherent vowels of the glyphs. This first paper showed many faults, and it was severely criticized by Thompson. In a paper written in 1953 but not published until 1955, Knorozov (1955a) put forward many new readings both of individual glyphs and of glyph groups. This paper has received considerable recognition among linguists who had little or no knowledge of the glyphs or of what was previously known but has been very coolly received among Maya scholars. Thompson has criticized Knorozov's work repeatedly, and I have defended it. Chapter 9 contains a restatement of my views on this, in the light of Thompson's criticisms.

A second group of scholars has insisted on the generally ideographic nature of the script and has worked a great deal with numerical, calendrical, and astronomical data. Numerical studies by Ernst W. Förstemann revealed the nature of the Venus calendar and eclipse tables in the *Dresden* during the 1880's, and similar work by J. T. Goodman in the United States showed the numerical character of the head variants of the numbers. Eduard Seler established many valid readings of glyphs and glyph groups, including those of the colors. Much of his work has more value than that of his successors working from the same premises because he insisted more rigorously on the importance of glyph compounds, rather than individual glyphs. Paul Schellhas's work has covered nearly the whole span of Maya studies to date; his first publication was in 1886 and his last in 1945. He first identified the hieroglyphs of many of the deities in 1897, a revised English version of his work being published in 1904. Schellhas began the system of identifying the deities by letters of our alphabet, because of the many differences of opinion as to which figure in the codices represented which known deity of the Maya pantheon.

Sylvanus G. Morley, who did more than any other man to collect and publish the many Maya inscriptions, made his main contributions to decipherment in recognizing variants of the calendrical and astronomical glyphs. The nature of the so-called Supplementary Series of the inscriptions was first clearly recognized by John E. Teeple, who was probably the most extreme defender of the view that the script was designed entirely to record calendrical and astronomical data and contained very little else. One of the most prolific writers on the Maya hieroglyphs was Hermann Beyer. His most important contribution was the recognition that the "variable element" of the Initial Series Introducing Glyph (see glossary) was actually the name glyph of the deity who ruled the particular month in which the inscription was erected. Beyer specialized in attempting to identify the original objects which the hieroglyphs portrayed, with little regard for the words and language involved. His identifications vary greatly in their value. His 1937 study of the inscriptions of Chichen Itza was of great importance for showing the existence and variability of parallel clauses, the first important work of that kind since Cyrus Thomas.

This group is best represented today by Günter Zimmermann and Thomas S. Barthel, of Hamburg. Zimmermann, in addition to his catalog (1956), has done very important work on the astronomy of the codices. Barthel's studies of the Chichen Itza inscriptions and of the Rain God passages of the *Dresden* have helped to elucidate the relationship between the codices and other types of data. He is now working extensively, trying to determine the linguistic equivalents of the glyphs.

Finally, a third group of scholars has emphasized the importance of knowing the linguistic corollaries of the glyphs and the fact that the script cannot be divorced from the language of the group that produced it; yet within this limitation these scholars have tended towards an ideographic interpretation. They recognize the phonetic use of glyphs with multiple meanings but tend to think of such replacement as being in all cases on the morphemic level, if I correctly understand their viewpoint. Daniel Garrison Brinton, whose *Primer of Maya hieroglyphs* (1895) is the model for the present work, William E. Gates, president of the Maya Society and author of *An outline dictionary of Maya glyphs* (1931), and J. Eric S. Thompson have been the three leaders of this group. Thompson's 1950 study presented a wealth of calendrical and mythological data, many new identifications, proof of the grammatical structure of the glyphic texts, and evidence that minor glyphic affixes could represent syllables and possibly longer words. There has been no published critical evaluation of this work, and its complexity makes it difficult for beginning students and people unfamiliar with Mayan studies to evaluate, as the ridiculous review by Archibald Hill (1952) clearly shows. In Mexico, César Lizardi Ramos has done important work in the tradition of this group.

I have elsewhere given a fuller summary of the history of decipherment of the Maya script (Kelley 1962a). In that work, I pointed out an initial trend to work extensively with the codices and to establish the Maya words for the glyphs, followed by a period in which attention was focused on the inscriptions and on calendrical data. A period of integration was inaugurated in 1943 by J. Eric S. Thompson's (1943a)

demonstration that some affixes represent grammatical particles, a finding that I regard as one of the four major discoveries of recent glyphic studies. Heinrich Berlin's demonstration that certain glyphs are typical for each site and Tatiana Proskouriakoff's evidence for a dynastic sequence at Piedras Negras virtually resolved the dispute over historical interpretations of the inscriptions. Yurii Knorozov's attempt to show that the Mayan script includes a phonetic element, which I regard as the fourth major discovery of decipherment, is still disputed.

Mention should be made of two developments of importance since my 1962 summary appeared (Kelley 1962a). The first is the rise of the so-called Mérida school of decipherment, established by Wolfgang Cordan. Although the group has a better knowledge of Yucatec and other Mayan languages than other scholars working with the glyphs, their work has suffered from separatist tendencies and a too ready acceptance of Cordan's work by others in the school. Most members of the group have little understanding of modern linguistic techniques, and their principles of decipherment have allowed inexact phonetic correspondences and the correspondence of an entire phrase to a single glyph. This makes appraisal of their results difficult. In general, I have cited the Mérida school only in those cases where they have suggested a reading that seems to me plausible. The other development is a recent interest in attempting computer decipherment of the Mayan script, initiated by three Russian scholars, E. V. Evreinov, Y. G. Kosarev, and V. A. Ustinov. The utility of the transcription and catalog produced by these Russian scholars (Evreinov, Kosarev, and Ustinov 1961b, vol. 3) is great, but the evidence supporting new decipherments seems weak, and the procedures have not been adequately explained. More recently, a number of scholars in Mexico and the United States have become interested in using computers for decipherment, and the Centro de Cálculo Electrónico of the National University of Mexico has done important preliminary work on this. Working with them, the Comisión para el Estudio de la Escritura Maya (CEEM) has produced another new catalog and inaugurated the first international symposium dedicated exclusively to the decipherment of Maya script in Mexico in December 1966.

It is surprising to find that at least two scholars of the University of Bujumbura, Burundi, are working on Mayan problems. L. de Sousberghe has produced an interesting and helpful study of Mayan kinship terms. More recently, Antoon L. Vollemaere has produced a series of working papers on the decipherment of the Maya script. Vollemaere is apparently working on principles which involve assigning phonetic values to parts of glyphs, in the tradition of Whorf and Héctor Martínez C. It is surprising that at one point Vollemaere regarded the order in which glyphs were to be read as uncertain.

Recent Developments

A growing body of important glyphic studies have not been taken into account in the body of the text, and some need brief mention here. Eric Thompson's continuing studies include a brief summary of his views in *Maya hieroglyphs without tears* (1972*a*) and his long-awaited and extensive study and edition of the *Dresden* codex (1972*b*), full of new ideas on specific decipherments and with some important general statements of his views. These show that the degree of agreement among scholars is now somewhat greater than when the text of my book was written but that there are still substantial differences. A publication by Michael Coe (1973) includes a new codex, of disputed authenticity, and many extremely important reproductions of texts and drawings from pottery. Coe has established the existence on ceramics of a "primary standard sequence" of glyphs in which glyphs recur in a fixed order, although there is substantial variation in which glyphs occur in any particular text. It is Coe's contention that all texts on pottery vessels refer to the land of the dead. In general he makes a good case for this view, but I am still not fully convinced that it is always true. Coe has identified God K as a Mayan equivalent of Aztec Tezcatlipoca, a view which is clearly correct and which throws new light on Ah Bolon Tzacab, as well as some reciprocal information on Tezcatlipoca.

Dumbarton Oaks Foundation has now published the results of the seminar on Mesoamerican writing systems which they sponsored; the volume, edited by Elizabeth Benson (1973), contains Floyd Lounsbury's important study of the "ben-ich" prefix, demonstrating that in many cases it is to be read *ah po* 'lord'. This demonstration affects our understanding of the Emblem Glyphs, as well as supplying one more phonetic glyph. In the same volume, my article, written in collaboration with K. Ann Kerr, gives preliminary results of my work on Mayan astronomy but has little of direct glyphic interest. At that time, I had not recognized the dominant Mercury interest of *Dresden* pages 69–73; unfortunately, despite this interest, I am still unable to recognize with certainty a glyph for Mercury. Elizabeth Benson also arranged an extremely profitable "mini-conference" on Palenque glyphs at Dumbarton Oaks in May 1974.

Here I can only allude to some of the most important results of that meeting. Lounsbury has established that the lid of the sarcophagus contains the death dates or burial dates of a series of Palenque rulers. Lounsbury, Linda Schele, Peter Mathews, and myself, working with rubbings supplied by Merle Greene Robertson, determined that a number of the rulers depicted on the sarcophagus are wearing their name hieroglyphs, in the style so familiar in the Mixtec codices. We also found what we regard as a phonetic rendering of the name of Lady Zac Kuk (White Quetzal), one of the Palenque rulers. The chronology of Palenque rulers, thanks to Lounsbury, Schele, and Mathews, has now been established with very little room for change. My Palenque chart should be modified considerably in the light of the new evidence. Our joint work also led us to recognize two glyphs, both apparently to be read *le* 'lineage', of considerable help in deciphering kin relationships. Lounsbury pointed out that the prefix T74:184, frequent as a title of Palenque rulers (as pointed out by Berlin), is to be read *makina* 'lord' (Landa's *ma* and *kin* are incorporated in the glyph). This same prefix is incorporated in the name glyphs of God GIII of the Palenque Triad, the remaining elements being a youthful head and a shield. I would suggest that the head is to be read *xib* 'youth', and the shield *balba*, Yucatec for 'to hide oneself' (cf. Yuc. *tacunba* 'to hide oneself, to shield oneself'). This rendering would make GIII's name read "Lord of Xibalba", the name given by the Quiche to the underworld, fully appropriate to my identification of him as a god of death. The fact that *balba* is a two-morpheme word apparently written by a single glyph should be taken into account in my discussion of the relationship of glyphs and morphemes. Lounsbury also drew my attention to *Madrid* 89a, which shows a god with sun-god characteristics and a macaw headdress. This is enough to suggest his identity with a Yucatec sun god called Kinich Kakmoo, Sun-Eye Fire-Macaw. The glyphs above read *ah kak(a) mo,* according to the Knorozov transcription, and furnish new strong evidence that the doubled glyph T669b:669b is to be read *kak* 'fire'.

Finally, I wish to mention a forthcoming study by Norman Hammond, Peter Mathews, and myself, in which we attempt to demonstrate that T630 is the Lubaantun Emblem Glyph and that the importance of Lubaantun, as indicated in the inscriptions, was considerably greater than anyone would have anticipated.

In general, the new studies have seldom invalidated specific interpretations of glyphs suggested in this book, and none has provided any major new breakthrough. They are, rather, additive to what is said here.

Nature of the Script: Agreement and Disagreement

While the emphasis differs, there are a great many points where agreement has been reached, and the purpose of this work is to show clearly where there are such agreements, to evaluate some points which are in dispute, and to point out the basis for reasonable disagreements.

The agreements may be summarized as follows:

1. Many glyphs have both a *geometric* or *symbolic* form, often unrecognizable as a depiction of a particular object, and a *head variant*, in which the glyph assumes the appearance of a human or animal head. At least some glyphs can also appear as complete figures of humans or animals (or deities), with no known change in meaning or, presumably, in the manner of reading.

2. The order of reading is usually clear and generally accepted. When head-variant glyphs face to the left, as they usually do, glyphs are read from left to right and from top to bottom. In the rare cases when head-form glyphs face to the right, the text is read from right to left, as on the "zodiacal" pages of *Paris*. In the codices, passages are most commonly of four or six glyph blocks, arranged as:

1   2
3   4

or as:

1   2   5
3   4   6

or perhaps sometimes as:

1   2   3
4   5   6.

Occasional passages are in the order:

1   2
3   4
5   6
7   8   etc.

In the inscriptions, the usual order is as follows:

1   2   9   10
3   4   11   12
5   6   13   14
7   8   15   16

save that the length of the columns is usually greater.

Within glyph blocks, the order of the individual glyphs may be as follows:

1*a*   1*b*

or:

1*a*
1*b*

or:

          1*b*
1*a*
          1*c*

Occasionally other variations are found, but they are usually obvious from the context.

3. The general content of certain sections of the codices and of the stelae is clear—for example, the eclipse table and the Venus table of the *Dresden* and some calendrical and astronomical calculations of the stelae.

4. A single idea or word may be expressed either by a single glyph or by two or more glyphs in a recurrent grouping, such as the group for 'dog'. The order of the glyphs within such groupings is standardized.

5. Some minor elements, attached to major glyphs as affixes, are grammatical prefixes and suffixes.

6. The nature of the script is mixed. Such pictographic elements as heads of birds or animals serve as the name glyphs of those animals; there are also ideographs that had a fixed meaning or content, however they might be read. Thus the glyph for 'seventh-day name' was the same whether read Manik or Che. Finally, there is some phoneticism, at least in the use of a single glyph for different meanings which are homonyms (e.g., *chac* 'red, great'). The latter is the so-called rebus writing.

7. Many specific glyphs or glyph compounds have been satisfactorily identified and generally accepted. These include numbers (normal and head-variant forms), day and month names, time-period glyphs, 'sun', 'rain', 'wind', 'sky', 'earth', 'moon', 'Venus', animal names, plant names, deity names, colors, directions, some verbs ("action glyphs"), and a very few grammatical elements. Occasional disagreements, even with respect to these, are discussed in succeeding chapters.

8. Some glyphs, at least in late times, could be read in more than one way, depending on context. Thus the *haab* 'year' glyph was also the glyph for the day Cauac, and presumably it was read in both ways.

9. The texts of the codices are written in a quasi-syntactical structure, to use Barthel's (1958) term. That is, like our labels, they contain grammatical

elements which correspond to spoken language but are probably considerably simpler than normal speech would be.

10. The publication of Thompson's *Catalog* (1962) makes it clear that the total number of glyphs is probably on the order of 750–850, a substantial increase over a previously widely accepted number of about 400 glyphs.

11. Teeple, Thompson, Barthel, and others formerly interpreted scenes and inscriptions on stelae, wall panels, lintels, etc., as usually ritual, religious, or astronomical. Recent work of Berlin and Proskouriakoff, summarized in Chapter 11, has demonstrated the essentially historical nature of many of the inscriptions, vindicating a position held on a priori grounds by Herbert J. Spinden, Knorozov, and myself. While there will certainly continue to be disputes about details in interpretation, this position has now been accepted in principle by such authorities as Thompson, Barthel, Linton Satterthwaite, and Alberto Ruz Lhuillier. As far as I know, it has not been rejected by anyone working with the materials.

There are still at least four major areas of disagreement:

1. The amount of phoneticism. Barthel formerly believed that even rebus-like usage was a fairly late and unimportant development of the script and argued that phoneticism is unlikely to be more prevalent in undeciphered portions of the script than in the deciphered portions. I, on the other hand, think that from the period of the earliest monuments the Mayas could have written any word in their language in a completely phonetic fashion. These two positions probably represent the extremes of disagreement on this point.

2. The use of ideographs. Thompson apparently still believes that a good many glyphs are "signs" without any necessary linguistic referent. While admitting that number glyphs belong in this category, I think that most or all of the remaining "ideographs" are logographs, representing words or parts of speech.

3. The kind of phoneticism. Knorozov believes that a single morpheme (such as *cutz* 'turkey') of consonant-vowel-consonant (CVC) form could be written phonetically by two CV glyphs, neither of which had any semantic relation with the CVC root. This is not merely rebus writing, but a true phonetic script. He has proved this point to my satisfaction, but phoneticism in this sense is not accepted either by Thompson or by Barthel. Full data on this point are presented in Chapter 9.

4. The existence of determinative glyphs. Knorozov has postulated the existence of determinative

glyphs, which were added to other glyphs to indicate which of two or more possible readings should be accepted, but which were probably not actually pronounced. Chapter 10 contains a discussion of this problem with reference to Knorozov's examples as well as some other possible cases. The existence of determinatives in this sense has been denied by Thompson and Barthel, with reference to Knorozov's examples.

Linguistic Discussion

There are many classifications of the Mayan languages, which generally agree as to relatively minor subgroups and recognize a number of larger groups but disagree as to the nature of the relationships of these larger groups. The subjoined classification is based primarily on my understanding of the glottochronological evidence. Table 1 gives the calculations of Morris Swadesh (as given in McQuown 1964, p. 60), presented in a somewhat rearranged form. The figures given represent the approximate number of centuries since divergence began, based on the concept that there is a regular loss of vocabulary in a fixed test list of one hundred words. Table 2 shows a family tree of the Mayan languages through time, as I understand it, based primarily on the glottochronological evidence and on the statements of various classifiers. Table 3 compares various classifications which have been made. (The Gates classification is from his study published in Morley 1920; Kroeber's classification is found in Kroeber 1939; the Swadesh scheme is from Swadesh 1961; and the Kaufman-McQuown version is from Kaufman 1964 and McQuown 1964.) It is clear from the figures given that Uspantec consistently shows more cognates than are expectable with all other branches, as does Tojolabal. Conversely, Tzotzil and Mam both show fewer cognates than would be expected with an absolutely constant rate of loss. Unrecognized cognates and unrecognized borrowings have undoubtedly caused some distortion, but either of these explanations would tend to result in an irregularity restricted to some branches of the Mayan family, rather than the consistent differences found. It therefore seems to me probable that there are, in fact, differences in the rate of preservation, so that Uspantec and Tojolabal have preserved more archaic terms, and Mam and Tzotzil have accepted more innovations. Because Mam shows thirty-six centuries of divergence from Huaxtec and no other language shows more than thirty-two, some authorities have assumed that the primary split was between Mam and Huaxtec and that Mam was somehow more divergent

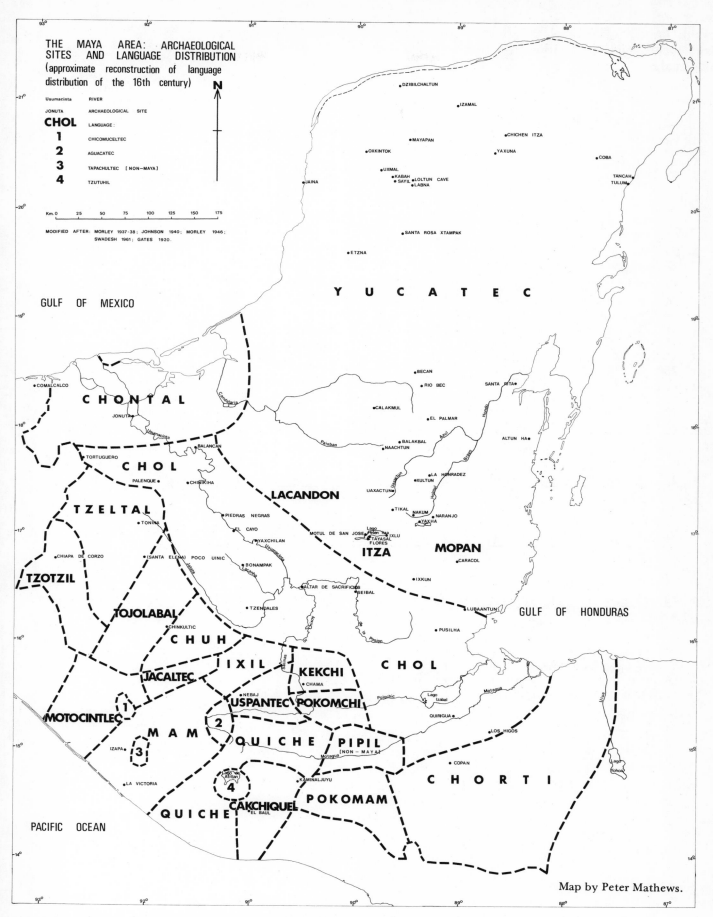

The Maya Area: Archaeological Sites and Language Distribution

Table 1
Glottochronological Relationships of the Mayan
Languages

```
Chicomuceltec
  6   Huastec
 26  24 | Lacandon
 25  22 |  6   Yucatec
 31  29  21  18 | Chontal
 30  27  17  16 |  7   Chol
 32  24  21  18 | 13  11   Chorti
 26  26  20  21 | 16  15  14   Toholabal  (Chañabal)
 32  29  19  20 | 19  16  17  14   Tzeltal
 29  27  24  24 | 21  19  18  13  19   Chuh
 26  27  27  25  24  23  20  17  21 | 15   Jacalteca
 23  26  26  24  21  24  21  17  24 | 15  12   Motocintleca
 26  27  24  24  22  22  20  18  21 | 18  13  14   Ixil
 30  29  23  26  25  27  23  21  26 | 18  16  15  11   Aguacateca
 29  26  26  28  27  26  24  21  25 | 22  20  17  15  16 | Quiche
 28  26  24  24  25  24  22  21  26 | 22  19  19  20  19 |  6   Rabinal
 30  25  28  28  26  24  22  21  26 | 22  19  17  16  22 |  8   7   Cakchiquel
 30  27  21  22  22  22  22  21  24 | 20  18  20  15  19 | 15  15  14   Pokomchi
 30  28  25  26  25  24  24  24  28 | 25  21  19  18  21 | 18  16  16  11   Pokomam
 26  27  27  28  26  24  24  21  24  24 | 22  24  17  20 | 20  17  19  19  15   Kekchi
 28 –26 + 25 + 26  25  24  23  22 – 26–22.5  20 –19 + 17 – 20 – (Jacaltecan group omitted from these averages)

   27+       25+            23+                    19

 24  29  22  22  21  16  16  18   7  22  25  30  27  30  27  30  29  26  30  27  Tzotzil
   26.5     22          18                      28+

 34  36  30  31  27  29  27  24  27  22  16  19  21  16  20  24  21  20  22  24  30 Mam
   35      30.5        27–                18                22–

 24  23  26  24  22  21  20  18  24  20  15  10  12  11   6   8   8  11  13  15  30  13 Uspantec
   23.5     25          21               12        7            13
```

Source. Rearranged from Swadesh (as given by McQuown
1964), with Tzotzil, Uspantec, and Mam removed from the
main chart to better show consistencies.

Table 2
Suggested Family Tree of the Mayan Languages

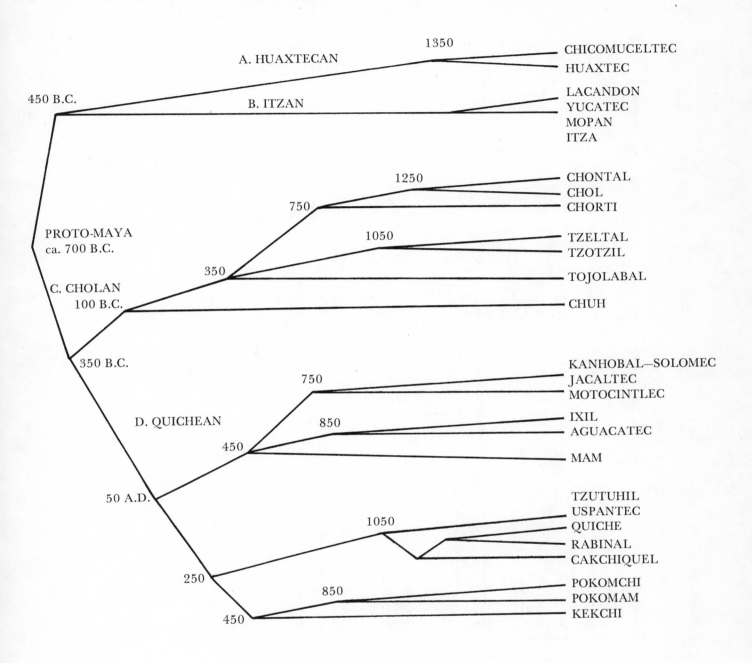

A. HUAXTECAN

1350 — CHICOMUCELTEC
HUAXTEC

450 B.C.

B. ITZAN

LACANDON
YUCATEC
MOPAN
ITZA

PROTO-MAYA
ca. 700 B.C.

1250 — CHONTAL
CHOL
CHORTI

750

1050 — TZELTAL
TZOTZIL

350

TOJOLABAL

C. CHOLAN
100 B.C.

CHUH

350 B.C.

KANHOBAL—SOLOMEC
JACALTEC
MOTOCINTLEC

750

D. QUICHEAN

850 — IXIL
AGUACATEC

450

MAM

50 A.D.

TZUTUHIL
USPANTEC
QUICHE
RABINAL
CAKCHIQUEL

1050

250

POKOMCHI
POKOMAM
KEKCHI

850

450

Table 3
Comparison of Mayan Linguistic Classifications

Gates	Kroeber	Kaufman—McQuown	Swadesh
VII. Huasteca	Huastec	Huastecano	I. Inik Huasteco
[4g. Chicomucelteca]	Chicomucceltec	Huasteco Veracruzano	Huasteco
		Potosino (omitted, K.)	Chicomucelteco
		Chicomucelteco [=Cotoque, Coxoh]	
I. Maya	Maya group	Yucatecano	II. Winik 1. Yaxque
1a. Maya	Maya	Yucateco	Maya
1b. Itza	Lacandon	Itza (omitted, K.)	Lacandon
1c. Lacandon	Mopan	Lacandon	
		Mopan	
III. Chol	Chontal group	Cholano	2. Yaxche
2c. Chontal	Chontal	Chontal	Chontal
3a. Cholti	Chol	Chol	Chol
3b. Chorti	Chorti	Chorti/Cholti	Chorti
II. Tzental	Tzotzil group	Tzeltalano	
2a. Tzental	Tzental	Tzeltal	Tzeltal
2b. Tzotzil	Tzotzil	Tzotzil	Tzotzil
2d. Chañabal [=Tojolabal]	Chañabal	Tojolabalano Tojolabal	Tojolabal
4f. Chuje	Chuj	Chuj	Chuj
4d. Solomeca [=Kanhobal]		Kanjobalano Kanjobal-Solomeco	3. Chaxque
4e. Jacalteca	Jacaltec	Jacalteco	Jacalteco
4h. Motocintleca	Motocintlec	Motocintleco	Motocintleco
4b. Ixil	(Ixil-Quiche group) Ixil	Mameano Ixil	Ixil
4c. Aguacateca		Aguacateco	Aguacateco
IV. Mame	Mame	Mame	4. Mame
4a. Mame			
V. Quiche	Ixil-Quiche group	Quicheano	5. Grupo Quiche
5a. Quiche	Quiche	Quiche	Quiche
5b. Cakchiquel	Cakchiquel	Cakchiquel	Cakchiquel
5c. Tzutuhil	Tzutuhil	Tzutuhil	
5d. Uspanteca	Uspantec	Uspantec (omitted, K.)	Uspanteco
		Achi [=Rabinal]	Rabinal
VI. Pokom	Pokom group	Kekchiano	Pocomam
6a. Pokoman	Pokoman	Pocomam	Pocomchi
6b. Pokonchi	Pokonchi	Pocomchi	
6c. Kekchi	Kekchi	Kekchi	6. Kekchi

Lowland Maya / Upland Maya

Kroeber's original diagram is overlapping and schematic but seems to group as above.

There seems to be no difference between Kaufman and McQuown at the level of the eleven groups on the left.

than any other Mayan language. However, its average divergence from the Jacaltecan group is only eighteen centuries, whereas the average divergence of Jacaltecan from Kekchi/Quiche is nineteen centuries, and the divergence of Mam from Kekchi/Quiche averages nearly twenty-two centuries, with no correction. If the Mam divergence is systematically reduced by five centuries, it comes in line with other evidence.

I think it is clear that nearly all students have recognized the major breaks between Huaxtecan, Itzan, Cholan, and Quichean, whatever they have been called. The glottochronology makes it clear that Cholan and Quichean make a major group as opposed to Huaxtecan. The position of Itzan, however, is anomalous. Its average divergence from Huaxtecan is 24.2 centuries; from Chuh, 24.0; from Quichean, 25.6; and from Cholan other than Chuh, 19.1. At first sight, these figures suggest a close relationship of Itzan to Cholan; this has long been a favored opinion and may be right. On the other hand, the position of Chuh here would suggest that it may show a truer rate of divergence and that the divergence from the other Cholan groups may have been partly diminished by extensive unrecognized borrowing. Since we know that in Itzan such important features as deity names and names of days of the calendar were borrowed from Cholan, this seems a distinct possibility. Conversely, it is unlikely that there has been any borrowing relationship in either direction between Huaxtecan and Itzan. I am, therefore, inclined to think that Itzan may actually have a closer relationship to Huaxtecan than to Cholan/Quichean. This view, shown in the relationships set up in Table 2, is far from being proved.

The problem of the degree of relationship between the various branches and the time depth of their divergence is intimately linked to the question of how best to use our linguistic data in attempting to decipher Mayan writing. It is clear that Cholan languages are now spoken or have been spoken in the recent past from Palenque on the north (Chol) to Copan and Quirigua in the south (Chorti). Swadesh has calculated the time depth between Chol/Chontal on the one hand and Chorti on the other at eleven to thirteen centuries, that is, a divergence that began about 600–800 A.D. While the correlation of the Maya calendar with our own is not yet settled, and the precise chronological value of glottochronology is still in dispute, this date seems a very good approximation for the end of Classic Period ("Old Empire") Maya. Thus, both distribution and chronology point to the derivation of Chol/Chontal/Chorti from the Classic Period language of the inscriptions. Using the chronology adopted in Table 2, both Tojolabal and Tzeltal/

Tzotzil would have started diverging from the ancestral Chontal/Chol/Chorti group within the period of the inscriptions. Itzan, on the other hand, probably began diverging as a language as early as 700 B.C. Inscriptions are known in the area of the modern Itzan languages, and there is a substantial probability that at least one and perhaps all three of the surviving Mayan books come from that area.

These alternative possibilities may then be set up: (a) Classic Period Mayan inscriptions record a single homogenous language, represented by modern Chol, Chontal, and Chorti; (b) Classic Period Mayan inscriptions record a single homogenous language, represented by modern Itzan (Yucatec, Lacandon, Mopan, and Itza); (c) Classic Period Mayan inscriptions record at least two languages, ancestral Cholan and ancestral Itzan, and possibly divergent Cholan languages. A remote fourth possibility is that the language of the inscriptions became extinct and that no existing languages are directly derived from it. We know from Bishop Landa that the writing system was being used to record Yucatec in the sixteenth century, and Thompson (1950, p. 16) has pointed out correspondences between material in the codices and Yucatec which suggest that the codices are closer to Yucatec than to the Cholan languages. He regards Cholan and Yucatec as very closely related and seems to think they might have a common origin as late as the time of the Classic Period inscriptions. This view seemed more plausible prior to the publication of the glottochronological evidence. At the present stage of our investigations, we need to utilize every source which may throw light on the inscriptions; even such distantly related languages as Mam and Huaxtec may contain words which have been lost in later times in the languages descended from the language or languages of the inscriptions.

For epigraphic studies, it seems desirable to use reconstructed linguistic forms wherever possible. Such hypothetical forms are normally marked in linguistic studies with an asterisk, a practice which will be followed throughout this book. The reconstructions are a useful device to make the cross references from one language to another more uniform. They should not be considered to mark exactly the true phonetic pattern of the words in early times. However, in the present state of Maya studies it is often more convenient to cite words directly from the various Maya languages, a procedure which may also have the advantage of suggesting a special relationship between the glyphs and some particular Mayan language or group of languages. If words are directly quoted as possible explanations for certain glyphs, this does not imply that I think the glyph was necessarily read with exactly the pronunciation of the particular quoted form.

Nonlinguists easily reach the stage of recognizing that certain changes are to be found between the pronunciation of a word in one language and its pronunciation in another, related language. However, they are often reluctant to take the next step and adopt the basic principle of modern linguistics, that all changes are regular—that, if a change of a sound occurs in one word under specified conditions, the same change will occur in all other words containing the same sound under the same conditions. This principle may not always be entirely true, but empirically it gives better results to act as if it were. For present purposes, the most useful list of reconstructions which has yet appeared is that of Terrence S. Kaufman (1964). Use has also been made of the reconstructions of Abraham Halpern (1942), Norman A. McQuown (1955), and Ronald D. Olson (1964, 1965). The reconstructions of McQuown and Kaufman probably incorporate a substantial number of distinctions which are not made in the script, and Olson's reconstructions, although probably less accurate linguistically, may well be closer to the distinctions made in the script. Each reconstruction implies that, by applying a strict set of rules, one can always know what pronunciation a form would take in any specified daughter language. The rules for the correspondences are given in Plate 1, together with the reconstructed original sounds, according to the various authors.

A final point should be emphasized. No nonscientific script anywhere in the world fully conforms to the linguistic distinctions in pronunciation made by the speakers in speech. We cannot impose a priori expectations on the script from purely linguistic evidence; however, once a distinction has been recognized as existing in the script, it cannot safely be ignored in the subsequent interpretations of particular glyphs.

Terminology

While Mayanists have evolved a fairly good descriptive terminology for the glyphs, there is a clear need for a more adequate and more explicit analytical terminology in Mayan glyphic studies. Mayan inscriptions are normally divided into columns with space between them and into vertical units, likewise usually with space between them. The columns are lettered from left to right (A, B, C, D, etc.), and the vertical units are numbered from top to bottom (1, 2, 3, 4, 5, etc.). This useful reference system was invented by Charles Rau. By combining letters and numbers (A1, B3, C10, etc.) one can refer to a physically distinct unit. This is the glyph block. Within it, there is normally a *main sign* and one or more *affixes*. With some exceptions, main signs are normally more or less rounded squares, taking up most of a glyph block, while the affixes are physically smaller units, relatively long and narrow and often irregular in outline. If they are to the left or on top, the affixes are referred to as *prefixes;* if they are to the right or at the bottom, they are referred to as *postfixes*. Occasionally, more than one main sign occurs in a single glyph block. Main signs are normally divided into two classes, *symbolic variants* and *head variants*, the two often showing a close relationship. Symbolic variants include all glyphs which do not represent a human or animal head. In general, most symbolic variants seem to have corresponding head variants, which are apparently read in the same way and have the same meaning. Occasionally, there are *full-figure variants*, which represent an entire human or animal figure. (See Fig. 3.)

Analytically, the existing terminology seems very inadequate, and the following terms are proposed:

1. For minimal graphic units, the term *grapheme* has recently been used both by Knorozov (1963) and by Barthel; it is obviously preferable to my attempt to use *hieroglyph* for the same unit (Kelley 1962*a*), since the latter term has normally been used in a much more extended way in Maya studies.

2. The existence of head variants and other indications that two or more glyphs might be used for a single word or sound have led Knorozov to propose the term *allograph* for two glyphs which are descriptively different but seem to be functionally identical.

3. In Maya writing, a grapheme may often be dissected into smaller units. Descriptively, these may be called *elements* of the grapheme. Analytically, such elements may be either parts which define the grapheme or, in some cases, graphemes placed physically within a larger grapheme. In the latter case, they have usually been called *infixes,* a term which has been used primarily in an analytical rather than a descriptive sense.

4. It was discovered early in Maya studies that regular sequences of two (or sometimes more) graphemes were found in contexts suggesting that they were names of objects or actions. Generally, such a grapheme sequence was called simply "a hieroglyph," with the implicit (and sometimes explicit) assumption that one of the two graphemes was "basic" to the meaning and the other "secondary." I attempted previously to use the term *glyph group* to apply to such sequences (Kelley 1962*a* and elsewhere). Unfor-

tunately, this conflicted with the varying uses that have been established for the term *glyph*, and it has been pointed out to me that it pre-empts the useful word *group* for a very restricted meaning. I have, therefore, coined the term *glyger* (from *glyph group*) to refer to such units. It should be emphasized that the glyger is an analytical unit, implying some sort of unitary reference, and is not merely a sequence of two graphemes, even if these are found together frequently. Thus, the two glyphs which recur together with the meaning 'dog' form a glyger, but the two recurrent glyphs read 'at the sky' do not.

5. A larger analytical unit is that which has been called a *clause*. This always contains two or more graphemes and may contain one or more glygers. In the past, clauses have been defined principally on the basis of repetition on various monuments. It will be pointed out, however, that they may also be defined on the basis of grammatical structure. In some cases a clause, however defined, may ultimately be shown to be a multigrapheme glyger. In spite of this possible overlap, the term *clause* is useful for an analytic unit which is normally larger than the glyger.

These units are recognized and used by all, or nearly all, of the scholars now working with the hieroglyphs; I hope that the terminology will help to solve problems of reference.

Scribal Variation

Zimmermann (1956) made the first attempt to show that minor variations in the form of one glyph in a particular section of the *Dresden* are generally accompanied by consistent variations in other glyphs. His analysis suggested that these are typical of different scribes and that at least eight or nine scribes worked on copying the *Dresden*. In general, such differences in handwriting do not seem to cause any difficulty in recognizing the glyph intended. In Classic Period inscriptions, regional, chronological, and individual variations of this sort may lead to greater difficulties in determining what is intended. Thus Thompson (1962, p. 215) has given the number 602 to a glyph found in the Palenque area; this is closely similar to glyph 586 and appears in similar contexts. Despite the separate numbers, Thompson thinks the two forms are merely regional variants of a single glyph. The most extreme variation of this sort is between the glyphs of the inscriptions and those of the codices. Here identity is often hard to demonstrate. When rather similar glyphs appear in similar contexts in inscriptions and codices, one must suppose that they were read in the same way. However, differences

in subject matter in the inscriptions and codices may create different contexts even for originally identical glyphs.

Another type of variation consists of using different glyphs to convey the same information. I have the impression that the scribe responsible for pages 45–63 of the *Dresden,* as well as some other parts of that codex, enjoyed showing his versatility and command of the script. I believe he deliberately put down unusual combinations of glyphs, as if to show his fellows that they still had a thing or two to learn. Conversely, I think the scribe of *Madrid* created false and misleading combinations (rarely, he produced enlightening ones) because of his frequent errors. These suggest to me the substantial possibility that the scribe suffered from some sort of partial dyslexia. For this reason, I believe that the *Madrid* scribe should not be relied on in making important theoretical points or unique decipherments.

Types of errors or variations made by the *Madrid* scribe include drawing glyphs backwards, reversing the elements of glygers, putting postfixes in prefix position, substituting glyphs of similar but nonidentical sound, omitting a glyph from a glyger, and, probably, using glyphs with the wrong meaning. On M20a, we find the *u* glyph drawn backwards, although it is in correct position in the same context on the previous page. The reversal of T19:59 to T59:19 in the "bird passages" (M94b–95b) is, I think, an example of element reversal which is psychologically explainable by the fact that T59 (*ti*) is normally a grammatical prefix. On M112c, we find *u* postfixed above the first picture and prefixed to the same glyph above the second and third pictures. T181 normally appears as a suffix, as it does on M108c; the parallel passage on the previous page shows it prefixed to the same glyph. On M108c, the normal elements of the glyger for 'east' appear in reverse order. I believe that M42c shows a very interesting and enlightening form of error. In Yucatec, an older *te* 'tree' was shifted in pronunciation to *che*. In five passages on M42c, we find the now widely accepted affix T87 for *te*, but a sixth parallel shows this glyph replaced by T219, for which I accept an older reading of *che*. Thus a "correct spelling" in a historic sense was replaced by what had become a phonetically more accurate form. On M6a, where we would expect the glyph for 'west' (T219:544), we find only T219. This may be an intentional abbreviation, but it may equally well be an example of dyslexic lapse. Use of glyphs with wrong meanings is hard to demonstrate, since our knowledge of the meaning is derived entirely from context. Nevertheless, there are some suggestive inconsistencies. T296 (cf. T159) seems to refer to a peccary (M93a); with 'seven' prefixed, it refers to an armadillo (M91a) and to an animal which may be either a deer or a peccary (M41b). Perhaps there is a word which has these varied meanings, but I am inclined to think that the scribe wrote the wrong glyph by error in one or two of these places. Taken together, there are enough well-documented examples of several kinds of inconsistencies and seeming errors to indicate that a very substantial degree of caution is necessary in utilizing the data from the *Madrid*.

Part One.
Decipherment of Specific Glyphs

Although it is highly desirable to establish objective criteria by which to appraise suggested decipherments, relatively little has been done in this regard, and decipherment still seems to be more an intuitive art than a science. As a very rough guide to my own appraisals of probability or improbability, the following criteria are implicit or explicit in many of my remarks on specific glyphs:

1. The identification of a glyph as a depiction of an object can be considered probable if:
   a. it has distinctive traits which are easily recognizable; and/or
   b. it corresponds closely to Mayan depictions of that object; and
   c. there is only one object to which it corresponds; or
   d. phonetic use supports the identification. Identification of the object may sometimes be made after a phonetic value has been established that suggests a particular identification.

Major disagreements usually indicate that at least one of the above characteristics is absent or has been ignored by one of the decipherers.

2. The meaning of a glyph can be considered as adequately established if:
   a. it is one of a series of parallel passages in which a changing glyph corresponds regularly to a changing depiction; and/or
   b. the glyph is regularly repeated with a particular kind of depiction; or
   c. it regularly recurs in a defined chronological context indicating a particular astronomical or historical interest; and
   d. it fits the grammatical structure of the writing.

3. The reading of a glyph phonetically can be considered probable if:
   a. there are two or more established meanings for which there are known homonyms in at least one Mayan language; and/or
   b. the glyph is clearly identified, and only one known Maya word is used for the object depicted; or
   c. it is one of an interlocking set of phonetic values.

Despite differences of opinion about basic principles, there has been a fairly steady accumulation of partial decipherments of specific glyphs. Some of these have received little attention, while others have been widely used. In the latter category, the most basic decipherments have been the glyphs for the numbers.

Chapter 1
Numbers

According to a marginal note in the *Book of Chilam Balam of Mani,* dated 1793 and written by a native Maya Indian, a bar or line in Maya stood for 'five', and a dot stood for 'one'. The validity of this system as applied to the codices was shown by Förstemann in the 1880's and has not been doubted or challenged at any time since. In the *Dresden,* Förstemann found that dates were marked in red and the intervals between them were marked in black. It was known from Landa and early colonial Maya books that the number permutation series in dates never went above 13. Applying this to such a sequence as that on D35c–37c, we find: black 9, red 9, black 11, red 7, (black glyph), red 1, black 10, red 11, black 15, red 13, black 9, and red 9, to be read as follows: (+9) = 9 (+11) = 20 (i.e., 13 + 7 of the next count) = 7 (+?) = 1 (+10) = 11 (+15) = 26 (i.e., 13 + 13 of the next count) = 13 (+9) = 9 (of the next count). Large numbers of such series provided clear-cut mathematical evidence of the validity of the system and also made possible the identification of intervening glyphs which did not obviously fit this pattern, such as the black glyph mentioned in the above series, which can be shown to have the value 20, Yucatec *kal.*

The number of such glyphs in the codices is small, but the known ones are shown in Figures 1 and 2 with the Mayan names of the numerals. Förstemann was also able to show that in some cases a series of numbers were written in vertical columns and that in such cases the different positions of the numbers indicated a place notation system, similar to our system, but with differing values. As used in dates, the bottom place marked days up to 20. When 20 was indicated, 1 was marked in the next position up, and a zero symbol was put in the bottom place. In this second place, the series ran only to 18, and when 18 periods of 20 days each were to be annotated, a dot (1) was put in the third position from the bottom, a zero in the second position, and a zero in the first position, thus indicating 360 days. This usage was apparently designed to approximate the length of a year, and all numbers above this follow the more regular vigesimal pattern of multiplying by 20. Dots which are part of a numeral with bars are put on the left or above the bars, immediately adjacent to them. Spacing is used to indicate place value. Dots following a numeral with bars (i.e., under or to the right) indicate that the bars are in a series, occupying the next position greater than the dots. Thus, ·‖ is 11, · ‖ is (1 × 20) + 10, i.e., 30, and ‖ · is (10 × 20) + 1, i.e., 201.

Studies in the inscriptions soon showed that the same system was used there. However, in this case the bar-and-dot numerals were often replaced by the

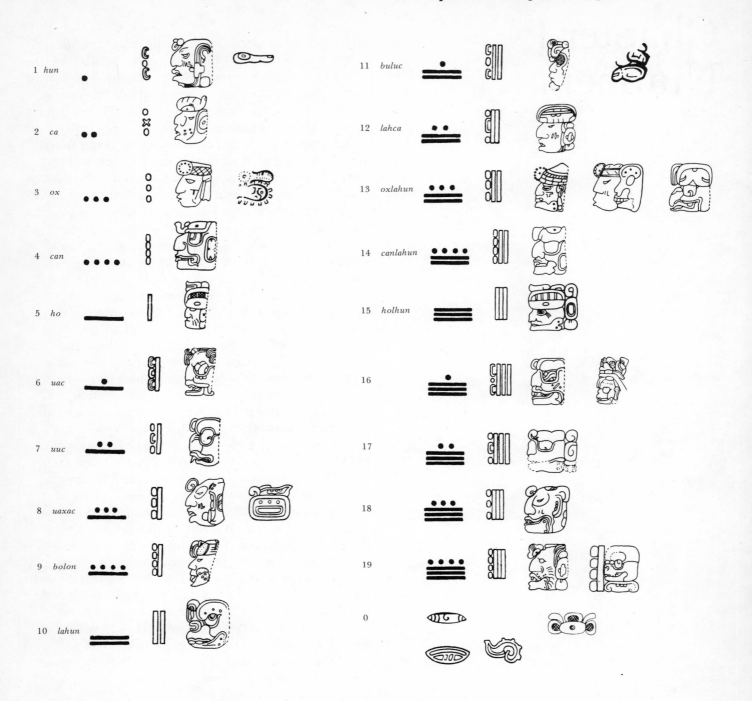

Figure 1. The Maya numerals (1–19).

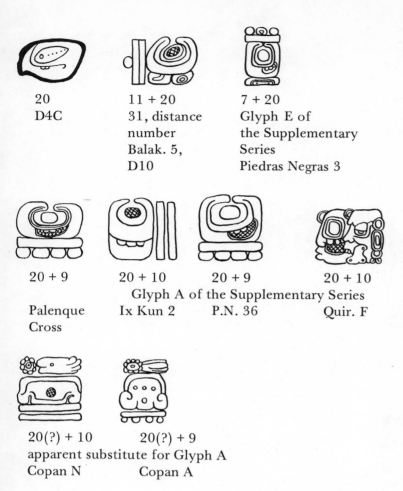

20
D4C

11 + 20
31, distance
number
Balak. 5,
D10

7 + 20
Glyph E of
the Supplementary
Series
Piedras Negras 3

20 + 9

20 + 10

20 + 9

20 + 10

Glyph A of the Supplementary Series

Palenque
Cross

Ix Kun 2

P.N. 36

Quir. F

20(?) + 10
apparent substitute for Glyph A
Copan N

20(?) + 9

Copan A

Figure 2. The number twenty (Yucatec *kal*, Tzeltal *tab*).

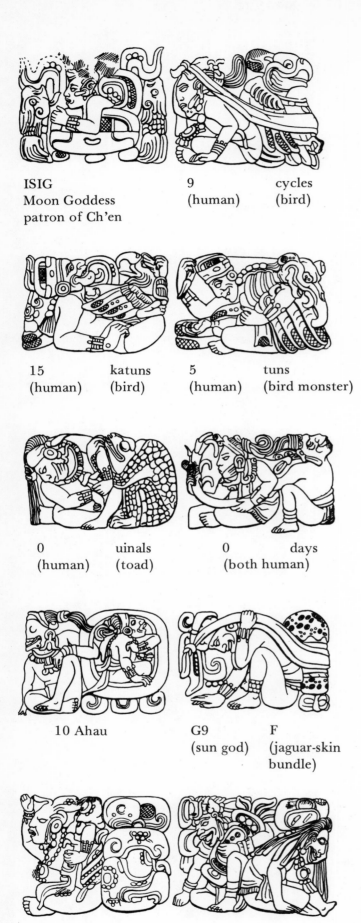

ISIG
Moon Goddess
patron of Ch'en

9   cycles
(human)   (bird)

15   katuns
(human)   (bird)

5   tuns
(human)   (bird monster)

0   uinals
(human)   (toad)

0   days
(both human)

10 Ahau

G9   F
(sun god)   (jaguar-skin
                 bundle)

8 Ch'en

Figure 3. Full-figure glyphs from Copan, Stela D. *See also* Figures 92 and 99.

heads of gods. Fortunately, it was early determined that the Mayas erected monuments indicating the number of days which had elapsed since a common base date, many centuries in the past. During the time that many of the monuments were being erected, nine periods of four hundred "years" of 360 days each had passed since the beginning date of Mayan history (a presumably apocryphal date). It was soon noticed that nearly all the monuments began either with a bar-and-dot numeral nine or with a bearded head of a god, and it was assumed that this head represented 'nine'. Since the resultant date could usually be read, it was often possible to calculate what the period number should have been, and with the large number of inscriptions, it immediately became possible to check these results. The decipherments by J. T. Goodman in 1897 were rapidly accepted by most students, with some modifications by Seler in 1899 (in Seler 1902–1923), and their self-verifying nature in the various Mayan inscriptions means that any beginning student can very rapidly check for himself the values of the different deity heads as numbers. However, some numbers have been found only in a very few inscriptions, and there still remains some doubt as to what their distinguishing characteristics are. An interesting feature is that the god for ten is the Death God, and gods for the numbers above this normally show the fleshless lower jaw of the Death God combined with the characteristics of the number which is to be added to ten to give the particular number. There are, however, also separate glyphs for eleven, twelve, and thirteen. Signs which indicate a zero in the sequence were the subjects of much argument, many scholars holding that to the Maya these glyphs stood for completion, rather than nothingness. This argument is still not adequately resolved and probably will not be until someone manages to decipher how these glyphs were actually pronounced by the Maya. For the purposes of the student, it only needs to be borne in mind that they indicate a return to a cyclical base, of the sort which we indicate by a zero, whatever the Maya conceptualization of this was. These 'zero' glyphs represent shells, for which the generic Yucatec name is *hub*.

The climax of elaboration in the Maya glyphs is to be found in the fantastic "full-figure" glyphs (Fig. 3), in which an entire animal or deity is shown to represent a single number or a single period. These sometimes show the numbers as bearers of the periods. Only a few such inscriptions are known, including one recently discovered at Palenque.

It will be noted that a glyger for 'eleven' determined from context, D19a (Zimmermann 1956, p. 109), consists of three graphemes, the first of which has been, unfortunately, destroyed. Presumably it should be read by some cognate of Yucatec *buluc* 'eleven'. See the phonetic discussion in Chapter 9.

The following linguistic reconstructions, derived from Kaufman 1964, may have some relevance to the glyphs which have been considered in this section. Reconstructions apply to the whole family unless otherwise specified. Periods are used to separate reconstructions for one meaning from reconstructions for the next.

One: **jun*. Two: **ka'; ka'ib*. Three: **'ox*. Four: **kyang*. Five: **ho'*. Six: **'waq*. Seven: **huq*. Eight: **waqxëq*. Nine: **beleng*. Ten: **lajung*. Eleven: (a) **buluk*, Tzel.-Tzo.-Chl.-Chr.-Yuc.; (b) **jun + lajung*, Kek.-Jac.-Mam; (c) **'us-luk*, Chu.-Kan. Twelve: (a) **laj-kaX-*, Tzel.-Tzo.-Toj.-Chu.-Kan.-Chl.; (b) **kab-lajung*, Pch.-Kek.-Jac.-Mam. How many: **jay*. Twenty: (a) **kw'al;* (b) **taxb;* (c) **'winaq* (=man). First(1): **nah*. First(2): **bah*. To count: **'aj*. To measure: **p'is*.

Chapter 2
Calendrical and Astronomical Glyphs

Landa gives a lengthy description of the calendar of the Yucatecan Maya as it was in his time, including glyphs for days and months. This calendar consisted of several permutation series, the most basic being a series of 20 named days. Each day had an accompanying number from 1 to 13, and both numbers and days ran in endless sequence, so that the same day name recurred with the same number only after 260 days. The calendar year was composed of 365 days, divided into eighteen periods of 20 days each, usually called "months," and one period of five days. This calendar year was distinguished from what might be called the "counting year" of exactly 360 days. Each of the eighteen periods of 20 days had its name and associated glyph or glyger.

Since the sequences and glyphs for both day names and month names were given by Landa, the quite similar glyphs of the codices were easily recognized and quickly verified, and there was little problem in going from these to the inscriptions. However, although it has been conventional to use Landa's Yucatec names for the day and month glyphs, variant lists of day names and month names from other groups sometimes made it clear that other names might be closer to the original way of reading the glyphs. The most striking cases were the months in which the glyphs had color prefixes but no color term was found in the corresponding Yucatec month name. The glyphs for the days are shown in Figure 4 with names from Yucatec, Chuh, and Quiche. These three of the many Maya lists represent all the recorded variations in names, although not by any means all of the variations in pronunciation. The nature of the variation between highland and lowland groups suggests to me that these lists may represent independent translations from a non-Maya original source. The glyphs for the months are shown in Figure 5. The variations in month names are much greater, and only a sample is shown. It should be kept in mind that the glyphs represented words and may be found in other contexts with their normal meanings. It is possible that day and month names were less fixed than ours and that some of the variation indicated the use of long-accepted alternatives.

Numbers, days, and twenty-day months all had their patron deities, as did longer periods of time. Dates were normally given in this order: day number, day name, date of month. In the later periods of Yucatán, the day which fell on the first of the month Pop was the first day of the year, and that day gave its name to the year. It will be seen that, since the least common factor of 260 and 365 is 5, the same day would not recur in the same month position until fifty-two years of 365 days had passed.

Yucatec	Chuh	Quiche, 1722	Codices		Inscriptions		
1. Imix	+ Imox	+Imox					
2. Ik	+ Ic	+ Ikh					
3. Akbal	(+Q) Woton	Akhbal					
4. Kan	+ Cana	Kat					
5. Chicchan	Abak	Can					
6. Cimi	(+Q) Toh	Ceme					
7. Manik	Ceh	+ Ceh					
8. Lamat	+ Lambat	Khanil					
9. Muluc	+ Mulu	Toh					
10. Oc	Elab	Tzih					
11. Chuen	Bats	+ Batz					
12. Eb	+ Ehub	+ Ee					
13. Ben	+ Been	Ah					
14. Ix	+ Iix	+ Iix					
15. Men	Tzikin	+ Tzicin					
16. Cib	Chabin	Ahmac					
17. Caban	Kixcab	Noh					
18. Etz'nab	Chinax	+ Tihax					
19. Cauac	+ Chavuc	+ Caoc					
20. Ahau	+ Ahau	Hunahpu					

Figure 4. Mayan day names and glyphs. Symbols: + indicates agreement between adjacent columns (Yucatec and Chuh or Chuh and Quiche); (+Q) indicates agreement between Yucatec and Quiche.

Yucatec	Kanhobal	Chol (??) Kekchi (??)	Codices	Inscriptions
1. Pop	3. Nabich	————		
2. Uo	4. Moo	Icat		
3. Zip	5. Bak	Chaccat		
4. Zotz'	6. Canal	————		
5. Zec	7. Cuhem	Cazeu		
6. Xul	8. Huachsicin	Chichin		
7. Yaxkin	9. Yaxacil	Ianguca		
8. Mol	10. Mol	Mol		
9. Ch'en	11. Khek Sihom	Zihora (?) (copying error for Zihom?)		
10. Yax	13. Yax Sihom	Yax		
11. Zac	12. Sah Sihom	Zac		
12. Ceh	14. Khak Sihom	Chac		
13. Mac	15. Mac	Chantemat		
14. Kankin	16. Oneu	Uniu		
15. Muan	17. Sivil	Muhan		
16. Pax	18. Tap (5 nameless days)	Ahkiku		
17. Kayab	1. Uex	Kanazi		
18. Cumku	2. Sakmai	Olh		
5 days without a name (uayeb)				

Figure 5. Month names. Both the names and their order are extremely variable. For additional lists and a discussion of variation, see Thompson (1950, p. 106). The third list is part of a Kekchi document but seems phonologically unlike Kekchi. Thompson has suggested it is Chol, also doubtful. In at least four cases, it seems to be closer to the monuments than the Yucatec list.

Examination of the inscriptions has shown that glyphs very similar to those given by Landa are found in mathematically related groups, indicating that their order is the same as that given by Landa and enabling recognition of occasional forms which vary from those given by Landa. Mathematical calculation of these inscriptions, particularly work by Förstemann and Goodman, has shown that the Mayas used an era, counting forward the number of days which had elapsed since a day corresponding to Yucatec 4 Ahau 8 Cumku. The Maya practice was to give the number of periods of four hundred counting years, the number of periods of twenty counting years, the number of counting years, the number of months, and the number of days which had elapsed from the (implied) date 4 Ahau 8 Cumku to the date written in the inscription. Such a date is conventionally written, for example, 9.6.10.0.0 8 Ahau 13 Pax and is called an Initial Series (IS) date. This is to be read as nine periods of four hundred years, plus six periods of twenty years, plus ten years, no months, and no days, from the base date, 4 Ahau 8 Cumku, to 8 Ahau, thirteenth day of the month Pax. The year might equally well be written Maya Era (ME) 3730. Glyphs for each of these periods were quickly identified, although determination of the Maya names of the various periods was much slower and still presents many difficulties. It was also discovered that there was the same type of alternation between relatively simple symbolic forms and quite complex forms representing animals or deities which is found in the numerals. There are certain other eras from which the Mayas occasionally calculated dates, sometimes apparently over millions of years. However, 4 Ahau 8 Cumku may justifiably be called "the ME."

It will be seen that the Maya Era gives us a functioning and unbroken system of days, corresponding closely to the Julian Day number used by our astronomers. The latter counts a continuous series of days from the date 1 January −4712 (of the astronomers, who insert a year 0; 4713 B.C. of historians). If one knew the true date in time of 13.0.0.0.0 4 Ahau 8 Cumku as "zero date," the Julian Day number of that date would give a constant. This constant, added to any Mayan day number, would immediately convert it to the Julian Day number. Hence one of the principal chronological tasks facing Mayanists has been the correct establishment of this constant. This has been variously referred to as the "Ahau equation" or the "correlation constant." The structure of the 52-year cycle continued in most of Mesoamerica until the arrival of the Spaniards, and parts of it continue to the present day. A count of *katuns*

(periods of twenty 360-day years) named for their ending days and known from the colonial period was usually thought to represent an unbroken series of katuns from the old zero date which had been forgotten. If the 52-year cycle of colonial and modern times accurately represents the old Classic Maya cycle chronologically, with no break or shift, then possible correlations must differ from each other by 52 years. If the katun count represents the old katun endings, then possible correlations must differ from each other by 5 × 52 years, i.e., 260 years (of 365 days). This interval was widely accepted as the true one, at which possible correlations must repeat. Two correlations based on this assumption have been widely accepted. The first is that of Herbert J. Spinden (1924, constant 489,384). The second is that of Thompson (in most detail, 1935, constant 584,285; revised, 1950, to 584,283). Any Maya date converted by Spinden's correlation falls 260 years earlier in our calendar than the same date converted by Thompson's correlation. It should be emphasized that the correlation of the 52-year cycle with our own calendar is within one day of being identical in these two correlations. Thus, both would make 7 Ahau 13 Ch'en fall on 5 March (or 4 or 6 March, according to Thompson's one-day revisions in opposite directions), 1339 A.D., but they would put this at different points in the Maya long count.

In spite of occasional dissidents who wished to put the dates either 260 years earlier still or, more frequently, 260 years later, these two correlations have enjoyed continuing support from Mayanists, with the majority favoring Thompson. However, there are certain major discrepancies between either of these two correlations (and, indeed, any correlation based on the sixteenth-century and modern data) and what seems to be the most obvious interpretation of the astronomical data in the codices and on the monuments. This has led to some rather strained interpretations by defenders of Spinden or Thompson and also to correlations which attempt to solve the problem entirely by astronomical data. Table 4 lists all possible correlations at 52-year intervals to a limit which would put the end of the Maya Classic Period at the time of the Spanish Conquest at one end (which we know is ridiculously late) and to one which would put the end of Maya Classic in the early centuries A.D., which seems far too early by most of our general archaeological criteria. Table 5 lists various correlations which have been suggested on astronomical or other grounds but do not agree with the colonial data. Unlike Table 4, it does not include all possibilities based on the same assumptions. Plate 2 shows

Table 4
Correlations Based on Criteria 1, 2, and 3

   356,523
+ 375,503
 *394,483 (modified Bowditch)
   413,463
   432,443
   451,423
   470,403
 *489,383 (489,384, Spinden)
   508,363
   527,343
   546,323
   565,303
+ *584,283 (Thompson, originally 584,285) (Goodman, 584,280; Martinez, 584,281
                                      both outside criterion 2)
   603,263
   622,243
   641,223
+ 660,203
 *679,183 (Vaillant, first preference, formerly preferred by Wauchope)
   698,163 (698,164, Dittrich — only one in this table which passes criterion 8, close
          on criterion 6)
   717,143
+ 736,123 (only one in this table which clearly passes criterion 6)
   755,103
 *774,083 (Vaillant, second preference)
   793,063
   812,043
   831,023 (impossibly late)

Note. Correlations which also pass criterion 4 are marked *;
those which pass criterion 5 are marked +.

Table 5
Variously Based Correlations Which Reject Criterion
2 or 3

438,906	(Willson, based on criteria 6, 8, and 11)
449,817 (?)	(Bunge, 1940, nowhere gives a correlation constant nor a complete double date in Mayan and Christian calendars, but from the data he gives, I believe this is his constant)
+482,699	(Smiley, preferred correlation)
+*489,138	(Makemson, 246 days off Spinden)
497,879/?8	(Dinsmoor)
500,210	(Smiley, second possibility)
588,466	(Mukerji, criterion 10)
626,927	(Kreichgauer)
679,108	(Escalona Ramos—believes that pre-Columbian calendar had a true leap-year, completely unrecorded and uncounted)
774,078	(Weitzel)

A great many other correlations might be derived from combining the
various criteria in different ways.

Note. Correlations which pass criterion 4 are marked *; those
which pass criterion 5 are marked +.

the nature of the archaeological and historical sequences to which the various correlations must be fitted.

The basic criteria for the correlations shown in Tables 4 and 5 are as follows:

1. The gross archaeological and historical evidence sets rough limits. An impossible late date is set by 831,023, which puts the contemporary Maya date 10.2.8.9.4 12 Kan 2 Pop on the lintel of the Temple of the Initial Series in 1553, after the Spanish Conquest. There is no correspondingly impossible early date, but 356,523 is about as far removed from currently preferred dates in the opposite direction. The majority of carbon-14 dates would support a correlation between 470,000 and 605,000. The carefully chosen material from Tikal supports a correlation near 580,000 (Thompson, Mukerji, etc.), but seemingly reliable material from Chichen Itza would support a correlation near 490,000 (Spinden, Makemson, etc.). If one accepts the view that the Plumbate Period ended by about 1200 A.D. and that it began after 10.4.0.0.0 of the Maya long count (as in Plate 2), one can reject all numbers greater than about 680,000.

2. Documentary sources make 12 Kan 1 Pop (shifted by one day from Classic 12 Kan 2 Pop) fall on 15 July 1553, plus or minus one day. Only Maud Worcester Makemson has attempted, unconvincingly, to deny this criterion.

3. It is assumed, for purposes of the correlations in Table 4, that there has been no calendrical shift of more than one day since the Classic Period. Correlations in Table 5 must assume the falsity of either criterion 2 or criterion 3.

4. Documentary sources put the conquest by the Spaniards in a katun 13 Ahau. It has been widely accepted, on quite inadequate grounds, that this is a katun-ending of the old long count. Those correlations which fit it are marked *.

5. The *Dresden* codex and the inscriptions alike suggest that 9.16.4.10.8 was at or near new moon. All correlations in Table 4 which fit this criterion are marked +. Spinden, of necessity, rejected this criterion in favor of a standardized lunar calendar, counting from full moon and differing widely from observations.

6. The *Dresden* codex suggests that 9.16.4.10.8 is the base of an eclipse table and that node passage is within one day of this date. Spinden and Thompson, accepting the eclipse function of the table, arbitrarily remove it from its base to the extent necessary to fit their respective correlations. Charles H. Smiley regards it as a lunar table without eclipse functions. The only correlation in Table 4 which passes this criterion is 736,123 or, better, 736,124. The next closest to passing this criterion is 698,164.

7. Makemson regards 9.16.4.10.8, 9.16.4.11.3, and 9.16.4.11.18 as two partial solar eclipses with a lunar eclipse between them. In this case, node passage would have to coincide closely with 9.16.4.11.3 rather than with 9.16.4.10.8. She uses these dates to argue that the apparent base of the eclipse table is not the real base, denying criterion 6. Nothing in the text justifies regarding these dates as a series of eclipses.

8. The *Dresden* codex suggests that 9.9.9.16.0 was a heliacal rising of Venus. A. Dittrich (1936) found that the only heliacal rising between 4712 B.C. and 1553 A.D. which fitted this and criteria 2 and 3 gave the constant 698,164. Various "late placements" of the table, shifting it from its apparent base, allow some leeway. The 584,283 correlation is off from the criterion by twenty days, which can be compensated in this way.

9. Smiley has good evidence, largely unpublished, that 9.16.4.10.8 was one of the stations of the solar year. This criterion does not coincide with any correlation in Table 4. It may be made to coincide with criterion 5 and either criterion 6 or criterion 7, but not both.

10. Dhirendra Nath Mukerji (1936) has suggested that the Maya date 4 Ahau 8 Cumku is an attempt to calculate the Hindu Kaliyuga Era and that it coincides with later Hindu attempts to do this without variation. This gives the constant 588,466, off forty-seven days from criterion 8.

11. R. W. Willson (1924) has suggested that 9.19.7.15.8 3 Lamat 6 Zotz indicates some noteworthy configuration of Mars, probably a stationary point. In terms of his analysis, it should have been the second stationary, 352 days before conjunction, but he is not this specific, and, indeed, he suggests it should be the first stationary, about 39 days before opposition. The criterion is not generally accepted, since 780, a close approximation to Mars's period, is exactly three periods of 260 days, and it was felt that this might be a simple multiplication table.

Since Spinden is the only scholar who has presented any substantial number of decipherments of glyphs which are directly dependent on his correlation, the problem is rather irrelevant in terms of the main purposes of this book, and this very condensed discussion must suffice. (See discussions of the Makemson, Weitzel, and Escalona Ramos correlations in Thompson 1950, pp. 306–310; of Vaillant, Bowditch, Goodman, Martinez, Spinden, and others in Thompson 1935; of many correlations, including the Kreichgauer correlation, in Andrews 1940; of Dinsmoor, Smiley, Makemson, and others in Satterthwaite and Ralph 1960; of the Wauchope correlation in Wauchope 1947; of the Vollemaere correlation in Vollemaere 1973; of the Bunge correlation in Bunge 1940. Fuller details and further references may be found in the cited studies.)

The phonetic value of the glyph for 'day' is known to be *kin* 'day, sun', first established by Brasseur de Bourbourg, the discoverer of the Landa manuscript. This value was substantiated not only by the glyph's numerical use in the codices, but also by its use in Landa's glyph for the month Yaxkin, and good evidence indicated that the glygers for 'east', *lakin,* and 'west', *chikin,* both contained this grapheme.

The month of twenty days, known to the Yucatec Maya and modern students as the *uinal,* is designated by the same glyph as the day called Chuen in Yucatec and Batz in other Maya languages. The true phonetic rendering is still unknown, or at least has not been established to the satisfaction of most scholars studying the glyphs.

The period of 360 days was known in Yucatec by two terms, *tun* and *haab,* the latter being widely spread in the various Maya languages as a term for 'year'. The first glyph for the 360-day period (T548) was read as *tun* by Seler and may represent a drum.

The alternate term for 'year', *haab,* has a meaning apparently derived from words for rain (Kekchi *hab* 'rain', Cakchiquel *hab* 'shower', Thompson 1950, p. 48; Huaxtec *āb* 'rain'). It was long known that in parts of the inscriptions other than the Initial Series an alternate glyph for 'year' (T528) was employed and that it was virtually or entirely identical with the glyph for the day called in Yucatec Cauac, corresponding to Aztec Quiauitl 'rain' and probably cognate with terms in other Mayan languages meaning 'storm' or 'rain'. It thus appears extremely likely that this glyph is to be read *haab,* as suggested by Thompson (1950, p. 49).

The *Dresden* distinguishes two glyphs, both used for the day Cauac but otherwise separate. I believe these stand for *haab* and for *cu,* which otherwise seems to be a third reading for T528 in the inscriptions.

The glyger for the period of twenty years of 360 days each incorporates the tun sign, and the name for this period in Yucatec was *katun;* since *kal* is 'twenty', it has often been supposed that *katun* was some sort of abbreviation of *kaltun,* but evidence for processes of this sort in Maya is rare, and the glyph for 'twenty' is well known and corresponds in no particular with this glyph (see Fig. 1). The so-called comb elements correspond to a form called *ca* by

Landa, and it was long suggested (first by Seler, apparently) that the unglottalized *ca* was written for the glottalized *ka.* There are, however, strong indications that this distinction between *ca* and *ka* was rigorously observed by the Maya, and at the moment there is little other evidence indicating how this glyph is to be read, although for convenience, normal usage will be followed in calling it the katun glyph. Barthel (1966*b*, p. 130) has suggested that it sometimes is used for 'war', which is also *katun* and would support the normal reading.

The glyger for the 400-year period consists of a doubled form of T528, sometimes with an affix or with a tun glyph below it. Since 'four hundred' in Maya is *bak,* this is usually referred to as the *baktun* glyph, but there is no evidence that this is the correct Maya term. Goodman called it the 'cycle' glyph, and I believe it corresponds to Yucatec *cuc* 'cycle'. Although these glyphs for the day, uinal, year, katun, and cycle were early recognized, inscriptions referring to higher periods are much rarer, and such forms were not as quickly recognized. Thompson (1950, Fig. 26) gives the now well-established glyph for 8,000 years in seven examples (one an error); he also gives six examples of the glyph for 160,000 years and one example of a probable glyph for 3,200,000 years, indicating the distinguishing characteristics of each. The basis of these glyphs is the 'cycle' glyph with differing affixes. These longer periods are called respectively *pictun, calabtun,* and *kinchiltun* in the writings of Mayanists, but these are terms composed by modern scholars, and the complete absence of the tun sign in these glyphs makes it seem highly unlikely that they correspond to the ancient names. In my opinion, pseudo-Maya readings are to be avoided wherever possible, but I have included these terms, as they are established in the literature. All these period glyphs are given in Figure 6.

The great majority of Maya monuments open with what has been called the Introducing Glyph (IG) or Initial Series Introducing Glyph (ISIG), which is followed by the date in the Maya Era, a regular series of glyphs including those identified above, usually starting with the 'cycle' glyph. This date, including both the era and the resulting day, is called by Mayan scholars the Initial Series (IS). The Initial Series is normally followed by another group of glyphs, which are generally constant in varying degree and have been called the Supplementary Series. Letters were given to the glyph blocks, according to their position in the sequence, by Morley (1916). Not all of these groups are present in all of the inscriptions, but, when they are, immediately following the day date of the IS come Glyph G and Glyph F. It has been determined by

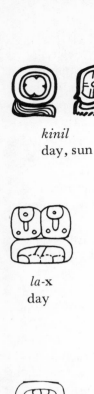  

kinil
day, sun   sun at horizon (*hatzcab*?)   day   day   day   day

la-x
day   *la*-x   *la*-x   *bix*?
day in
counts of
5 or 7   head
allograph
of *bix*?   *kin*
head
allograph

uinal
(20-day
period)   uinal
allograph   tun
(360-day
period,
year)   tun
head
allograph   katun
(20 tuns)   katun head
allographs

20 katuns
so-called
baktun,
cuc
(400 tuns)   baktun
head
allograph   20 baktuns
so-called
pictun
(8,000 tuns)   pictun
head
allograph   20 pictuns
so-called
calabtun
(160,000 tuns)   20 calabtuns
so-called
kinchiltun
(3,200,000 tuns)

half of a period
shell
prefixed   shell
infixed
—note
ma
prefix   one
shell period   lacking,
to go   *haab*
year, period
water, rain
—synonym
of *tun*

Figure 6. Period glyphs.

Thompson (1929) that these indicate which deity in a sequence of nine gods was ruling at the given date, and these glyph groups are discussed more fully in connection with the deities (Chapter 4). Such terms as "Glyph G" are retained because they are well established in the literature, but the student should realize that there is no single glyph corresponding to Glyph G, nor even a single glyger, but instead a series of nine glygers which can occupy the same position in this series. Glyph F, on the other hand, consists of a small group of variants, which all seem to indicate the same word or short phrase.

The remainder of the Supplementary Series is now generally set apart as the Lunar Series, because it is known that it has to do with data on the moon. This was early recognized by Morley and has been adequately demonstrated and generally accepted by all subsequent students. The sequence of glyphs is as follows: E, D, C, X, B, A. Two additional glyphs, Y and Z, are occasionally inserted at some points in this sequence. D normally has a numerical coefficient, and occasionally glyphs intervene between D and its coefficient, apparently indicating a certain number of nights or days, a reading often assured in other contexts. One of the most surprising things about the Lunar Series is that the factor which brought about its recognition almost certainly involves a misinterpretation of the evidence. Both Glyph E and Glyph A represent a crescent moon, and, with the prevailing ideographic interpretation, it seemed logical to assume that this indicated a lunar count. However, in an editorial note in *Maya Research* 3, no. 2:212, Beyer points out that, "Paradoxically, we might say: Glyph E represents the moon, but has nothing to do with it. The moon-sign of Glyph E undoubtedly is used as nothing but a numeral. It is, in this series, as it is in the tzolkin divisions of the codices, the symbol for 20." Hence, when Glyph E is found, it is simply part of the coefficient of Glyph D. Long series of computations have shown that Glyph D, with its coefficient (including Glyph E as part of the coefficient if the number is twenty or above), indicates the age of the current moon. Glyph A consists of the same glyph as Glyph E, i.e., the 'twenty' glyph, and always has a number postfixed, either 'nine' or 'ten'. This indicates that the lunar month under consideration is of either twenty-nine or thirty days, a meaning which was recognized by Willson in 1915, Morley subsequently showing that the month in question was the month in which the accompanying IS date fell (Morley 1920, pp. 554–555).

Glyph D consists of approximately seven "variants" (actually completely different glyphs) (Fig. 7).

Teeple (1930, p. 48) showed that the accompanying coefficients gave the current age of the moon. He showed a remarkable and effective congruence with calculated average lunar ages, but with disturbing discrepancies of greater variation than would be expected. Thompson (1937, pp. 67–68) believed that the count gave the current age in a manner comparable to our counting from new moon. Subsequently, he argued (1950, pp. 237–239) that the different variants all refer in different ways to the mythical "death" of the moon at conjunction. Because of the necessity to fit this data to his own correlation, Spinden (1928d, pp. 42–43) argued that the count was from full moon, and that it included a cumulative error which was not corrected.

Recent evidence suggests that the Mayas counted from at least two slightly different bases, indicated by different glyphs. One of these is a hand glyph which seems to correspond, at least sometimes, to the hand which may be read *lah* 'to complete, to end'; in this case, we may suppose the count is from the first night of lunar invisibility or, just possibly, from the last night of visibility. On the other hand, Proskouriakoff has shown that another of the Glyph D variants, the upended frog head (T740) is associated with "initial dates" (see Chapter 11, where these are identified as birthdays), and Barthel has pointed out that Pokomchi *pok'* is 'be born' and 'frog'. Since Thompson (1937b, pp. 67–68) points out that both Kekchi and Pokomchi refer to the (visible?) new moon as 'the moon is born', it seems clear that T740 is to be read *pok'* and represents a count from visible new moon. Thompson (1950, pp. 47–48) had earlier suggested a connection with the possibly related root *po,* referring both to frogs and the moon; although this seemed plausible at the time, Barthel's interpretation is preferable. This evidence clearly opposes Spinden's view. The variation in base will probably adequately account for the previous disturbing discrepancies.

Judging by its "lunar postfix," Glyph C is a verb with a deity name as the so-called variable element. Several different hand glyphs may be involved. One of them is clearly *lah* 'end'. No one has yet adequately defined the pattern of occurrence of the deity names. The identities of these deities are discussed in Chapter 4, where their glyphs are given.

Glyph X is actually a series of glyph groups of obviously different meanings. Certain typical forms recur (Fig. 8), but, again, the pattern of their recurrence has not been accurately determined. There is a possibility that they represent deity names.

Glyph B shows an animal (agouti?), often with a "long-bone" suffix, under a bent glyph which has

1.    So-called lunar postfix read by Thompson *u*. Thompson reads 'completion of the moon'.

6a.   Thompson points out that *po* may be either 'moon' or 'frog'. Believes should mean 'disappearance of moon'.

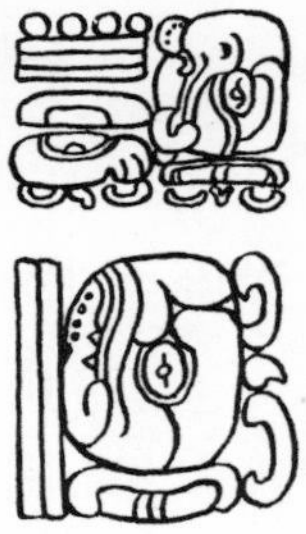

6b.

2.   Read by Thompson simply 'completion'.

3.  Beyer identifies infix as an 'eye'—not the circle of the 'twenty' glyph. Beyer reads 'shining moon'; Thompson, doubtfully, 'death of moon'.

4.   Prefix identified by Beyer as 'jade'. Thompson agrees, but says it symbolizes water. Beyer reads 'shining moon'. Thompson reads 'dead moon (?) in the heaven of the rain gods'.

7.  Skull in moon read by Thompson 'death of moon' and whole combination read as 'completion of death of moon'.

5.  Thompson follows Beyer in regarding main glyph as 'Death'. Thompson reads whole group as 'The Dead One in the Land of the Rain Gods'.

8.  Thompson suggests 'old moon's light lost to view at disappearance or conjunction'.

Figure 7. Glyph D of the Lunar Series, with some suggested interpretations. Thompson believes that all of these glyphs indicate disappearance or conjunction of the moon, to which the preceding coefficient is added to indicate the actual lunar age, and read '*n* days after completion of moon'. The glyph groups shown above certainly indicate the age of the moon, but all these readings seem very doubtful.

X1
cf. glyphs
for god
of Pax
and G7

X1
alternate

X2
cf. G1
May have
a number
prefixed.

X3

X3
alternate?

X4

X4a

X5
Essential feature
is head of rain
god with varying
affixes, here
(sky, earth) *ca*
and an affix.

X6a
kan (yellow)
with prefix

Figure 8. Glyph X of the Lunar Series.

been called the "elbow" glyph. Teeple (1930, pp. 62–63) has suggested that the "elbow" may represent a house and that the glyph indicates that "this moon ends its residence in its last house in either 29 days or 30 days, whichever is shown by Glyph A." This is interpreted more astronomically (ibid., p. 115) as meaning disappearance of the moon at conjunction. I have seen no justification for regarding the "elbow" as a house and no indication that the animal stands for the moon. Moreover, since the glyph is a standard part of *all* Lunar Series, it is certainly not associated by context with conjunction. The "elbow" in double form surrounds a *kin* glyph on Santa Elena Poco Uinic Stela 3; and, by analogy, Teeple (1930) suggested that "this would mean disappearance of the sun which could scarcely be anything but solar eclipse." The date is 9.17.19.13.16 5 Cib 14 Ch'en, which was a new-moon date (hence a possible solar eclipse). In the 584,286 variant of the Thompson correlation this was a total eclipse, visible in Chiapas shortly after noon. Whatever the meaning of Glyph B, it is certainly found in the *Dresden* eclipse table and elsewhere in that codex in apparently astronomical contexts. Hence the plausibility of the suggested meaning as 'solar eclipse' is not necessarily to be judged entirely by what seems to me the faulty concept of "the moon in her house." Ultimately, this interpretation will depend in large measure on what correlation finally proves acceptable.

One of the most interesting early identifications was Förstemann's decipherment of the glyger for the planet Venus (Fig. 9). On pages 46–50 of the *Dresden* he noted the repetition, five times, of the numbers 236, 90, 250, and 8, totalling 584 days. An accompanying table in the codex shows the dates of these critical points of the Venus cycle, starting from a base 1 Ahau 18 Kayab and re-entering at 1 Ahau 18 Kayab after 104 years, or sixty-five revolutions of Venus, with a small variation. Förstemann recognized 584 days as a remarkably close approximation to a Venus year, with inferior conjunction calculated as 8 days, and identified a glyger which recurred in all the columns associated with this calculation as the name glyph for Venus. In all these calculations, this glyph has the prefix which has been identified as *chac* 'red, great', and a Yucatec name for Venus is *Chac Ek* 'Great Star'. Thompson (1950, p. 218) shows that Great Star is a common Maya designation of Venus in several different languages, although the particular words meaning 'great' are different, as are the particular words meaning 'star'. It would seem fairly obvious that, if the glyger for Venus consisted of the 'great' glyph and another glyph, and the name for Venus is Great Star, then the second glyph should mean sim-

ply 'star', probably Yucatec *ek* 'star' or *kanal* 'star'. Strangely enough, however, the second glyph, has, instead, been taken to mean 'Venus', wherever it occurs. It is possible that Venus was considered "the star" par excellence (if no prefixes are present). Thompson (1950, p. 229) notes that "Venus glyphs in the inscriptions are not reviewed in detail because there is full evidence that no pattern of significance will emerge whatever correlation is used." This seems easily understandable, if glyphs which do not refer to Venus at all, but rather to other planets or constellations, have been included in the calculations.

It is curious that the 'Great Star' combination is so rare in the inscriptions. At Ca3–Cb4 of the north panel of the east door of Temple 11 at Copan, the combination occurs as part of a passage which is very similar to the Venus passages of the *Dresden.* The opening verb seems to be the same, a hand with a shell above it. In the codices this is normally followed by a direction glyph and then by a deity name. The second and third groups of this passage at Copan may well be the name of a goddess, as the third group seems to be a female head.

Thompson (1950, pp. 227–228) has drawn attention to an inscription from a block reused in the Hieroglyphic Stairway of Naranjo, with a count from 9.7.14.10.8 3 Lamat 16 Uo forward 2.5.7.12 to 9.10.0.0.0 1 Ahau 8 Kayab. The interval is 16,352 days, which is twenty-eight synodical revolutions of Venus and is only a day and a half less than forty-one synodical revolutions of Jupiter. It involves both the day 3 Lamat, which is the basis of an important table in the *Dresden* codex, and the day 1 Ahau, believed to be particularly associated with Venus. Another count in the Hieroglyphic Stairway is from 9.9.18.16.3 7 Akbal 16 Muan forward 1.1.17 to 9.10.0.0.0 1 Ahau 8 Kayab. The interval of 397 days is slightly less than 2 days short of a synodical revolution of Jupiter. Both inscriptions contain the so-called 'Venus' glyph (here regarded as simply a 'star' glyph), and it is possible that one of the glygers which contain the 'star' glyph refers to Jupiter. Since they are not the same, it is unlikely that both of them do.

The inscription of Stela 3 at Caracol throws particular light on this Naranjo inscription and is of additional interest because of the repeated references to another star or planet. In this inscription at Caracol, the date 9.9.18.16.13 7 Akbal 16 Muan recurs, as at Naranjo, with a similar count forward to 9.10.0.0.0 1 Ahau 8 Kayab. In the Caracol case, the "crossbands" and "smoke" glyphs found with the Naranjo inscription recur, but the glyph also includes a shell-like element. This glyph recurs with the 'star' glyph at Palenque on the Middle Tablet of the Tem-

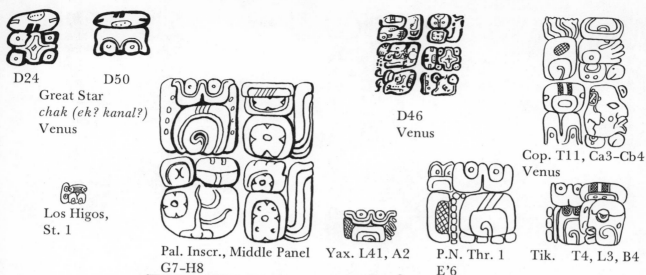

D24   D50
Great Star
chak (ek? kanal?)
Venus

D46
Venus

Cop. T11, Ca3–Cb4
Venus

Los Higos,
St. 1

Pal. Inscr., Middle Panel
G7–H8

Yax. L41, A2

P.N. Thr. 1
E'6

Tik.   T4, L3, B4

?

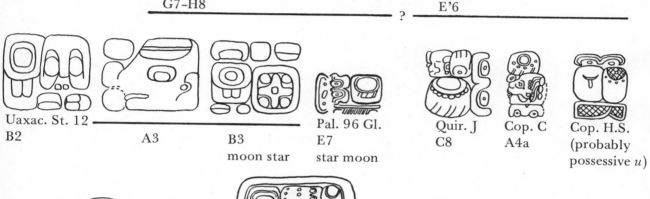

Uaxac. St. 12
B2

A3

B3
moon star

Pal. 96 Gl.
E7
star moon

Quir. J
C8

Cop. C
A4a

Cop. H.S.
(probably
possessive *u*)

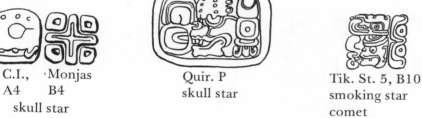

C.I.,   Monjas
A4   B4
   skull star

Quir. P
skull star

Tik. St. 5, B10
smoking star
comet

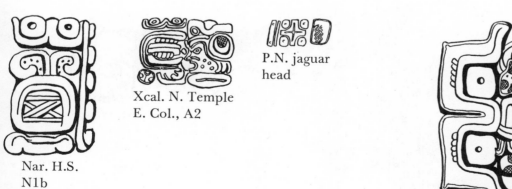

P.N. jaguar
head

Xcal. N. Temple
E. Col., A2

Nar. H.S.
N1b
Jupiter?

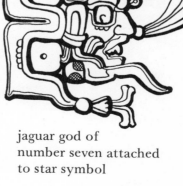

jaguar god of
number seven attached
to star symbol

Figure 9. Star glyphs.

P4
—sun, —moon,
falling star

D58b
falling star
associated with
sun and moon glyphs

D57b

M59c

D68a

Pal. Cross,   reversal,
D15   sky-binding

Pal. Inscr. Middle
Panel, G9–H9

Figure 10. Astronomical passages.

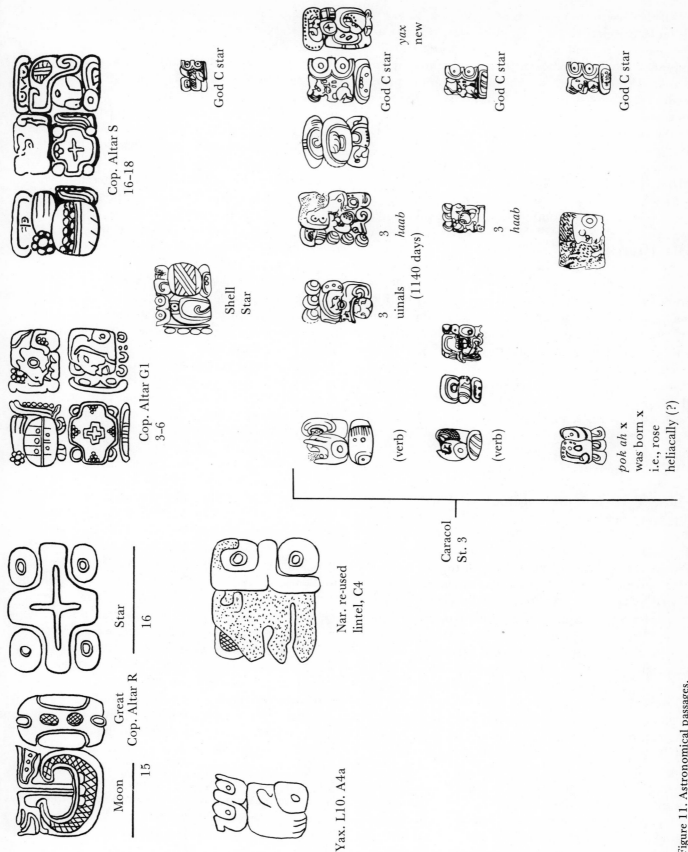

Moon ———— Star
15   16

Great
Cop. Altar R

Nar. re-used
lintel, C4

Yax. L10. A4a

Cop. Altar S
16–18

God C star

Cop. Altar G1
3–6

Shell
Star

God C star   *yax*
              new

3   *haab*
uinals
(1140 days)

3   *haab*

God C star

God C star

(verb)

Caracol
St. 3

(verb)

pok ah x
was born x
i.e., rose
heliacally (?)

Figure 11. Astronomical passages.

ple of the Inscriptions (passage G7–H9), at Tikal (Temple 4, Lintel [L] 3, B4), at Piedras Negras (Throne 1, E'6), and at Yaxchilan (on L41). I suspect that Shell Star is a particular planetary name but cannot yet demonstrate this. The other compound, which recurs four times in the inscription, is 'star' preceded by a deity head with a deformed mouth and Chicchan (snake) markings on the face. (This is called "God C Star" in Figure 11.)

A very interesting occurrence of a 'star' glyph is at B10 of Stela 5, Tikal. This is preceded by a human head with a tubular pipe in its mouth and smoke coming from it. The combination could easily be read 'smoking star' (Yucatec [Yuc.] *budz ek*), a term for 'comet' (Brinton 1895, p. 35).

There is, of course, the possibility that some inscriptions which contain the 'star' glyph nonetheless do not refer in any way to astronomical events. Some deity names, such as Ah Chicum Ek (Barrera Vásquez and Rendón 1948, p. 82), contain the word 'star', and, even if they were originally star deities, they might be referred to in a nonastronomical context. Place names and personal names might also include the word 'star'. Stela 18 from Etzna has a 'star' glyph associated with a female head and a glyph with typical Emblem Glyph prefixes, suggesting that 'star' is, here, part of a woman's name.

Some other passages with 'star/Venus' glyphs seem worthy of brief comment (see Fig. 10). On D58b, a human figure is shown hanging, head down, from two glyphs of 'sun' and 'moon', each in large double frames, one of which is darkened. The head of the falling figure is a 'star' glyph. This being is clearly represented by the opening glyph of the passage above, which shows a figure, head downward, followed by the 'star' glyph. The glyph recurs on page 4 of the *Paris* in an apparently similar context. Thompson (1950, p. 233) has suggested that this refers to the Maya equivalent of the Aztec Tzitzimime, monsters who are said to have plunged to earth during eclipses. This seems plausible but far from certain. The glyph has also been suspected of referring to the revolutions of Venus or Mercury, and the 702-day interval from the preceding picture, which also shows the same glyph, suggests the possibility of connections with Mars.

Considering some of the statements which have been made about Maya astronomy, it is surprising how little solid information is available. The Venus table of *Dresden* has provided the glyger for 'Venus' and, by my reinterpretation, the glyph for 'star'. It has likewise provided the structure of a conventionalized pattern of the movements of Venus. The *Dresden* also contains a similar lunar-solar table,

which apparently deals with eclipses. The table consists of sixty-nine groups of either 5 or 6 lunations in a group, totaling 405 lunations and reaching a total of 11,958 days (probably meant to be a partly recurring cycle, starting from a day 12 Lamat, and reaching a day 12 Lamat again after 11,960 days). Directly preceding the table proper occurs the date 9.16.4.10.8 12 Lamat (1 Muan), and all early investigators assumed that this was the base of the table. However, Teeple (1930, p. 98) argued that the changes in the astronomical phenomena dealt with in the lunar table and in the Venus table were such that both tables must be early (in this case, at the 9.16.4.10.8 date) or that both tables must be late. He presented some evidence that the Venus table was late (at 10.10.11.12.0 1 Ahau 18 Kayab rather than at 9.9.9.16.0 1 Ahau 18 Kayab, a date given in the codex). This argument has been widely accepted, as it solves the difficulty that at 9.9.9.16.0 1 Ahau 18 Kayab, there is no heliacal rising of Venus in the Thompson correlation. Teeple (1930) also showed that the possible eclipse dates clustered rather sharply in the tzolkin in a way that permitted calculation of the base date at which the sun's path crossed the moon's path (draconic node passage, which defines the dates on which eclipses may fall and occurs slightly over twice a year). This showed that 12 Lamat, the base date of the table, was one day after node passage. The date 9.16.4.10.8 12 Lamat 1 Muan is associated with three others—one being, unfortunately, structurally impossible as it stands. The remaining two are 9.16.4.11.3 1 Akbal 16 Muan and 9.16.4.11.18 3 Etz'nab 11 Pax, i.e., respectively fifteen and thirty days later than the 12 Lamat date. Makemson (1943, p. 189) argued that they must be either a pair of solar eclipses with a lunar eclipse between or a pair of lunar eclipses with a solar eclipse between. The evidence of any eclipse function is based solely on the eclipse-table context and on the dates, and I would not think that two dates each fifteen days apart, with no associated glyphs, would provide any evidence for their meaning. It is only the context of the eclipse table which gives the suggestion any plausibility whatsoever. It may be pointed out that the inscriptions show that 9.16.5.0.0, some 152 days later, had a recorded age of 4 days. This would put 9.16.4.10.8 at new moon. Since solar eclipses must occur at new moon, within about eighteen days of node passage, and lunar eclipses at full moon, *if* Makemson's interpretation were correct, this would have to be a pair of solar eclipses with a lunar eclipse between (as she notes, 1943, p. 193). Teeple has shown that the 12 Lamat which is the base of the table must be at or very near node passage. He, however, doubts that this 12 Lamat is the 9.16.4.10.8 12 Lamat 1 Muan which appears directly prior to the table with nothing between. Makemson's interpretation would make 9.16.4.10.8 about fifteen days before node passage and hence certainly not the table base. In spite of Teeple and Makemson, I prefer to think that the table base is 9.16.4.10.8, which is recorded at the point where the table base should be, and hence is a new moon at node passage and a possible solar eclipse. It should be pointed out that this is contrary to both the Spinden and the Thompson correlations.

The eclipse table is interrupted by ten pictures. The first occurs 502 days after 12 Lamat, and the succeeding intervals are 1,742 days, 1,034 days, 1,211 days, 1,742 days, 1,034 days, 1,210 days, 1,565 days, 1,211 days, and at the end of the table, 708 days. According to Willson (1924, p. 10), central eclipses do repeat somewhere on the earth after 1,033, 1,211, 1,388, and 1,565 days and may repeat after 1,742 days. He also says that at least one eclipse must repeat somewhere on earth every 177 days (1924, p. 11). His study indicates that the picture intervals should be interpreted as referring to eclipses potentially visible in the local area, whereas the other intervals simply refer to possible eclipses somewhere. Unfortunately, there is no series of nine or ten eclipses which were visible in Yucatán and which coincide with the recorded intervals. Hence, this is a prediction table rather than a record of past events.

With glyphs associated with each picture and with each of the subsidiary sixty-nine potential eclipses, one would think that it ought to be possible at least to recognize glyphs for eclipses. However, there is no glyph or glyger which repeats with each of the sixty-nine groups, nor is there even any single glyph which recurs with every one of the pictures. Attempts, however, have not been wanting. Teeple's suggested glyph for 'solar eclipse' has already been mentioned. Another glyph (T326) consists of two large frames, one black and one white, with a 'sun' glyph or 'moon' glyph in the interior (Fig. 12). This glyph recurs with seven of the ten pictures of the eclipse table (if the two glyph blocks associated with the terminal date of the picture are included) and is shown as part of one of the remaining three pictures, although not in the text. It was early regarded as representing an eclipse (Willson 1924, p. 33), a view still shared by Makemson (1943, p. 191), who said, "There seems to be no good reason for rejecting the obvious interpretation of these as symbols of solar and lunar eclipses, which they clearly suggest." Thompson (1950, p. 272) has suggested a general meaning of 'sun darkened' and 'moon darkened', the context indicating whether the

darkening was due to an eclipse, to rainy weather, or to lightning storms. The frame occurs once (D45b) surrounding an *akbal* glyph, with a frame surrounding a *kin* glyph. Since *akbal* is normally 'night' and *kin* may be either 'sun' or 'day', one is first tempted to think of an alternation here of 'day' and 'night'; 'night darkened' could conceivably be a reference to a stormy night or a lunar eclipse. Since both sun and moon appear in the texts above a single picture, an explanation of both as eclipses implies that the text talks about more than the actual days associated with the picture, since solar eclipses are always at new moon and lunar eclipses always at full moon. In the *Paris* zodiac, to be considered shortly, this glyph, with the *kin* infix, is associated with a series of pictures which differ from each other by 168 days. The distance from eclipse intervals (177, 178, 148) seems too great to believe that this is in any sense an eclipse series.

Another glyph for which the meaning of 'eclipse' has been suggested (Spinden, 1930, p. 76) is a compound of *kin* ('sun, day') and *akbal* ('night, darkness') with a suffix. In the codices, the glyph normally occurs in divinatory almanacs, and Thompson (1950, p. 260) has again suggested a general meaning of 'sun darkness', perhaps extended to the darkening of the sky before a storm—in short, a general term for 'dark day' rather than a reference to 'day and night'. He goes on to suggest that, if this is a correct interpretation, divinatory passages also occur on the monuments, where the compound is "of common occurrence." This would seem to be the strongest argument against an otherwise reasonable suggestion, as it is quite likely that the "old farmer's almanac" would predict "dark days" but highly unlikely that a monument would be erected to say that they occurred or would occur.

Spinden (1930, p. 76) also interprets as 'eclipse' a glyger found in varying form with Eclipses 50 and 51 of the *Dresden* table. In terms of the arguments presented in the chapter on phoneticism, the first consists of *pa* and *lu* with *kin* infixed in *lu*, while the second shows *pa* infixed in *lu* with *kin* preceding. According to Thompson (1950, p. 236), a Yucatec term for 'new moon' is *pal u* (literally, 'child moon'). This might indicate that *pal u kin* or *kin pal u* could be read as 'sun (at) new moon', which would be appropriate for an eclipse. It should be pointed out that the glyph transcribed *lu* above is widely read as 'sacrifice'. It should also be pointed out that the glyphs associated with some of these tables seem to take on a rather inelegant aspect, in which grammatical niceties are not always observed.

Spinden (1930, p. 76) also believes that the knot

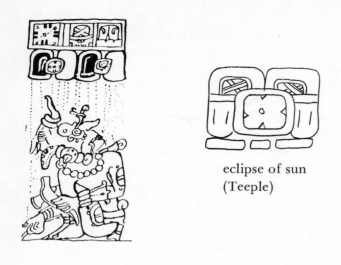

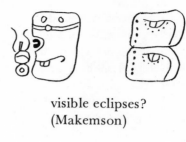

eclipse of sun
(Teeple)

visible eclipses?
(Makemson)

x–sun   x–moon   verb   God B   day–night   x-earth-sky

introduction
to Venus
table and
Serpent #5

x

*chibil< *chabil< *cab-il*
eclipse (Knorozov)

half-darkened
ahau

half-darkened
kin

reversal of
the seasons
(Spinden)

synonyms, formerly
suggested 'equinox'

Figure 12. Alleged glyphs for eclipse, reversal, equinox.

glyph (T684), which ought, more properly, to be classed with the affixes, means 'eclipse' when found with the moon glyph. It appears to have the reasonable meaning of 'capture' or 'hold prisoner' or something of the sort in the codices. Proskouriakoff has shown that in the inscriptions it is associated with inaugurations. We now know that it is to be read *hok.* T684 *may* be a slightly different version of the "wreath" associated with "ring numbers" in the *Dresden.* Brinton (1895, p. 36) points out that the phrase *hunbalan u,* literally, 'the moon roped', is said to mean 'lunar conjunction'. If so, the knot might conceivably have a meaning of 'conjunction', and the particular head would indicate what star, planet, or constellation is referred to. Since we do not know what factors governed inauguration, the two meanings need not be incompatible. The glyph occurs with the same head form infrequently, and mathematical analysis of the repetitions would probably be inadequate for proof or disproof of any possible astronomical meaning. It does not occur in the codices in a convincing astronomical context.

Knorozov, more linguistically oriented, noted that a variant of the *caban* glyph is found in the eclipse table. Since initial **k* sometimes becomes **ch,* he postulated that Yucatec *chibil* 'eclipse' derived by assimilation from earlier **chabil,* from **cab-il.* Presumably this would be literally 'earthing', which is particularly appropriate for lunar eclipses. This is, however, unlikely unless the word is a Cholan borrowing, since the root *cab* remains as such in Yucatec.

Makemson (1943, p. 202) thought that the Maya eclipse table might have involved predictions of which eclipses would be visible as well as which might occur. She suggested two glyphs which might stand for visible eclipses. The first (Fig. 12) was found with Eclipses 14, 15, 24, 30, and 44, all of which were visible in her placement of the table and in the Thompson correlation; it was also associated with numbers 17, 23, 29, and 40, which were not visible. Her second glyph was found above Eclipses 41 and 47, both visible, using the same criteria.

Förstemann (1906, pp. 212–215), writing prior to the discovery of the eclipse function of the table, drew attention to a pattern of repetition in the glyphs, involving intervals of seven. This is shown graphically in Figure 13. He maintained that the glyphs had no connection with the associated dates, but, instead, were placed at 13-day intervals, so that every seventh group would recur after 91 days, making up the stations of the 364-day year. It seems clear that the suggested pattern of recurrence at intervals of seven groups is valid, at least in part, but the inter-

pretation of the glyphs as unrelated to the accompanying dates is in such striking contrast to the association of glyphs and dates elsewhere in the codices that only overwhelming proof could support it. This is not forthcoming. Förstemann also draws attention to the glyger which occurs with Eclipses 16, 19 (picture), 32, and 64 (Fig. 13), which he thought might represent the sidereal lunar month of nearly 28 days, conventionalized as exactly 28 days. His basis for this opinion is not clear to me. Barthel (1968*b*) has been able to establish that the deity sequence of D4a–10a represents the gods of successive sidereal lunar months of 27 and 28 days.

Another table whose structure is partially understood is the so-called zodiac of the *Paris.* Here we find a table of dates, 28 days apart, starting, like the *Dresden* eclipse table, with a day 12 Lamat. This sequence of days re-enters after 1,820 days (5 × 13 × 28; 65 × 28; 5 × 364; 20 × 91). The days of the cycle are Lamat, Cib, Kan, Eb, and Ahau, which are also potential days of heliacal rising of Venus in the *Dresden* table. Above the table proper are seven pictures, one of which is almost completely effaced. These show animals hanging from a so-called planetary band, the body of the "two-headed dragon." Each of them is attached to one of the 'darkened-sun' glyphs. Between each picture and the next is the number 8.8 (i.e., 168 or 6 × 28). Beneath the table are an additional three animals, a skeleton, and a destroyed area, which has usually been regarded as having had two additional pictures. The interval here was probably normally 8.8 as well, although in at least two cases inspection alone would suggest merely 8, and there seem to be some other variations. It has been suggested (Spinden 1916) that these pictures represented a sort of Maya zodiac, consisting of thirteen constellations at 28-day intervals (13 × 28 = 364 = one line of the *Paris* table). Later, Spinden (1924, pp. 54–55) attempted a placement of these relative to our signs of the zodiac. The most clear-cut evidence for such an equation was the third sign, Turtle, since the Motul dictionary identified the Maya turtle constellation as coinciding, in part, with our Gemini. From this, Spinden went on to identify the other constellations in the same order as the pictures, which I shall try to show was an error. Seler (1902–1923, IV, 638–642) had already shown the virtual identity of part of this sequence with another, from the Casa de las Monjas at Chichen Itza. The two, slightly rearranged, are shown together (Fig. 14). In the latter, the animals are shown with the glyph then regarded as 'Venus', and Seler said this should represent a series of conjunctions of Venus with various constellations. Spinden

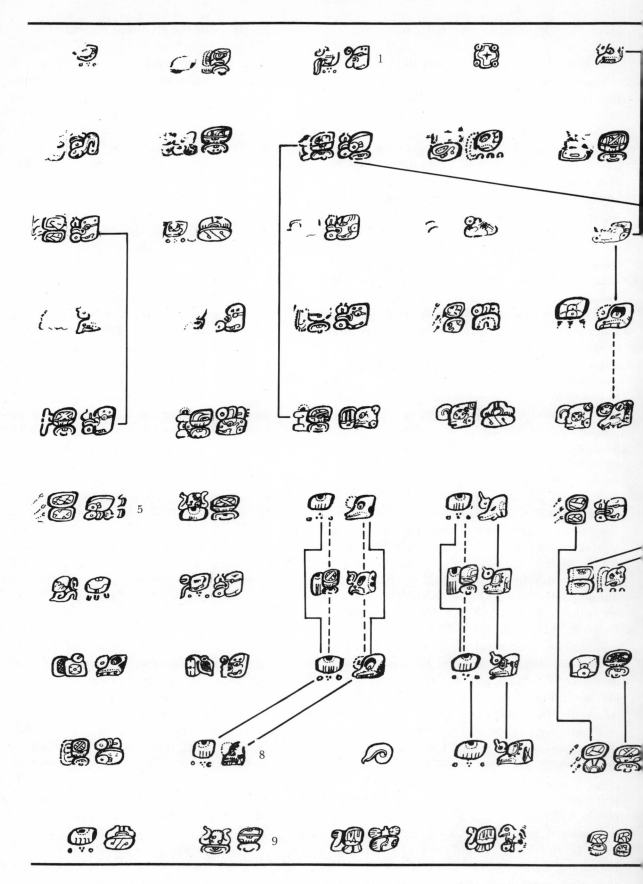

Figure 13. Pattern of repetition of *Dresden* eclipse-table glyphs by sevens. Solid lines indicate repetition. Broken lines indicate variation. Numbers refer to pictures in the eclipse table.

pointed out that Venus is always near the ecliptic, and hence that the constellations might correspond in function to our zodiacal signs, which are along the ecliptic. Since I regard the glyph as meaning simply 'star', the Monjas sequence could be interpreted as a series of constellation names, without necessary reference to Venus or to the ecliptic. However, the apparent lunar interval of 28 days does suggest that they are probably ecliptic constellations, since the moon also tends to remain near the ecliptic.

Certain comments need to be made on the comparisons between the *Paris* sequence and the Chichen Itza sequence, as well as on the identifications generally. Seler pointed out the sequential correspondence of Turtle, Scorpion, Bird, and Reptilian Monster in both series (Fig. 14, numbers 3–6). The scorpion appears in humanoid form, but with the unmistakable tail at Chichen Itza. The counterpart of the bird in the codex, regarded as an eagle by W. Stempell, looks more like a vulture at Chichen Itza. Seler, believing them to be identical, suggested that the local 'pheasant' or *cox* bird best reconciles the two depictions. The reptilian monster in the *Paris* has a rather crocodilian head, a serpentine body, and a split fishtail. The Monjas picture has a similar head but a serpentlike tail. If one assumes that the crossed elements (part of the 'sky' glyph) at Chichen Itza are to be ignored, the depiction preceding the turtle is a 'star' glyph without any other symbols. The depiction preceding the turtle in the *Paris* is a rattlesnake, with two heads facing in opposite directions, which is immediately reminiscent of the so-called Venus monster, and of the Feathered Serpent (always a rattlesnake), who was identified as god of Venus. This suggests that 'star' here is "the star" par excellence, Venus. To this extent, the older identification would hold. The bird, which precedes 'star Venus' at Chichen Itza, should correspond to the badly eroded first animal of the *Paris* sequence.

Thus far, the correspondence is fairly clear and not too difficult. The remainder presents a more complex problem and needs to be considered separately for the two series. Number 8 of the *Paris* sequence is a badly eroded animal, which Spinden thought might be a frog. Villacorta and Villacorta (1930, p. 221) identify the same animal as a deer, because of his front hooves. The hooves are not very clear, but they certainly look like hooves in the Villacortas' drawing. These might equally well serve as identification for a peccary, which is clearly present at the Monjas. The identity of the following animal of the *Paris* seems to be a bat. The 'night' glyph is in his eye, he is shown with claws, and he has wings. Seler (1902–1923, IV,

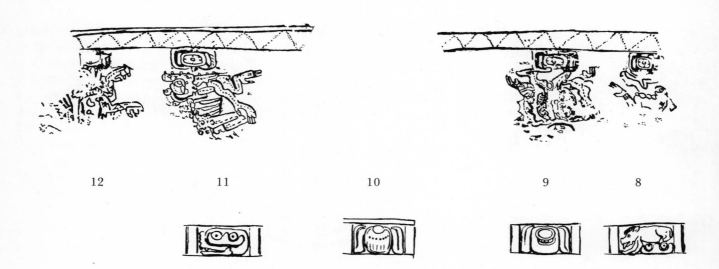

Figure 14. Zodiacal signs from the *Paris* codex compared with an inscriptional series from Chichen Itza.

727) identifies this animal with one from *Madrid* page 8, I think correctly, and regards both as butterflies. The *Madrid* figure has the typical upturned nose of the leaf-nosed bat. Spinden has suggested it may be a deer, to which it bears no resemblance. Possibly his reference has somehow reversed *Paris* numbers 8 and 9, since number 8 does seem to have hooves, and the peculiar shape of number 9 might suggest a frog. After the destroyed space there appears a humanoid skeleton with some animal characteristics, particularly the crocodilian mouth. Finally, there is a badly destroyed animal with apparent claws and spots. Spinden identifies this last animal as the peccary. Villacorta and Villacorta call it an ocelot (*tigrillo*), which seems to me to agree much better with the visible characteristics.

The Monjas sequence is, unfortunately, damaged at two critical points and uninformative at two others. The second square still has the 'star' glyph preserved and hence was a constellation name. The first square is apparently completely destroyed and may have been either the simple crossbands or another constellation. If the first square was not a constellation, then only eleven are given in all. Following the destroyed constellation is the Peccary constellation. Then a 'moon' glyph appears, with affixes and without a 'star' glyph. It is followed by a *naab* glyph with affixes, again with no 'star' glyph, and finally by a skull with a 'star' infix.

If we assume that Peccary corresponds to *Paris* number 8, and Skull to *Paris* number 12, then there is only one erased constellation at the Monjas, corresponding to the unidentified bird of *Paris* number 7. This would suggest that Bat, of *Paris,* corresponds to the 'moon' glyph at the Monjas, a suggestion that seems reasonable but is unproven, and that one of the two animals missing in *Paris* corresponded to the *naab* of the Monjas. The most puzzling feature of this reconstruction would be that Ocelot, which would be number 13 of *Paris,* is completely missing at the Monjas, which would have only eleven constellations. However, since the Monjas sequence—Skull, Bird, Star Venus, Turtle—is fixed and without room for another, this is implied in any case.

If one accepts the identification of the Turtle constellation (Ac Ek) as Gemini, one can reconstruct a zodiacal sequence with fair reliability. It should be pointed out that one of Thompson's informants told him that the Turtle was the square of Orion (Thompson 1950, p. 116). For the rough approximations of the present attempt, a shift from Gemini as base to the neighboring Orion would involve a change no greater than the range of error of the method. The suggested correlation is shown in Table 6.

For a full understanding of Table 6, it is necessary to understand both the Monjas-*Paris* "zodiacal" sequence and the table of 1,820 days which accompanies this sequence in the *Paris.* The 1,820-day period was set down in thirteen columns of five rows each. Each row is read horizontally from right to left and implicitly totals 364 days, including the 28-day interval between dates of one line and those of the next. In five of the columns, most or all of the glyphs are now completely illegible. They can, however, easily be restored from the mathematical structure of the surviving parts. The mathematics and the available space combine to suggest that the zero date of the table was 12 Lamat in the upper right hand corner. The interval between any two adjacent dates in the same row is 28 days and the interval between any two adjacent dates in the same column is 364 days. After going through all five rows of the table, a count of 28 days from the last date in the bottom left takes one back to the first date in the upper right hand column, so that the table is a re-entering 28-day table. At the end of the period of 1,820 days, the table is about six days short of five sidereal years.

If one starts with the day 12 Lamat at the base of the table, assuming that it is to be associated with the badly damaged bird at the right of the animal sequence and counting forward by the 168-day interval marked between Bird and Rattlesnake, one reaches 11 Cib at the end of six sidereal lunar months (of 28 days each). Presumably, 168 days will reach six-thirteenths, or nearly halfway, around the sky. A further 168 days takes one 336 days from the base. This is 29 days less than 365 days. Hence alternate pictures are one-half to one-third of the sky apart and should roughly correspond to successive zodiacal constellations, in the reverse of the normal order. The combination of the 'darkened sun' glyphs, which also appear in the *Dresden* eclipse table with the day 12 Lamat which is the base of that table, and the interval of 168 days suggests that this table is also particularly concerned with eclipses. The 168-day interval is slightly over 5 days less than the 173 1/3 days of the "eclipse half-year" and 9 days less than the 177-day interval at which eclipses most frequently recur (the other possibilities being 178 days and 148 days). Hence a solar eclipse in a certain constellation will be followed by another solar eclipse in a constellation of the opposite side of the sky. If the intent of this sequence was as I suggest, these constellations will normally follow each other in the order given in *Paris.* Six periods of 168 days make 1,008 days, while six periods of 173 1/3 days make 1,040 days. Hence, an eclipse in the first constellation would, after six intervening eclipses, be followed by an eclipse in the fifth

Table 6
Suggested Correlation of Our Constellations with the
Paris Zodiacal Sequence

Western Zodiacal Constellations	Series of 13 Maya Constellations	Day-Names Reached From 12 Lamat Table Base	
(Cancer)	(1. Bird)		
	12. Skeleton/Skull	1 Cib	
		+ 336 (2 X 168)	↑
Leo	10. (*naab*)	3 Ahau	
		+ 336	
Virgo	8. Peccary	5 Kan	
		+ 336	
Libra	6. Fish Snake	7 Lamat	
		+ 336	
Scorpio	4. Scorpion	9 Eb	
		+ 336	
Sagittarius	2. Rattlesnake/Venus	11 Cib	
	* — — — — — —	↑	
Capricorn	13. Ocelot	13 Kan	↑
		+ 336	
Aquarius	11. ??	2 Lamat	
		+ 336	
Pisces	9. Bat/Moon	4 Eb	
		+ 336	
Aries	7. Bird	+ 168 6 Cib	
		+ 336	
Taurus	5. *Cox* bird?	8 Ahau	
		+ 336	
Gemini	3. Turtle	10 Kan	
		+ 336 (2 X 168)	
Cancer	1. Bird	12 Lamat	

Note. This tentative identification is based on the equation of the Maya Turtle constellation with our Gemini. The day names given at the right are those which would be reached with a fixed interval of 168 days from the base 12 Lamat. The Maya section is to be read from bottom to top. The interval of 336 days has the effect of moving forward eleven steps in the series of zodiacal constellations, which is equivalent to moving back one step.

constellation rather than in the seventh constellation. The uncorrected 168-day cycle would reach the seventh constellation. Partial destruction of the manuscript makes it uncertain whether any correction was applied at this point.

When repeated, the cycle would gradually shift away from the constellations. The 12 Lamat table provides a re-entering cycle for the 168-day period, but only after six repetitions of the table or nearly thirty years. Since the cycle shifts away from the constellations at the rate of approximately 6 days on every repetition of the table, the base would have shifted by 36 days and would be in a different constellation on each repetition of the cycle. This may have been one of the ways in which the table was used and would explain why there was no direct tie-in between the constellations and the accompanying 1,820-day table.

There are, however, indications of corrections which are not clear to me. Just before the Skeleton constellation is a number in two unaligned parts (or two numbers). If intended to be read together, they would read 8.14, i.e. 174 days. This 6-day correction would just bring the constellations back in step with the 28-day table after one use, at the expense of reaching day names which are not contained in the table, so that it could not continue to be used. Between the Skeleton and the Ocelot, there seem to be two eights side by side and a sixteen midway between and below them. Conceivably this represents 336 (8 X 20) + (8 X 20) +16, but it would be a very unusual way to represent such a period. In any case, it suggests something unusual about the end of the sequence. Because of the destruction of some of the numbers and uncertainties of interpretation of others, the identification of the constellations proposed in Table 6 must be considered tentative. Some of the details may be wrong even if the general outline is correct.

Documented references in the inscriptions to these constellations seem very rare. Lintel 3 from Temple IV at Tikal shows in B4 the glyger 'shell star' followed immediately by *yax* and a turtle head, then by 'east'. I suspect a reference to Gemini but am far from certain. The glyphs resembling Emblem Glyphs (see Chapter 11) found in astronomical contexts may refer to locations in constellations, but this is also doubtful.

Spinden, at various times, has suggested the identification of various glyphs and glygers which he supposed were of an astronomical nature. None of these has been adequately verified; some depend directly upon his correlation, and some have since been disproven, but the student would do well to be able to recognize them. For some time, Spinden held the hypothesis that the variable central element of the ISIG referred to the principal subject of the following inscription. However, Beyer was subsequently able to show that it indicated the deity ruling the month of the Initial Series date. Spinden identified one of these glyphs as a glyph for the summer solstice. According to his correlation, the summer solstice fell in Zec during much of the Classic Period, and Beyer's subsequent evidence showed that this was the glyger of the patron deity of the month Zec.

Spinden (1924, p. 189) suggested that a glyph in a Palenque inscription with the number 'one' prefixed indicated 'one tropical year'. No evidence was presented for this view. Thompson (1950, p. 194) suggested that "the sign must mean something like 'period completed'." He gives a list of occurrences with the prefix 'one' and points out that this also occurs in connection with the "half-period" glyph. The dates given neither support Spinden's view nor suggest any alternative. In the same passage is a glyph which Spinden (1924) thought might refer to "one solstitial round" or to "solstitial or equinoctial division points of the year." It is actually the Emblem Glyph of Palenque (see Fig. 72) and has no astronomical meaning.

Another interesting hypothesis of Spinden's dealt with the "half-darkened" *kin* sign (Fig. 12), which, in at least one case, is found in the same context as the half-darkened Ahau. Charles P. Bowditch (1906a) had suggested that this was a glyph for the equinox, and Spinden found that it was present in a long inscription at Palenque associated with a date which was, in his correlation, an equinox. Moreover, this same inscription apparently dealt with a period of about 753 years, in which the sun would move halfway around relative to the stars, and in which the natural measuring points are the solstices and equinoxes. Spinden's correlation put one of these points at the winter solstice. This was excellent supporting evidence for the correlation, and, if the correlation were accepted, the interpretation would seem plausible. However, Thompson (1937, p. 89) pointed out that there were other occurrences of the half-darkened *kin* and that the intervals between them were such that it would be impossible for all or even most of them to be equinox intervals, and hence that the decipherment was wrong. Spinden has indirectly responded to Thompson's criticism by saying, in effect, that if a text made reference to the equinox in a glyph, it need not also always make reference to it in a date. In English we might refer to one event as occurring at a certain date and to another, related event as occurring "at the last equinox." While Spinden's statements are nowhere as explicit as this, his interpretation of various uses of this glyph suggests this is what he intended. Although this is certainly possible, it is equally clear that Thompson's criticism greatly weakens the case. It may also be pointed out that the half-darkened Ahau remarkably resembles the Hopi kachina called *ahul,* the sun kachina, with stars painted on half of his face (Fig. 12). This kachina was particularly associated, not with the equinoxes, but with the winter solstice.

Spinden (1924, pp. 183–184) also drew attention to a glyph resembling an S on its side. He pointed out that it is found in *Dresden* with two figures facing in opposite directions, on one of whom water is falling, and suggested that it meant the reversal of the seasons from dry to wet. It is also found with dates in the Temple of the Cross and the Temple of the Sun at Palenque. In the latter two, it is associated with dates about 753 years after the Maya Era. This is the time necessary for the vague year to shift halfway around the seasons; thus a date 15 Ceh, which was a summer solstice at the earlier date, would be a winter solstice at the later date. In fact, this date 15 Ceh, given in the text, is a winter solstice in Spinden's correlation. Spinden regarded the glyph associated with this 'reversal' glyph as identical with what we now know is the patron of Zec, which he regarded as the summer solstice. Hence, for him, the combination read 'reversal of the summer solstice'. Comparison with other passages at Palenque shows clearly that this glyph is simply a variant of the normal 'sky' glyph, with the knot affix read by me as *tab. Caan tab* 'the tying of the sky' would be a reasonable phrase for the solstices or equinoxes, and so we are back at Spinden's interpretation by a different route and without specific reference to the summer solstice. For those who reject the reading *tab,* just 'reversal of the sky x' would be very reasonable in this context. The same glyph sequence is found with the date 19 Ceh, four days later, in the Temple of the Sun; of course, both cannot be solstice dates.

Another glyph which Spinden tried to read as 'summer solstice' is the so-called hand sprinkling water (Fig. 59). Thompson pointed out that this glyph recurs at the end of time periods. There has been considerable dispute as to whether it normally represents a hand sprinkling water or a hand sowing grain. Linguistic evidence suggests that there may be little difference in these interpretations. Quiche *malah* is 'scatter, cast, strew'; *malik* is 'scatter, cast, corn for divining'; Tzeltal *mal* is 'to sprinkle'; one or the other of these could easily account for the hand, and, indeed, either of them might have been drawn to be read *mal;* Yucatec *mal* is 'pass', which agrees with the use of this verb with the ends of time periods. All three meanings are closely related conceptually, and all were probably in use in Classic Maya. Spinden's meaning seems to have been derived inappropriately from some association with a particular time period which was at or near a summer solstice in his correlation.

One curious glyph compound was read by Spinden as 'winter solstice'. I have no alternative to suggest but see nothing in the context to warrant Spinden's interpretation, even in terms of his own correlation.

Another very interesting glyph read by Spinden (1924, p. 221, Fig. 58) as 'reversal of the seasons' (Fig. 12) is in the same passage with the supposed 'winter-solstice' glyph and the *mal* glyph. Here reference is made to a date 12 Ahau (13 Kayab) and to two 'reversals of the seasons' plus 13 uinals, reaching 9.11.0.0.0 12 Ahau 8 Ceh. 'Reversal of the season' should, then, be a calendar round or multiple of calendar rounds. I believe that 'rounds of the seasons' would be more accurate than 'reversals of the seasons' and that this refers to 2 X 1,507 vague years (=1,506 tropical years), which is the period which had elapsed from the important early dates at Palenque. Such a suggestion must be tentative, for there is no supporting evidence.

Both Willson and Förstemann have suggested that various other glyphs had astronomical meanings, but none have received wide acceptance. Some are shown in Figures 9–12; if any of them are valid, it will have to be shown through new work. The same figures (9–12) show a number of glyphs of unknown meaning which tend to recur in connection either with long periods of time or with astronomical calculations.

The stylized body of the two-headed dragon or planetary band is frequently pictured where the text has the 'sky' glyph. This band has on it a varying series of symbols, which include the glyphs for 'night', 'moon', and 'star'. Other symbols on this planetary band have been variously assigned to particular planets with little supporting evidence.

In sum, we may say that there has been a considerable utilization of calendrical data in dating monuments and that a few of these glyphs may be read adequately in Maya. Unfortunately, the reading of the calendrical glyphs as Maya words has not received nearly as much attention as the problems of dating monuments. In the terrain of astronomy, about which much has been written, we know with reasonable probability only the glyphs for 'sun', 'star', and 'Venus', and the latter two have normally been confused. Despite the fact that most scholars working on the material have accepted the *Dresden* lunar table as a mechanism for predicting eclipses, there is no generally accepted glyph for 'eclipse'. Our knowledge of the mechanism of various astronomical tables and of the calendar is quite adequate, but our understanding of the associated glyphs has lagged far behind.

The following linguistic reconstructions, derived from Kaufman 1964, may have some relevance to the glyphs which have been considered in this section. Reconstructions apply to the whole family unless otherwise specified. Periods are used to separate reconstructions for one meaning from reconstructions for the next.

Sun, day, time: *q'iing. Star: (a) *'eeq', Tzel.-Yuc.-Chl.-Chr.; (b) *q'anal, Tzo.-H.-Toj.-Chu.; (c) *ch'umil, etc., Pch.-Q.-Jac. (Mam?). Night: *'aq'ab. Year: *ha'b, ha'b-il. Yesterday: *'ewey. Tomorrow morning: *kabej. Day before yesterday: *kab(e)jey. Within three days: *'oxej. Three days ago: *ox(e)jey. Within four days: *kongej. A year ago: *jun-ha'b-ey. Early: *sajb/sehb.

Chapter 3
Directions
and Colors

It was Léon de Rosny who originally determined the glyphs which stood for the directions and Eduard Seler who first correctly determined the colors. The two are treated together here, since the Mayas, like many American Indian groups, associated particular colors with particular directions. The codices frequently give a series of four directions and associated color glyphs, and the general meanings of these were recognized early in the history of decipherment. Figures 15 and 16 summarize the evidence and the present interpretation. The series of glyphs which expressed the directions have long been clear, but there was at first a great deal of doubt as to which glyphs were associated with which directions. The *kin* sign, early recognized, was found in two of these directional glyphs, and the Yucatec words for 'east' and 'west' are respectively *likin* and *chikin.* There was agreement that these two glyphs were the east-west directions, but there was much argument as to which was which. Similar difficulties prevailed with the other two directions.

Despite various attempts to sort out the directions, direct evidence was not forthcoming; emphasis shifted to the association of specific colors with directions, a line of inquiry which eventually furnished evidence which satisfied all Maya students. Objects associated with directions are listed in *The Book of Chilam Balam of Chumayel* (Roys 1933, pp. 64–65): red flint stone, red ceiba tree, red corn, red bees, and red flowers are associated with the east; white stone, white ceiba tree, white corn, white bees, and white flowers, with the north; a similar series of black objects, with the west; and, finally, yellow objects, with the south. Three different series of associated color-directional glyphs are found in the *Dresden* (30b–31b, 29c–30c, and 30c–31c). The same color glyph is associated with the same directional glyphs, and the sequence is the same, in the three cases, although the opening point is not. Two of these series have deities drawn below the color-directional glyphs, and in each of these two series one of the deities is colored black. It seems reasonable to suppose the color black should be associated with the west, as in the *Book of Chilam Balam of Chumayel.* The associated direction glyph contains the *kin* sign and hence is already indicated as being either 'east' or 'west'. If the black-west relationship is valid, the glyph associated with the other *kin* sign should be 'east'; again, assuming that the association with directions is the same in the *Dresden* as in the *Chumayel,* the associated color should be red. The Yucatec word for red is *chac,* which also means 'great'. This color glyph is the same glyph as the first element of the glyger for the planet Venus, generally known in Mayan languages as 'the great star' (Yuc.

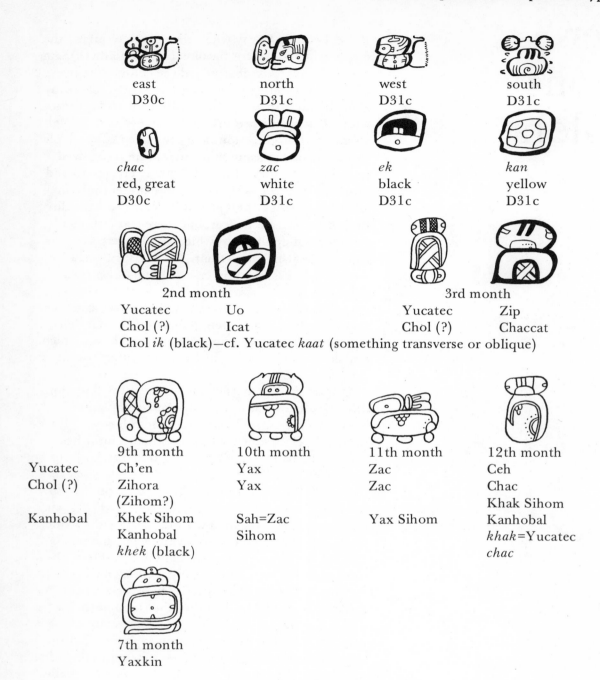

east D30c	north D31c	west D31c	south D31c

chac red, great D30c	*zac* white D31c	*ek* black D31c	*kan* yellow D31c

2nd month

Yucatec   Uo
Chol (?)   Icat
Chol *ik* (black)—cf. Yucatec *kaat* (something transverse or oblique)

3rd month

Yucatec   Zip
Chol (?)   Chaccat

	9th month	10th month	11th month	12th month
Yucatec	Ch'en	Yax	Zac	Ceh
Chol (?)	Zihora	Yax	Zac	Chac
	(Zihom?)			Khak Sihom
Kanhobal	Khek Sihom	Sah=Zac	Yax Sihom	Kanhobal
	Kanhobal	Sihom		*khak*=Yucatec
	khek (black)			*chac*

7th month
Yaxkin

Figure 15. Glyphs of the directions and colors.

chac ek). The same color glyph is occasionally associated with the name hieroglyph of a goddess, depicted in a brownish-red color; the glyph is also prefixed to the name glyph of the jaguar, who is called variously *chac mol*, *chac ekel*, and *chac balam*. The view that the color glyph represents *chac* 'red, great' seems fully justified.

Further support is to be found in the sequence of month glyphs. The Yucatec month names Uo and Zip show no correspondence to the glyphs for these two months, each of which contains a color prefix and a crossed-band glyph, but the equivalent months of a list believed by Thompson to be Chol (see Fig. 5) are Icat and Chaccat ('black *cat*' and 'red *cat*', *cat* perhaps corresponding to Yuc. *kaat* 'something transverse'; the associated color glyphs correspond to those above determined as, respectively, 'black' and 'red'). There is another group of four names which also supports these color values. The successive Yucatec months are Ch'en, Yax, Zac, and Ceh; the equivalent ones in the putative Chol series are Zihora (probably an error for Zihom—see the following series), Yax, Zac, and Chac; the Kanhobal list gives Khek Sihom, Sah Sihom, Yax Sihom, and Khak Sihom. Kanhobal *khak* corresponds to the Yucatec and Chol *chac* and likewise means 'red'. Kanhobal *khek* corresponds to Yucatec *ek* 'black'. All four of these months contain the same basic element with differing prefixes, and the first and fourth correspond to the glyphs determined as 'black' and 'red' previously. *Yax* and *zac* are also both color names, corresponding respectively to 'blue-green' and 'white'. They are found in this same order in Yucatec, the Chol (?) list, and in Pokomchi. In the Kanhobal list, *sah* corresponds to *zac,* and the order is reversed. Here we again get good evidence as to which sequence is correct, as there is another month, called Yaxkin in Yucatec, with equivalent names in Tzeltal, Tzotzil, Kanhobal, and Ixil. The glyph for this month consists of a *kin* sign with a prefix corresponding to the prefix of the glyph for the first of the two months corresponding to Yucatec *yax* and *zac*. This means that the prefixed glyph for the remaining month of this series should have the meaning 'white' and be read *zac*.

Returning now to the color-direction sequence of *Dresden,* the glyphs following 'red-east' should be those for 'white' and 'north', if *Dresden* corresponds with *Chumayel;* we find that, in fact, the first color glyph after 'red-east' does correspond to that given for the month Zac. The remaining direction must be presumed to be 'south' and the remaining color, 'yellow', Yucatec *kan*. One would expect to find confirmation that this glyph is *kan* either in the day

glyph corresponding to Yucatec Kan or in the month glyph corresponding to Yucatec Kankin, but these are different glyphs. The remaining material is so well attested that this last identification has nonetheless been generally accepted.

According to Landa, the years were called after their beginning days, which at that time were Cauac, Kan, Muluc, and Ix. Landa says that the years were assigned to directions and ruled in succession by four different deities called the Bacabs. The Black Bacab of the west ruled the Cauac years. Similar evidence associates the Yellow Bacab, south, and the Kan years; the Red Bacab, east, and the Muluc years; and the White Bacab, north, and the Ix years. In the *Madrid* codex (pp. 34–37), new-year ceremonies similar to those described by Landa were first recognized and studied at length by Cyrus Thomas (1882, pp. 59–92). Thus, M34 has the Cauac years and the glyph for 'west' as previously determined; M35, the Kan years and the glyph for 'south'; M36, the Muluc years and the glyph for 'east'; finally, M37 has the Ix years and the glyph for 'north'. A parallel series of new-year ceremonies is also to be found in *Dresden* (pp. 25–28). Here the year-beginning days differ by one from those of the *Madrid,* and the year-ending days of the previous year are also given. The partly illegible glyphs associated with the gods of the year's end give 'black' associated with Manik and 'red' associated with Caban, while the direction glyphs indicate an association of Akbal and 'west', Lamat and 'north', Ben and 'east', and Etz'nab and 'south'. These differences from the colonial period should be noted here, but possible explanations are not pertinent enough to the immediate problem of glyph deciphering to warrant a lengthy consideration (see Thompson 1934, pp. 223–224, and 1950, pp. 249–252).

It is, therefore, possible to identify the Mayan glyphs for the colors *chac* 'red', *zac* 'white', *ek* 'black', *kan* 'yellow', and *yax* 'blue, green'. Presumably these glyphs were read approximately as given, with some minor changes in pronunciation. All of them can be shown to be proto-Mayan, on linguistic evidence. It should be emphasized that each glyph represented a word and hence was a logograph. These glyphs might have the meaning of any Mayan homonym, and there is no reason to suppose that the color meanings are primary. T109 is to be read *chac*, but whether it is to be translated 'red' or 'great' depends entirely on context.

We are not in such good position with respect to the directional glyphs. It has usually been accepted that the 'east' and 'west' glyphs correspond respectively to Yucatec *likin* and *chikin. Likin* is an assimi-

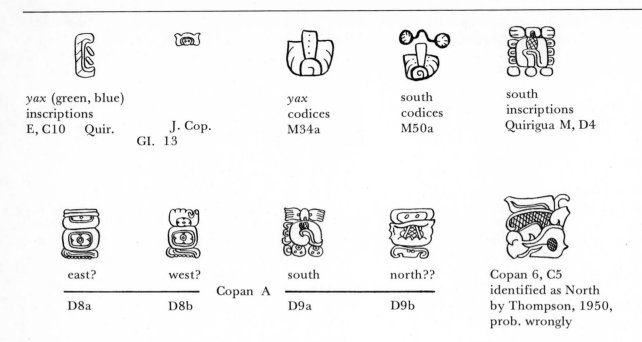

Figure 16. Glyphs of the directions and colors.

lated form of an older *lakin,* and it has been assumed that this is the correct form for the glyph.

In the case of *chikin* the evidence is by no means clear (see the discussion in Chapter 9). Even the basic assumption of correlation with Yucatec may be unsound. Since the sun (*kin*) moves from east to west, several Mayan languages have distinct forms for 'east' and 'west' incorporating the word *kin,* and their presence in Yucatec and in the glyphs is not proof that Yucatec is an adequate explanation of the glyphs. Moreover, the glyphs in the codices and those in the inscriptions differ in a number of respects. The best evidence for a complete direction series of glyphs on the monuments is from Copan A; compare *Dresden* pages 8a–9b. The glyphs which have been presumed to stand for 'east' and 'west' both have *kin* signs in them, but the other elements are distinct from those in the codices. There is a hand glyph in one of them, as there is in the 'west' glyph of the codices, but the position of the hand is quite different from that in the codices, and I would assume that it represents a different word or prefix. The presumed 'east' glyph likewise has a different prefix. The glyph for 'south' is recognizably the prototype of the form in the codices, the central element being an inverted shell, corresponding to the "shell variant" of the *kin,* save that the latter is not inverted. In the codices, this central element of the 'south' glyph and the glyph for *yax* are drawn in nearly or quite identical forms, both reasonably resembling their prototypes in the inscriptions, which, however, do not resemble each other.

Possibly some factor was operating to make them seem more similar conceptually. The glyph presumed to be 'north' shows no similarities to the form in the codices. This is probably a "six-direction" series, since 'earth' (down) and 'sky' (up) are also included.

Occasionally in Maya texts we have references to 'earth-center', in a cosmological and directional sense. In the *Chumayel* (R. Roys 1933, Maya text p. 32, translation p. 100) a directional series is given, omitting the red ceiba tree of the east and replacing it by a green ceiba "in the center [of the world]." In 1889, Seler had pointed out what seemed to be a series of five directions in which the *cab* 'earth' glyph appeared, with the associated color *yax* 'green'. He suggested a meaning of 'center, vertical, up or down'. This seems entirely valid. In the *Dresden* and, more rarely, in the *Madrid,* the *cab* glyph is found followed by T663. Knorozov (1967, no. 155, p. 92) read T663 as *tan* 'middle', apparently without cosmic implications. However, *tan* would normally be prefixed to *cab* rather than suffixed. Thompson (1950, p. 271) read the glyph as *pakal* 'seed', partly because of a frequent agricultural context, partly because of the association with the *cab* 'earth' glyph, and partly because of agricultural associations of some associated glyphs. However, the combination appears in no less than three of the picture sections of the *Dresden* eclipse table, and its other associations seem to me more cosmological than agricultural. I think that the associated "agricultural" glyphs are found because of their grammatical meanings rather than their

agricultural connotations, and the agricultural context, when valid, probably refers to ceremonial or divinatory associations. The Maya term which Roys translates 'in the center' is *tu chumuc*. The Evreinov, Kosarev, and Ustinov catalog (1961*b*, III, 153–155, no. 175) shows that the *cab*-T663 combination appears with *ti* 'at' prefixed, with the locative read by Thompson as *yol* 'in' prefixed, and with *tu* prefixed in the form without crosshatching. The *tu* prefix with crosshatching appears with T663, without *cab*. This latter use would seem to correspond fully with the cited *tu chumuc*. Without either a demonstrated homonymic use or known cognates in other Mayan languages, a suggestion that T663 should be read *chumuc* must be very tentative but, I think, is preferable to either *pakal* or *tan*.

Thompson (1950, p. 251; Fig. 4, 1–4; Fig. 41, 5–6, 7–8, 19–20, 21–22, 28–29) has shown that glyphs for the directions are found in a standard phrase on several monuments, which he translates approximately as 'to *n* direction the count of the year'. The glygers for 'east', 'west', and 'south' in these inscriptions agree with the series from Copan Stela A. Thompson tentatively identified a glyph for 'north' on Copan Stela 6 (glyph block 17) (Fig. 16), apparently on the basis that it was not any of the other directions and that it occurred directly preceding the 'count of the *haab*' clause. However, he failed to note that the normal 'south' glyger appears earlier in the same glyph block, and this inscription is apparently a case of inserting a couple of words in a clause.

Thompson (1943*b*, pp. 137–151; 1950, pp. 212–217, Fig. 35) had shown the existence of a cycle of 819 days and the fact that it was accompanied by a regular, although somewhat variable, set of clauses. Heinrich Berlin and I noted that these clauses contain both color glyphs and directional glyphs and that "dates which differ from each other by multiples of 4 × 819 share a common explanatory glyph, which we regard as a direction glyph" (Berlin and Kelley 1961, p. 11). This was the first demonstration of an association of colors and directions on the monuments of the Classic Period in a form approximating that of the codices. Thompson assigned the letters A–G to the originally known examples of the 819-day count. Berlin and I added three more texts recognized by Thompson, which were lettered H, I, J (Berlin and Kelley 1961). Of these, B, I, and J contain 'east'; G and F contain 'south'; C, D, and H contain a head resembling the codex head for 'north'. The chronological variation between these texts suggested that the days of the 819-day count were assigned to directions as follows:

East	North	West	South
Imix	Ik	Akbal	Kan
Chicchan	Cimi	Manik	Lamat
Muluc	Oc	Chuen	Eb
Ben	Ix	Men	Cib
Caban	Etz'nab	Cauac	Ahau

This assignment of days to directions allowed Text A to be assigned to the west, and Text E to the north. The latter has a very unusual glyger in the place where we would have expected 'north' (Fig. 17). It may be a synonym for 'north', but that cannot yet be demonstrated. Texts I and B, assigned to the east, have glyphs which seem to be variants of *chac;* Texts C and D, assigned to the north, both contain a glyph which is apparently *zac* 'white', and a more doubtful *zac* appears in Text H (north); Text A, assigned to the west, has a clear *ek* 'black' glyph; and Text G, assigned to the south, has a clear *kan* 'yellow' glyph. Despite the doubtful identification of some of these color prefixes, the consistent associations in the same order as that which persisted into colonial Yucatán seem sufficient to justify the conclusion of continuity of color-direction symbolism from the Classic Period. The consistency also seems adequate to justify recognizing the 'north' glyph of these passages. Their general structure seems to parallel that of offering texts in the *Dresden,* including the same introductory verb. The same verb or a closely similar one occurs with passages associated with the Initial Series of the tablets of the Temples of the Cross, Foliated Cross, and Sun, at Palenque. Here direction glyphs are also found, 'north' with the Temple of the Sun, 'west' with the Temple of the Foliated Cross, and 'south' with the Temple of the Cross.

In addition to the texts considered above, Thompson (1962, pp. 216–217) has suggested, on the basis of similar glyphs, that two partly destroyed stucco texts at Palenque may have contained this clause. These have been included in Figure 17 as texts K and L. Neither color nor direction glyphs nor dates have been recognized among the preserved fragments; so the texts cannot be assigned to directions. Proskouriakoff (1964*a*, p. 192) has tentatively recognized a date of this series on Yaxchilan Stela 4. The text (M) is badly damaged, and I have been unable to recognize either color or direction glyphs (which should be 'black' and 'west' if correctly deciphered). Berlin (1965*a*, pp. 340–341) has recognized still another certain case of the 819-day count at Pier A of House A, Palenque (Text N). This one is identified by both date and glyphs but is unfortunately destroyed in the glyph blocks where color and direction glyphs would

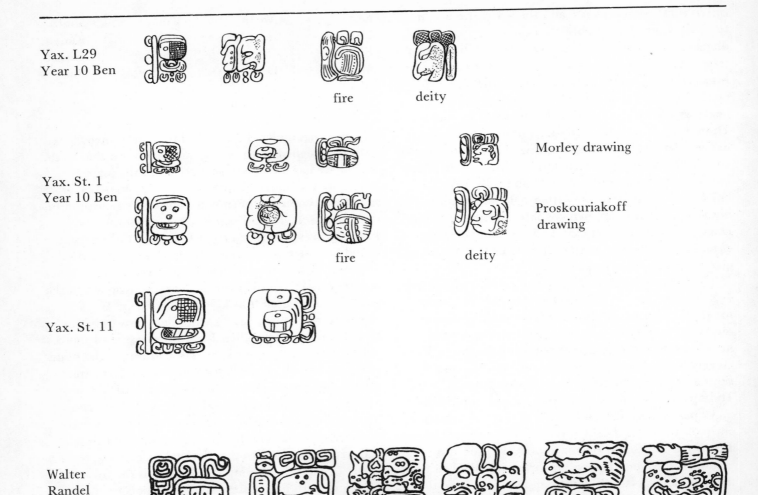

Figure 18. Supplementary texts associated with the 819-day count. Abbreviation: Yax., Yaxchilan.

be expected. Finally, an unpublished memo from Linton Satterthwaite points out another example on the recently discovered Walter Randel Stela (Text O). This one may be recognized by both the date and the accompanying glyphs. These include the introductory offering glyph, the glyph of God K, and a glyph of a deity head with *kan* 'yellow' infixed. This is the expected color glyph, but 'south' is not recognizably present.

Several of the Initial Series associated with these dates seem to refer to births. Text F may refer to the birth of a deity, and Texts B, H, and A seem to refer to the births of human rulers. Text O contains the 'emergence' glyph which I have postulated as a synonym of 'birth'. Texts B, D, and O contain texts, apparently associated with the IS, which seem to share a deity glyph and a 'fire' glyph.

The Initial Series of Texts B and D fall in years in which 11 Etz'nab was the first of Pop, while the 819-day count of these texts fell in years 10 Ben 1 Pop. In Text O, the IS fell in a year 10 Ben 1 Pop, while the 819-day count fell in a year 9 Lamat 1 Pop. It is noteworthy that the "birth of the gods" at Palenque also fell in a year 9 Lamat 1 Pop and that the accompanying texts include 'fire' glyphs. The year 9 Lamat would correspond in part to an Aztec year 7 Tochtli (Rabbit) and to a Mixtec year 6 Rabbit because of the different days from which Aztecs and Mixtecs named the year. The Mixtec *Vienna* Codex shows the ceremonies accompanying the inauguration of new rulers (Burland 1947). These occurred at approximately fifty-two–year intervals in one of the successive years 5 House, 6 Rabbit, or 7 Reed and were accompanied by the drilling of new fire. This corresponds with the evidence of Ixtlilxochitl, who tells us the Toltec rulers had reigns of fifty-two years each and shows the beginning dates as 5 House, 6 Rabbit, or 7 Reed, except for Topiltzin. Interestingly, the *Annals of Cuauhtitlan* (Velásquez n.d.) put the accession of Topiltzin Quetzalcoatl in a year 7 Reed. While the details and context are obviously different in some ways, the fact that 'fire' glyphs appear in the Mayan inscriptions in years which are the equivalents of the Mixtec-Toltec new-fire ceremonies implies a basic unity. This correspondence greatly increases the probability that these glyphs refer to fifty-two—year new-fire ceremonies.

Another example of associated color and direction glyphs is to be found on Copan Altar Z at B4–A5, where 'black' is prefixed to a badly eroded glyph in B4 and 'west' appears with a knot prefixed in A5. An interesting series showing color symbolism with no demonstrated association with directions is found in a lengthy inscription from Yaxchilan (analyzed in detail, Chapter 13), which shows, at structurally similar points of repeated clauses, the glyphs for 'white', 'red', and 'yellow' in that order. In this inscription, 'white' is associated with the Piedras Negras Emblem Glyph, 'red' with the Tikal Emblem Glyph, and 'yellow' with an unknown site.

The glyger T1030o:23 is apparently a deity name, which is known to appear on various Mayan monuments with the prefixes 'white', 'black', and 'yellow'. At Tikal, it precedes a glyger also found at Yaxchilan with the other series just mentioned (see Figs. 92, 93).

Both color and direction glyphs are common on the monuments, but no adequate study of their distribution has yet been undertaken. Despite the fact that we can now recognize the direction glyphs on the monuments and know something of their religious connotations, we are still uncertain as to how any of them should be read. The codex glyphs for 'east' and 'west' make good sense as *lakin* and *chikin*, corresponding to the Yucatec names, but they are not the same as the glyphs in the monumental inscriptions, which retain the *kin* grapheme but are otherwise dissimilar. There is no good reason for reading the 'north' glyph in the codices as *xaman* (Yuc. 'north'), but, *if* it is read that way, the head form for

'north' on the monuments is probably also *xaman*, as the two seem to be identical. The glyph for 'south' on the monuments is clearly the prototype of the 'south' glyph of the codices, despite the resemblance which the latter bears to *yax*. This glyger includes a prefixed *ma*, which makes it seem quite unlikely that it is to be read *nohol*, which is Yucatec for 'south'. Napoleon Cordy (1946, p. 112) has suggested a reading *ma yam*, which would agree with the superfixed *ma* grapheme. He assumes that *yam* was represented by *yax*, the two sharing the element *ya*; however, as I have pointed out above, the inscriptional prototype of the 'south' glyph does not resemble *yax*. In any case, I would not expect (or accept without very good evidence) a variation between *yax* and *yam*. Cordy may be correct, but his decipherment in this case must rest entirely on the *ma* element, as far as present evidence goes.

Thus, we seem to have adequate evidence for the reading of the color glyphs and can at least identify glyphs for the directions, even though we are uncertain as to how to read them in Maya. Preliminary utilization of these glyphs in studies of the monumental inscriptions shows a considerable time depth for patterns of color-direction symbolism known from colonial Maya documents and gives us fuller information on the calendrical associations of this symbolism.

The following linguistic reconstructions, derived from Kaufman 1964, may have some relevance to the glyphs which have been considered in this section. Reconstructions apply to the whole family unless otherwise specified. Periods are used to separate reconstructions for one meaning from reconstructions for the next.

Red: *kyëq, etc. White: *sëq. Green: *yë'x. Yellow: *q'ën. Black: (a) *k'aq, Pch.-Kek.-Toj.-Chu.-Kan.-Jac.-Mam-Q.; (b) *'ejq', Tzel.-Tzo.-Yuc.-H.-Chl.-Chr.

Chapter 4
Deities

Deity glyphs were early recognized in the codices, especially in the classic studies of Schellhas (1897, 1904). Many of the glyphs are pictographic, and, as in the case of the animals, an association of the picture of a certain deity with a very similar pictograph soon becomes obvious. Because of difficulties and disagreements as to the identification of many of these deities in the codices with deities known from colonial Maya sources, Schellhas assigned a series of letters to the deities, and these have been used, with some modifications, ever since. Distinguishing the glyphs for the deities is obviously only a first step towards decipherment, but the disagreements about identification persist. The Schellhas letters still have considerable utility, except in cases where it has been shown that he grouped together depictions and glyphs which should have been kept apart. Seler early suggested some modifications of the Schellhas scheme, and Thompson has also made some modifications. The Seler and Thompson modifications are not consistent, and a certain amount of confusion has thus resulted. Recently, Zimmermann (1956) has abandoned the whole system in favor of a numbered series, prefixed by the letter G (*Gott* 'god'), because it has become apparent that there are more deities than there are letters in the alphabet. Unfortunately, he preserves a system of subletters, giving G1, G1a, G1b, G2, G2a, G2b, etc., for forms where separate numbers for each would have been more consistent. No single system can deal adequately with the fact that some gods are animals. Conceptually I would favor incorporating animals with other deities, since the Maya did not separate them in their deity series, but in practice I have often found it more convenient to separate them.

Gods A, B, C, D, E, G, K, L, and P of the Schellhas enumeration still seem to be acceptable in the form in which he defined them and with the glyphs that he assigned to them, except for minor modifications. Gods that he designated F, H, I, O, M, and N require some modification, usually because he lumped together deities that should be distinguished. The accompanying Figures 19–37 illustrate the deities, grouped under the Schellhas letters, together with glyphs and representations from the inscriptions which seem to refer to the same deities.

This material may be summarized as follows:

God A: The Death Gods

The basic glyger for the Lord of Death was recognized by Schellhas, although some of the frequently associated glyphs which he gives do not seem to be

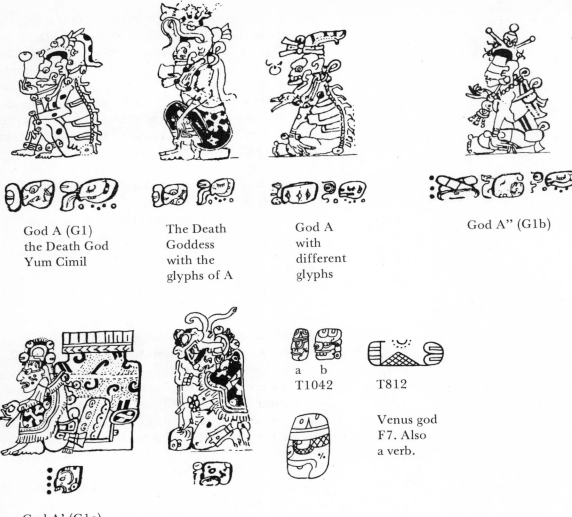

God A (G1)
the Death God
Yum Cimil

The Death
Goddess
with the
glyphs of A

God A
with
different
glyphs

God A" (G1b)

a   b
T1042

T812

Venus god
F7. Also
a verb.

God A' (G1a)
Uac Mitun Ahau
according to Seler

Palenque
TFC, G7

God R. Not a
death or war god
but originally
confused with God Q
as God F.

God Q, originally
lumped with God R
as God F. A god of
war and death.

Figure 19. Gods of death.

God G: The Sun God (Zimmermann's G5)

The main reason for the identification of this deity (Fig. 20) is apparently the use of the *kin* sign, 'day, sun', as the central element of the name glyger and its occasional occurrence on the deity's body. He appears rarely in the codices but is commonly represented in inscriptions.

God K: The God with the Ornamented Nose (Zimmermann's G8)

This deity (Figs. 20, 34) seems to have been quite prominent. He has some obscure connection with Gods B and D. His glyph, in several variants, is frequent in the inscriptions. God K is shown as the regent of the year Ben in the *Dresden* new-year ceremonies. The ceremonies depicted correspond in part to those of the *Madrid* codex, and the latter correspond in surprising detail with the new-year ceremonies described by Landa. In both Landa and the *Madrid* there was a one-day shift in the calendar, so that the ceremonies fell on the days Cauac, Kan, Muluc, and Ix, rather than on Lamat, Ben, Etz'nab, and Akbal, as in the *Dresden*. Other correspondences suggest that the *Dresden* Ben years correspond to Landa's Kan years, with which he associates a deity called Bolon Zacab. Seler (1902–1923, I, 376–377) therefore suggested the identity of God K and Bolon Zacab, whose name appears more correctly in the *Books of Chilam Balam* as Ah Bolon Dzacab (Tz'acab) or Ah Bolon Tzacab. The glyph in the codices does not have *bolon* ('nine') prefixed, but this number is prefixed to the glyph of God K at Chichen Itza, at Copan, and sometimes at Palenque. It is possible that he corresponds to God G1 of the Nine Lords of the Night (Fig. 31), but the usual glyph of God K has not been found in this context. Thompson (1934, pp. 224–226) pointed out that, as year regent, Bolon Tz'acab seemed to correspond to the Aztec Cinteotl, the Maize God.

God P: The So-Called Frog God (Zimmermann's G11)

Schellhas's identification of this deity (Fig. 21) as a frog god is based on his strange-shaped fingers. The *tun* sign is apparently part of his headdress. He wears a shell necklace and has two black marks at the corner of the eye. His name glyph in the *Madrid* is a pictograph, showing the two marks near the eye. Tozzer and Allen (1910, p. 310) say that "the knob-like finger tips at once suggest one of the tree toads"

and that the lines suggest the species *Hyla eximia*. However, in the accompanying figure, it will be seen that the "fingers" seem to be a removable implement of some unusual sort, as the lines of the right hand cross over the alleged "hand," part of which is dangling below. Moreover, in the accompanying scenes, there is a deity identical in every respect except that he lacks the "fingers." In the *Dresden* (p. 4a) the deity who opens a series of twenty deities has the same peculiar headdress, a round earplug with marks on it which may once have been identical with those in *Madrid*, and the same shell necklace. He has a serpent staff in his hand, and a quetzal bird is worn as an appendage on the back; however, the lines around the eye are quite differently drawn. The identifying glyphs are almost identical with those of God H. Seler identified God P as Kukulcan, the Feathered Serpent or Quetzal Snake; this was denied by Schellhas (1904, pp. 39–40). Seler's basis for the identification was threefold: first, Father Hernández said that a list of twenty gods was headed by Kukulcan, and this figure is the first of a twenty-god series in *Dresden*; second, the serpent staff and the quetzal on the back suggest the quetzal snake; third, the shell necklace is typical of representations of the Feathered Serpent in manuscripts from southern Mexico of the "*Borgia* group" of codices. The first of the two glygers is virtually identical with one of the name glyphs originally assigned to God H by Schellhas, which has been read as Kukulcan by Knorozov (1955*b*, p. 89). This leads us directly to the disagreements about God H.

God H: The Chicchan God, of Schellhas

Although Schellhas steadfastly maintained that this was but a single deity, most of the other scholars who have studied the problem have reached the conclusion that at least two deities are represented. The first of these, whose glyphs relate him to God P, is Zimmermann's G14. According to Zimmermann, he is a god of good omen. There are several minor variations in his hieroglyphs, and he sometimes has the number 3 or 6 prefixed to his name. His hieroglyph on D4c (Fig. 21) is of particular interest, as it clearly shows the two lines back from the eye, otherwise characteristic of the glyph of God P. The representations, however, are quite unlike those of God P and differ markedly among themselves. Seler (1902–1923, I, 695–699) sets these representations apart as those of a "young god" and does not relate him to Kukulcan. It has been suggested that the designation H be reserved for this deity.

The other deity has been called by Seler CH (Fig.

God H (G14)
Note variant
glyph from D4c
with eye-markings
of God P.

God P from *Dresden*
with glyphs almost identical
to those of God H. Note
tun headdress, shell necklace.

God P from *Madrid* with
pictograph. Note removable
"hand," tun headdress, shell
necklace, lines behind eye.
(G11)

God CH with variations of name
glyphs. Cf. Venus table god P19.

Compare
prefix with
that of
God H.
Note beard.

Compare body markings
of snake, above, with
infix in glyph of
God CH.

Glyphs of god
of number nine
from the
monuments.

Figure 21. Snake gods.

21); in this he has been followed by Zimmermann, who calls him also G7. This god's representations are found in situations of ill omen, and he is shown with death symbols (D3a, D7b, D50, Zimmermann 1956, p. 163). His name hieroglyphs include *yax* and a head variant with the *chic-chan* glyph infixed. Schellhas (1904, pp. 29–30) thought that this head variant was sufficiently similar to that previously mentioned that the distinctions made by Seler "cannot be satisfactorily proved, and must be regarded as an arbitrary assumption." I, on the other hand, feel that the arbitrary assumption is the identity of two sharply and consistently distinguished forms which take different affixes and different infixes. The *chic-chan* glyph was shown by Seler to be a normal Maya representation of markings on a serpent body (Fig. 37). Beyer showed that on the monuments this glyger occurs as the name of the god of the number nine, frequently represented as bearded. For a further discussion of the relationship of Gods P, CH, and H, with evidence suggesting the correctness of the association with Kukulcan, see "The Palenque Triad" below.

God F: The God of War and Human Sacrifice

Here Schellhas has grouped together three deities (Fig. 19). All three were distinguished by Seler (1902–1923, IV, 570–573), but his distinctions were generally ignored. The God of War and Human Sacrifice described by Schellhas has been called God Q by Thompson and G3 by Zimmermann. Brinton (1895, pp. 125–126) had already utilized the designation Q for a completely distinct deity and the letters R, S, T, U, and V for the animal gods, respectively *muan* bird, dog, vulture, jaguar, and turtle. Brinton's designations never came into general use. The number ten is prefixed to the name of Thompson's God Q, and a dot above this was long interpreted as a one, making the total eleven. Other examples show that originally it was a not a dot but a "death eye" (Fig. 19). A line runs down nearly the entire face, passing through the eye, both in the representations and in the glyph. This resembles that of the Maize God and of the Aztec god of flaying, Xipe, who is also believed to have been originally a maize god. Flaying the skin of a human seems to have been symbolic of husking corn.

Schellhas combined the God of War and Human Sacrifice with a death god shown on D5b, D28b, and elsewhere. This deity's characteristics are the 'night' symbol in the eye, the 'death' symbol on the cheek, a cloak with crossbones, a peculiar headdress, and a necklace, both of the latter with the so-called death

eyes. Seler (1902–1923, I, 381) calls this deity Uac Mitun Ahau and Zimmermann assigns him the number G1a (see Fig. 19). Seler relied here on the parallel between Landa's account of the new-year ceremonies and the representations of those ceremonies in the codices. Some representations of this god have probably been confused with those of God A. This god's head used as a glyph (T1042) appears as part of a verb at Palenque. It appears in the *Madrid,* with the back of the god's head as the base of the glyph. In this context, Thompson has given it a separate number (T812).

Schellhas also erred in regarding these gods of war and death as identical with a god whose hieroglyph *does* have 'eleven' (*buluc*) prefixed. This god has a curved line passing in back of his eye, resembling that found in the glyph *cab/caban* (Fig. 4). His name should therefore begin with Buluc and might contain the word *cab*. His associations are entirely benevolent (Thompson 1950, pp. 131–132; Zimmermann 1956, p. 167). Thompson has called him God R (see Fig. 19), and Zimmermann, G16. Barrera Vásquez and Rendón (1948, pp. 82, 85) identified an undifferentiated God F with the known deity Buluc Ch'abtan or Chabtan, which might easily be a borrowing of a Cholan name which would be *cab-tan* in Yucatec. It is presumably the combination of Buluc and Chab in association with God R which has led to this identification by Barrera Vásquez and Rendón, as well as by Knorozov. Buluc Ch'abtan is the deity who piles up skulls and bones and who causes 'seven years of wars and droughts'. These characteristics are appropriate for God Q, whose name however does not have 'eleven' prefixed or *cab* infixed. They are completely inappropriate for God R, whose name does have 'eleven' prefixed and *cab* infixed. The initial combination of the two gods by Schellhas as God F must be largely responsible for this identification, unless one assumes that there had been a very marked change in the characteristics of God R.

The Goddesses I, O, and Others

Because Schellhas mistakenly identified the glyphs of a young goddess, whom he did not describe at all, as those for an old goddess, whom he called I, a considerable confusion has arisen in the literature. It seems to me that separate hieroglyphs and separate characteristics can be recognized for several goddesses, all of whom have been involved in the confusion which started with Schellhas and was later compounded by other scholars, including Zimmermann. Schellhas (1904, p. 31) describes his Goddess I (Fig. 22) as "an

Goddess O
of Schellhas
Zac—?

alternate
glyphs of
weaving goddess
M102d—cf.
Fig. 58

Goddess I of Schellhas,
mistakenly called O
by Thompson and Zimmerman
Chac Chel

   See also the
   goddess L18 of
   the Venus table,
   whose glyphs identify
   her as the Moon
   Goddess, patron of
   the month Ch'en.

Zac — ?
glyphs of young goddess,
mistakenly called I by
Thompson and Zimmerman

Figure 22. Goddesses.

old woman with the body stained brown and claws in place of feet. . . . She wears on her head a knotted serpent and with her hands pours water from a vessel." He suggests that her glyphs are those of a female head with *zac* 'white' prefixed but says this "cannot be proved with certainty." As these glyphs belong to a young goddess who has none of the characteristics described by Schellhas, this is certainly an error. Schellhas (1904, p. 38) says his Goddess O "is distinguished by the solitary tooth in the underjaw as a sign of age . . . she is represented working at a loom . . . she never wears the serpent, but a tuft of hair bound up on her head and running out in two locks." Her glyph has *zac* prefixed to an aged female head. Zimmermann uses the Schellhas system and adds his own number system. He calls the young goddess Goddess I because she is associated with the hieroglyphs that Schellhas incorrectly suggested were associated with *his* Goddess I. The Zimmermann number for this young goddess is G22. Zimmermann gives the number G24 to the old goddess described by Schellhas under the label "Goddess I" and correctly associates her with her hieroglyphs. However, he calls her Goddess O, apparently confusing the two old goddesses correctly distinguished by Schellhas. In his text, Zimmermann (1956, pp. 167–168) discusses I and O together, indicating that they are only two aspects of a single goddess. In this, he follows Thompson (1939), who identified most Mayan goddesses with the Moon Goddess. Whatever conceptual or theological identity there may be between them, I would distinguish four goddesses.

The first of these, Schellhas's Goddess I *as described* (Zimmermann's G24), is associated with flood, destruction, serpents, and the Black God of War. She is depicted in a reddish brown color, and her name has the glyph *chac* 'red' prefixed. Sometimes a female head follows, sometimes a glyph which has been variously regarded as a knot or an agave plant (Yuc. *chelen;* Knorozov 1955a, p. 69, no. 56). This usually has suffixed to it Landa's *le.* It seems highly probable that the goddess's name is to be read Chac Chel and that she is the predecessor of the later Mayan goddess Ix Chel. Thompson (1939, p. 148) points out that in the *Ritual of the Bacabs* there is a reference to *chacal* Ixchel 'red Ix Chel' and *zacal* Ixchel 'white Ix Chel'. While Thompson (1939) considers Ix Chel a moon goddess, the word *chel* means 'rainbow'; the Yucatec Ix Chel is a goddess of healing; and healing is frequently associated with rainbow deities in other cultures. Ix Chel was also patron of childbirth and divination. It must be admitted that, aside from possible connotations of the name Red Rainbow, there is nothing to suggest that Ix Chel was

connected with floods. Brinton (1895, p. 63) regards this goddess as a personification of the thunderstorm, called in Maya *pecchac.*

The second goddess, Schellhas's O, normally has the *zac* grapheme (T58) prefixed to a deeply wrinkled female head. The goddess herself is shown weaving. Thompson (1939, p. 132) suggests that the *zac* grapheme is to be understood here as indicating *zacal* 'weaver', an interpretation which seems highly likely.

The third of these related goddesses, Zimmermann's G22, is the young goddess called "the White Lady" by Gates. Like the goddess just mentioned, her name usually has the prefix *zac* (T58), but in this case I suspect it means 'white'. She seems indistinguishable from a goddess who has the *caban* curl (T171; see Fig. 4) as a prefix and, occasionally, the "bundle" affix (T103). The female head which is the second grapheme of her glyph may be read simply *ch'up* 'maiden'. She is the goddess of the number one and of the day Caban.

Finally, the fourth is the goddess with the moon sign in her hieroglyph, the Moon Goddess par excellence. She appears frequently in the inscriptions as the goddess of the month Ch'en. In the codices, her glyphs appear only in the deity list of the Venus table. Barthel (1952, p. 98), examining the sequence of repetition of these deities, was able to show that these glyphs stood for a goddess shown on D49a, emptying a vase of water. Barthel surmised that she was a water goddess. The glyphs seem to indicate that she was primarily a moon goddess. Thompson (1950, p. 223) seems correct in regarding the suffix as a moon representation, although I do not think that the glyph is *normally* read as referring to the moon (see Chapter 10 for suggested readings as a verbal suffix).

Gods L and M of Schellhas, with Zimmermann's Y and Z (the Black Gods)

Schellhas recognized only two black deities in the codices, Gods L (Zimmermann's G4) and M (Zimmermann's G20) (see Fig. 23). Thompson (1950, p. 76) separated out a series of representations of a black god in the *Madrid.* Zimmermann has called this deity G15 or God Z. The representations show an intimate relationship with God M, since God Z upon occasion has the same drooping lip, and his eye appears as the name of God M. According to Schellhas, his God L does not appear in the *Madrid.* Zimmermann (1956, pp. 164–165) believes that God Z (or G15), to whom he attributes negative characteristics, and God L (G4), to whom he attributes positive characteristics, are the

a merchant god from *Fejervary Mayer*, probably an equivalent of Yacatecuhtli—compare nose with God M

God M with scorpion tail

Madrid codex, p. 33b: God Z with head of God M at waist

glyph of third god of Palenque Triad

God M with spear and merchant's pack

God M and glyph

alternate glyph for third god of Palenque Triad?

god of month Uo

god of number 7

Tablet, sanctuary, Temple of the Sun: central shield and spears. Note humanized jaguar traits of face.

Figure 23. The black gods.

Mixcoatl, with the shield and spear of war

God Z

God L as warrior

glyphs of God L

Dresden codex, p. 14c: God L, distinguished by fleshless lower jaw, white forehead. Note feathers (?), bird, and maise plant in headdress.

Tablet, Temple of the Sun: *a*. seven-black-(deity); *b*. note similarity of clothing to deity at right and headdress like God L and deity at right.

Tablet outside sanctuary, Temple of the Cross, Palenque. Old man smoking. Note jaguar-skin garment and jaguar ears. Headdress has feathers (?), mythical bird, and maize plant. In latter, note inverted head with death symbol.

same. He points out the close parallel between the *Dresden* flood page (D74), which shows God L, and the *Madrid* page (M32a–b), which shows God Z. In the *Madrid,* God Z is shown with spear in hand, or waving an axe and firebrand, or hunting. At Palenque, a god with the typical headdress of God L is shown supporting shield and spears in the miscalled "Temple of the Sun." All these associations suggest a war god; he may be the equivalent of the Aztec Mixcoatl, who was the first warrior and an important hunt god. For a further identification, see "The Palenque Triad" below.

Cyrus Thomas (1888, p. 358) identified God L with the Black God, Ek Chuah, who has more usually been identified with God M. Thompson in turn identifies God M, rather than God L, with a Maya equivalent of Mixcoatl. God M is depicted with a remarkable long nose, and the Aztec god of merchants who corresponds to Ek Chuah is Yacatecuhtli 'Nose Lord'. Both God L and God M are frequently shown with a scorpion's tail, and it has been pointed out (Brinton, 1895, p. 67) that Ek Chuh means 'Black Scorcher', a name of a large black scorpion. The pack on the back of God M seems to me to confirm his merchant status and equivalence with Ek Chuah (Chuah is probably a derivative of Chuh); Thompson has argued that the pack might equally well pertain to a hunter. God M is the god of the number seven and likewise appears in Glyph C of the Lunar Series and as the deity of the month Uo (see Thompson 1962, p. 282, for a discussion of the substitution of the normal glyph of God M for the usual head variant and Kelley 1962a, pp. 29, 39, for the identification of God M as Ek Chuah and the parallel identification of the god of Uo as Ek Chuah).

God Y (Zimmermann's G13) was recognized by Seler, although not given a separate designation by him. His face markings are closely similar to those of God L, and he seems to be a deer god (Seler 1902–1923). He is the regent of katun 12 Ahau (*Paris,* p. 10) and is apparently shown as the husband of a deer goddess (*Dresden,* p. 13c). Thompson (1950, p. 76) points out that in Yucatán the chief god of hunting, especially of the deer, is Zip or Ek Zip ('Black Zip'), although he seems inclined to identify this deity with God M or God Z. The glyphs of God Y (Fig. 25) show a 'seven' (Yuc. *uuc*) prefixed, and Zimmermann (1956, p. 164) suggests a connection with the deity Ah Uuc Yol Zip. Zimmermann's identifications of God Y in the *Madrid* overlap with those by which Thompson originally established the deity whom Zimmermann calls Z. This Black Deer God of the codices, associated with the number seven, is certainly likely to be the equivalent of Ah Uuc Yol Zip.

If so, T146 is apt to be *yol.* Other contexts do not seem to support this identification, and Thompson regards T96 as *yol.*

God N

Zimmermann's Gods G2, G2a, and G2b seem to be a series of closely related gods. Any of these gods is normally shown with a net on his forehead and a conch shell or turtle shell on his back. Zimmermann's G2 includes gods whose hieroglyphs are T63 or 64 or 65:528, with either a 'four' or a 'five' prefixed. He distinguishes them from G2a, which has a 'five' prefixed to T63/64/65:548. T528 is *haab* 'year', and T548 is *tun* 'year'; in the Venus deity series, they substitute for each other in the name of God N. I regard them as fully equivalent and hence feel that Zimmermann has made a false distinction in separating G2 and G2a. On the other hand, the 'four' and 'five' lumped in G2 are not equivalent and should be distinguished, whatever their relationship. The glyph for G2b lacks a numerical prefix, and the net is directly attached to the conch shell (T210) or to the turtle shell (T626). In the latter form, it occurs as part of the name glyphs of the rulers of Piedras Negras. The gods called N seem to be the gods of the end of the year, the unlucky five-day period called *uayeb;* yet their characteristics seem to be good ones, and they are not directly associated with that period. Knorozov (1955b, p. 72) read the net glyph as *vay, vaay,* as a derivative of *bay* 'net', but there seems to be no adequate evidence for this postulated phonetic change. Interestingly, in the *Madrid,* God N is sometimes represented simply as a turtle. He upon occasion wears the tun sign as a headdress, which identifies him with the old god of the number five. Since the gods of the end of the year among the modern Maya are the Mams, Thompson (1950, p. 133) identified the N Gods as Mams. In a recent paper devoted to these gods, he maintains that they are Bacabs, supporters of the sky, rather than Mams. The association of Bacabs and turtles has long been known, and the new identification seems preferable to the old. I identify the Mams with the opossums associated with the year's end in the *Dresden* new-year ceremonies (Fig. 88); I am therefore inclined to doubt that they were also turtles. Quite probably, the modern deities called Mams have many of the functions and characteristics of the N Gods.

Schellhas also identified an isolated deity on *Dresden* page 20b, to whom he assigned two nonconsecutive glyph blocks. Brinton (1895, p. 125) called this deity Q and said he was "probably a mere person-

N' (G2a)
5 net tun

net shell

N'' (G2b)
net turtle shell
(cf. Fig. 25)

N (G2)
5 net *haab*

4 net *haab*

Figure 24. God N and variants.

age." Zimmermann has called him God U, or G26, and accepts the glyphs shown in Figure 25 as his name. It is not impossible that he is the same as a deity on *Dresden* page 20c, called by Thompson "the White Lord" (Fig. 25), since comparable though not identical glyphs occur with God U.

Thompson (1950, p. 56) has identified the glyphs of a rather obscure deity known in Yucatán as Bolon Yocte (from earlier *bolon oc-te*) (Fig. 25). *Bolon* is the well-known number 'nine', Oc is a known day sign, and Thompson's brilliant decipherment of *te* is discussed in Chapter 10. This deity is apparently among those fighting God N on *Dresden* page 60. He is known as a regent of katun 11 Ahau, and this page is devoted to a katun 11 Ahau. His glyphs appear fairly frequently at Palenque.

Several studies by Seler were of importance in identifying glyphs of gods found in series at various places in the codices. Thus, on pages D46–50, dealing with the Venus calendar, one finds three sections of

text above pictures of deities. In the center section, deities are shown with spears and spear throwers (Fig. 26), and in the bottom section gods are shown pierced by the spears. The first six glyph blocks in the center section are parallel on all five pages. First comes a verb, then glyphs indicating the direction, then a name glyph, then the glyphs for Venus, then another name glyph, and then the sequence T1.568. On D46, the god throwing the spear is God L, and the god being speared is God K. The first name glyger is that of God L, and the second is that of God K. It is, therefore, highly likely that the same relationship holds in the other cases. On D47, the glyphs are 'Ten Sky', and Ralph L. Roys (1933, p. 101) has pointed out that the deity depicted corresponds to descriptions of a deity, Lahun Chan, which would be Cholan for 'Ten Sky' and might be a borrowing in Yucatec. Thompson (1950, pp. 218–219) presents a series of roundabout arguments reinforcing the identification of the deity throwing the spear with Lahun Chan,

b   d

T 1028

probably a different
glyph from T 1028a, c
T 1028d may be
a goddess.

c   a

T 1028
God U

God Y
Note deer horn
headdress
God of Katun 12 Ahau

glyph of
Bolon-oc-te
from
Palenque

Deer Goddess
wife of God Y,
above

God N
in his
turtle shell

spearpoint
and shield
indicating war

Bolon-oc-te,
one of the two
attacking gods

glyph of
God of Katun
13 Ahau
apparently an
alternate name
for God E

God W
G28
glyphs
not
known

God X
G30
glyphs not
known

the "White Lord"
carried by
the goddess

Figure 25. Miscellaneous gods.

although the glyphs themselves remain the most telling evidence for this view. The deity struck is an animal which has been identified as a puma, and the glyphs which should indicate his name are apparently those of the jaguar. This is somewhat disconcerting, but should almost certainly be considered a correspondence rather than a discrepancy. On D48, the deity struck is the Maize God, and his glyphs appear, in accordance with hypothesis, in the fifth glyph block. This is enough support to warrant the conclusion that the other deities are named in the corresponding passages, and these identifications are assumed in Figure 26. Thompson (1950, pp. 218–220) regards all of these gods as Venus gods, but while the glyphs and dates certainly imply some sort of identification with Venus, I do not think that adequate evidence has been presented for regarding them as basically Venus gods, rather than as secondarily identified with Venus. D25 lists some of the same deities, in association with the date 4 Ahau 8 Cumku, with a different verb. The first two deities with spears are given and then all five of the deities speared, in the same order, with some slight variation in glyphs. Seler (1898) has drawn attention to the remarkably close similarity to passages from the *Borgia* group of codices of southern Mexico (Plate 3) and to a passage from the Aztec *Annals of Cuauhtitlan* (Velásquez n.d.) indicating that the morning star spears the following groups on different days: the aged, the children, the great lords, the rain (causing drought).

The identification of the hieroglyphs of the deities on these pages of the *Dresden* was finally completed by Barthel in 1952. It has long been realized that hieroglyphic passages to the left of the pictures on each page, associated with the changing dates of the Venus cycle, give the successive names of twenty deities in two parallel lists. In the first list, there is a verb (the same one found with the pictures), which is followed by direction glyphs, then by a deity name, and then by the glyphs for Venus. The only difference in the two lists is that the verbs on D46 and in the last column of D50 lack the past-tense suffix (T181) found on the other pages. The presence of a considerable number of known deity names makes it likely that the other glyphs are also deity names. Those glyphs associated with the east are also found, in the same order and associated with the same verb, in the introduction to the Venus table, D24. It should be noted that the deities referred to on D24 are different from the deities associated with the east in the pictures in the central section of the following pages, with whom the same passages seem to occur.

In the bottom section, D46, the first deity name (associated with the east) seems to have the same

elements which appear in the headdress of the deity at the top of the page. The deity at the top of the second page is a death god, and the deity glyphs in the comparable position are of God A, the Death God. At the top of the third page is God N, and the glyphs in comparable position are of the God N variant with 'four' prefixed. At the top of D49 is a goddess, and the glyphs are those of a goddess with the 'moon' suffix. Finally, at the top of page 50, the Maize God appears with a death god. The glyph is that of a deity with the *chicchan* spot on his head, a quite appropriate identification for the death god shown. Thus, all these deities can now be recognized by their proper glyphs, thanks to the work of Seler and Barthel.

Seler (1904a; 1902–1903, pp. 289–290), in his usual penetrating fashion, drew attention to the close parallel between the five gods shown with spears in the central section of the *Dresden* Venus almanac and the gods of what he identified as the five Venus periods in the *Borgia* and *Vaticanus 3773* codices. The precise geographical origin of the *Borgia* group codices, to which these two belong, is still disputed. They closely resemble the Mixtec manuscripts of Oaxaca but lack the calendar names so typical of the latter group. Strangely, only four deities are shown in the latter two codices; these are assigned by Seler to the cardinal directions; he assumed that the deity of the center was omitted. The identification is based on the associated day glyphs, which emphasize the possible initial days of the Venus periods of a 104-year Venus cycle. Of these four deities, Tlaloc (the Rain God) and Xipe Totec (god of flaying) present no problems in identification. A third deity was originally identified by Seler as Tlahuizcalpantecuhtli (the god of the morning star). He later identified this deity from a mass of parallel representations as Mixcoatl, god of hunting and war, who often has the same face painting as Tlahuizcalpantecuhtli. The fourth deity he identified at one time as Tepeyollotl (1904b; 1904a, p. 367), at another (1901–1902, pp. 145–146) as an obscure Mixtec deity with the calendar name Four Snake, and finally (1902–1903, p. 286) as a specialized aspect of Quetzalcoatl as ruler of Tula; he referred to the latter as Quetzalcoatl-Huemac.

Strangely enough, although Seler correctly recognized the generic parallel between these deities and those of the five Venus periods of *Dresden*, he seems to have completely confused the identification of the respective deities in his final analysis. In his 1898 study (translated in 1904a), he identified the deities by implication because of their assumed association with the directions. This assumption was wrong, since

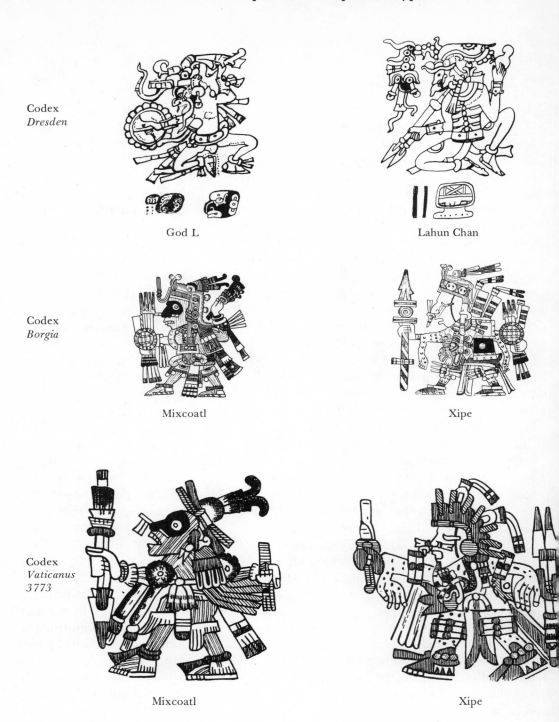

Codex *Dresden*

God L

Lahun Chan

Codex *Borgia*

Mixcoatl

Xipe

Codex *Vaticanus 3773*

Mixcoatl

Xipe

Figure 26. Spear-throwing deities. *See also* Plate 3.

unidentified gods

Tlaloc

Four Snake

Tlaloc

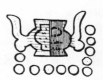

Four Snake

all five of these Maya gods are explicitly associated by the accompanying glyphs with the east. However, this did involve associating the deities of the *Borgia* in a specific order with those of the *Dresden* as follows: *Borgia* upper left: D46b; *Borgia* lower left: D47b; *Borgia* lower right: D48b; *Borgia* upper right: D49b. This order, completely rejected in Seler's later studies, seems to me correct. I have argued elsewhere on other grounds that Mixcoatl (*Borgia* upper left) corresponds to God L (D46b). The second parallel between Lahun Chan (D47b) and Xipe Totec (*Borgia* lower left) is rather unexpected, but convincing on analysis. Xipe Totec, as god of flaying, is usually believed to have originated as a god of husked maize (Thompson 1933, p. 145). Lahun Chan, represented with his ribs bare, as befits a god of flaying, wears the typical ear-of-corn headdress of the Maya Maize God. In the third parallel, the animal god of D48b is shown wearing a small disk with three dots on it, which is otherwise typical of the frog deity of the inscriptions. Thompson (1950, p. 219) suggests that he is the same as the deity of D37a, who likewise has animal features and wears a similar disk with three dots as an earplug. Seler identified the latter as a frog, apparently because of his rain associations and the disk with the three dots placed in his ear. Zimmermann (1956, p. 168) has given the latter god the designation X and considers his identity with the god of the Venus pages doubtful. God X is drawn in a fashion remarkably similar to the fishing god depicted in the canoe texts from Tikal (Fig. 80), and I think they must be the same. Thompson (1950, p. 219) suggested that the deity of D48b might be the equivalent of the Dog God, Xolotl, the twin of Quetzalcoatl, but this seems to depend on his hypothesis that all five deities are specifically Venus planetary gods. As a parallel to Tlaloc, the Rain God (*Borgia* p. 25, lower right), a frog god seems quite reasonable, and, indeed, *Madrid* page 12b shows God B, the Rain God, in the form of a frog.

The fourth parallel, in many ways the clearest of all, is likewise one of the most interesting. The deity of *Borgia* page 25, upper right, is shown with a snake emerging from just below the nose and with a bird headdress. Behind his eye are two curved lines going in opposite directions. The deity of D49b likewise shows a snake emerging from the vicinity of the mouth and wears a bird headdress. The name glyphs of this deity in the *Dresden* include a head-variant glyph which has two curved lines going back from the eye in opposite directions. While the bird headdress is fairly common among deities, both of the other traits seem to be rare. Surprisingly, the deity of the *Vaticanus* lacks all three of these traits shared by the

Borgia and *Dresden* representations but does share face and body paint, as well as knives in the mouth, with the *Borgia* representation. Seler (1902–1903, p. 288) describes the figure in *Borgia* as combining "*Quetzalcouatl's* face-painting and beard with the Sun God's dress badges." He describes the deity of D49b as having face painting like that of the Mexican Tezcatlipoca rather than like that of Quetzalcoatl. In 1901, Seler (1901, pp. 145–146) concluded that the *Borgia* deity "unmistakably" corresponded to a deity Four Snake depicted in the *Vienna* and other codices which we now know to be Mixtec. The trait upon which this identification rests, namely the snake emerging from behind the mouth, seems specific enough to fully validate this conclusion. In the *Vienna* (Fig. 27), Four Snake is represented with Nine Wind (Quetzalcoatl), and both deities have their accompanying name hieroglyphs. That of Four Snake depicts a monster carrying a sun disk on his back. In the *Nuttall* codex, page 37, Four Snake appears carrying a Venus staff, and he is associated, here and elsewhere, with certain rain gods. In the Mixtec manuscripts, his headdress is customarily of entwined rattlesnakes. Four Snake normally appears with a deity Seven Snake, who is often represented in a very similar way, but who never has the snake emerging from behind the mouth. Seler (1902–1903, pp. 287–288) finally rejected the identity of the *Borgia* deity as Four Snake in favor of the identity with Seven Snake and further suggested that this was a special form of Quetzalcoatl, called "Quetzalcoatl-Huemac, of Tollan [Tula]" as mentioned earlier, to be distinguished from Nine Wind Quetzalcoatl. I see no reason to reject the original identity of this *Borgia* deity with Four Snake, indicated by the snake behind the mouth, but would admit the possibility of some sort of conceptual relationship to Quetzalcoatl. Thompson (1950, p. 220) once suggested "with some assurance" that the deity of D49b was to be identified with Quetzalcoatl-Kukulcan. He thought that the snake projecting from behind the mouth, coupled with a bird appearing as an ear ornament, suggested a rebus for the name "Quetzal snake." As weakening his case, he pointed out the fact that the deity does not have the face painting of Quetzalcoatl. This no longer seems of much weight, since the *Borgia* deity, who seems to be parallel, does have the face paint of Quetzalcoatl. My major objection to this identification is that the bird does not seem to me to correspond to normal representations of a quetzal. In terms of the Mixtec parallels, we may add that the snake appears, but the bird does not, making a rebus use less likely, and that Four Snake seems to have a completely different name (Sun-Carrying Monster).

, p. 5

Seven Snake	Four Snake

Vienna, p. 30   Four Snake
sun-carrying monster   Nine Wind

Figure 27. The god Four Snake.

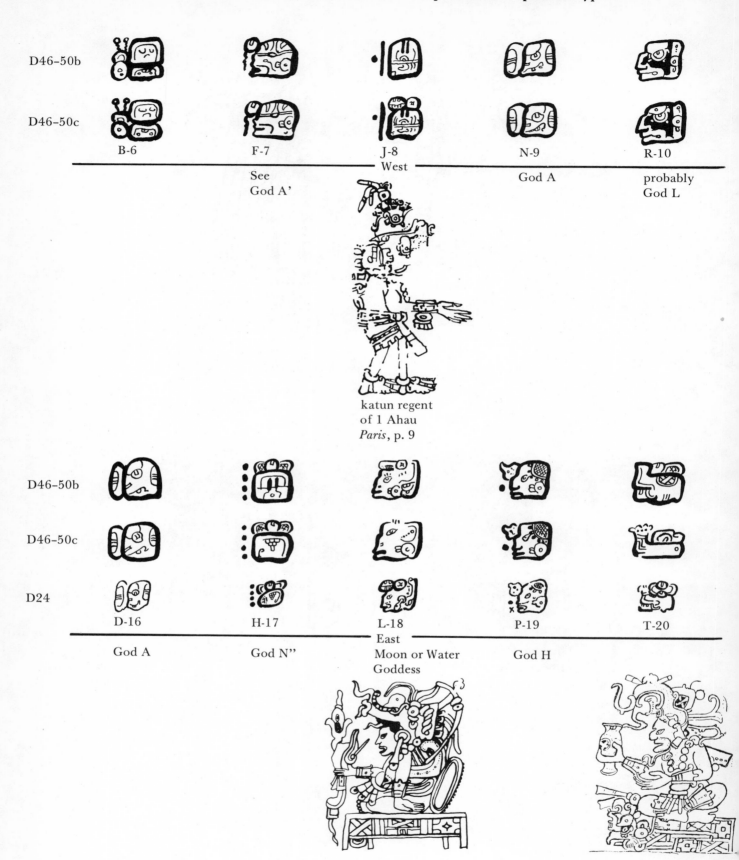

	B-6	F-7	J-8	N-9	R-10
D46–50b					
D46–50c					

West

	See God A'		God A	probably God L

katun regent
of 1 Ahau
Paris, p. 9

	D-16	H-17	L-18	P-19	T-20
D46–50b					
D46–50c					
D24					

East

| God A | God N'' | Moon or Water Goddess | God H | |

Figure 28. Deity glyphs in the *Dresden* Venus passages.

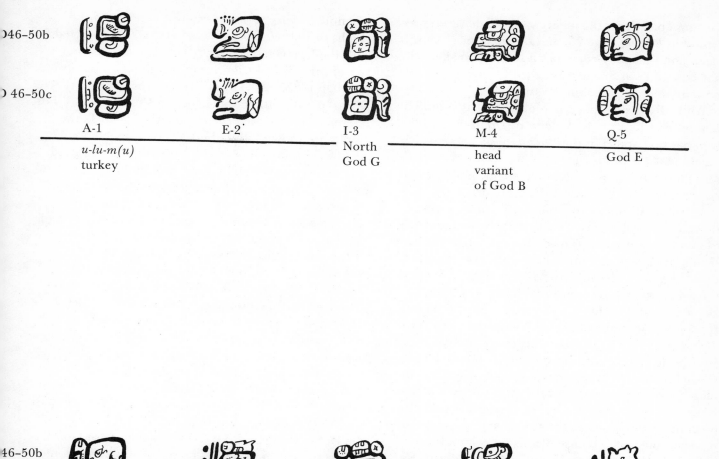

046–50b

046–50c

A-1

u-lu-m(u)
turkey

E-2

I-3
North
God G

M-4

head
variant
of God B

Q-5

God E

46–50b

46–50c

C-11

G-12

muan
bird

K-13
South

O-14

God K

S-15

peccary

To sum up, I think the identity of the deities represented in *Borgia,* page 25, and *Dresden,* page 49b, is clear, and that they correspond to Four Snake. I do not believe Four Snake was called Quetzalcoatl but do think he had some similar functions.

While discussing this group of deities, it should be pointed out that the fifth deity of *Dresden* (p. 50b), who has no parallel in the *Borgia,* has a name which I would read Ca-ca-tu-?-l(a) (see Fig. 62). If a corresponding deity name could be recognized, it would give the value of the unidentified glyph.

It will be seen that these identifications imply a strict sequential correspondence of the two series. If the same requirement is made for the series of deities struck by spears, as I think it must be, we find that three of Seler's identifications seem sound, but that the other two are reversed. (See Plate 3. To further aid comparative studies, a virtually identical series from *Bologna* is also included.) Thus the Corn Goddess is the first of the *Vaticanus* series, and the Corn God is the third of the *Dresden* series (D48c). The second of the *Dresden* series is the puma (or incompletely drawn jaguar?), and the fifth of the *Vaticanus* series is the jaguar. The eagle in the third *Vaticanus* position corresponds to the *Borgia* shield and spear, representing war. Because of this correspondence, Seler argued that the eagle also symbolized war. He further argued that the fifth deity in the *Dresden* series (D50c) also represented a warrior, since he is the only one of the pierced figures carrying a spear.

Seler did not utilize the fixed sequence implied by these three equations in comparing the remaining two pairs of deities. He apparently thought that a more meaningful correspondence was achieved by transposing these deities, so that Bolon Tzacab was equated with Chalchihuitlicue and the animal-headed figure of *Dresden* page 49c with the throne as a symbol of royalty. However, the correspondences resulting from a strict sequential comparison likewise show some symbolic similarities. With such a comparison, the animal-headed figure wearing a jade necklace and having a half circle of dots over the eye must correspond to Chalchihuitlicue 'Jade Skirt', the Water Goddess. A full circle of dots is shown on her skirt in the *Vaticanus.* A similar association of jade and dots with water is found among the Mayas (Thompson 1950, p. 277). The glyph of the animal-headed god is composed of the turtle-head grapheme and the small headless human figure on D49b, although on D24 only the latter is present.

The complex associations of God K are such that he might be equated either with the throne or with the Water Goddess. The characteristics of God K are shown in Figure 34.

Another deity series of interest consists of the glyphs of the twenty deities of D46–50, connected with the Venus table (Fig. 28). This series is given twice, with slight variations in the glyphs. Thompson (1950, pp. 223–224) has discussed the entire series, which he calls "directional gods in Venus tables." For reference, he assigned them the letters A to T; the glyphs are shown as numbers 1–20 of his Figure 42. To avoid any possible confusion with other series, I will identify each one in discussion by both letter and number. It has already been pointed out that the five glygers occurring in the first position of the lower series, associated with the direction east, are those of the five deities pictured in the upper compartments of the same pages, as shown by Barthel. These are, respectively, D-16, the Death God (God A); H-17, God N; L-18, the Moon or Water Goddess; P-19, the Chicchan Death God (God H); and T-20, the deity who wears the headdress of the long-snouted monster with crossbands in his eyes. Tikal Stela 31 shows the head of this monster substituting for the so-called Venus monster as patron of the month Yax.

Glygers of clearly recognizable deities are I-3, the Sun God (God G); M-4, a head variant of the glyph of God B; Q-5, the head of the Corn God (God E); N-9, the Death God (God A); O-14, the glyger for God K. This series certainly shows no particular indication of being primarily Venus gods; instead major deities of the regular pantheon appear to be associated in some way with Venus.

A plausible case can be made for the identity of certain other deities here. A-1 consists of the glyphs which, following Knorozov, I read *u-lu-mu,* i.e., *ulum* 'turkey' (see Fig. 61); Barthel (1955a, p. 18) has read the same glyger as *ubech* 'pheasant', one of the major birds of sacrifice. This is based on interpreting the Knorozov *lu* as 'sacrifice' and the Knorozov *mu* as 'bird' and on an identification by Seler of this series with a *Borgia* series which shows a turkey. Thompson has suggested that the A-1 glyger represents some god of the underworld, a suggestion based entirely on associations of the *lu* glyph. He mistakenly refers to the *mu* glyph as a "bundle."

S-15 is the glyger for the peccary, with 'seven' prefixed (see Chapter 5 for a contrary identification with the macaw). G-12 is regarded by Thompson (1950, p. 224) as "a deity of the 13 skies or the thirteenth layer of heaven"—more specifically, I regard it as the *muan* bird, which has these associations, although the glyger is not fully identical. R-10 is called by Thompson "the black-headed variant of God D." The glyph is, in fact, identical with that of God L, save that it lacks the *imix* prefix characteristic of the glyger of that deity. The *imix* normally has two lines of dots suspended from it, and these appear as an infix to the earplug in R-10. If the deity intended is not God L, it is probably one of the other closely related black gods. F-7 is a deity whose glyph has 'night' infixed, a death sign on the cheek, and a death eye. In short, the name glyph has the characteristics of Zimmermann's deity G1a (God A'). J-8 is the katun regent of *Paris* page 9, a Katun 1 Ahau (see following discussion). This leaves unidentified only E-2, B-6, C-11, and K-13. Both E-2 and C-11 have the *etz'nab* infix, and K-13 is *akbal* infixed in the serpent-scales glyph with an unidentified prefix and *ben-ich*.

Katun Gods in the Paris Codex

Another series of deities whose name glyphs occupy a regular position and are hence identifiable is that of the katun gods of the *Paris* codex, as recognized by Seler. The codex shows, for each katun, a god seated on a sky band and another god approaching with an offering. On P11, the approaching god is God D, and the glyger for God D appears at the top of the second column of glyphs; on P8, the god is shown with a bird head, and a bird-head pictograph heads the second column of glyphs; on P7, the approaching god wears a headdress with a crossband on it, and the glyph heading column 2 is a head with a crossband; on P6, the approaching God is God N, in his conch shell, and the glyph heading the second column is his well-known glyger, in the turtle-shell variant. Contrary to expectation, the glyger heading column 2 on P4 is that of God C, whereas the deity approaching with a gift wears the headdress of God P, whose name glyphs do not seem to appear at any point on the page. On P3, there is also a problem, since the Corn God is apparently represented, and the glyph is not the normal glyph of God E. However, in this case, it is not known to be the glyph of any other deity and may be a synonym for God E or the name of another closely related god. Despite the one clear discrepancy, on present evidence it seems useful to hypothesize, with Seler, that the other glygers heading the second columns of glyphs on these pages are the names of the approaching gods. Strangely, the colonial "prophecies" for the various katuns contain relatively little which is helpful. Perhaps the most striking correspondence is that the deity Yax Coc Ah Mut, the latter part of whose name contains the element *mut* 'bird', is said to be the 'face in heaven' of the katun 3 Ahau, which has the previously mentioned bird deity. Seler's conclusion that the glyph represents the name of the deity subsequently known as Yax Coc Ah Mut

seems quite likely, but the glyph is probably some earlier synonym and not to be read *yax coc ah mut*, since I doubt that a single pictograph could represent four morphemes.

Twenty Deities in the Dresden

On pages 4–10 of the *Dresden* appear a series of twenty deities, with six glyph blocks above each deity. The meaning of the opening verb, identical in all twenty passages, has not been ascertained; it is followed in all cases by a glyger which I read *tu cech* (earlier *tu cec*). This is followed in all cases where identity can be established by the glyger of the deity represented below—always in the third glyph block, sometimes with an additional name or title in the fourth glyph block. The remaining two glyph blocks are probably augural. The deities are associated with dates either two, three, or four days apart. While most of the deities are well known, some appear only in this sequence. Zimmermann (1933) has suggested that an additional series of seven deities mentioned, but not depicted, above the body of the two-headed dragon on D4–5 may raise the total of this sequence to twenty-seven deities. In this case, each deity is referred to by a name in the second glyph block and by a verb in the first glyph block which is identical to the opening verb in the passage under discussion. Unfortunately for this hypothesis, the top table re-enters at a day 10 Imix, whereas the second one starts at 12 Ix. There have been various attempts to associate this list of twenty deities with other lists of twenty deities, such as the gods of the twenty day names and the deities of the Venus table, but the associations are seldom fully convincing. Förstemann (1904, pp. 569–571) noted that the jaguar and the vulture appear as deities on page 8 and that they are separated by two days. The general Mesoamerican Day of the Jaguar is followed after two days by the Day of the Vulture. However, if one starts from the day 10 Imix as base of the table, the days reached are not Jaguar and Vulture. Förstemann suggests that they should be and that the base of the table ought to be Cib instead of Imix. By making such unwarranted changes in the base, it is possible to explain almost anything. Taking the table at face value, several days appear more than once, with different gods; other days do not appear at all, and the order does not coincide with that which one would expect. Nonetheless, there are enough similarities to the sequence of day-name gods to make one wonder if some common organizing principle may not have been used. Barthel (1968*b*) has now shown that the intervals associated with this deity sequence are those of sidereal lunar months.

Seler (1904a, p. 216), approaching the problem differently, has regarded these twenty gods as a consecutive series and has compared them with the deities of the twenty day names, as shown in the *Borgia* and related codices from southern Mexico. He equated the first deity of the sequence with the god of the day Cuetzpalin (Maya Kan); considering that Kan was one of the possible year bearers, this forms a logical beginning point for a sequence. Unfortunately, this was true of sixteenth century Yucatán, but it was not true in the *Dresden*. Moreover, these deities are associated with nonconsecutive dates, and the first one is associated with Akbal, not Kan. There are a number of similarities but not, I think, enough to counterbalance the structural unlikelihood.

Isolated Deity Figures

Besides these legitimate comparisons of different series of deities, there are also occasional isolated deity figures whose hieroglyphs may be recognized from the general grammatical structure of the passages in which they occur. Few of these have clear-cut characteristics. Thompson (1950, p. 56) discusses a deity known in colonial times as Bolon Yocte, of whom little is known. *Bolon* is 'nine', and the glyph for *oc* has long been known as one of the day names. *Yoc* is a grammatical derivative of *oc*. Thompson points out a repeated deity-name glyph containing 'nine', *oc,* and a third glyph (T87), also found with the meaning 'tree' and as a numerical classifier with month names. The morpheme *te'* has the meaning 'tree', and *te* is a numerical classifier, as Thompson points out; so the glyph *bolon-oc-te* is almost certainly read correctly.

Another deity has been called "the White Lord" by Thompson (1958, p. 303) because his glyphs have 'white' as the first grapheme and *ahau* 'lord', infixed in an unusual frame, with the bundle affix.

The Mams

The new-year pages of the *Dresden* show the last days of the old years and the first days of the new years, in four groups. Associated with the ends of the old years are opossums, carrying deities. The structure of the lengthy text above them seems to say "[color] [opossum] *u mam,* [deity] *u cuch*"; in the text, the color of the opossum varies in the four different kinds of years. From the context, the glyph for the opossums seems quite clear. The phrase *u mam* 'its Mam' is based on Landa's *ma,* also found in other contexts where this interpretation is reasonable. This phonetic rendering means that the Mams should be, or include, the opossums shown below. This seems plausible, for the Mams are gods of the year's end. Moreover, the Tzeltal months Alauch and Mucuch seem to be the Big and Little Opossum months. They correspond to Cakchiquel Nabei Mam and Rucab Mam, Great Mam and Little Mam. Whatever this may mean, it seems to indicate that in some circumstances Mam and Opossum were at least partly interchangeable. This does not necessarily mean that all Mams, who are conceived of as a large class of ancestral gods, were necessarily opossums, nor does it mean that the opossum never played any other role in Mesoamerican mythology.

Month Deities

In addition to these deity names from the codices, a certain number of names are known from the inscriptions, including many which cannot easily be equated with those of the codices, as well as some that are clearly "identical," in the sense of being chronologically separated ideas about a god who represents a historical continuity. The fullest and most important set is the list of month deities. Beyer was able to show that the "variable element" of the Initial Series Introducing Glyph (what Spinden called the "title glyph") varied regularly according to the month in which the Initial Series date occurred. Beyer hypothesized that the name given was that of a deity of the month. Thompson (1950, pp. 105–107) discusses these patrons of the months on the basis of their glyphs. Morley (1947, p. 234) lists them even more briefly. Strangely, no one has attempted to equate them with the month deities mentioned by Landa, although Morley (1947, pp. 247–256) discusses these only a few pages later and does list both together in his Table VI. Neither has anyone made any formal published attempt, as far as I know, to equate the Aztec deities with Mayan deities of equivalent months. Plate 4 shows the glyphs of the month deities, in sequence, with Morley and Thompson identifications compared with deity lists for the months from Landa and Bernardino de Sahagún. Such a comparison immediately reveals several interesting congruences, and suggests modifications or corrections of a number of identifications made by Morley and Thompson.

There is no dispute about the jaguar as patron of Pop, the Sun God as patron of Yaxkin, the Moon Goddess as patron of Ch'en, the Venus God or Star God(?) as patron of Yax, and the Wind God as patron of Mac. The fact that the birth of Huitzilopochtli was celebrated on the Aztec equivalent of Mayan Yaxkin ('New Sun') throws more light on the origins of that famed Aztec War God than it does on the glyphs. It is of interest to find that Tititl, the equivalent of Ch'en, was the feast of the young Moon Goddess, as this offers some support for the view that month gods, like other aspects of the calendar, derive from an ancient common prototype.

Morley's statement that the patron of Zip was a "serpent-god" is probably based entirely on the rather reptilian head. The correctness of Thompson's identification of the head as being that of the so-called Mars beast may be seen by comparing the glyphs of the two. The association of this reptilian peccary or deer with the Moon Goddess of the Aztecs or with Ix Chel of the Mayas is not clear. Morley's remarkable idea that the patron of Zotz was the bat is an example of how easy it is to see what we expect to see. Since *zotz* means 'bat', he expected a bat. The deity is, however, a fish—probably, as Thompson suggests, the *xoc* fish. The patron deity of Ceh is neither New Fire (a view in which Morley follows Spinden) nor the Sky God, as Thompson maintained in 1950. The glyger, which recurs elsewhere, still has a completely unknown referent. The Sky God has also been associated with the month Zec, where an alleged 'sky' glyph alternates with the *cab* 'earth' glyph. The glyph is certainly very like 'sky' and sometimes seems to occur at Palenque substituting for the regular 'sky' glyph. Nonetheless, it is normally distinct, as may be seen in Figure 54. According to Landa, this month was dedicated to Hobnil, who was a bee god. Since *cab* may mean 'bee' as well as 'earth' (Fig. 37), I suspect that 'bee' is intended here, although Thompson suggests that there may be some connection with the 260-day cycle. It may be mentioned that the Aztecs made sacrifices for "the birth of the mountains" during their equivalent month, Tepeilhuitl. This might suggest that *cab* has here the 'earth' meaning, but this interpretation does not seem likely.

The patron of Zac is represented as some sort of reptilian or amphibian monster, variously regarded as a toad or frog and probably equivalent to the god of the twenty-day period. Tlaloc, the Rain God, is patron of the Aztec equivalent, and it has been shown that God B, a god of rain, is sometimes represented in frog form. Taking these facts together, I am inclined to believe that this deity represents the Rain God in frog form and may explain the general absence on the monuments of the glyph for God B as found in the codices. Barthel (1955a, p. 7) has pointed out an exceptional instance of the God B glyph appearing on a monument at Chichen Itza.

The patron of Pax is represented by an anthropomorphized feline head, rather resembling the head of the patron of Uo, accompanied by a representation of a paw. Thompson suggests it may stand for *chac mol* 'giant paw', a name for the jaguar. He points out that Landa puts a feast to the god Cit Chac Coh 'Great Father Puma' in this month, but he tends to regard it as coincidental. I am inclined to think that this patron of Pax known from the inscriptions is related somehow to Cit Chac Coh, although no *chac* glyph appears in the name. Certain similarities to the glyph of the seventh deity of the Nine Lords of the Night are apparent. They do not amount to identity, and it is not clear whether they refer to the same or a related deity. There are also similarities to the first form of Glyph X of the Lunar Series.

The related patron of Uo can be identified with some assurance as Ek Chuah and God M, as well as the patron of the number seven (see Fig. 23). The glyph typically has the eye which appears alone as the glyph of God M in the codices. A recently discovered inscription shows M's glyph for the patron of Uo. The identity of God M as Ek Chuah has been challenged, but a consistent series of indications support it. The month Uo corresponds to the Aztec Ue Micailhuitl, in which there is a feast of the merchants, associated with the death of the god Yacatecuhtli. The birth of Yacatecuhtli is celebrated by the Aztecs in Toxcatl, corresponding to Maya Muan. The month Muan was the time of a festival celebrated by the owners of cacao plantations, dedicated to Ek Chuah. Cacao beans were used as money and are especially connected with the merchants. Both Yacatecuhtli and Ek Chuah are merchant gods. Yacatecuhtli is represented as a black deity with a long nose (the name means literally 'Nose Lord'), and God M is likewise represented as a black deity with a long nose. God M is also normally shown with a bundle on his back, similar to that of the merchants. Finally, he is also shown at times with a scorpion's tail, and *ek chuh* is a Yucatec term for 'scorpion' (cf. Kelley 1965, p. 102). Thompson's (1950, p. 76) identification of God M as a Maya deity corresponding to Aztec Mixcoatl is based on associations with war and hunting and on a substantial overlap of characteristics between Mixcoatl and Yacatecuhtli. Actually, the Maya seem to have had both a black god of hunting and a black

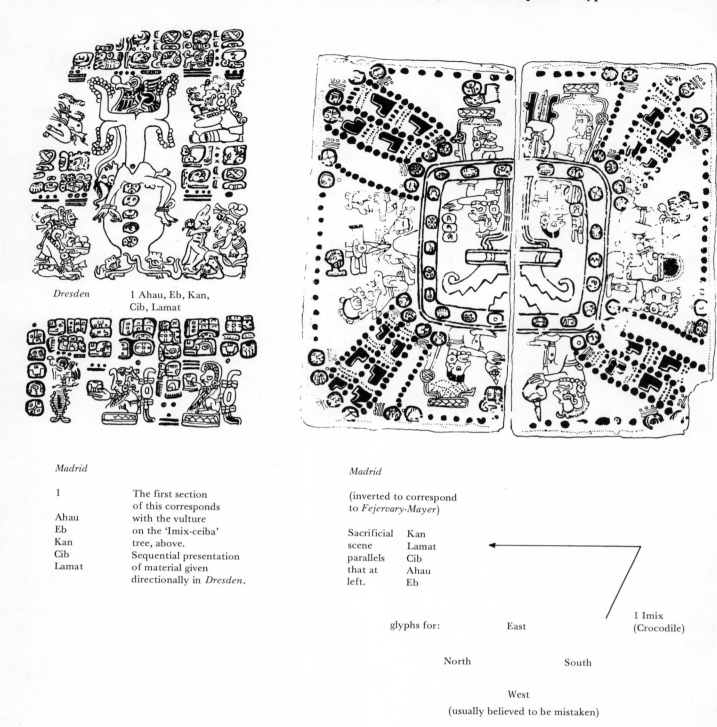

Dresden 1 Ahau, Eb, Kan,
  Cib, Lamat

Madrid

1

Ahau
Eb
Kan
Cib
Lamat

The first section
of this corresponds
with the vulture
on the 'Imix-ceiba'
tree, above.
Sequential presentation
of material given
directionally in *Dresden*.

Madrid

(inverted to correspond
to *Fejervary-Mayer*)

Sacrificial   Kan
scene   Lamat
parallels   Cib
that at   Ahau
left.   Eb

glyphs for: East   1 Imix
                              (Crocodile)

     North   South

        West
(usually believed to be mistaken)

Figure 29. Direction gods from *Dresden*, *Madrid*, and *Fejervary-Mayer*.

Fejervary-Mayer

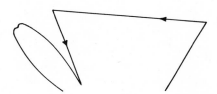

(1) Reed

(1) Crocodile

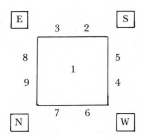

Directional placement of the Nine Lords of the Night. Their normal sequence is indicated by the numbers. See Fig. 31.

war god (whom I identify with God L), but neither of them seems to have been God M. In any case, references to a group of seven black gods suggest that they may have included several deities who shared a considerable number of traits.

The patron of Kayab is a goddess, whom Thompson (1950, pp. 116–117) regarded as the young Moon Goddess. She is the patron of the number one and of the day Caban, apparently. The equivalent Aztec month, Tecuilhuitontli, was the feast of the death of Huixtocihuatl, a goddess of salt.

Of the five remaining months, the forms for Mol and Cumku are so variable as to suggest that several different deities may sometimes have presided over those months, none clearly identifiable. The deity of Muan is sometimes represented by a head, which may represent a goddess, and sometimes by a bird, which I suspect is the owl called *muan*. The animal skull of the Kankin patron is still not clearly identified, and the deity of Xul has a head which does not correspond clearly to that of any of the deities known in the codices. Thompson has valiantly tried to associate Mol with God D, Cumku with the Itzamnas as sky lizards, and Kankin with an earth monster; the arguments are roundabout and rest in part on the assumption that the glyphs of the months represent their mythical associations, whereas I regard them simply as names. The month Mol corresponds to Tzeltal/ Tzotzil Mux, which suggests two Huaxtec terms, *molbēl* 'moisten' and Muxi', name of a god of water (cf. Quiche [Q.] *muxan* 'swim'; *muxilih* 'wash oneself'). The equivalent Aztec month, Atemoztli 'Falling Water', is the festival of the Tlalocs, or rain gods, who descend at the time of the feast. Taken together, this suggests that the patron should be Chac, the Rain God, but nothing in the glyphs seems to justify this view.

Nine Lords

Another series of deities, first recognized as such by Thompson (1929), are the nine gods who rule successively over the different days. The Aztecs have a known series called the Nine Lords of the Night. Unlike the Maya series, which ran endlessly, the Aztec series ran for only 260 days and started over again on 1 Cipactli (corresponding to 1 Imix) with the god Xiuhtecuhtli. Roberto J. Weitlaner (1958) has recently shown that a similar series is still functioning in Oaxaca as the sole surviving remnant of the ancient calendar. Here the nine lords follow each other in daily succession for 259 days. On the 260th day, two lords rule together, and the series begins again on the 261st day with the first lord.

A possible clue to the identity of the Nine Lords of the Night may be found in the close resemblance between pages 75–76 of the *Madrid* and page 1 of the *Borgia* group codex *Fejervary-Mayer* (Fig. 29). The latter shows the Nine Lords of the Night, with the first lord in the center and two deities assigned to each of the directions. The beginning point in the *Fejervary-Mayer* is with the day (1) Crocodile. The days progress counterclockwise, reaching the day (1) Reed, a year bearer, in the upper left. All our sources associate Reed years with the east.

The pages of *Madrid* are shown upside down in Figure 29, in order to conform with those of the *Fejervary-Mayer.* In this position, the count starts with Hun Imix (the Mayan equivalent of 1 Crocodile) in the same position as in the *Fejervary-Mayer.*

The Maya glyph for 'east' is associated with this quadrant in agreement with the *Fejervary-Mayer.* It has been supposed that the directions have been transposed here, but the structural similarity suggests there is no error. The direction assigned by the scribe to the north includes the days Lamat, Kan, Ahau, Cib, and Eb. These days recur with a similar scene of human sacrifice on *Dresden* page 3a. Seler (1902–1923, IV, 604) has drawn attention to a parallel passage in *Madrid* (p. 91c). The day 1 Ahau is an important base in the Venus calendar, which is probably involved in this parallel. While the *Madrid* deities do not seem directly comparable to those of the *Fejervary-Mayer,* the parallel suggests that they may ultimately derive from the Maya series of Nine Lords of the Night, with additions and modifications. A completely different series of Mesoamerican directional gods, also intimately tied to the calendar and probably representing a similar cosmological scheme, may be seen in Figure 30.

Figure 31 shows representations of the nine lords from the *Borgia* group codices, with their Aztec names and the names and characteristics of the Oaxacan equivalents. Unfortunately, no one has yet managed to satisfactorily equate the Aztec deities with the Maya glyphic series. The only fully satisfactory identification in the Maya series is of G9 with the Sun God—probably the old Sun God, who was associated with the jaguar and the underworld. G7 sometimes has 'seven' prefixed and once has *ek* 'black' infixed. The G7 glyphs resemble those of the god of Pax. Cit Chac Coh, Landa's Great Father Puma, associated with Pax, received offerings to obtain victory in war. The number 'seven' and the 'black' infix suggest connections with the seven black deities associated with merchants, hunting, and war; this is far from clear, and none of the Aztec deities is directly and obviously a war god or god of hunting. Tepeyollotl

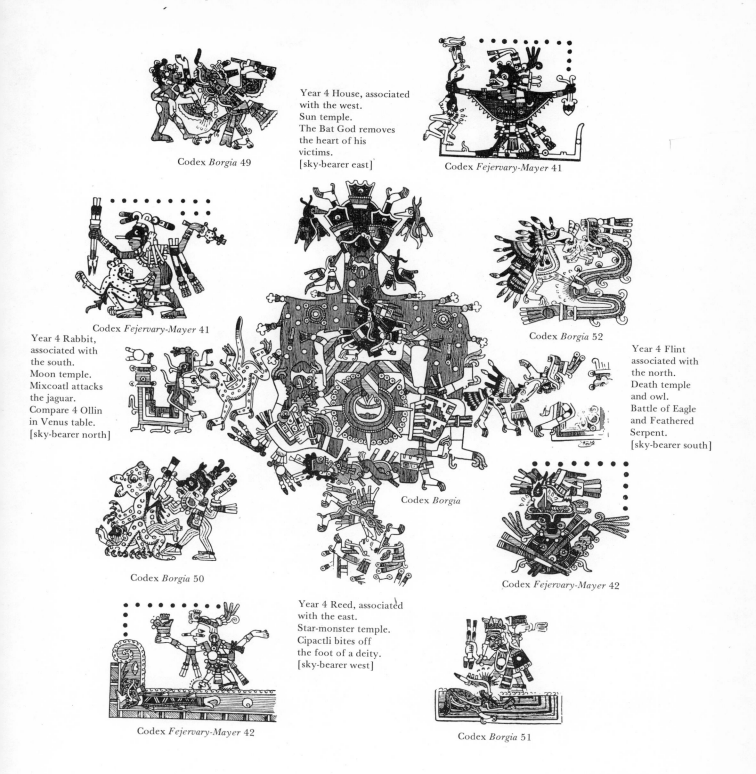

Codex *Borgia* 49

Year 4 House, associated
with the west.
Sun temple.
The Bat God removes
the heart of his
victims.
[sky-bearer east]

Codex *Fejervary-Mayer* 41

Codex *Fejervary-Mayer* 41

Year 4 Rabbit,
associated with
the south.
Moon temple.
Mixcoatl attacks
the jaguar.
Compare 4 Ollin
in Venus table.
[sky-bearer north]

Codex *Borgia* 52

Year 4 Flint
associated with
the north.
Death temple
and owl.
Battle of Eagle
and Feathered
Serpent.
[sky-bearer south]

Codex *Borgia*

Codex *Borgia* 50

Codex *Fejervary-Mayer* 42

Year 4 Reed, associated
with the east.
Star-monster temple.
Cipactli bites off
the foot of a deity.
[sky-bearer west]

Codex *Fejervary-Mayer* 42

Codex *Borgia* 51

Figure 30. World Ages, directions, and associated myths. Compare with Maya constellation sequences, Figure 14.

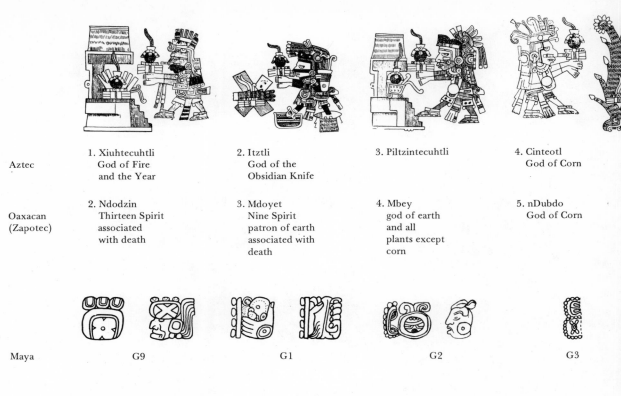

Aztec

1. Xiuhtecuhtli
   God of Fire
   and the Year

2. Itztli
   God of the
   Obsidian Knife

3. Piltzintecuhtli

4. Cinteotl
   God of Corn

Oaxacan
(Zapotec)

2. Ndodzin
   Thirteen Spirit
   associated
   with death

3. Mdoyet
   Nine Spirit
   patron of earth
   associated with
   death

4. Mbey
   god of earth
   and all
   plants except
   corn

5. nDubdo
   God of Corn

Maya

G9

G1

G2

G3

Figure 31. The Lords of the Night. The alignment of the Maya glyphic series with the others is not certain. The Aztec and Zapotec names are correctly aligned with the deity representations from the Codex *Fejervary-Mayer*.

Mictlantecuhtli
God of Death

6. Chalchihuitlicue
Jade Skirt, Goddess
of Water

7. Tlazolteotl
Earth Goddess

8. Tepeyollotl
Heart of
the Mountain

9. Tlaloc
God of
Rain

Kedo
God of Justice

7. Mdan
Goddess of the Sea
Supreme Deity
God of Ancestors
(bisexual?)

8. Mše
the thirteen
messengers,
'police'

9. Mbaz
Earth God
Guardian of Animals
a seven-headed
serpent
Mother Earth

1. Mdi
Four Rain Gods
at the
cardinal
points in
iguana shape

G4
Seven Moon
or Twenty-seven?

G5

G6
cf.
North

Seven
White?

G7

(not
G3)

extremely variable
glyphs

G8
cf. Cum
of Cumku
(month)

'Heart of the Mountains', a deity of the underworld with some jaguar associations, is the most likely equivalent, as Thompson (1950, p. 210) notes. Thompson (1929) originally suggested that Glyph G1 corresponded to Cinteotl and so on through the sequence, but, in 1950, he merely said that there is little profit in comparing them, because of the uncertain Maya identifications. The Oaxacan series can be compared with the Axtec, since the identity of two of the deities is clear. Cinteotl corresponds to nDubdo and Quiauitecuhtli (Tlaloc) to Mdi, fixing a sequential correspondence. On the basis of Hindu parallels, I have recently argued that G1 corresponds to Itztli and so on through the sequence (Kelley 1972).

One error in Thompson's placement of the glyphs of the nine lords has been followed by Knorozov and should be pointed out. Thompson (1950, Fig. 34, no. 20) shows, as an example of G3, a glyph from the Xcalumkin IS at A9. The date is clear, and it should be accompanied by G3. However, this glyph is completely distinct from the well-known shield glyph of G3 and is identical with Thompson's Figure 34, number 32, an example of G7. I think there can be very little doubt that this is an example of error on the part of either the sculptor or the original scribe.

Deities in the Lunar Series

Another series of deities is to be found in connection with Glyph C of the Lunar Series. As has been pointed out, this glyph is a verb. The subject (or object?) of this verb is represented by a miniature head or glyph, which is apparently in all cases a deity name (Fig. 32). The pattern of repetition of these deities—and hence the order of the series—and the number of deities involved are still unknown. Apparently the deities are not directly tied to the long count, for Morley (1920, p. 560) gives examples of different gods appearing when the same date is recorded at two different sites, although there are also examples of agreement between different sites. Morley recognized among these the goddess of the number one, the axe-eyed deity of the number six (a goddess, judging by her forelock), the Corn God (E) of the number eight, the Chicchan God (CH) of the number nine, the Death God of the number ten, and the god of the number seven, called by Morley, puzzlingly, God K, although I can see no resemblance between them. There is also a deity regarded by Morley as the god of the number four—a reading which seems to me unconvincing. The eye glyph of God M (Ek Chuah) is also present. An animal skull resembling that of the Kankin patron, a head glyph

resembling that for the god (or goddess?) of Muan, a bird god, a glyph which resembles the codex glyph for God H, a glyph which may be a symbolic form of the name of the same deity, and several glyphs for still unidentified deities round out the sequence. At least fourteen deities must be involved, and I suspect more. Unfortunately, the glyphs are so small that erosion of detail takes more toll in this series than elsewhere, and recognizing significant elements is often difficult.

Glyph X of the Lunar Series, so called because of its great variability, is actually a series of glygers recurring at a fixed point in the Lunar Series (Fig. 8). The pattern of repetition has been partly established, but the reasons for it are not yet known, although E. Wyllys Andrews (1934) once thought he had determined the mechanism of repetition. The head of God C between the jaws of a reptilian head (X2) rather resembles the glyphs of God G1, while X1 resembles the god of Pax and G7. X5 is apparently a bird head with Cauac/*haab* infix which probably represents the Rain God, found also elsewhere in the inscriptions. X6 is the head of a rain god with varying affixes. Possibly it should be read *cauac* or *haab*. Glyph X6a is *kan* 'yellow', here with the *ben-ik* superfix which I believe is normally associated with places. X4 shows the moon under crossed human legs, which one would think should apply somehow to the phases of the moon. I am not convinced that this series of glyphs does refer to deities, although it may. Discovery of the mechanism of repetition and the full meaning of these glyphs might throw considerable light on the Lunar Series.

Number Deities

Another series of clear-cut deities consists of the gods of the numbers (see Chapter 1). The heads of the numbers above thirteen consist of a fleshless lower jaw, indicating 'ten', with the head of the appropriate deity of the numbers from one to ten. The nature of this correspondence appears clearly in Figure 1. Most of these deities are known in other contexts as well. Goodman, Seler, and Thompson have all pointed out that the first thirteen numbers seem to correspond to the deities of thirteen of the twenty days, in sequence, starting with One as Caban, representing the Earth Goddess. Most of the deities are fairly well known. Thompson (1950, p. 132) regards Two as a god of sacrifice, related to Aztec Xipe and perhaps the same as God Q. Two has a human hand infixed in his head and lacks the 'ten' prefixed to the name of God Q; so if he does repre-

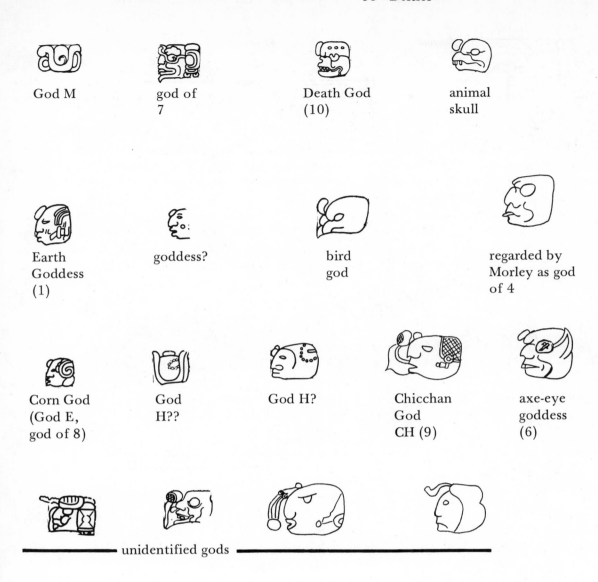

God M

god of
7

Death God
(10)

animal
skull

Earth
Goddess
(1)

goddess?

bird
god

regarded by
Morley as god
of 4

Corn God
(God E,
god of 8)

God
H??

God H?

Chicchan
God
CH (9)

axe-eye
goddess
(6)

unidentified gods

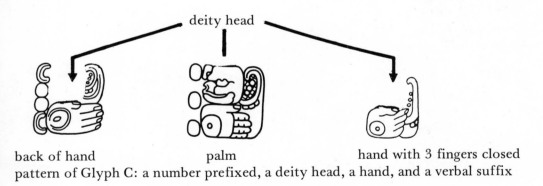

deity head

back of hand

palm

hand with 3 fingers closed

pattern of Glyph C: a number prefixed, a deity head, a hand, and a verbal suffix

Figure 32. Deity glyphs from Glyph C of the Lunar Series.

Tula. Representation of Tlahuizcalpantecuhtli, i.e. of Quetzalcoatl as morning star, according to Saenz.

Copan. The two-headed dragon. The Venus monster as front head, with crossed bands in eye.

Chichen Itza. Representation of Quetzalcoatl according to Seler. Note crossed bands above eye.

Dresden, pp. 4–5. The absence of the primary characteristics of the two heads on the monuments makes the identity less certain, but the deity figure in the front mouth is reminiscent of the inscriptions.

Venus monster from external decorations, Temple of the Cross, Palenque. Note crossed bands in eye.

Figure 33. The two-headed dragon.

Temple of the Foliated Cross, Palenque. Front view of rear head of two-headed dragon.

Another view of the rear head of the two-headed dragon.

Glyph X1 of Berlin, identified by Spinden as glyphs for the rear head of the two-headed dragon, from the Temple of the Inscriptions, Palenque.

Two-headed dragon, inverted for ease of comparison. Planetary band as body.

sent the same deity, he is not identified by the same glyphs. Three has the *ik* 'wind' glyph infixed and is presumably a wind god. Thompson suggests he is also a rain god, primarily because of the circlet of dots on his forehead of a type often associated with water. The equivalent day is Cauac, Day of Rain. Four is the Sun God (God G), Five is God N, Seven is probably God M (as previously suggested), Eight is the Corn God (God E), Nine is the Chicchan Serpent God, and Ten is the Death God (God A). Axe-Eye, the goddess of Six, is so far known only through this number; the corresponding day would be Ik 'Wind, Life', which has no obvious connection. The deity of Eleven has the *caban* curl behind the eye, rather resembling the head of God R. The latter has 'eleven' prefixed to his name. Thompson (1950, p. 135) says that the deity of Eleven is "clearly masculine." Considering the parallelism of the numbers 4–9 with 14–19, I think that Thompson dismisses too easily the possibility that this is a feminine head and that the deity of Eleven is, like the deity of One, an earth goddess. The head of the deity of Twelve sometimes wears the 'sky' glyph infixed and hence should represent a celestial deity. The number is parallel with the day Lamat, associated with the Venus God, and one of the Venus deities is Lahun Chan, probably 'Ten Sky', a fact which leads Thompson to postulate that the god of Twelve is Lahun Chan. This seems to me to be going far beyond the evidence, since the number ten is not associated with this deity in any way. The deity of Thirteen seems to be a reptilian monster, with the *uinal* glyph sometimes infixed.

The Two-Headed Dragon

An important deity of Classic times who falls outside the usual categories is the two-headed dragon (Fig. 33). This unusual monster or group of monsters shows a great deal of variation. His body sometimes becomes the "sky band"; at times it is apparently a snake body; at other times, the body is heavy; the feet may be shown with large claws or, sometimes, with hooves like a peccary. The front head is the Venus monster, with crossed bands in the eye or over it and the 'star' glyph somewhere on it. The back head has a fleshless lower jaw and the 'sun' glyph on its forehead, with three glyphs attached. These elements are found at Palenque as a glyger, clearly the name of the rear head of the dragon, as first pointed out by Spinden (1924, p. 201). Frequently a human head looks out of the front mouth of the monster; it is usually referred to as emerging, although it seems equally likely that the monster is finishing a good

meal. Thompson (1939, pp. 152–161) argues that the sky monsters correspond to the Itzamnas. This is an addition to the view that God D is Itzamna, not an alternative suggestion or a rejection of that identification. Presumably this interpretation is parallel to the view that Kukulcan is (*a*) any feathered serpent or (*b*) a humanoid deity named Feathered Serpent. The arguments seem to me quite convincing but are too complex to reproduce here in their entirety. The front head of the monster is apparently the prototype of the Toltec figure identified by César A. Sáenz (1964, p. 71) as Tlahuizcalpantecuhtli 'Lord of the Dawn', a morning-star deity. At times, the monstrous front head is that of a feathered serpent. This association of Venus and feathered serpent immediately suggests the later concept of Kukulcan. I have recently suggested (Kelley 1965) that Kukulcan, rather than being an imported Mexican concept, was an important deity of the Classic Period.

The Palenque Triad

The evidence for the importance of Kukulcan during the Classic Period derives from a study by Berlin (1963) in which he showed the existence of a triad of deities, referred to both together and separately, and identified their glyphs and associated dates. The latter are 1.18.5.3.2 9 Ik 15 Ceh, 1.18.5.3.6 13 Cimi 19 Ceh, and 1.18.5.4.0 1 Ahau 13 Mac. These dates fall about 2,700 years before the earliest historical monuments which we know from the Maya area and are clustered in a period of eighteen days. Obviously, they have an important mythological function. Throughout Mesoamerica, the most important date associated with gods or humans is that of the birth date which gives the person or deity his calendar name. The upturned frog's head or "initial date indicator" seems to indicate birth and is associated with the date 1 Ahau 13 Mac. Another glyph, found on a representation of a snail shell, with God K and the Corn God emerging from the shell, is repeated in association with all three dates. I believe it means 'emergence'; the snail shell has been recognized as a symbol of birth by Seler, Förstemann, Tozzer, Brinton, and others. Taken together, I think these factors indicate that the dates are the birth dates of deities. This view was held, but never fully justified, by Seler. I have attempted to show that Nine Wind (9 Ik) was widespread as a name of Quetzalcoatl/ Kukulcan (Fig. 33), that One Flower (1 Ahau) was a name of Cinteotl, the Aztec Corn God (Fig. 34) and of certain sun gods, and that Thirteen Death (13 Cimi) was the name of a war god (Fig. 23). I have also tried to show that iconography of the Palenque temples associated with these dates (9 Ik, Temple of the Cross; 1 Ahau, Temple of the Foliated Cross; 13 Cimi, Temple of the Sun) agrees with these deities. In this case, the study of the iconography was done in conjunction with my belief that the emphasized dates were the birth dates of the gods. This text suggests that 1 Ahau was the birth date of God K and offers some support to his identification as (Bolon) Tzacab (Fig. 34). It also indicates that 13 Cimi was the birth date of God L, a war god (Fig. 23).

The iconographic evidence may be summarized very briefly. The so-called Temple of the Sun features a tablet showing a shield and crossed spears, the normal Mesoamerican symbols of war, associated with a deity whose headdress identifies him with God L of the codices, frequently shown, with spear, in warlike attitude (Fig. 23). The Temple of the Foliated Cross emphasizes a stylized corn plant, showing also representations of the Corn God and of God K, whose attributes indicate a special connection with agriculture (Fig. 34). The Temple of the Cross shows a planetary band, the rear head of the two-headed dragon (Fig. 33), and a stylized tree cross with serpent heads projecting from it. The exterior of the temple shows a figure corresponding closely to representations of Tlahuizcalpantecuhtli, the Venus God as morning star. It may be noted that the *yax* glyph, often associated with the god of the number nine, is prominent as a decorative element around the stylized cross.

It should be pointed out that, elsewhere in Mesoamerica, Nine Wind is sometimes the name of twin deities and that twin myths are widespread in many parts of the world. Frequently the twins represent a dichotomy in which one stands for war, the other for peace, or one is stupid and the other clever. It is not impossible that the differences in associations of Gods H and CH reflect this dichotomy.

Dieter Dütting (1965*b*), starting from Berlin's 1963 work, studied the iconography in terms of different premises. He concluded that the iconography reflected a fundamental grouping of the three elements: water, earth, and fire. I believe that the different conclusions reached by Dütting and myself reflect different analyses and emphases rather than complete disagreement. The deity called GI by Berlin (Nine Wind, the Venus God, or Quetzalcoatl, in my study) is regarded by Dütting as a sky god, associated with water because of the associated *chicchan* 'serpent' glyph. Berlin's GII (One Flower, god of vegetation and the sun, to me) is regarded by Dütting as a god of vegetation, and, hence, of the earth. Finally, we both associate GIII with the old god in the jaguar skin (Fig.

23) and with fire. Dütting did not recognize the identity of the god in the jaguar skin with God L. For him, the association with fire is basic, while for me it is a natural but peripheral association of the War God. Barthel's subsequent evidence that the upended frog is **pok'* 'be born' makes it virtually certain that the date associated with each of the three gods is a birth date and gives the calendar names of the deities, as I have maintained. My analysis adds a near synonym for 'birth' in the 'emergence' glyph, as well as giving us information about the nature of the deities referred to by these glyphs.

Places Associated with the Gods

Besides the deities themselves, we have a series of glyphs associated with places in which the deities appear. Since the Aztecs had concepts of thirteen heavens, and other Mesoamerican groups may have believed in nine or ten heavens, with nine underworlds, it is reasonable to suspect that these concepts are involved in some of the place names associated with deities. Figure 35 shows the Rain God in thirteen different localities from *Dresden* pages 65c–69c. The glyphs for the localities were first identified as such by Cyrus Thomas, who wrote:

> Comparing the second character (b) of each group with that upon which the god is seated or standing, we find sufficient evidence to satisfy us that this symbol is the one which is used throughout to indicate this object. For example, the second symbol in the group on Plate 69 [Fig. 35, no. 13] is an exact copy of the object on which the deity is seated. The same thing is substantially true of that in the left hand [error for middle] group of Plate 66 [Fig. 35, no. 5], the middle [error for left] group of 67 [Fig. 35, no. 7], and the right hand group of 68 [Fig. 35, no. 12].
>
> Assuming, on account of the remarkable regularity of this series and the fact that the deity is in each case seated or standing on something, that this rule holds good throughout, we have a clew to those corresponding symbols which are not simple copies of the things they are used to indicate. (Thomas 1888)

The clew was not followed up in print until 1953, when Barthel tried to show that these glyphs were, in fact, the glyphs of the thirteen heavens. This he did by comparison with Aztec hymns preserved by Sahagún. Unfortunately, these do not constitute a direct and ordered sequence of heavens; so there is ample room for variation in their interpretation.

Glyphs of GII of the Palenque
Triad. Variant of God K with
muc(a) (?) prefixed to name.

glyphs of God K

God K as Manikin
Scepter, a symbol
of authority. Note
that element infixed
in forehead seems
to be a tubular pipe.

God K in the
mouth of a
serpent. Note
kin (sun) glyph
in forehead.

God K offering a sacrifice

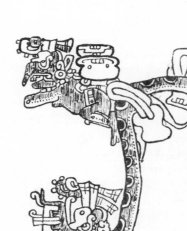

glyph of God K
as a deity with
bolon (nine) prefixed

glyph of
God K as a verb

God B, the Rain God, on
a serpent whose head
seems to be a variant
of God K

God K
as a
turtle?

Palenque TFC   *pok'* xx   GII   emergence
                   was (?) born ruler   (date 1 Ahau)

Figure 34. God K, GII of the Palenque Triad, identified as
(Bolon) Tzacab and as Hun Ahau (One Lord, Aztec One
Flower).

God K in the mouth
of a serpent whose body
forms the so-called
Ceremonial Bar.
Note the serpent
foot of God K.

Manikin
Scepter

the serpent-footed
God K as Manikin
Scepter

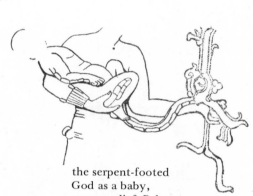
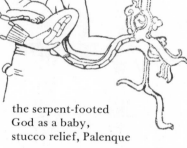

the serpent-footed
God as a baby,
stucco relief, Palenque

bearded variant of
God K presented to
Maize Tree, Palenque
TFC

Manikin
Scepter

emergence of God K
variant with Corn God
from a shell, symbol
of birth

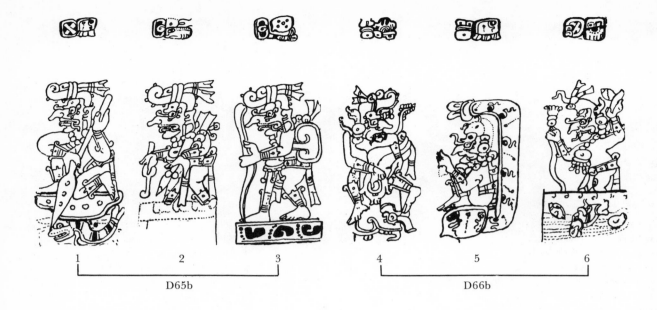

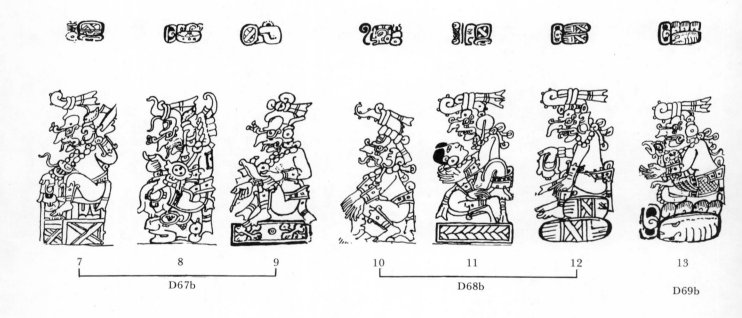

Figure 35. Localities of the Rain God: a single sequence. The thirteen heavens?

Figure 36. Isolated localities of the Rain God.

Nonetheless, Barthel was able to show some rather striking parallels. He was also able to show that in other sequences the same glygers recurred in association with the same types of scenes, thus verifying the identifications of the locative glyphs proposed on structural grounds.

Figures 35 and 36 include the locative prefixes as well as the glyphs themselves. In Figure 36 several other "locality" glyphs are shown besides the series of thirteen from *Dresden* pages 65c–69c suggestive of the thirteen heavens (shown in Fig. 35). The association of the *cab* 'earth' glyph with the god in a canoe is puzzling. The alternate glyph for this locality is *imix* (identified as a water lily, Yuc. *naab*) with 'in' prefixed. A meaning of 'water' for the *imix* glyph is now widely accepted, and I have suggested (Kelley 1962a, p. 28) that *naab* 'water lily' is being used for *nab* 'lake, lagoon, sea'. The three glyphs for what Thompson has called 'jewel water' show interesting variations, two of them involving an outstretched hand. Knorozov (1955a, p. 66, no. 16; p. 90, no. 177) has suggested that *naab* 'palm of the hand' is here being used for *nab* 'ocean'. This type of substitution seems to me the best possible evidence that these glyphs are correctly read. Unfortunately, it is often difficult to tell whether a hand glyph does or does not show the palm. The footprint grapheme in the second 'jewel-water' glyph may be read *be* (as in Landa, edited by Tozzer [Tozzer 1941], p. 170) or may simply be a phonetic determinant for *nab*. The head substituting for this in the third glyph for 'jewel water' may change the meaning slightly or may be another way of writing *be*.

The second locality is regarded by Barthel as 'sand'; the graphemes are unexplained. The third locality is the place of footsteps (T585:186). Knorozov (1955a, p. 87, no. 139) has read T585 as *col* 'field' and T186 as *tah,* making the whole read 'cultivate the field', a phrase that has no relevance in this context. Thompson's identification of T585 as *bix,* a numerical classifier, seems sound; proto-Maya *bix* is apparently 'dance', and I am inclined to regard this glyph as meaning 'place of dancing'. It should be noted that it has the 'in' prefix. The fact that the footprints are shown going in opposite directions and turning back upon themselves may support this view somewhat. This would indicate that T186 is some sort of locative suffix, probably corresponding more to our 'place of' than to our 'at'. The fourth locality is simply the normal 'sky' glyph with an unusual locative prefix. The head of a rain god is the fifth locality. Perhaps the accompanying glyphs should be regarded as a deity name rather than a locality, but the glyger is found only in this context and, surprisingly, has the

'in' prefix. The sixth locality is the place of crossed bones, interpreted by Barthel as a cist; it is interesting to find it represented by the little figure without a normal head (T227, probably the same as T703), which frequently appears in astronomical contexts. T227 also appears with the head of the *muan* bird as the glyph for the *muan* bird's head, as a place.

The seventh locality is the ceiba tree with the crocodile head for base, the so-called *imix* ceiba, and the accompanying glyphs read *ti-yax-te* 'at the ceiba'. The *zac-cab* ('white-earth') glyphs of the eighth locality are interpreted by Barthel (1953, pp. 94–95) in a metaphorical sense as the morning light associated with dead warriors; in this he is following known Aztec metaphors. The ninth locality shows the ocean, and the glyphs include *nab,* but the accompanying elements are unclear. The tenth locality shows the god drumming and a head with a speech scroll (perhaps for song) as the glyph. The eleventh locality seems to show a sexual relationship between the Rain God and the Moon Goddess, and Barthel associates it with the heaven where the sons of men are created. The glyphs do not include a locative prefix, but rather the supposed agentive *ah.* This is another context where the reading *hitz* 'dead' is inappropriate. Locality 12 is regarded by Barthel as the place of the two reed bundles, which does not help much. I would be more inclined to think that in this case the place was one which could not easily be represented; so its name was put in place of a drawing. The name might well be represented by some term in which initial and final consonants are identical. The thirteenth locality is regarded romantically by Barthel as the "place of eagledown feathers." The prefix is identified as down feathers and the head as an eagle, following Seler. Neither of the identifications seems to me at all well established, though I have no alternative to offer.

Concluding Remarks

In sum, we can recognize the glyphs of many of the gods and associate them with particular representations in the codices. In a few cases, these identifications can be extended to the inscriptions. A good many other deity names can be recognized in the inscriptions, but we are frequently unable even to determine what kind of deity is referred to. The arbitrary Schellhas letters for the gods are still of value because of our continuing inability to read the names of most of the gods in Maya. We are also able to recognize references to mythical places, but our understanding of the places referred to is still very vague, and few such names can be read in Maya.

A large number of deities are known chiefly from the colonial *Books of Chilam Balam*. It is often not clear that a deity is referred to, for nothing marks off a deity name from the rest of the text. This means that what one scholar takes for a deity name may be regarded by another scholar as a phrase to be translated. It is also clear that the Mayas were fond of puns, and even deity names do not seem to have escaped the transformations caused by this fondness. For these reasons, any list of the more obscure deities is apt to be quite erroneous. The following list represents the considered judgment of Alfredo Barrera Vásquez, one of the leading scholars in this difficult area. (The list and Spanish translations are from Barrera Vásquez and Rendón 1948, pp. 81–85; the English versions are mine.)

Ah Ahsah, El-estrella-de-la-mañana [The Morning Star]

Amayte Kauil, Cuadrado-deidad [Squared Deity]

Ahau Can, Señor-serpiente [Lord Snake]

Ahau Caan, Señor-del-cielo [Lord of the Sky]

Ahau Tun, Señor-labrado-en-jade [Lord Carved-in-Jade (Lord Stone)]

Bacab, Vertedor [Pourer]

Ah Bacocol, El-vertedor-de-vasijas-de-cuello-angosto [He, the Pourer from Narrow-Necked Jars]

Ah Bolon Am, El-nueve-piedra-labrada [He, the Nine Carved-Stone]

Bolon Buth, Nueve-ahito [Nine Surfeit (Very Full)]

Bolon Chooch, Nueve-amarga [Nine Bitter (Very Bitter)]

Ah Bolon Dzacab, El-nueve-fecundador (*Yax Bolon Dzacab*, Gran-nueve-fecundante) [Nine Procreator (He of Many Generations); Great Fertile Nine]

Ah Bolon Kanaan, El-nueve-precioso [He, the Precious Nine]

Ah Bolon Kin, El-nueve-sol [He, the Nine Sun]

Ah Bolon Mayel, Nueve-perfumado [Nine Perfumed (He, the Much-Perfumed)]

Bolon ti Ku, Nueve-deidad [Nine Deity]

Ah Bolon Yocté, El-nueve-pata-de-palo [He, the Nine Leg-of-Stick]

Ah Bolon Yocteil, El-nueve-de-la-pata-de-palo [He, Nine of the Stick Leg]

Ah Buluc Ahau ti Yocté Tok, El-señor-once-pata-de-palo-con-pedernal [He, Lord Eleven Stick Leg with Flint (Knife?)]

Buluc Chabtan, Once-ayunador [Eleven Faster]

Buluc Am, Once-piedra-labrada [Eleven Carved-Stone]

Ca Kinchicul, Dos-sol-signo [Two Sun Sign]

Ah Can Ek, El-cuatro-oscuridad (o El-estrella-serpiente) [He, Four Darkness (or He, the Snake Star)]

Ah Cantzicnal, El-de-los-cuatro-rincones [He of the Four Corners]

Ah Cap Uah Tun, El-que-ordena-los-tunes [He Who Puts the Stones (or the Years) in Order]

Ah Cantzicnal Bacab, El-vertedor-de-cuatro-rincones [The Pourer of the Four Corners (of the Sky)]

Cilich Colel, Sagrada-señora [Holy Lady]

Cit Bolon Ua, Decidor-grandes-mentiras [Speaker of Great (or Many or Nine) Lies]

Ah Coctun Numya, El-empedernido-que-da-desgracia-y-dolor [The Stoned One Who Gives Disgrace and Sadness]

Ah Commayel, El-ofrecedor-de-perfume [The Giver of Perfume]

Ah Cup Cacap, El-que-quita-el-resuello-apretando [He Who Squeezes Out the Breath]

Chac Bolay Can, Gran-carnicera-serpiente [Great Carnivorous Snake]

Chac Bolay Ul, Gran-carnicero-caracol-terrestre [Great Carnivorous Land Snail]

Ah Chac Chibal, El-gran-devorador-de-carne [He, the Great Devourer of Meat]

Chac Hubil Ahau, Señor-muy-revoltoso [Very Revolting Lord]

Chac Ek, Negro-chac (o Estrella-roja) [Black Rain God (or Red Star or Great Star)]

Chacmitan Choc, Gran-podredumbre [Great Decay]

Chactenel Ahau, Señor-de-la-flauta-roja [Lord of the Red Flute]

Chan Tokil, Poderoso-del-pedernal [Powerful of the Flint]

Ah Chicum Ek, El-estrella-guiadora [The Guiding Star (North Star)]

Ah Chichic Soot, El-que-agita-la-sonaja [He Who Shakes the Rattle]

Ah Dzundz, El-enjuto [The Lean One]

Ek Coc Ah Mut, El-estrella-tortuga-anuncio [The Star Turtle Sign]

Ekel Nok Canal, Paño-de-estrellas-celestiales [Banner of Celestial Stars]

Ek Chuuah, Negro-escorpión [Black Scorpion]

Ah Ektenel, El-de-la-flauta-negra [He of the Black Flute]

Hahal Ku, Deidad-verdadera [True God]

Hapai Can, Serpiente-tragadora [Swallowing Snake]

Hom To Chac, Hundido-en-la-lluvia [Submerged-in-the-Rain]

Ho Habnal Tok, Cinco-pedernales-afilados [Five Sharpened Flint-Knives]

Hun Ahau, Uno-señor [One Lord]

Hunab Ku, Unica-deidad [Sole God]

Hun-Uitzil-Chac, Uno-chac-de-las-montañas [One Rain God of the Mountains]

Hun Yoppol Ik, Viento-reseco [Scorching Wind]

Itzam Cab Ain, Brujo-del-agua-tierra-cocodrilo [Witch of the Water-Earth-Crocodile]

Ah Itzam Caan, El-brujo-del-agua-celestial [He, the Witch of the Heavenly Water]

Itzamná Kauil, Sagrado-brujo-del-agua [Sacred Witch of the Water (or Lizard House God)]

Itzamtzab, Las-cabrillas-del-brujo-del-agua [The Rattles of the Witch of the Water]

Itzmal Kauil, Sagrado-brujo-del-agua [Sacred Witch of the Water]

Ah Itzmal Thul, El-brujo-del-agua-a-chorros [The Witch of the Gushing Water]

Ix Bolon Yol Nicté, La-nueve-corazón-flor-de-mayo [The Nine Heart *Plumiera*]

Ix Chancab, La-poderosa-mielera [The Powerful Honey-Maker (or The Female Snake-Bee)]

Ix Chuah, La-llenadora [She, the Filler]

Ixma Chucbeni, La-incompleta [She, the Incomplete One]

Ix Dziban Yol Nicté, La-flor-de-mayo-de-corazón-pintado [She, the *Plumiera* of the Painted Heart]

Ix Dzoy, La-flaca [She, the Lazy One]

Ix Kan Citam Thul, La-preciosa-jabalí-conejo [She, the Precious Peccary-Rabbit]

Ix Kan Itzam Thul, La-preciosa-bruja-del-agua-a-chorros [She, the Precious Witch of the Gushing Water (or The Precious Lizard-Rabbit)]

Ix Kanyultá, Preciosa-garganta [Precious Throat]

Ix Pucyolá, La-destructora-del-corazón-del-agua [She, the Destroyer of the Heart of Water]

Ix Saclactun, La-que-está-en-Piedras-Blancas [She Who Is in White Stones]

Ix Tab, La-de-la-cuerda [She of the Noose]

Ix Tan Yol Chulul, La-que-está-en-el-corazón-del-agua-llovediza [She Who Is in the Heart of the Showery Water]

Ix Tan Yol Ha, La-que-está-en-el-corazón-del-agua [She Who Is in the Heart of the Water]

Ix Tol Och, La-ventruda-zarigüeya [She, the Big-Bellied Opossum]

Ix Ual Cuy, La-tecolote-de-alas-extendidas [She, the Barn Owl of Extended Wings]

Ix Ual Icim, La-tecolote-de-alas-extendidas [She, the Horned Owl of Extended Wings]

Ah Kay Kin Bak, El-que-vende-carne-para-el-sol [He Who Sells Meat for the Sun]

Ah Kinchil, El-de-rostro-solar [The Sun-Faced One]

Ah Kinchil Cobá, El-chachalaca-de-rostro-solar [The Sun-Faced Chachalaca]

Kinich Kakmó, Guacamaya-de-fuego-de-rostro-solar [The Sun-Faced Fire Macaw]

Ah Koh Bacab, El-vertedor-de-la-máscara [The Masked Pourer]

Ku Caan, La-deidad-del-cielo [God of the Sky]

Ku Citbil ti Caan, Señor-deidad-del-cielo [Lord Sky God]

Ku Likul Caanal, Deidad-del-cielo [God of the Sky]

Ah Kukulcan, El-serpiente-quetzal [The Quetzal Snake]

Ah Kul Itzam Caan, El-santo-brujo-del-agua-celestial [The Holy Witch of the Heavenly Water (or The Sacred Sky Lizard)]

Lahun Chaan, Diez-poderoso [Ten Powerful (or Ten Sky)]

Ah Maax Cal, El-mono-vocinglero [The Shouting Monkey]

Ah Maben Tok, El-de-la-caja-de-pedernal [He of the Flint Box]

Ah Masuy, El-agostador [The Parcher]

Ah May, Pezuñas-del-venado [Deer Hooves]

Ah May Cuuc, El-venado-ardilla [The Deer Squirrel]

Ah Miscit, El-barredor [The Sweeper]

Ah Misnilacpec, El-que-mueve-barriendo-con-las-narices [He Who Moves Sweeping with his Nostrils]

Ah Mol Box, El-juntador-de-cortezas-para-preparar-el-vino-ceremonial [The Gatherer of Bark to Prepare the Ceremonial Wine]

Ah Mucen Cab, El-que-guarda-la-miel [He Who Guards the Honey]

Ah Ni Poop, El-de-la-nariz-como-estera [He with a Nose like a Mat]

Ah Nitoc, El-bastardo-narigudo [The Nosy Bastard (The Big-Nosed Bastard)]

Ah Okol Koh, El-de-la-máscara-que-llora [He of the Weeping Mask]

Ah Ox Kokol Tzek, El-tres-amontonador-de-cráneos [The Three Heaper-up of Skulls]

Oxlahun Citbil, Trece-ordenador [Thirteen Arranger]

Oxlahun ti Ku, Trece-deidad [Thirteen God]

Pahool Chac, Chac-destructor [Destroyer Rain God]

Ah Pauahtun, La-erguida-columna-de-piedra [The Erect Column of Stone]

Pizlimtéc [Piltzintecuhtli] [Lord Noble Prince (Aztec name)]

Ah Sac Dziu, El-tordo-blanco [The White Thrush]

Sactenel Ahau, Señor-de-la-flauta-blanca [Lord of the White Flute]

Sac Uacnal, Blanco-prominente [Prominent White]

Ah Siyah Tun Chac, El-chac-que-hace-nacer-piedras-preciosas [The Rain God Who Causes the Birth of Precious Stones]

Sum Ci, Cuerda-de-henequén [Henequen Cord]

Ah Toc Dzudzil, El-bastardo-marchito [The Faded Bastard]

Ah Tooc, El-quemador [The Burner]

Tupem Caan, Atronador-de-los-cielos [Thunderer of the Skies]

Thuul Can Chac, Lluvia-de-serpientes-flacas [Rain of Lazy Snakes]

Ah Tzay Kanché, El-certero-escabel [The Sure Footstool]

Tzintzin Bac Toc, Hueso-musical-tostado [Toasted Musical Bone]

Tzintzin Coc Xul, Concha-de-tortuga-musical-de-vara [Musical Turtle Shell for Beating]

Uac Chuuahnal, Seis-vertedor-de-calabazas [Six Pourer from Gourds]

Ah Uaxac Yol Kauil, El-ocho-corazón-sagrado [The Eight Sacred Heart]

U Colel Caan, Señora-de-los-cielos [Lady of the Skies]

Ah Uooh Puc, El-signo-destructor [The Destroyer Sign]

Uuc Chapat or *Ah Uuc Chapat,* Siete-ciempiés-escolopendra [Seven Centipede]

Ah Uucté Chapat, El-siete-ciempiés-escolopendra [He, Seven Centipede]

Ah Uuc Chuah, El-siete-alacrán [He, Seven Scorpion]

Ah Uuceb, El-siete-montañas [He, Seven Mountains]

Ah Uuc Kin, El-siete-sol [He, Seven Sun]

Uuc Satay, Siete-muerte [Seven Death]

Ah Uucté Cuy, El siete-tecolote [He, Seven Barn Owl]

Ah Uuc Tut, El-siete-de-la-ocarina [He, Seven of the Ocarina]

Uuc Suhuy Sip, Siete-virgen-ofrenda [Seven Virgin Offering]

Uuc Uitzil Chac Ek, Siete-chac-estrella-de-las-montañas [Seven Great Star of the Mountains]

Ah Uc Yol Sip, El-siete-corazón-ofrenda [He, Seven Heart Offering]

Ah Xixteel Ul, El-rugoso-caracol-de-tierra [The Wrinkled (or Bumpy) Land Snail]

Xobil Tun, Piedra-preciosa-que-se-cuenta [Precious Stone Which Is Counted]

Yax Aclam, Verde-tortuga [Green Turtle]

Yax Coc Ah Mut, El-del-anuncio-tortuga-verde [Green Turtle of the Omen]

Yaxal Chac, Lluvia-verde [Green Rain]

Yaxal Chuen, Gran-mono-artífice [Great Pseudo-Monkey]

Yax Dzoy, Gran-flaca [Great Lazy One]

Yubte Takin, Palio-de-oro [Canopy of Gold]

Yuma Netziuit Kuk Yaxum, Señor-del-agua-arruinador-de-la-cola-del-quetzal-arruinador-del-pájaro-verde-yaxum [Lord of the Water Who Ruins the Tail of the Quetzal, Who Ruins the Green Bird, the Yaxum]

Yumil Caan, Señor-del-cielo [Lord of the Sky (Father in Heaven)]

Yumil Caan Yetal Luum, Padre-del-cielo-y-de-la-tierra [Father of Sky and Earth]

The following linguistic reconstructions, adapted from Kaufman 1964, may have some relevance to the glyphs which have been considered in this section. Reconstructions apply to the whole family unless otherwise specified. Periods are used to separate reconstructions for one meaning from reconstructions for the next.

Holy thing, god: *k'uh* (Hua.?). Wicked spirit: *lab* (Toj.-Chu.?). Nagual/witch: *way* (=dream). Fast: *ch'ahb*. Heart, soul: *pixan*, *kw'ux* (=love).

Chapter 5
Animals
and Plants

Besides sporadic, sometimes important, identifications of particular animals or glyphs for animals, there have been three systematic studies of animal representations in the Mayan codices and inscriptions. The earliest, by W. Stempell (1908), treated the problem entirely from a zoologist's viewpoint. Seler (1909), who worked on the same problem slightly later, viewed the matter from the light of a thorough knowledge of the nature of the conventions of Meso-american writing systems and took into account Mexican representations as well as Mayan ones. Tozzer and Allen (1910) worked as a team, Tozzer supplying the knowledge of the Mayanist and Allen doing the biological identifications. In some cases, clear-cut identifications were possible, and there was no disagreement among any of the scholars. In many others, conventionalization had proceeded so far that marked disagreement occurred among the scholars.

Combinations of different animal attributes in mythology are given expression in glyphic and pictorial representations. Deities may be represented with human bodies and animal heads, and human heads are sometimes shown on animal bodies. In such circumstances, strict insistence on biological accuracy of representation before attempting an identification seems unrealistic. In other cases, it is possible to make a generic identification, even when a specific identification is not possible. If the use of a glyph indicates that a particular word corresponds to the glyph, even if some of the glyphs are not clear representations of the object, it seems useful to accept the identification. Many logographic identifications are based on this principle. When only a head is involved, identifications may be very precarious, and arguments may range from insects to mammals; in some cases, full-figure variants enable clear-cut identifications. The absence of a relative size scale is often a considerable handicap, as in the case of a bird variously identified as a hummingbird, a tern, a frigate bird, and a pelican.

The identification of the day names and glyphs and of the month glyphs furnished a certain number of animal glyphs also (Fig. 37). Thus, the month called Zotz in Yucatec shows a head identifiable as that of the leaf-nosed bat, called *zotz* in Yucatec. Cognate forms in other languages show that this is an ancient word for 'bat' (Tzeltal [Tzel.] *sots'* 'bat'; Manche Chol *zutz* 'bat'; Palencano Chol and Chontal *zutz'* 'bat' [cf. Thompson 1950, p. 108]; Huaxtec [H.] *thut'* 'bat'; Q. *zotz'* 'bat'—the consonants all correspond regularly, but the vowel shift to -*o*- in Yucatec, Tzeltal, and Quiche is still unaccounted for).

The month *Muan* shows a strange head, which is in some cases that of a bird. Carl Hermann Berendt

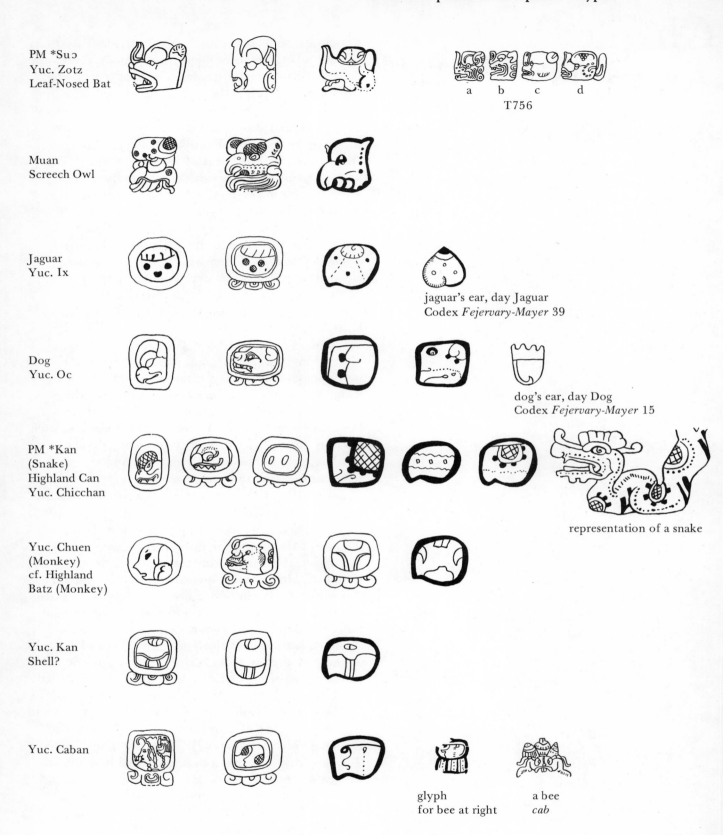

Figure 37. Animal glyphs from the day-name sequence.

found the name *moan* applied to the crested falcon (Brinton 1895, p. 74), and in Chol *muhan* is 'kite' or 'sparrow hawk', but representations in the codices have generally been accepted as the Yucatecan screech owl (see below), and Thompson (1950, p. 114), without giving his source, says that *moan* in Yucatec is 'screech owl'.

The Mayan glyph for the day called Ix in Yucatec is extremely similar to glyphs from the Mexican codex *Fejervary-Mayer* for the equivalent day, but has a slightly less conventionalized form, which is clearly the ear of a jaguar. In the other language groups of Mexico which share the calendar, this is normally the Day of the Jaguar, and, in Kekchi, *hix* is 'jaguar'. The Quiche name for the equivalent day, Balam, also means 'jaguar'. In any case, it seems that the glyph is a jaguar's ear and means 'jaguar', although it is not so clear whether the original reading was *ix* or *balam* (cf. Thompson 1950, p. 82; Seler, 1902–1923, I, 487). In the case of the day sign for Yucatec Oc, a head variant is most common, representing a not easily identifiable animal, which alternates in some cases with another glyph which seems to be an ear. This identification again seems assured by the use of an ear for the equivalent day in the non-Maya *Fejervary-Mayer* codex. In the other languages where the calendar is found, the equivalent day is usually that of the dog, and Palencano Chol *ok* is 'dog' (Thompson 1950, p. 78). Huaxtec *oc* is 'fox'. The reading *oc,* with the meaning 'wild dog' or 'coyote', seems the most probable original form. This *oc* glyph has frequently been confused with an animal glyph used for the month Xul, discussed later.

The highland day name Can means 'snake', and it has been pointed out that the design, while not obviously snakelike in any way, shows a form which is frequently found on the backs of representations of snakes in the codices. The equivalent Yucatec day name should also be Can (which is the Yucatec for 'snake'), but it is actually Chicchan, apparently borrowed from some Cholan dialect where proto-Mayan **kan* became *chan*. The Chicchans are known as giant rain serpents among the Chorti (Thompson 1950, p. 75). Similarly, the normal glyph for the day known as Chuen among the Yucatec and as Batz in other Maya dialects is not visually identifiable. It is presumably to be read as 'monkey', since the names *chuen* and *batz* both mean 'monkey', and the equivalent days in other groups are represented by a monkey. Moreover, one head variant looks like a monkey.

The day Kan is represented by a glyph which Brinton (1895, p. 110) identified as a polished stone, shell pendant, or bead, pointing out that one meaning of Yucatec *kan* is 'shells or stones used as money or

for necklaces'. Thompson (1950, p. 75) says that it is too conventionalized to be recognized. Knorozov (1955a, p. 68, no. 49) says that it is a shell, and I think this interpretation is likely to be correct, as the glyph shows a decided similarity to the "shell variant" of the *kin* glyph. There are other, clearer, examples of shell glyphs (see below), but they cannot be read as satisfactorily.

The Yucatec day name Caban corresponds to highland Maya Noh, to Tzeltal (?) Chic, and to Chuh Kixcab. The element *cab* means 'earth', and the equivalent Aztec day is called Movement or Earthquake. It had already been noticed by Léon de Rosny (1878) that the glyph with an affix was regularly associated with certain passages in the *Madrid* apparently referring to bees and beekeeping, and, since Yucatec *cab* also means 'bee', it has been generally accepted that this glyph is to be read *cab* and to be understood either as 'earth' or as 'bee'. There are certain difficulties in connection with suffixes to this glyph which can be better treated in connection with grammatical features of the script.

The identification of calendrical glyphs led fairly directly to recognition of almost all of the glyphs above. Another very early group of identifications were those associated with offerings (Fig. 38). These normally consist of a glyph representing the head or forepart of the animal offered. In the case of fish and iguanas, the whole body may be offered, and, in the case of deer, a haunch is normally recognizable. The head of the ocellated turkey (Maya *cutz*, Tozzer and Allen 1910, p. 326) is frequently shown. Other types of turkeys were known to the Maya, and several different names are translated simply 'turkey'. *Dresden* page 23 shows a descriptive passage, including a fish glyph, above a picture of a female figure holding out a bowl with a fish resting on it. Parallel passages (without pictures) refer to other offerings, including turkey and a venison haunch. On D29–31b there are two sets of passages, apparently describing offerings, in which there is a close parallelism. Thus, the first set is in the order:

1 2
3 4
5

in which 5 was always the offering glyph. In the second set, the order was as follows:

1 2
3 4
5 6
7 8

a   b
T588
offers, gives

apparently refers
to the sprinkling
or offering of
bird blood

T1038b
its
offering

ocellated
turkey
cutz

iguana
Yuc. *hu*

fish
PM *key*
Yuc. *cai*

T795
deer
(haunch,
Yuc. *hau*)

T799

possibly
iguana

tzab ca-ca-aan (?)
[verb]   [objects in
           dish below]

Figure 38. Offering glyphs.

and again 5 was always the offering glyph. In the latter set, the normal offering glyph was replaced by a glyger which, from the parallels, should stand for 'turkey', as de Rosny pointed out long ago when he interpreted this group as 'turkey' and read it *cutzo*. Its identity in the offering glyphs was emphasized by Cyrus Thomas (1888) and is backed up by its occurrence in *Madrid*, page 91a, above a picture of a turkey in a noose. Offerings of turkey, iguana, fish, and deer are also shown on D29c–30c. D40c–41c shows a series of six passages in which the fourth glyph is always an offering glyph—three of these have not been identified, but the remaining three are fish, turkey, and deer. In these series, the deer offering is normally represented by a haunch, for which Thomas suggested the reading *hau*, Yucatec 'deer haunch'. In most cases, the offering sits upon a glyph which is the same as the day sign Kan, perhaps due to an association with the meaning of Yucatec *kanan* 'precious', or perhaps due to an association with corn and, by extension, food in general (cf. Thompson 1950, pp. 75, 281). Whorf, taking one of these offering glyphs entirely out of context, suggested that the iguana was a "double writing" of the Kan sign below it, since Kan corresponds to the Aztec day name Lizard. He does not explain why fish, deer, or other offerings should be written 'lizard'.

Two famous parallel passages are to be found in the *Dresden* and *Madrid* (Fig. 39). A series of six phrases on *Dresden* pages 16c and 17c consists of four glyph blocks each; each of the first three is accompanied by a picture of a woman (or goddess) and a bird. The fourth phrase exactly parallels one on D17b, above a similar picture of a woman and a bird. In the *Madrid*, there are eight phrases, and each of them is accompanied by a picture of a woman and a bird. The first picture in *Dresden* shows the *muan* bird, and the first glyph in this group shows the head of the *muan* bird. The fifth phrase begins with the head of a vulture, also found in other passages above the picture of a vulture, and long recognized as the glyph for 'vulture', and the sixth phrase begins with the glyger suggested above as that of the turkey. The second picture in *Dresden* shows the quetzal bird, and the same bird is in the second picture of *Madrid*. The two glyphs do not at first look very similar, but comparison with forms in the inscriptions shows their common origin. The macaw is shown in the third phrase in *Dresden* and the first phrase in *Madrid*. Thomas, in commenting on this passage, writes, "From these facts we conclude that the first symbol in each of these groups denotes a bird, and, as no two are alike, that they refer to different species, the one at *g* [the third phrase in *Dresden* and

the first phrase in *Madrid*] corresponding with symbol No. 24 [the macaw glyger], the bird beneath being the great parrot or ara" (Thomas 1888). He therefore reads this group as *moo*, the Yucatec name for a macaw. A second glyph (a head variant) accompanies this first symbol in the *Dresden*, and it is only the second glyph which is found in the *Madrid* as the name glyph of the macaw. The identification of these name glyphs as those of the birds below does not seem to have been challenged at any time, although Thompson (1958a) has suggested that the glyphs actually refer to certain types of illnesses symbolized by the birds, rather than to the birds themselves. This hypothesis will be criticized in detail later, but it does not seem pertinent here, where the association of certain glyphs and certain birds is apparent.

The third bird in *Madrid* is identified as a king vulture by Tozzer and Allen (1910) and as a crow by Villacorta (Villacorta and Villacorta 1930). Seler (1909, IV, 556) has also identified this bird as a vulture. However, the probable identifying glyph looks like *yax*. Quiche *raxon* (from **yax-*) is 'blue dove', or a gray bird with blue wings. The fourth bird is very interesting, as the glyger which should correspond to its name is identical with that of the dog (see below). The bird is identified as an owl by Seler (1902–1923, IV, 612) and as a "Yucatan screech owl or Moan-bird" by Tozzer and Allen (1910). However, the *muan* bird is found as the eighth bird of this series, and this bird lacks the typical spotted tail of the *muan* bird. Villacorta calls it a *paujil* ('guan'), one of the Cracidae. Seler and Villacorta both identify the fifth bird as an eagle; the glyph is like that of the black vulture of D17b, which Seler also identifies as an eagle, but it lacks an infix in the mouth which the latter has. Perhaps the Mayas, like the Aztecs, classed eagles and vultures together. The sixth bird of *Madrid* is an owl, identified by Seler as the *muan* bird, but by Tozzer and Allen as an *icim* owl. The first glyger above is apparently that of the owl, although Barthel thinks the second glyph is that of the owl. He draws attention to the use of this glyger in connection with the *muan* owls of D7c and D10a (personal communication), but I believe that the true glyph of the *muan* owl proper in these cases is one which might be read 'Thirteen Heaven'—it is worth noting that the number thirteen is prefixed to the *muan* bird's head as part of its glyph on D16c. The first glyger in *Madrid* begins with Landa's *i*. The seventh bird is a turkey, but the name glyph, if present, is completely different from the one in *Dresden* or elsewhere in *Madrid*. The final bird is the *muan* owl, here called only by a title that was normally applied to God D (see Chapter 4).

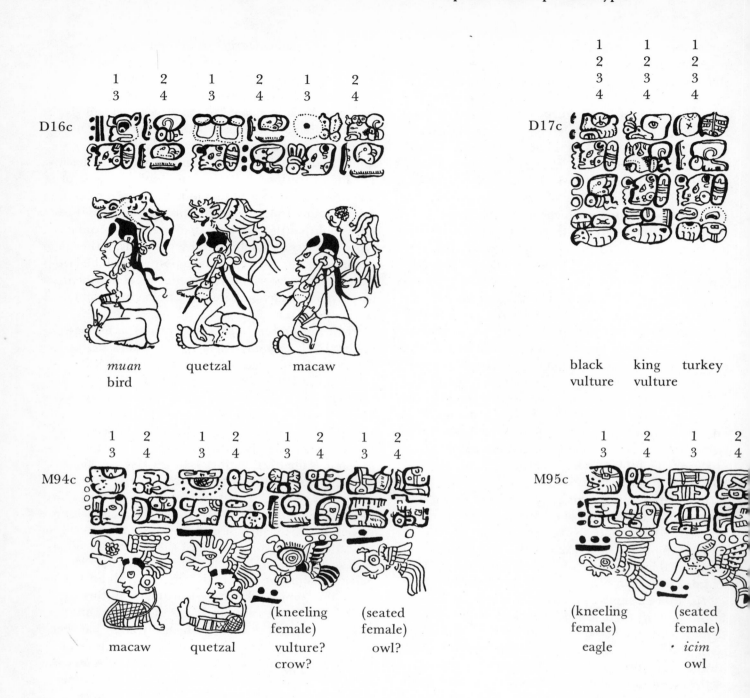

Figure 39. Parallel passages from the *Dresden* and *Madrid* co-dices. The first glyph block in each of the *Dresden* passages is that of the accompanying bird. This is usually, but not always, true in the *Madrid*.

D17b

1 2
3 4

black
vulture

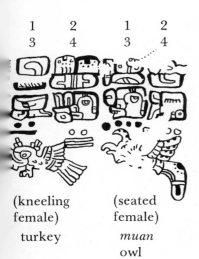

1 2   1 2
3 4   3 4

(kneeling   (seated
female)   female)
turkey   *muan*
               owl

The name of the bird in these passages is usually followed by *u* and a glyger composed of T19 and T59. Seler thought that the spiral glyph, T19, represented a bird's beak and suggested at various times that either T19 and T59 together or the former alone should be read *mut* 'bird, tidings'. T59, the glyph identified by Thompson as *ti,* is seemingly universally accepted. Cordy (1946, p. 114) read the glyph T19 as *koch,* suggesting that T59, found as an affix to the vulture head, read *kuch* 'vulture' and that this was not to be distinguished from *cuch* 'burden', which was, in turn, the same as *koch* in the meaning 'to carry on the head or shoulders'. He suggested that the two together were "double writing" (i.e., determinatives, as defined in Chapter 10). Thompson (1958*a,* p. 301) has a lengthy discussion of the glyph T19 and also concludes that it is to be read *koch,* which, he argues, means 'divinely inflicted sickness or punishment'. This is part of his contention that the birds here pictured actually refer to diseases. Neither Thompson's nor Cordy's arguments seem to me acceptable. Knorozov has read T19 as *mu* in what I regard as the probative context of the month name Muan. I therefore accept the reading *mu-t(i)* 'bird'.

Thompson (1962, p. 164) has argued that the bird pictographs (or, at least, some of the pictographs lumped as T236) are sometimes to be read simply as *chich,* which, like *mut,* has the dual meanings of 'bird' and 'tidings'. The use of T236 as the prefix to the 'tun' or 'year' glyph to form a glyger meaning 'tidings of the year' seems highly plausible.

In both *Dresden* and *Madrid* we find the glyger T604:671 associated with representations of the vulture (Yuc. *kuch*) in the appropriate position to indicate the bird's name, rather than the previously mentioned pictograph. The glyger was first recognized as that of the vulture by Cyrus Thomas (1888, p. 353).

I think that T212 may represent a feather, since it looks rather like one and is found in a compound with the *can* 'snake' glyph in a passage which I believe refers to the birth of the Feathered Serpent. It is, however, not demonstrably like any Mayan representation of feathers known to me.

Cordy has drawn my attention to a glyph of a turkey head and another glyph which apparently replaces Glyphs D and E of the Lunar Series and hence should indicate the current lunar age (on Stela F, east side, Quirigua). Thompson (1950, p. 240) says that "the left glyph is hard to identify," but the long wattle hanging down over the beak seems to me unmistakable evidence that a turkey is involved. The reference is apparently to a moon age of zero days or thereabouts. Thompson identifies the right-hand element

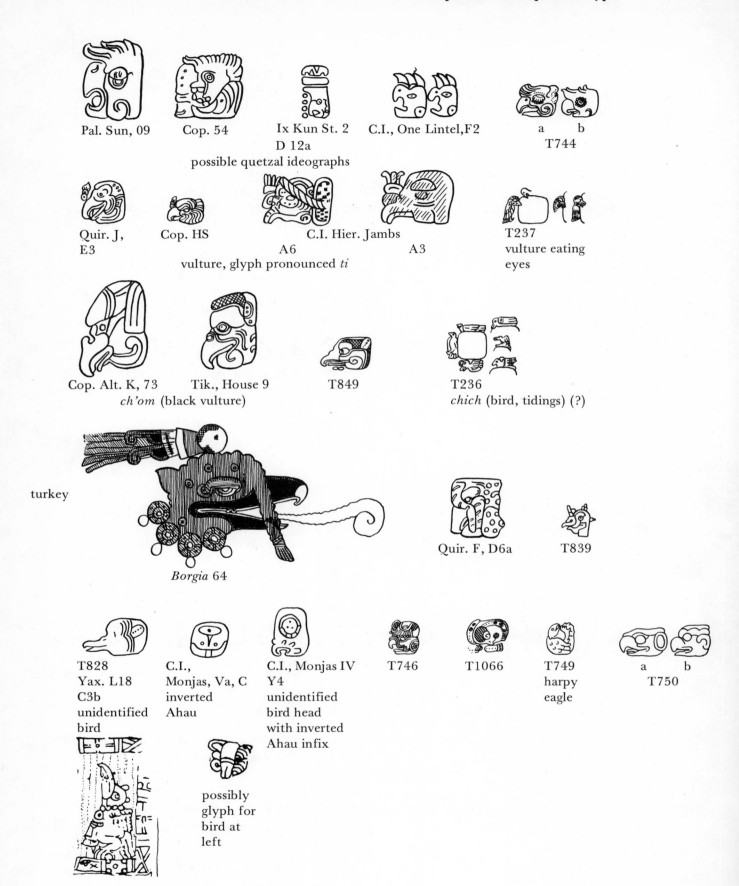

Pal. Sun, 09   Cop. 54   Ix Kun St. 2   C.I., One Lintel,F2   a   b
                           D 12a   T744
                   possible quetzal ideographs

Quir. J,   Cop. HS   C.I. Hier. Jambs   T237
E3   A6   A3   vulture eating
          vulture, glyph pronounced *ti*   eyes

Cop. Alt. K, 73   Tik., House 9   T849   T236
ch'om (black vulture)   *chich* (bird, tidings) (?)

turkey

Borgia 64

Quir. F, D6a   T839

T828   C.I.,   C.I., Monjas IV   T746   T1066   T749   a   b
Yax. L18   Monjas, Va, C   Y4   harpy   T750
C3b   inverted   unidentified   eagle
unidentified   Ahau   bird head
bird   with inverted
                             Ahau infix

                 possibly
                 glyph for
                 bird at
                 left

Figure 40. Bird glyphs.

as the "upturned frog head." I know of no word for 'turkey' which might be plausibly connected with the lunar count, nor of any mythical connection between the moon and turkeys.

Pictographs of quetzals, vultures, and macaws are not uncommon on the monuments, and the 'vulture' and 'macaw' glyphs are also found in the codices. One of the liveliest controversies arose when G. Elliott Smith (1924) declared that some supposed representations of macaws (according to Tozzer and Allen 1910, pp. 343–345) instead depicted elephants (Fig. 41). The difficulty of some of the identifications is abundantly clear from the mere possibility of such a controversy. To back up his position, Elliott Smith pointed out that some Indian representations of elephants show an unrealistic spiral near the mouth, and others show a circle around the eye. Both traits are associated in the Maya area on such a disputed representation as that from Stela B, Copan, but both also appear on unmistakable macaws.

Seler (1902–1923, IV, 557) showed that a deity on D40b, variously identified as a macaw or a turtle, was one of a series which was paralleled in the *Madrid* (Fig. 87). The parallel deity of *Madrid* page 12a (the eighth deity from the left in Fig. 87) has claws and tail feathers. This should have made it clear that the ring of circles around the eye was the typical feature distinguishing the macaw from the turtle. However, Seler himself contributed to the confusion (1902–1923, IV, 668) by identifying a glyph with the ring around the eye (T744) on Copan Stela B as a turtle. The glyph apparently refers to the large carvings on the same stela, which were also regarded by Seler as turtles. These are the same ones which Elliott Smith calls elephants. As if a three-way argument over identification as macaws, turtles, or elephants were not ridiculous enough, it has also been suggested that the animal shown is a tapir. No competent professional has taken the latter opinion seriously, but it still finds occasional supporters among those who are unwilling to believe in trans-Pacific trading of elephant art and yet cannot quite believe Stela B shows macaws.

Elliott Smith suggested that a conventionalization first applied to elephants was shifted to macaws by Mayan artists copying art objects showing elephants, with which they were, even in his view, unfamiliar. The small human figures associated with the head on Stela B, taken out of context, seem to support Smith, but anyone familiar with the treatment of subordinate figures on the Maya monuments will not find this convincing. In any case, the macaw with a human arm in its beak (represented in both the *Madrid* and the *Borgia*) must have been conceived as a very large bird.

Animal heads appear frequently as parts of names in the inscriptions, but, even where their identification is certain, the reading of the name may be doubtful. The known occurrence of only a single name for a particular animal in widely distinct languages may suggest a particular reading. Such tentative readings are included with the figures. In other cases, varying evidence may suggest several different possible readings for a glyph or glyger. At least three terms, and possibly more, seem to have been in use for dogs. *Oc,* a wild dog, is known from the day signs, as previously mentioned (see Fig. 37). The month name Xul is represented by a closely similar head. Gates (1931, p. 33) points out that the *oc* form in the codices has a dark spot over the eye, and two blobs on the ear, both normally absent in the *xul* form. The two different forms occur in different compounds as well as in the two distinct calendar contexts noted. The distinction is minor but highly consistent, and certain rare apparent exceptions may be due to copying errors. The *oc* animal in the inscriptions seems more variable, and such a consistently definable difference from *xul* has not been pointed out there. The *xul* animal closely resembles the animal of Glyph B of the Lunar Series, and Thompson (1962, p. 356) lumps them as T758. Thompson (1950, p. 109) has suggested that *xul* may have been an ancient word for 'dog', from which Aztec Xolotl, name of the canine deity, is derived. No Mayan term of similar meaning has been pointed out, save that Kekchi *xul* is a generic name for 'animal'. The *xul* glyph in the codices frequently takes the infix *akab/akbal* 'night', and Gates (1931, p. 33) suggests that the *xul* was a predatory night animal. The glyger for the dog in the codices was first recognized by Seler (1902–1923, I, 477) and has been read *tzu-l(u)* by Knorozov, *tzul* being a rare Yucatec term for 'dog' (see fuller discussion, Chapter 9). Thompson has read the glyger as *pek* because this is the commonest Yucatec word for 'dog' and because it enables him to make a connection with the Yucatec use of the word *pek* in connection with droughts. No one has yet suggested *ah bil* or *bincol* for any of these 'dog' glyphs, although these terms also appear as Yucatec terms for 'dog'.

The *xul* animal usually has T7 infixed on the monuments, and T759 is a very similar (or identical?) animal with the flint-knife glyph infixed. The Glyph B animal (lumped by Thompson with the *xul* animal as T758) seems normally to have a snout sharply divided into upper and lower sections. Full-figure representations throw some light on this animal. A representation from Quirigua Stela B shows the animal as Glyph B of the Lunar Series. The body is generally anthropomorphized, but the rear foot is shown

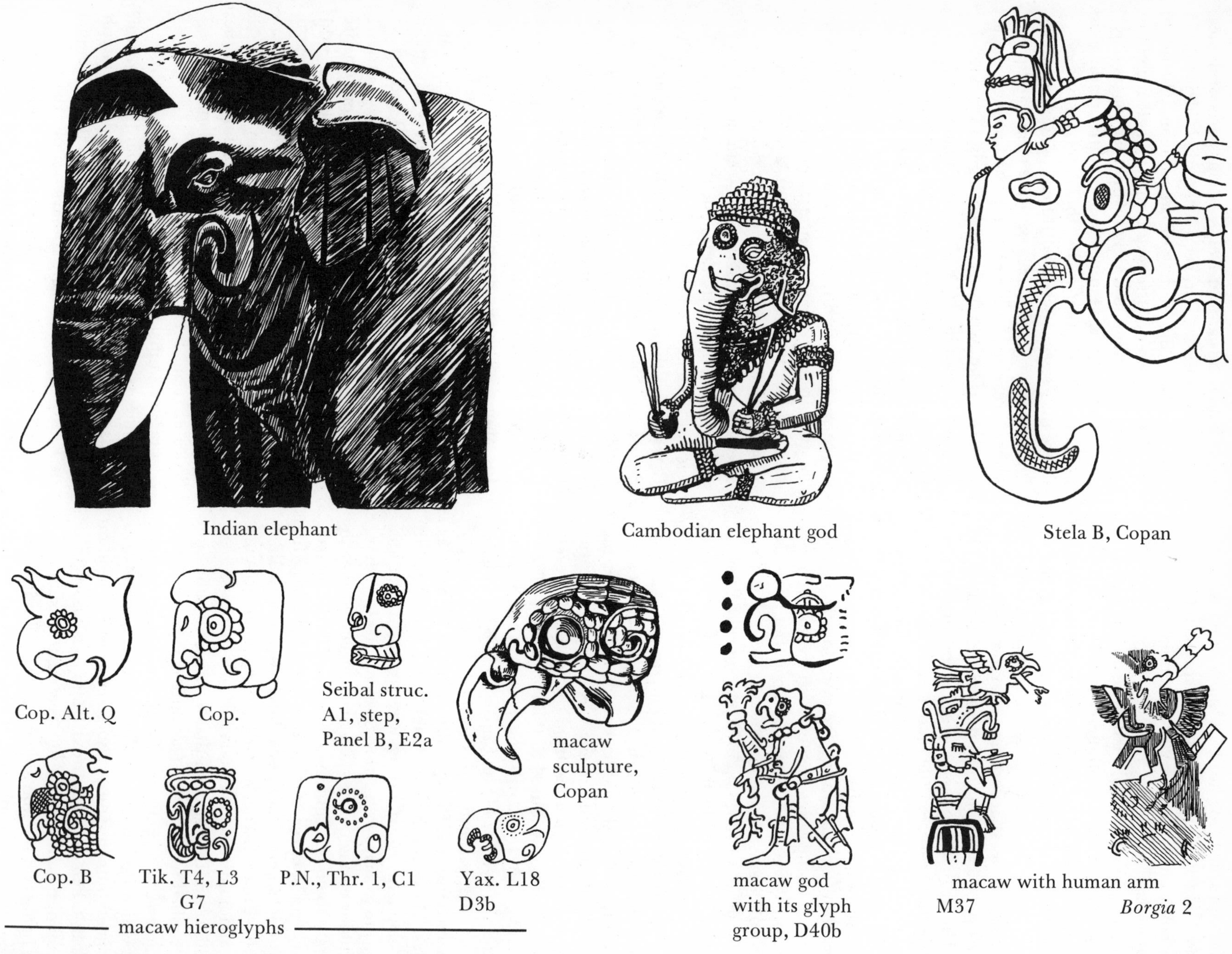

Stela B, Copan

macaw with human arm
Borgia 2

M37

Cambodian elephant god

macaw god
with its glyph
group, D40b

macaw
sculpture,
Copan

Yax. L18
D3b

Indian elephant

Seibal struc.
A1, step,
Panel B, E2a

P.N., Thr. 1, C1

Cop.

Tik. T4, L3
G7

Cop. Alt. Q

Cop. B

—— macaw hieroglyphs ——

Figure 41. Elephants and macaws.

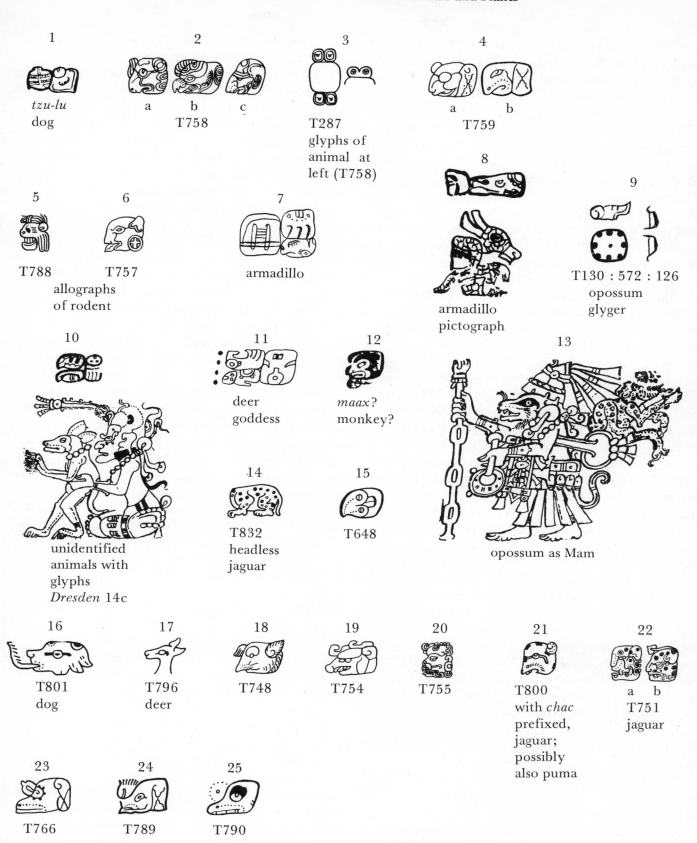

1

tzu-lu
dog

2

a   b   c
T758

3

T287
glyphs of
animal at
left (T758)

4

a   b
T759

5

T788

6

T757

allographs
of rodent

7

armadillo

8

armadillo
pictograph

9

T130 : 572 : 126
opossum
glyger

10

unidentified
animals with
glyphs
Dresden 14c

11

deer
goddess

12

maax?
monkey?

14

T832
headless
jaguar

15

T648

13

opossum as Mam

16

T801
dog

17

T796
deer

18

T748

19

T754

20

T755

21

T800
with *chac*
prefixed,
jaguar;
possibly
also puma

22

a   b
T751
jaguar

23

T766

24

T789

25

T790

Figure 42. Animal glyphs.

with only three toes, as opposed to the five fingers of the hand. Morley has identified the animal as an agouti, a large rodent, and the agoutis have five toes in front but only three in the rear. They are primarily nocturnal (agreeing with the 'night' infix of the *xul* animal), and the agouti snout seems to me quite like that of the Glyph B animal. Lizardi (1941) has shown that a doubled glyph (T287) substitutes for the name of T758. In terms of the principles which I accept, this suggests that T287 is a phonetic glyph and that the initial consonant and final consonant of the animal's name are identical. Unfortunately, this does not apply to either of the Yucatec terms for 'agouti', *haleb* (the large red-yellow agouti [Tzel. *jalaw*]) or *tzub* (the smaller gray-and-white agouti).

Thompson (1962, pp. 354–362) thinks that the lolling tongue typical of T757 suggests that it is a dog; it normally has the *kan* cross infixed. It has also been supposed to be a jaguar, and Thompson, in deliberate ambiguity, coined the term "jog" for this and similar animals. Proskouriakoff (1968) has shown that T788 is simply an early version of T757, a fact which would certainly not be suspected from the "type examples." Intermediate forms and context indicate this identity. Barthel (1963, p. 191) read T788 as *balam* 'jaguar' and implicitly identified it on Tikal Stela 31 as a title, a suggestion previously made by William Coe. Proskouriakoff has demonstrated that the animal of T757/788 is neither a dog nor a jaguar, but a rodent, pointing out the large cheeks, small eyes, and projecting teeth. She thinks the animal is probably a paca, an agouti, or one of the larger gophers. There is considerable terminological confusion among these animals, but roots in *hal-* seem to refer to the paca; *tzub* is, at least sometimes, an agouti; and *ba/bah* is applied to gophers (in Quiche, to the mole). Because of its general context preceding personal names, Proskouriakoff (1968, p. 249) thinks T757/788 should read " 'Here is portrayed (or recorded) . . . ,' 'In commemoration of . . . ,' or some such phrase directing attention to the subject of the accompanying picture." I think it is merely some sort of title. More recently, Barthel (1968a, pp. 147–148) has discussed the colonial Maya equation of agoutis and gophers with rulers and sorcerers, and now he prefers to read T788 as *tzub*, which he regards as equivalent to the title *kulel*.

Proskouriakoff also shows that T757 is an allograph of the Imix-variant T558 (see Chapter 9 for a discussion of the confusion on this glyph in the Thompson catalog), which I have suggested should be read *ba*. While *ba* would fit nicely as 'gopher', I know of no title *ba* and am less willing than Barthel to accept symbolic substitution. T788 is accompanied in

some cases by a knot glyph (T60) which suggests tying (*tab*), and the two together suggest the known title *batab*. However, I think it is not T60 but another knot glyph, T102, which is to be read *tab*, and T60 is prefixed to T788. To read *tab-ba* as the known title *ba-tab* would involve an inversion which I am not ready to accept without other evidence. In any case, this would not explain the fact that the animal head frequently appears without the knot. In short, I must concur with Proskouriakoff's view that the reading *ba* is dubious, without finding Barthel's *tzub* entirely convincing.

Glyger number 7 in Figure 42 may be accepted as that of the armadillo, on the basis of its occurrence in a "marriage" passage (*Dresden,* page 21b). In this section, the male figure is a deity or animal, with his hieroglyphs in the third place. Only the dog is actually shown in this section, but Seler (1902–1923, IV, 525) has pointed out that a parallel passage (*Madrid,* pages 91d–92d), with the same calendar structure, shows the same "husbands" in the same order, showing, however, an armadillo in the third phrase of the series. In *Madrid,* the armadillo is represented by a pictograph (Fig. 84); in *Dresden,* it is apparently represented by a phonetic glyger, which should be read *i-ba-ka,* according to decipherments which I accept. This is not a known name for the armadillo, but **ib, *ibach,* and **iboy* are found as armadillo names.

Another animal is represented on *Dresden* page 14c (Fig. 42). It has not been certainly identified. It was regarded by Stempell and Seler as a deer and by Beyer (1929) as a dog. This picture is another representation of mythical marriages—Deer Goddess and Deer God, Vulture Goddess and Dog, White Goddess and God L—and the animal is shown with God D; hence it is to be understood as a female. The name of the female appears in the first position in the other three cases, where the identity is otherwise attested, and the normal regularity of passages in the *Dresden* makes it likely that the glyger in first position here is that of the animal. Knorozov (1955a, p. 92, no. 197) reads *ch'amac* 'fox', but neither the phonetic elements nor the identification of the animal seem certain enough for one to be sure of this.

The Deer Goddess of the same passage is represented by the complex glyger (Fig. 42) found in the other previously mentioned marriage passage, but with the glyphs in a different order. In the latter case, the *Dresden* implies that the deer is a buck. Knorozov (1958a, p. 470) has read the deity name as Can Cheknal, although this does not agree with the order of the glyphs in either of the passages. Knorozov's argument that this case of glyphic inversion is in accordance with specified rules is not convincing. The *manik* glyph, here read *che* by Knorozov, is the hand glyph for the day name which corresponds to the day called Deer throughout the rest of Mesoamerica. In Yucatec, 'deer' is *ceh,* and cognate forms are present through most of the family. The *manik* glyph by itself appears to refer to 'deer' (*Madrid,* p. 91a), and I believe it is here to be read simply *ceh.* However, in view of the apparent tendency to abbreviation and inversion shown by the scribe of *Madrid,* this might represent, as Zimmermann (1956, p. 160) suggested, an abbreviation of the glyger under consideration.

As mentioned earlier, the glyph for the day Ix or Balam seems to represent the ear of a jaguar and to be read 'jaguar'. The pictograph of the jaguar's head, often accompanied by the water lily which so well typifies this great water-loving cat, also seems to be read 'jaguar'. On D47c, a large cat pierced by a spear (Plate 3) has been identified as a puma by Stempell (see Seler, 1902–1923, IV, 469–470); however, the absence of spots which suggested it was not a jaguar may be due to the fact that this section of the *Dresden* is not completely painted. The hieroglyph of the head (Plate 3) does have spots. It also has the prefix *chac,* found with several different names for the jaguar, but also with at least one name for a puma god (Chac Cit Coh 'Great Father Puma'). Seler (1902–1923, IV, 469–470) has pointed out that the same glyger is found with the undisputed jaguars of D8a and D26a. *Chac balam* seems a likely reading. A glyph depicting a headless jaguar (T832) is also known from the inscriptions (Fig. 42). At Palenque, this glyph is found in passages which seem to refer to the War God. No one has suggested a plausible meaning or reading for this headless-jaguar glyph.

A number of suggestions have also been made regarding monkey glyphs. The day called variously Chuen or Batz corresponds, throughout Mesoamerica, to a day called Monkey in the local language, as has been mentioned. The same glyph is found to indicate the period of twenty days, known from Landa as the uinal (i.e., *win-al*). 'Month', however, appears in the Motul dictionary as *uen,* and *chuen* might be a compound *chu-uen.* No plausible reading has yet been suggested covering both meanings, 'monkey' and 'month'. Knorozov (1955a, p. 65, no. 7) has read the glyph phonetically as *ke,* but this does not explain the apparent use to mean 'monkey'. Pictographs of monkey heads or full figures of monkeys sometimes replace the glyph for *kin* 'day'. This usage has been explained in terms of the associations of the Sun God with monkeys (Thompson 1950, p. 143), but I would prefer a word meaning both 'monkey' and 'day' (or 'night').

Thompson (1958a, pp. 304–305) has identified glyph number 12 in Figure 42 as a monkey glyph, from its shape; from the context it should be either an animal or, just possibly, a deity. He reads it as *maax* 'monkey', and, since it is part of a disease almanac in his interpretations, he indicates that it refers to *chac nich' maax* 'an inflammation of the gums'. Without following him in the entire reading, the identification still seems quite possible. In referring to T648, which is found as the head of the death manikin, Thompson (1950, p. 268) said, "I think the simian features of this figure with its crest and 3-shaped design on the temple . . . are undeniable." This glyph is known to have associations with evil in the codices; so Thompson suggested the reading *kaz* 'bad, perverse, stupid, roguish', pointing out that *maax* 'spider monkey' enters into several Yucatec words meaning 'rogue' or 'ruffian'. T648 had previously been identified as an owl head until Beyer (1929) devoted an entire paper to trying to prove it was a dog. Beyer pointed out the close resemblance of this glyph to the head of the animal shown in Figure 42, number 10, which he regarded as a dog, and which is certainly not a monkey. The identification seems to me still questionable, and I would be happier with a more pedestrian correspondence between the identity of the glyph as a depiction and its meaning, although *kaz* has been accepted by Knorozov (1967, p. 91) in preference to his earlier *mu.*

I believe that the glyger T130:572:126 may be identified as referring to the Opossum Gods of D25–28 (Fig. 42). The identification of the animal as an opossum was first made by Stempell. This was doubted by Tozzer and Allen (1910, p. 347), who, however, thought the identification "very possible." Further evidence of other representations of opossums in Mesoamerica, given by Seler (1902–1923, IV, 506 ff.), made it virtually certain. It seems accepted by all the present generation of scholars. Analysis of the lengthy phrases above these representations shows that they have the form . . . X *u mam,* Y *u cuch* . . . , in which Y represents the god carried by the opossum (*u cuch* 'his burden'), and X must, therefore, represent the opossum, who is, I think, here identified as one of the Mams, or gods of the end of the year. The glyger may be a compound giving the name of an opossum god, rather than simply the word 'opossum'. The name is probably some cognate of the Yucatec *och* 'opossum', Quiche *'uch.*

Another glyger which I think may be identified substitutes at Naranjo in what may be a lineage name for a rodentlike head (Fig. 43). I believe the head is a squirrel (Yuc. *cuc*) and have other reasons for reading the glyger as *cuc.* The major reason for doubting the reading is the presence of unexplained affixes. Since

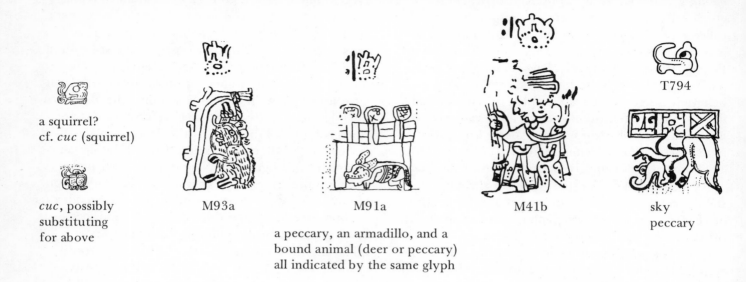

a squirrel?
cf. *cuc* (squirrel)

cuc, possibly
substituting
for above

M93a

M91a

M41b

T794

sky
peccary

a peccary, an armadillo, and a
bound animal (deer or peccary)
all indicated by the same glyph

Figure 43. Animal glyphs.

the glyger is also used for the so-called baktun, the various heads that substitute for the latter should also represent animals called *cuc* or synonyms for baktun. The most obvious possibility here is that some of the rather amorphous birds may be doves (cf. Q. *quku*, H. *cucu'*). The clearest of these representations is identified by Tozzer and Allen as a black vulture, and the hooked beak eliminates the possibility that this particular glyph shows a dove.

The glyger shown after *cuc* in Figure 43 was, strangely, unidentified prior to Knorozov's work. Regarding the animal represented as a peccary, he originally read '*7 citam*' (Knorozov 1955*b*, p. 53, no. 9), but later adopted the reading *ken*. Because of a superficial similarity of the glyph to the macaw glyger and the presence of the number seven, associated with the macaw in the *Popul Vuh*, Seler (1902–1923, IV, 557–558) thought that this was a macaw glyger. It occurs twice in the *Dresden*, once among the Venus gods and once as the name of a deity associated sexually with the White Goddess (D19b). Contextual evidence for identity is lacking in both cases. The full glyger, with '7', is found twice in *Madrid*, and the glyph without the '7' element appears once (Fig. 43). In the latter case (M93a), a clear-cut peccary is shown, caught in a trap, and the associated glyphs include only the 'trap' glyph and the glyph under discussion. In another passage dealing with trapping (M91a), the glyph of the figure shown is always in the third compartment. Here we have the full glyger. The animal shown seems to have hooves, a peccary snout, and an armadillo's ears and body. On M41b, the full glyger likewise appears. The sentence structure is

unusual (see p. 188) but seems to me to indicate that the glyger refers to a captive animal shown below. The figure is of a hoofed animal, which has been generally regarded as a deer or peccary. The variation in the three figures is disconcerting, but certainly in no case is there any indication of a macaw. A generic word which might apply equally to peccary, armadillo, and deer would be welcome, but if it is necessary to choose between them, I would, like Knorozov, pick 'peccary'.

Another glyph, T794, represents an animal which is shown hanging from the sky in *Dresden* and *Madrid* (Fig. 43). It has been called the Mars beast because of its association with a table of multiples of 780 days. Thompson (1950, p. 105) identified it with the patron deity of the month Zip. Tozzer and Allen (1910) regarded the animal as a conventionalized peccary, while Thompson (1950, p. 105) thought it might be a deer. Seler (1902–1923, IV, 551) drew attention to a representation which shows it with a quite long tail and a rather serrated back (Fig. 43), as well as the hooves and elongated snout of the other representations. He thought it was a composite "lightning beast" with mixed characteristics. He also compares it with the crocodilian sky monster of *Dresden*, which is also depicted with hooves. Sky associations and peccary characteristics seem dominant, and I prefer to call it simply a "sky peccary."

A pictograph of a bird's head appears on *Madrid* page 28c, where it seems to refer to a bird shown below, attacking the Corn God. The bird seems to be a crow, according to Seler (1902–1923, IV, 580–581), but the pictograph is not a crow (Fig. 44).

ideograph
for bird
below?

crow?
hoh
M28c

turkey
ulum

T613
eagle?
shark?

T612
le

bird god
Yax Coc Ah
Mut, with
turkey head

T743

a   b
T626

T625

turtle head,
turtle shell
(side), and
turtle shell
(back) glyphs

M17a

T207
rattlesnake
rattles

T206
worm or
snake

T327

centipede
head

T737
insect
larva

Z729
larva
glyph

Z759
snake, sometimes
confused with
T737

centipede

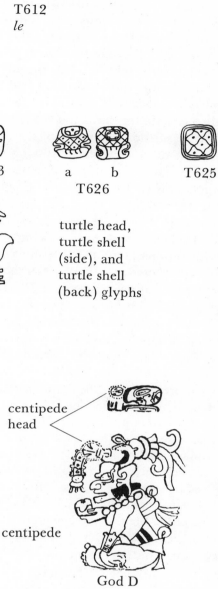

God D

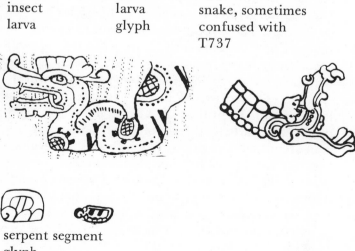

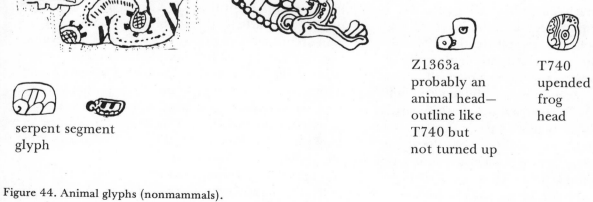

serpent segment
glyph

Z1363a
probably an
animal head—
outline like
T740 but
not turned up

T740
upended
frog
head

Figure 44. Animal glyphs (nonmammals).

Perhaps the artist made a mistake, or perhaps the names of the two birds are homonyms. The Mayan name for crow is *hoh.*

A glyger which Knorozov has read *ulum* 'turkey' opens the names of the Venus gods. Independent attempts by Seler and myself to align this series of twenty deities with those in the *Borgia* produced different alignments, but both lists suggest that this day was ruled by the turkey. Barthel (1955a, p. 18), who thinks that what Knorozov and I regard as *-m(u)* is actually a generic for 'bird' and that Knorozov's *lu* is 'sacrifice', reads this as 'its bird of sacrifice' and then compares the *ubech* 'pheasant' with the turkey as a bird of sacrifice. For a fuller discussion, see the section on God N (in Chapter 4) and Chapter 9.

Seler (1902–1923, IV, 591–592) has drawn attention to the strange headlike glyph (T613) for the day Men (Fig. 44). This seems to show some interchangeability with another glyph (T612), and they have often been considered as variants. Seler showed apparently similar use for what is probably T612 at Palenque and for a bird head. Since the day Men can be indirectly associated with the eagle, he argued for the identity of the bird head at Palenque with the eagle (cf. Tzel. *jumen* 'vulture'). Unfortunately, the identity of use consists of being found with the water-group prefixes, and the context indicates that the head, which is the Palenque Emblem Glyph (EG) (Fig. 72), is not actually substitutable for the T612 glyph. Seler also argues that the Palenque bird head is the forerunner of the bird head of D17b, which is part of the name glyger of the bird below. The latter is identified by everyone else as a vulture, but Seler maintains that it could be an eagle. The evidence for identifying either Men or the Palenque EG as an eagle head seems scanty. Tozzer and Allen suggest Men is a shark, a reading that seems equally uncertain.

A glyph for a mythical bird is identical with that for the vulture, save for a notch at the back of the head. The glyph refers to a deity shown as regent of katun 3 Ahau (*Paris*, p. 8), with a bird head and a human body: Seler (1902–1923, IV, 625–627) points out that Yax Coc Ah Mut, a bird deity (Fig. 44), is associated with katun 3 Ahau in the *Books of Chilam Balam* (see Barrera Vásquez and Rendón 1948, p. 106) and that Landa associates this deity with the Muluc years. A turkey appears in a place of honor in the *Madrid* representation of the Muluc year, and the bird deity of katun 3 Ahau is shown with a wattle, which looks remarkably like a turkey wattle, hanging down over the beak. It would seem that the glyph stands for a turkey god who was known as Yax Coc Ah Mut to the colonial Maya. However, I strongly doubt that the glyph can be read as *yax coc ah mut*

and suspect that it gives a different name of the god.

There are pictographs of a turtle head (T743) and a turtle shell (T626) (Fig. 44). The turtle-head glyph is found in a context (M17a) where it seems to mean 'turtle'. In the Landa alphabet, it occurs with the value *a;* since 'turtle' is *aac,* it has been assumed that Landa's informant simply gave him a glyph beginning with *a.* Interchangeability with other glyphs and use in context suggest that Landa's *a* may be correct. The turtle-shell glyph, with Landa's *ma* prefixed, is one of the glygers for the month Mac. Following Knorozov, I have supposed this glyger was *ma-aac.* However, Thompson (1962, p. 244) points out that one of the Yucatec words for 'turtle shell' is *mac,* which might indicate a partially phonetic reading, *ma/mac.* Barthel (1955a, pp. 21–22) points out that *coc ac* is a name for turtle and that *coc* is 'miserable'. With the tun glyph, the turtle shell is found on D73b, where the context supports the meaning 'miserable year'. Thompson (1967, p. 8) gives the same reading.

Interestingly, turtle shells and other types of shells seem to typify God N. He may wear either a turtle shell or some sort of marine shell (*Fasciolaria gigantea,* Tozzer and Allen 1910, pp. 296–297). The accompanying glyphs likewise have either a turtle shell or a marine shell but do not always agree with the representations. In one case (M13a), a turtle appears instead of the god. Shells appear in other cases as glyphs, again with marked variability. The normal 'zero' glyph is a shell (see Chapter 1).

Several other animal glyphs (in Fig. 44) may be passed over rather quickly. The rattles of the rattlesnake (T207) were identified by Tozzer and Allen (1910, p. 312, and probably earlier), and a representation of glyph and snake side by side is adequate proof of the identification. Knorozov (1955a, p. 69) has read the glyph *cuc,* on grounds which are not clear to me. The glyph is used in connection with time periods. More recently, Knorozov (1967, p. 82) has suggested *tzub,* comparing *tzab* 'rattles of a snake' with *tzutzubtah* 'to add, to supplement'. The worm or snake (T206) used for an anterior date indicator is likewise quite identifiable as a glyph but not recognizable as a particular snake or worm. This glyph could represent a cognate of Quiche *niih* 'a worm used for lining pots, to stink' (*nih* 'varnish worm'; *ni* 'stink'). Hauxtec *nihuihuíl* 'oloroso' ('odorous') and *nijiy* 'olor de cal' ('odor of lime') are probably related. It is not impossible that Landa's *-n-* represents this *ni/ne* rather than *ne* 'tail'. A snake, associated with very long time periods, is referred to by T327:17 (see Fig. 89).

Under T737, Thompson (1962, p. 316) has lumped at least a "naturalistic snake," "a headless snake," and "probably . . . a larva." These should have had separate numbers. Zimmermann assigned the numbers 729, 759, and 1363 to glyphs lumped as T737 by Thompson and did not include either the "naturalistic snake" or the "headless snake." (See Fig. 44.)

Full-figure forms of the uinal glyph represent a frog or toad and are quite similar to T740, the so-called upended frog head (Fig. 44). Thompson (1950, pp. 47–48, 239) suggested that *po* 'frog, toad' substitutes for *po* 'moon' in the Lunar Series. Then Proskouriakoff demonstrated the use of T740 for "initial dates," and I interpreted them as birth dates. Finally, Barthel (1968a, pp. 134–135) has demonstrated that the true reading is **pok'* 'to be born', 'frog'. This reading seems to me convincing. Use of this glyph in the Lunar Series seems to refer to a count from the "birth" of the moon.

Tozzer and Allen (1910, pp. 363–364) show to my satisfaction that God D is particularly associated with the centipede and that a conventionalized centipede head forms part of his glyger (see Figs. 20, 44), a fact which seems to me to substantiate their view.

Finally, there must be some discussion of three fish glyphs and their equivalents. T608, called by Beyer and Brinton a mollusk and by Barthel a penis (an interpretation already specifically rejected by Brinton in 1895), seems to me the headless body of a fish. The same identification is given by Knorozov (1967, p. 103, no. 374), who reads *dzu (tz'u)*. Comparison with fish in the codices and on the "bones text" from Tikal shows a virtual identity. The identity as a mollusk was suggested by the frequency with which this glyph is associated with another, resembling two shells. The identity as a penis involves utilizing the more cursive representations and regarding the two shell-like objects as part of the glyph, in spite of the fact that they occur prefixed to other groups and that T608 also occurs with other glyphs. Its shape is very unusual and corresponds so well to Landa's -*m*- that I think the two are identical. I would suggest that T608 is to be read *me* (cf. Q. *mech* 'bearded fish').

One of the discoveries which did the most to reopen some of the important questions about the nature of the Maya script was Thompson's (1944) demonstration of the great likelihood that *xoc* 'count' was represented in the inscriptions by the head of a large fish, the *xoc* or 'shark'. Substituting for this in many inscriptions was the hieroglyph T511, also found for the day Muluc. Since the *xoc* shark is a patron deity of the day Muluc, Thompson assumed that the *xoc* head was the head form of the *muluc* glyph. Reasonable as this seems, it implies both a straightforward rebus use for *xoc* and a symbolic secondary meaning for *muluc*, which he appar-

ently thinks should also be read *xoc* in this context, "the symbol for water or rain representing the creature which inhabits water and in all probability gave rain to the earth" (Thompson 1950, p. 163). This view neglects the fact that there is a perfectly good allograph or head variant of *muluc*, which is not the *xoc* fish, but rather the so-called *kan* dog. While the Yucatec day is named Muluc, equivalent days in the other languages are simply Mulu (or, in the highlands, Toh). The Quiche language seems to offer a clue to this labyrinth with the definition of *mul* as 'time, turn, rotation, revolution'. The counting of the year might easily appear in another context as the turning of the year. Although I have not checked all occurrences, this meaning would certainly fit most of the contexts with which I am familiar.

Thus I believe that Thompson's brilliant decipherment of *xoc* 'shark' for *xoc* 'count', which I fully accept, was overextended in the attempt to apply it to T511, which I think should be read simply as *mul(u)*. I also think it was overextended in another direction when Thompson attempted to go from this fully valid identification to other fish glyphs, which he then said symbolized counting. In particular, I am convinced that a very common fish head is to be read simply *ca*. In Figure 45, I have shown both *ca* and *xoc* in typical contexts. One of these fish heads shows consistent interchangeability with the so-called comb (T25), which Landa said was *ca*, and with the fish (T203). The "comb," however, never appears with the affixes typical of the *xoc* fish. This creates a distinction in context which supports the other reasons for separating *xoc* 'shark' from *ca* (cf. *cai* 'fish'). Despite their descriptive similarity, the *ca* head seems to show a distinctive form. It is also clear that the *xoc* head has certain infixes not associated with the *ca* head. Most notable of these is the glyph T501. Thompson (1950, p. 72) has shown that this represents a water lily, Yucatec *naab*. Figure 46 shows the artistic representations which warrant this conclusion. *Naab* is also the word for 'ocean', and I believe that here it is merely meant to indicate that the *xoc* is an ocean fish and is not intended to be read.

The *naab* glyph leads to a consideration of some other plant glyphs, although identified plant glyphs are still very few. Thompson has shown that affix T87 is frequently shown where trees are referred to, appears as a numerical classifier, and is found as a deity name following the glyphs for *bolon-oc*. Since *te* means 'tree', is a numerical classifier, and completes the known deity name Bolon Yocte (in which the *y* of *yoc* reflects late Yucatecan grammatical processes), this may be considered one of the best documented of all decipherments. This decipherment

T203

substitutability of
comb—fish head—full fish
ca
Note relatively
small size of
mouth.

compounds with
xoc fish head

Figure 45. *Ca* fish and *xoc* fish.

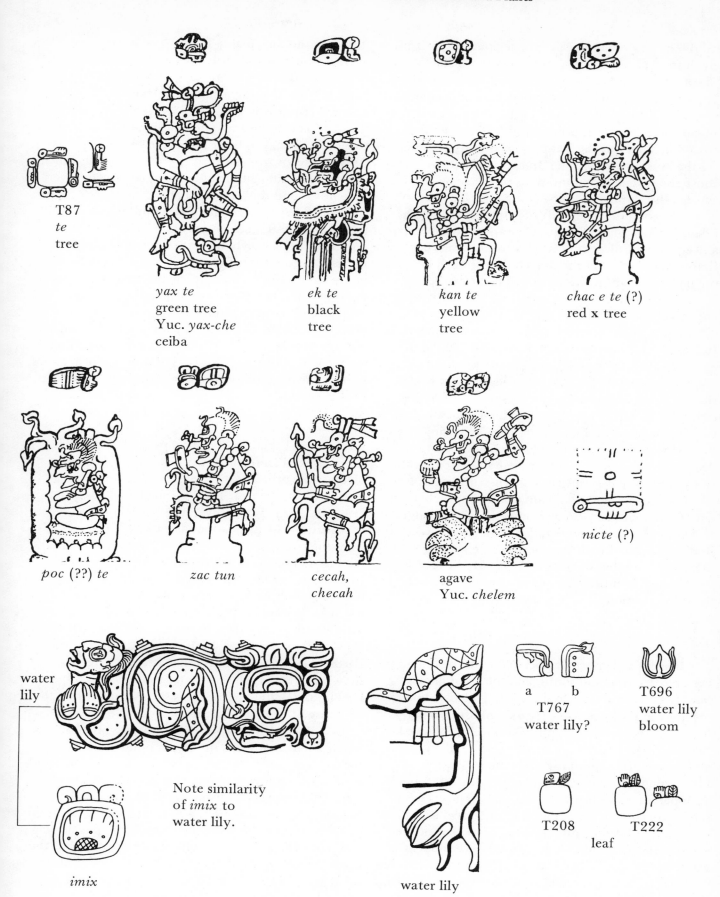

T87
te
tree

yax te
green tree
Yuc. *yax-che*
ceiba

ek te
black
tree

kan te
yellow
tree

chac e te (?)
red x tree

poc (??) *te*

zac tun

*cecah,
checah*

agave
Yuc. *chelem*

nicte (?)

water
lily

imix

Note similarity
of *imix* to
water lily.

water lily

a   b
T767
water lily?

T696
water lily
bloom

T208

T222
leaf

Figure 46. Plant glyphs.

led directly to the more specific decipherment of the glyph for 'ceiba'. The Yucatec name for 'ceiba' is *yaxche* (from earlier **yax-te*), literally 'green tree'. The *yax* glyph is one of the earlier known decipherments, and the ceiba tree is recognizable, not only as a plant, but because it is normally depicted with a crocodilian head at the bottom, apparently standing for the mythical *imix*-ceiba. In appropriate places above the several representations of the ceiba tree appears the glyph *yax* followed by affix T87, *te*.

Thompson (1939, p. 138) suggested that the *kin* ('day, sun') glyph represents a four-petaled flower, or a five-petaled flower converted to four petals, because four is the number of the Sun God. Although he originally thought it was a five-petaled tobacco flower, he revised his opinion to suggest that it was the equally five-petaled *Plumiera*. The latter is of great erotic and religious importance in Mesoamerica. In Maya, it is known as *nicte*. Knorozov (1955a, p. 83, no. 85) reads as *nicte* a glyger composed of the glyph Z1341a with T87 (*te*) affixed. Z1341a is identical with the ordinary *kin* glyph, save that it has a dotted outline. The glyph is found with apparent offering passages in the *Dresden* (pp. 12c, 15c). Barthel regards this as the only one of Knorozov's decipherments which is fully acceptable. Neither the context nor the descriptive similarity of the glyph to a flower seems to me adequate to warrant such acceptance, although the reading is moderately plausible.

A passage starting on *Dresden* page 30c shows God B associated with various places, including a substantial number of trees and plants. The locative glyph which identifies the plant seems always to be in the third position:

1 2
3 4

The first four plants are associated with the directions east, north, west, and south, and the plant names have the color prefixes 'red', 'white', 'black', and 'yellow', in the latter two cases simply followed by *te* 'tree'. The *zac* 'white' glyph is, strangely, followed by the tun glyph rather than the *te* glyph, and an extra glyph (postulated as *e*) precedes the *te* glyph in the first example (to be read *chac e te*?). In D32c appears an apparent agave plant, named by two heads with the locative *ti* prefixed. Yucatec for 'agave' is *chelem*, and the first head might conceivably be that of the goddess (Ix) Chel, although I would have thought it was simply a glyph for 'woman'. The unlikely-looking plant on D33c is identified as T563a with the *te* affix. Knorozov (1955a, p. 85, no. 115) read this as *pocte*, translated as 'desierto con arboles, matorral' ('desert with trees'). This hardly seems a likely reading for

this water-holding plant. Tzeltal *pok* is 'resin', and 'resin tree' would be a slightly better meaning. In 1967, Knorozov compares his reading to Yucatec *poc che* < **pok te*, to which the meaning 'thicket' is assigned (Knorozov 1967, p. 93). However, evidence that T563a is to be read *poc* is scanty. The second tree on D33c has a glyger (preceded by the locative *ti*) which Knorozov has read *checah* (a reading which I accept), presumably from earlier **cecah*. However, I have not found this as a tree name.

Glyph T696 looks to me like a budding flower, but there is no contextual support, nor are there flower representations which make it undeniably clear that this is a correct identification. A leaf glyph is found in the composite affix to which Thompson has given the single number 208, as well as in the composite affix given the single number T222. Thompson (1959, p. 359) argues that Landa's second *l* glyph is a leaf and stands for *le* 'leaf'. Knorozov has identified it with T568, which he reads *lu*. The identity of Landa's poorly drawn glyph is of relatively little moment. Both *xaq* and *le* are widespread Mayan terms for 'leaf', and the leaf glyph probably represents one or the other of them.

T663 has been read by Thompson (1950, p. 271) as *pakal* 'seed', a reading which seems to me completely unjustified (see Chapter 3 for a fuller consideration of this glyph). T767 is called by Thompson (1962, p. 368) "water lily." The representation seems to justify the identification, despite its difference from the *imix/naab* glyph. Still a third glyph (T625; see Fig. 44) seems to me to be sometimes derived from the water lily. The view of the side of a water lily (Fig. 46, bottom center) makes it clear that this is possible. Thompson (1962, p. 243) calls T625 a turtle shell and the turtle (M17a; see Fig. 44) supports this view, already expressed by Beyer (1937, pp. 67–68). Barthel (1955a, p. 16) says that *Dresden* page 2d shows that the glyph must refer to the woven object held by the deities below. This seems required by the structure of the sentence. Knorozov (1967, p. 94) reads T625 as *box*, one of the Yucatec words for 'turtle shell', and reads the glyger pointed out by Barthel as *boxih* 'clothing', good support for the turtle-shell interpretation in this case. At Chichen Itza, T625 appears with *zac* prefixed, and Barthel suggests that *zac*, in this context, is probably 'weave'.

There seem to be three recognizable glyphs dealing with corn (Fig. 47). The stylized corn plant forms the head of the Corn God (T1006). The related or identical affixes T84, T85, and T86 seem to represent a corncob in its foliage. T130 seems to represent maize foliage or an immature ear of corn. All suggested interpretations of these glyphs seem to reflect agree-

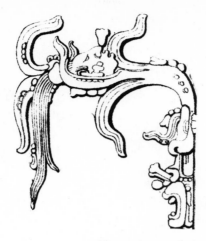

The Corn God from *Dresden*. Compare head with T84–86 below. A stylized form of the head is T1006, the name glyph of the god.

Two views of the Corn God as a corn cob from the TFC, Palenque. Note the leaf structure.

Compare with T84 below.

The growth of corn (*Madrid*, p. 28b).

The corn seed (?) being protected from a crow.

Growing corn being protected from a mammal.

The mature corn.

The context suggests that the *kan* glyph here means 'corn seed'.

T84
Read by
Knorozov
nal
ear of corn

T84   T85   T86

T130
Read by
Knorozov
aan
young ear
of corn

Figure 47. Corn.

ment that they represent plant motifs and, more particularly, corn motifs. For a fuller analysis of their grammatical functions, see Chapter 10, where their identification as words is considered.

Thus it appears that a substantial number of animal glyphs have been long identified and that recent work is refining upon many of the identifications. Readings in Maya are still relatively rare, but an increasing number of plausible suggestions are being made. Animal glyphs are so numerous that this will remain a promising field of study for many years, and the main problem is differentiating similar glyphs. Plant glyphs are much fewer, and the promising identifications which have already been made are unlikely to be greatly extended.

The following linguistic reconstructions, derived from Kaufman 1964, may have some relevance to the glyphs which have been considered in this section. Reconstructions apply to the whole family unless otherwise specified. Periods are used to separate reconstructions for one meaning from reconstructions for the next.

Dog: (a) *peqw', Yuc.-H.-(Zapotec?); (b) *tzw'i', others. Turkey: (a) *'akw'ach, Pch.-Kek.-Chu.-Kan.-(Agc.)-Chl.; (b) *'akw', Mam-Q.; (c) *kutz, Tzel.-Yuc.-Chr.-(H.?). Cat: *mis/mes (<Nahua?)(H.?). Domestic animal: *'alaq'. Roar: *woj. Jaguar: *bah-lĕm, Yuc. balam (H.?). Opossum: (a) *'uch, Tzel.-Tzo.-Yuc.-Chl.; (b) *'uhchum, Toj.-Tzel.-Chu.-Kan.-Jac.; (c) *huhty', H.-Kek.-Q. (Q. vuch) (Mam?). Rat: (a) *ch'oh, Tzel.-Tzo.-Pch.-Kek.-Q.; (b) *ch'o', Yuc.-(Chr.); (c) *ch'o'w, Toj.-Chu.-Kan.-Jac.-(H.?)-Chl.; tzuk<MZ. Rabbit: (a) *t'u'l, Tzel.-Tzo.-Yuc.-Chl.-Chr.; (b) *chich, Toj.-Chu.-Kan.; (c) *'imul, Pch.-Kek.-(Agc.)-Q.-H.; koy<MZ. Mole: (a) *baah, Tzel.-Tzo.-Yuc.-H.-Pch.-Kek.-Jac.-Chl.-Q.-Chr.-Mam; (b) *kwo'n, Chu.-Kan. Armadillo: (a) *'ib, Tzel.-Tzo.-Jac.-Chl.; (b) *'ib-ach, Yuc.-Chu.-Kan.-Chr.; (c) *'ib-oy, Pch.-Kek.-Toj.-Mam-(Cak.) (H.?). Puma: *kooj (Mam?). Squirrel: *ku'k (H.?). Deer: *kyehj (H.?). Weasel: *saqbin. Spider monkey: (a) *ma'x; (b) *k'oy. Howler monkey: *batz'. Coatimundi: (a) *tz'utz'; (b) *kohtom; (c) *sis. Coyote: (a) *'oq; (b) *xo'j. Paca or tepezcuintle: *halaw; Dasyprocta punctata chiapensis: haleb, tzub. Porcupine: *k'i'x + *'uch/huhty' (zarigüeya). Tapir: (a) *tzimin; (b) *tixVl, Cak. Skunk: *pahëy. Fox: (a) *wa'x (Mixean?); (b) *wetw (Zoquean?). Peccary: (a) *kitam; (b) *'ahq. Bat: *sootz'. Bird: (a) *mutw, Tzel.-Tzo.-Toj.-Chu.-Yuc.-Chl.-Chr.; (b) *tz'ikwin, Yuc.-H.-Pch.-Kek.-Kan.-Jac.-Q. (Mam?). Crow: *jooj (Yuc.?). Vulture: (a) *hos, Tzel.-Chu.-Kan.-Chl.; (b)

*'usej, Toj.-Chu.-Jac.-Chr.; (c) *k'uty, Pch.-Kek.-Q.-Mam-H.-Yuc. Sanate: (a) *tz'ok/ch'ok, Kek.-Pch.-Kan.-Jac.-Mam-Q.; (b) *k'a'aw, Tzel.-Toj.-Chu.-Yuc.-(Chl.?). Hummingbird: *tz'unu'n. Owl: *xooch'. Owl: (a) *tuhkuru; (b) *'ikin. Male bird: *'aj-tzo'. Duck: *pech. Macaw: *mo'. Hawk: (a) *likw; (b) *t'iiw; (c) *xi(h)kw; (d) *kwot. Parrot, parakeet: *ky'el. Flea: *ky'ĕq. Bee, honey: *kaab. Fly: *'us (Pch.-Kek. 'utz') (H.?). Grub: (a) *hĕ'h, Tzel.-Tzo.-H.-Pch.-Chl.-Mam; (b) *ha'y, Chu.-Kek.; (c) *haja', Kan.-Jac. Ant: *sanik, etc. Spider: (a) *'am, Yuc.-Tzel.-Tzo.-H.-Pch.-Kek.-Chl.-Q.-Chr.; (b) *xim, Mam-Chu.-Kan.-Jac. (Toj.?). Louse: *'uk'. Tick: *siip (Yuc.?). Butterfly: (a) *pehpen; (b) *nam. Cricket: *chül/xiil, Q. centipede, not cricket. Firefly: *kwuk-way. Cockroach: (a) *pewal; (b) *peek'. Mosquito: *xe'n. Wasp: (a) *xuux; (b) *hoonon. Scorpion: (a) *sina'ng; (b) *tzek. Toad: (a) *'wo', Yuc.-H.-Kek.-Toj.-Chu.-Mam; (b) *peq/poq, Kan.-Jac.-Tzel.-Tzo.-Chl.-Chr.-Q.-Pch. Frog: (a) *'aj-muuch (Tzel.-Tzo.) Yuc.-H.-Kek.-Chl.-Chr.; (b) *pajtza', Chu.-Jac.-Kan.; (c) *ch'uch', Tzel.-Tzo.-Toj.-Mam (Q.?). Fish: *kĕy (H.?). Crocodile: *'ahyin, Jac.-Kan.<Spanish. Large turtle: (a) *'ahkw; (b) *peety (or *peetz). Small turtle: *kwokw. Crab: (a) *twĕp; (b) *nep'. Iguana: (a) *intam (not Mayan?); (b) *huuj/hiij. Worm: cf. stop, bow, bend, twist, *luqum, etc. (Mam?). Snake: *kan (Pch.-Kek.?). Shell: (a) *puy; (b) *xoch; (c) *kw'o. Root: (a) *xe', Kek.-Kan.-Jac.-Mam-Q.; (b) *yab, Pch.-Q.; (c) *'ib, etc., Tzo.-H.-Toj.-Chu.-Chl.-Tzel. (<'eb) (Yuc.?). Nut: (a) *neeq'/nahq', Yuc.-Pch.-Kek.-Q.-Chr.; (b) *bĕq', Tzel.-Tzo.-Chl.-Jac.-Mam (Q.) (H.?). Thorn: *k'i'x. Seed: *hing('). Resin: (a) *q'ol; (b) *xuch'. Flower: *ngik. Leaf: *xaq. Avocado: *'oong. Coyol: *mĕĕp. Chili pepper: *'ik. Chocolate: *kakaw, kokow, kĕkĕw<Nahua. Sapodilla: *muy'. Pineapple: (a) *kw'ewex; (b) *pak. Guava, pata, etc., MZ. Zapote: (a) *twulul; (b) *ha'as. Jocote: *po'on, etc. Tree: *tyee'. Pine: *tya'ng, (H.?). Ceiba: *'inup. Palm: (a) *xa'ng; (b) *'apak'. Achiote (Bixa orellana, a plant for red dye): *ho'ox. Willow: *toq'oy. Fir: *kw'isis. Cork: *bĕĕty. Oak: *jih. Yellow squash: *h'uXm. Potato (?): *'iis. Bean: (a) *kinaqw', Tzel.-Tzo.-H.-Pch.-Kek.-Toj.-Q.-Mam; (b) *bu'ul, Yuc.-Chl.-Chr.; (c) *tut, Chu.; (d) *hup'al, Kan.-Jac. Tomato: (a) *pix; (b) *koya,<MZ. Blackberry: (a) *tok-an; (b) *makom. Vine: *'aaq'. Gourd: (a) *mukwun; (b) *tz'ohl. White squash: (a) *q'ooq'; (b) *mĕy. Grape: *tz'usub. Nettle: *lah (Mam?). Herb: (a) *'aq, Tzel.-Tzo.-Yuc.-Kek.-Toj.-Chu.-Chr.; (b) *k'im, Kek.-Pch.-Kan.-Q.-Jac. (H.?). Amole (various agave plants, particularly those whose roots are used for soap): *ch'upaq. Reed: (a) *'aj; (b) *jalal. Fern: *tzihb. Greens: *'ityaj. Cotton seed: *tux. Cotton: *tinĕm,

etc. Sunflower: *su'n*. Henequen: *kih*. Manioc: *tz'iXn*. Bromelia: *'ek'*. Squash (chayote): (a) *pehtwaq;* (b) *pajk'ak'*. Pineapple: (a) *pajk';* (b) *matzajti'* (not Mayan?). Corn: (a) *'i'm*, H.; (b) *'ix + i'm,* others. Corn cob, dried ear: *ngal*. Green corn: *'ajan*. Ripe ear of corn: *bëqël*. Fresh corn: *hih/hi'*.

Pinole, a corn drink: *ky'aj,* (Tzel.-Tzo.?). Leached corn: *buuch* (=ashes). To shell corn: *q'uty*. Corn drink: *maatz'* (=to suck). Corn dough: *q'oy*. To grind corn: *juch'*. Atole, a corn gruel: (a) *'ul*<MZ?; (b) *sa';* (c) *joch'*. Leaves of corn: *joj/joq*. Chewing tobacco: *kw'uhtz*. Cigar: *siikw'*. Tobacco: *mëhy'*.

Chapter 6
Artifacts

A preliminary step in decipherment is, in many cases, the identification of the object represented. While this is certainly true of deities, animals, and plants, it becomes of vital importance when considering glyphs representing artifacts. Although presumably the glyph may, at least in most cases, stand for the object represented, it may also stand for various homonyms. The meaning must, therefore, be determined by the context and by known homonyms of words for the objects. As a general principle, it should be borne in mind that the identifications should base themselves as much as possible upon Maya models rather than upon a priori conceptions derived from our own culture. It has also frequently been suggested that an object may have a "symbolic" value, based not upon phonetic homonyms but rather upon the associations which the object has in Mayan culture or even, more broadly, in Mesoamerican culture. Although I am inclined to doubt this, I have made a rough attempt to group artifacts shown as glyphs into use or association categories.

A series of affixes which occurs frequently seems to show various types of knots. Many of these seem to have grammatical functions. In one case, the so-called toothache glyph (T684, Fig. 56), the knot extends around a human or animal head of some sort and has been supposed to mean 'capture' but is associated with the inauguration of rulers. Knot glyphs have been the subject of a special paper by Dütting (1965a).

Two glyphs have been recognized which depict bundles. Z61 (which equates partially but probably not entirely with T103) is shown to be a merchant's pack by comparison with M91a (Fig. 48). This is a good example of the necessity for examining the Maya sources, as an a priori identification of this glyph would have been difficult, if not impossible. Z61 is the subject of a special paper by John Fought (1965), who has proposed for it the reading -al. For a consideration of the grammatical aspects of this identification, see Chapter 10. I know of no Maya word for 'bundle' which directly corresponds to al, but it may perhaps be relevant that in Huaxtec alchic is 'heavy' and alem is 'weight'; Tzeltal al is 'weighs, heavy'; and Quiche 'al is 'heavy, weight'.

The second bundle glyph (T609) shows the wrapped-up skin of a jaguar, as demonstrated by Thompson (1950, p. 212); the full-figure glyph from Copan Stela D shows the identity of the glyph. This glyph appears as Glyph F of the Supplementary Series in one of its forms. No reading has yet been proposed.

The glyph T601 was identified as a carrying device by Beyer. Comparison with the representation of

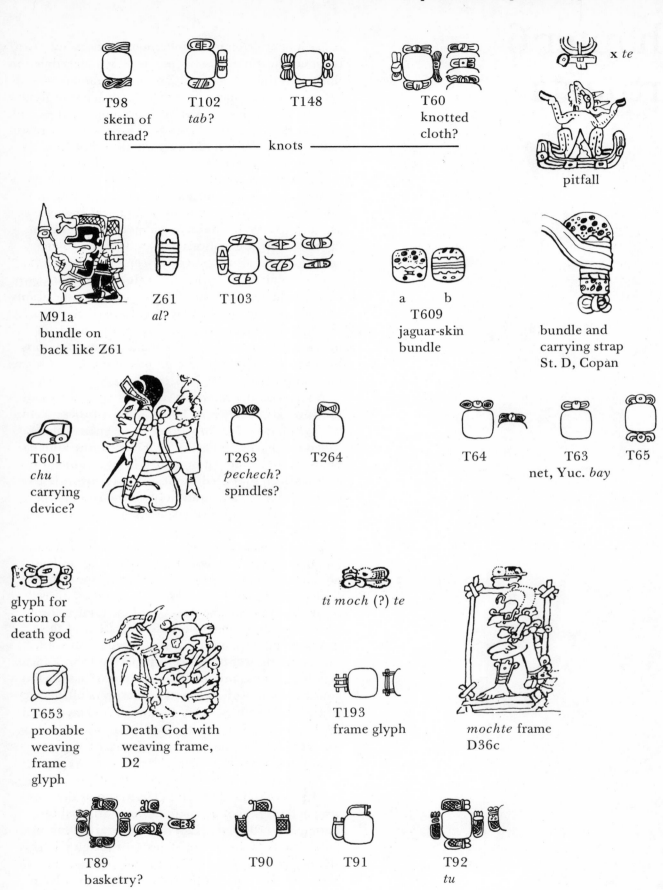

T98
skein of
thread?

T102
tab?

T148

T60
knotted
cloth?

— knots —

x *te*

pitfall

M91a
bundle on
back like Z61

Z61
al?

T103

a   b
T609
jaguar-skin
bundle

bundle and
carrying strap
St. D, Copan

T601
chu
carrying
device?

T263
pechech? spindles?

T264

T64

T63
net, Yuc. *bay*

T65

glyph for
action of
death god

T653
probable
weaving
frame
glyph

Death God with
weaving frame,
D2

ti moch (?) *te*

T193
frame glyph

mochte frame
D36c

T89
basketry?

T90

T91

T92
tu

Figure 48. Artifacts.

carrying devices in the *Dresden* and *Madrid* makes the identification seem plausible but far from certain. Thompson, followed by Barthel, has read the glyph as *cuch* 'burden', but the meaning 'burden' is conveyed by a glyger of which this is only the second element; it seems, instead, to be a phonetic glyph, *chu* (see discussion, Chapter 9). The original meaning of *chu* in this context is not yet determined.

Barthel (1955*a*, pp. 16–17) has identified T263 as representing spindle whorls; Beyer (1937, p. 70) had earlier referred to them as "spindle-shaped objects." Barthel tentatively suggested the reading *pechech* 'spindle' as indicating *pech* 'tick'.

Hieroglyph T653 seems to be a weaving frame, with a bone awl inserted in the process of weaving. It is compared, in Figure 48, with a representation of a weaving frame in use, from the *Dresden,* page 2. Another type of wooden frame, of unknown use, is the prefix T193, which should be compared with the scene from D36c (Fig. 48).

Various types of crosshatched and looped elements seem to indicate different conceptions. Crosshatching on the monuments may correspond, in the codices, to a solid black, to crosshatching, or, in glyphs which seem otherwise identical, to a blank white area. In cases where black in the codices corresponds to crosshatching on the monuments, the black seems to represent the original concept more appropriately than the crosshatching, as, for example, in portraying jaguars' spots. In some cases, the crosshatching seems to correspond to a representation of netting of some kind. Knorozov (1967, p. 84, no. 071) has identified T64 as a net (Yuc. *bay*) and suggested a reading *uay*. T63 and T65 seem to me, from their distribution, and from the compounds which they form, to be merely the variants of T64 without crosshatching. The glyphs identified by Thompson as T89, T90, T91, and T92 (Fig. 48) appear to represent some sort of frame with netting across it and to be equivalent in all cases. The identification of T92 by Thompson as *tu* is discussed in Chapter 10. The scene from M93a (Fig. 49) seems to represent some sort of net cage or trap but has no close equivalent in the glyphs. Crosshatching is also frequently used in the codices to indicate woven garments (or decoration on them?). Looping seems frequently used for matting and thatching. In its most general form, this is found as T192, which may represent a simple mat (Yuc. *pop*). With posts below, as in T614a (which I regard as distinct from T614b), Brinton (1895, p. 96) suggested that this represented a canopy. More likely, it represents a house. It appears as the central glyph of the glyger for 'house, temple', and Knorozov has suggested a reading *otot* (Yuc. *otoch* 'house'). I am unwilling to accept this reading

until the other elements of the glyger can be adequately explained. A probable linguistic identification of a glyph for a frame or cage, on *Dresden* 36c (Fig. 48), has been made by Floyd G. Lounsbury and Michael D. Coe (1968). In this section of the *Dresden,* God B normally appears in a temple, but in this one picture he is in a rather crude frame or cage. A glyph in the third position above has the locative prefix *ti,* followed by the dotted-circle glyph which is the first element in *moo* 'macaw', then by a crosshatched element, and finally by *te,* as identified by Thompson. The locative prefix suggests that this glyph sequence refers to the crude structure below. Lounsbury and Coe note the Tzeltal term *mochilte* 'jaula' ('cage'), which might suggest that the unidentified crosshatched element was to be read simply *chil.* However, in investigating modern Tzeltal and Tzotzil terms, they found reference to a special platform for San Juan which was called the *mochtee* or simply *moch,* literally 'basket'. They therefore suggested that the crosshatched element was to be read as *moch* 'basket', with the preliminary *mo* as a phonetic determinant, and wavered between the view that *te* was to be read and the view that it might be simply a semantic determinant. I am inclined to accept the reading *ti (mo) mochte.* A possible complicating factor is that on the frame below is a representation of a dish with something in it, of which the first element looks strikingly like the *mo* above. What this may mean is quite obscure. The mat throne glyph from Tikal Stela 31 is closely comparable to the representation from M88b (Fig. 49), save that the 'earth' glyph has replaced the bottom part of the glyph in the latter representation.

As a separate glyph, the tubular pipe occurs only once, prefixed to the 'star' glyph (Tikal St. 5, B10; see Fig. 9). Compare the representation of God L smoking (Fig. 23). I have suggested that the combination is to be read *budz ek* 'smoking star', a known Yucatec term for comets. The inscriptions suggest that the pipe has been infixed into the head of God K, though the infix has been so conventionalized in the codices that it is no longer recognizable as a separate element.

The fan glyph (T627, Fig. 49) has been identified by Barthel (1964*a*, p. 228), who shows it associated with the jawbone, apparently as a symbol of rank, both in a vase painting and in a glyphic representation from Chichen Itza. It may perhaps be read **wa* or **wal.* Brinton (1895, p. 94) pointed out that the *yax kukul,* a green feather ornament attached to a staff, was probably the original of the *yax* glyph. Another glyph which can easily be identified is T24, which represents a shell ornament, as pointed out by W. J.

M93a net trap

T192
thatch?

a b
T614
building with
thatch roof?

house, temple
cf. T614a

M88b — mat throne

Tikal St. 31
mat throne

a b
T627
fans

jawbone
and fans
—both on
figure at right

T24
shell
ornament
(tinkler)

shell ornaments
on belts

receptacles for blood offerings —
mussel shells? —paper?

T149

T548
tun
wooden
drum

T549
pax
to break;
wooden drum

tun type
drum from
Duran

a b c
T686
T686c is
a pottery
drum.

T190
axe
baat

T333
compound
axe + *ca*

T361
spear thrower

T678
helmet

T112
spear point
—see figure
at right

a b
T594
checker-
board
shield

a b c
T624
complex
shield,
pacal; see
figure at right

T152
round shield
with hanging
ornament

T685
pyramid
Yuc. *mul*

T150
stairway

T697
stairway?
ladder?

Figure 49. More artifacts.

de Gruyter (1946, p. 25; cf. Spinden 1913, p. 84). De Gruyter implies a connection with the bar for 'five', which he cites as *hob,* comparing with *hub* 'large sea shell'.

On the basis of an apparent association with stones in the codices, Cyrus Thomas (1882, pp. 74–75) suggested that T548 was a "stone heap" possibly to be read *piz,* "a stone serving to form the divisions in a Katun or cycle" or *ppic,* "stones placed one upon another, serving to count the intervals in the cycles." Its use for the 360-day period (Yuc. *tun*) was a factor in leading Seler to regard the glyph as a "precious stone" (Yuc. *tun* 'stone'). This position is not essentially different from that of Thompson (1950, p. 144), who has suggested that the glyph is a stabilized compound of a glyph for 'jade' (Yuc. *tun* again) and the prefix *yax* 'new, green'. Comparison with the *yax* glyph leaves me unconvinced.

The *tun* glyph was identified as a wooden drum by Brinton (1895, p. 92), and Marshal H. Saville immediately accepted it. Figure 49 shows the Aztec drum representation relied on by Brinton to demonstrate his point. It was not then known that an ancestral Mayan word for drum was **tun:* Yucatec *tunkul* 'divine drum' (?); Quiche *tun* 'hollow log drum'; Chorti *tun* 'hollow log drum' (Wisdom 1940, pp. 175–176). The glyph is nearly the same as that for the month Pax (T549), except that the top part of the latter is split or divided by two curving lines. Brinton, without referring to the Pax glyph, identified the *tun* glyph as the drum called in Yucatec *pax che (pax* 'musical instrument'; *che<*te* 'wooden'). Yucatec *pax* means 'broken, disappeared', and Quiche *paxih* means, among other things, 'split, divide, break, separate'. It would seem that the dividing lines on the Pax glyph may have been used as a semantic/phonetic determinative indicating that the drum should be read *pax,* not *tun* (cf. de Gruyter 1946, p. 27). Thus, one may expect that this glyph was used elsewhere meaning 'to break' and possibly for 'medicine' (Yuc. *pax,* Tzel., Tzo. *pox*).

The Maya also used a pottery drum. This is included by Thompson in his glyph 686, which is actually a whole series of glyphs, sharing only the fact that they seem to be pottery representations. The glyph for 'pottery drum' was first identified by Brinton (1895, p. 91). No readings have been suggested for this series of glyphs.

Several glyphs show artifacts used in warfare, and some of these seem to be used to refer to 'war', in what seems to be a more ideographic usage than I tend to think was common. The axe glyph (T190) was pointed out by Thomas (1882, p. 126) and by Brinton (1895, pp. 103–104), who suggested the reading *bat,* based on Yucatec, with known meanings 'axe' and 'hail'. Cognates with both meanings are now known to be present in widely separated Mayan languages. A Yucatec term for a subordinate ruler was *batab,* which may be translated, perhaps too literally, 'hatchet man'. T190 is frequently found in a compound with T25 (*ca*) both in the codices and in the inscriptions. Thompson has, strangely, given this a separate number, T333. Berlin (1958, p. 114) has suggested that on the monuments of Tikal, followed by the katun glyph with a numerical prefix, the combination was to be read *batab n* katun(s), or *n batab* katun(s). While willing to accept the fact that the axe glyph is *bat-* and had here taken on secondary meanings associated with rule, I suspect that the true reading should be *batac* or *batca.* Cordy has suggested the reading *cabat,* with the meaning 'fall', and the positioning of the glyphs is unusual enough that this sequence may be possible. The meaning fits the context in the codices.

The atlatl (spear thrower) held in the hand (T361) is so far known as a glyph only from Tikal Stela 31. The Teotihuacanoid figures on the sides of the monument are shown carrying such atlatls. No reading has been suggested. The helmet glyph (T678) was identified by Morley (1937–1938, III, 96–98). He pointed out that the glyph was found in the text on Lintel 2 at Piedras Negras and that a similar glyph was found at Palenque associated with a record of 'one moon'. Since the figures in the accompanying scene at Piedras Negras wore helmets, Morley argued that the glyph referred to them and hence that the entire scene had an esoteric astronomical significance. This interpretation now has only historic interest, as a demonstration of the way in which a preconceived view about the nature of the inscriptions delayed valid decipherment. The identification of T678 as a helmet remains valid.

The leaf-shaped chipped-stone object (T112) has been called a "flint knife" since the time of Brinton (1895, pp. 88–89), who suggested the reading *ta* 'flint knife'. Knorozov has suggested instead a reading *tok* 'flint'. The object might equally well be called a spear head (Thomas 1882, p. 145; see Fig. 49), although the distinction was probably minor. In Quiche, *tok* is 'flint, lance, knife' among others. T112 is distinguished from the *etz'nab* glyph (Fig. 4) only by the greater conventionalization of the latter.

Several shield glyphs appear in the codices and inscriptions. T152 is a round shield with hanging ornaments. Most of the other glyphs (T583, T594, T624) show a shield having the shape of a slightly rounded square, with a cross, "propeller," or "checkerboard" design in the center. These sometimes appear without the normal border but in the same distribution and with the same affixes. The "checkerboard shield" is so designated by Beyer (1937, p. 123). On the basis of Yucatec *maaxcinahba* 'escudarse' ('to shield oneself'), Knorozov has suggested *maax* as a reading for the shield glyph. The association of the glyph with scenes of fighting in the codices is frequent enough to support Jean Genet's (1934) contention that the shield glyph means 'war', but no one has yet suggested a reading which fully confirms this. I have tried to show that, on the monuments, most of the shield glyphs (with the probable exception of T152) are to be read *pacal* 'shield' (see Chapter 9).

Araujo, Rodríguez, and Solís (1965, pp. 19–20) point out that the initial glyph on some of the canoe scenes of the "bones texts" from Tikal (Fig. 80) shows what they regard as a reduplicated representation of a canoe. The bottom part of the glyph is a tipped-up representation of a canoe, as can be seen by comparison with the accompanying scene. They are probably correct in regarding the top element of the glyph as a canoe also, although the linear element is going in a different direction. In any case, the glyph is not a simple reduplication, since the two parts are at different angles and a string of dots is added. Because of the reduplication, Araujo, Rodríguez, and Solís (1965, p. 30) doubt that Yucatec *chem* 'canoe' is involved and reconstruct a form **kukup* 'canoe', suggesting connections, which are not entirely clear to me linguistically, with Kekchi *huyub* 'canoe' and Chontal-Chol *hukup* 'canoe' (cf. Q. *hukub* 'boat'), as well as with Kekchi *huyub* 'paddle' (?) and *huyuk* 'to paddle'. They mention Yucatec *baab* 'to paddle' without pointing out that it may well be a reduplication. They seem to regard this initial glyph as a noun, whereas its position is that of a verb, and the immediately following glyph is that of the deity doing the paddling. I would therefore regard the glyph as meaning approximately 'to paddle' and as probably related to one of the forms cited, but I doubt the specific reconstruction of Araujo, Rodríguez, and Solís.

Finally, there are various glyphs which seem to represent constructions of some sort. T685 (Fig. 49) is a pyramid and has been read *mul*, Yucatec 'pyramid', by Knorozov. At Palenque, with T12 (which Knorozov has read *ah*) prefixed and with various suffixes, it is probably to be read *ah mul-* 'the pyramid builder', referring to the individual responsible for the Temples of the Sun, Cross, and Foliated Cross. T150 may

represent some sort of platform (or, in some cases, perhaps some sort of bundle). T697 may represent a stairway or ladder.

The identification of glyphs depicting artifacts is still in its preliminary stages, and the number of adequate readings in Maya is still far smaller than may be expected in the future. The codices have provided good evidence on how the Mayas depicted artifacts, and these representations will continue to be important. The matching of these identifications with possible readings from the dictionaries of the Mayan languages is progressing, but use as homophones is needed as proof of such readings.

The following linguistic reconstructions, derived from Kaufman 1964, may have some relevance to the glyphs which have been considered in this section. Reconstructions apply to the whole family unless otherwise specified. Periods are used to separate reconstructions for one meaning from reconstructions for the next.

Salt: **'aatz'am* (Yuc.?). Mortar: **këë'*. Griddle (*comal*): (a) **sa'm;* (b) **saamVt;* (c) **xoht*. Bowl, cup, gourd: **tzuh*. Chocolate cup: **tzima,* <MZ (Yuc.?). Tray: **jukwub/hukwub*. Bowl: **johm*. Basket: (a) **mo'ch;* (b) *chakach;* (c) **xu'kw*. Jar: (a) **p'eht;* (b) **p'in;* (c) **pat;* (d) **xij;* (e) **q'i/eb*. Net bag: **chim*. Cotton, cloth: **nooq'* (Chl.?). Shoe, sandal: **xëngëb* (to walk) (H.?). To sew: **tz'is* (Yuc.?). Trousers: **weex* (H.?). Necklace: **'uh*. Skirt: (a) **'uhq;* (b) **chang*. Clothing: **q'u'*. To weave: **jal*. Spindle: **peteht*. Comb: **xih-ab*. To scrape: **xih*. To sweep: **mes* (H.?). Cord: **k'ëjang/k'ëham*. Bench: **twem* (H.?). Mat: **pohp* (H.?). Road: **beh*. House: **'otyoty,* etc. (Tzel.-Tzo.?). House: **ngah* (H.?). To nail: **baj*. File: **ju'x/hu'x*. Axe: **'ikyaj,* Yuc. *baat*. Sweat bath: (a) **twuung;* (b) **pus;* (c) **'ikwah*. Hut: (a) **pat;* (b) **pasel;* (c) **kabal*. Stairway: **'eb*. Gallows: **'oy*. Bridge: (a) **q'ë . . . ;* (b) **pam* (flat) + **tyee'* (wood). Bed: (a) **ch'aht;* (b) **ch'aakw*. Hammock: **'ab*. Blowgun: (a) **puhb;* (b) **'up';* (c) **tuhk'*. Cement (wall): **tz'aq*. Wall: (a) **pahkw';* (b) **p'itz'ap'*. Adobe: **xan*. Boat (canoe): **tyem*. Pine(?) incense: **pom*. Mask: **kw'oox* (H.?). Drum: **'wejb*. Play, toy: **'alas*. Music: **son*. Dance: (a) **'aQ'ot;* (b) **xaj*. Rattle: **so'ty*. To sing, song: (a) **Q'ay;* (b) **bix*. To jump: **p'ity*. Flute, whistle: (a) **su'/sub;* (b) **'amëy;* (c) **xul*.

Chapter 7
A Selection
of Body-Part
Glyphs

A wide range of human and animal body parts are used as glyphs. The commonest, by far, are heads. Where these are of animals or deities, they seem to be read, directly, as the names of those animals or deities. They may also be used for homonyms, so that the shark head, *xoc,* is used for *xoc* 'count'. Recognized deity heads have been included in the section on deities, and recognized animal heads have been included in the section on animals. To give here a wide range of additional heads, without context or identification, seems fruitless. It should, however, be emphasized that even the use of Thompson's *Catalog* would not allow the recognition of all classes of head glyphs, since many quite distinctive heads have been lumped together under the same number. Many head glyphs seem to correspond fully in function to glyphs which are not head glyphs, to such an extent that we normally speak of *head variants* of glyphs. It is well within the range of possibility that a majority of the head glyphs correspond to simpler glyphs which might also be used in the same contexts and read in the same way (i.e., that they are, in Knorozov's term, allographs).

Other body-part glyphs, human and animal, are included here in the belief that it should be possible to identify many of them with considerable probability. Various forms of hand glyphs are extremely common. The day Manik is represented by a hand (T219) probably read *chi, ci, che,* or *ce.* It might also be read *ceh.* De Gruyter (1946, p. 14) has suggested derivation from *chiic* 'to gather', a reading which seems plausible.

Another hand grapheme (some of the glyphs cataloged by Thompson as T217) is frequently used in the inscriptions in connection with the ends of time periods. This hand normally has two or three fingers held straight and the others bent. Thompson (1950, p. 280) points out that *lahal* means 'to end, finish' and 'to buffet with the palm of the hand, or with two or three fingers held straight'. However, he preferred a reading *tz'oc* (Thompson 1950, p. 186) because that was the term for 'end, complete' normally used in colonial documents with the end of a katun. *Tz'oc* has no obvious connection with 'hand', and hence I would prefer his alternate, *lahal.* This is a composite form, and the glyph itself may simply be read *lah.* Because of the use of this hand grapheme in this way, many investigators assumed that the hand itself "symbolized" ending and hence that any hand glyph in any context meant 'end'. I must emphasize again my belief that glyphs were to be read as logographs or phonetic components of words and that belief in this sort of "symbolism" is equivalent to denying that Maya hieroglyphs were true writing.

Figure 50. Various hand and pseudo-hand glyphs.

The palm of the hand was *naab,* and Knorozov has pointed out apparent use of a glyph (K263) showing the palm being used for the near homonym *nab* 'ocean'. This glyph coincides in part with T713, which, however, includes other graphemes. This may be the hand glyph used in the Venus table of *Dresden.* A Tzeltal derivative, *nabuy,* means 'to measure' (a semantic development comparable to the use of "hand" in English as a measure of height for horses), and I would not be surprised to find that some uses of the hand in the codices and inscriptions involved this meaning. It is very difficult in the codices to distinguish between the outstretched palm and the outstretched back of the hand, which one would expect to represent a different grapheme. The grapheme *naab* has also been confused with that probably read *lah.*

Still another hand glyph (T669) is a fist made into a pseudo face. It has been read by Barthel (1964*a,* pp. 224 ff.) as *kab* 'hand'. The reasons for preferring the phonetic rendering *ka* may be found in the discussion of phoneticism (Chapter 9). It is not impossible that an original *kab* was later read *ka.*

Knorozov in 1955 read T667 as *mac,* a reading based partly on the belief that it was Landa's *m,* while Zimmermann (1956, p. 16) read it as *em* 'descent', a reading later adopted by Knorozov (1963, p. 299). I strongly doubt that it is Landa's *m* and would prefer *et* 'to hold', a reasonable interpretation of a closed hand. An example of homonymic use would help to make this more certain.

The hand with the thumb separate (T670) has been read by de Gruyter (1946, p. 34) and, apparently independently, by Knorozov (1955*a,* no. 15) as *dza* 'to give', a reading which has been tentatively accepted by Barthel. This is entirely plausible in context (Fig. 50); however, Knorozov (1963, p. 302) seems to have abandoned it. De Gruyter points out its use in the name of God GI of the Lords of the Night, alternating with the fish-in-hand glyph (T714, Fig. 57), both prefixed by 'nine'. A small fish is *tzac* in Maya, and de Gruyter regards both glygers as indicating the deity name Bolon Tzacab. As reasonable as this seems, I would doubt that *dza (tz'a)* is to be equated with *tza.* Nonetheless, either of these readings by itself looks plausible. De Gruyter's further analysis of this glyph assumes a degree of variation in the phonetic relationship of graphemes and the meanings derived from them which I am completely unwilling to accept.

Thompson (1962) recognizes some nineteen graphemes representing different sorts of hand glyphs, and Knorozov (1963) distinguishes fifteen distinct graphemes. Neither of these attempts seems to me to adequately distinguish all probably meaningful hand glyphs. It should be pointed out that apparent similarity of use may have blinded us to significantly different hand glyphs. Thus, Glyph C of the Lunar Series always shows a hand glyph, the form of which is extremely variable. I would have expected these hands to represent at least three different verbs and probably more. I think we have all assumed that they form only one grapheme because of the regularity of the appearance of a hand grapheme in this context, but a postulate that they represent significant variations should probably be examined.

There are also glyphs of a single finger, with the meaning 'one', and of the whole arm (T224, Fig. 51; perhaps also some, but not all, examples of T234). Knorozov (1955*a,* nos. 9, 10) regards all these as upraised arms, suggesting for the less realistic form the reading *kuul* 'divine' and for the more realistic, *ch'a* 'to take'. Neither seems to me strongly indicated, and I doubt that the glyph read *kuul* is actually an arm.

A leg is represented by T768b; Thompson insists, unconvincingly, that T768a is also a leg. One would expect T768b to read *acan* 'foot, leg', but it is very rare, and evidence is inadequate to verify this reading. There is also a glyph of crossed legs (T701), prominent in astronomical contexts. A headless body (T703), an upper body (T704), and the lower parts of the body (T700, T702), as well as a body with a cut(?) across it (T705) all appear as glyphs. None has yet been deciphered in any meaningful sense beyond recognition of what is represented. T705 could represent a human sacrifice, but the glyphic context does not seem adequate to show whether it does or not.

At least one glyph represents an eye (T680) and functions as the name glyph of God M. It cannot be read. Knorozov (1955*a,* no. 6) has identified T96 (Fig. 65) as an eye, reading it *ich,* which is both 'in' and 'eye'. The glyph almost certainly means 'in', and it is sometimes found infixed in the eyes of various figures. However, *yol* seems to be the correct reading. For the same reason, the occurrence of T534, the inverted *ahau* (=T178), which is believed to be read *la* (Fig. 62), in the mouth of a deity suggests that it may represent a tooth, but this is far from proven; the glyph has also been regarded as an anthropoid mask and, by Knorozov (1955*a,* p. 72, no. 91), as a blowgun. The human lower jaw (T590, Fig. 51) has been read by Cordy (1946, p. 109) as *lah* 'end, die' in the compound *lahca* 'twelve'. The regular use of the fleshless lower jaw in the head variants of the numbers above ten (*lahun*) offers some support for the view. The fact that a hand glyph has also been read *lah* does

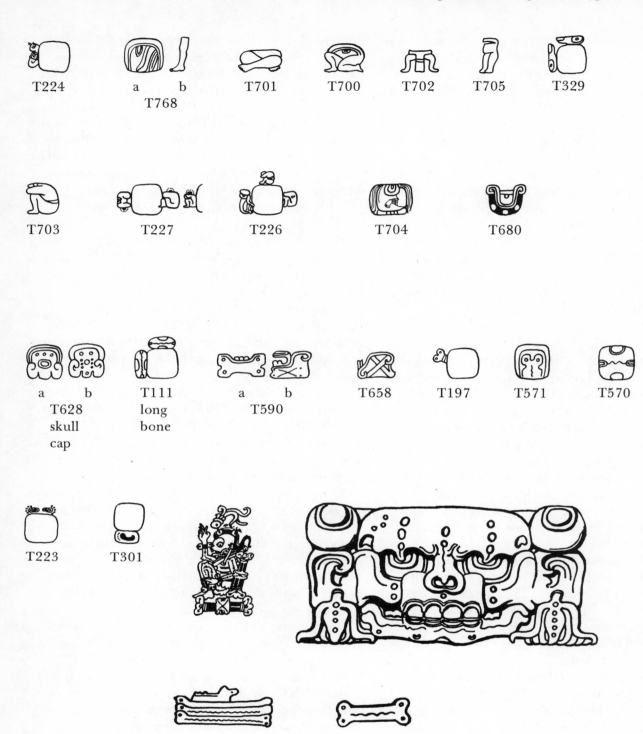

Figure 51. Body-part glyphs.

not necessarily argue against this view, for there is beginning to be a fair amount of evidence that two glyphs might each represent the same phonetic sequence. Barthel (1964a, p. 228) has drawn attention to the association of this lower-jaw glyph with the fan glyph, suggesting that both are symbols of authority on the basis of a representation of a ruler holding a fan and wearing a trophy jaw.

The following linguistic reconstructions, derived from Kaufman 1964, may have some relevance to the glyphs which have been considered in this section. Reconstructions apply to the whole family unless otherwise specified. Periods are used to separate reconstructions for one meaning from reconstructions for the next.

Tail: *ngeeh. Wing: (a) *xiikw', Tzel.-Tzo.-Yuc.-Pch.-Kek.-Kan.-Jac.-Mam-Q.; (b) *wech', Toj.-Chl. (H.?). Horn: (a) *'uk'a', etc., Pch.-Jac.-Kan.-Mam-Q.-H.; (b) *xul.ub, Tzel.-Yuc.-Toj.-Chu.; (c) *xukw.ub, Kek.-(Cht.) (<xuhkw, flank, corner). Egg: (a) *ngolop', Toj.-Chu.-(Agc.); (b) *mol, Pch.-Kek.-Q; (c) *xos, Kan.-Jac.-Mam-Q.-Yuc. (he'); (d) *tun/ton (stone) + mutw (bird), Tzel.-Tzo.-Chl. (H.?). Feather, quetzal bird: *q'uuq' (H.?). Crest, comb: *t'eel. Nest: *sook. Honeycomb: *'okwong, *'aqang. Bone: *baaq. Blood: *kik'. Tongue: *'aaq' (H.?). Hand/arm: *qw'ëb. Ear: *xikwin/chikwin. Belly: (a) *k'u . . . /k'o . . . , Jac.-Kan.-Tzel.-Tzo.-Mam-Chu.; (b) *pam, H.-Pch.-Kek.-Q.; (c) *nëk', Yuc.-Chl.-Chr. Nose: (a) *ngi'/ngu', Tzel.-Tzo.-Yuc.-Pch.-Toj.-*k'u . . . /k'o . . . , Jac.-Kan.-Tzel.-Tzo.-Mam-Chu.; Kan.-Jac.-Mam-Q. Nose, mucus: *sahm/sihm/tzwa'm. Jaw: (a) *cha'am, Yuc.-Tzel.-Tzo.-Toj.-Chl.-Kan.; (b)

*ka' (=grindstone), Pch.-Kek.-Chu.-Jac.-Mam-Q. (H.?). Tooth: *'eh, H. tzooh = Yuc. ko, Yuc./'e/ = 'point'. Claw, paw: (a) *'ihky'aq, Tzel.-Yuc.-H.-Chu.; (b) *'ixKy'aq, Pch.-Kek.-Q.-Mam; (c) *'isky'aq, Kan.-Jac.; (d) *'ech (Chu./ch'a'ak/ = horn), Toj.-Chu. Knee: (a) *ch'ehk, Pch.-Q.-Mam; (b) *penekw, Chu.-Kan.-Jac.; (c) *pi'x, *pi'x (knee) + *jo'l (head) = knee, Tzel.-Yuc.-Chl.-Chr. (H.?). Face, eye: (a) *wëty, Yuc.-Pch.-Kek.-Chl.-Chr.-Q.-Mam; (b) *sat, Tzel.-Tzo.-Toj.-Chu.-Kan.-Jac. (H.?). Mouth: *tyii' (H.?). Head: (a) *jo'l, Tzel.-Tzo.-Yuc.-Chl.-Chr.; (b) *joolom, Pch.-Kek.-Toj.-Chu.-Kan.-Jac.-Mam-Q. (H.?). Shoulder: (a) *tehleb; (b) *kehleb. Cheek: *koh. Internal organ: *tzuqu . . . /kuqu . . . Breast: (a) *'im; (b) *chu'. Side: *xuhkw. Jaw: (a) *kahlam, etc.; (b) *kawa, etc. Brains: *kiXn. Skin: (a) *tz'uhum/tz'u'um; (b) *'oot'. Eyebrow (and related meanings): (a) *mëtzab; (b) *metz'. Buttocks: (a) *'it; (b) *twop/yo'p. Liver: *seh. Neck: *qul/qal (qwël?). Lungs: *sot'. Hair (and related meanings): (a) *xi'l; (b) *tzo'tz; (c) *'sim; (d) *tzon. Shoulder: (a) *pat; (b) *'i'j. Navel: *muux. Genitalia: (a) *'at (male, female); (b) tux (female); (c) kun (male, female); (d) lu'/lolis (female). Thigh: *'ë'. Leg: *aqan. Foot: *'oq, *'oq-etw = tripod B. Side: *tz'eh. Left hand: (a) *kw'exam; (b) *tz'eh (=side). Summit, top: *wi'. Excrement: *tzwë'/të'. To defecate: *kis/tzis/tis. To sneeze: h/'−a−t'/tz'−i−s/x. Urine: *chu . . . Saliva: *tyuhb/tzuhb. To sleep: *way. To close the eyes: *mutz'. To rest, to live: *kwux. To tire: *lub. To sweat, burn: *kiq/kiq'. To belch: *qeb. To die: *këm. Dumb: (a) *mem; (b) *'uma'. Deaf: (a) *twakwan; (b) *kohk. Hunchback: *p'us. Force: *'ip. To kill: *mil.

Chapter 8 Miscellaneous Glyphs, Particularly Verbs

Besides the specialized glyphs which have already been considered, a substantial number of glyphs are known which refer to actions (basically verbs), activities, objects not relevant elsewhere, natural phenomena, or abstractions. The order of glyphs normally seems to correspond to spoken word order, and the glyph indicating the nature of the activity shown is normally in first position. Despite clear definitions of much of this material from its context in the codices, the glygers have seldom been used in attempting to read the inscriptions. Even when individual occurrences have been noted, systematic tabulation and analysis have not been carried out. The presence of these glygers here should encourage such studies.

Among the earliest glyphs recognized were those for offerings, which were frequently pictorial in nature. A complete fish and iguana, the head of an ocellated turkey, and the bound haunch of a deer, appearing in the glyphs as well as in accompanying scenes showing these animals being offered, made the meaning clear (Fig. 38). Generally these were combined with the *kan* glyph, for reasons not yet clear. These passages frequently began with or included the glyph T1038b (Fig. 38), preceded by *u*. Barthel (1953, p. 98) says the meaning is certainly 'darzubringendes Opfer, Spende, Gabe' ('proffered sacrifice, offering, gift'), for which he suggests the reading *ziil.* Knorozov (1955*b*, I, 31) suggests *bol* 'porción de comida' ('portion of food'), comparing it with Brasseur de Bourbourg's *bool* 'sacrificio' ('sacrifice'), which is to be compared with Quiche *bol* 'roast'. Zimmermann (1956, p. 39) suggests it is the 'Träger' ('bearer') of the offerings. None of these readings attempt to explain why the glyph should be a human head without a lower jaw. Thompson (1966*a*) devotes a page and a half to glyphs lacking the lower jaw. He concludes that the intent was to refer to biting. This particular glyph he thinks refers to eating or divine food, and he suggests *hanal* 'food, to eat' as the reading. Zimmermann's suggestion does not seem to accord with the grammatical structure of the relevant passages; any of the others seems possible. Barthel's analysis of the meaning seems to best fit the context but to take least account of the head itself.

The verb associated with the offering passages is transcribed by Thompson as 588.181:140. (See Fig. 17; the verb is number 1 in each sequence.) However, this transcription seems to me entirely misleading, since T181 is the verbal suffix of the past tense (Fig. 66), and the physical form seems to suggest that it is affixed to 588:140, which constitutes a glyger. Knorozov (1955*a*, no. 91) reads the combination as *zil-* 'to offer'. The context strongly supports some such meaning as 'offer, give, sacrifice' or even 'pay', since this is the action glyph referring to the pictures of a deity holding out a bowl with an animal sacrifice on it. The meaning of this verb and of the noun represented by T1038b should be closely parallel. I suspect that one of them is the *zil/ziil* term but doubt that both are, as I would then expect virtual identity in the glyphs, aside from the affixes. I have drawn attention (Appendix to Berlin and Kelley 1961) to the close parallel between certain offering passages in the *Dresden* and a set of clauses in various inscriptions associated with dates of the 819-day count. These clauses, first pointed out by Thompson, open with the verb under discussion and include color and direction glyphs, with an apparent reference to God K.

Considering the ceremonial nature of many of the activities depicted in the codices, it is not surprising to find a number of verbs which refer directly or indirectly to ceremonials. Landa describes a Mayan baptismal ceremony, which he calls *caput zihil* 'to be reborn' (Tozzer 1941, pp. 102 ff). A scene in *Madrid* shows women apparently sprinkling water on children (Fig. 52). De Rosny (1883) and Thomas (1882, pp. 154–155) independently recognized the initial glyger above these scenes as 'baptize'. Knorozov (1955a, p. 91, no. 189) read *che-hi-i* (cf. *chehi* 'riega' ['sprinkles']); Fought (1954, pp. 261–262) points out that the Motul dictionary gives *oc haa* 'enter water' for 'baptize', but he finds that neither this term nor Landa's seems to coincide with the form of the glyger. He prefers *tsehali* 'it is sprinkling, she is sprinkling', deriving from *che(h), al,* and *i*. The readings *che* and *i* are discussed in connection with phoneticism (Chapter 9) and the reading *al* as a grammatical particle (Chapter 10). I would have expected a beginning in *ce* rather than *che* and am not fully satisfied with any of these readings, but the meaning seems clear from the context.

Barthel (1955a, n. 95) draws attention to a representation on *Madrid* page 96b which shows a man piercing his tongue with a thorn. The action glyph is apparently in the second glyph block, with possessive *u* prefixed. This is Thompson's "inverted fist," T667. A note in the Villacorta edition of *Madrid* refers to it as 'sacrificio', and the scene is described as 'sacrificio de la lengua' ('sacrifice of the tongue'). It might be more correctly described as the drawing of blood from the tongue for a sacrifice. Despite some variation, this seems to be the same glyph found, as T712, at Yaxchilan, where it is associated with scenes of a rope set with thorns being drawn through the tongue, as was pointed out by Proskouriakoff (1950, p. 470). No one has yet suggested a Maya equivalent. Cordan's reading (1963a, p. 55), *kamil,* misidentifies the glyph

as the hand (T669); elsewhere (1963a, p. 44) he reads T667 as *cha* (doubled as *chach*).

T667 is found doubled or with a slight variant in the infix of the second glyph on page 38a of the *Madrid*, where it is identified by Villacorta as a deer haunch. Villacorta thought it meant 'to hunt with a spear', since the glyph accompanies representations of hunters with spears. Whorf (1942, p. 489) believes it reads *lo-m-ma-n,* i.e., *loman* 'something speared or stabbed, pierced, wounded, or killed, by a dart or spear'. As a stem, this is reasonable, but Whorf's contention that the glyph is a hand is doubtful, his belief that all hands were read *ma* is incorrect, and I see nothing to support his view that the infix was a separable glyph reading *lu, lo*. However, a root in *lom* with a meaning 'pierce' would seem applicable to the tongue-piercing ceremony as well.

The glyph (T589) meaning 'drill' was first recognized by Seler in 1897 (see Seler 1902–1923, I, 396–397). Brinton (1895, p. 93) had referred briefly to previous identifications by A. Pousse (1884) and Thomas (1882, pp. 127, 148) as 'making fire' or 'grinding paint', but Brinton identified the glyph as representing a drum. Seler showed that it referred to the drilling of fire, thus indirectly relating to the previous interpretation as 'making fire'. He showed from comparative Mexican material that the object shown in the scenes and regarded by Thomas as a mortar is actually a fire drill. Whorf (1942, pp. 493–496) suggested that the glyph should be read *hax*, the only word for 'drilling' that he knew in Maya. At least two other words meaning 'drill' are now known in Mayan languages. As in the case of the *lom-* root just considered, Whorf analyzed the glyph into its component parts, assigning phonetic values to each minor part. Representations of this glyph at Chichen Itza were identified by Beyer (1937, p. 120) as showing drilled shells, probably of the Spondylus. He wrote, "There exist archaeological specimens of this shell in which perforations correspond to the circlets." This suggests that the glyph was supposed to indicate the word 'drill' by showing a drilled object, an interpretation which seems much more likely than Whorf's contention.

Thompson (1950, p. 265) apparently identified this glyph independently, without remembering that it had been done before, and likewise considered the probable reading as *hax*. He suggested that the affixes represented what was drilled and were sometimes of a highly symbolic nature. Thus, an affix identified as a dog's head was said to stand for the drilling of fire because the dog is connected with fire in mythology. The close association of the dog with fire is well es-

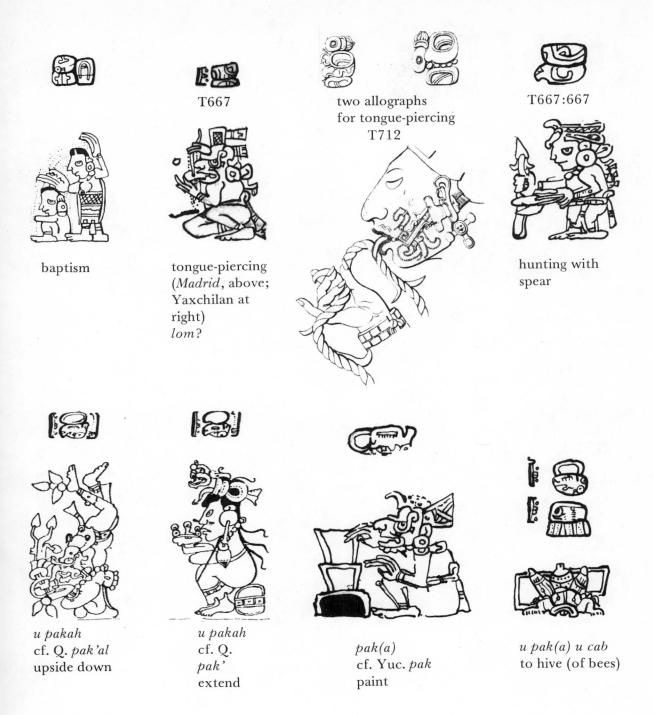

baptism

T667

tongue-piercing
(*Madrid*, above;
Yaxchilan at
right)
lom?

two allographs
for tongue-piercing
T712

T667:667

hunting with
spear

u pakah
cf. Q. *pak'al*
upside down

u pakah
cf. Q.
pak'
extend

pak(a)
cf. Yuc. *pak*
paint

u pak(a) u cab
to hive (of bees)

Figure 52. Various activities.

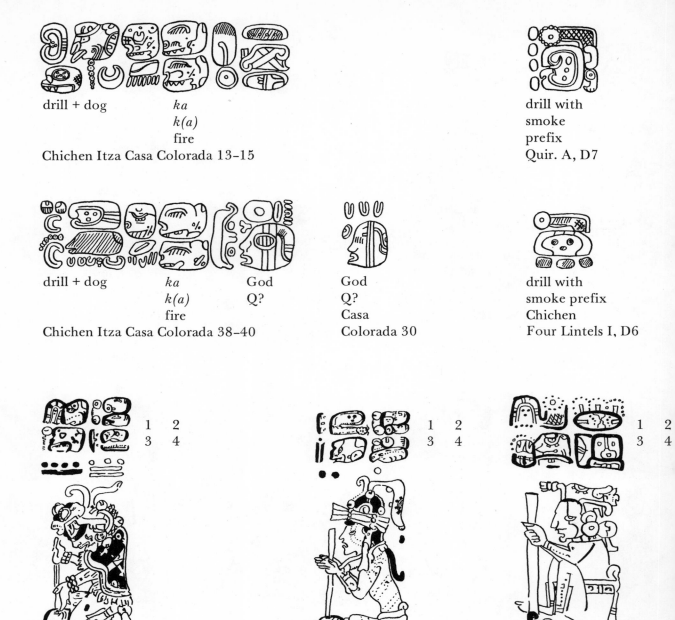

drill + dog   *ka*
                     k(a)
                     fire
Chichen Itza Casa Colorada 13–15

drill with
smoke
prefix
Quir. A, D7

drill + dog   *ka*   God
                     k(a)   Q?
                     fire   God   drill with
Chichen Itza Casa Colorada 38–40 Q?   smoke prefix
                                   Casa   Chichen
                                   Colorada 30 Four Lintels I, D6

glyph 1: drill + dog

D5b

glyph 3: God Q
(shown here)
D6b

glyph 1: drill + supposed smoke suff
glyph 2: T49:112
M38c

Figure 53. The drilling glyph (T589). Yucatec *hax* 'to drill',
Quiche *bak* 'drill, pierce'.

drill

Chichen
Four Lintels II, C1–C2

drill + *mul* suffix

Casa
Colorada 41   Four Lintels II, E4

1 2
3 4

glyph 2: its fire (T122.563a)

M38b

1 2 3
4 5 6 or

1 2 5
3 4 6

drill + *mul* suffix
(jade, according to Thompson)
D8b

tablished; however, unless it can be shown that the Mayas used an expression such as 'drill dog' when they meant 'drill fire', the coupling of these glyphs does not seem to be adequately explained. The 'drill' glyph is also found with the affix which Thompson identified as *mul* 'jade', an association which suggested to him a reference to drilled jade in a representation on D8b–9b. Nothing in the context either supports or disproves this possibility. Representations on M38b and M38c have 'drill' with a 'smoke' affix, as on D5b; only those on M38b show drilling of fire; those on M38c apparently show the drilling of a flint knife (Fig. 53).

Barthel (1955a, pp. 14–15) made an important contribution by showing that a glyph at Chichen Itza, formally similar to the *Dresden* and *Madrid* examples mentioned above, was found with the same affixes, including 'dog', 'jade', and 'smoke' (Fig. 53). The latter, which Thompson believed stood directly for 'fire', was found prefixed rather than suffixed; this placement suggests that it had considerable semantic independence from the stem, unlike the usual verbal affixes. Thompson (1950, Fig. 33, no. 11) shows the 'drill' glyph among the examples of his "shell-hand" glyph, an equation that is almost certainly an error.

In the codices, the glyph for 'drill' is sometimes closely associated with the glyger for 'fire', T122: 563a (Fig. 54). The latter was defined by Seler in the same paper in which he defined the 'drill' glyph. The first glyph (T122) was soon confused, particularly in Spinden's writings, with a completely different glyph (T44), which formed a glyger with T563b. The meaning was soon extended to a variety of glygers which had either T44 or T122 as a prefix and either T563a or T563b as a "main sign." Thompson (1950, p. 166) further confused T563 with T561, the 'sky' glyph, and defined a lengthy series of "variants" of the 'sky' glyph. In 1950 he condemned Spinden for not recognizing the "identity" of 'sky' and 'fire'. He had extricated himself from this confusion by 1958 but still maintained the identity of T563a and T563b in his *Catalog* (1962). In a recent paper, I have tried to consider the various glyphs and glygers which have been called 'fire' (Kelley 1966a). It will be seen that T122:563a refers to the torches brought by the macaw deity on D40b and must mean either 'fire' or 'torch'. On M38b (Fig. 53) the same group is found with the 'drill' glyph above a representation of the drilling of fire and must mean either 'fire drill' or 'fire'. The two representations taken together make it quite clear that the correct meaning must be 'fire'. Thompson (1958a, p. 303) has read the glyger as *kak*, which is the normal Mayan word for 'fire'. T122 seems to be 'flame' or 'smoke'. On D17a and D19c

the Moon Goddess is shown with this glyger as her burden, and the representation obviously coincides both with the glyph in the accompanying passage and with the flames represented elsewhere in the codex (cf. D36a, the torch in the hand of a dog). Spinden (1924, p. 202) identified T563a as a bundle of firewood; this identification was accepted by Beyer and, later, by Thompson (1962, p. 186). Supporting evidence for this identification is not convincing. Such an assumption suggests that 'flames' plus 'wood' created a picture of a fire which might be read directly as 'fire'. I know of no comparable glyphic formation and consider this extremely doubtful. Whorf (1942, p. 493) read the glyger as *to kak*, which he reinterpreted as *tok k'ak'* (i.e., in conventional Yucatec orthography, *tooc kak*). This would mean that T563a by itself could mean 'fire', although I know of no shred of contextual evidence to support this view. Knorozov (1955a, sec. 2, no. 111) read both elements of the compound as *poc*, supplementing each other. He gives *poc* the meaning 'fire', but this meaning is not directly derivable from 'to heat', which he quotes, and he has subsequently withdrawn this reading. Cordan (1963a, p. 60) identifies T122 as *ak, uk, ok* 'tongue' and reads the glyger as *cha-ak* 'lightning'. He maintains, wrongly, that the glyger is always associated with storm and rain. The reversal of the glyphic elements is unexplained.

The glyger appears as the upper part of a deity(?) head in passages which may refer either to 'the fire god' or simply to 'fire'. If the glyger is to be interpreted as referring simply to 'fire', the combination might be considered the head variant of T122:563a. If the deity head is to be read separately, it should not be designated a head variant. Thompson (1962) has given the combination of this head with the 'fire' glyger a separate number, T1035. Possibly this combination simply indicates that fire is a deity, without implying that one reads a word meaning 'deity' or giving the name of a fire god.

Another glyger which may refer to 'fire' or 'torch' is T49:110, which is found on D40b in a passage which is structurally very like that accompanying the Macaw God in the preceding passage. The accompanying picture shows a dog with torches. T49:110 is also found on D36a with God B holding torches. Knorozov (1955a, p. 87, no. 129) reads *toc* (actually *tooc*) 'to burn', likewise suggesting the same reading for T49:112 (1955a, p. 86, no. 128). In the latter case, T112 is the flint knife, a near homophone of 'to burn', since in some Mayan languages it is *toc* (Q. *tok* 'stab, wound, flint, lance, hurt, knife'). Brinton (1895, pp. 88–89) thought that T112 and T110 were variant representations of the flint knife, for which he

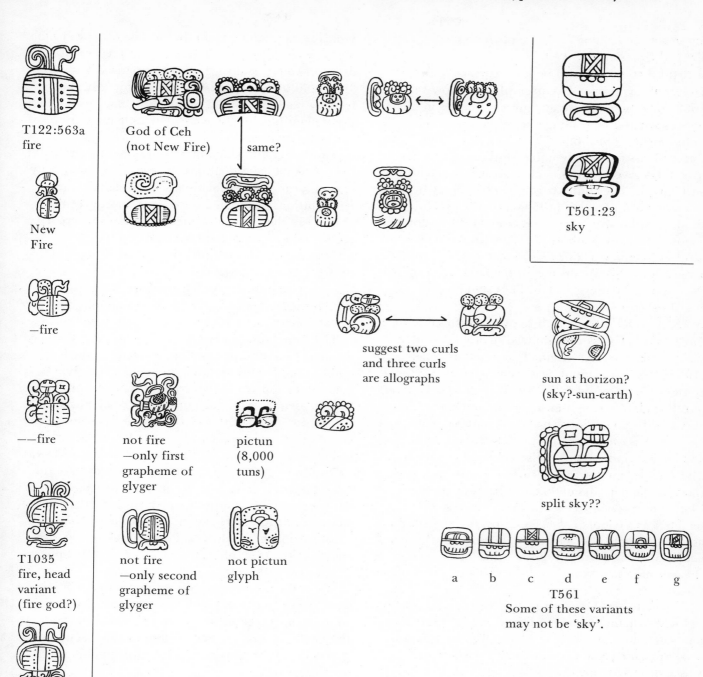

T122:563a
fire

New
Fire

—fire

——fire

T1035
fire, head
variant
(fire god?)

fire (god?)

fire (god?)

God of Ceh
(not New Fire)   same?

not fire
—only first
grapheme of
glyger

pictun
(8,000
tuns)

not fire
—only second
grapheme of
glyger

not pictun
glyph

suggest two curls
and three curls
are allographs

sun at horizon?
(sky?-sun-earth)

split sky??

T561:23
sky

a   b   c   d   e   f   g
T561
Some of these variants
may not be 'sky'.

Figure 54. Fire and sky glyphs.

suggested the reading *ta*. None of these readings explains the presence of T49.

A third glyger which I believe represents 'fire' is T669:669. Knorozov has attempted to show that T669 corresponds to *ka* and gives examples in the codices where this reading seems plausible. This would make T669:669 *ka-k(a)*, i.e., *kak* 'fire'. This glyger recurs repeatedly in inscriptions at Chichen Itza and is several times in close association with the 'drill' glyph. The context seems to be one of fire ceremonialism. Barthel (1955a, pp. 13–14), following an ideographic interpretation, compares this doubled hand with death symbols (T669) with the doubled hand of Manik type (T219/671; see Fig. 50) found in association with fire drilling in the *Dresden*. I regard the doubled Manik (T671:671) as standing for *cech* 'sacrifice' (see Chapter 9).

T563, misconstrued as 'fire', was confused with T561, 'sky'. This confusion leads us to a consideration of the latter. As originally defined by Seler (1902–1923), the glyph was recognized as 'sky' in a context where it had T23 affixed (Fig. 54). This very puzzling affix is sometimes present and sometimes absent with no obvious change in context. T561 had been read as *caan* 'sky', on the basis of its context and its association with the so-called planetary band. The decipherment of its occurrence with 'ten' prefixed as the deity name Lahun Chan (an apparent Cholan borrowing) seems to verify the suggested reading *caan* (Cholan *chan*). Occurrence in paired association with the 'earth' glyph and with the *naab/nab* 'sea' glyph further supports this meaning, as does the astronomical 'reversal of the tying of the sky' (see Chapter 2).

The fact that the glyph read in calendrical context as the day name Caban contained the root *cab* 'earth' and was found in contexts where this was an appropriate meaning as well as in contexts where *cab* 'bee' was appropriate meant that this was one of the earliest glyphs defined. The identification of the Imix glyph as a water lily, *naab*, was not made until Thompson's analysis of 1950, and the recognition of it as a homonym of *nab* 'sea, lake, lagoon' was still later (see discussion, Chapter 5). It is fairly frequent in the inscriptions with the locative prefix *ti*, and the validity of the decipherment seems clear.

The prefix T137 consists of three large dots with extended lines of smaller dots coming from them (Fig. 55). It is usually found in *Dresden* in association with the wavy green lines which seem to indicate water, and it was suggested by Cyrus Thomas (1893, p. 263) that the glyph was to be read *haa* 'water'; it is normally associated with a sky glyph tilted on its side, and Thompson (1950, pp. 272–273) feels this

indicates rain falling from the sky. Knorozov (1955a, sec. 1, no. 126) identifies the glyph as representing drops of water, and suggests a comparison with *toz* 'dust' and *tozhaa* 'rain'. Later (1963, p. 280) he preferred a reading *ch'ah*. The meaning 'rain' seems entirely plausible, but I have seen no adequate proof of any suggested reading.

Another glyph which may sometimes mean 'rain' is the Cauac day glyph, also read as *haab* 'waters, rainy season, year', and probably as *cu*. While the water connotations of the name are clear, I know of no context in the codices or the inscriptions where it seems to have the specific meaning 'rain'.

Thompson, who defined the "water group" of prefixes, has suggested that they sometimes refer to rain, but we now know that they are the normal prefixes associated with the Emblem Glyphs, and any direct connection with rain seems highly unlikely.

The day glyph Ik (Fig. 4) is found in the "weather-almanac" sections of *Dresden*, a location which seems appropriate for the meaning *ik* 'wind'. The glyph sometimes appears in this context with the prefix *zac* 'white, pseudo, artificial, pure', and *zac ik* is a name for the east wind (Brinton 1895, p. 41), although the color white is normally assigned to the north, while red is assigned to the east. Proskouriakoff has drawn attention to the use of this glyph (*ik*) in the inscriptions (where it is likewise frequently associated with the prefix *zac*) in contexts which suggest an association with death. Here the meaning of *ik* as 'soul, spirit' seems most relevant. Proskouriakoff has also shown that the glyph T76 (??):575 normally appears in a clause with *zac ik*.

From the calendar glyphs we know that T509 is *cimi* 'death', and the glyph appears frequently as part of the name glyger of the Lord of Death. However, the glyph has not yet been found in a clear-cut context referring to the death of an individual in the inscriptions.

Birth is also treated in the inscriptions, and it now seems that T740, the upended frog's head, is to be read **pok'* 'be born' (Q. *poq'oh* 'sprout, multiply, be born, hatch, burst open, split'), following recent studies of Barthel (1968a, pp. 134–135). This is a small but significant change from Thompson's reading *po* 'frog, moon'. At Palenque, T740 alternates with the glyger T74:565 (with varying affixes); T74:565 seems to be the action glyph referring to the emergence of God K from a shell (Kelley 1965, pp. 95–97). It was generally accepted at the turn of the century that the shell indicated 'birth' (Brinton 1895, p. 75; Förstemann 1904, pp. 427–428, citing evidence from Seler 1890). I think it may be safely assumed that here the compound is a synonym for 'birth' with, perhaps, the

T137
rain

rainy
sky??

cauac
rain,
storm

T503
ik
wind

zac ik

T76
T575

u

zac
ahau
ik

zac ik
death phrase
(*ahau* may be
infixed in *zac*
or separate)

T509
cimi
death

T740:24
pok'
be born

T74:565:178.117
emerge

emerge
(allograph)

T47.552:24
marry

T47.565:24
allograph
or
synonym

T115.614:601
synonym
also means
temple

Figure 55. Various natural and social phenomena and processes.

more literal meaning of 'emergence'. Figure 55 also shows the compound with T565 replaced by its head variant. Since I accept T74 as *ma* and T565 as a serpent segment, it should be easy to determine this 'emergence' glyger, but I have not yet been able to do so.

No clear-cut glyph for 'marriage' has yet been determined, although there are three plausible candidates. The crossbands, T552, appear with T47 prefixed and T24 suffixed in passages showing an apparent sexual relationship between male and female deities or animals. In passages of similar content, T565 substitutes for T552, with the same affixes. Occasionally, although not in this context, T552 appears as an infix of T565. Förstemann called T552 'conjunction' (of stars) or 'sexual union' and thought T565 "may denote coition" (Förstemann 1906, p. 101); Knorozov (1955*b*, III, 17–19) read both glygers *hicham, hichan,* or *hich'am,* translated 'husband'. For a fuller discussion of both references, see Kelley 1962*b*, pp. 324–325. I there pointed out that T115. 614:601 (M92c), which also means 'temple', appears in a passage which is a parallel to a *Dresden* passage with T47.552:24 and that T565 appears on the monuments with differing affixes between what seem to be personal names. In two cases these seem to be a female name coupled with a male name, but in one case there are what I believe to be two females, and in others sex is not determinable. Closer study of the affixes or a satisfactory decipherment of T565 may ultimately resolve this problem. For T552, de Gruyter (1946, pp. 28, 54) suggested a reading *kaat,* based upon the facts that the months corresponding to Uo and Zip in "Kekchi" (probably actually a Chol list) are Icat and Chaccat (*ic* 'black'; *chac* 'red'), that the main element of the month glygers is T552, and that they have prefixed the glyphs for, respectively, 'black' and 'red'. The common element *cat* corresponds to Yucatec *kaat* 'atravesado de por medio' ('crossed in the middle'), a good description of the glyph. Since *kat* means 'wish, desire', this seems to me a likely example of the use of a near homonym. It seems unprofitable to discuss de Gruyter's interpretation of the full glyger at length, and I merely point out that he thinks T47 is read *buhul* and that it indicates the stem *bok* 'to bore fire with the fire sticks', which he thinks was "loaned for" *oc* 'copulate'; this sort of reading overlooks a number of basic principles of decipherment and linguistics. Thompson (1950, pp. 107–108) suggests the reading *kaat,* without mentioning the meaning 'desire' or the association with sexual activity. Knorozov (1955*a*, p. 70, no. 75) reads *cha,* which he compares with *ch'etal* 'cruzarse' ('to cross each other'). Although I was originally inclined to accept the latter, *kaat* now appears to me a better reading.

Besides the major themes of birth, death, and marriage, warfare is generally important in most cultures. A number of Mayan glyphs seem to reflect this preoccupation, directly and indirectly. The earliest of these to attract attention was the knotted glyph, T684, which Thompson has called the "toothache glyph." Seler (1902–1923, I, 565–566) drew attention to the use of this glyph with T682 infixed, particularly on D67a, where God B is shown with a sling carrying God K. Here glyph and representation seem to coincide closely. On M91a, the glyph appears with pictures of an armadillo in a deadfall, a black god with a spear, and a turkey and a deer caught by nooses. On page 92a it accompanies two pictures of deities, and, in a continuation of the same passage on page 93a, a peccary is shown in a noose and a turkey in a net trap (?). Some meaning such as 'capture' seemed clear to Seler, despite the cases where the deities' action was not obviously relevant.

This rather reasonable interpretation seems at complete variance with a passage on *Dresden* page 23b, where the same glyger appears as the verb for a picture of the young goddess holding out a bowl with a fish on it, in a context which should mean roughly 'offer'. Proskouriakoff (1960, pp. 456–457 and elsewhere) has shown that certain dates which seem to be associated with the beginnings of reigns are accompanied by the "toothache glyph" with a wide variety of infixes, including the *kal* glyph. Cordan (1963*a*, pp. 45, 49) suggests the "toothache glyph" is *hok* + *kal* (Ticul dictionary, *hokal* 'bound together'; Tzotzil *hokol,* assimilated form, 'hung up'). More recently, Barthel (1968*a*, p. 136) has pointed out that *hok* is found as a Yucatec root meaning 'to put in office'. This makes it virtually certain that the reading *hok* is correct. If the offering scenes are connected with divination, it may be relevant that Tzeltal *-jok'iy* is 'preguntar' ('to ask a question').

Another glyger, T601:25, is found on D3b, M41b, and elsewhere, associated with pictures of bound deities or animals. Thompson (1962) has given a separate number, T512, to what is almost certainly the inscriptional equivalent of T601. Proskouriakoff (1960, p. 470) shows that T512:25 (with affixes) and sometimes T512:25.25 are associated in the inscriptions with scenes of the capture of prisoners. Knorozov (1958*a*, p. 471, no. 15) has read the glyger as *chuc-,* 'asir, prender' ('to grab, to take, to seize, to capture'). This Yucatec word meaning 'capture' has cognates in the Cholan group with the meaning 'tie, bind'. For the phonetic consistency of T601 as *chu* and T25 as *ca,* see Chapter 9.

young goddess with
fish in bowl
D23b

God B with God K in sling
D67a

Black God holding bundle

armadillo in deadfall
M91a

Black God with spear
M91a

turkey in noose
M91a

deer in noose
M91a

Figure 56. *Hok* 'knotted moon' (T684) in first position in all
texts.

chu-ca-h
tie, bind

chu-ca-h
inscriptional
versions

T1.108:764
glyph which indicates
relationship between
a captor and a captive
(ordinarily faces left)

Black God
of War

327:17

black
snake

fish-in-hand
glyphs and
God B with
a fish in
his hand

tzab
ce(h) fire

tzab	*ce*	*u*	*ca*
	x		*ca*
			aan

(offering context)

tzab-ce
(other
context)

Figure 57. Verbs.

Proskouriakoff (1963, pp. 150–151) points out the presence of glyphs on the thighs of prisoners shown on a lintel at Yaxchilan; in the accompanying inscriptions, these same glyphs immediately follow the *chuc* glyger. These glyphs recur in later texts as part of the titles of the individuals doing the capturing and are there preceded by T108:764, which therefore denotes a captor/captive relationship (see Chapter 11 for a fuller discussion).

Cyrus Thomas (1888, p. 371) drew attention to a "representation of an idol head in a vessel covered with a screen or basket." Above it was the glyph also found for 'twenty', Yucatec *kal,* and he pointed out that *kal* also "signifies to 'imprison' or 'inclose' which is certainly appropriate to what we see in the figure." It may be pointed out that Tzeltal shows a comparable semantic parallelism, for *tab* is both 'twenty' and 'tie'. However, 'inclose' is the more relevant term here, and Yucatec *kal* seems a preferable reading. It may be pointed out that the 'twenty' glyph appears at Yaxchilan as an apparent epithet of the ruler Bird Jaguar. Yucatec *kal* is cognate with Huaxtec *ts'ale* 'king' and with Quiche *q'alel,* a title, the head of a group, and is probably included in Yucatec *ixikal* 'señora principal' ('noble lady'). I would, therefore, read the Yaxchilan title as *ah kal chac* and translate it 'the great ruler'.

An interesting parallel between *Dresden* and *Madrid* is to be found on D33b–35b and M3a–6a; these passages show a serpent coiled around what seems to be a body of water. The glyger for what is happening is T207:671. T207 is the rattle of the rattlesnake (*tzab*?), and T671 is the Manik hand probably to be read *ce* (occasionally *ceh*?). It is interesting to find the glyger T207:671 at Yaxchilan (L31, B4) directly followed by the glyger for 'fire' in an apparently ritual context. T207 alone is followed by 'fire' in a similar context on the Walter Randel Stela, whose original provenience is unknown (Fig. 18).

A glyph which should give us substantial information on various Maya cycles, if it could be fully deciphered, is T327:17. This is found in *Madrid,* pages 18a–20a, above pictures of deities seated on the mouths of serpents. They might be considered to be emerging from the serpent mouths, being swallowed by the serpents, or simply sitting. The same glyger appears on D61 (see structural analysis, Chapter 13), directly preceding the figures of serpents with deities seated on their jaws, which accompany extremely long calendrical calculations. However, without the aid of *Madrid,* it would have been impossible to associate the glyph with the serpent figures. The Black God of War appears on D69, seated on the mouth of a serpent with a similar

accompanying text. In this case, T327:17 does not appear until the following page, but the validity of the association is indicated by the fact that it there has the prefix *ek* 'black', as it does on D73a.

Proskouriakoff (1960, p. 470) has also drawn attention to the fact that the fish-in-hand glyph (T714) normally occurs (with verbal suffixes) in association with representations of a serpent which has in its mouth a head and torso of a human or deity. It is normally associated with dates "far in the past," and she suggests that it "represents a rite performed in memory of a dead hero." A more mundane interpretation is suggested by D65a, where this glyph appears in the first position, appropriately for a verb, with God K represented below holding a fish in his hands. To confuse the issue still further, this glyph appears as G1 of the Nine Lords of the Night with a prefix of 'nine', substituting for the more usual figure of a hand in a different position, holding the head of God C. Thompson formerly identified G1 as a glyph for the deity Ah Bolon Tzacab (whose name might better be written Tz'acab or Dzacab). De Gruyter (1946, p. 34) pointed out that *bolon* is 'nine', that *tzac* is a small fish, and that *kab* is 'hand', suggesting that *bolon tzac kab* was written for Bolon Tz'acab. He also pointed out that *tz'a* is 'to give, hand over, place, concede', and *tz'aac* is 'that which is given'. The deity name has usually been interpreted as *dzacab* 'generations'. There is also the possibility of a connection with *dzacah* 'to heal by magic rites' (Brinton 1895, p. 144). Despite apparent confusion between *dza/tz'a* and *tza,* it does seem as if the term for 'small fish' may somehow be associated here. My own decipherment premises would not allow writing *kab* for *cab* (see Chapter 9); so I would be inclined to think that 'giving' is what is intended by the hand.

Cyrus Thomas pointed out in 1892 that the glyger T612:542 is found on M91a, following the 'capture' glyph just discussed, above the picture of a turkey in a snare. Both are found in the Landa "alphabet," with the respective values *l* and *e.* Since *le* is Yucatec for 'noose', Thomas felt that this proved the alphabetic nature of the Maya writing. The Landa "alphabet" actually gives glyphs for the Spanish names of the letters, and the vowels probably represent glyphs with an unrepresented initial glottal stop. Hence, I would read this sequence *le-ʔe,* for *leʔ,* just as I read the sequence T87:542 as *te-ʔe* for *teʔ* 'tree', although I recognize that T87 appears without suffixes in *Dresden* as 'tree'. The context is not absolutely clear, and there are few additional examples (see further discussion, Chapter 9). Villacorta and Villacorta, commenting on M42c, read the glyger T283:558 (501?) as 'cacería por lazo' ('snaring') and T219:542/

T1.612:542
u le- ? (e)

T283:558
normalized
glyger for
snaring, M42c

hok + kal
catch,
snare?

T219
deer

le
noose

at right a
very similar
scene of
deer-snaring
but with a
different glyph,
cf. Fig. 56

cuch
burden

T146:542b.181.1.515:515
verb   *u -po-p(o)* (?)

verb   *ti te- ? (e)*

verb   *ti te- ? (e)*

its mat
M102c

at the
tree
(post)
M102b

at the
tree
M102d

T227.504
nak?

to smoke

M86–87b

Figure 58. Hunting, weaving, and other activities.

T87:542 as 'cacería por trampa' ('trapping'). Whorf (1942, p. 487) misidentifies T219 by drawing it like T62, which he identifies as a loop and reads *le* 'noose'. The 'trapping' glyph of the Villacortas (T219/T87) is, in fact, what I read as *che-te*. Whorf's reading of T219:542/T87:542 as *le* seems much less convincing than Thomas's reading of T612:542 as the same word, *le*. The 'snaring' glyger of the Villacortas consists of a glyph which I now regard as unidentified and T558, which may be intended for T501, which I have read *ba*. Be that as it may, the glyger should certainly refer in some way to the use of a tree snare.

Another glyger of substantial importance in the arguments about phoneticism is T528:601, which normally appears when an individual, frequently a deity, is shown carrying something on his or her back. Seler (1902–1923, I, 562) read the glyger as *cuch* 'burden'. Whorf (1933, pp. 21–22) showed that a wide range of Maya words associated with carrying began with *cu* and hence that the glyger should begin with *cu* but did not commit himself further, although he suggested that it was possibly the verb *cumah*. Thompson (1950, p. 267) suggested *cuch haab* or *cucuch,* in both cases reading T601 alone as *cuch* 'burden'; he later suggested that T528 is sometimes read *ku* 'god', and hence the glyger is *kucuch* 'god-burden'. These suggestions ignore the fact that when T601 appears in other compounds it does not, from the context, mean 'burden'. Moreover, when the White Goddess is shown with 'fire' on her back, accompanied by T528:601, it hardly seems likely that fire may be properly called a deity. Although Thompson (1950, pp. 267–268) was the first to distinguish two forms of Cauac, he lumps both together as T528 in the *Catalog.* I have shown (Kelley 1962c, pp. 283–284) that both of these forms appear in the *Dresden* for the day Cauac but that only one appears in any given glyger. The glygers for 'eleven', 'turkey', 'pictun', and 'burden' consistently contain one form, while the glygers for the months Yax, Zac, and Ceh, the glyger for 'year', the glyger for God N, and the glyger for 'drought' consistently have a different form. I accept Knorozov's reading *cu* for the first form and Thompson's reading *haab* for the second form. Knorozov's reading of the 'burden' glyger as *cu-chu,* i.e., *cuch,* seems to accord best with the evidence. Thompson's view that T528 has another value, *ku,* is based partly on Landa (who says it is *cu* and distinguishes it from another glyph which he says is *ku*) and partly on alleged associations with deities (*ku* 'god'), which seem to me susceptible of other interpretations. It has been suggested that T601 represents a carrying device, which has been one of the reasons for assigning an ideographic inter-

pretation to it, reading this glyph alone as *cuch*. The identification seems plausible but far from proven, and I would not regard the interpretation as disproving its identity as a phonetic glyph, *chu*.

A verb form which may be identified with some assurance is T515, which appears with verbal suffixes on D2b and D2c; the pictures below show deities making mats or nets with a needle (Barthel 1952, p. 46). In doubled form, the glyph refers to the object being made on M102c (Fig. 58). Although Villacorta and Villacorta describe this as a scene of spinning, it seems rather to show a woman working at a horizontal loom. Thompson (1950, p. 57) draws attention to words in various Maya languages beginning with *po-* referring to 'sewing' and 'huipil' (cf. also Q. *pot* 'blouse'). *Pop* (*po* reduplicated) is widely spread in Mayan languages as the word for 'mat'. Hence, Knorozov's reading of T515 as *po* seems quite reasonable and just short of proof. Thompson had suggested that T740 could be read *po;* Barthel's demonstration that T740 is to be read *pok'* rather than *po* has eliminated this one alternative. Cyrus Thomas (1897, p. 237) had suggested a reading of T515 based on Yucatec *chuyah* 'sewing'. Cordan (1963b, p. 31) reads T515:515 as *chuch* 'Fadenknauel' ('hank of thread'). This certainly is reasonable, and if the Villacortas are right in thinking that spinning is shown, this would be the most plausible interpretation. Moreover, T515 bears a substantial similarity to T601, which I regard as *chu*. The similarity is not an identity, however, and the two do not appear in the same contexts. Lounsbury, in a paper presented at the American Museum of Natural History in 1970, has shown that *chuch* is used in a way that corresponds closely with a careful technical description of the activity shown on M102c and has made it almost certain that T515 is merely an allograph of T601, despite the apparent contextual differences.

The glyger which gives the verb identifying the activity of the woman who is making the mat or spinning is T146:542b. Knorozov (1955a, p. 85, no. 108) once read *piɔbil* 'tejer' ('weave'). Unfortunately, the meaning is not directly derivable from the elements from which it is composed. Cordan (1963a, p. 51) points out that *pidzbil-* can mean 'peinar la lana, deshebrar, partir' ('to comb the wool, divide'). This does not seem strong support for the meaning 'weave'. Araujo, Rodríguez, and Solís (1965, pp. 62–63) accept Knorozov's reading but seem to regard it as equivalent to *piz,* a root for 'measure'. Such phonetic looseness is unjustified at the present stage of analysis, and their attempts to support the reading in this way rather weaken it. Knorozov (1963, p. 285, no. 060) now reads T146 as *ppu,* but none of his

---

examples seem probative. Villacorta and Villacorta also identify another glyph on M102b (T812 with the verbal suffix T181) as meaning 'tejer' ('weave'). This glyph is the head of a death deity (T1042) given a quarter turn from its normal position. It seems clear that the meaning is approximately correct.

Three representations of a deity smoking a tubular pipe appear on *Madrid* pages 86–87b (Fig. 58). The initial glyger in the accompanying texts is T227:504; Seler pointed out that this glyger probably meant 'smoking'. T227 is a seated man; *nak* in Tzotzil is 'to sit'; the second glyph is the well-known glyph for 'night' (Fig. 4), Yucatec *akbal*. Knorozov (1955a, p. 65, no. 1) reads T227 as *nak*, citing only Yucatec *nak* 'belly'. For the combination T227.561:23, Knorozov (1955a, p. 83, no. 84) reads *nak chaan*, citing Motul *nak caan* 'capa del cielo' ('layer of heaven'), a plausible reading. T504, the *akbal* glyph, is read by Knorozov simply *ak*. Cordan (1963b, p. 64) follows this reading completely, giving *nakak* 'to smoke'. This seems to be entirely a derived meaning, for which he cites the comparative evidence of Yucatec *nakba* 'to burn' and Chontal *nuk'um* 'he smokes'. If the latter is due to assimilation from an earlier **nak'um,* it would certainly support the reading of T227 as *nak*, although not necessarily the interpretation of T504 as *ak*. Tzeltal *nak'* 'to hide' may account for the use of this glyph in astronomical contexts, where it may indicate occultation.

Seler (1893) was first to determine the meaning of another glyger, T90:829, shown accompanying musical activity, especially drumming (M22b) or rattling (Fig. 59). I believe the first glyph is *tu* and that the overall meaning should be *tun* 'drum'. If so, T829 should be *n(u)*, assuming synharmony (see glossary). Various glyphs identified as T829 on M22b are not clearly rendered; representations of T829 elsewhere seem to represent an animal head. On M22b, the glyph T829(?) appears once, face downwards. This is suggestive, since Tzeltal *nujaj* is 'ponerse boca abajo' ('to put oneself face down'). The glyph is not regularly in that position, however, and I have no suggestion to make as to why it might be *nu*.

Elsewhere I have discussed the reasons for regarding the hand sprinkling water or sowing corn as *mal* 'to sprinkle' or 'to pass'. The use of the hand with the meaning 'end' and reading *lah* (or, less likely, *tz'oc*) has also been discussed. Thompson's identification of the *xoc* shark as meaning *xoc* 'to count' and its frequent substitution for the *muluc* glyph (*mul* 'time, turn') has been amply discussed. A few other verbs, acceptable in context, have been established with some degree of probability from a prior reading of their phonetic elements (see Fig. 62).

Another verb which Thompson has attempted to identify is T573, originally called the Distance Number Introducing Glyph because of its usual occurrence in the inscriptions prior to notations of the number of days which passed between one specified date and the next. Thompson (1950, pp. 160–162) pointed out that this should be a word connected in some way with counting or adding and suggested it might be *bukxoc*, a term used to refer to the wheel of the year bearers (but restricted, according to the examples quoted, to a count of years), or *hel* 'to move, to exchange', or, as a noun, 'successor in office'. He preferred the latter, and it has been accepted by authorities as different in their basic assumptions as Knorozov, Barthel, Fought, Cordan, and the Mérida school. Moreover, a reference to 'successor in office' seems much more appropriate in terms of our present concept of the subject matter of the inscriptions than it did when Thompson wrote. Nonetheless, although I have no alternative to offer, the interpretation still seems to me to rest on shaky grounds. The glyph does not particularly suggest turning or rotation to me, and the context would indicate a more direct association with counting. Thompson does not show *hel* used in colonial times in this way, nor is there any satisfactory homonymic use.

A few other verbs may be identified approximately from context. M11b shows God B sowing or planting with a dibble. The first glyger of the accompanying passage is T16:506 with the past-tense verbal suffix (T181). T16 is *yax*, and T506 is *kan*. We can therefore postulate that *yaxkan* could have the meaning 'sow'.

On D44b–45b and on M2a we find a verb consisting of T190.25 and the verbal suffix T181. T190 is the axe, *bat*, and T25 is *ca*. The verb should be read *batca* or perhaps *batac* or *bataca*. It is followed immediately by the name glyph of the subject, the sky peccary, patron of the month Zip. The accompanying pictures show this deity apparently hanging from the sky. From the *Dresden*, I would have suspected that the verb meant something like 'descend', but the more anthropomorphized deity of *Madrid* is shown twice with axes in his hand and once with a torch; a fourth representation is too worn for identification of the object in the hand. Since *bat* is 'hail', one wonders if this is not a storm deity and if the reference is not to 'hail'. The axe glyph also occurs as part of a glyger in which various deities are shown working on what seem to be the heads of wooden idols (M95d–96d, M97a, M97b). On M97a, T190 seems to be directly followed by the verbal suffix T181 and hence to be read *batah* 'axed', and this is probably what is intended on M96d, although T181 is shown there in a very degenerate form. On M97b, the glyger is

u hel **x**

x *hel aan*

hel with
ti (at)
prefixed

yax kan to sow

T90:829

shaking
a rattle?

T90:829

drumming

hand sprinkling
water or
scattering grain
mal (to pass)

his fire at heaven   of   *bat ca ah*
Chac

Note
unusual
word
order.

T190.25.181
bat ca ah

T190:181
batah

M97a

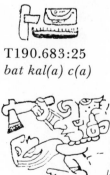

T190.683:25
bat kal(a) c(a)

M97b

D39b
water
pouring

Figure 59. Verbs.

T190.683:25. T683 is the moon glyph which stands for 'twenty' and is apparently to be read *kal*. I suspect that here the word represented by the glyph is a cognate of Quiche *k'al-* 'to fell a tree', although this meaning is not directly relevant. In any case, the glyphs are probably to be read *bat(a)kal(a)c(a)*. The glyger T190.25 occurs not infrequently in the inscriptions.

Another verb which may be identified with some probability is to be found on D39b. Here the old goddess with the serpent headdress is shown emptying a jar of water. It seems fairly certain that this represents heavy rain. The first glyger in the passage above has the verbal suffix, T181. In other parts of this sequence, the first glyger is not always a verb, but here the verbal suffix indicates it is. If so, it should mean either 'rain' or 'pours out water'. The glyger consists of an animal head (T791b) and an affix which I cannot surely identify but think is T251.

Throughout the Venus passages of *Dresden*, we find a verb consisting of the prefix T24 and an outstretched hand (T713; Thompson also includes glyphs of hands in other positions under this classification; see Fig. 50). The verb seems to indicate an association of Venus with some deity and is associated with all four positions of the Venus cycle. I suspect that the root is *naab-* 'palm of the hand'. T24 (Fig. 49) seems to be a shell ornament, but an adequate reading is difficult to find.

The identification of verbs has progressed substantially in the past fifteen years, and there is every reason to expect a great deal more progress. The recognition of verbs as a separate class of glyphs has now reached a high degree of reliability. The meanings of many verbs are known and the codices provide contextual evidence for a substantial number of verbs in addition to those for which there is already good published evidence. The publication of Mayan dictionaries is enabling us to determine, on a broad comparative basis, the most likely readings for those verbs whose meanings have already been determined. Thus, this is one of the most productive areas in glyph decipherment at the present time.

The following linguistic reconstructions, derived from Kaufman 1964, may have some relevance to the glyphs which have been considered in this section. Reconstructions apply to the whole family unless otherwise specified. Periods are used to separate reconstructions for one meaning from reconstructions for the next.

To sow: **aw; *tz'un*. To harvest: **jach'/hach'*. Field: (a) **kol;* (b) **'abix;* (c) **kw'al;* (d) **'alVj;* (e)

*aw-Vl. Hoe: **'aq'in/'aq'en*. To grind: **ke'*. To fry, toast: **k'il*. To chew, bite: **kw'ux* (H.?). To eat meat: **tzi'/twiw*, (H.?). To drink: **uk'*. To eat: **we'/wa'*. Tortilla: **waaj/wah*. Hunger: **wa'/we'/wi'*, (H.?). To whistle: **xuub*. To eat fruit: **lo'*. To lick: **leq'*. To swallow: **biq'/buq'*. The neck, to swallow: **nuq'*. To eat soft foods: **maq'*. Tortilla: (a) **'o'tw;* (b) **lej/loj*. Cooked, ripe: **tyaq'-ang*. Raw: **tzeh*. Ashes: **tya'ng*. Firewood: **si'*. Fire: **q'aXq'*. Smoke: (a) **tap'*, Toj.-Chu.; (b) **ngup'*, Kan.-Jac.; (c) **sib*, Mam-Q.-Pch.-Kek.; (d) **butz'*, Yuc.-Chl.-Chr.; (e) **ch'ahil*, Tzel.-Tzo. (H.?). Live coals: (a) **aq'al*, Tzel.-Tzo.-Toj.-Q.-Chr.-Chu.; (b) **aq'*, Pch.; (c) **q'al*, H.-Mam (Yuc.?). Hot: (a) **q'ix/q'ax*, Tzel.-Tzo.-H.-Pch.-Kek.-Toj.-Chu.-(Chl.); (b) *tëqëw*, etc., Yuc.-Lac.-Chl. Lime: (a) **chuun*, Pch.-Kek.-Mam-Q.; (b) **tya'ng* (=ashes), Yuc.-Chl.-Tzel.-Tzo.-Toj.-Chu.-Kan.-Jac.-H. Cold: (a) **siis;* (b) **si'kw;* (c) **ke'*. Soot: (a) **bëq;* (b) **si'* (firewood) + **bëq*. To put out (a fire): **tyup/tyup'*. To burn (something): **kw'at*. To burn (up): **til*. To vomit: **xeh/xap'*. Pus: **poxow*, (H.?). Cough: **oj(o)b*. Sick: **'yah/'ya'*. Strangle, breathe: **jiq'/jaq'*, (Yuc.?). Pain, painful: **q'ux*. To see: **il* (H.?). To shine: **lem*. Sweet: **ki'*. Sour: (a) **pëj*, Tzel.-Tzo.-Yuc.-Toj.-Chu.-Kan.-Jac.-Chl.-Chr.; (b) **ch'am*, Mam-Q.-Pch. (H.?). Stinking: **tyu'h*, (H.?). Bitter: **k'ah*. Hot: **yah*, (H.?). To hear, feel: **'abiy/'ubiy* (H.?). To smell, to kiss: **'utz'*. To come: **tyal*. To arrive (there): **hul/'ul*. To leave: (a) **el*, H.-Pch.-Kek.-Toj.-Chu.-Kan.-Jac.-Mam-Q.; (b) **loq'*, Tzel.-Tzo.-Kan.-Chl.-Chr.-Yuc. To return: **sut* (H.?). To enter: **'ok*. To take, to carry: **k'am* (H.?). To walk: **xang/xe'*. To arrive (there): **q'o(ch)*. To carry, burden: (a) **'iq;* (b) **'ihqatz*. To call, bring: **'iq'*. To pass: (a) **q'ax;* (b) **sol;* (c) **'ek'*. To fall, descend: (a) **kwo/kwu;* (b) **'em*. To run, flee: **'ahn*. Stopped: (a) **tekw'*, Tzel.-Toj.-Kan.-Q.; (b) **wa'*, Tzo.-Yuc.-Chl.-Chr.-Mam; (c) **ling*, Chu.-Jac. (H.?). Stooped: **qot*. Below: **'ahlang*. Earth, land: (a) **'ulew*, Pch.-Q.; (b) **lu'm*, Tzel.-Tzo.-Yuc.-Toj.-Chu.-Chl.-Chr.; (c) **ch'och'*, Kek.-Kan.-Jac.-Mam (H.?). Dust, sand: (a) **poq*, Yuc.-H.-Pch.-Kek.-Chu.-Jac.-Kan.-Mam-Q.; (b) **hi'*, Tzel.-Tzo.-Chl.-Chr. Metal, money: (a) **taq'in*, Tzel.-Tzo.-Yuc.-Toj.-Chl.-Chr.; (b) **ch'ihch'*, Pch.-Kek.-(Agc.)-Q.; (c) **puwaq*, Pch.-Kek.-Mam-Q.; (d) **ky'e'n*, Chu.-Kan.-Jac. Hole, well, cave: (a) **ky'e'n*, Tzel.-Tzo.-Toj.-Yuc.-Chl.-Chr.; (b) **job/jul*, Yuc.-H.-Pch.-Kek.-Chu.-Mam-Q. Stone: (a) **'abaj*, Pch.-Kek.-Mam-Q.; (b) **ton/tun*, Tzel.-Tzo.-Yuc.-Chl.-Chr.; (c) **ky'e'n*, Chu.-Jac.-Kan.-H. Mountain: **witz*, (H.?). Mud: (a) **lo/uuq/q'*, Yuc.-H.-Mam-Toj.; (b) **'anam*, Chl.-Chr.-H. Glass, mirror: **nen*. Field, plain: **twëq'ang*. Water: **hë'*. To bathe: **'atw-in*. Dry: **tyaq-ing*,

(H.?). Drop (n.): *t'uj/tz'uj. Rain: *ngab. Swim: *nux/mux/nox. To get wet: *tz'aj. Lake: (a) *najb; (b) chh; (c) *pam (plain) + *ha' (water). Get wet: *'ak'. Air, wind: *'iq'. Cloud: (a) *tyoq, Tzel.-Tzo.-H.-Kek.-Chl.-Chr.; (b) *suutz', Pch.-Q.-Kan.; (c) *muyal, Yuc.-Jac.; (d) *'asun (<MZ), Toj.-Chu.-Kan.-Jac. Hail: *baty (H.?). Sky: *kya'ng (H.?). Moon: (a) *'uh/'uj, Tzel.-Tzo.-Yuc.-Chu.-Chl.-Chr.; (b) *'iik', H.-Q.; (c) *poh (<MZ), Kek.-Pch.; (d) *'ix-'ajaw, Jac.-Kan.-Toj.-Mam. Shade: (a) *'ax; (b) *muung; (c) *'eng. Thunder: *kyah(o)q. To buy: (a) *man, Tzel.-Tzo.-Yuc.-Toj.-Chu.-Kan.-Chl.-Chr.; (b) *loq', Kek.-Pch.-Jac.-Mam-Q. To sell: *k'ay, Yuc.-H.-Pch.-Kek.-Mam-Q.; to lose: *k'ay, Tzel.-Tzo.-Toj.-Kan.-Jac. To pay: *toj, (H.?). To write: *tz'ihb (H.?). Paper: *hu'ng. To grow, do business: *p'ol. Town, city (tribe): *'amaq'. Market: *k'iwik. Property: *q'in. To sell: *kong. To lose: *saty. To laugh: *tze'. To cry: *'oq'. To answer: *tyaq'. To tell someone: *'ut. To say: *kih. To say something: *hal/'al. Visitor, stranger: *hulë'/'ulë'. It is well: *kwo. Let's go: *qong. To call out: *'aw. To send: *taq. To send, messenger, work, service: (a) *'ab; (b) *'ab-aty; (c) *'ab-ty-el. To explain, put in line: *chol. To seek: (a) *say/sa'/sah, Tzo.-Chu.-Kan.-Jac.-Chl.-Chr.; (b) *sik', Pch.-Q.-Kek.; (c) *leh, Tzel.-Yuc.-Toj. (H.? Mam?). To fear: *xi'/xi'w, (H.?). To think, to know: *na', (H.?). To encounter, obtain: *twah/twa'/twaw. To mark, draw: *'ehtw-Vl. To know, recognize: *'ojtyaq. To be ashamed: *kw'ix. To take: *tzaq. To hate: *'il (=see?). To become accustomed to: *q'ay. To lend: (a) *mat; (b) *mahtan. Gift: *si. Change, exchange: (a) *kw'ex; (b) *jel/jal. To accept a loan: *maj-an. Lazy: (a) *ky'aj; (b) *'saj. Good: *'utz. A bad action: (a) *mul; (b) *mahk. Robbery: *'eleq'. Tax, tribute: *patan. To signal with a finger, finger: (a) *ky'ut; (b) *ky'ut-ub. To jump, save, help: *kwol. To like, need, ask for, love: (a) *q'an; (b) *'aj. Slave: *mun. Companion: *'ety. To roll, coil: *bal. To bury, hide: *muq (H.?). To pound, strike: *ten/t'en/net'. To beat: *q'oj. To fold: *q'och. To scratch, gnaw: *jot'.

To rip out: *boq. To skin: *poch'. To turn: *tz'ot. To open: *jap. To damage, a debt: *kw'as. To cut: *boj. To stop cutting: *q'aj. To divide: *q'ep. To cut asunder: *xet'. To grab, to prepare: *chap. To join, complete: *tz'aq. To pile up: *bus. To collect, join together: (a) *mul/mol; (b) *tzob. To squeeze, make a fist: *mich'/much'/moch'. To shake: *ngik. To fan, a fan: *wel/wal. To mix: *kwap. To give, place: (a) *'aq'; (b) *'ya'. To paint, dye: *bon. To be full: *noj (H.?). To rot: *q'a'/q'ah. To grow: *ky'ih (H.?). To end: *laj. Contents: *bahal/ba'al. To swell up: (a) *sip/sit'; (b) *mal. To fill: *but'. To remain: *hil. Heavy: *'a(h)l. New: *'ak' (H.?). Long: *naqt. Fat: *pim. Soft, slow: *q'u'n. To make a ball: *kw'ol. Strong: (a) *kew; (b) *tulan. Big: (a) *niw/nim; (b) *niwan; (c) *niwaq. Spherical: *wol. Narrow: *lahtz'. Circular: *set. Thick: *tyëty. Much: *yab. Hard, strong: *tzëtz. Ripe, seasoned: *yij. Dirty: *tz'i'il/tz'iil. Thin: *jëy. A ball: *pis. Deep: *tyam. Correct: *tyoj. Little: *ch'in, etc.

The decipherment of specific glyphs is the foundation upon which our understanding of the nature of the script must be built. To know the meaning of even two or three glyphs may be enough to establish some general principle which is an aid in further decipherment. At a different level of understanding, the ability to recognize such glyphs as 'star', 'fire', 'offer', 'be born', or 'conquer', all now known, may enable us to determine in rough outline the entire meaning of a text, or at least to recognize its general subject matter. Suggestions are accumulating very rapidly; widely accepted specific decipherments are fewer but are still approaching a tenth of the glyphs known to us. The importance of a relatively small number of these glyphs in our texts means that we can now understand the general tenor of considerably more than one-tenth of the inscriptions. In the process, the Mayas have been humanized and appear to us in a much more realistic light.

Part Two.
General Problems in Decipherment

Chapter 9
Phoneticism

Until very recently, discussions of phoneticism in the Maya script have been hindered by inadequate terminology and imprecise definitions of the problem. Disagreements as to interpretation persist, but the problem has emerged much more clearly. All the works of Yurii Knorozov have contributed greatly to our understanding, and I have published one paper defending his general position (Kelley 1962b). Thomas Barthel (1958) published one paper which was extremely critical of Knorozov. Eric Thompson has opposed the entire idea of a phonetic system; his criticisms and comments have, in a review (1953a), in two articles (1959, 1963c), in the introduction to his *Catalog* (1962), and incidentally in many other articles, helped to clarify where the differences of opinion lie.

In the past, the term *ideograph* was applied to any glyph which was assumed to convey an idea, whether that idea was nebulous and fuzzy or precise and clear-cut. *Ideographic* was regarded as the opposite of *phonetic,* and the *kin* glyph was used to "prove" that there was "some phoneticism" in the Maya script, since it appeared both with the meaning 'day' and as part of the glyphs for 'east' (*likin/lakin*) and 'west' (*chikin*) (Bowditch 1910, pp. 255–256). It should have been clear that the example proved too little or too much, for *kin* is also 'sun'. If it had not been known from Landa that T544 was *kin,* it might have been worked out that it represented the "idea" for 'sun', because the sun marked the days, and that it was used in the directional glyphs because the directions marked the path of the sun. The varied use of the *kin* glyph is, in fact, evidence that an idea was conveyed; but it was conveyed through graphemes representing words. As long as the word has not been identified, such a glyph may seem to be an ideograph in the older use of the term, divorced from any linguistic reality. Such a glyph is, in fact, both ideographic, in the sense of conveying an idea, and phonetic, in the sense that it corresponds to a particular phonetic sequence. For such glyphs the term *logograph* has been used in this book and will be used in the following discussion. The logographs sometimes conveyed several different meanings, which were homonyms in the language. Thus, Brinton (1895, p. 109) pointed out that the color terms might be used also in other contexts with other meanings which corresponded with other meanings of the words *kan* 'yellow', *chac* 'red', *zac* 'white', and *ek* 'black'. Similarly, Bowditch (1910, p. 255) pointed out that *yax,* as well as being 'green, blue', was also 'new'. Brinton referred to this as "rebus-writing," and the term has been widely used since. We would now say that this was a logograph with multiple referents. Barthel, who has recently done a great deal of work on logographs and established a number of important examples, was still inclined, as late as his 1958 paper (presented in 1956), to regard even "rebus" use as relatively late and unimportant.

Seler's reasons for identifying T548 as *tun* 'stone, year' and Thomas's argument that *kal* stood for both 'twenty' and 'imprison' show that logographic use was widely recognized at the turn of the century. Despite this recognition, scholars made few attempts to go beyond the already established logographs. For this reason, Thompson's demonstration that *xoc* 'shark' was used for *xoc* 'count' was a considerable surprise to many Mayanists. Thompson's work opened the door to a very considerable number of new logographic decipherments and effectively demolished the claims of Beyer and Teeple that there might be little or no linguistic element in the script.

Work has now progressed so far in this regard that I view with considerable skepticism any claim that Mayan glyphs, other than the numbers, can be divorced from the linguistic background of those who produced them. In this respect, they differ sharply from the Mixtec-Aztec script, which is genuinely ideographic-pictographic. The conventions of the latter script (save in the period of degeneration under Spanish influence) were virtually free of linguistic connotations. In my opinion, the Mixtec-Aztec script was deliberately designed to convey certain types of economic and historical information across the many language barriers of ancient Mesoamerica. Using a few simple conventions, a monolingual Mixtec scribe could produce a tribute roll which could be read by a monolingual Aztec scribe. It is usually believed that this important and useful trait is proof of the "primitive" nature of the script and the relative backwardness of the highland Mexicans. It seems to me more plausible to regard it as one of the crowning achievements of Mesoamerican culture, which might well be adopted, with appropriate modifications, for international commerce today.

The contrast between this true ideographic-pictographic script and the Maya script is tremendous. Everything we know about the latter indicates that it was language bound and could not be used for cross-linguistic communication. Within the culture it could convey a great many kinds of information that could not be conveyed by the Mixtec-Aztec script. I believe that everyone now accepts the fact that logographs play a very important role in the Maya script. Phoneticism, in this sense, is no longer in dispute in Mesoamerican studies. There is, however, still dispute as to whether the Mayas ever used more than one glyph to write a single morpheme, or word. Writing of

this sort is phonetic in the sense that it excludes whatever meanings (if any) the individual graphemes have, and the meaning is determined solely by the sequence of sounds indicated by the graphemes. Throughout this chapter, the word *phonetic* will henceforth be used in a restricted sense to refer to this type of writing. The particular type of phonetic writing postulated by Knorozov consists of the use of two or more graphemes, each representing a given consonant-vowel combination, to write a single morpheme or a series of morphemes.

It should be emphasized that those of us who believe that the Mayas were capable of writing phonetically have explicitly and repeatedly affirmed that much of the script is logographic. Many of the general arguments which have been presented against phoneticism seem to presuppose a completely phonetic script. As far as I know, there are no living defenders of the existence of a completely phonetic script; so arguments against it are merely attacking straw men. There are certain a priori arguments which can be made about the nature of the script. J. Friedrich attempted to give some general principles for the decipherment of unknown scripts. In considering the number of glyphs, he wrote: "A script consisting of less than thirty signs will presumably turn out to be alphabetic; the probability of its decipherment is higher than that of a more complicated system. Scripts containing fifty, a hundred, or even several hundred different symbols may justifiably be regarded beforehand as more or less complicated syllabic systems of writing, perhaps employing also word-signs, and their decipherment can be expected to involve more considerable difficulties" (J. Friedrich 1957, p. 152). In the case of the Maya, it is hard to make a clear-cut estimate of the number of glyphs which were in use, because of difficulties of weighting minor variations, because of the many nearly or quite illegible inscriptions, and because of the obviously specialized nature of the surviving sources. Thompson (1958*b*, p. 46) once suggested that there were less than 400. Writing about 1961, Knorozov (1967, pp. 34–35) estimated about 350–450 graphemes. The Thompson *Catalog* (1962) made it clear that these were substantial underestimates and that the true number was probably closer to 750 or 800 graphemes.

Friedrich's "word-signs" in the previous quotation correspond to what are here called logographs, which certainly are present in large numbers in the Maya script. However, if the script were entirely logographic, even allowing two or three meanings to a grapheme, the maximum number of meanings would only be on the order of two thousand. It seems unlikely that any group which had so many graphemes would be satisfied with such a small percentage of their total vocabulary. Conversely, there are far more signs than would be necessary for a syllabary of consonant and vowel (CV) type or for a true alphabet. Kaufman (1964, p. 84) reconstructs thirty-eight consonants and six vowels for the proto-Mayan system. If all these sounds were distinguished in the script (which is highly unlikely), a true alphabet would require 44 graphemes, and a CV syllabary would require 228 graphemes. The total number of graphemes, then, strongly suggests a mixed system. Thompson (1962, pp. 19–20) refers to comparable quantities of glyphs for an unspecified stage of Egyptian writing and seems to feel that this indicates that the Mayan script is "pictographic or ideographic." However, the Egyptian script was basically logographic, with a full set of alphabetic glyphs with which the scribes could have written any Egyptian word. No one could deny the pictographic nature of much Egyptian writing, but there is no indication that it was ideographic in the sense intended by Thompson.

Thompson (1962, pp. 20–21) lists the thirty-three most frequently used graphemes and shows that many of them are of known meaning and were obviously used in a nonphonetic way. At some time prior to the publication of Thompson's work, Knorozov (1967, p. 49) was pointing out that it is a general rule of "naturally formed codes" to have a balance which will tend to make the text as short as possible. In a mixed logographic-phonetic script, it saves effort to write the most commonly used morphemes by a single grapheme and to write infrequently used morphemes syllabically. Thus, Thompson's finding is in entire accord with the basic theoretical premises upon which Knorozov's work is based. Thompson went on to show that there is no evidence that any of these glyphs was used acrophonically—that is, in no case is there evidence that the glyph considered stood for the initial sound of the whole morpheme which the glyph represented. Since it was already clear that most of these glyphs were used morphemically rather than phonetically, it would have been very surprising if any evidence of acrophony had been found. In point of fact, plausible as acrophony seems, there is almost no supporting evidence for it, and I know of only two glyphs which even suggest it (*ka* might be from *kab, ca* from *cai*). As far as I know, no serious scholar has suggested that acrophony had anything to do with the presence of phonetic glyphs in the Maya script (I do not consider Werner Wolff a serious scholar). Hence, Thompson's attempt to demonstrate its nonexistence, on materials which should not show the principle even if it were in use, is essentially irrelevant. No one denies that T526 is *cab/caban* 'earth', that T561 is *caan* 'sky', or that T528 is Cauac (with exceptions). No scholar has suggested at any time within the past twenty years that any of these was read *ca*. It *has* been suggested that T25 was read *ca,* as Landa said it was. An attempt to seriously consider acrophony (or any other aspect of the script) ought to start with a consideration of the suggestions which are taken seriously by those who believe in the principle.

Implicit in Thompson's view of the relationship of logographs and phonetic glyphs is the assumption that phonetic glyphs are obviously superior and that evolution tends towards phoneticism. Thus, he writes, "There remains the possibility that the Maya system was originally ideographic and pictographic, but in time changed to syllabic" (Thompson 1962, p. 20). This suggestion is in sharp contrast with the development of Egyptian writing, which he has just cited. All the phonetic glyphs were in use in Egypt at a very early date, originally accompanied by a relatively small number of logographs. In the Egyptian script, new logographs were constantly being invented until, as Thompson points out, they numbered in the thousands in the Ptolemaic period—but the Egyptians could still use the phonetic glyphs to write the names of the Ptolemies or any other word if they wished to. The logograph has one great advantage over phonetic writing, in that meanings tend to remain more stable in logographic systems than do sounds in phonetic systems. Hence, developments through time with a phonetic script must, sooner or later, tend to the emergence of "spelling" in the English sense of an incongruous pairing of partly or wholly unlike elements. I strongly suspect that when the script was invented or developed, some or all of the Mayan languages still preserved a final vowel on words which now end with a consonant. Thus linguistic evolution may lead to obvious discrepancies between the script and the language in their later stages.

Besides such secondary discrepancies, there are bound to be primary discrepancies, caused by the difference in recognition of important distinguishing characteristics of the language by a native speaker without linguistic training and by a linguist. There has been a great deal of bootless a priori argument among Mayan scholars as to whether the Mayas distinguished in their script between the two sounds written in modern Yucatec *c* and *k,* or between other more or less similar sounds. In fact, no known script (other than those devised by linguists) distinguishes adequately, either phonetically or phonemically, between all the sounds found in the language being recorded. However, in deciphering, one should neither assume that a particular distinction is made nor assume that it is not made, but wait for clear-cut evidence in the glyphs themselves as to which sounds were distinguished. In this particular case, there is abundant evidence that the Mayas did distinguish the *c* sound from the *k* sound in the script, as will be seen.

Another factor of importance in the script which seems to be frequently misunderstood by opponents of phoneticism is that, in such a mixed script, a scribe may frequently write words in one way at one time and in another way at another. This has long been recognized in the Maya script with respect to the so-called symbolic and head-variant forms, which are, in Knorozov's term, allographs. The number 'eleven' may be written with two bars and a dot, it may be written as a deity head, it may be written as a full-figure representation of a deity, or it may be written with a three-grapheme glyger which, following Knorozov, I interpret phonetically. However these differences are interpreted, the fact of variation is clear. Again, 'dog' may be written either with a dog's head or with a glyger which seems to be phonetic. The two uses are parallel. In Egyptian script, one may find in a single inscription a word written in one place by a logograph alone, in another by alphabetic symbols alone, and in a third by a logograph accompanied by one or more of the glyphs for the sounds of the word. Thompson (1963*c*, p. 128) expresses surprise that the Mayas would write 'fire' phonetically according to my interpretation when "otros estudiosos [other students]" had identified "ideo-pictographic" glyphs for 'fire'. This is exactly parallel to the two different ways of writing 'dog'.

Another general factor which needs to be taken into account in any attempt at phonetic decipherment is the degree to which there is a normal and necessary order in the graphemes composing a glyger. Thompson (1963*c*, p. 130) repeats that a uniform order is essential in phonetic writing. This is, in fact, untrue, for in early Sumerian the order of writing graphemes varied freely without regard to fixed sequence. However, the more vital point is that in Mayan one does have uniform order with relatively few exceptions. Among the exceptions are a number of cases from the *Madrid* which I would now explain by the partial dyslexia of the scribe. Thompson's (1963*c*, p. 131) criticism of another attempt at phonetic decipherment may be translated from his text: "For example, the glyphs 630.568 [actually 559.568] which he [Knorozov] reads *tzu-l(u)* appear in reverse order on *Dresden* page 39a and should, therefore, indicate *lutz(u),* 'fishhook', but they appear above the figure of a dog." Thompson does not point out that the dog is the only figure shown

and hence should be the subject of the sentence; yet the supposed 'dog' glyph appears in the first position, where one would normally expect a verb. He further assumes that the Yucatec meaning 'fishhook' is the only possible meaning of *lutz*. However, the Tzeltal dictionary shows -*luts'* 'meter abajo de' ('place below'). Anticipating an objection, I point out that Tzeltal *ts'* frequently seems to correspond to a Yucatec nonglottalized *tz*. This by no means provides an adequate translation of the passage, but it is much more promising than either 'fishhook' or 'dog'. The dog on this page may well be appearing as a *nagual* or animal body of Chac, the Rain God, whose glyphs appear in the third position, appropriately for the subject of the action. Where the 'dog' glyger appears in its expected position, there is usually abundant reason to be sure that it refers to 'dog', and it retains the appropriate order of glyphs. The fact that one cannot explain every case, when dealing with such obscure material, does not invalidate interpretations based upon an overwhelming majority of cases. The glyger for 'dog' is T559.568 and not T568.559. Completely aside from any question of phoneticism, the appearance of the former sequence in all cases where the meaning is clear-cut should lead us to be very dubious about any claim that the meaning is the same when the elements are reversed.

Thompson's further contention (1963*c*, p. 132) that shifting of affixes, such as *ti,* from the first position of one glyph block to the last position of a previous glyph block invalidates reading *t(i)* on the end of a glyger is a misinterpretation of the unit of study, confusing glygers with glyph blocks. The important thing is that the order of sequence is the same and that the morphemic breakdown is the same. It is conceivable that even a two-grapheme glyger might sometimes be divided between two adjacent glyph blocks without changing the reading of the glyger.

Similar confusion mars Thompson's argument (1962, pp. 25–26) that the percentage of prefixes to suffixes in the glyphs (i.e., glyph blocks) is too high to agree with known grammatical prefixes in the Yucatec language "on the assumption that main signs correspond to stems." He then goes on to demolish an argument which he spent a page and a half building, by pointing out that main signs do *not* correspond to stems—as has been known for the past seventy years. His discussion of the verbal affixes of *Dresden* (Thompson 1963*c*, p. 27) points out that a relatively small number of affixes are attached to verbs. He writes, "Yet, if these signs [the verbs] are phonetic, in contrast to the largely ideographic nature adduced for the Imix group, one might reasonably expect an increase of affixes with them" (ibid.). If I understand him correctly, he is intimating that there should be more affixes because the verbs would consist of phonetically written glygers. This ignores the fact that the commonest pattern for verbs in Mayan is not CVC (the minimum which can be written phonetically with a CV syllabary), but CV. Hence the affixes should be only the verbal affixes of the language. The CV glyphs which function as logographs when they are verbs may, to be sure, function as phonetic glyphs in another context.

The affixes figure largely in another basic problem, the reason for doubling of glyphs. Beyer (1926) argued that doubling of glyphs was for aesthetic purposes. Thompson has repeatedly urged the same view. Even Knorozov (1967, pp. 64–65) admits "decorative duplication, often found in inscriptions." Even though many cases of duplication cannot be adequately explained phonetically at the moment, and it would be premature to offer an explanation in many cases, I still hold the a priori view that doubling, whenever and wherever it occurs, is functional. Thompson's most basic argument is that the different shapes of affixes and main signs make it impossible to substitute one of them for the other without marked distortion. To avoid this, affixes are doubled when "functioning as main signs," and main signs are doubled when functioning as affixes. Now there is no doubt that affixes in the main-sign position are frequently doubled. Affixes are frequently grammatical particles, and one of the commonest patterns which they have is CV. The glyphs which Thompson has read *ti, tu,* and *te* are all independent morphemic logographs, which may also function, following Knorozov's interpretation, as phonetic glyphs of CV type. Put differently, phonetic glyphs should be substantially more frequent among the affixes. One would, therefore, expect doubling to occur in many cases. In a syllabary, doubling is essential to represent doubled sounds but should not occur when the sounds are not doubled. Thompson (1962, p. 10) says that all of the evidence of the glyph catalog supports Beyer's view that doubling does not normally affect the meaning. He then goes on to say that he thinks certain signs vary their meanings on becoming affixes! He moreover points out that, in one of the few cases where we control the meanings to a certain extent, "The Cauac sign (528) doubled becomes the baktun glyph" (Thompson 1962, p. 11); i.e., it changes its meaning. Conversely, when the color glyphs are made main signs preceding the *te* 'tree' glyph, none of them are doubled. Thompson's glyph 287 actually consists of one glyph repeated twice, appearing in Glyph B of the Lunar Series under the "elbow." It is here functioning as a main sign in Thompson's terms, yet still

appears doubled. As an affix it is also doubled. I do not think it is a serious distortion of the Thompson-Beyer position to say that the statement "there is no evidence of change of meaning" through doubling is simply an expression of the fact that usually we do not know the meanings, either doubled or single.

There are actually fewer examples of doubling than are needed to supply convincing evidence that doubling is due to an aesthetic function, according to the alleged aesthetic rule. Thompson (1963c, p. 122) says that of thirty affixes which appear as main signs at least four times, seventeen are sometimes duplicated. Put differently, thirteen of these are not known to appear in duplicated form, and the others are not always in duplicated form. A "general" aesthetic principle which is followed only half the time or a little more does not seem to me an adequate explanation of the data. Thompson (1962, pp. 39–68) lists some sixty-one affixes which also appear as main signs. Of these, nineteen appear doubled on some occasions, although they may also occur as main signs with other affixes, rather than doubled. Some of the others are rare, but some are common. It seems to me significant that in the case of the color glyphs, where we know meanings and readings and where doubling would be nonsensical, it does not occur. Given the facts that in several cases doubling produces what seem to me sensible and valid readings (see Fig. 61) and that we still do not know readings for most of the affixes, I would suppose that in all cases doubling is functional rather than aesthetic. To say that there is no change of meaning when the meaning is completely unknown seems to me to be going far beyond the evidence. In point of fact, the large number of cases in which doubling does not occur shows clearly that the Mayas were capable of solving the aesthetic problems caused by a change in the normal position of the glyph without resorting to doubling and without getting distortion of an unrecognizable nature.

Although there is some doubling of CVC morphemes in Yucatec speech and I would expect logographs of this sort to be doubled on occasion, I continue to believe that doubled glyphs are usually good indicators of phoneticism. I would not expect nearly as many doubled glyphs as are found if doubling were entirely due to reduplication of logographs.

It is also worthwhile to point out some of the historical and structural reasons why ideographic and pictographic interpretations have played such a large role and why many of the most competent scholars working on the material have been so reluctant to recognize phonetic elements in the script. I believe that the first factor, psychologically perhaps the most important of all, was the apparent discrepancy between the Yucatec day names and month names given by Landa and the glyphs he gave for them. The glyph he called Chouen (=Chuen) appeared with the meaning of 'twenty-day period', which he called *uinal;* the glyph he called Manik appeared as the first element of the glyger for 'west', but no word for 'west' contained the word *manik*. The glygers for Pop and Uo were found to contain similar glyphs; yet the names were markedly distinct. The constant habit of referring to the days and months by the names given by Landa (so pervasive that it has even been continued here, despite its obvious incorrectness for earlier periods of the script) has continued to impress all students of the glyphs with the disparity between the glyphs and the names for them. The first things that the beginning student learned were these Yucatecan names, and the obvious disagreements between names and script led to attempts to explain the differences through ideas inherent in the glyphs, derived, usually, from Maya mythology. There seems no reason to doubt that Landa correctly gave the names as used by the Yucatecans of his day, but many of them seem to correspond to our writing *lb.* and reading *pound.*

Side-by-side with this emphasis on the disparity between the names of glyphs and the glyphs themselves went an emphasis on the pictographic glyphs. They were easily recognizable, and, in the codices, where the head of a particular animal or deity was regularly accompanied by a representation of the same animal or deity, it was obvious that the pictograph was also an ideograph for the name of the animal or deity. It was not nearly as clear how these pictographs should be read. The introduction of the Schellhas system of letters to refer to the deities, because of the disagreements about identification, tended also to discourage really attempting to read the pictographs as Mayan words, while their meanings became quite obvious. The unsatisfactory results of the early attempts at phonetic readings, ending with Cyrus Thomas's renunciation of his famous "key," contrasted strongly with the very satisfactory results which were being obtained in the calendrical studies. Thereafter, with the exception of occasional general statements by Gates, the better scholars all tended to concentrate on ideographic studies. Occasional positive statements about "phoneticism" actually referred in most cases to the few accepted logographs. Decipherment thenceforth took on something of the nature of a self-fulfilling prophecy. Determinations of meaning and logographic decipherments increased, and their presence was then supposed to prove that there were no other elements in the script.

Another factor of importance has been the reluc-

tance of Mayanists to get adequate training. Minimal competence should require a basic understanding of the principles of modern linguistics, reasonable familiarity with the glyphs both in the codices and in the inscriptions, a good knowledge of at least one Mayan language, and some knowledge, whether direct or indirect, of the previous literature. Even today, no scholar working on the material has these minimal qualifications. There are, of course, good reasons, both in terms of the history of Mayan research and in personal terms, for this situation. Until very recently, most students of the glyphs have been trained in archaeology, which is a demanding professional field; if they had additional training, it was apt to be in ethnology, or a general background in anthropology. The range of their interests and capabilities was often extensive—but it was not adequate to do extended linguistic decipherment of the Mayan glyphs.

Two final factors lie in the relationship between script and language and in the nature of the available sources. Knorozov (1967, p. 49) has pointed out that, in a mixed script, it is more economical to write common terms logographically and rare terms phonetically. This means that contextual proof and verification are inevitably going to be easier to find for logographs, a fact which would bias decipherment towards the logographs even without the historical factors which have been mentioned. The other contextual factor is the relationship between inscriptions and codices. The inscriptions are usually substantially longer, and the associated context is usually not as clear. Much of the material in the inscriptions consists of calendrical glyphs; a few verbs are frequently repeated; and much of the remainder consists of personal names and titles. Since most personal names of men are animal names, and since animal heads are one of the commonest types of logographs, we can expect an even higher percentage of logographs in these texts than in the codices. It was in the inscriptions that most of the early work was done. Given these conditions, the codices still furnish the most promising terrain for further phonetic decipherments, although I expect some to be made in the inscriptions. Painted glyphs on pottery are, in some ways, more like the codices and may be expected to furnish some solutions when serious work is done on them.

Considering all factors together, it is not remarkable that recognition of the phonetic element in Maya took so long, and it was entirely expectable that it would be recognized by an "outsider" who had not had any formal training in Mayan studies. Yurii Knorozov's first paper (1952) was a strong attack upon bourgeois decipherers and particularly upon Eric Thompson. It had little data and much of that was incorrect or poorly presented. With respect to the problem of phoneticism, it was also the most important paper which had been written up to that time. His much more moderate and extremely sophisticated presentation in 1963/1967 made his premises explicit, gave the basic documentation, and presented the source materials for an intensive study of the Maya script. However, most of the results had already been printed in two papers in 1955, and anyone studying the material seriously and sympathetically could have determined many of the premises.

Despite the weaknesses of Knorozov's first paper, he presented enough details to make it quite clear that the Maya script included a phonetic syllabary. Many of Knorozov's readings depended in part on the famous Landa alphabet (Fig. 60), but the details are self-verifying and need no justification from Landa. The proof of the readings is the context and not Landa, who is, at best, a sometimes helpful guide. Figure 61 shows the interlocking relationships of many of the readings established by Knorozov. A good starting point is furnished by the interlocking glygers for 'eleven', 'dog', and 'turkey'. The 'eleven' glyger formerly consisted of three graphemes, but one has become illegible. It now reads x.T568:528. The word for 'eleven' in all the languages from which this material might come is *buluc* or some cognate. T568 has been called an ideograph for 'sacrifice', and T528 has been associated with rain, but no one has yet suggested why x-sacrifice-rain should stand for 'eleven'. Phonetically, T568 would have to be either *l-*, in an alphabetic script, or *lu* in a syllabic script, and T528 would have to be *c-*, or *cV*, where V represents an undetermined vowel. The normal glyger for 'dog' consists of T559.568, and the glyger for 'turkey' consists of T528.559. If they are phonetically constituted, there has to be a word for 'turkey' beginning with *c* and ending with a consonant which begins a word for 'dog' ending with *l*. This is satisfied by the words *cu-tz* and *tzu-l*. Assuming a syllabic script, T568 must be *lu*, T528 must be *cu*, and T559 must be *tzu*, and these sounds must fit into other occurrences of the glyphs. Before discussing such other occurrences, there must be some consideration of certain objections which have been made by Eric Thompson. In discussing the 'dog' glyger, Thompson (1959, p. 359) wrote that there are four strong arguments against the reading *tzul*: (*a*) *tzul* is a rare term for dog; (*b*) the element read as *lu* is almost certainly not Landa's *l* (*ele*); (*c*) the order of the two components is once reversed; (*d*) there is good evidence that the compiler of the *Dresden* codex assigned the value *pek* to this term. To the first objection we may answer that, in accordance with a general theory of

mixed scripts, it is precisely the rarer terms which tend to be written phonetically. Perhaps the scribe of *Dresden* had some particular reason for using the word *tzul* and knew that the pictograph for 'dog' would normally be read *pek*. The second "strong argument" has no basis whatsoever, since the reasons for identifying *lu* are independent of any ideas about the Landa alphabet (logically, if not historically). The reversal argument has already been considered and dismissed. This leaves only the "good evidence" for the value *pek*. This consists of the argument that *pek* 'dog' stands for *pek* 'water tank' and, since water tanks are used during a drought, for 'drought'. Thompson likewise attempts to show that the dog is associated with drought and that in colonial usage the word used for 'dog' in this context was *pek*. He further argues that the dog shown in the codices, holding blazing torches, must likewise be a symbol for drought. I will support the latter opinion by pointing out that the *kintunhaab* 'drought' compound, upon which Thompson and I agree, is found on D40b with a picture of the Macaw God holding torches. Hence, holding torches is a reasonable symbol for 'drought', although earlier scholars had usually associated the torches with lightning (cf. Brinton 1895, p. 71). Thompson himself has more recently decided that the 'drought' interpretation was an error and that the reference is rather to relatively rainless lightning storms (Thompson 1964, p. 152). In the same paper, he argues that *tzul* was probably originally a seal and was applied to the new type of domestic dog brought in by the Spaniards. This made it necessary to use the term *tzula* 'water *tzul*' for the seal. He quotes some similar cases to establish the possibility of the process.

I am perfectly willing to admit the association of a dog deity with either drought or lightning but find this inconsistent with the alleged homonymic use for 'water tank'. Thompson's additional argument that the dog glyph is used "rebus fashion" for *pek,* a skin infection, simply seems to me further proof that his thesis of disease divination is incorrect, resting here, as in many other cases, upon a very weak foundation. It may be pointed out that Thompson (1963*c*, p. 119) says that the elements *tzu* and *le* would, in Knorozov's interpretation, be read *tzul*. While this is perfectly true, it should be pointed out that, in that case, Knorozov and I would be most reluctant to accept the meaning 'dog', since 'dog' is composed of *tzu* and *lu,* and available evidence suggests that the "mute" vowel at the end of a word was always the same.

Thompson (1959, pp. 359–360) has also argued that *cutz* was a name for a female turkey, not a male.

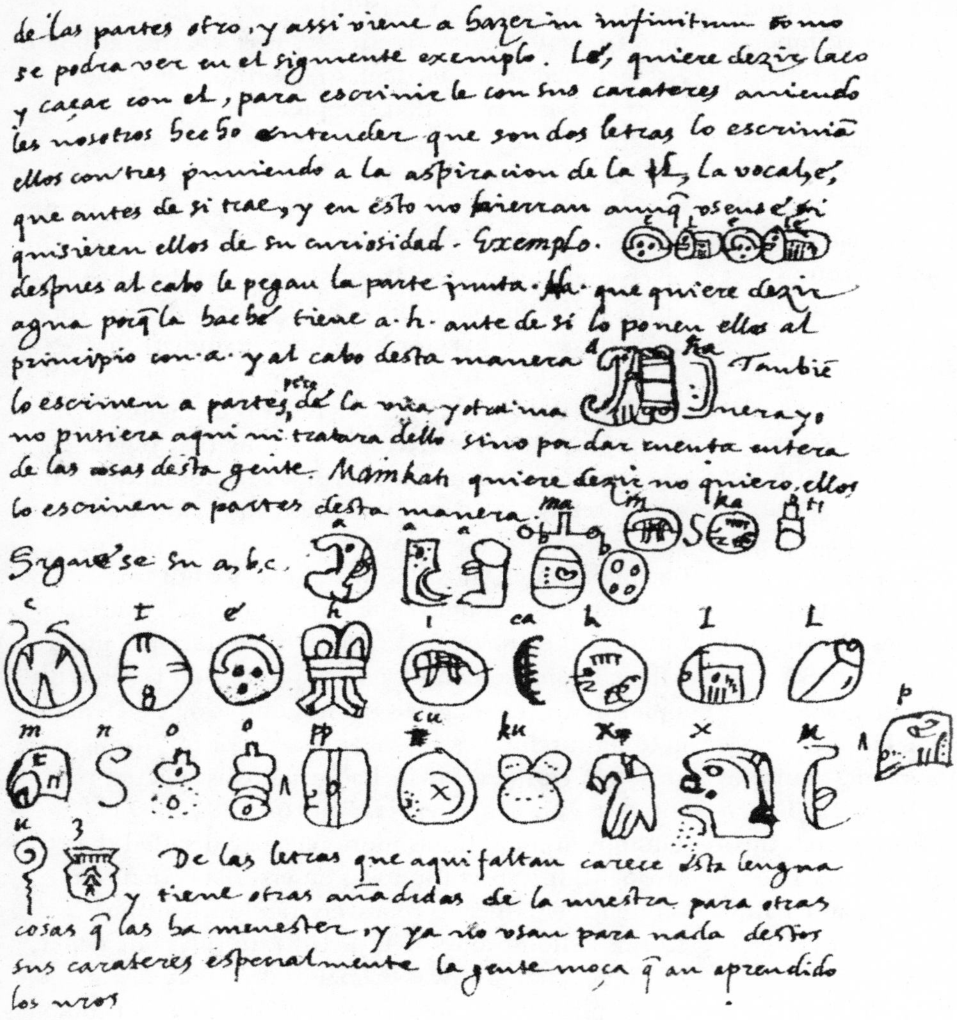
de las partes otro, y assi viene a hazer in infinitum como se podra ver en el siguiente exemplo. Le, quiere dezir laço y caçar con el, para escrivirle con sus carateres aviendo les nosotros hecho entender que son dos letras lo escrivian ellos con tres poniendo a la aspiracion de la h, la vocal e, que antes de si trae, y en esto no hierran aunq̃ usen de e si quisieren ellos de su curiosidad. Exemplo. despues al cabo le pegan la parte junta. Ha que quiere dezir agua porq̃ la hache tiene a. h. ante de si lo ponen ellos al principio con a. y al cabo desta manera Tambiē lo escriven a partes de la una y otra ma nera yo no pusiera aqui ni tratara dello sino por dar cuenta entera de las cosas desta gente. Ma in kati quiere dezir no quiero, ellos lo escriven a partes desta manera.

Siguese su a, b, c.

De las letras que aqui faltan carece esta lengua y tiene otras añadidas de la nuestra para otras cosas q̃ las ha menester, y ya no usan para nada destos sus carateres especialmente la gente moça q̃ an aprendido los nuros

Figure 60. The Landa alphabet.

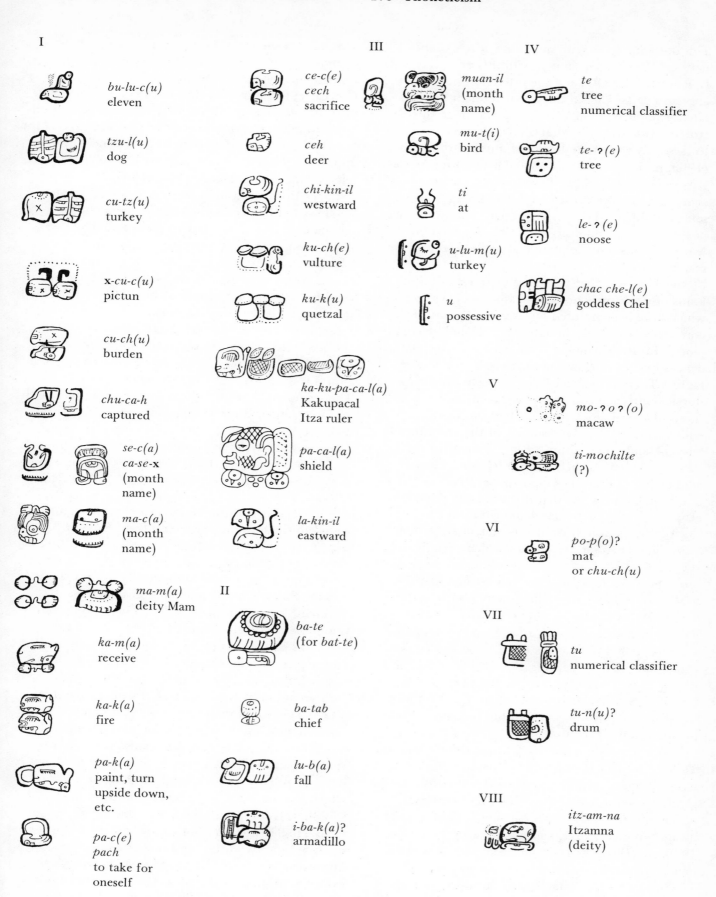

I

bu-lu-c(u)
eleven

tzu-l(u)
dog

cu-tz(u)
turkey

x-*cu-c(u)*
pictun

cu-ch(u)
burden

chu-ca-h
captured

se-c(a)
*ca-se-***x**
(month name)

ma-c(a)
(month name)

ma-m(a)
deity Mam

ka-m(a)
receive

ka-k(a)
fire

pa-k(a)
paint, turn upside down, etc.

pa-c(e)
pach
to take for oneself

II

ba-te
(for *bat-te*)

ba-tab
chief

lu-b(a)
fall

i-ba-k(a)?
armadillo

III

ce-c(e)
cech
sacrifice

ceh
deer

chi-kin-il
westward

ku-ch(e)
vulture

ku-k(u)
quetzal

ka-ku-pa-ca-l(a)
Kakupacal
Itza ruler

pa-ca-l(a)
shield

la-kin-il
eastward

muan-il
(month name)

mu-t(i)
bird

ti
at

u-lu-m(u)
turkey

u
possessive

IV

te
tree
numerical classifier

te-?(e)
tree

le-?(e)
noose

chac che-l(e)
goddess Chel

V

mo-?o?(o)
macaw

ti-mochilte
(?)

VI

po-p(o)?
mat
or *chu-ch(u)*

VII

tu
numerical classifier

tu-n(u)?
drum

VIII

itz-am-na
Itzamna
(deity)

Figure 61. Phonetic compounds (glygers).

This does not agree with modern Yucatec dictionaries, where *cutz* is simply 'wild turkey' (cf. also R. L. Roys 1957, p. 97, and the reference, p. 80, to the ancestral deity, Cit Ah Cutz, which might be translated 'Honoured Father Turkey'). Kaufman reconstructs *kutz* as the Tzeltal-Chorti-Yucatec word for 'turkey'. Even more tellingly, Munro S. Edmonson (1965, p. 63) lists *kutz* as a Quiche word for *Meleagris ocellata,* the wild turkey. In any case, *cutz* was some sort of word for 'turkey', and even if a minor semantic shift had occurred (which Thompson must postulate, in the opposite direction, for modern Yucatec), this is inadequate reason for rejecting the reading.

The mere fact that it is possible to establish the kinds of similarities between script and language which have been pointed out is virtual proof of the correctness of the decipherment. It would be completely futile to attempt to show such correspondences for any language except one of the Mayan family. There is no English word for 'turkey' in which the second syllable or consonant is the same as the first syllable of any word for 'dog'. No word for 'dog' ends with the second consonant of the word for 'eleven', and no word for 'turkey' ends with the same consonant as the word for 'eleven'. Those who maintain that the supporting evidence is stretched to the point that it is unusable should attempt to make a similar demonstration for English or Spanish or Nahua by similar stretching. The evidence so far presented is a mere fraction of the total, which I regard as furnishing far more adequate proof of particular decipherments than the most certain previous decipherments, such as the logograph for *kin*. It should be emphasized that Knorozov and I, accepting the general principles enunciated and the glygers for 'eleven' and 'turkey', would have had to read the 'dog' glyger as *tzul* or at least *tz Vl* whether or not it was found in any dictionary. The fact that such a word is recorded for 'dog' is the strongest possible support, but it is not necessary to the reading *tzul*.

In the previous statements, I have simply said that T528 is *cu*. This is an oversimplification of one of the more complex glyphic problems. T528 is also the day glyph known in Yucatec as Cauac and known by cognate forms in the other calendars. These words mean 'thunder, storm, lightning, rain' (Thompson 1950, p. 87). In the *Dresden* codex, T528, as a day name, appears in two forms, which we may call T528a and T528b. The distinction was first made by Thompson (1950, pp. 267–268), although he did not recognize its full importance and did not make any differentiation in the numbers of his *Catalog*.

Throughout the *Dresden,* the two forms are kept completely distinct except when used for the day Cauac. The glyphs for the months Yax, Zac, and Ceh/Chac; the glyph for God N; the glyph for the year of 360 days; the 'drought' glyph; and the glyger T122.87:528a all contain only T528a. The glygers for 'turkey' and 'burden' contain T528b, which also appears in the unique occurrence of the glyger for 'eleven' and in the so-called pictun glyph.

Cauac does not usually seem to be an adequate reading of either T528a or T528b outside of the day-name series; so we may suppose that T528 was read in more than one way, depending on context. Thompson (1950, pp. 122, 190–191, 269) suggests that T528 must be read *haab,* as the only term besides *tun* which might apply to the 360-day year. He points out that *haab* may consist of *ha* 'water' plus an instrumental (or, better, an agentive) suffix and that the glyph itself seems to represent a segment of the body of the celestial rain dragon. Such an interpretation is fully consistent with the meanings of Cauac. The supposed 'drought' glyph contains *kin, tun* (with an affix), and T528a. Thompson compared it with Yucatec *kintunyaabil,* a known term for 'drought'. Knorozov (1967, p. 30) objected that *yaab* is 'much' and *haab* is 'year', so that Thompson's interpretation is inconsistent. However, the *Book of Chilam Balam of Chumayel* repeatedly uses *yab-* forms where the context makes it abundantly clear that they correspond to the meaning 'year' (cf. R. L. Roys 1933, p. 21, *tu yabil,* translated, p. 81, as 'in that year'). Knorozov (1955a, p. 56) suggests that T528 sometimes appears as an unread determinative for 'time, period'. Since it seems that *haab* in *kintunyaabil* 'drought' cannot mean, literally, 'a year', this interpretation is basically similar to Thompson's. Moreover, it is clear that in Landa's month lists there is no morpheme corresponding to *haab* in the month names Ch'en, Yax, Zac, and Ceh, although the glygers for these months contain T528. I would, therefore, accept Thompson's reading *haab* 'year', with, sometimes, a more indefinite meaning 'period' and a clear possibility that, at least in late times, it was sometimes an unread determinative. Since this glyph appears with 'year' and 'drought', it must be T528a which has the value *haab*. Since 'turkey' contains T528b, this form must have the value *cu*. Knorozov (1967, p. 91, written prior to my article of 1962) confused the two forms and suggested that *cuil* was a Maya word for 'year', although there is no lexical evidence to support this idea. Since the distinction between T528a and T528b is not found on the monuments, one must suppose that context determined whether to read *Cauac, haab,* or *cu*.

In an extensive critique of my defense of Knorozov (Kelley 1962c), Thompson (1963) repeatedly made it clear that he still did not distinguish between T528a and T528b, although that had been one of my important points. Thus, he pointed out at Chichen Itza a glyph for the month Yax with a reduplicated T528 and said that to read it Yaxcuc, "following the thesis of Kelley," is absurd (Thompson 1963, pp. 127–128). I am by no means certain that the glyph is, indeed, reduplicated, but, in any case, the *Dresden* makes it clear that this is T528a, which I read *haab*, following the thesis of Thompson. No doubt, *Yax haab-haab* is equally absurd, but, if it is an unread determinative, reduplication would not affect the meaning. Again, Thompson (1963c, p. 122) says that T528 represents the year of 360 days, whereas when T528 is doubled it stands for 400 of those years. However, it is T528a which is the glyph for the year of 360 days, whereas it is T528b which appears in the pictun glyger, from which one may reasonably assume that it would likewise appear in the baktun glyger.

This leads directly to another element of the dispute over the reading *cu* for T528b. I have said (Kelley 1962b, pp. 281–282) that the reduplicated form T528b:528b found in the pictun glyph must be read *cu-c(u)*, i.e. *cuc*. This follows inevitably from the reading 'turkey' and from the reading 'burden', shortly to be considered. I have gone on to point out that the reduplicated T528 was found for the period which Goodman (1897) called "the cycle" and which modern scholars have called the baktun (see Chapter 2). Thompson points out that Goodman's name is a modern invention and, implicitly, admits the lack of evidence for *baktun* even as a Maya term by his roundabout efforts to defend it. If Goodman could conceptualize the period of 400 tuns as a cycle, I see no reason to think that the Mayas were necessarily more precise. *Cuceb* is found as a term applied to a series of years, and it is a derivative of *cuc-*, which, in Yucatec, refers to roundness and circular movement. Alfredo Barrera Vásquez (Barrera Vásquez and Rendón 1948, p. 167) entitles the series "Cuceb o rueda profetica de los años tunes de un katun 5 Ahau [*Cuceb* or prophetic cycle of the *tun* years of a Katun 5 Ahau]." Thompson (1963c, pp. 125–126) refers to this as the "21 year-bearers," but it seems to me that the scribe may have regarded the twenty tuns forming a katun as a unity which he called a *cuceb*, although the names are those of the year-bearers. My appraisal of this particular source is very different from Thompson's. I believe that the existing copies derive from an original written in 1596 (miswritten 1544 in the existing copies) and that, allowing for copying error, it is one of our most important sources for the

mythology of the calendar system. The fact that its katun sequence disagrees with that which is necessary for the Thompson correlation does not seem to me as clear-cut evidence of the ignorance of the original writers as it does to Thompson. R. L. Roys (1949, p. 165) translates the heading *cuceb* as 'that which revolves'. If the tuns of a katun could be 'that which revolves', I see no reason to think that a baktun might not also be 'that which revolves'. Neither one is a cycle in the strictest use of the term. Thompson's assumption that the recorded tuns are merely part of a fifty-two—year cycle, to which the scribe should have applied the term *cuceb*, and that *cuceb* therefore could only be applied to a re-entering cycle is simply an assumption. I have also pointed out the apparent substitution of T528.528 for an animal head in the supposed glyphs of a ruler at Naranjo. Here *cu-c(u)* may be replacing *cuc* 'squirrel' as a lineage name. Absence of proof that the animal is a squirrel and the presence of unexplained affixes reduce the plausibility of this contention. Thompson (1963c, p. 126) argues that T528:528 should be read *baktun,* because *bakhaab* was used in colonial sources for this period and, I suppose, because he reads T528 as *haab.* Given his premises, I would have expected him rather to suggest that *bakhaab* was a preferable reading. I see no reason why two *haab* glyphs should indicate *bak* 'four hundred', a reading which seems to me in complete contrast with the importance which the Mayas normally gave to numbers. To write *bakhaab* or *baktun* without the *bak* seems to me as strange as, apparently, many of my suggestions seem to Thompson.

Thompson goes on to argue that *if* the "duplicated cauac" is phonetic, then the katun glyph should also "logically" be written phonetically. I have seen no evidence whatsoever that this type of logic is a factor in the use of phonetic glyphs rather than logographs, in the Maya script or any other script. In any case, I see very little evidence that the Classic Period name for this period was *katun.* The katun glyph on D60b and on D61 has T528a rather than T528b; so it corresponds to *haab* rather than *cu* in terms of my premises. Thompson's attempt to read, for me, *cacuac(a)tun* is, therefore, a misrepresentation of my position. I suspect that the entire top half of this glyph forms a single grapheme, and I doubt very much that it was read either as *ka* (since I think T669 is *ka*) or as *kal* 'twenty' (since the 'twenty' glyph is well known). I am also unwilling to believe that *katun* derives from **kaltun,* as postulated by Thompson (1963c, p. 127).

As a further complicating factor, Thompson has also suggested that T528 is sometimes read *ku* or *kul.*

This leads directly to a consideration of T528b.601. T601 has been considered an ideograph for 'burden' and has been read *cuch* by Thompson (most recently, 1965a, p. 4). The discussion in Chapter 8 has shown that Seler regarded the entire glyger as meaning 'burden'. Certainly, the glyger is repeatedly found in contexts where some such meaning is demanded. Insofar as I know, T601, when it does not have T528 preceding it, is never found in a context where the meaning 'burden' is plausible. Thompson argues that the burden is always a divine one when T528 is present and, therefore, that the probable reading is *ku* 'god, divine'. He also bases the reading on the representation of posts (D26–28; Thompson 1964, p. 150) which, he says, have the *cauac* sign in them. This is somewhat misleading, as they have only the "grapes" element, which is the factor distinguishing T528a from T528b; the entire glyph is not present. If one assumes that this distinguishing feature is adequate to suggest a connection with T528, it should be with the *haab* series, rather than with the *cu* series, of which the 'burden' glyph is a member. The fact that the scribes were careful to keep T528a and T528b apart seems to me adequate to demolish Thompson's weakly based suggestion that both should be read *ku*. An earlier suggestion of Thompson (1950, p. 267) that T528b.601 might be read *cuch haab* may be dismissed, both because it implies that T601 alone may be *cuch* and because it confuses T528a, *haab*, with T528b, *cu*. It is, instead, clear that this is a typical syllabic reading, with T528b as *cu* and T601 as *chV*.

The inherent vowel of T601 must be *-u*, giving *chu*, since the glyger T601:25 with affixed 181 (miswritten by Thompson, 1962, p. 225, with 181 between the two graphemes of the glyger) is found above pictures of bound individuals. The inscriptional equivalent, which should have the same number, is T532:25, found associated with representations of captives. Tzotzil *chuk* 'ties, imprisons' and Chorti *chuki* 'to tie, capture' are clear contextual equivalents. Some possibility of variation is suggested by Quiche *chuq'abah* 'take by force, seize, violate', which has a glottalized form.

T25 is also the terminal grapheme of the glygers for the months Mac and Zec (in the *Dresden*). For this reason, *cV* is preferable to *kV* in the sequence T601:25. Delaying for a moment the consideration of Mac, I should point out that the normal inscriptional form of the glyger for the month corresponding to Yucatec Zec is in reverse order. I have suggested (Kelley 1962b, pp. 284–285) that this corresponds in part to the equivalent Chol name for the month, Cazeu. There is no *u* element in the glyger, and T130 is usually, but not always, present. The latter should be read *aan*. Hence, the usual inscriptional form should be Cazeaan, rather than Cazeu. Since this is clearly a compound form, apparently derivable in both instances from a root *caze-*, a certain amount of minor variation is expectable. The presence of *caze* in Cazeaan and Cazeu suggests that T25 should have the value *ca*, which is the value given it in the Landa alphabet. By the same token, Z1331a (misread as two graphemes by Thompson) must be *se* (Yuc. *ze*). It corresponds to Landa's letter *c* (pronounced in Spanish *se*). Thompson (1963c, p. 133) points out that Landa's version of the glyger for Zec seems to have *-aan* and lacks T25; so presumably it should be Zean, if this is not another one of Landa's errors.

In a similar way, T74, the initial grapheme of the glyger of the month Mac, is Landa's *ma*. However, here we get into a more complex problem. The glyger appears in a number of different forms. Frequently, T74 is followed by T626, the turtle shell. I had assumed that this stood for *ma- aac*, the shell of the turtle standing for *aac* 'turtle'. Thompson (1963c, p. 137) points out that the turtle shell was called, in Yucatec, *mac;* it was also sometimes called *box,* and *coc ac* was a name for 'turtle'. Barthel (1955a, pp. 21–22) had read the turtle-shell glyph as *coc* in a plausible context. It may, therefore, be that *ma* is used as a phonetic supplement to show that one should read *mac* rather than *coc*. In many cases, T74 is followed by the fish-head glyph or the fish glyph, two allographs of T25 (Fig. 45). Here I presume the simple reading *ma-c(a)*. In some cases, T74 is replaced by T502 (=T557), which I regard as an allograph or near allograph of T74, possibly differing in vowel length; in these examples T502 is followed by T25, and I again assume a reading *ma-c(a)*. Occasionally one finds the combination T74:626:25.25. Anticipating my willingness to adopt *mac*, Thompson (1963c, pp. 137–138) points out that this would give *(ma)mac(caca)*, with three phonetic determinants for one easily recognizable main sign, also identifiable by context. He suggests that this would be a great exaggeration—a suggestion with which I must agree, only pointing out that it is the Mayas' exaggeration, not mine, since it is quite clear that they could and did represent the month, frequently, by only two graphemes. I have no functional explanation to offer for the reduplicated *ca,* but neither does it correspond with Thompson's formulation of aesthetic doubling.

Thompson suggests that the older name of Mac was Chantemac, known from Pokomchi and Kekchi calendar lists, and that this would correspond to a hypothetical Yucatec *Tantemac. He then reads T74 as *tan* and T626 as *mac*. The known *te* glyph does not appear, nor is there any possible allograph for it. The combination of T74 as *tan* with the fish head (confused with the *xoc* fish and given the meaning 'count') contains no element which can be read *mac* by Thompson's interpretations, suggesting that phoneticists are not the only ones who must occasionally stage Hamlet without the Prince of Denmark.

The reading of T74 as *ma* is found in doubled form on the new-year pages of *Dresden*. It can only be read *ma-m(a)*. This glyger is preceded by *u*, preceded in turn by a glyger which, from the structure of the phrase, must refer to the opossum below, which is assigned a different color in each of the four years. The passage must be read 'Opossum *u* Mam'. Thompson (1963c, p. 125) says that a reading 'its Mam' has no meaning and is ungrammatical, since *u* 'its' always goes with the object possessed, and not with an individual. In this case, the relationship is attributive, with *u* indicating membership in a class for a particular year: 'The Black Opossum is the Mam *of the year*', or words to this effect. The grammatical construction seems to me as plausible in Maya as its parallel in English. Thompson argued that the Mams are malignant and that the associations of the opossum are with abundance and fertility; hence the two cannot be identical. Earlier, he had written (Thompson 1950, p. 133), "Mam . . . is generally regarded as an evil god in the Alta Verapaz, although in southern British Honduras, where he is merged with the mountain-valley gods, his aspect is benignant." *The Book of Chilam Balam of Chumayel* (R. L. Roys 1933, p. 153) calls the *tolil och,* the 'actor opossum', "he who lies in wait for you on all fours" and classes him with the "fox chieftain," the "blood-sucking chieftain," and the "avaricious ones of the town." It would seem that there was a certain ambivalence about Mams, opossums, and Bacabs, with whom Thompson identifies the opossums. The Mam is specified as the deity of the five days ending the year, and these passages refer to the ending period of the year. In context, the meaning 'Mam' makes excellent sense. Thompson's reading, *u tan* 'the time of', does not make sense in the whole passage cited. I have attempted to show that Mam and 'opossum' are legitimate equivalents because the Tzeltal months 'little *uch*' and 'big *uch*' (*uch* being Tzel. for 'opossum') correspond to Cakchiquel Nabei Mam and Rucab Mam (Kelley 1962c). Thompson disingenuously argues that the correspondence does not prove anything, because it is not sure that the months correspond, although he himself thinks they do. I think it is not impossible that there is some degree of correspondence between Mams and Bacabs. Thompson (1950, p. 133) notes that the Kekchi bury a Mam at Easter, and colonial sources

(Barrera Vásquez and Rendón 1948, p. 100) indicate that Bacab was somehow identified with Christ and was killed by being tied on a pole, indicating that Mams and Bacabs were somewhat equated in colonial times. Thompson cites good evidence for identifying opossums with Bacabs. This evidence seems no better than the evidence for the equation of Mams and opossums. Perhaps the relationship between Bacabs and Mams may explain this apparent discrepancy. In any case, I do not think the *mam* reading can be rejected.

Thompson's reading of the 'south' glyph as *tan-yax* has nothing to recommend it and is no support for the identification of T74 as *tan* rather than *ma*. The inscriptional prototype of the second grapheme is not *yax*, and there seems to be no good evidence that a word *tan-yax* could possibly have the meaning 'south' even if the combination is grammatically possible. For possible use of T74 as an independent grapheme, *ma* 'no, not', see Chapter 10.

T74 is also found, inverted, following T669. Thompson (1963c, p. 145) has suggested the reading *lah* 'end' for T669, a grapheme showing a hand with death infixes. He had previously (and, I believe, correctly) suggested *lah* as a possible alternate reading of a different hand glyph (see Chapter 7). Barthel (1964a, p. 224) read T669 as *kab* 'hand', having finally rejected an earlier Thompson suggestion, *et*. Knorozov (1955a, p. 88, nos. 149, 150) read T669:74 as *kam-* 'to receive'. Another earlier Thompson alternate suggestion for this glyger had been *kamac* 'to receive' (Thompson 1950, p. 266). The Thompson suggestion was based largely on context. Knorozov, however, was simply combining T669, identified as Landa's *ka*, with T74, Landa's *ma*, giving *ka-m(a)*. Barthel's arguments in favor of his logographic reading are too lengthy and complex to reproduce here but revolve around the combinations T669.122 and T669.604. The affix T122 seems to be a representation of smoke or flames, and Barthel reads the combination as *kab-kak* 'fire hand', a Yucatec name for an incense burner. T122 is, however, frequently found in contexts where the reading *kak* seems inappropriate (see fuller discussion, Chapter 8). Barthel reads the second sequence as *kab-ku* 'god hand', a euphemism for the sacrificial knife. Both of these are reasonably appropriate in the general context of the ceremonial inscriptions of Chichen Itza but seem to me inappropriate in the particular contexts in which they are found. I regard the sequence T669:604 as a part of the much longer glyger *ka-ku-pa-ca-la* (see further discussion near the end of this chapter).

The best evidence in favor of the Knorozov reading *ka* is in a context first pointed out by Barthel

(1955a). Here we find the reduplicated form T669.669, in the inscriptions of Chichen Itza (Fig. 112), associated with passages which contain the 'drill' glyph and which closely parallel passages in the codices. Barthel argued that the Chichen Itza passages referred to the drilling of fire, as the codices certainly do. Strikingly, the logographic(?) glyger for 'fire' is entirely absent at Chichen Itza. Instead, Barthel has to depend on the presence of various affixes which seem to have grammatical functions which make it unlikely that they would also convey the meaning 'fire'. In Knorozov's interpretation, T669.669 would be read *ka-k(a)* (proto-Maya **k'ak'* 'fire'). The evidence is not quite as good as that which we find for some glygers in the codices, but it is very good.

We also find the sequence T74:669 (sometimes with grammatical affixes). Thompson has used this reversal of the order of T669:74 as proof that the order of glyphs was not always fixed in a glyger and, hence, that phonetic values were probably not involved. In this case, reversing *ka-m(a)* 'to receive' gives *ma-k(a)*. Among the meanings of Yucatec *mak* are 'handle, manipulate, adjust' (Whorf 1933, p. 14). I do not think that any of these is actually the meaning of the glyger T74:669, which, like T669:74, refers to the action of a god who is holding out his hand with something on it. These meanings do suggest that cognates with not too dissimilar meanings could express the action and that a phonetic rendering *mak* should not be ruled out.

One of the clearest evidences in favor of phoneticism is supplied by the redoubled glyger T604.604, found in *Dresden* as the name of the quetzal. The proto-Maya for 'quetzal' is **k'uk'*, showing the doubled consonant which must be present if the glyger is phonetic. T604, in the inscriptions, is regarded by Thompson as a single grapheme. The equivalent form in the codices was transcribed by Zimmermann as two graphemes, Z84:1302. Although Z84 does occur as a separable grapheme, I think the phonetic evidence supports the view that T604 is only one grapheme. The glyph consists of two dotted ovals above and a basket-shaped element below, which is crosshatched in the inscriptions and blank in the codices. The lower element is outlined by a series of dots, which are on the outside in the codices and on the monuments except at Chichen Itza, where they are surrounded by an outside line. Landa gives for *ku* a simpler glyph, consisting of two dotted ovals above and a near circle below, with a line of dots marking off the circle. Thompson (1963c, p. 128) argues that there is only a superficial similarity between T604 and Landa's *ku,* since the latter consists of a prefix and a main sign, and the main sign is not

like T604. In this, he is opposing not only Brasseur de Bourbourg, Cyrus Thomas, Knorozov, and myself, who might be presumed to be prejudiced in favor of phoneticism, but also Seler, Zimmermann, and Barthel, all of whom regard T604 as identical with Landa's *ku*. Presumably to them, as to myself, the dotted near circle of Landa seems like the dot-outlined blank of the codices, with the line on the outside, as at Chichen Itza, rather than on the inside, as in the codices.

With this establishment of independent evidence for Landa's *ca, ka, cu,* and *ku,* it seems appropriate to consider the nature of the Landa alphabet, since these glyphs are crucial to understanding what degree of acceptance we may give to that important document (Fig. 60). When Landa came to the letter *k* (pronounced *ka* in Spanish), his informant supplied two glyphs. The first, Landa transcribed *ca;* the second, he transcribed *k;* however, the latter is transcribed, in an example, as *ka*. When Landa came to the letter *q* (pronounced *ku* in Spanish), he was again given two glyphs: the first he transcribed *cu* and the second *ku*. The distinction between *ca* and *cu* on the one hand and *ka* and *ku* on the other, as used in all later documents, is that the latter two are glottalized. This is likewise the distinction in the previously proposed decipherments. The convention of writing *c* and *k* for the sounds which a modern linguist would write *k* and *k'* had already been established by some of the more linguistically minded Spanish missionaries when Landa arrived in Yucatán (Durbin 1969). Despite the difficulty which Spanish speakers would have had in distinguishing these sounds, where they were found in paired opposition, as in this case, it should have been possible to recognize the difference. This strongly suggests that Landa's informant insisted on the paired opposition of these sounds with reference to the native writing system. That Landa was frequently unable to hear this difference and subsequently misrecorded many words is not really relevant to decipherment. When Thompson argues, in spite of this distinction, that Landa's *cu* may really have been *ku,* because Landa did misrecord in other instances, he seems to me to completely miss the importance of Landa's evidence.

There is likewise an important lesson to be learned from Landa's recording of a distinction between *ca* and *cu,* or between *ka* and *ku*. The names for *k* and *q* are the only instance in the names of the letters for the Spanish alphabet where a single initial consonantal sound is followed by a different vowel. The distinction, then, implies both that different vowels required completely different glyphs, i.e., that Landa was recording part of a syllabary, and that the glyphs given corresponded to the names of the Spanish letters, rather than to the sounds represented by the Spanish letters. The latter conclusion can be reinforced by other data. Landa's first *b* is the footprint between two lines, T301, long held to represent Yucatec *be* 'road' (Tozzer 1941, p. 170), and corresponding to the Spanish name for the letter *b*, which is *be.* Landa likewise gives three examples of how the glyphs were used, but the authoritarian Spanish bishop had to explain to his informant how one should write, and the end result indicates that both parties were quite confused. Landa writes (Tozzer 1941, pp. 169–170), "*Le* means a noose and to hunt with it; in order to write it with their characters, we having made them understand that there are two letters, they wrote it with three, putting as an aspiration of the *l*, the vowel, *e*, which it has before it"; as finally written, the example has four characters, rather than the one which the informant clearly wished to write, the two which Landa considered correct, or the three which represented the informant's next attempt. The example gives Landa's letter *e* (labeled *e*), then Landa's letter *l*, (labeled *l*), next Landa's letter *e* again (still labeled *e*), and finally Landa's letter *l* again (this time labeled *lé*). The example suggests that when Landa asked how they would write *le*, the informant simply wrote T612 (the *l* of the alphabet). Then Landa impatiently "explained" that there were two letters (Spanish *l e*, pronounced *ele e*). The informant proceeded to write three—Landa's *e* (T542), Landa's *l*, and, finally, *e* again "putting as an aspiration of the *l*, the vowel, *e*, which it has before it." Landa then, apparently, in the time-honored tradition of European spelling, asked whether one spelled 'noose' as *l e*, *le* (which he would have pronounced *ele e*, *le*). The informant, doubtless wondering if Landa was not a little crazy, would then have written what was, for him, *e le e le*. Thompson (1959, p. 351) has a beautifully imaginative picture of the scene between Landa and his presumed informant, Nachi Cocom. He suggests that Landa's *e* is actually *elel* 'to burn' and argues against the view that T612 is *le*, suggesting that the whole sequence was *elel le elel le*. This seems to me to make nonsense out of what can be explained rather easily from what Landa himself writes. When, in the alphabet, the informant was asked how to write *ele* in one character, he simply took the latter part of the sequence and wrote *le*.

The same relationship is found between the letter *h* of the alphabet and Landa's second example. Landa writes: "*Ha* means water, and, because the sound of the letter *H* has *a h*, in front of it, they write it at the beginning with *a* and at the end in this way. . . . They also wrote it in parts, but in both ways" (Tozzer

1941, p. 170). The sound of the letter *h*, in Spanish, is *ache*. The labels of the three graphemes used by the informant to write what he thought was wanted are misleading. Landa's *a* and Landa's *h* have jointly been labeled *a;* clearly, they should have been labeled *a-che*, that is, the informant's attempt to write *h*, with which Landa apparently told him that *ha* began. We are then left with one grapheme, which is labeled *ha*, as if it represented the whole word, but which may be the informant's attempt to represent the *a*, which he must have been told was part of the right way to write *ha*. However, it is not one of the three graphemes which the informant gave as *a* in the alphabet.

One of the glygers for a goddess who has been identified as (Ix) Chel is T109.145:612 (Fig. 61). The glyph T109 is the logograph for *chac*, probably here intended for 'red', a known prefix of the name of the goddess Ix Chel in colonial times. Nothing in the glyger corresponds to Ix. T145 is very similar to Landa's *h;* if the same, it should be read *che*; T612 is Landa's *le*. Read together, phonetically, they give *che-l(e)*. In the *Madrid*, T145 sometimes appears without T612; I do not know whether this indicates that it was sometimes a logograph for *chel* or whether it is another example of the supposed dyslexia of the *Madrid* scribe. Landa's *le* also appears, followed by Landa's *e*, above a picture of a turkey in a noose, on M91a. Cyrus Thomas naturally regarded this as proof of the alphabetic nature of the script, reading *l-e*, much as Landa might have done. I, on the other hand, think that the supposed vowel glyphs should actually be understood as CV-type glyphs, in which C is the glottal stop (ʔ). We know that this is true of the glyph for *u*, which is actually *ʔu*, the possessive particle. Assuming that *e* is really *ʔe*, I would assume that 'noose' was here written *le-ʔ(e)* or *leʔ*. This is, in fact, the correct form of the word for 'noose'. The Thompson *Catalog* (1962, no. 612) indicates that this is the only occurrence in the codices of this combination, although Thompson (1959, p. 351) says that the same glyger is found on the next page above a picture of a deer caught by a deadfall. The latter does not seem to me to be the same glyph, but the glyph is quite badly eroded, and it is hard to be certain. Thompson writes, "Of the approximately 99 other occurrences of Landa's *le* element, not one seems to belong in the fold with the one occupant pictured on Madrid 91 *a*" (ibid.). Since none of the other ninety-nine have the final glottal stop indicated, this is not surprising. I suspect that a convention of ignoring a final glottal stop was used in the area where the *Dresden* codex was produced, for the *Dresden* scribes have T87 (*te*) as 'tree', where a more correct rendering would be *teʔ*. In the *Madrid* in approximately similar contexts we find T87:542, which I would interpret as *te-ʔ(e)* or *teʔ*, in full agreement with the similar recording of *leʔ*.

Similar evidence is provided by Z1331a, already discussed as being in what seems to me a probative context in the month Zec/Cazeu. This is Landa's *c*. It has already been pointed out that this letter is called in Spanish *ce*, i.e., *se* (which would be written in Yucatec *ze*). This is one of the few cases where Knorozov originally misunderstood what happened. Although his *Catalog* (Knorozov 1967, p. 100) correctly has *se*, his text discussion (Knorozov 1967, p. 23) was apparently written earlier, when he supposed that Spanish *ce* corresponded to Yucatec *ce* (linguistic *ke*), for he explains that Landa's copyist mistakenly wrote *t* for the next letter (following *c* in the alphabet) when he should have written *k*, giving *ce/ke* as a parallel to the *ca/ka* and *cu/ku* examples. Actually, *c* is *se*, and the *t* which follows it is as close as the informant could come to Landa's *d* (named *de*). Since *d* is somewhat closer to the glottalized form, this probably represents *t'e*, especially since Thompson has shown that T87 is *te*.

There is little to say of the rest of the Landa alphabet at the present time. Landa's *i* appears at the beginning of glygers for a certain type of owl (*icim*) and for the armadillo (*ibach*), but there are difficulties in both readings. Landa's first *o* appears, doubled, as part of the glyger for the macaw in the *Dresden* (T582.296.296). I formerly suggested a reading **mo-ʔoʔ(o)* (Kelley 1962b, p. 307), based on Yucatec *moo*, following Manuel J. Andrade's (1955) statement that a double vowel at the end of a word always indicates the presence of a glottal stop. I would now suggest the possibility that the Yucatec convention of writing double vowels at the end of a word reflected, at least in part, a convention of the native writing system and that the glyger T582.296.296 may stand rather for **moʔ(o)*. The principal difficulties with this interpretation are that it is inconsistent with the writing of *te* in the same manuscript and that one would think the presence of a glottal stop was adequately indicated by *o/ʔo* itself. Lounsbury and Coe (1967) have shown that T582 is to be read *mo* in the glyger *mochilte*. For the special complexities of this reading, see Chapter 6. The glyph is very similar to that for the month Mol, the latter being distinguished by an infix resembling or identical with the glyph for 'black'. Quiche *mol* 'ring' seems descriptively apt for the glyph. It has not been demonstrated that the two glyphs are used interchangeably in any contexts, and their partial phonetic similarity may be accidental.

I regard Landa's *m* as being T608, which I regard, in turn, as a section of the body of a fish. Knorozov (1967, p. 103, no. 374) makes the same identification of T608 as a fish but reads *tz'u* (Yuc. *dzu*). The vowel is probably derived from the principle of synharmony (see below), since most of the compounds of T608 are with glyphs ending in -*u*. If the identification of T608 as Landa's *m* is acceptable, T608 should read *me*, in accordance with the general interpretations of the Landa alphabet here proposed. For other identifications of T608, see Chapter 5.

Landa's *n* is an S-shaped figure which has long been regarded as a tail (Yucatec *ne*). There is, however, some possibility that it stands for 'stink worm'.

A few of the Landa glyphs cannot be equated with known glyphs from the codices or monuments, but most of them are recognizable. I now think that virtually all of the Landa glyphs are correct representations of Mayan CV glyphs and that any error present has been introduced through misunderstandings between Landa and his informant. Even those Landa glyphs for which there is no good contextual support from other sources have been introduced at the appropriate points in Figure 62, which gives a summary of known syllabary readings. By observing the compounds which these glyphs form with others, it is possible to establish a fair probability of the inherent vowels of still undeciphered glyphs, in accordance with the principle of synharmony. This principle was first established by Knorozov, who pointed out that in most cases where there is a reading of CV^1-CV^2, the second vowel, V^2, is identical with the first, even though the second vowel is not pronounced. A check of the cases which seemed to be best established showed that this principle held in about five out of six cases. Thus, if an unknown phonetic glyph appears in glygers with *bu, cu, chu, tzu, mu,* and *te*, it is highly likely that the vowel of the glyph is -*u*. The reliability of this principle decreases markedly with fewer cases, but it may still furnish a useful lead or suggestion. Because of this type of interlocking, decipherments tend to fall into phonetic groups linked by a common final vowel.

Knorozov formerly believed that this was a purely graphic device, as it may be, but Dell Hymes drew to my attention the fact that Whorf thought that the Mayan language family was related to the Penutian languages of California; in these languages, the typical phonetic pattern for nouns is CVCV, in which the second vowel is normally but not always the same as the first. Adequate comparative studies to check this have not been made, but when they are, it will be of great interest to see whether the recorded silent vowel implicit in the CV syllabary in Maya agrees with the final vowel of presumed cognates in the Penutian languages.

A certain number of additional glyphs seem to have been correctly deciphered (Fig. 61). Thompson has shown the correctness of *ti* (T59), from Landa's third example, and first established the readings of *te* and *tu* (see Chapter 10). I have maintained that T89, T90, T91, and T92 are nonmeaningful variants (allographs) of a single glyph, to be read *tu*. The glyger T90.829 is found on M22b with a picture of drumming and on pages 89d–90d with a series of seven pictures, one of which is drumming; none of the others are, and Seler's association of the glyger with music seems inadequately based, as does my own suggestion that T829 might be *nV*, from *tu-nV* 'a drum, to drum'. Also on M22b is T90.608, *tu*, plus the glyph I read *me*, which would give *tum(e)*, a term which might also be appropriate. These are, at best, only plausible suggestions.

The inverted *ahau*, T534, appears preceding the *kin* glyph in the glyger for 'east', *likin* in modern Yucatec, assimilated from an earlier *lakin*, also recorded in colonial texts. A reading *li, la* has long been accepted, although not absolutely proven (see Chapter 3). Similarly, the glyph for the day Manik, T671 (=T219), which normally corresponds to days named Deer in other Mesoamerican calendars, is found in the glyger for 'west', Yucatec *chikin*. It also sometimes seems to mean 'deer', Yucatec *ceh*, Quiche *ceh, cieh*, Cholan *chij*. The glyger T604:671 means 'vulture'; the first glyph is *ku*, and a known word for vulture is *kuch*. R. L. Roys (1957, p. 130) points out that the place name Tikuch is also sometimes written Kuche, which normally means 'cedar'. However, *che* is one of the four possible interpretations of T671, the others being *ce, chi*, and *ci*. The *che* of 'cedar' derives from an earlier **te* and is presumably distinct in origin both from the *che* of Chel (see above) and from T671. The latter may well represent an earlier *ce*, as McQuown has suggested to me that a former **k* (=Yucatec *c*) became *c* initially and *ch* finally in Yucatec, becoming *ch* initially and finally in Quiche. T671:671 appears in scenes of sacrifice and offering. I believe it represents Yucatec *cech* 'sacrifice', and Ximénez's dictionary of Cakchiquel, Quiche, and Zutuhil (Ximénez n.d.) gives *chech* 'sufrir y pedir algo a mano' ['to suffer and to ask for something by hand'], a reasonably clear cognate. *Che* seems slightly more likely than other suggestions.

Knorozov has read T715 as *pa*. The crosshatched version of the same glyph is called T586 by Thompson and is an allograph of T1023 and of T602. It is found in a glyger T715:671, which Knorozov reads *pach* 'to take for one's self'. In the glyger T715:669, *pa-k(a)*, it is found in appropriate contexts for the meanings 'to paint, varnish' and 'to swarm' (of bees),

as well as probably 'to bring honey'. Despite the lack of a fully probative context, it seems a highly likely decipherment.

The five-grapheme glyger, or clause, T669.604. 586:25.534, found repeatedly at Chichen Itza, can be read, in terms of previous identifications, as *ka-ku-pa-ca-l(a)*. It appears in contexts which suggest it is a personal name, and Kakupacal was reputed to have been a "valorous Itza captain." The name means 'Fire His Shield'. The sequence T602.25:534, with variations in position and use of allographs but with no change in sequence, is found repeatedly at Palenque in association with a pictograph for a shield, which it sometimes seems to replace completely. This constitutes contextual support for the meaning 'shield', which follows inevitably from the reading *pa-ca-l(a)*. Occasional reduplication of the final T534 is probably grammatical, although this cannot yet be certainly shown from context. It will be noted that three of these glyphs are given by Landa (although one is challenged by Thompson), that one was long accepted because of its use in *likin, lakin*, and that only *pa* depends on a reading first established by Knorozov. Two of the glyphs, *ka* and *ku*, are established by reduplication in near-probative contexts, and there is good evidence for *ca*. The obtaining of a sequence of this length which is meaningful and appropriate is the best possible type of evidence in favor of the correctness of the decipherment and of the general principles upon which it rests. Barthel's different reading of the first two graphemes of the sequence as *kab ku* has been mentioned. He attempts to establish something of the context of the last three but does not suggest readings.

Thompson's *Catalog* identifies his T515 with Z1363a, a reading which seems to me rather doubtful. The glyger Z1363a:1363a appears in the context of work on a loom(?) and has been read by Knorozov as *po-p(o)*, i.e., *pop* 'mat'. The main reason for preferring this to *chu-ch(u)* is that a different (though similar) glyph has already been read *chu* on what seem to me better grounds (see above).

The month Muan is written at one point in the *Dresden* by T19:130:116. T116 also appears suffixed to the head of the *muan* bird as the name of this month. Reasons for accepting Knorozov's reading *-il* for this affix are given elsewhere but are not relevant to the reading of T19:130, which must correspond to the head of the *muan* bird. Since there is very good evidence for regarding T130 as *aan*, T19 must be *mu*. In the bird passages, we find the name of a bird followed by *u* and the glyger T19:59. T59 is Landa's *ti*, so that the combination must read *u mut(i)* 'its bird' (or 'tidings'). This is a thoroughly convincing con-

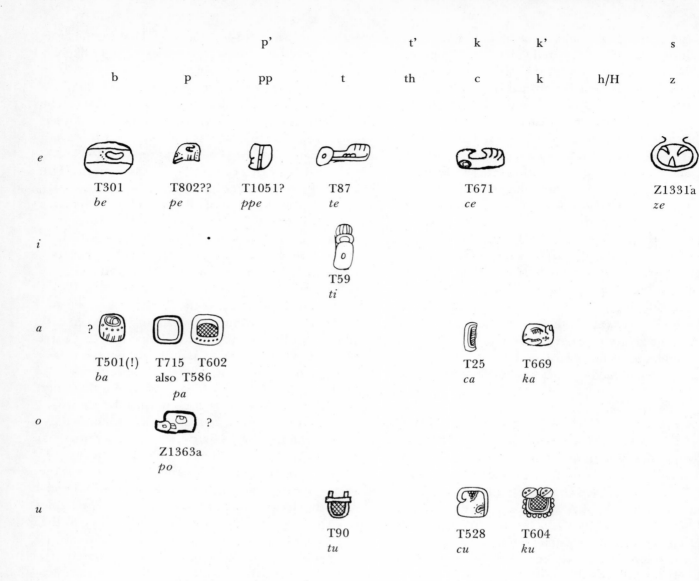

Figure 62. The Maya syllabary: a tabular summary of known CV readings.

		c		ɔ'	č	č'	w		ʔ
n	m	l	tz	dz	ɔ	ch	čh	u	y

ne

T608
me

T612
le

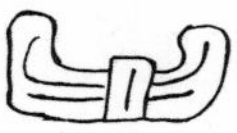

T145
che

T542
ʔe

T679
ʔi

T23
na

?

T74
ma

or

T534
la

T238   T15   T743
ʔa

T582
mo

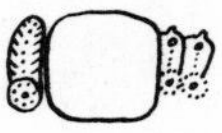

T99
ʔo

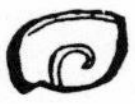

T19
mu

T568b
lu

T559
tzu

T532
chu

T1
ʔu

Figure 63. Glyphs read as CV by Knorozov; validity not adequately demonstrated.

text. In the list of deities in the *Dresden* Venus table, we find the glyger T1.568:19. This must read *u-lu-m(u)*, i.e., *ulum*, another name for 'turkey'. Reasons for thinking that this deity may have been a turkey god are given elsewhere (see Chapter 4, section on God N).

The glyph T23 is one of the more puzzling affixes. It is one of the few affixes which are sometimes present and sometimes absent without obvious changes either in grammatical structure or in meaning. It is the last grapheme of the glyger of the deity usually identified as Itzamna, and here it is virtually always present. This strongly suggests a reading *na*, which has been Knorozov's reading. Barthel's reading *al* seems to me unlikely. If Knorozov is correct, T23 may be present on such glyphs as *caan* 'sky' as a phonetic determinant. However, it appears so commonly in such contexts, and other glyphs appear so rarely in such contexts, that this explanation does not seem likely. Its use in the glygers T23:25:23 and T25:556:23 offers some support for the *na* reading; since T25 is *ca*, these glygers seem to be phonetically composed, and the principle of synharmony would suggest that T23 ended in *-a*.

The glyph labelled T556 above is involved in one of the more complex confusions of the Thompson *Catalog*. Zimmermann correctly distinguished Z1321, the *imix* glyph of the calendar, sometimes to be read *naab*, from Z1360 and from Z1361. T558 is the equivalent in the codices for T556 of the inscriptions and corresponds to Z1360. It also corresponds to the type glyph which Thompson uses for T501. Under T501, however, Thompson includes the *imix/naab* glyph, which comprises most of the occurrences of T501. Z1361 corresponds to T557 of the codices, of which the inscriptional form is T502. I have suggested that this is an allograph of T74, *ma*. Thus, Thompson has given five numbers to three graphemes but has still not adequately distinguished among them.

I have arbitrarily used T558 both for the codical occurrences of Z1360 and for the inscriptional form T556. T558 in this combined sense is found in the glyger T669:558.35 (*ka*-x-x), in T586:25:558 (*pa-ca-*x), in T25:558:23 (*ca*-x-*na[?]*), in T558.25:558 (x-*ca-*x), in T679.558:669 (*i*-x-*ka* 'armadillo'), in T558:102 (a title), and in T568.558 (*lu*-x). Knorozov (1967, p. 94, no. 181) read T558 as *bu*, apparently because of its use with T568 in a glyger where the meaning 'fall' (*lub*) was appropriate and because of the principle of synharmony. However, if it is in harmony with *lu*, it is out of harmony with all the other identifiable phonetic glyphs with which it is found. T568.558 could equally well be read *lu-b(a)*, and still convey the meaning 'fall'. The reading *ba* would best fit the 'armadillo' word, since *ibach* is Yucatec for 'armadillo', but *ka* is then unexplained. There is no clear context for the other examples of use of T558, except T558:102. This is a title of rulers in the inscriptions. T102 is a knot glyph, which I believe should be read *tab* 'tie, bind'. The rendering *batab* gives one of the best-known titles of rulers. The frequent glyph for rulers, T558.25:558, would be read *ba-ca-b(a)*, i.e., *bacab*. This is known in later times as a deity name and a lineage name, but I have not found it as a title. I would say of this glyph that the glyphic contexts in which it is found strongly suggest that it is a phonetic glyph, and that the principle of synharmony indicates it should end in *-a*. Read as *ba*, it fits well in a number of cases, but the evidence falls short of good proof. The rodent head, T757/788, sometimes appears as an allograph of T558.

Figure 63 shows a very considerable number of graphemes interpreted by Knorozov as having definable or probable CV readings. In a few cases, I am convinced he is wrong. In many cases, no evidence is presented, and there are no obvious probative contexts. The forty or more suggested readings in these categories would fill many of the blank spaces of Figure 62 if correct, but it seemed wiser to separate them at this time. In no case have I personally found the evidence for any of these readings as plausible as that for those which I have previously given, but a few of them seem promising.

Despite the reluctance of many competent Mayanists to accept the evidence of the existence of purely phonetic glyphs in the Maya script, the data which support this conclusion seem to me overwhelming. We already know a substantial number of such glyphs which seem to me adequately established. Unfortunately, glyphs of this type are by no means the only kinds of glyphs, and the various classes of glyphs are frequently hard to distinguish on a priori grounds. The relative rarity of phonetic glyphs in the deciphered material means that they do not automatically lead us to a cumulative series of new decipherments. However, as other scholars take up this aspect of decipherment, we should be able to determine most of the phonetic glyphs.

Chapter 10
The Grammar
of Maya Writing

It is obvious that a description of the grammar of a language as determined from its writing system will differ in significant ways from a grammar based upon actual speech patterns. When the writing system is as little known as that of the Classic Maya inscriptions and it is not even certain what language was being written or how much it has changed through time, one cannot hope to write a real grammatical description. Nonetheless, certain characteristics of the Maya script can be recognized and do conform with known characteristics of Mayan languages. Unfortunately even the latter have not been adequately studied.

Although Eduard Seler (1902–1923, I, 65–126) attempted a comparative study of some aspects of the grammar of the various Mayan languages, no modern study is available. Principles of linguistic analysis have become ever more sophisticated; descriptive materials, vocabularies, and texts have been accumulating; and some valuable comparative studies of vocabulary have appeared; but a modern comparative grammatical synthesis has not been attempted.

For those with a deep interest in the subject and an adequate command of the terminology and concepts of modern linguistics, the studies of Classical Yucatec by Norman McQuown (1967) and of Classical Quiche by Munro Edmonson (1967) give some comparative basis. It should be emphasized that *Classic* in this context refers to sixteenth-century speech and not to the Classic Period of the archaeologists. An introduction to Yucatec Maya in more traditional form by Tozzer (1921) is somewhat fuller and probably easier for a nonlinguist to understand. It is also more than adequate for our present state of knowledge of the Maya writing. Distinctions which were too subtle for Tozzer to recognize or points where he erred in interpretation would certainly elude us in studying the script.

For present purposes, the following salient points of Mayan grammar should be mentioned. McQuown divides all morphemes into nouns, verbs, and particles. In Yucatec, adjectives are classed grammatically by McQuown as nouns, taking many of the same suffixes. There are also some specifically adjectival suffixes. Edmonson points out that, in Quiche, "numerals, colors and similar elements" (i.e., adjectives) have inflections of noun type in some cases but also show grammatical distinctions from typical nouns. From the standpoint of the vocabulary, it is my impression that the adjectives do not show the interchangeability of use which one frequently finds between roots used as grammatical verbs in one case and as grammatical nouns in another.

Word order is quite different from English, as verbs with their various affixes normally come first; in the case of a transitive verb, it is followed first by the object and then by the subject. Adjectives normally precede nouns. Extensive series of particles tend to appear in fixed orders in both Yucatec and Quiche at the present time, but cognate particles do not always appear in the same order in the two languages, a fact which suggests more freedom of usage at an earlier date.

An intensive comparative study of the order of elements in modern Mayan languages, of the particular roots which must have specified affixes, and of the necessary co-occurrence of specified grammatical features would be extremely helpful in decipherment. I believe that such a study would enable identification of a wide range of still-elusive affixes in the script, which, in turn, would provide us with components of phonetically written words and would considerably restrict the classes of morphemes which could possibly fit in particular contexts. For purposes of use in decipherment, grammatical particles should be accompanied by lists of morphemes with which they can be associated.

In the absence of such a comparative study, and with much fuller grammatical references for Yucatec than for the Cholan languages, comparisons will usually be made with Yucatec in the following material. This does not necessarily imply that Yucatec is either different from or the same as Cholan unless so stated. The references are intended only to show a general congruence between grammatical features in the script and in at least one of the Mayan languages.

Eric Thompson, in his great work on the Maya script (Thompson 1950), presented an extensive analysis of the principles of the writing system as he understood them at that time. He has amplified and somewhat changed his viewpoint on certain matters in the preface to his *Catalog* (1962). Although my conclusions are often different, I have drawn heavily on these statements, which should be read by all students of the script. As will be seen, I have also relied on the very important grammatical identifications of specific elements and general statements of Yurii Knorozov (especially 1955*a* and 1967).

An interesting attempt to determine the rules of Maya writing was made by Nap Cordy (1946). Much of this is concerned with phoneticism, but certain more general statements are made, including the allegation that the script contains "double, corroborative, or determinative" writing, a point that is still in dispute. Cordy likewise maintains that the order of writing did not always correspond with the order of speech, another still-debated point.

The first general attempt to determine the struc-

tural nature of Mayan writing was made by Whorf (1933). While his conclusions as to specific readings have generally not withstood the test of time, his analysis of the relationship between texts and pictures in the codices showed the normal order of occurrence of various classes of glyphs. Verbs come first and are followed by a reference to the grammatical object, if any, and then by a reference to the grammatical subject.

Sometimes there is no verb, in our sense, in a sentence, as in the "burden" passages, where the structure is "its burden of **x** [the carrier] (is) **y** [the object carried]," in which neither the glyphs nor spoken Maya contain any equivalent of the parenthetical *is*. Other passages have the structure "relationship (of male) **x** (to female) **y**" or "(female) **y** relationship (to male) **x**." Direction glyphs, when found, may either precede or follow verbs in sentences which are otherwise like the first category mentioned. In general, the structure of sentences in the codices is fairly easy to determine and agrees with what we know of spoken Yucatec. There are greater difficulties in determining the structure of sentences on the monumental inscriptions, but many of them show these same kinds of sentences.

It is apparent from the types of identification made that this principle of structural analysis had already been recognized by Cyrus Thomas and by Seler, but they do not seem to have fully recognized its general applicability.

Thompson has preferred to use the term *action glyphs* for Whorf's "verbs," thus avoiding a precise grammatical interpretation. He and Barthel both accept Whorf's structural analysis. Figure 64 shows some instances of the glyphic sequence *verb-object-subject* and of other typical sentences. Their order coincides with that in Yucatec speech.

The order of some subordinate elements is also clear. Thus, adjectives normally precede nouns. Specifically, the color glyphs always precede the glyphs which name the objects to which they refer. This remains true even for those color glyphs which sometimes function as main signs. This order is likewise true of spoken Yucatec, though not for all words translated as English adjectives. Numbers also precede time periods. Locative glyphs (Figs. 35, 36, 65) precede glyphs for the places to which they refer, and the possessive *u* precedes the glyphs for the object possessed (or the action performed), both usages corresponding with spoken Yucatec. The identified and generally accepted glyph for the numerical classifier *te* (Fig. 65) falls between the numeral and the objects classified, as it does in Yucatec speech.

I believe that this constitutes the full series of

hok kal ah	God K	**x**	God B	**x** *caan*	God E
				sky	(plus other
verb	object		subject		elements)

God B noosed God K

u	*ti caan*	*can* **x** *kin*	*tun*
		mo haab	
possessive	fire at sky	Four **x**	drought
		Macaw	

the Macaw God's fire in
the sky : drought

drill - **x**	*u*	God D
	his fire	
verb	object	subject

6 tun(s)

can te (Zec)
fourth (of the month)
Zec

ek caan	*chac ek*	*ek te*
black sky	Great Star	black
	(Venus)	tree

goddess	sexual	dog	(augury)
	relation-		
	ship		
	(noun?)		

sexual	god	goddess	(augury)
relation-			
ship			

Figure 64. Typical sentences.

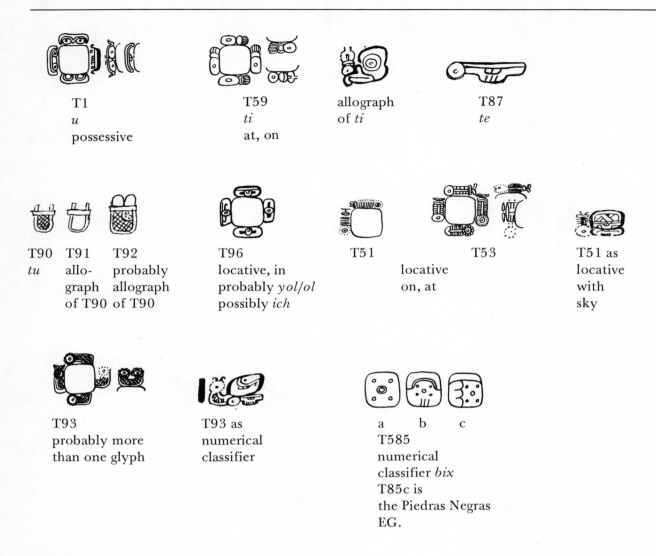

Figure 65. Identified grammatical particles.

elements on which there is agreement. It will be seen that in all cases there is a correspondence between the glyphic sequence and the sequence in Yucatec speech. This creates a strong presumption that the same is true for undeciphered elements, and only a very strong case would be construed as valid evidence against this presumption. Thompson has suggested several alleged differences between the order of glyphs and the order of speech. Each of these will be considered individually. I think there are valid reasons for rejecting all of them over and above their disagreement with this general criterion. While I think the presumption of agreement with Yucatec grammatical order is a useful and generally valid criterion of correct decipherment, this should not be construed as meaning that there is no possibility of a discrepancy in order between the writing system and the spoken language which it represented, which, in itself, probably differed in some respects from Yucatec as we

know it, even if it was ancestral Yucatec. There are such differences in nearly all writing systems (cf. English *$2.00,* representing spoken *two dollars*), and we may expect to find a few of them eventually in Mayan. The point is that the available evidence suggests that they should be few and that any such alleged case should require very good evidence before being accepted.

There are still only a few grammatical glyphs which are widely accepted with little or no dispute, but they are very important for the light they throw upon the nature of the script.

Brasseur de Bourbourg recognized that the glyph given by Landa in his "alphabet" for the letter *u* (Fig. 65) was found in the codices intervening between two noun groups in ways that seemed to indicate its use as the Maya possessive particle *u.* This was established by the 1890's to the satisfaction of scholars as diverse in their viewpoints as Cyrus Thomas and Eduard Seler, but a later generation of epigraphers, led by Morley and Beyer, read this glyph in the inscriptions simply as an "ending sign." Whorf (1942, pp. 496–497) again insisted on reading this glyph in the codices as *u* but made no reference to it in the inscriptions, and it was left for Thompson (1950, p. 188) to show that the so-called ending sign of the inscriptions was actually the *u* possessive and that its use on the monuments corresponded to the various uses of the morpheme *u* in Mayan. This is accepted by Zimmermann, Barthel, Knorozov, and probably all of the present generation of scholars.

In his third example, Landa gives another glyph, *ti*. The inscriptional form of this glyph (T59) was recognized as the Landa *ti* by Thompson, who showed that it corresponded to the use of the Maya locative *ti* and could often be translated 'on' or 'at'. He also showed that a vulture's head (with this glyph attached to its nose) frequently substituted for this glyph and was almost certainly to be read in the same way (Thompson 1950, p. 58).

Another important identification by Thompson was of a glyph (T87) found between numerals and month glyphs. In Yucatec, the particle *te* is used in a similar way, and he showed that the same glyph occurred with the apparent meaning 'tree', which is *te* in most Maya languages, and was also found as a postfix to a deity name, of which the first two elements were Bolon-oc. Since Bolon Yocte is a Maya deity name (*yoc* being a Yucatec variant of *oc*), the value seems fully confirmed.

Thompson also recognized in the inscriptions a particle, used with periods of time, which he identified as *tu* (T92). This affix is found in inscriptions at Chichen Itza, immediately followed by a number and then by a month name. He distinguished this from a somewhat similar-appearing glyph (T90), also associated with numbers, because the latter appeared between the number and the period referred to, and because the former has three dots not found with the latter (Thompson 1950, pp. 196–197). For this second numerical classifier, he has suggested the value *piz* or *p'el*. However, if his identifications are correct, these objections do not seem to be validated. In his Figure 4, number 22 shows the glyph *with* the infix of three dots standing between the number and the period glyph, and numbers 21 and 35 show forms which he read *tu* which apparently did not have the infixed dots. I have suggested that the form read by Thompson as *piz/p'el* is to be read in the codices as a phonetic CV glyph with the value *tu*. To me, this supports the identity of the two forms and the value *tu* for both. Knorozov has not accepted *tu* as a reading for either of the forms distinguished by Thompson. Like myself, he thinks T90 and T92 are mere variants. He suggested a possible reading *ten* in 1955, later read *tem* (Knorozov 1967, p. 101, no. 334). I do not know of any convincing context for this reading.

Besides these cases, where fairly clear-cut and acceptable identifications have been made, there are many other suggested interpretations of varying value. There are some glyphs whose functions we are able to recognize without being able to give an absolutely clear-cut identification. Cyrus Thomas made a very acute study of the glyphs for places associated with God B in the *Dresden* (see Figs. 35 and 36). A variable series of prefixes, including that now known to be *ti*, is found with these place names. A fuller study by Barthel (1953, p. 91 and elsewhere) of the places visited by the Rain God included the recognition of two additional glyphs as locatives, because of their position preceding the place-name glygers. One of these (T96), which he read *yol* 'heart of', is also read by Knorozov as a locative, *ich* 'within' (Fig. 65). Knorozov regards the glyph as representing an eye, Yucatec *ich*, and the glyph is found as part of the eye of various gods and animals. However, glyphs are frequently infixed in the eye, and this is not adequate proof, though it offers minor support for Knorozov's view. Thompson (1965a) pointed out that the morpheme *yol* is used with 'sky' and 'earth' and that he did not find *ich* used with them. Since T96 is prefixed to the widely accepted glyphs for 'earth' and 'sky', this is excellent support for a reading *yol*. There is at least one case of *ich* preceding *caan* 'sky', in the compound place name Ich-caan-zi-ho. However, the rarity of the usage still supports Thompson's view. Thompson also points out that *u* is prefixed to T96; *u yol* is correct, but *u ich* is not (unless *ich* is understood as 'eye, face' rather than as the locative). Taking these facts together, I now think T96 must be *ol/yol*. T96 also occurs with *naab* 'sea', with what may be 'sand' (Fig. 36), with 'jewel water', and with the 'place of footsteps'. It occasionally occurs suffixed, but the only decipherable example known to me is following *kin* (M100c). *Kinich* is a known Yucatec compound, forming part of the name of the deity Kinich Kakmo 'Sun-Eye Fire Macaw', but it seems to have no relevance in this passage. I do not know of any occurrences of *kin-ol*, *kin-hol*, or *kin-yol*.

The other locative (T51, and I think also T53; see Fig. 65) is "translated" by Barthel (1953, p. 91) as 'auf' ('on'? 'at'?), but no Maya equivalent is suggested. On D66b it is clearly a place locative, but in inscriptions at Chichen Itza it appears following the *haab* 'year' glyph and preceding a statement of '(katun) *n* Ahau', where its use must be at least slightly different. Thompson (1950, Figs. 38, 39) indicates a rough meaning of 'on' or 'at'. Evreinov, Kosarev, and Ustinov read *ti* 'at', which is reasonable if one is willing to believe that two completely distinct glyphs, having only a slight physical similarity, are to be read in the same way. The glyph is called by Thompson the "centipede affix," a quite possible identification. In the codices, it normally appears with two antennae and six legs, if that is what they are, suggesting rather an insect. If one is willing to accept the view that the codices have preserved a more archaic form than the monuments, a view for which there is little evidence, I would prefer the meaning 'insect' to 'centipede'. Knorozov in 1955 (1955*a*, sec. 1, no. 149) read this glyph as *lem*, a numerical classifier for 'times'. He apparently abandoned this unsupported reading by 1963 (p. 285). A locative which can be used with places and times and has an additional meaning of 'insect' or 'centipede' should be easy but has so far eluded identification. It may be pointed out that cognates or ancient homonyms of Yucatec *can* 'snake' appear with the meanings 'centipede' and 'insect'.

The use of numerical classifiers between numbers and the objects counted makes them fairly easy to recognize, once the possibility has been recognized, although this does not always lead immediately to a correct decipherment. On D26a, 27a, and 28a, we find numbers prefixed to T93 (Fig. 65), which is followed by a moon glyph (*kal*?) to which is affixed *te* (T87). Thompson (1962, p. 277) says that T93 can be identified "with little hesitation" as sparks and smoke, an opinion I am unable to share. He points out its regular occurrence prefixed to T672, which he calls 'fire fist' (previously 'shell hand') and which sometimes has numbers prefixed. T93 also occurs in other contexts, frequently prefixed to apparent verbs on the monuments (hand glyphs, the 'drill' glyph, etc.). It is one of the relatively few affixes which occur both as prefixes and as suffixes. Cordan (1963*a*, p. 20) reads it as *ka* and the combination in *Dresden* as *kakalte* 'child', giving the numbers a symbolic meaning. Since he has read the glyphs of this passage in the wrong order (see Chapter 13), the context does not seem convincing; it is, furthermore, implausible in at least some of the other contexts. Evreinov, Kosarev, and Ustinov have read T93 as *chac*, for reasons not apparent to me. Knorozov (1967, p. 102, no. 350) reads T672 as *chuh* and maintains that it represents a burnt offering; both suggestions seem unlikely. Whorf identifies T672 as a representation of woven work on a loom, Maya *sakal*, and

from this gets *s*, *sa*—a dubious identification based on a very dubious procedure.

A numerical classifier which I think has been correctly identified by Thompson (1950, pp. 170–171) is T585 (Fig. 65). He suggests that this is *bix*, a classifier used with the numbers five and seven. The glyph is found followed by T186 in the codices as the locative for the 'place of footsteps'. Huaxtec *bixnel* 'a dance' and *bixom* 'be dancing' suggest the same root, supporting Thompson's view; cf. Quiche *bix* 'sing', *bizah* 'dance'. Cyrus Thomas (1893, p. 246) and Whorf (1942, p. 484) identified the glyph in question as Landa's second *b*, which has only four dots, unlike the five dots of T585. The design appears on earplugs from the Preclassic Period on. Knorozov (1967, p. 89, no. 122) originally read *col* 'field' and later *ba*. Neither reading seems as plausible as Thompson's.

One of the more important affixes in spoken Yucatec is *-il*, which occurs with nouns, pronouns, adjectives, verbs, and adverbs. Thompson (1950, pp. 269–271) has identified T24 (Fig. 66) as *-il*. His supporting arguments come mainly from the occurrence of two glygers. The first of these is composed of T544, *kin*; T548, *tun*; T528, *haab*; and T24. The order of the elements sometimes varies. There is a Yucatec word which contains these morphemes, which is *kintun-yaabil* (with normal *-y-* from **-h-*) 'drought'. The glyger appears in the various augural passages in contexts where this meaning seems appropriate. See especially D40b, where the compound, without affix T24, is associated with a picture of the Macaw God holding torches, and the associated glyphs read 'his fire at heaven (of) Macaw God'. This, therefore, suggests that T24 should represent the missing grapheme *-il*. However, the morpheme *-il* is attached to *haab*, whereas T24 is found, in this glyger as in other contexts, affixed to T548, *tun*, and is seldom affixed to T528, *haab*, here or elsewhere. Thompson (1962, pp. 134–142) lists only three instances of this affix on the second commonest of all Maya glyphs. In spoken Yucatec, and indeed in all branches of the Mayance family, the affix *-il* is exceedingly common with *haab*, to the extent that *haabil* rather than *haab* is frequently cited as the "word" for 'year'. This is a negative reason for doubting this identification, but, I think, a valid one.

Thompson's second argument for reading T24 as *-il* depends on the identification of what he regards as an augural glyph, a glyger composed of T533, *ahau*, with T24 both prefixed and suffixed. This, he thinks, is *ahaulil* 'rule, reign', derived from *ahau* 'ruler'. The glyger, found with the glyger for Itzamna, has been regarded as a second name of that deity, but it is also found in places where Itzamna is, apparently, not referred to. The resultant grammatical structure of some of the passages seems to be awkward in spoken (or read) Yucatec, and I am not entirely satisfied with the meaning in many cases. T24 is *prefixed* to the names of the Death God and the Corn God. Thompson reads their names as Yum Cimil and Ah Uaxac-Yol-Kauil, or possibly just Kauil. In both cases *-il* is suffixed, although the glyph is prefixed, one of the reasons leading Thompson to suppose that glyphic order need not coincide with spoken order. In the case of Yum Cimil, there is no glyph to represent *yum* in Thompson's explanations.

Knorozov (1955*a*, sec. 1, no. 90) suggested alternate readings of *om, un, hun*, which were neither consistent nor adequate. As prefixed to the names of Death God and Corn God, I would incline to the readings Yum Came (cf. Yuc. Yum Cimil—the absence of an element corresponding to *-il* here is an objection to my reading, just as the corresponding absence of *yum* was an objection to Thompson's) and Yum Kaax, a known name of the Corn God. The fact that these two deities share a common prefix, *yum* 'lord, father', which is not found with other deity names, suggested this view. However, Yum-Ahau-Yum 'Father-Lord-Father' for T24.533:24 does not seem very Yucatec in sentiment or grammar. Knorozov (1967, pp. 86–87) reads T24 as *um* and this compound as *um-la-um*. However, the *ahau* is not inverted as it is in the examples which, following Knorozov, I read *la*. The problem is a difficult one, and I am not yet ready to accept any identification suggested for T24.

While I think that Thompson's reading of T24 as *-il* is wrong and that Knorozov's as *um* is at best doubtful, I think that Knorozov's identification of T116 as *-il* is certainly correct. T116 (see Fig. 66) is commonly found with *kin* 'sun', and Thompson (1950, p. 142), in an imaginative flight of fancy, suggested that it corresponded to the Maya concept of the 'cords of the sun', read *u tab kin*. Barthel (1955*a*, p. 16) reads simply *tab*. A connection of the sun cord with *haab* 'year' or 'rain' seems unlikely; yet T116 is the commonest of all affixes to T528, *haab*; Thompson (1962, pp. 134–142) lists sixty-one certain occurrences, without other glyphs intervening. *Haabtab*, while very euphonious, does not seem a promising reading. The difficulties of the combination of *haab* and the "suntail" have been obscured by the habit of referring to this combination as the "winged Cauac." As I have pointed out, *-il* is the commonest affix to *haab* in spoken Mayan. Affixed to the glygers for 'east' (Yuc. *lakin*) and 'west' (Yuc. *chikin*), T116 would convert them to *lakinil* 'eastward' and *chikinil*

'westward', making very good sense in context. *Lakin-tab* 'east cords' does not seem to me to make sense. *Kin-il* is a very frequent expression, fully accounting for the sun's "cords" in my opinion. Again, T116 is affixed to the grapheme of the *muan* bird as the glyph for the month Muan. Muan-tab 'Owl Cord(?), Rain Cord(?)' does not seem likely—Muanil, on the other hand, is 'Rainy', certainly a plausible month name.

There are also certain agentive or nominal prefixes which can be recognized with some probability. Proskouriakoff (1961, pp. 16–17) shows two types of feminine heads. The first (T1002), found frequently in the inscriptions, is apparently an indicator of references to adult women; the second (T1000a), with a long lock of hair coming down the side of the head, is apparently a reference to younger women or girls (see Fig. 66). The second type apparently corresponds to the well-known glyph of the Moon Goddess in the codices. The glyph also appears in the inscriptions for the presumably equivalent patron goddess of the number one. Knorozov (1955*a*, sec. 2, no. 200) has suggested for this glyph, in the codices, the reading *ch'up* 'maiden'. Berlin (1959, p. 6) apparently does not distinguish the two types, but suggests the reading *ix*, the Yucatec feminine prefix. I am inclined to accept *ch'up* for the glyph with the long lock of hair and *ix* for the female head without the long lock of hair. There is, unfortunately, little in the way of adequate proof for these readings based on Yucatec.

One male head (T1037; see Fig. 66) has been plausibly read as *xib* 'youth' (Barthel 1953, p. 92). The best contextual evidence is in a series of references (D29c–30c) where T1037 has color prefixes and is followed by the glyph for God B. Since God B's name has usually been read Chac and since the head is obviously that of a man or youth, this series has been identified with the deities known from Landa as Zac-xib-Chac, Ek-xib-Chac, Kan-xib-Chac, and Chac-xib-Chac.

The more strictly grammatical masculine prefix is *ah*, which may also appear as an agentive, without necessary reference to sex. Knorozov (1955*a*, sec. 2, nos. 3–10) has identified T13 as *ah*. The same glyph was identified by Beyer (1937, p. 151) as "death eyes"; Thompson (1950, p. 45), who regards the Beyer identification as "reasonably sure," emphasizes that this circle element is an attribute of the Death God, whether or not Beyer is correct. Thompson regards this as the symbolic form of a small death's head. There is no doubt that T13 and the death's head occur in many of the same contexts, but I am by no means certain of their identity. Thompson (1950, p. 189) reads both of them as *hitz'* 'death

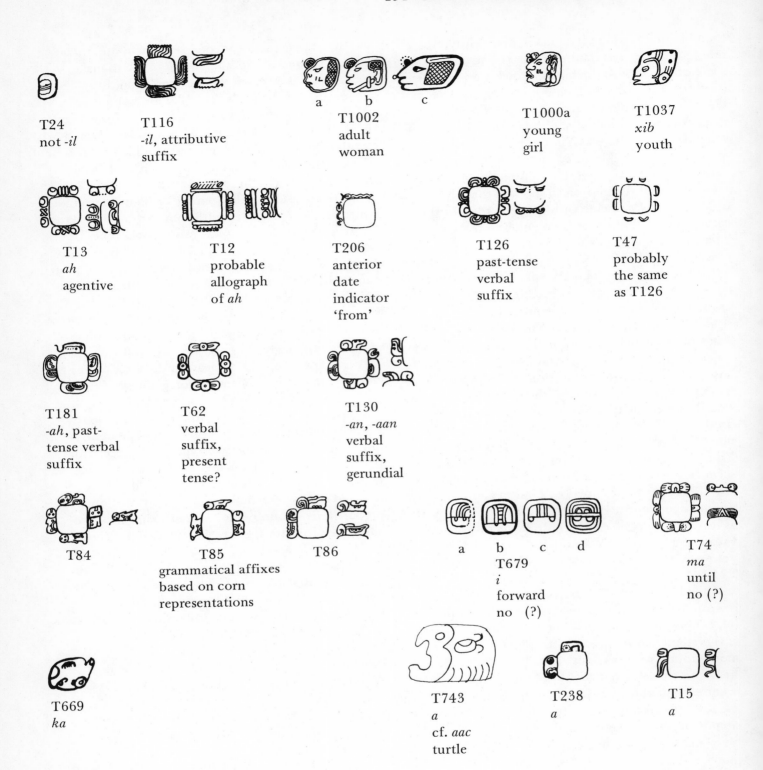

Figure 66. Suggested grammatical particles.

T140
-*l(a)*?
-*lal*

allograph
of T140,
classed
by Thompson
as T178

T178

T139
probable
allograph
of T140

T23
not -*al*
-*na*?

T103
-*al*?

T25
ca

T186
probably
not
tah

T558
ba?
reflexive

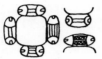

T110
not
ta
long
bone?

T109
chac (red, great)
grammatical
functions unknown
Some examples
of *yax* (green)
are mistakenly
included in T109.

T172
not
yetel

throes, expiration, end' (the last an extension of meaning not found in the dictionaries). This reading makes sense in terms of the apparent identification of the object shown, but it does not coincide with its use in the inscriptions or in the codices. One frequently finds T13 present in name glyphs (Figs. 74–83). Knorozov reads it with a whole series of glyphs in the codices, where it makes very good sense as *ah* and very poor sense as *hitz'*. The most interesting example is to be found on D19c. Here we find a sequence of glyphs which may be transcribed approximately as 'Fire' *zac ch'up ah cuch,* i.e., 'the White Maiden, the bearer of fire', which is shown below. 'White Maiden, death burden' does not coincide in any way with the representation. Moreover, the order of the glygers shows a very interesting variation from neighboring passages. Thus, the immediately previous passage may be transcribed 'God Q' *u cuch zac ch'up,* i.e., 'God Q, her burden (of) (the) White Maiden'. This inversion of order is precisely what one would expect in changing from *u cuch* to *ah cuch.* The use illustrates the agentive, not necessarily masculine, character of the prefix.

Another case where the evidence seems to support Knorozov is to be found in *Madrid,* pages 40b–41b, where we have a series of hunting scenes, in which T13 precedes the Manik/Ceh glyph. Barthel (personal communication) has suggested the reading *hitz' ceh* 'dead deer', which makes sense as an isolated remark in the general hunting context. However, 'dead deer' in such a context should be consistently the object of the sentence, and this does not seem to be the case. The order of the glygers rather suggests that it is sometimes the subject and sometimes the object. Knorozov reads *ah ceh,* the standard term for 'hunter', which seems to me to fit the grammatical context better. T12 frequently appears in similar contexts and may be an allograph of T13 (see Fig. 66).

Thompson (1950, p. 164) points out that T206, a "wiggly creature, perhaps a snake or an eel or even a tadpole" (probably a snake, since it has a forked tongue) is usually attached to a day sign to indicate that the date of which it is part is earlier than another date in the same calculation. This may be called an *anterior date indicator.* It may appear between the numeral and the day sign, or it may appear before the numeral, while in one known case it is attached to a tun glyph rather than a day glyph.

Thompson (1950, p. 163) has drawn attention to a postfix (T126) which functions as an anterior date indicator when affixed to *xoc-ti;* i.e., it indicates "that the CR [Calendar Round] date to which it is adjacent is the earlier of two dates joined by a dis-

tance number." The approximate meaning of the phrase *xoc-ti*-T126 must be 'count *back* to'. Since *xoc* is a verb, T126 must be some sort of verbal suffix. This is fully verified by its frequent use with known verbs or action glyphs and by its appearance as an affix to the first glyph in the codices and to the first glyph following dates, many times, on the monuments. It is also found as the postfix of periods of distance numbers but is not postfixed to Initial Series. Occasionally, it is found as an element in glygers, where it seems to have a purely phonetic use. Knorozov (1955a, p. 59) reads it as *hi,* the past-tense suffix, third person singular, of inchoate verbs, neuter voice (cf. Tozzer 1921, p. 74). Since nearly all verbs on the monuments must be referring to past events when associated with past dates, it is highly likely that this is some past-tense suffix. Barthel regards it as -*ah,* the commonest of all past-tense suffixes. This is very reasonable if one rejects Knorozov's reading of T181 as -*ah,* discussed below. Moreover, Barthel regards this glyph as identical with one prefixed in contexts where the agentive *ah* is expectable. This double context would reinforce the identification in a very plausible way, but it has not been definitely proven that the prefix and suffix are actually identical, and I still favor the Knorozov readings. A clear demonstration of association with a verb known to take this suffix would support Knorozov's view. His readings of the glygers which he identifies as *zihil* 'birth' and *hicham* 'husband' are not impossible, but they are far from conclusive.

T126 is often found with another verbal affix, T181, identified by Thompson as a representation of half of the normal moon glyph, for which it seems, rarely, to substitute. With this, I am in full accord, although Knorozov disagrees. Since one of the words for moon is *u,* and since *u* (T1) is found as a prefix to certain verbs/action glyphs, Thompson argues that this postfix is also to be read as *u.* This "lunar postfix" is one of the examples which lead him to conclude that glyphic order does not coincide with linguistic order. The two glyphs are normally found in complementary distribution only on what seem to be verbs. T1 is found in a whole series of contexts where T181 never appears. The known use of *u* with verbs to indicate an action done by someone is simply an extension of the possessive to actions—his action (verb) (of) *x'.* Since T181 is often found without T126 following verbs which refer to events in the past, it should be a past-tense suffix. Knorozov (1955a, sec. 1, no. 127) has read it as the commonest of all past-tense verbal suffixes, Yucatec -*ah,* attached to transitive verbs, a suggestion already made by Seler (1902–1923, I, 698). Barthel (personal communication,

December 1966) reads *-ic,* a present time suffix to transitive verbs. Since T181 is found on the monuments attached to verbs which refer to actions which occurred in the remote past, I cannot accept the view that it is a present time suffix. Knorozov's reading is in full accord with the evidence, insofar as I know it. Figure 67 shows those glyphs which take this postfix in the codices (rearranged from Evreinov, Kosarev, and Ustinov 1961, pp. 41–45). Although the glyph is found, rarely, as a prefix and is occasionally found in nonverbal contexts, it is by far the best indicator of verbs. Figure 68 shows those glyphs from the monuments which take this affix (following Thompson 1962, p. 84, omitting doubtful examples, and arranged to show known action verbs first). I believe that nearly all of the glyphs in these two figures will be found to be verbs on more detailed analysis, although some of them doubtless have other functions as well. T181 is sometimes found doubled, on the monuments, which has been among the reasons for regarding such doubling as purely aesthetic. According to Tozzer (1921, p. 33), *-ah* is doubled to indicate the distant past in the intransitive verb. This usage does not, of itself, explain its occurrence with *chuc(a)* (Fig. 61), which is a transitive verb, but it does suggest that the doubling was probably syntactical. Minor changes in usage may well have occurred during eight or ten centuries, even if the script of the monuments is ancestral Yucatec.

Barthel (1954, p. 46) draws attention to an interesting passage from *Dresden* page 2c, which shows deities using a needle in "the making of a mat or net." He points out that when the action is being performed, one finds the affix Z73 (= T62; see Fig. 66). He does not make any specific interpretation, but this passage would suggest the possibility that the affix represents a present-tense suffix. He points out that the other passages have different affixes, which should also be tense indicators. One of these is T126, already discussed as a possible past-tense suffix.

The other is Z76 (= T130), which is found with a picture showing God D "sitting inactive in front of the object holding the needle upright in his fist. Here the action evidently has not yet started" (Barthel 1954, p. 46). This affix is found in a glyger for the month Muan (see Fig. 5). Following Knorozov, I believe that the only adequate explanation of the two graphemes making up this glyger is that the first represents *mu* and the second (T130) stands for *-an.* The suffix *-an* is used in making past participles or verbal nouns (Tozzer 1921, pp. 88–89: *mentaan* 'hecho' ['made']; *nakan* 'a thing fallen'). This would suggest that God D had finished, rather than that he was waiting to start. This is Thompson's "postfix A" (1950, pp. 281–

282), which he associates with maize, and which he suggests should be read *ak,* a term referring to 'fresh or tender or new' vegetation; it also means 'humid'. The word for 'ear of green corn' throughout the entire Mayan family (Kaufman 1964, p. 99) is **'ajan,* which would give Yucatec *-aan.* Knorozov (1967, p. 47) points out that T130 is the only grapheme which is affixed to glyphs for both transitive and intransitive verbs and that *-an* is the only morpheme affixed to both transitive and intransitive verbs. In light of this, I have no hesitation at all in regarding Knorozov's reading as correct, in spite of the difficulty of explaining its use with the months conventionally called Pop, Zec, Kankin, and Kayab (see Fig. 5). T130 seems to be added frequently when the so-called *ben-ich* prefix (see Chapter 11) is found (see Thompson 1950, pp. 291–292). I suspect that it has several grammatical functions on the monuments which were no longer in use at the time our earliest information on Yucatec was written.

Thompson writes of T84 (Fig. 66): "It is composed of two parts, the second of which is the same as the identifying characteristic in the codices of the maize god, and which is set on his head, a vegetal motif. The other is what may be a small face attached to the base of this vegetal motif" (Thompson 1950, p. 285). He goes on to suggest that this indicates the Maize God (or Corn God), but that the latter was probably a general god of vegetation and that "One would be inclined to accept it as a symbol for maize alone were it not that it appears in a number of contexts where the restricted meaning of 'maize' would hardly fit, but the more general term *te* is applicable" (ibid.). He therefore argues that this is another glyph for *te.* The glyph closely resembles T85 and T86; the basis of all three appears to me to be a ripe ear of corn. This affinity is recognized both in Knorozov's reading, *nal* 'ear of maize' (Knorozov 1967, p. 83, no. 066), and in Barthel's reading *tzuc* 'cornsilk'. Knorozov's term is attestable as ancestral Mayan, probably not shared by Huaxtec, and is found in several apparent deity names, where *nal* seems slightly more appropriate than *tzuc.* It is quite possible that the three related glyphs, T84, T85, and T86, may include both the *nal* and the *tzuc* terms. Knorozov originally equated *nal* with *mal* and *mol,* as alternate readings for which there seems to be no justification. *Nal* is found as a noun suffix indicating 'possessor of, he of', which seems appropriate for its use in deity names.

Thompson has identified the function of another grammatical prefix (T679). Prefixed to *xoc-ti* (instead of being suffixed, like the anterior date indicator) it indicates that the calculation is going forward to a

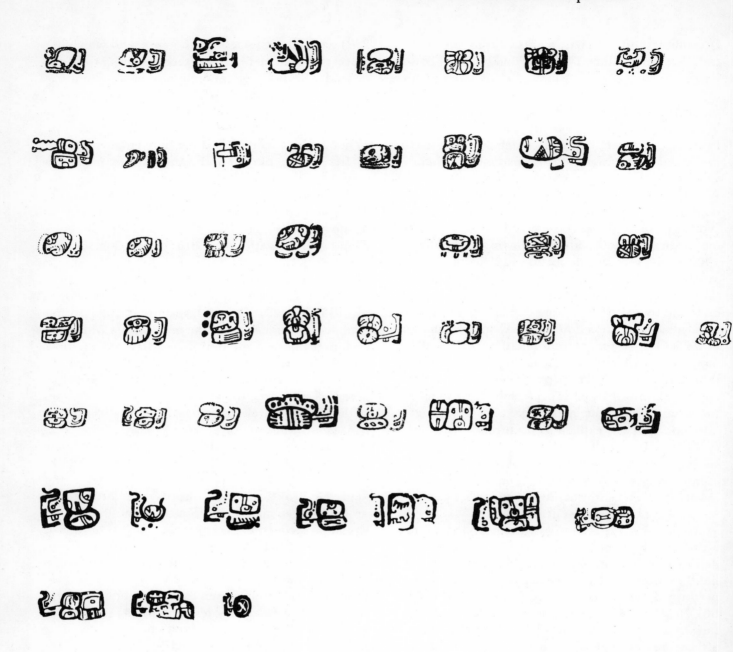

Figure 67. The *-ah* suffix (T181) in the codices.

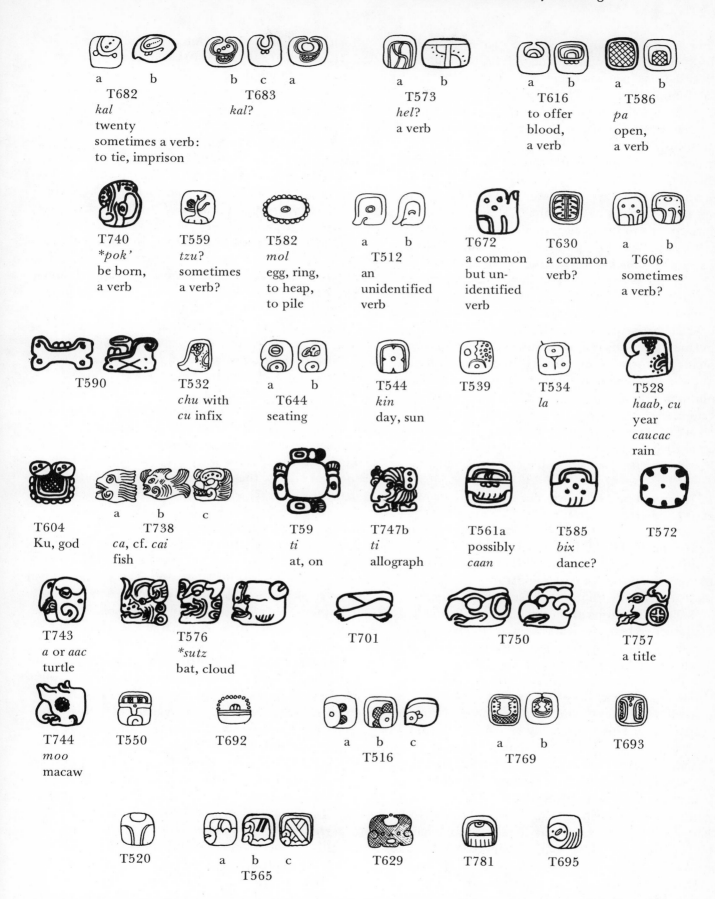

a   b   b   c   a   a   b   a   b   a   b
T682   T683   T573   T616   T586
kal   *kal?*   *hel?*   to offer   *pa*
twenty   a verb   blood,   open,
sometimes a verb: a verb   a verb
to tie, imprison

T740   T559   T582   a   b   T672   T630   a   b
pok'   *tzu?*   *mol*   T512   a common   a common   T606
be born,   sometimes   egg, ring, an   but un-   verb?   sometimes
a verb   a verb?   to heap,   unidentified identified   a verb?
                        to pile   verb   verb

T590   T532   a   b   T544   T539   T534   T528
            chu with T644   *kin*   *la*   *haab, cu*
            cu infix seating   day, sun   year
                                                                          caucac
                                                                          rain

T604   a   b   c   T59   T747b   T561a   T585   T572
Ku, god   T738   *ti*   *ti*   possibly   *bix*
            ca, cf. *cai*   at, on   allograph   *caan*   dance?
            fish

T743   T576   T701   T750   T757
a or *aac* *sutz*   a title
turtle   bat, cloud

T744   T550   T692   a   b   c   a   b   T693
moo   T516   T769
macaw

T520   a   b   c   T629   T781   T695
            T565

Figure 68. Glyphs in the inscriptions that take T181 as a suffix, according to the Thompson *Catalog*. Not checked against the originals. Does not include those glyphs that appear in the co- dices (Fig. 67). Occasionally, these glyphs may be part of a glyger, and sometimes the order may be somewhat different than the Thompson transcription implies.

later date. He has suggested some such meaning as 'leading to, forward to, falling on'; his attempted "translations" show a decided preference for 'forward to'. Berlin (1965a, p. 336) points out that when T679 is prefixed to T713, the calendar-round date to which reference is made comes at the end of the passage, thus showing another context in which some such meaning as 'forward' seems indicated. I believe that this glyph is Landa's *i*, a resemblance that was first pointed out by Beyer and later by Thompson. I do not know any use of a grammatical particle *i* which corresponds to those suggested for the glyph. Fought (1965, pp. 261–262) points out that T679 follows T103, which he identifies as *al* (see below). Since it is known that -*i* is one of a very limited number of morphemes which follow -*al*-, this is good supporting evidence if T103 is indeed *al*. The commonest use of *i* is as a negative (Huaxtec *i* 'no', Tzotzil *ʔiʔi* 'not'), and in Huaxtec *i* is also 'our'. Neither of these meanings seems pertinent in the contexts under discussion. Some supporting evidence for reading *i* comes from phonetic readings in compounds. There is also some evidence of interchangeability with T74, which I regard as the negative *ma*, suggesting occasional use as a negative. Knorozov (1967, p. 90, no. 139) reads *i* 'until', which is also a possible early meaning of *ma*.

Barthel (1964a, pp. 234–235) has argued that T679 should be read *ch'en* 'llega, se termina' ('arrives, ends'). He attempts to identify Chichen Itza as derived from T59.679:8, read *Ti-ch'en-(Itza), and points out that T679 is one of the prefixes of Landa's glyph for the month Ch'en. This reading fits well with the use as a posterior date indicator but is in complete disaccord with my understanding of the Landa alphabet. The supposition that the *chi* of *chich'en* could derive from *ti* ignores the facts that *ti,* as a locative prefix, remained *ti* in Yucatec and that Landa reads T59 as *ti,* not *chi*.

T74 is universally admitted to be the glyph to which Landa assigns the value *ma*. It is found repeatedly in contexts where a phonetic rendering *ma* seems likely. This glyph, early recognized both in the codices and in the inscriptions, has been largely neglected. Whorf (1933, pp. 13 ff.), arguing that the glyph represented hands (which seems unlikely), attempted to show that the Maya might once have had a word *ma* meaning 'hand'; he spent most of his labor on trying to show that all recognizable hand glyphs (including those which I believe should be read *ce, ka,* and *lah*) should be read *ma*. He made no attempt to show that the glyph corresponding to Landa's *ma* was used in the inscriptions in ways similar to known meanings of the morpheme *ma,*

which would have been a potentially more profitable study. Barthel (1953, p. 100) suggests that *ma* prefixed to a *kan* glyph should be read 'no . . . maize'. Contextual evidence that either supports or refutes this contention has not been brought to light.

One place where I think the *ma* glyph may be read with some plausibility is in the 'count of the year' clause (Thompson 1950, p. 251). In this clause, a directional glyph is followed by a group composed of T74, *ma;* T528, *haab* 'year'; and T511, *muluc,* here with an approximate meaning of 'turn' (Q. *mul* 'time, turn, rotation, revolution'). Thompson believes the meaning is approximately 'to the east (north, west, or south) the count of the year', an interpretation which ignores T74. In Huaxtec, *ma* means 'until', a meaning apparently cognate with its 'no, not' meanings in other Mayan languages, and probably to be understood as 'not (yet)'. A translation 'until the year turns' seems to be fully reasonable in this context.

Some such meaning as 'until' may also be involved in the use of T74 with the "half-period" glyphs (Thompson 1950, Fig. 32, nos. 46–55; cf. Fig. 6 in this book). Where the *ma* glyph is absent, I suspect that the meaning is at least slightly different, although this is not demonstrable from context. We should, at any rate, be wary of assuming that T74 does not change the meaning here. Again, in the clause (or glyger?) which Thompson doubtfully reads '*haab* completed' (his Fig. 32, nos. 56–60), a *ma* appears prefixed in one case and *i* in another. Thompson translates the latter as 'forward to', but I think it is quite possible that *ma* 'no' and *i* 'no' are being substituted one for the other, and that the meaning in these two cases may be directly opposite to that in the other three cases shown by Thompson. A full analysis of all occurrences of T679 and T74 might prove to be extremely helpful.

Another glyph whose identification is derived from Landa is T669. It is generally agreed that this glyph is identical with one given by Landa as *ka,* and the glyph is found frequently in glygers where this value seems to be wholly acceptable, e.g., *ka-k(a)* 'fire', Kakupacal, and others. The glyph represents a hand with a death-eye infix; Barthel has argued that it is to be read *kab* 'hand'; Evreinov, Kosarev, and Ustinov give *kab* and *ka* as alternate possible readings. However, I am not yet satisfied by any of the alleged occurrences of T669 as *kab* (see fuller discussion, Chapter 9). Occurrence as a grammatical particle is rare and doubtful, but expectable; so it is included here. Barthel (1955a, p. 15) read this glyph alternately as *et;* reading T122 as *el,* he read the glyger T669:122 as *etel,* Yucatec *yetel* 'and'. He has informed me (personal communication, December 1966) that he no longer regards this as a valid reading.

Landa gave the phonetic value *a* to three glyphs. The first of these, T743, is universally recognized as a turtle, which, in Maya, is *aac.* The second is identified by Zimmermann as his glyph 28 (T238) and the third as his glyph 3 (T15). Zimmermann (1956, p. 15) points out that both T238 and T15 can very well be glyphs for the subject pronoun and possessive pronoun of the second person singular, Maya *a,* and that they show substantial interchangeability in use. He also points out that T15 shows interchangeability with T743 in inscriptions at Chichen Itza, and so suggests reading both of them *ac.* This is accepted by Barthel (1955a, p. 20), who thinks that the context suggests sacrificial connotations and hence that these glyphs stand for *ac,* the grass used to draw blood from the tongue for sacrifice.

Since T238 does show functional correspondence with Maya *a* and interchangeability with both T743 and T15, I would prefer to follow Landa and read all three of them as *a,* recognizing that T743 may well have been read *aac* at an earlier date and keeping this in mind as a possible alternative. The reading *a* for T238 goes back to Brasseur de Bourbourg. Knorozov has read both T238 and T15 as *a* but retains the conventional *aac* for T743. Knorozov's contextual readings of *a* for T15 offer substantial support for reading T743 also as *a,* since the two interchange at Chichen Itza.

T140 (Fig. 66) affords a good example of the disparate results that stem from differing approaches to the problems of decipherment. Suggestions as to its meaning range from a multimorpheme phrase to short grammatical particles. T140 consists of a pair of circles with three dots forming a triangle between them. In the more elaborate forms, the inverted *ahau* (T178) appears as the outer pair of circles. T140 is affixed to a skull, which seems to be a subsidiary name or attribute of the Death God, and Thompson (1950, p. 268) suggests that the three dots in the postfix stand for *multun,* since *multuntzek* 'heap of skulls' is a Yucatec phrase for mass death; the affix also appears with *imix,* for which Thompson suggests a translation of 'heaped-up abundance'. Thompson's interpretation involves the view that a single glyph may be used to represent an entire phrase or, at least, a word which the Mayas could easily have seen was composed of more than one morpheme. I think *multun* would have been represented by the two known glyphs *mul* and *tun.* Without very good evidence, I would reject a priori the view that a single glyph may represent two or more obviously distinct

morphemes. I except such forms as *haab* or *balam,* whose etymological origin may well have been obscure to the Maya even when the script was coming into existence.

Barthel has suggested that T140 should be read *ban* 'lots of', an interpretation which retains Thompson's idea that the suffix refers to quantity, but puts it into a single morpheme, which I find much more acceptable. Knorozov (1955a, p. 76, no. 146) regards T140 as the suffix *-l,* which forms nouns and neuter verbs. From the fact that it substitutes for the final glyph (T178) in the glyger which I read Kakupacal, I assume that it is largely or entirely substitutable with T178, the inverted *ahau,* which I read *la.* I therefore think it is also to be read either *-l(a)* (which, in essence, agrees with Knorozov's reading) or *-lal(a),* in which the doubled occurrence of the inverted *ahau* indicates a repeated value. In this case, we would get a form Kakupacalal(a), which is a grammatically possible sequence. However, I am unable to demonstrate that the occurrence of this form in the texts is in grammatically appropriate contexts.

When one considers the paucity of papers on Maya grammar, it is surprising to find that two papers have been devoted to the grammatical affix *-al,* related to the suffix *-l,* just discussed. Barthel (1954) considered that T23 was *-al,* while Fought (1965) rejected this view and argued that T103, the bundle glyph, was *-al.* I have suggested that T103 is, in fact, a bundle (which Fought had doubted) and that it could stand for an early Maya **ɔal* 'heavy'. The argument is multifaceted, for Thompson had considered that T23 was another glyph to be read *te,* while Knorozov thought that T23 was *na* and that T103 was, perhaps, *-n* or *-h(e).* The basis of Knorozov's reading *na* for T23 is its occurrence in the glyger for God D, whom he, like most modern scholars, regards as Itzamna. This occurrence is left unexplained by Barthel's reading, a factor largely responsible for Fought's rejection of that reading. Thompson's argument that T23 represented a second *te* can probably be ignored; no one has adopted it, and its author has abandoned it for Barthel's reading. Barthel considered four contexts where T23 as *-al* seemed to him plausible. Fought points out that none of these is clear-cut and that in one case the proposed interpretation disagrees with the glyphic sequence. In another of these contexts, T23 is affixed to T561 'sky', generally accepted as Maya *caan.* The affixed form *caanal* should mean 'on high', according to Barthel himself. However, if one compares the passages where T23 is affixed to T561 with those where T561 occurs alone, both seem to mean 'sky' or 'heaven', rather than 'on high'. Figure 110 shows a passage from Copan with 'four' prefixed, where the reference is surely to the fourth 'heaven' rather than to the fourth 'on high'. The *kin* glyph likewise does not seem to change its meaning in any obvious way when T23 is affixed; *kinal* would be 'heat', and this could be the meaning in some cases, but it is not required by the context in any case. To say that there is no obvious change does not, of course, mean that the affix is necessarily devoid of meaning; it indicates, rather, that decipherment is difficult; I doubt that *-al*, which has such strong and obvious effects on meaning, can be the correct decipherment of T23. On the other hand, while the context of T23 in God D's name glyger gives strong support to a reading *na*, it does not really seem to explain adequately many other occurrences of the glyph.

Fought's consideration of T103 is both the most comprehensive consideration of a glyph in all contexts and the most linguistically sophisticated study which has yet been published. On the whole, I am inclined to think that his reading is preferable to Knorozov's *-h(e)*, and it is certainly preferable to Knorozov's *-n*. None of the readings resulting from Fought's identification are implausible, insofar as I can tell.

It should be pointed out that Fought's reading for the 'baptize' glyph, *chehali* 'it, or she, is sprinkling', contains an unexplained *-h-*. Fought says that Knorozov's reading, *chehi*, ignores T103 entirely, but this is untrue. Knorozov is here reading T103 as *-h(e)-*, thus explaining the *-h-* which is not accounted for in Fought's reading. On the other hand, it is not explained why this reading would not give *che-he-i*, since T103 would here be internal. The use of T103 with offerings is perhaps the most difficult context to explain, and such a form as *xocal*, read for 'fish' and suffixed T103, must be rejected as not relevant to a fish offering, since *xoc* is a shark and depictions of fish offerings suggest rather small fish. I strongly doubt that sharks were usually offered to the gods by the Maya. See Chapter 5 for some distinctions between *xoc, ca,* and possibly other fish glyphs. (Reasons for the phonetic rendering of the "comb" (T25) and its allographs, the fish head and small fish, as *ca* have been given in Chapter 9. Possible grammatical functions will be considered below in connection with the count group, of which it is a member.)

Another suffix apparently represents a knot (T186). In 1955, Knorozov (*1955a,* sec. 1, no. 70) identified the grapheme as a 'manojo de ramas' ('bundle of twigs') and read it phonetically *tah,* a past-tense, active-voice suffix to applicative verbs (ibid., p. 59). Two morphemes are presumably involved: *t* and *ah,* the latter being the past-tense suffix previously discussed. Knorozov now maintains that a single glyph could not express two morphemes; this probably is the reason that he has withdrawn the reading (Knorozov 1963, p. 287). In any case, it is by no means clear that this glyph is a verbal suffix. It occurs most frequently with T585 as the locative for the 'place of footsteps' and is found both as a prefix and as a suffix. As a prefix, it is found only in the *Madrid,* and I have given elsewhere my reasons for thinking that the *Madrid* scribe is not to be trusted in such matters without some sort of external controls. I regard this grapheme as still undeciphered.

Few of the other readings of grammatical particles which have been suggested are convincing, although some warrant discussion. Knorozov (*1955a,* no. 71) thought that T558 was *bal,* a present passive suffix to verbs. T558 appears compounded with *lu,* and Knorozov, following the principle of vowel synharmony, later thought it must be *bu.* I have shown that in four other glygers it appears compounded with *pa, ca, ka,* and the probable *na,* and that therefore *ba* is a more likely reading, which has some contextual support. *Ba* is a reflexive particle used with pronouns or verbs. I know of no evidence applying to grammatical functions with the latter reading.

Knorozov (*1955a,* no. 89) has read the "long-bone" suffix (T110) as either *ta* or *toc* and T109 as *chac* (long known) or *ta.* Despite the grammatical importance of *ta* in verbal affixes, there seems to be little or no grammatical support for the readings. I am inclined to think that T109 has some sort of grammatical function in some cases, but I doubt that it is *ta.*

An important grammatical glyph is T172. Knorozov (*1955a,* no. 128) has read this as *et,* represented by Yucatec *yetel* 'and'. On D24, the glyphs of the five deities pierced by spears in the Venus table are shown in order. All five glygers have T172 prefixed. The first follows mention of two of the five deities who do the piercing. I would have expected something like 'against' rather than 'and' in this context. On D72a, T172 follows *bat* of the sky peccary (see Fig. 85) and precedes *cab* 'earth', where some such meaning as 'toward', 'at', or 'on' would seem more appropriate than 'and'. In some cases, it seems to connect unlike things, as on D66a, where it precedes the name of the Corn God and follows an elaborate glyph which has an unknown meaning but does not seem to be a deity name. Although I have nothing better to propose, Knorozov's reading is not what I would have expected from these contexts. Barthel (1965a, p. 154) has read T172 as *hul.* Barthel believes that the glyph represents the feathers of an arrow shaft, standing for *hul* 'arrow', and indicates 'shot' in the previously mentioned passage from the Venus table. While this interpretation is semantically reasonable in that passage, I do not know of parallel use of *hul* in later texts; it does not seem to fit semantically in other passages; and the occurrences suggest to me a grammatical prefix. The visual identification is not implausible, but neither is it very obvious.

Knorozov's attempt to read the *yax* glyph (T16, T17, some examples of T109) as *hal*, a root suffix of inchoate verbs, present tense, neuter voice, depends largely on the glyger for 'south'. Grammatical context offers very little support insofar as I have been able to determine. It may be that two originally distinct glyphs have been drawn more and more alike until they are indistinguishable in the codices, in which case there may well be two values for *yax*, but I see nothing to support the reading *hal*. As of 1963 (p. 295, no. 164) Knorozov preferred a reading *h(o)*.

An important analysis by Thompson which should ultimately lead to the decipherment of several grammatical glyphs was the recognition of a certain degree of interchangeability in two groups of affixes, which he called the *count group* and the *water group*. Figure 69 (rearranged from Thompson 1950, Fig. 5, with additions) shows the various elements of the count group. It will be seen that there is a very substantial overlap in the distribution of the various glyphs which occur as prefixes here. This overlap is more than adequate to suggest that all these glyphs have somewhat similar functions. Only one of them is known and accepted without dispute, and this is the possessive *u* (T1). This glyph appears in a substantial number of other contexts where most of the count group do not. A fish head appears in some few cases in this group and is one of the reasons Thompson called this the count group. Having correctly made the important decipherment of *xoc* 'shark' as a rebus for *xoc* 'count', he went on to argue that all fish glyphs represented counting. I have argued that the *xoc* glyph can be distinguished from the fish head which substitutes for the "comb" and that the latter is to be read *ca*. In the contexts of counting time periods, *ca* probably should be translated 'then'. Thompson maintained that the glyphs I read *xoc* and *ca* were substitutable with the upended fish head, which he likewise included in the count group. I am by no means certain that this head represents a fish rather than a reptile. In any case, I doubt very much that it represents either *xoc* or *ca*. Finally, Thompson associated the *muluc* glyph (Fig. 4) with this group. I have argued in Chapter 5 that this glyph represents *mul* 'turn, rotate, revolve' and that the *xoc* fish is not the head form of *muluc/mul*. Here it need merely be pointed out that *mul* occurs inside the Glyph B "el-

bow" (a fact which may ultimately be important for the decipherment of that glyph) but not as a prefix to it and that it is found as a prefix to the *cab* verb. The latter is the only case where *mul* overlaps with the members of the count group in the stricter sense.

One other decipherment of a member of this group can, I think, be made with some probability. Knorozov (1955a, no. 136 and p. 59) suggested that *ca* 'two' substituted for *ca* 'and'. The dots with a cross between them have been confused with the death-eyes glyph, but are apparently nothing more than *ca* 'two'. In the count group, they probably stand for *ca* 'then'.

A puzzling factor in this series is the occurrence of the manikin death's head and the (partly?) equivalent death eyes. I have defended Knorozov's interpretation of the latter as the agentive *ah*, but in this context Thompson's reading *hitz'* 'extinction' seems slightly more likely on present evidence. It may be noted that Tzeltal *-ajtay* is 'to count' and *ajtal* is 'calendar, date', while Huaxtec *ajib* is 'fiesta'; these words suggest that some former meaning of *ah* may be relevant. Possibly this is a grapheme with multiple readings.

From another viewpoint, one finds that these glyphs are attached, first, to temporal units (to tuns, katuns, and cycles) and to glygers which seem to refer to cyclical units. I have the impression that they are attached to these time glyphs as points in time, rather than as periods of time, but this interpretation is largely dependent on the interpretation of *ca* as 'then'. These particles are likewise associated with what seem to be verbs. Glyph C of the Lunar Series certainly seems to be a verb, as does the *cab* glyph with T126. Context indicates that the "knotted death" combination (Fig. 69, col. 10) is also a verb. Taken together, it seems likely that most of the glyphs of the count group function as temporal locatives.

One glyph for which I would, very tentatively, suggest a possible reading is the bracket with a line of dots (T11; see Fig. 69, row 3). Thompson (1950, p. 187) points out rare cases of substitution of T11 for T25, the "comb," which leads him to suppose that the two glyphs are fully equivalent; their rarity leads me to presume that some change of meaning or reading is involved. In one case, T11 replaces T25 in the *imix*-comb-*imix* combination (T558.25:558), for which I have suggested the reading *bacab(a)* and the meaning of a title. If T11 is distinct, one would expect another word, *ba*-x-*b(a)*, which is also a title. This expectation would be fulfilled by *ba-ta-b(a)*. *Ta* is a known locative, closely parallel in function and meaning with *ti*. It is known to be used with periods

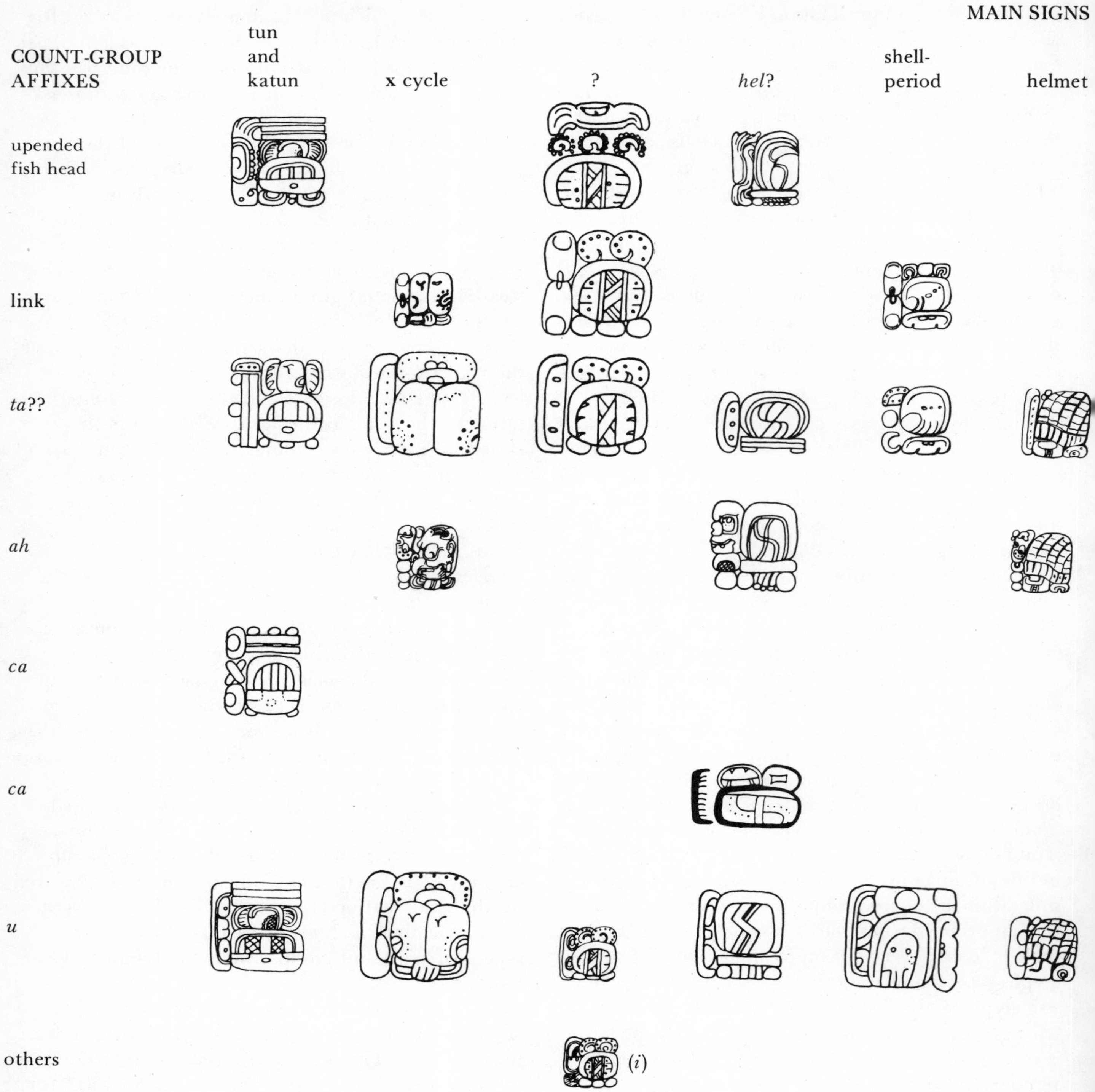

Figure 69. The count group and related affixes.

God C in "elbow"	Glyph B ("elbow")	*tup(a)*	"knotted death" verb	cab x verb	*haabil?*	others

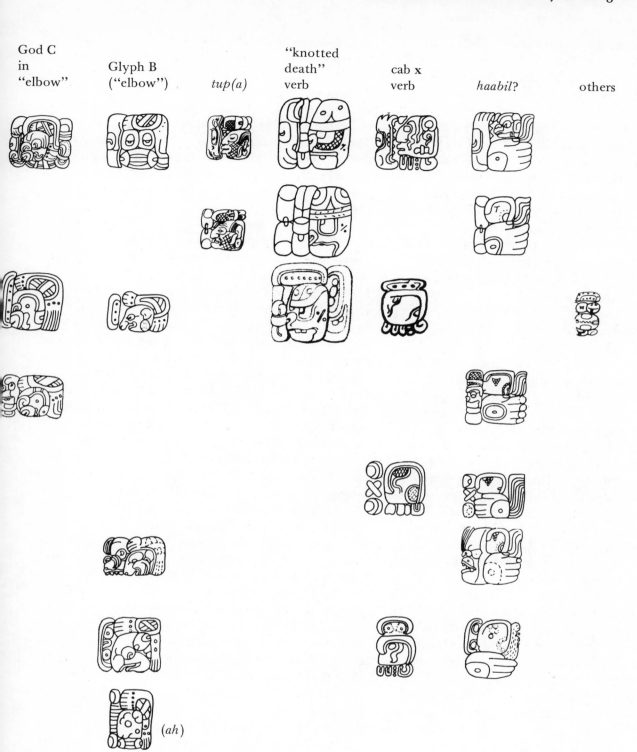

(ah)

of time. Moreover, the bracket with a line of dots occurs once (Palenque, TFC, 017) prefixed to the Palenque Emblem Glyph. This suggests that it can be a locative with places as well as with time periods. While far from conclusive, this interpretation is quite possible. It has been suggested that *ta* and *ti* both derive from a single original morpheme. This interpretation is possible, but it is equally possible that two different original morphemes are involved.

From contextual usage, the "link" glyph seems to be a member of the count group, but I know of no adequate evidence for its reading or meaning.

The water group of affixes consists of the various prefixes found with the Emblem Glyphs (Fig. 72). Their conceptual unity is higher than that of the count group, for most of them do show plausible connections with water. This fact is considerably more puzzling since the discovery of the function of the Emblem Glyphs (see Chapter 11) than it was previously. One would expect the water-group affixes to represent some sort of fairly standardized prefix, perhaps a locative particle, perhaps a phrase such as 'in the town of' or 'of the lineage of' or whatever local phenomenon they represent. It is hard to think of any phrase with water connotations which might be appropriate. The infixed elements *yax* 'blue' and *kan* 'yellow' might suggest color-direction symbolism, but nothing else seems to point in that direction, and none of the prefixes as a whole is deciphered. Barthel (1966c) has discussed this group at length. His interpretations may be found in Chapter 11 below. A number of his suggestions seem to support the view that lineages are referred to.

The so-called *ben-ich* superfix (T168; see Fig. 72), present with this group, is likewise a puzzle. Thompson (1950, pp. 200–201) argues that the second element of this superfix is a conventionalized center from a Lamat glyph, pointing out that some early compounds show a *ben-lamat*. He also points out that Lamat is the day of Venus and that Venus is called Noh Ich, or Nohoch Ich 'big eye' or 'big face'. He suggests that the superfix, when found as an element in the name of the Sun God, may convert *kin* to Kinich, a known later name of the Sun God. This is, of course, one of the examples he can use to support his position that glyphic order does not invariably coincide with spoken order. The *ben* has to be ignored in his explanation of the prefix. Cordy (1946, p. 111) read *ben* as its calendar equivalent *ah* and the second element as *au*, hence *ahau* 'lord, ruler' or 'he of the *milpa* [cornfield]'. Knorozov once read *behla*, *be(n)hele* 'now' (Knorozov 1955a, sec. 2, no. 60) but now reads *bentzil* (Knorozov 1967, p. 86). Cordan (1963a, pp. 40–41) regards the basic glyph as a fire

and reads *kich-ben*. The two elements interchange their positions, one is equivalent to *ben*, and they are used with the Emblem Glyphs in a way which makes me suppose that they are a locative. Nonetheless, I am not satisfied with any of the suggested transcriptions. Barthel (1966c, p. 161) points out that *ben* 'high' is equivalent in meaning to *ich* 'high' and thinks that this may be some sort of morphemic parallelism. This hypothesis nicely explains the variability of order of the glyphs. (For further discussion of T168, see Chapter 11.)

From these decipherments, I must turn to a consideration of the general question of whether or not the Maya possessed determinatives, and, if so, what kind. Cordy (1946) was the first to declare fully and explicitly that they did. His nicest example, in my opinion, is the identification of the *ti* glyph as *kuch* 'cotton thread', used with the pictograph of the head of the vulture, *kuch*. Unfortunately, this was prior to Thompson's demonstration that the glyph was actually *ti*. Without the latter, I would certainly have regarded this example of Cordy's as a valid and important decipherment, showing how two elements might be used together to indicate a particular word.

Although it has never been explicitly pointed out, the orthodox use of Yucatec day and month names is suggestive of some examples of determinatives. The months called Ch'en, Yax, Zac, and Ceh (Fig. 5) contain a glyph (T528) identical with the Cauac day sign, which, following Thompson, I recognize as *haab* 'year'; yet no one has suggested that the months be read as Ek-haab, Yax-haab, Zac-haab, and Chac-haab, as would be appropriate in this case. Anyone who accepts the Yucatec forms for these names without further doubt thereby also accepts some sort of determinative for these months. This decipherment is also bound up in several other problems. Knorozov maintains that *haab* is etymologically a compound (it is probably *haa* 'rain' plus agentive, rather than *haa* plus plural, as suggested by Lounsbury in Fought 1965, p. 262) and that a single grapheme could not represent two morphemes. Hence he regards the *haab* glyph as an unread determinative for a period of time. This has support from the Yucatec month names Yax and Zac as recorded in colonial times (see Fig. 70). On the other hand, the *Dresden* compound which Thompson deciphered through Yucatec *kintunyaabil* 'drought' is regarded by Knorozov as simply *kintun*. In this case, spoken Yucatec supports the view that the glyph is *haab* and was read. There is no basic disagreement on the meaning of the glyph, for *haab* may refer to a period of time other than a year and, indeed, other than a rainy season, as *kintunyaabil* for 'drought'

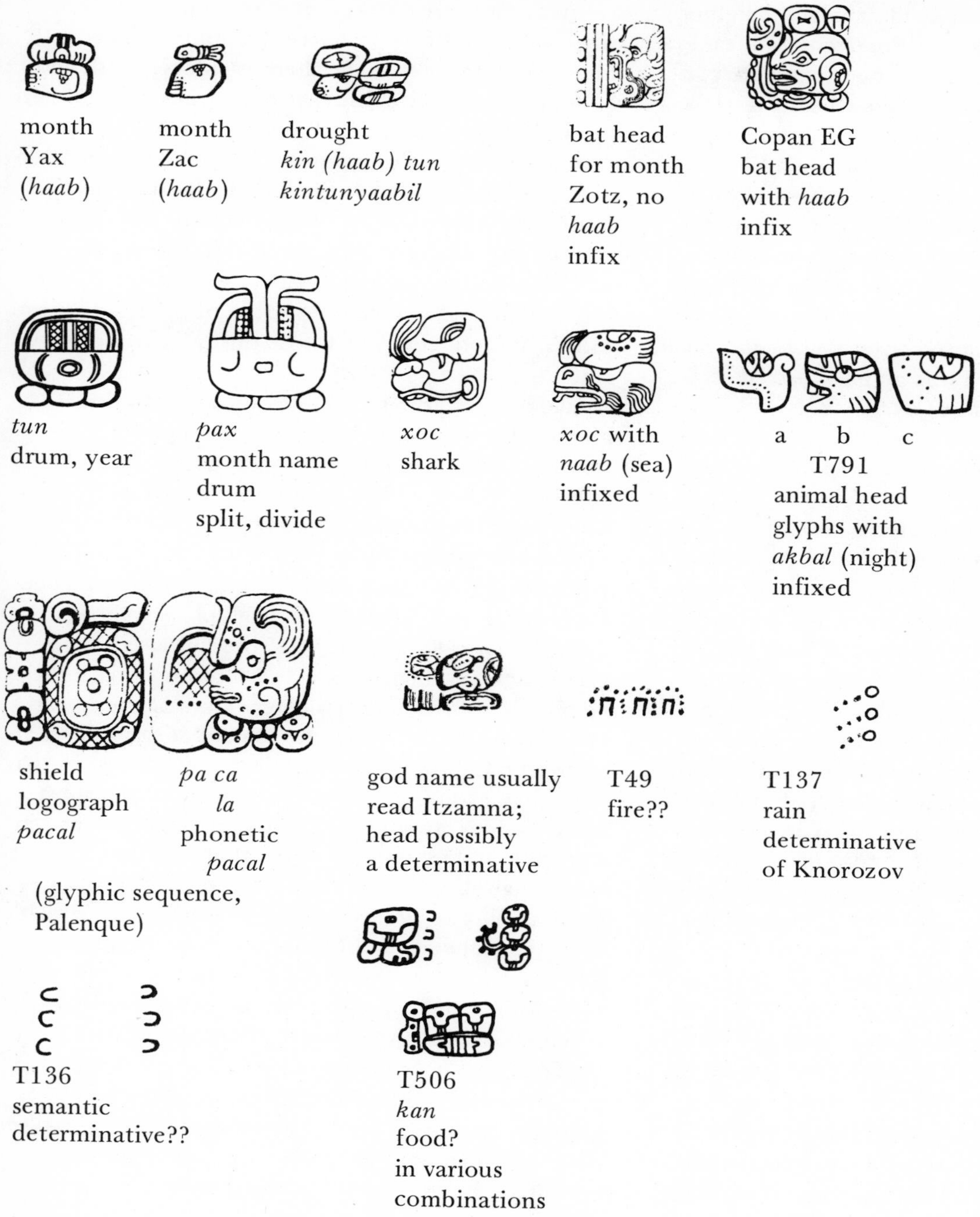

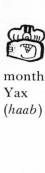

month
Yax
(*haab*)

month
Zac
(*haab*)

drought
*kin (haab) tun
kintunyaabil*

bat head
for month
Zotz, no
haab
infix

Copan EG
bat head
with *haab*
infix

tun
drum, year

pax
month name
drum
split, divide

xoc
shark

xoc with
naab (sea)
infixed

a   b   c
T791
animal head
glyphs with
akbal (night)
infixed

shield
logograph
pacal

*pa ca
la*
phonetic
pacal

(glyphic sequence,
Palenque)

god name usually
read Itzamna;
head possibly
a determinative

T49
fire??

T137
rain
determinative
of Knorozov

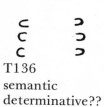

T136
semantic
determinative??

T506
kan
food?
in various
combinations

Figure 70. Determinatives.

adequately demonstrates. As a day name, the glyph was read Cauac in Yucatec. In the *Dresden*, it takes two forms as a day name. These two forms are consistently found in different glygers when it is not a day name, although no corresponding difference is determinable on the monuments. In one set of glygers, context suggests the meaning 'period of time' and the reading *haab* (following Thompson); in the other, the glyph is found where the phonetic value *cu* is appropriate (following Landa; see Chapter 9). The suggestion is that on the monuments the one glyph T528 was read, according to context, as *Cauac, haab,* or *cu* and that in *Dresden* one glyph was read as *Cauac* or *haab,* the other as *Cauac* or *cu,* while, at least by late times, the *haab* variant was sometimes not read at all and hence was a determinative in the strict sense.

The same glyph is also apparently found as a determinative in a different sense in Classic Period inscriptions. Barthel (1955*a*, p. 29) has pointed out that in some highland Maya languages the word for 'bat' is a homonym of a word for 'clouds' (although Quiche shows vowel variation, *zutz'* 'cloud, storm', *zotz'* 'bat', some Mayance languages show -*u*- in the 'bat' word). Barthel suggested that the Copan Emblem Glyph (not then recognized) is a good example of the use of a bat pictograph to mean 'cloud'. Supporting this is the presence of T528 as an infix in the bat head. Here, I would suggest, the root *haa* 'rain' is involved and used solely as a determinative to indicate that the 'cloud' meaning of **sutz* rather than the 'bat' one is basic.

A very interesting type of variation is the difference between *tun* 'drum' and *pax* 'drum'. The splitting of the latter apparently corresponds to *pax* 'split, divide, break' and thus differentiates the synonyms *tun* and *pax.*

Another example, both of multiple referents for a single grapheme and of the use of a grapheme as a determinant, probably not read, is to be found in the *imix* glyph (T501, for which the "type" is, in fact, aberrant). Cognate forms in other languages suggest that the day name was originally **Muxi* or **Moxi,* with metathesis and assimilation giving the Yucatec form. Thompson showed that the glyph represented a water lily, and Barthel drew the logical conclusion that it could be read as *naab* 'water lily' and in such compounds as *nabte* 'spear'; I have extended this to use as a homonym, *nab* 'ocean, lagoon, lake', an interpretation with which Barthel tells me he concurs. The water-lily glyph with this meaning also seems to substitute for a hand glyph read by Knorozov as *naab* 'palm of the hand'. Thompson shows that the shark (Yuc. *xoc*) was used as a homonym for *xoc* 'to

count', and the *naab* glyph is sometimes infixed in the head of this fish. I believe it is simply a determinative to show that the shark is an ocean fish and help avoid possible confusion with other types of fish heads.

Another probable example of an ideographic determinant may be found in the 'night' glyph (T504) frequently infixed in the eyes of certain animal-head glyphs. The probable purpose of this was to indicate that the animal was an animal active during the nighttime, helping to prevent confusion of the head with others. I doubt very much that this infix was directly read.

The only clear-cut example of a phonetic/ideographic determinant which I think can be fully recognized is a glyph or series of glyphs with several variants which appears at Palenque. In some places, a conventionalized shield glyph appears (T624); in similar contexts, the sequence T602.25:139 appears; and in still other cases, both appear. 'Shield' in Yucatec Maya is *pacal,* and the three glyphs are those I read phonetically as *pa-ca-la* in the supposed name Kakupacal at Chichen Itza. As I interpret this, either *pa-ca-la* is a phonetic supplement to distinguish between two possible words for 'shield', or the shield ideograph is a supplement to distinguish between two possible meanings of *pacal.* The nature of the substitution here is strong support for the reading *pacal,* in my opinion. It should be noted that *pacal* is probably etymologically a compound, *pac* + *al*; the shield ideograph is, thus, evidence against Knorozov's view that a single grapheme could never represent two morphemes.

Knorozov has suggested the use of several other determinatives. In the glyger usually regarded as that of Itzamna, the grapheme T1009 (but not all the glyphs considered variants of this by Thompson) has no phonetic role to play in Knorozov's interpretation. Knorozov suggests (1955*a*, no. 26) that, here and elsewhere, it is an unread ideographic determinative for 'god'. Barthel, originally inclined to accept this statement, wrote me in October 1956 that he preferred rather to regard it as 'brujo' ('witch'). If Knorozov's phonetic reading is accepted, we must consider T1009 a determinative or an epithet of Itzamna.

Knorozov (1955*a*, no. 116) regards T49 as a determinative for 'fire'. It is certainly found in two different glygers for 'fire', but in my opinion neither of them can be read well enough to make it seem at all likely that T49 is not a phonetic element of some word or phrase for 'fire'.

An affix which suggests raindrops and occurs in rain contexts is T137. This glyph is regarded as a "rain determinative" by Knorozov but may equally well be a word for rain. Its meaning is almost certainly 'rain'.

The *kan* glyph (T506) appears repeatedly as an element in offering glyphs. Despite its known reading, *kan*, no one has suggested what seems to me a really plausible reason for this use. Knorozov (1955a, no. 49) suggests that it is a determinative for 'food'. He has accepted Thompson's identification of the glyph as a shell and amplified it by pointing out that one meaning of *kan* is 'shell'. The unexplained difficulty here is the reason why a shell (or a phonetic *kan*) should stand for 'food'. If this could be explained, the context would make Knorozov's explanation seem quite plausible.

Finally, Knorozov (1955a, no. 150) has suggested that T136 has the very remarkable quality of being a "determinador de sentido [determinant of meaning]." Judging by his examples, this means a glyph used to distinguish between two possible readings of a single grapheme. Thus, when *yax* 'new, green' is accompanied by T136, it becomes 'south' in the codices; however, on the monuments the 'south' glyph has a main element which is quite different from the monumental form of *yax*—yet the "hooks" (T136) are present. It is hardly likely that the hooks distinguish 'south' from 'green' when the two are already completely different. Other examples seem to me equally unconvincing. I suspect that T136 is, rather, some normal grammatical suffix.

Although it is not directly a question of grammar, some consideration of the methods of glyph composition used by the Mayas seems appropriate here, as these methods have played a certain role in the general question of the importance of affixes, and as some processes, such as infixing, present problems in reading the glyphs. Thompson (1950, pp. 37–46; 1962, pp. 25–28) has presented more detail on this problem than anyone else. Following Beyer, he defines as affixes those glyphs which always join their main signs with their bases (defined by superfix position). One of the most important conclusions of his study was that the order of elements is far more important than the particular way in which they are arranged in glyph blocks. Thus, some affixes may occur to the left of a main sign or above it, both being interpretable as prefixed elements; others may occur to the right or below, both being suffixed elements. Occasionally, affixes shift from one glyph block to another or from one main sign to another without obvious changes in meaning. Thus, Thompson (1950, p. 39) writes, "A very common glyph . . . is composed of two Imix signs, the second of which

has the comb prefix . . . but in one text this prefix becomes a postfix without seemingly any change in general meaning." The statement does not make it clear that the element normally prefixed to the *second* glyph becomes postfixed to the *first* glyph, so that no change in order of the elements of the glyger is involved. Again, Thompson points out that the *tu* glyph may appear either suffixed to *kinil* or prefixed to the month glyph, with no change in order. He compares this to "wrong punctuation," but it seems to me more like breaking a word at the end of a line. Despite the plausibility of the rule that meaning does not change if order remains constant, Berlin (1963, p. 94) has demonstrated an important apparent exception to it. The glyger appears in the two forms shown in Figure 71, upper right corner. When it appears in the first form, it is used with the glyph of only one of the three deities forming Berlin's Palenque Triad. When it appears in the second form, it is used with the glyphs of all three of the deities. It is possible that a change in order is actually involved here, since I would normally read the four graphemes of the second variant in the order Tiii.597.43:59, whereas I would read those of the first variant in the order iii.597:59.43; the fact that the graphemes themselves do not change and that they obviously share most of their meaning would suggest, however, that no change in order is involved. This very acute observation of Berlin's shows that we should be wary of assuming that apparently minor changes do not involve grammatical changes or minor shifts in meaning.

The nature of infixes is a difficult problem. In three cases I have suggested that they functioned as ideographic determinants and were not read. Sometimes a glyph which is normally prefixed above or to the left may be infixed. T679, *i* (Fig. 66), is an example (Fig. 71; Thompson 1950, p. 37). Or a glyph which is normally postfixed may be infixed in the head form of what is normally a prefix (Fig. 71; Thompson 1950, p. 38). This suggests that the order of reading of infixes was not invariable; yet such glyphs would almost certainly have been read. Generally, head variants are not infixed. In an analytical sense, it is often difficult to decide whether a recurrent element of several glyphs, also found independently, should be considered an infix of those glyphs or simply a part of them.

Glyph fusion, in which the elements of one glyph or glyger are combined with those of another, sometimes occurs (Fig. 71). No one has yet demonstrated any resultant change either in meaning, reading, or context.

Duplication of affixes is presently a matter of considerable dispute. Beyer and subsequently Thomp-

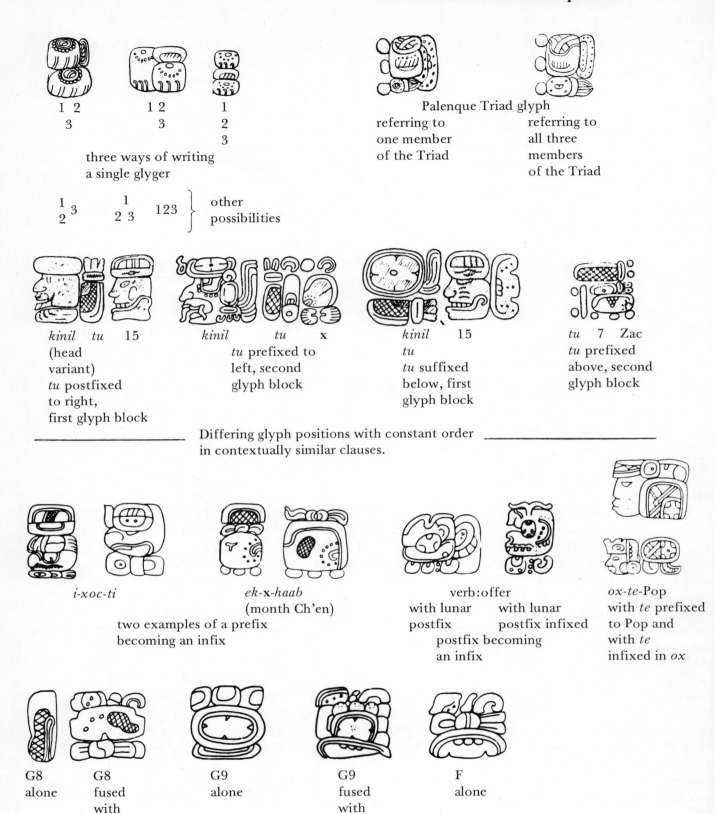

1 2
3

1 2
3

1
2
3

three ways of writing
a single glyger

Palenque Triad glyph

referring to
one member
of the Triad

referring to
all three
members
of the Triad

$\frac{1}{2}$ 3 $\frac{1}{2 \, 3}$ 123 } other
possibilities

kinil *tu* 15
(head
variant)
tu postfixed
to right,
first glyph block

kinil *tu* x
tu prefixed to
left, second
glyph block

kinil 15
tu
tu suffixed
below, first
glyph block

tu 7 Zac
tu prefixed
above, second
glyph block

—————————— Differing glyph positions with constant order ——————————
in contextually similar clauses.

i-xoc-ti

*ek-**x**-haab*
(month Ch'en)

two examples of a prefix
becoming an infix

verb:offer
with lunar   with lunar
postfix   postfix infixed
postfix becoming
an infix

ox-te-Pop
with *te* prefixed
to Pop and
with *te*
infixed in *ox*

G8
alone

G8
fused
with
F

G9
alone

G9
fused
with
F

F
alone

Figure 71. Glyph composition.

son have maintained that such duplication is purely aesthetic and involves no change in meaning. To me, it seems strange that Thompson, who has been primarily responsible for showing the futility of the view that affixes are mere decorative elements, should try to retain this view with respect to one type of affixing. (See the full discussion in Chapter 9.)

Finally, we must consider the relationship between graphemes and morphemes. At present, it seems to be universally admitted that in some cases a single grapheme may be read as a single morpheme, with single or multiple referents. Examples are the glyphs read *tun*, translated variously as 'year', 'stone', 'end', and *kal*, which may be read as 'twenty', 'imprison', 'ruler'. The occurrence of single graphemes with multiple linguistic referents seems to be accepted in principle by everyone, although it is hard to find examples acceptable to all. I have suggested that the readings *cauac/haab/cu* for T528 and *imix/naab* for T501 are valid. It is also generally accepted that a glyger consisting of two graphemes may represent two morphemes with a single meaning. The best example is the glyger for 'ceiba', consisting of *yax* 'green' and *te* 'tree', in combination *yaxte*, i.e, Yucatec *yaxche* 'ceiba'. Thompson, Barthel, and others with a largely ideographic approach apparently consider that all examples of glygers with a single meaning are of this type. I, however, follow Knorozov in regarding such glygers as those for 'dog' and 'turkey' as being composed entirely of phonetic glyphs which have no separate semantic components—e.g., *tzu-l(u)* and *cu-tz(u)*. Put differently, these are two-grapheme glygers each of which represents a single morpheme. Another disputed question is whether a single grapheme may under any circumstances represent more than one morpheme. Knorozov (1958b, p. 290) has said flatly that this is impossible, rejecting a number of his own earlier readings because of this principle. I hold the intermediate position that an old and stabilized compound which comprised a single "word" to the Mayas may be represented by a single grapheme, despite the fact that it is etymologically composed of more than one morpheme. *Pacal* 'shield' and *haab* 'year' seem to me good examples of this. Thompson goes farther and maintains that a single grapheme may represent an object or group of objects which would normally be referred to by a series of obviously distinct morphemes. Thompson's *mul-tun* for T140 has been accepted by the Mérida school, but I am still unable to accept that there are any valid examples of this process.

One surprise, to me, was the discovery that apparently a word might be recorded phonetically in a way that did not coincide with its etymological origins, although there are still so few examples that they are denied by many scholars in the field. The most striking is the often-mentioned glyger for Kakupacal. Etymologically, this is clearly *kak-u-pacal* 'Fire His Shield'; phonetically, it was rendered *ka-ku-pa-ca-l(a)*. It may be noted in passing that this is good evidence that final vowels had been lost by the time of the Chichen Itza inscriptions which contain this glyger. Another example, suggested by Michael Coe, is *mochilte* 'cage'. Etymologically, this is *moch* + attributive -*il* + *te* 'wood'; phonetically, it is *mo* + x + *te* (Lounsbury and Coe 1966).

We also know that some morphemes which are phonetically identical in Yucatec may be represented by two distinct graphemes, associated with different meanings. The best example is the difference between the glyphs for *kan* 'yellow' and Kan, a day name. We do not know how common such glyphs are, nor whether they may reflect a time when the pronunciation was at least slightly different. It is generally accepted that a single word may be represented without any obvious change of meaning or use by either a symbolic glyph or its head variant, but there is no clear example of two different symbolic graphemes read in precisely the same way.

Despite the gaps in our knowledge, we have advanced greatly in the past twenty years, and the basic nature of the relationship between script and speech seems fairly clear.

The following linguistic reconstructions, derived from Kaufman 1964, may have some relevance to the glyphs which have been considered in this section. Reconstructions apply to the whole family unless otherwise specified. Periods are used to separate reconstructions for one meaning from reconstructions for the next.

Reflexive pronoun: (a) **bah*, Tzel.-Tzo.-Yuc.-H.-Kan.-Chu.-Chl.-Chr.; (b) **'ib*, Q.-Pch. (Mam?). Demonstrative: **ha'*. What? (a) **tu/ti*; (b) **bi/ba*. Definite article: **te*. This: **'in*. Emphatic pronoun: **tukw*. Plural suffix: **tyaq*. SERIES A: First person singular: **'in/w*. Second person singular: **'a*. Third person singular: **y*, (H.?). First person plural: **q*, (Jac.-Kan.?). Second person plural: **e*. Third person plural: **ky*. SERIES B: First person singular: **'in*. Second person singular: **atw*. Third person singular: **nulo*. First person plural: **'ong*. Second person plural: **ex/ox*. Third person plural: **eb/ob/ab*. Negative: **ma*. In, at: **tyë*. There is: **'ë'y*. Where: **bëy*. And: **'ix/'ax*. There: (a) **te/ti*; (b) **le'*. Yes: **me/mi*. Still, yet: **toh/toj*. Perhaps: **wa'n*. Of, for: **y-u'un/y-u'uj*.

Chapter 11
Places
and People

Prior to 1958, most Mayan scholars thought that there was little or no historical information in the Mayan inscriptions. Despite nearly a century of study, no one had discovered glyphs for place names or for names of historical individuals. The lengthy dates and calculations which made up most of the inscriptions were believed to deal principally with elaborate attempts to record changes in calendrical or astronomical calculations. A few individuals, such as Spinden, reiterated the contention that the scenes of battle and representations of individuals on the monuments suggested preoccupation with warfare and dynastic matters, but such statements did not lead to any detailed studies.

A major change in orientation occurred with the publication of a paper by Berlin in 1958 dealing with a series of glyphs which he called Emblem Glyphs (EGs), which showed direct associations with particular sites. Berlin gave them this name because he did not wish to commit himself as to whether they were names of local deities, dynastic names, place names, or other localized phenomena. This paper was followed very closely by another brief paper of Berlin's (1959) trying to show the presence of glyphs for individuals on the famous Palenque sarcophagus, and by a very detailed and convincing presentation of data from Piedras Negras by Proskouriakoff (1960), showing evidence for a historical interpretation of the monuments at that site in terms of a dynastic sequence.

Thus, the whole problem was removed quickly from the realm of a priori argument to that of specific interpretation of particular glyphs. Four additional papers by Proskouriakoff (1961a, 1961b, 1963, 1964a), one by myself (Kelley 1962b), another by Berlin (1965a), one by Barthel (1966c), one by Coe and Benson (1966), and one by Jacinto Quirarte (1968a) added a wealth of detail in support of the general contention that much of the subject matter of the inscriptions is historical. Thus far, there has been no attempt to disprove this interpretation, which seems widely accepted in principle, if not in detail.

Interestingly enough, Bowditch (1901) had remarkably anticipated Proskouriakoff's work in some brief notes on the recently published monuments of Piedras Negras. Although he did not recognize personal glyphs, birth glyphs, or inaugural glyphs, and although he wrote only of Stelae 1 and 3, he did suggest a fully historic interpretation: "Let us suppose the first date of Stela 3 to denote the birth; the second the initiation at the age of 12 years 140 days, or the age of puberty in those warm climates; the third, the choice as chieftain at the age of 33 years 265 days; the fourth his death at the age of 37 years

60 days" (Bowditch 1901, p. 13). After a parallel interpretation of Stela 1, he asks, "Could the two men represented on these stelae have been twins having the same birthday?"

If Bowditch or some contemporary scholar had gone on to check the glyphic context of this acute idea, scholars studying the Mayan writing might have been saved some sixty years of dubious astronomical interpretations.

There is still some disagreement as to the role of the Emblem Glyphs. I have maintained that they are simple place names, Proskouriakoff thinks they are probably dynastic names, and Berlin remains uncommitted. In general, the Emblem Glyph appears at the end of inscriptions when it relates to local affairs. It has a prefix of what Thompson called the water group plus the so-called *ben-ik/ben-ich* prefix (Fig. 72). With some few exceptions, when a "foreign" EG appears at a site, it is either (*a*) accompanied by glyphs including the heads of females, (*b*) associated with what seem to be the names of captives, or (*c*) associated with other foreign EGs. Among the prefixes, the head of the god of the number nine, a *kan* cross, and a *yax* glyph with additional elements are identifiable. In a very few cases, EGs appear with known locative prefixes. The standard prefixes frequently do not appear in early texts and are often not present with foreign EGs, especially when feminine heads are prefixed.

Barthel (1968*c*) has recently published a very interesting study of EGs with a well-integrated set of hypotheses about their meaning. The hypotheses fall into two general groups, one dealing with the relatively constant elements, the other with the variable local glyph. The following discussion draws heavily but not exclusively upon Barthel's paper. Some of his ideas are omitted, and occasionally relevant data have been added.

One of the distinctive features of the EG is the presence of the superfix T168. Despite the single number, this is composed of two glyphs, separately catalogued as T584, the glyph for the day called, in Yucatec, Ben and, in the highlands of Guatemala, Ah and as T687a. Either of the two may appear first. Since the order is variable, I would not be willing to accept the idea that T584 can be, here, the suffix *ben* or the masculine or agentive prefix *ah*. Barthel points out that Kekchi *ben* is 'Spitze, das Oberste, Erste' ('peak, supreme, first') and that *benil* is 'Erster, Oberster, Häuptling' ('first, highest, prince'), i.e., that the term may refer to high rank.

The interpretation of T687a has varied greatly. Seler read it as *kak* 'fire' and Cordan as *kich* 'warm oneself, incense burner', probably in part because of representations of the glyph amidst flames in the codices. Knorozov (1967, p. 86, no. 100) reads it as *tzil* for reasons which are not entirely clear to me. Thompson (1950, pp. 200–202) argued at some length for a reading *ich* 'eye, face, within'. In particular, he thought that the use of T168 prefixed to the *kin* glyph and with a suffix added might correspond to Kinich Ahau, a name of the Sun God. He also pointed out one case in which Lamat substitutes for T687a, which resembles the center of the Lamat glyph. The facts that Lamat is the day of Venus and that another name for Venus is Noh Ich 'Great Eye' seemed confirmatory. Moreover, T168 is prefixed to katun glyphs; Thompson suggested that here *ich* could correspond to the colonial Yucatec use of *ichil* 'within' as a prefix to katun names.

Barthel points out that *ich* derives from proto-Mayan *wéty,* which gives Quiche *vach,* which also means 'before, in front of'. Similar forms are found in other highland languages. This meaning corresponds well, in a metaphorical sense, with that previously given for *ben*. Hence, Barthel argues that *ben* and *ich* are both correct and that they form a synonymous pair. This is a common Mayan literary construction, but not normally found with the synonyms directly repeated in this fashion. This does explain the variability in order and makes the reading *ich* from *wéty* seem very plausible, suggesting that it indicates rank in this context. On the other hand, *ich* as a simple locative 'in' might coincide better with EGs as place names, but this interpretation would leave *ben* essentially unexplained.

T130 (Fig. 66), for which the reading *aan* seems to me best, often appears as a suffix to the EG, although its presence is not obligatory. It is presumably derived from *'ajan* 'green corncob' and may coincide with *'ahn* 'run, flee'. Barthel, pointing out a Chorti practice described by Rafael Girard in which a priest runs before the group in rituals, suggests that T168 prefixed and T130 suffixed may indicate 'he who runs before'. This seems to me semantically plausible, but the order of the graphemes seems grammatically wrong for this interpretation. I would rather suspect that T130 functions here as a locative suffix (a possibility suggested by Barthel), although I know of no evidence for *-aan* with this function.

The EG prefixes of the water group consist of a series of dots (T32 or T35), usually supposed to indicate a liquid, with various infixed elements. Barthel interprets the latter as various ornaments: a shell pectoral, a turquoise plaque, a bone pendant, and the *yax* glyph. Although Barthel does not mention it, Brinton long ago suggested the identity of *yax* with a feather ornament for a staff. Barthel points out that the highland Mexicans used terms like 'necklace', 'jade', and 'flower' for children and draws attention to the use of all these ornaments of the EG prefixes at Palenque in association with representations of babies. Seler's identification of the EG prefixes T32 and T35 as 'blood' might be correlated with highland Maya *qiqel 'blood, relatives', but Barthel prefers to read *pul*. Edmonson (1965, pp. 92–93) shows Quiche *pulih* as 'spill water, draw water' with Yucatec cognates and Quiche *pulub* as 'foam'. As a root, *pul*- may also mean 'born, to be born, to grow'. The double meaning fits very well here. In this case, the combination of *yax* with *pul* might well be read as 'first-born'; the other forms might express other relationships or equivalents. The interpretation seems to me highly likely. The EG proper, following 'first-born prince' or whatever other interpretation seems best, could still be a lineage, a tribe, or a place. Barthel, without reaching a firm decision, gives suggestive evidence in favor of tribes, which will be summarized later.

It should be borne in mind when working on this material that the original Maya names of nearly all the archaeological sites are unknown and that the names now used for most sites have been given during the last century. Even in Yucatán, where many native names survive, they often seem to be descriptive of the sites after they reached their present ruinous condition.

The EGs themselves are quite enigmatic. The bat head of Copan with its 'rain' infix (Fig. 72) is apparently to be read *sutz* with the meaning 'cloud'. This could refer to a cloud deity or conceivably to a bat deity or to the ethnic group later known as the Zotzil, as well as to a place name. No EG can be read or recognized as a definite, known deity name, a fact which seems to me to be strong evidence against that hypothesis. Neither can any of them be read as a known Maya family name, nor, by and large, do they have the character of known Maya family names. Among the Lacandones, all known names of lineages are animal names (Tozzer 1907, pp. 40–41), and among the Mayas of Yucatán, animal and plant names greatly outnumber all others, although there are a substantial number of other types of names. While our sample is small, animal heads are obviously a small minority among the known EGs.

The most convincing evidence that the EGs are not dynastic names comes from Quirigua. Here, an individual whom I identify as a local Quirigua ruler, Two-Legged Sky (Quirigua Ruler I, also called Twelve Earthquake; see Fig. 76), is consistently associated with the Copan EG; a woman who is associated with him (perhaps his wife?) is associated with the Quirigua EG; later rulers at Quirigua have names which

resemble those of Two-Legged Sky but are associated with the Quirigua EG. At other sites, the same EG continues in use, even when there are suggestive reasons for suspecting a change in dynasty. The situation at Quirigua is easy to explain in terms of an individual from Copan marrying a local woman of Quirigua, with his or their descendants remaining at Quirigua. It is hard to explain in terms of the descendants of a woman taking her dynastic name rather than their father's, when other available evidence points to patrilineal inheritance of names.

There is a final reason for regarding the EGs as place names, which I personally find very convincing. We now know a great deal more about the glyphs than we did even a few years ago, and, if the EGs are not place names, then there seems to be no possibility that there is a major unexplored category of glyphs which could be place names. The later Mayas put a considerable emphasis on place names in migration legends and in other types of historical references. The Mixtec codices nearly always identify people in terms of their place of origin. Finally, otherwise comparable inscriptions from all over the world do contain place names. Other categories of glyphs strongly suggest that they are patronymic or dynastic names, and there are glyphs which may refer to local deities, so that these subjects may be treated in the inscriptions even if the EGs are not interpreted as referring to them. On a priori grounds, there ought to be place names in the inscriptions, the EGs function as if they were place names, and there is no other known body of glyphs which could furnish place names; hence, I regard the EGs as place names.

Two further points should be made about the Emblem Glyphs. First, since the Mayas used meaningful names, any glyph appearing as an EG may also appear with its basic meaning; second, an EG may sometimes appear in its EG function without the prefixes which first led to its recognition. Thus, when a glyph which is a known EG in other contexts appears in a text without the usual prefixes, further analysis must be done before one can decide whether it is or is not functioning as an EG.

A still unresolved problem is posed by the presence together of two Emblem Glyphs both at Yaxchilan (Y1 and Y2) and at Palenque (P1 and P2). Proskouriakoff (1960, p. 468) has identified the Y2 Emblem Glyph at Yaxchilan as the Piedras Negras EG, but it lacks the unique prefix taken at Piedras Negras and in an earlier inscription at Yaxchilan (Figs. 92, 93). Moreover, the four dots surrounding the central cavity of the Piedras Negras EG in the Y2 glyph, as drawn from Yaxchilan Stela 12 (Proskouriakoff 1960, p. 467), look rather like natural cavities in

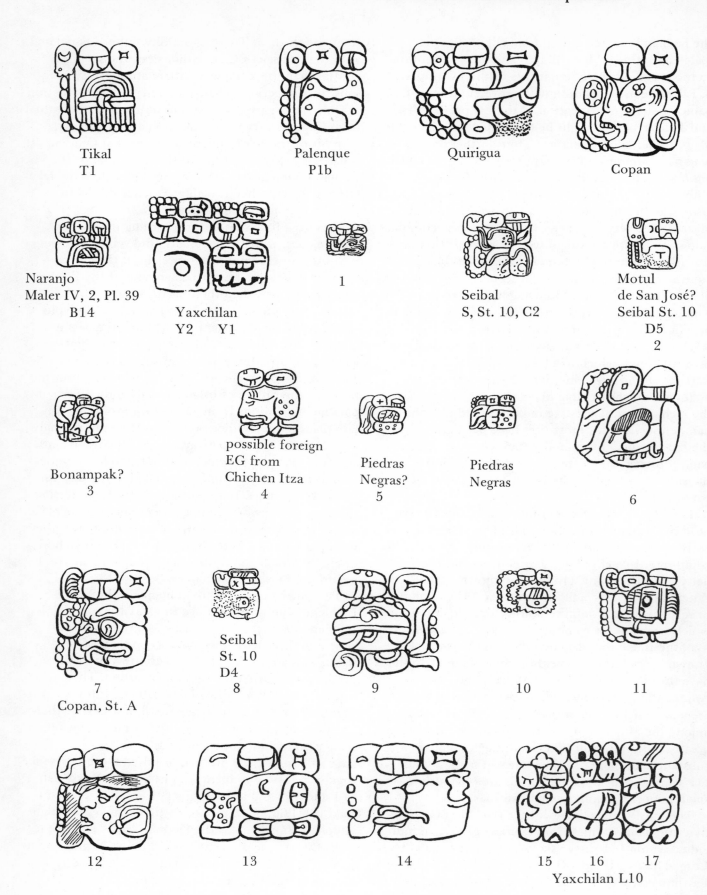

Tikal
T1

Palenque
P1b

Quirigua

Copan

Naranjo
Maler IV, 2, Pl. 39
B14

Yaxchilan
Y2   Y1

1

Seibal
S, St. 10, C2

Motul
de San José?
Seibal St. 10
D5
2

Bonampak?
3

possible foreign
EG from
Chichen Itza
4

Piedras
Negras?
5

Piedras
Negras

6

7
Copan, St. A

Seibal
St. 10
D4
8

9

10

11

12

13

14

15   16   17
Yaxchilan L10

Figure 72. Certain and probable Emblem Glyphs.

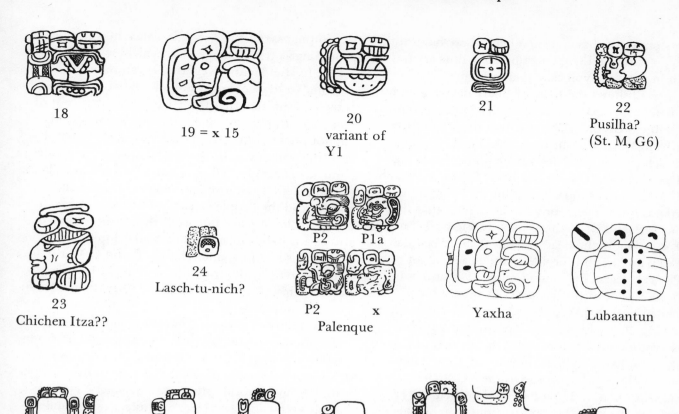

18

19 = x 15

20
variant of
Y1

21

22
Pusilha?
(St. M, G6)

23
Chichen Itza??

24
Lasch-tu-nich?

P2   P1a

P2   x
Palenque

Yaxha

Lubaantun

T36   T37   T38   T39   T40   T41

affixes of the so-called water group normally found with Emblem Glyphs

unusual variant of
prefixes with Naranjo EG

T168 (=T584.687a)
ben-ich prefix

Maler's photo of that stela and hence may have nothing to do with the EG. (These possible dots are not shown in the Y2 glyph as drawn in Figure 72.)

Figure 72 shows the EGs originally determined by Berlin and some other EGs recognized more recently. The Emblem Glyphs marked with a single question mark from Motul de San José, Bonampak, Pusilha, and Lasch-tu-nich (the latter from photographs supplied by Dana and Ginger Lamb; cf. Lamb and Lamb 1951) are found at those sites, but the epigraphic material is insufficient for us to be certain that they are not foreign EGs at those sites. In Figure 72, number 1 is probably the head variant of the Yaxchilan EG (Y1); number 6 is probably the head variant of the Piedras Negras EG; and number 11 is probably the head variant of the Tikal EG. A phrase from Yaxchilan L10 (Fig. 72, nos. 15, 16, 17) shows three glyphs together with a *ben-ich* prefix but without a water-group prefix, followed by the *u-cab*-x phrase (see below). I suspect that they are EGs but cannot be sure. Stela A at Copan shows the EGs of Tikal, Palenque, Copan itself, and an unidentified site (Fig. 72, no. 7). The latter is also mentioned on Seibal Stela 10 (Fig. 72, no. 8) with Tikal, Seibal itself, and the putative Motul de San José. Foreign EGs are particularly common at Seibal, where Stela 8 has one and Stela 7 has at least four and possibly five. John Justeson (1973) has recently demonstrated that T743 functions as the Emblem Glyph of Yaxha. In a forthcoming study with Norman Hammond and Peter Mathews, I will argue that T630 is the EG of Lubaantun. The considerable historical importance of this identification cannot be considered here.

Barthel's study of the EGs goes on from the structure to a consideration of particular EGs. Here he suggests that T570 (P1b) is the equivalent of proto-Maya *baaq* 'bone' (Yuc. *baac*). This is one of the Palenque EGs, and the identity of the glyph as a bone has long seemed likely. Another of the Palenque EGs, T1040 (P 1 a), is a skull, and Barthel suggests reading *tzek* (Yuc. 'skull'). A rather dubious tradition said that the Palenque area had formerly been inhabited by a tribe called the Tzequils, and Barthel suggests that this should be interpreted as 'Skull People', coinciding with the EG. The spelling of an isolated name in a Spanish source can tell us nothing of whether the name was glottalized or not, and there is phonetically nothing to oppose this identification. The same tradition refers to the Chanes or 'Snakes' as another tribe, and an EG referring to an unknown place or tribe is the 'snake' EG (two allographs, Fig. 72, nos. 6, 18). The possible equation, at least in name, of *sutz*, the EG of Copan, with the Zotzil tribe has been mentioned. Despite these agreements, particularly impressive in the case of the Tzequils, other EGs seem less promising as tribal names. *Bix* (which, with Barthel, I accept for the Piedras Negras EG) can refer to 'day' or 'song' or 'dance' but is not a known tribal name. I agree with Barthel that the Tikal EG is a topknot of hair (Yuc. *t'uch* is applied to female topknots) but am not prepared to accept *tuch* (Yuc., Chol 'navel') as a true homonym, however appropriate the latter name may seem for Tikal. 'Cleft Sky' for Yaxchilan is a dubious interpretation, although not impossible. I would read the "triple Cauac" of Seibal as x *haabil cuc* 'x cycle of years' but see little reason to regard this as a tribal or lineage name, and it looks almost as unlikely as a place name. The EG found at Motul de San José is *ik* 'wind, soul, life' and might be compared with such Mexican names as Ehecatepec 'Mountain of [the] Wind [God]'.

When Barthel goes on from the sporadic and dubious evidence offered by these examples and his interpretations of some others to postulate a "cosmo-sociological" system in which Palenque is associated with the underworld, priests, and teachers, Piedras Negras with earth's surface, warriors, singers, and dancers, and Yaxchilan with the sky and merchants, I feel that the evidence no longer adequately supports him. An alleged parallel system in the south merely serves to weaken the case. I would not deny in principle that cosmological-ordering principles may sometimes have been superimposed on such mundane matters as settlement patterns and craft specialization, but if there is any validity to this hypothesis, it will need much better evidence to show it.

The material from Chichen Itza presents a special problem, as it is abundant enough so that an EG should be known, and yet none has been suggested. With some hesitation, I draw attention to Beyer's "isolated" "Ahau variant 1" and "Ahau variant 2" (Beyer 1937, p. 89, Figs. 304–319). All but one of these has the *ben-ich* superfix, and one has prefix T35, which may be related to the water-group prefix, T36. In no case is the context conclusively like that of the EGs at other sites, but neither is it conclusively unlike. This *may* be the Chichen Itza EG (Fig. 72, no. 23). Barthel (1964a, p. 233) suggests that the compound T59.679:8 is to be read *ti-ch'een* and that this became Chi-ch'een (Itza). A substantial difficulty is to be found in the fact that T59, *ti*, is found in Yucatec as *ti* and did not become *chi*, Yucatec *chi* having a completely different origin. I am also very doubtful that T679, Landa's *i*, is to be read *ch'en*. In a number of cases, this compound follows the glyger which I read *pacab* 'lintel, sill, bench', which is found as a family name (R. L. Roys 1940, p. 43); at present this fact is not particularly helpful. The context does not seem to me to suggest that this compound is a place name.

Turning from the Emblem Glyphs to personal names and titles, we are now in a position to recognize glyphs standing for the subject of a verb and others standing for the object of a verb, from the general structure of the inscriptions. Proskouriakoff's work on the Piedras Negras inscriptions gave the first indication that this was possible within a strictly historical framework. She showed that, at Piedras Negras, dated monuments fall into series in which all the monuments of one series are associated in time and space. In each series, dated monuments cover a time span not greater than a lifetime and are located near each other within the site. In each series, a particular glyph (T684; see Figs. 56, 73), a verb, is associated with representations of a man seated in a niche and with a particular date, which is, thereafter, marked by anniversaries. Proskouriakoff calls dates marked by T684 "inaugural dates." In each case, another glyph (T740, the upended frog's head; see Figs. 55, 68, 73) is associated with a date several years before the series began, such that it could be a birth or baptismal date. A very striking example on Stela 3, back, shows a woman and a girl. Glyphs with female heads (one of the *ix* type for women, one of the *ch'up* type for girls; see Chapter 10) are associated with T740 and with two separate dates, one thirty-six years before the date of erection of the monument, the other three years before the erection of the monument. Apparently, the dates refer to the births of mother and child, or to some ceremony associated with birth. The name of the mother, identified by its association with the initial date (see below) includes the katun glyph. This is particularly convincing because, where the same woman is shown on Lintel 1, she wears a katun sign in her headdress. The Mixtec manuscripts repeatedly show individuals wearing headdresses which contain the elements of their names, and we may assume that the same was true of the Mayas. This gives us another clue which may be followed in trying to determine appellative glyphs.

Because dates marked by T740 are always the earliest dates in a series, Proskouriakoff calls them *initial dates*. The fact that birth dates were generally quite important in Mesoamerican cultures led me to believe that these initial dates were probably true birth dates. Barthel has now shown that T740 is almost certainly *pok* 'be born' (linguistic *pok*'). As a birth glyph, T740 has the affix T126 in all cases known to me and usually has the affix T181. Both seem to be past-tense suffixes (Fig. 66).

Before discussing specific names and sites, it seems desirable to outline what seem to be the best indicators that one is dealing with historic personal names or titles. The most basic prerequisite is that the structure of the text being studied must allow this interpretation, grammatically. Practically, this eliminates verbs in most cases, as well as certain glyphs and clauses of known meaning. In some cases, the only glyphs left may be personal names. However, it may be difficult to distinguish historical names from deity names (especially as the names of some individuals seem to incorporate deity names, as they do in most other cultures) or from other grammatical subjects; without knowing a considerable amount about a text, it may be even more difficult to determine the nature of a grammatical object than that of a grammatical subject.

There are certain clear indications. Directly after the IS date and subsequent Lunar Series, a verb with affixes, occupying a single glyph block, normally appears; it is usually followed by a name. Among these verbs are T740 and T684. T740, the upended frog, meaning 'was born', and T684, the toothache glyph, meaning 'was inaugurated', are excellent indicators that the following glyphs are the names of local rulers, as Proskouriakoff pointed out. However, the upended frog and the toothache glyph occur also in other contexts. T740 occasionally occurs as a substitute for T60, a knot glyph, in Glyph F of the Lunar Series; another substitute for the same glyph in the same context is T609, the jaguar-skin bundle, and a third substitute is a still unidentified bird head (Fig. 73); in all cases the prefix and suffix remain constant, suggesting either that all four of these glyphs have the same phonetic value or that all four of them are verbs having the same verbal prefixes and suffixes; the suffix is T23, with a doubtfully suggested value of *na*. The deity-head glyph T1030o substitutes for the glyger T740:23 both in Glyph F and in an interesting clause at Palenque. Berlin (1963, p. 96) indicated doubt about the equivalence of these forms at Palenque, but the Glyph F examples verify the substitution. Since verbs normally precede nouns, it is puzzling that Glyph F, an apparent verb, follows Glyph G, with which it is normally associated, although the latter is a nominal glyph for one of the Nine Lords of the Night. The repeated "birth" of deities at nine-day intervals is in full accord conceptually with statements from Aztec sources that gods were "born" every year on particular dates. This may be related to the fact that the first appearance of heavenly bodies in a particular cycle was called their "birth."

The peculiar knot T684 designates an event connected with an inauguration, as Proskouriakoff has

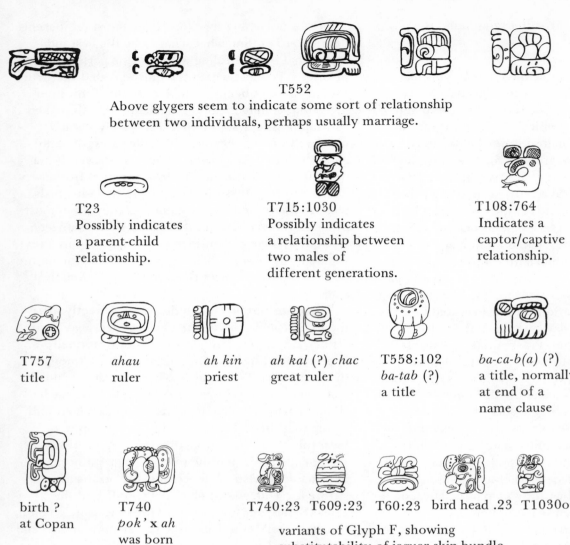

T552

Above glygers seem to indicate some sort of relationship between two individuals, perhaps usually marriage.

T23
Possibly indicates
a parent-child
relationship.

T715:1030
Possibly indicates
a relationship between
two males of
different generations.

T108:764
Indicates a
captor/captive
relationship.

T757
title

ahau
ruler

ah kin
priest

ah kal (?) *chac*
great ruler

T558:102
ba-tab (?)
a title

ba-ca-b(a) (?)
a title, normally
at end of a
name clause

birth ?
at Copan

T740
pok' x ah
was born

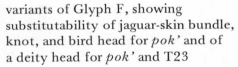

T740:23 T609:23 T60:23 bird head .23 T1030o

variants of Glyph F, showing
substitutability of jaguar-skin bundle,
knot, and bird head for *pok'* and of
a deity head for *pok'* and T23

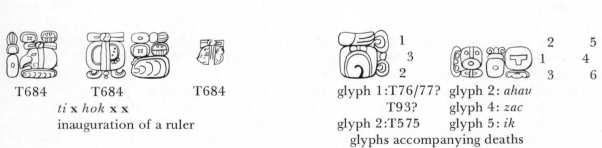

T684   T684   T684
       ti x *hok* x x
       inauguration of a ruler

	1				2	5
	3			1		4
	2				3	6

glyph 1:T76/77? glyph 2: *ahau*
       T93?   glyph 4: *zac*
glyph 2:T575   glyph 5: *ik*
glyphs accompanying deaths

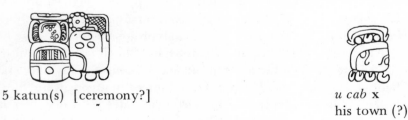

5 katun(s) [ceremony?]

u cab x
his town (?)

Figure 73. Indicators of personal names.

shown. On *Dresden* page 67a (Fig. 56) the knot is around a moon glyph, followed by a verbal affix and by the name glyph of God K in the object position. The picture shows God K surrounded by a rope held by Chac. This suggests a rather literal interpretation which is hard to reconcile with the inaugural use. The use of T684 as the verb on M55a, where God M holds a package by a rope, is in accord with this literal interpretation. Its use in the trapping passages, M90a–93a, suggests the meaning 'caught, trapped'. On *Dresden* page 23b, the knot with moon infixed appears in an offering passage, where it seems to refer to an offering of fish (Fig. 56). It has now been shown by Cordan (1963a) and Barthel (1968a) that the true reading of T684 is *hok* 'bind, hang up, inaugurate' (see Chapter 8).

Besides 'birth' and 'inauguration', one would expect to find glyphs indicating 'marriage' and 'death'. The former have not yet been discovered, but the *cimi* 'death' glyph has long been known because of its use in the day-name series. However, its use to indicate the death of a ruler does not seem to have been demonstrated, and Proskouriakoff has pointed out another glyger which seems to have this function. Thompson identifies the first glyph of this glyger as T793. This is denied by Proskouriakoff (1963, p. 163), who identifies it as a "serpent-wing." Thompson (1962, p. 99) also says it is sometimes T1021. The second glyph is the inverted shell, T575. The first glyph in these eroded examples seems to me to resemble T76 and T77, and I would be inclined to regard T76 and T77 as identical with each other. Both T76 and T77 appear in similar contexts. This glyger normally occurs in a clause which also contains *ahau, zac,* and *ik* (Thompson 1962, p. 99). Proskouriakoff points out that *binam ik* is translated 'muriose, fuésele el espíritu o el alma' ('died, spirit or soul left') and *ikal* is 'spirit'; the first phrase implies that *ik* itself could be read as 'spirit'. The "highly conjectural" nature of Proskouriakoff's interpretation is considerably strengthened by other cases which she did not consider in print. The presence of T23 (misread T24 by Thompson) affixed to *zac-ik* offers some support to the Barthel reading of that affix as *al*, since *ikal* is the later form of 'spirit', but the contrary evidence suggesting it should be read *na* still seems to me stronger.

In the case of the glyger T601:25, which, following Knorozov, I read *chuc* 'tie, bind, capture' (see Chapter 8 and Fig. 57), the name glyph or glyphs directly following the verb are normally those of a captive, and the name of the captor normally follows this; without other clues, it may be difficult to tell where one name clause ends and the next begins.

In general, when the EG of a particular place appears at the end or nearly at the end of an inscription, it is directly preceded by name glyphs of a local ruler. When the EG is followed by the *imix*-comb-*imix* glyger (T556.25:556—but see the discussion of these numbers in Chapter 9), the EG is preceded by what I regard as name glyphs in all instances known to me, whether at the end of a text or internally. I have drawn attention to a phrase commencing *u cab* (with an apparent verbal suffix) which seems normally to be followed by name glyphs (Kelley 1962b, p. 329). Another phrase, involving the so-called shell-hand glyph (T93:672:142) and a reference to 'five katuns', is associated with a ruler's name at Yaxchilan and Quirigua.

Some glygers involving possible indications of relationships have been postulated. In the codices, T126.565:24 seems to appear between the known glyphs of animals or deities who are represented as different sexes; so does T115.192:601, which also seems to mean 'house' or 'temple'. The crossbands (T552), which sometimes appear on the monuments as an infix of the serpent segment (T565), may substitute for the serpent segment in these passages. See Chapter 8 for a reading of T552 as *kaat* 'wish, desire'. Knorozov (1955a, p. 101) has read both these glygers as *hicham*, modern *icham* 'marido' ('husband') but gives no evidence for loss of initial *h-* and has to read the suffix T24 inconsistently. The serpent segment occurs on the monuments with varying affixes between personal names, but there are problems about even the few known examples. This glyph occurs frequently in other contexts, and, as an indicator, it should be used with caution.

I have suggested (Kelley 1962b, p. 328) that T715:1030 (Fig. 73) indicates a relationship between a male of a later generation and one of an earlier generation, such that its meaning should be 'son', 'grandson', 'nephew', or something of the sort if my interpretation of the Quirigua dynastic sequence is correct. T715 is the glyph which, following Knorozov, I read *pa*, but without knowledge of the other elements involved, this is probably not much help.

Proskouriakoff has drawn attention to a glyger (T108:764; see Fig. 73) which she originally thought indicated family relationships. She has subsequently shown (Proskouriakoff 1963, p. 152) that it indicates that one individual, whose name glyph or glyphs directly follow it, was the captive of another, and that these glyphs were incorporated into the name and titles of the captor. The glyger is thus a good indicator of names or titles but does not indicate family relationships.

I have suggested (see below) that T23 (Fig. 66)

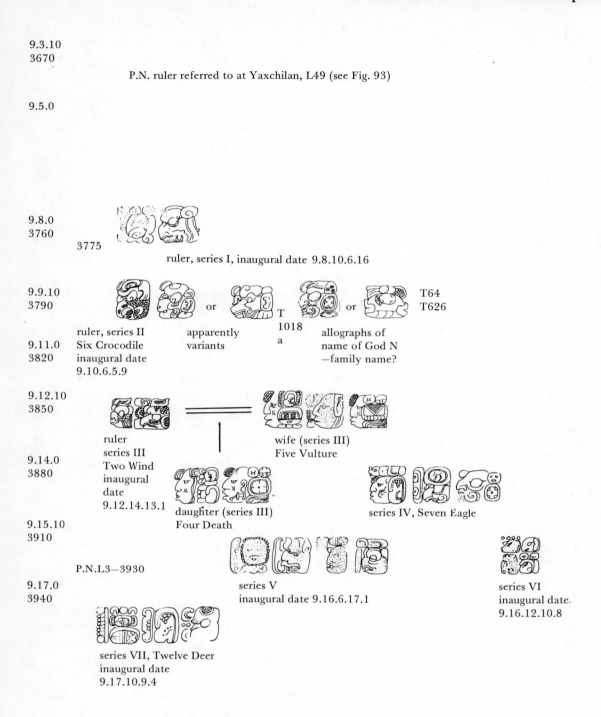

9.3.10
3670

P.N. ruler referred to at Yaxchilan, L49 (see Fig. 93)

9.5.0

9.8.0
3760

3775

ruler, series I, inaugural date 9.8.10.6.16

9.9.10
3790

or   T   or   T64
                 1018   T626
                  a
ruler, series II   apparently   allographs of
9.11.0   Six Crocodile   variants   name of God N
3820   inaugural date   —family name?
        9.10.6.5.9

9.12.10
3850

ruler
series III   wife (series III)
9.14.0   Two Wind   Five Vulture
3880   inaugural
        date
        9.12.14.13.1

                 daughter (series III)   series IV, Seven Eagle
                 Four Death
9.15.10
3910

        P.N.L3—3930

9.17.0   series V   series VI
3940   inaugural date 9.16.6.17.1   inaugural date.
                                                          9.16.12.10.8

series VII, Twelve Deer
inaugural date
9.17.10.9.4

Figure 74. The dynastic sequence at Piedras Negras.

prefixed to names may be read, at least sometimes, as *na* 'mother'; this depends on the recognition of name glyphs and cannot serve as a basis for recognizing them, at the present time.

A few generalized titles may be recognized (Fig. 73). *Ahau* 'lord' has long been known and sometimes seems to occur as a ruler's title, although more rarely than would be expected on a priori grounds. T757, the so-called jog or *kan*-dog, is almost certainly a title; it is particularly frequent at Copan and Palenque, but also found elsewhere; normally it is followed by name glyphs. The *kin* glyph is often found in name clauses, where it is probably to be interpreted as 'priest' or 'priestess' even when it lacks the agentive or masculine prefix *ah*. Its other meanings ('day, sun, feast') and its frequent use in other contexts make it a poor indicator of names. The title I read *ah kal chac* 'great ruler' or 'great king' occurs, to my knowledge, only at Yaxchilan and only as a title of Bird Jaguar. However, the complete moon glyph, *kal* 'king', may sometimes occur as a title elsewhere. The glyger or phrase T558:102 occurs on the bones texts of Tikal in contexts which indicate it is a title. Like the *kan*-dog, it is preceded by possessive *u* and followed by names. T558 is the glyph for which I have tentatively suggested a reading *ba* (Kelley 1962c, pp. 305–307), and T102 is a knot. Since *tab* is 'tie', I would suggest that this glyger be read *batab,* the well-known title of the town rulers or lesser chiefs at the time of the Spanish conquest.

Some more general indications of the occurrence of names may be pointed out. Female head glyphs, corresponding probably to *ix* (T1002) and *ch'up* (T1000a) are good markers for women's names (Fig. 66). The masculine prefix *ah,* as I follow Knorozov in reading T13, is normally a good marker of masculine names. The latter frequently include animal or human heads, sometimes to the exclusion of other types of glyphs. Several head glyphs together normally comprise all or part of a personal name.

For historical purposes, it is necessary to have a chronological framework; since the Maya dates are certain, while the correlation with our calendar is not, I have used Maya year dates in the accompanying chronological tables (Figs. 74–76, 78–79, 82–83; Plate 2). These dates are given in the number of tuns of 360 days which had passed at the time of the date referred to, calculated from the base date of the normal Maya Era, 4 Ahau 8 Cumku. (See Chapter 2 for a fuller discussion of Maya calendrics.) All figures use the same chronological scale, except the more general Plate 2. In accordance with general historical and genealogical usage, earliest events and people are placed at the top of the figures, rather than at the bottom, as is more customary in archaeological tables.

The seven series of glyphs which Proskouriakoff isolated from the monuments of Piedras Negras (Fig. 74) probably represent six generations, judging from their chronological relationships, and cover a period of 195 years. In the glyphs of Series II and Series IV, there is a glyger composed of a net (T64) and a turtle shell (T626). In the *Dresden* codex, this glyger sometimes appears as the name of God N (see Fig. 24). In these series from Piedras Negras, this glyger alternates with an anthropomorphized head (T1018a), which Proskouriakoff (1960, p. 471) thought had jaguar characteristics, but which seems to me reptilian (compare with reptiles in Fig. 44) because of the *kan* cross (normally associated with the turtle) and the curled mouth. The ear contains what is apparently the number seven (≗). This head is probably that of God N. In some instances, the net–turtle-shell glyger occurs alone as a reference to a ruler. The glyphs of God N define the Piedras Negras dynasty in the same way that the jaguar head defines the Yaxchilan dynasty, the sky glyph defines the dynasties of Tikal, Copan, and Quirigua, and the shield glyph defines the Palenque dynasty. Whether God N's name is also a family name or whether he should be considered a patron deity must remain an open question. This glyger allows us to recognize the names of other individuals of the dynasty, mentioned more casually. Figure 74 includes some clauses which I regard as names which are not mentioned by Proskouriakoff. None of them is associated either with an initial date or with an inaugural date, but all of them include the anthropomorphized reptilian head, and all occur structurally in places where they should be nouns.

Berlin's study of the famed sarcophagus from the crypt in the Temple of the Inscriptions and his far fuller study of the inscriptions from the Temple of the Cross at Palenque begin to give us the outlines of a history of Palenque comparable to that of Piedras Negras. Berlin was able to make the basic points that on the sarcophagus the sculptured figures of individuals, accompanied by glyphs, seem to be repeated, and that when a similar figure recurs, it is accompanied by similar glyphs, with some variation. This is the same type of recurrence that has been used in the codices to determine the name glyphs of animals and deities, and it is convincing even in the restricted number of cases here.

On the sculptured slab of the Temple of the Cross, Berlin was able to isolate some nine "topics" of Category I, which includes all glyphs associated with T713

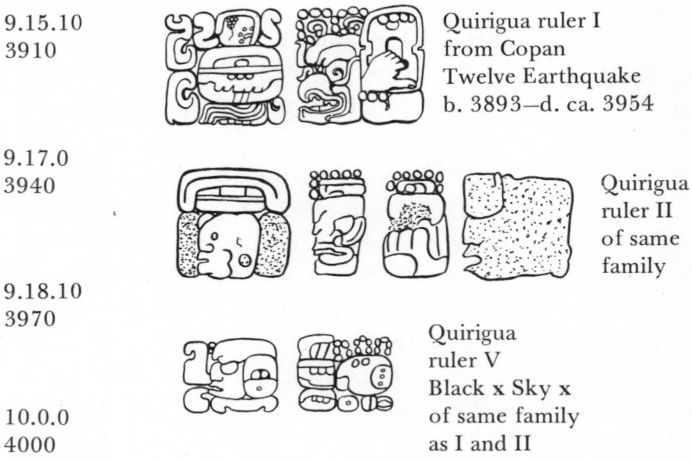

9.15.10 3910			Quirigua ruler I from Copan Twelve Earthquake b. 3893—d. ca. 3954
9.17.0 3940			Quirigua ruler II of same family
9.18.10 3970			Quirigua ruler V Black x Sky x of same family as I and II
10.0.0 4000			

Figure 76. Quirigua rulers.

or T757 (Fig. 75). Topic 7 was one of the glyphs he had previously isolated on the sarcophagus as a personal name. Topics 1 and 2 are associated with dates in the remote and presumably mythical past and recur in connection with dates over what seems to be a considerable period of time. The remaining seven topics occur associated with dates of the historical period, and no topic covers a span of time longer than a man's lifetime. The first two topics are those which I independently suggested to be the name glyphs of a goddess, not definitely identified, and of the god Kukulcan (Quetzalcoatl). There is, then, a strong presumption that the other glyphs Berlin has identified are also personal names. Berlin writes: "This tablet was hardly meant to be seen by the general public. It may indicate mythological descent from divine ancestors in the remote past. Such a belief seems to have existed among the Mixtecs and Zapotecs. Even the Aztec rulers claimed a mythological descent from nebulous Quetzalcoatl" (Berlin 1965a, p. 338). My hypothesis is in full agreement, and I have suggested that the temple was dedicated to that "nebulous Quetzalcoatl" himself.

The general hypothesis is further verified by the fact that most of the topics also recur in connection with the upended-frog or birth glyph. Within this general area of agreement, there is still room for some disagreement as to details. With respect to Topic 3, I accept Q5 as a personal name, but do not believe it goes with Q9, which I think is a (mythical?) place name (see the structural analysis, Chapter 13). I remain vaguely uneasy about Topic 5 for reasons I am still unable to define, and there seems to be an obscure and puzzling relationship between Topic 6 and

Topic 8. Finally, the T757 clause appears twice in connection with Topic 9, whereas it only appears once with each of the other topics. Moreover, the prefix to the animal head of Topic 9 is different in T10 and U16 from that in U13 and N1, although the heads themselves are closely similar and probably intended for a single animal. This would suggest to me that two individuals are jointly under discussion in these passages.

Certain additional things may be pointed out about some of the individuals referred to. The Hieroglyphic Stairway of Building C of the Palace at Palenque contains the IS 9.8.9.13.0 8 Ahau 13 Pop, followed by the birth glyph and the glyphs of a woman. The same inscription mentions a certain Shield Jaguar, whose name is followed by the Yaxchilan EG. This may be her husband. Her birth is likewise noted in E2—F2 of the west tablet of the Temple of the Inscriptions, where events of her life seem to be tied in to tremendous calculations which cover more than a million years. In this connection, it seems significant that she has the same calendar name, Eight Flower, as the goddess of Topic 1 of the Temple of the Cross. As to whether the importance of the goddess was enhanced because an important historical individual had the same calendar name, or whether the woman became important partly because of the importance of the goddess, I could not even guess, but I suspect that there was some relationship. On the same tablet, at T5, the date 6 Etz'nab 11 Yax appears, with a notation of the event in S6; a distance number of four katuns, one tun, ten uinals, and eighteen days leads back to the initial date 9.8.9.13.0 8 Ahau 13 Pop. On the south of the sarcophagus, in the same

glyphs of a woman, perhaps the wife of Quirigua ruler I

glyphs of a possible fourth ruler Quirigua

Quirigua ruler III of a different family?

temple, one finds the same two dates, 8 Ahau 13 Pop (with the birth glyph) and 6 Etz'nab 11 Yax, not placed in the long count. The dates are over eighty-one years apart, and the most likely explanation is that the latter date is a death date, since there does not seem to be any later date recorded in connection with the woman's life. The fullest account is to be found on the Tablet of the Palace, J10–I14, following the date 6 Etz'nab 11 Yax. This opens with the glyger for which Proskouriakoff (1963, p. 163) had already proposed the meaning 'death' in connection with inscriptions at Yaxchilan, the *sac* with *ahau* infixed, and the *ik* glyph (for which Proskouriakoff's tentatively proposed translation 'spirit' seems very reasonable). A full version of Eight Flower's name follows, with a reference to four katuns, which helps to verify the view that these isolated katun references are indications of age, since we know she was eighty-one tuns old.

The glyph in I13 is of exceptional interest, since it is the name glyph of Topic 9b with a half moon (T181) and T23 prefixed. As a suffix, I have accepted the reading -*ah* for the half moon, but I doubt that that is relevant here. T23 has been read by Knorozov as *na*. This passage is support for his reading, as *na* means 'mother' and I suspect this means that Lady Eight Flower was mother of the ruler Topic 9b. It should be pointed out that this would imply that the dates 1 Imix 4 Zip, 7 Kan 17 Mol, and 11 Chicchan 13 Ch'en should be placed one fifty-two–year cycle later than Berlin's brilliant analysis had suggested. Berlin's reconstruction would associate Topic 9 with dates at least 109 tuns apart (ME 3741/3742–3851), s opposed to fifty-seven tuns apart in my reconstruc-

tion; the latter therefore seems to me chronologically preferable as well as agreeing with the postulated relationship of Topic 9b with Eight Flower.

The passage ends with the agentive *ah* and a pyramid glyph with suffixes. I am not sure whether it refers to Topic 9b or to his putative mother. I suspect it is to be read 'the pyramid builder', and it may refer to responsibility for the building of the Temples of the Cross, Foliated Cross, Sun, and Inscriptions, although these were probably not dedicated until about eight years later, at 9.13.0.0.0 (ME 3860).

The date 8 Oc 3 Kayab, associated with Topic 9b, occurs with closely similar glyphs on the west Tablet of the Inscriptions, just after the date 6 Etz'nab 11 Yax. The glyph which occupies the same position in this clause as Topic 9b does in the Temple of the Cross is considered to be a slight variant of the same name. On the Palace Tablet, the date also recurs following 6 Etz'nab 11 Yax, but the accompanying glyphs in I15–J15 preceding the date seem quite distinct from those in the other inscriptions. A much more lengthy passage following the date, which apparently refers to deities, also seems to be associated with it.

An unidentified animal head, somewhat anthropomorphized, seems to serve as a personal name in the tablets on the jambs of Temple 18, judging by its occurrence with the birth glyph and with the *u cab* phrase. Similarly, the Tablet of the Slaves has, as its second date, 9.11.18.9.17 7 Caban 15 Kayab (ME 3838), which is apparently the birth date of someone called Chac Zotz 'Great Bat'. The glyphs are indistinct at this point, but the three-katun anniversary is specifically counted from a birth, and the Chac Zotz glyphs recur frequently through the tablet: with *kan*-dog in C2b–D2a, with an apparent variant of the *u cab* phrase in D3b–E1a, and at F4a and G2a.

Elsewhere, our information is less full, but some fairly clear-cut identifications have been made. At Quirigua (Kelley 1962*b*), I tried to show that nearly all the major monuments covering a period of about forty years contained the glyphs of a single ruler referred to, for convenience, as Two-Legged Sky (ruler 1, Fig. 76). His glyphs are normally associated with the Copan EG rather than with the Quirigua EG, and there is mention of a Copanec ruler whom I suspect to be his father (see below). In connection with these names, I noted a phenomenon I have called "capitalization," in which the apparent name glyphs of rulers take up a larger space than any other glyphs (Fig. 76). This was not consistent in the inscriptions of any of the rulers but did occur with these two. Although the names were not postulated because of similarities between them, comparison showed that four of the suggested rulers of Quirigua had names including the 'sky' glyph, that three of them had the first glyph of Thompson's 1030i or a regular substitute for it, and that both 'sky' and 1030i or its substitute occurred likewise among the name glyphs of contemporary rulers at Copan. This helps to verify the suggested sequence. While I regard the context as adequate for rulers I, II, and V, rulers III and IV should probably be considered somewhat more doubtful.

Proskouriakoff (1963, 1964*a*) has attempted the first detailed historical study of a Maya site, giving her interpretation of the happenings at Yaxchilan. The site is unique in its tremendous number of lintels with brief inscriptions associated with sculptures showing the striking events commemorated. One of the most interesting and enlightening of these is Lintel 8 (Fig. 77). Here a ruler and his companion are shown with prisoners, each of whom has his name written on his thigh. Both of the names appear in the accompanying text, one following the 'capture' glyph, the other following a glyger which appears frequently in appellative clauses (T108:764). Comparison of this text with others shows that where this glyger occurs, it is normally followed by what seems to be the name of somebody indicated elsewhere as a captive; Proskouriakoff has, therefore, suggested that it be read simply 'captor'. It indicates that the immediately following glyph is that of an individual captured by someone indicated by later glyphs—comparison with English grammar would tend to justify the rendering 'captor', but in Maya grammar the prefixed *u* found with this glyger strongly suggests to me that a rendering '(his) captive *X* (of) *Y*' is preferable to 'his

captor (of) *X*–*Y*'. With this very minor modification, I fully accept the Proskouriakoff demonstration. She is fully right in saying that these glyphs *designate* the Yaxchilan princes as captors, which is the important thing in the present context. The writing of the names on the thighs of the individuals is perhaps the strongest argument yet that the interpretation of the various text glyphs as names is correct.

From studying these various lintels, Proskouriakoff was able to show that the vast majority of the monuments at Yaxchilan referred either to a ruler called Bird Jaguar or to another called Shield Jaguar. These names recur in most of the contexts which mark names. Interestingly, while most of the monuments belong to the reigns of only two individuals of this name, there seems to be good reason to postulate the existence of at least two earlier individuals named Bird Jaguar and of an earlier and a later individual named Shield Jaguar. An early record (Lintels 34, 35, 36, 37, 47, 48, 49, analyzed at length in Chapter 13; see Figs. 92–93) refers to a Bird Jaguar (I) and to a Knotted-Eye Jaguar, while Lintel 21 refers to an early individual named Water Jaguar. The Hieroglyphic Stairway at Palenque refers to an individual named Shield Jaguar, whose name is followed by the Yaxchilan Emblem Glyph and who is somehow associated with the woman Eight Flower of Palenque. He is probably too early to be the Shield Jaguar whose reign is discussed at length by Proskouriakoff; so we should probably assume at least three individuals of this name at Yaxchilan. This particular type of name repetition is interesting but puzzling, as there seems to be nothing quite like it at other sites. Proskouriakoff has suggested that Jaguar should be regarded as a clan name and that the prefixes refer to lineages within a clan. I would be inclined rather to suspect that they may be *naal* names (derived from the mother's family) and indicate preferential marriage patterns. 'Jaguar' is probably to be read as one of the known Yucatec terms for the jaguar, perhaps *balam*, which is a known family name among both Yucatecs and Lacandones. It also means 'priest' and, of course, there may be occasional references to jaguars as animals or deities. I would not, therefore, expect jaguar glyphs outside Yaxchilan to refer to this family, unless the Yaxchilan EG or the full form of one of the Yaxchilan names appears. Proskouriakoff (1961, pp. 18–21) has drawn attention to the importance of the jaguar deity at Tikal and has suggested possible connections with Yaxchilan, but this seems to me tenuous at best. At Aguateca, she points out, there is a phrase *kin* Jaguar, which is also found at Tikal. Here I merely point out that *kinil* (as I read it) is probably to be related to *ah kin* 'priest, diviner', and *balam*

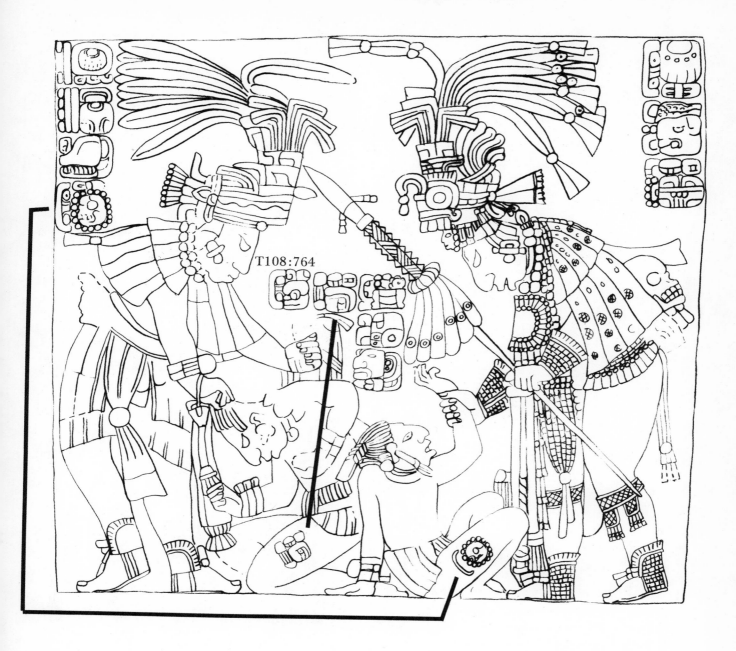

T108:764

Figure 77. Bird Jaguar and a subordinate capture two enemy
rulers. Yaxchilan Lintel 8, 9.16.4.1.1 7 Imix 14 Zec (ME3924),
ff. Tatiana Proskouriakoff. Note recurrence in text of glyphs
on thighs of prisoners. (Heavy black lines link corresponding
glyphs.)

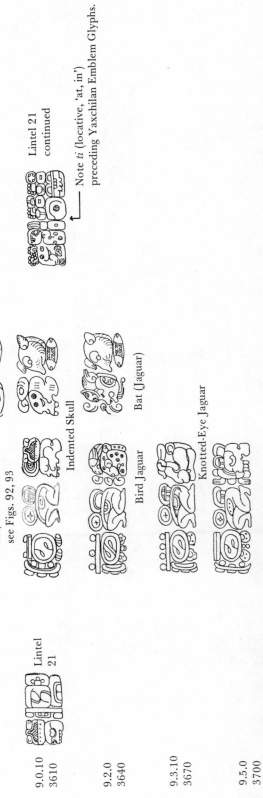

Lintel 21
continued

← Note *ti* (locative, 'at, in')
preceding Yaxchilan Emblem Glyphs.

Lintel 18
list

Structure 12
list, abstracted
see Figs. 92, 93

Indented Skull

Bat (Jaguar)

Bird Jaguar

Knotted-Eye Jaguar

Lintel
21

8.16.0
3520

8.17.10
3550

8.19.0
3580

9.0.10
3610

9.2.0
3640

9.3.10
3670

9.5.0
3700

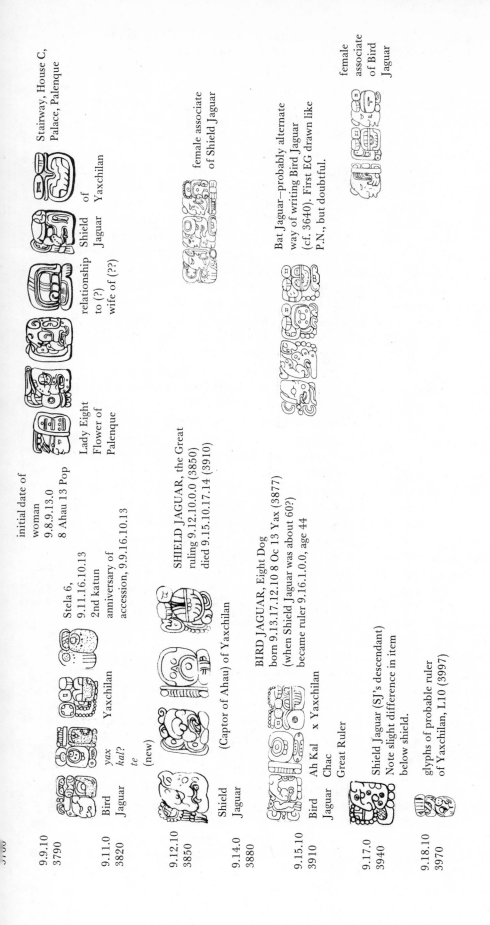

9.9.10 3790	Bird Jaguar	*yax kal?* te (new)	Yaxchilan	Stela 6, 9.11.16.10.13 2nd katun anniversary of accession, 9.9.16.10.13	Lady Eight Flower of Palenque	initial date of woman 9.8.9.13.0 8 Ahau 13 Pop
9.11.0 3820					relationship to (?) wife of (??)	Shield of Jaguar Yaxchilan
9.12.10 3850	Shield Jaguar	(Captor of Ahau) of Yaxchilan		SHIELD JAGUAR, the Great ruling 9.12.10.0.0 (3850) died 9.15.10.17.14 (3910)		female associate of Shield Jaguar
9.14.0 3880						Stairway, House C, Palace, Palenque
9.15.10 3910	Bird Jaguar	Ah Kal Chac Great Ruler	x Yaxchilan	BIRD JAGUAR, Eight Dog born 9.13.17.12.10 8 Oc 13 Yax (3877) (when Shield Jaguar was about 60?) became ruler 9.16.1.0.0, age 44	Bat Jaguar—probably alternate way of writing Bird Jaguar (cf. 3640). First EG drawn like P.N., but doubtful.	female associate of Bird Jaguar
9.17.0 3940		Shield Jaguar (SJ's descendant) Note slight difference in item below shield.				
9.18.10 3970		glyphs of probable ruler of Yaxchilan, L10 (3997)				

Figure 78. The Yaxchilan dynasty. . Abbreviations: P.N., Piedras Negras; SJ, Shield Jaguar.

might be a partly redundant term for 'priest'. If *kin* is taken as 'priest' and *balam* as 'jaguar', the phrase would be Jaguar Priest, perhaps appropriate at Tikal where the giant jaguar deity appears. Conversely, if *kin* were taken as 'sun' and *balam* as 'priest', we would have Sun Priest, also possible. The glyger preceding the title of the *kinil balam* at Aguateca, for which Proskouriakoff suggested a possible meaning of 'relative' in 1961, is none other than that which she later showed to be the captor/captive glyger and indicates that someone had captured the *kinil balam*.

The repetition of female heads among name glyphs is frequent at Yaxchilan, nearly always accompanying representations of female figures in the reliefs. Women seem to have played an important role in Yaxchilan, particularly in ceremonial activities, and the glyphs of several have been isolated by Proskouriakoff. Certain ones recur repeatedly in association with names of particular rulers and may well be their wives, although this is far from certain. Polygamy is strongly suggested by the fact that what seem to be several different female names may be associated with the glyphs of a single ruler. This is not surprising if one assumes that the Maya political structure was like that of the Aztecs or Mixtecs, where polygamy was normal in the ruling families.

Certain subordinate male figures recognizable at Yaxchilan seem to be associated with the rulers in various activities, particularly warfare. There are also certain individuals represented as enemies or captives. Their name glyphs suggest that some of the subordinate associates belong to the same family as some of the enemies, as Proskouriakoff has pointed out in connection with what she calls the "moon-sign family." Members of the latter family also appear at Piedras Negras, in connection with the name of Bat Jaguar of Yaxchilan, an individual who has the same initial date as Bird Jaguar. Hence, either this is another name for Bird Jaguar, or he had a twin. Figure 78 shows the sequence of rulers at Yaxchilan with some names of associated women.

For the rest, the Maya dynasties still remain quite obscure, although individual glyphs can be recognized. Figure 79 shows glyphs which I regard as giving names of individuals at Tikal. The interesting material from Stela 31 seems to contain references to several individuals. The clearest interpretation can be made for the two sides (Fig. 108). Both open with *u* and an animal head (T788) at I1 and M1. Thompson and Barthel have called this a jaguar (Barthel, 1963, p. 191, reads *u balam*). Proskouriakoff has shown that it is the early form of T757 and represents some large rodent. William Coe thought that the context here suggested a title, a suggestion which agrees with my

interpretation of T757. In I4, the Tikal EG appears without a water-group prefix and with an animal head (T844) directly preceding it in J3. The same head appears in N2 with *yax* and a knot glyph prefixed. Taken in conjunction, these glyphs suggest to me that the two sides represent two successive individuals bearing the name (or additional title) T844. Interestingly, and possibly suggesting a more mythical interpretation, the figure looking down from the sky on the front of the stela (Plate 6) has this animal as a headdress, with the *yax* prefix on its nose. A passage on the front (F10–E12) contains many of the same glyphs which appear in N1–N2, and associated glyphs also appear at other points throughout the inscription. Barthel (1963, p. 191 and elsewhere) calls T844 a "sky-dragon" and the nagual of the Fire God. It is true that, in the Venus table of *Dresden*, a head which seems to be that of this animal is the name glyph of the god (T20 of the Venus Series), shown sitting on a sky band, D46a, but the beast is depicted in a considerably more realistic manner at Tikal. In any case, deity and animal names appear as parts of personal names and titles. The prefix *yax* 'new, green' (in N2) is obvious if it refers to a title, but more difficult if it refers to a deity; if *yax* were being used as a color prefix, one would expect some color prefix also in J3, where none is found.

A number of passages in this text on Stela 31 have what may be name hieroglyphs, but the context is not adequate to define them yet (see the structural analysis, Chapter 13; Plate 6; and Fig. 109). However, one very common glyph, an animal skull (T846) with various affixes, seems to recur in apparent name contexts (for example, following the upended frog in E14). It is particularly common in a passage with the 'sky' glyph and a bone glyph (T571) which Barthel reads *baac* 'bone'; affixed to T571 is T23, which he reads *-al*. He suggests the whole is to be read *baacal* 'to pour liquid from an upturned vase'. As the *Dresden* "flood" page (D74) shows, the Mayas thought that inundations were caused when deities poured liquids from an upturned vase. With all due reservations as to affix T23, it seems that this may well be the root intended here. If so, there is a distinct possibility that glyph T846 and its affixes may be a deity name, not otherwise known; in that case, his "birth" at such a late date may refer to some astronomical phenomenon.

An animal head (T754) which seems, from its pattern of occurrence, to be the probable name glyph of an early Tikal ruler is found on Stelae 13, 9, 7, 3, 26, and, according to Thompson (1962, p. 341), at C5 of Stela 4. Except in the last case, wherever it is clear and uneroded, it has a three-pronged ceremonial chipped flint around its eye and an unidentified double curl on the top of the head. No context is clear-cut, but the glyph's presence directly preceding the Tikal EG at the end of the inscription of Stela 9 seems to me good evidence. Here the preceding three glyphs, all heads, may also be names or titles of the ruler, but the extensive use of head variants on Stela 26 warns us to be careful of assuming this. The head preceding the EG on Stela 26 is probably still connected in some way with the "Triad" passage preceding it and is not to be interpreted as a human name. If the identification as a name glyph is correct, it is highly likely that Stela 26, like the others, dates from ME 3620 (9.1.0.0.0). The absence of this glyph on Stela 31 would tend to support the view that that monument was earlier than 3620.

The head on Stela 4 seems to me to be at least somewhat different and certainly has different affixes; it is associated with an inaugural-date glyph, and the suggested possible dates are 8.17.2.16.17 5 Caban 10 Yaxkin and 9.3.1.10.2 5 Ik 10 Yaxkin (ME 3542 and 3661) (Proskouriakoff 1960, p. 469). If the latter is correct, the same individual may be referred to on Yaxchilan L37 (see Fig. 93), associated with a date 1 Cauac 7 Yaxkin—unfortunately, also unplaced in the long count (9.3.13.12.19, ME 3673, is a possibility). Here, however, the head seems different, and while each has a three-element prefix, they do not seem to be the same.

On Stela 23, the initial date 8 Akbal 11 Mol (ME 3669, 9.3.9.13.3) is associated with a female head, followed by what seems to be the Tikal EG. Nothing more is known of this woman.

The first ruler whose glyphs can be recognized with complete assurance is associated with the most impressive group of Tikal monuments. His glyphs occur on the lintels of Temple I, on the carved bones from Burial 116 sealed beneath Temple I, on the lintels of Temple IV, on Stelae 16 and 5, and finally on Lintel 3 at Piedras Negras. He has two glyphs which are normally associated with the "moon-sign family" at Yaxchilan, although there they appear in reverse order. These are followed by the 'sky' glyph and by the head of God K, which, taken together, I would read as caan tz'acab, i.e., of the caan maternal lineage. This ruler's glyphs appear with the so-called batab katuns (see Fig. 80). Berlin (1958) has suggested that each batab katun was made up of five ordinary katuns. These glyphs normally follow the Tikal EG, which in turn follows a name glyph. The batab is indicated by a head with a hand holding an axe postfixed. Since bat is 'axe' and batab is 'chief', Berlin thought the two might be related. The head with the axe postfix also has the te glyph postfixed, but there

is nothing to indicate -ab. It therefore seems more likely that this is to be read bat-te (or bate). Without pretending to explain this grammatically, I think bat is probably used here as the root for 'chief, ruler'. However, it seems to me that rather than indicating that this is a 'chief katun', somehow different from an ordinary katun, the glyph rather indicates that these are the katuns 'of the chief'. The structural pattern (name, EG, x number of katuns) is exactly parallel to statements of "isolated katuns" elsewhere. Evidence is accumulating that such statements refer, in some instances, to the number of completed katuns or, in other cases, to the current katun counted from a ruler's birth. Both are probably indicated by grammatical particles which we do not yet understand. It is possible that the suffix te is here to be understood as Yucatec -e, of future time, and indicates that the katun so marked is not yet completed, i.e., that it is to be read 'fourth katun' rather than '(after) four katuns'.

If one examines the known cases of the bat-te katuns at Tikal, one finds that several are associated with the glyphs of our moon-sign ruler. On the Temple of the Inscriptions (T6), any possible name preceding the EG is not legible. As an exception, on Stelae 22 and 19 (ME 3940 and 3960, 9.17.0.0.0 and 9.18.0.0.0) one finds a name different from that of the moon-sign ruler in a completely parallel statement. Although the dedicatory dates of these two stelae are one katun apart, it is probable that the reference dates are somewhat less than this. In any case, both have an indication of 'fourth bat-te katun'. Stela 21, which has a clear record of 'fourth bat-te katun', is broken directly above the EG, and hence the expected name is not to be found. Since the date is ME 3905 (9.15.5.0.0), one may predict that if the rest is ever found, it will have the name glyphs of the moon-sign ruler directly preceding the break. Including this case, there are references to 'fourth katun' on Stela 21 (3905); on Temple 4, Lintel 3, at H8 (3912); on Stela 5 (3913); and on Temple 4, Lintel 2 (3915). 'Third katun' appears on Stela 16 (3880). There do not seem to be 'fourth katun' records on Lintel 3 preceding H1, nor in D2, nor on Lintel 2 of Temple 4 at C2. All of these references are consistent with a beginning date between 3835 and 3840 (9.11.15.0.0 and 9.12.0.0.0).

The names of the ruler appear in full on the bones texts, MT51A and MT51B, and in abbreviated form in the parallel passages from MT38A and MT38B. These are the canoe scenes, with their highly mythical flavor. The texts in parallel form and the associated drawings are reproduced in Figure 80. It will be seen that the name of the moon-sign ruler occurs, pre-

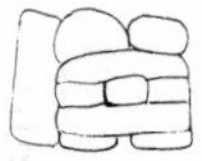

cf. possible names of
Tikal rulers on St. 31
(Plate 6, Fig. 109)

cf. Yaxchilan L37
(Fig. 93)

9.0.10 3610		T754
9.2.0 3640		T754
9.3.10 3670	St. 4 9.3.1.10.2 (3661) or 8.17.2.16.17 (3542)	T754?
9.5.0 3700	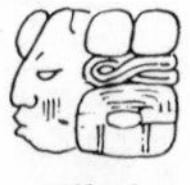	Six House apparently a female ruler Tikal EG?
9.6.10 3730		
9.8.0 3760		
9.9.10		

a female ruler (or priestess?) at Naranjo from Tikal

possible wife of moon-sign ruler

3 versions of the glyphs of moon-sign ruler

name of a ruler?   Tikal EG?

possible glyphs of a Tikal ruler, Seibal St. 10

9.12.10
3850

9.14.0
3880

9.15.10
3910

9.17.0
3940

9.18.10
3970

10.0.0
4000

Figure 79. Probable names of rulers associated with Tikal.

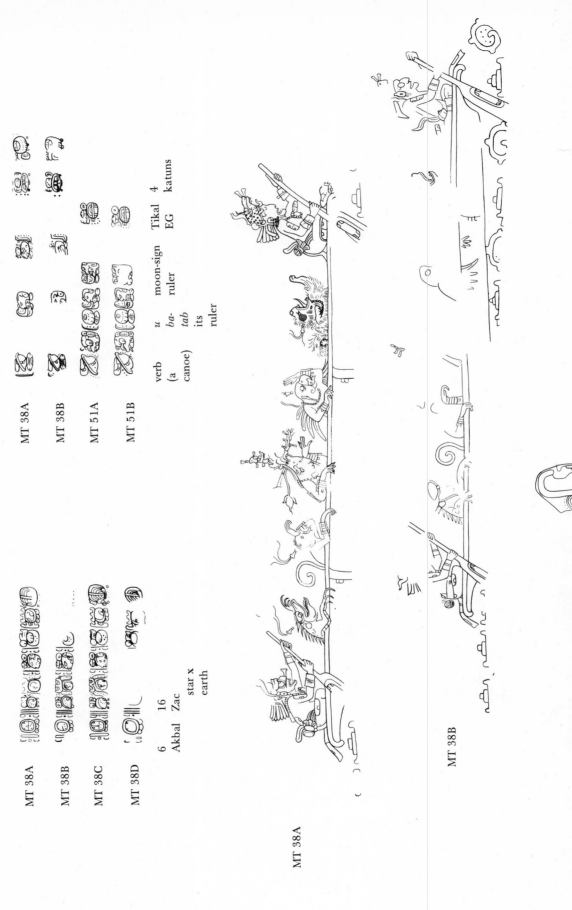

MT 38A

MT 38B

MT 38C

MT 38D

6
Akbal

16
Zac

star x
earth

MT 38A

MT 38B

MT 51A

MT 51B

verb
(a
canoe)

u
ba-
tab
its
ruler

moon-sign
ruler

Tikal
EG

4
katuns

MT 38A

MT 38B

MT 38C

MT 38D

MT 51A

MT 51B

Figure 80. Canoe texts from Tikal carved bones.

ceded by the phrase which I have suggested is to be read u batab and followed by the Tikal EG in MT51A and MT51B, while in MT38A and MT38B the name occurs with other glyphs and with 'four katuns' (without the bat-te reference). These references would certainly suggest that the ruler was in his fourth katun at the time of the burial and that, in all probability, the burial is that of the moon-sign ruler himself. This presents a problem, since Temple I is posterior to the sealed burial beneath it, and the lintels of Temple I have dates which have been read by Satterthwaite (1961b, pp. 64–72) as 9.13.3.0.0 9 Ahau 13 Pop, 9.13.3.7.18 11 Etz'nab 11 Ch'en (both ME 3863), and 9.12.9.17.16 5 Cib 14 Zotz (ME 3849). The other references to 'fourth katun' cluster from 3905 to 3915. If one accepts what seems to me the clear historical evidence, either these dates of Temple I must refer to a considerably earlier time than the period when Temple I was erected, or they must be placed fifty-two years later. Either of these solutions agrees much better with the stylistic evidence than does Satterthwaite's view. Style dating suggests that Temple I is, if anything, slightly later than Temple IV. It should be noted that the lintels of Temple I do not contain any 'bat-te katun' references which would make Satterthwaite's reading of the dates impossible.

Now it is necessary to turn briefly to the possible meaning of the obviously mythical scenes associated with the apparently historical text of these bones. The animals shown are some sort of dog, a parrot (anthropomorphic), a spider monkey, and an iguana. The first two are associated together by the prognostication for the day Oc ('Dog', originally 'Coyote'), which is Ix Kili 'Small Parrot' (Barrera Vásquez and Rendón 1948, p. 193), and by the Popul Vuh (Recinos, Goetz, and Morley 1950, p. 166), where it is said that four animals brought maize—yac, the mountain cat; utiu, the coyote; quel, a small parrot; and hoh, the crow. The Annals of the Cakchiquels (Recinos 1950, p. 50) say that the only two animals who knew where to get maize were Coyote (utiuh) and Crow (koch). One may presume that this is an old myth, for the Great Basin Shoshoneans say that Coyote and Crow stole pine nuts for mankind (Kelly 1938, pp. 395–403). The replacement of Coyote by Dog among the Mayas is also found in other stories. Both the Popul Vuh and the Annals of the Cakchiquels say that corn was brought from Paxil, and the Popul Vuh goes on to explain that the corn was then used to make man. Paxil is said by Recinos in a footnote to mean 'separation, spreading of the waters, inundation' (Recinos, Goetz, and Mor-

ley 1950, p. 165; see the glyph pax, Fig. 49 of this book).

The presence of two of the same animals and the Inundation place name suggest to me a connection with these scenes of animals in canoes. Their association with the maize from which man is created, on the one hand, and with what seems to be a fully historical accompanying text, on the other, suggests the possibility that this is a birth. The accompanying date is 6 Akbal 16 Zac, and Satterthwaite (unpublished communication) has suggested a long-count date 9.11.19.4.3 (ME 3839), assuming the latest possible date before the dates on the lintels of the temple above the burial. Without accepting either of these premises, the date seems likely to be correct, since it falls within the limits 3835–3840 previously suggested for the birth of the moon-sign ruler. It should be pointed out that Aubrey Trik (1963) says that the god shown is God B and that his name glyph appears before the EG, i.e., as part of the name of the moon-sign ruler by the present interpretation. However, the glyph incorporated in the name of the moon-sign ruler is that of God K, not that of God B, and the deity is probably neither B nor K, but rather Zimmermann's God X. I do not believe that another glyph in this text identified by Trik and Satterthwaite (in Trik 1963) as a glyph of God B actually belongs to B, K, or X, although it might belong to the latter.

The presence of the glyphs of the moon-sign ruler on Lintel 3 at Piedras Negras (without the Tikal EG) creates a possible chronological problem. Unfortunately, they are not associated with dates in any direct way. The IS (9.15.18.3.13 5 Ben 16 Ch'en, ME 3918) is the first-katun anniversary of a ruler who must have been a younger contemporary of the moon-sign ruler, but dates continue to a substantially later time. Perhaps the moon-sign ruler is indicated as genealogically related in some fashion to the Piedras Negras rulers, since the Piedras Negras EG appears shortly before in the same text. It should be noted that the female glyphs on Tikal Stela 5 are followed by an EG (Fig. 72, no. 12) and that the same EG is associated with the wife of the Piedras Negras ruler; so there was probably a relationship through females. It should also be noted that the names of near-contemporary females at Etzna and at Naranjo are followed by the Tikal EG and probably designate close relatives of the moon-sign ruler.

Several other bones texts are of interest here. The texts of MT42A and MT42B contain four clauses of three glyph blocks each. In third position is an EG; in second position, the presumed title for which I have suggested the reading batab; and the glyph in the first

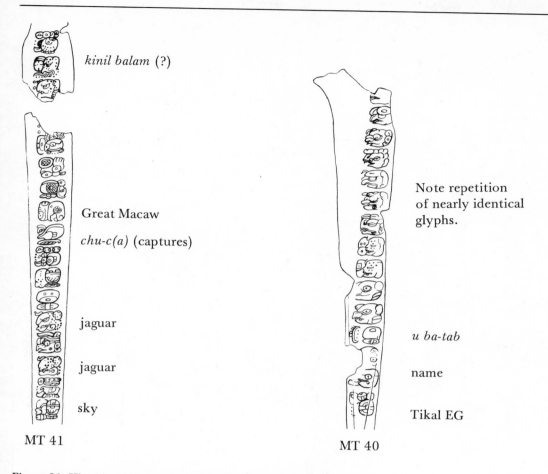

kinil balam (?)

Great Macaw

chu-c(a) (captures)

jaguar

jaguar

sky

MT 41

Note repetition
of nearly identical
glyphs.

u ba-tab

name

Tikal EG

MT 40

Figure 81. Historical information in the Tikal bones texts (miscellaneous texts).

position varies. In terms of the premises which have been explained in this chapter, I think that this variable element is the principal name or title of a contemporary ruler. The first phrase deals with Copan and the last with Palenque, but I have not been able to identify the glyphs with those of known rulers at those sites. The sites to which the other two EGs refer are not known.

MT40 has a clause which is parallel in structure (Fig. 81). Here the EG is Tikal, and the *u batab* phrase has two glyph blocks following it before the EG. The bone is broken, but at least eleven glyphs precede the *u batab* glyph block. These have the characteristics of a list rather than a normal text. In four places a glyph is repeated, differing, if at all, only in the affixes, and in three of these cases the glyph is repeated in the next glyph block. Every one of the glyphs is an animal or anthropomorphic head like those normally found in names. There is no obvious grammatical structure of any sort in the first eleven glyphs. In the light of the *u batab* phrase and the Tikal EG, the best explanation is that this is a list of ancestors or predecessors as rulers of Tikal. Verifi-

cation or disproof of this idea must come from a fuller knowledge of early Tikal rulers' names.

MT41 (Fig. 81) has the *chuc* 'capture' glyph near the middle, directly preceded by Chac Moo 'Great Macaw'; jaguar glyphs appear later in the text. It is contrary to all we know of the structure of the writing to think that either a subject or an object would precede the verb; so this is probably not a direct record of the capture of Macaw by Jaguar or vice versa. Nonetheless, it seems quite likely that this text refers in some way to the enmity between Macaw and Jaguar families which Proskouriakoff has suggested may have resulted, much later, in the downfall of Yaxchilan.

Both MT43 and MT44 start with *u batab*, follow with the glyph group of the moon-sign ruler, then have an otherwise unknown glyph block and the Tikal EG. In MT44 this is followed by 'westward', three unknown glyph blocks, and the Tikal EG again. MT44 has no other glyphs which I can interpret. MT55 ends with a female head with a star glyph and a suffix. Preceding this is a jaguar glyph. This is suggestive of Stela 18 from Etzna (ME 3840—9.12.0.0.0),

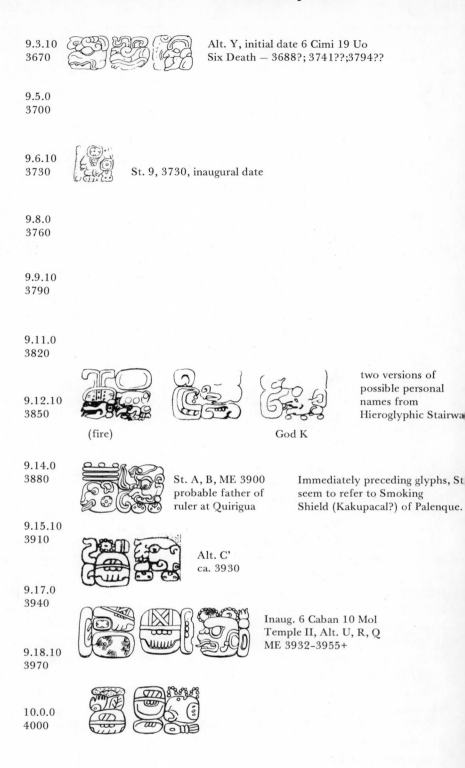

9.3.10 3670		Alt. Y, initial date 6 Cimi 19 Uo Six Death — 3688?; 3741??;3794??
9.5.0 3700		
9.6.10 3730		St. 9, 3730, inaugural date
9.8.0 3760		
9.9.10 3790		
9.11.0 3820		
9.12.10 3850	(fire) God K	two versions of possible personal names from Hieroglyphic Stairwa
9.14.0 3880		St. A, B, ME 3900 probable father of ruler at Quirigua Immediately preceding glyphs, St seem to refer to Smoking Shield (Kakupacal?) of Palenque.
9.15.10 3910		Alt. C' ca. 3930
9.17.0 3940		Inaug. 6 Caban 10 Mol Temple II, Alt. U, R, Q ME 3932–3955+
9.18.10 3970		
10.0.0 4000		

Figure 82. Copan rulers.

re)   God K   (fire)   (God K)

Alt. K, 9.12.16.7.8
3 Lamat 7 Yax (3856).
Glyphs probably are
or include name of
ruler, 4th katun.

 Apparent variant.
Substitution in
last glyph block
seems usual.

which has a star glyph in M2, a female (?) head in L3, and what I take to be the Tikal EG in M3. A jaguar glyph appears in A1. If the two "star women" are identical, MT55 must refer to an earlier generation than that of the moon-sign ruler; if not, there is an interesting suggestion of name repetition.

MT50 shows a canoe with the character of a bearded feathered serpent and *lamat* glyphs on the side, with the normal star glyph in the opening text. One is reminded of Quetzalcoatl and his serpent raft and how, after death, he became the morning star. If the other canoe scenes represent the birth of the ruler, this one probably represents his death, but unfortunately there seems to be no date by which to check this interpretation.

We have little information on later rulers of Tikal. The glyphs with the 'fourth *bat-te* katun' on Stelae 22 and 19 furnish a close parallel to those of the moon-sign ruler, as previously pointed out. They probably represent one of his successors. Seibal Stela 10 has a Tikal EG in B8, preceded by two glyph blocks which might be a name or title of the ruler of Tikal (Fig. 79). The Seibal EG precedes these glyphs, and similar phrases including two additional EGs follow them, but none of them are demonstrably references to rulers. Finally, Tikal Stela 11 has a series of possible name glyphs preceding the EG, but they are rather indistinct in published photographs.

One of the first possible indications of political control extending beyond the local area is found on a vase, believed to be of Tepeu 1 or 2 date, from Cerro Ecatepec, Chiapas (Culbert 1965, p. 22). This vase shows the Tikal and Piedras Negras EGs together (without EG prefixes), separated by one glyph from a bat-head glyph which might be the Copan EG. At Copan, the latter normally has *haab* infixed, but this was not necessarily the practice elsewhere. The scene shows individuals bringing textiles (as tribute?) to a ruler whose name is accompanied by an apparent Tikal EG.

One of the biggest puzzles in terms of historical information is presented by Copan. Here, there are many long inscriptions, covering a very considerable time period. Representations of human beings on stelae seem to show the traits of individuality in detail coupled with similarity in concept which mark historic personages at other sites. Despite these advantages, identified personal names are few in number. Proskouriakoff (1960, p. 468) was able to identify only one inaugural date and two initial dates in terms of association with the glyphs typical elsewhere. It seems quite possible that different glyphs were used to indicate these events. I was able (Kelley 1962b, p. 333, Fig. 7) to show that two sets of name glyphs at Copan shared elements with each other and with postulated name glyphs from Quirigua. The 'sun-at-horizon' glyph with 'new' prefixed and followed by 'sky' would, except for its association with an inaugural date, normally be supposed to have some sort of connection with astronomy. Its other associations support the view that it is part of a name. I also postulated a ruler called Eighteen Kan Dog; the glyphs I now suspect are simply a title meaning approximately 'the eighteenth (local) ruler', without other identification. The glyphs of this ruler appear frequently at Copan, and I now think that some of the preceding glyphs in some of the inscriptions may be personal or family names or titles. I think that the glyphs on Altar K (Fig. 82) almost certainly include the names of a ruler of Copan, as they are followed by a Copan EG and the '*bat-te* four katuns' phrase, but I cannot tell which of them are which. The 'fire' glyger head variant may be a name in this context. Altar Q seems to refer to Macaw (Moo) and New Macaw in a grammatical context which makes them names, in the broad sense, but it is not yet clear whether they are or are not titles, whether they refer to humans or deities, and whether they are or are not especially connected with Copan. Similar references appear elsewhere at Copan. The jaguar (*balam*) glyph also appears in similarly ambiguous contexts.

At Naranjo, inscriptions cover a relatively short period of time. The glyphs of the male and female rulers are given in Figure 83, following Proskouriakoff. The female ruler was apparently from Tikal. Proskouriakoff (1950, pp. 465–467) thought that the names on Stela 20 should be separated from her Series 1 because of certain differences. I have suggested (Kelley 1962c, p. 282) that the animal head in her Series 1 is a squirrel (Yucatec *cuc*) and that the doubled Cauac (T528) of Stela 20 is to be read phonetically *cu-c(u)*. The differing affixes, which formerly puzzled me, I would now regard as having differing or parallel grammatical functions, but this is not certain. The plausibility of this suggestion depends both on one's appraisal of the phonetic evidence and on the likelihood that the animal head is indeed a squirrel. Probable names from several other sites are also given in Figure 83.

Finally, I must draw attention to what I regard as a name sequence from Chichen Itza, a five-grapheme glyger (T669.604:586:25:178) which I read Kakupacal (Kelley 1962c, p. 304). This series occurs fourteen times at Chichen Itza. On the Halakal lintel, it precedes T565, the serpent segment, which I think may indicate relationships between individuals (see above). In the Casa Colorada, the glyger is followed, after three intervening glyphs (part of a glyph block),

Figure 83. Rulers at Naranjo and elsewhere.

by Knorozov's *ah* (Thompson's *hitz*), which is frequently found with name glyphs; by some other glyphs, which may be one or two additional titles; and by the presumed Chichen EG (see above). This passage opens with a fish-in-hand glyph, normally associated with historic figures in the Classic Period inscriptions to the south. Structurally, in this passage, these glyphs seem to me to be the most likely grammatical subject, although those immediately following cannot be entirely ruled out.

From the phonetic viewpoint, it suffices to point out that *ka, ku,* and *ca* are the glyphs given by Landa as having those values; that *la* is the initial grapheme of 'east' (Yuc. *lakin, likin*), the second being the known glyph *kin;* and that *pa* was established by Knorozov and accepted by me on the basis of its occurrences in the codices. *Pacal* means 'shield', and the latter three glyphs appear at Palenque in a context which has suggested to me that they are phonetic determinants for the associated ideograph of the shield. For a further discussion of these phonetic values, see Chapter 9.

From the historic viewpoint, Kakupacal, the "valorous captain of the Itzas," is one of the few Mayas known to us by name from the colonial documents. None of the surviving documents can be taken at face value as history, and their chronology is quite contradictory (see Barrera Vásquez and Morley 1949, Jakeman 1945). The Third Chronicle of Chumayel (in Barrera Vásquez and Morley 1949) says that Kakupacal and Tecuilu conquered Chakanputun in a katun 8 Ahau. According to this source, this would have been between 1183 and 1202 A.D.; it is connected here with the establishment of the Itzas in Mayapan in 1189. This source puts the abandonment of Chichen Itza by the Itzas in 1125 and the plot of Hunac Ceel between 1084 and 1104. This plot is apparently placed by the *Mani-Tizimin*–First Chronicle of Chumayel in a katun 8 Ahau, usually identified as running from 1185 to 1202, and Kakupacal is not mentioned. The account of Gaspar Antonio Chi, reconstructed and translated by M. Wells Jakeman (1945, p. 97) says that "the inhabitants of the said town of Itzamal were conquered by Kak-u-pacal and Uilu, valorous captains of the Itzas, formerly of the city of Mayapan." No date is given. Kakupacal is also said to have conquered Motul, 140 years after it was founded (see Tozzer 1941, p. 24). I do not think that these sources can be relied on in any way for a date. They do, however, show that there was a native tradition of an important Itza warrior named Kakupacal who, with his companion Bilu (or Uilu), conquered Chakanputun, Motul, and Itzamal.

The texts at Chichen Itza which contain the glyger I read Kakupacal all fall in a katun 1 Ahau (10.2.0.15.3–10.2.12.2.4, ME 4040–4052) (Thompson 1937, p. 186). The Thompson correlation would put them at 869–881 A.D., the Spinden correlation at 610–621 A.D. It is clear that any contention that the same individual is referred to is certainly not supported by the chronology. However, there is the possibility that more than one Itza captain was named Kakupacal, as well as the fact that there are major problems in the chronological interpretation of the chronicles and in the placing of the Maya Era relative to our era. There is also a difficulty for those who do not think that the Itzas were in Yucatán during the time of the Mayan inscriptions at Chichen Itza. The identity of the Itzas is a subject too far removed from glyph decipherment to be treated here, and I will merely say that it seems to me expectable to find the name of an Itza warrior in the Mayan inscriptions of Chichen.

Mention should be made of an attempt by Barthel (1964*a*) to read this glyger in a very different way. He regards T669.604 as reading *kab ku* 'hand of god', a euphemism for the flint knife of human sacrifice. The remainder (T586:25:178) is regarded by him as an explanatory term for the sacrificial knife. Neither the associations nor the grammatical structure seem to me to support this view (see Fig. 112).

There is one other series of glyphs at Chichen Itza which I regard as containing a personal name or title. The doorway lintel of the Akadzib opens with my proposed *batab* (Fig. 83). This is followed by a glyph read by Barthel *ah kalaan* (I accept *kal* and *aan*, but not *ah*). Then comes a glyger which seems to be the most basic part of the name, followed by a glyger beginning *bat-* 'axe, ruler', then by a glyger read by Barthel *nabte* (which I accept), and finally by the glyger which I have suggested may be the Chichen Itza EG. The structure of the phrase is closely parallel to those from Tikal already considered, and it is one of the best evidences for regarding the closing glyger of the phrase as the Chichen EG. Barthel (1964*a*, pp. 228, 241) has drawn attention to the fact that the combination of mandible and fan appears on the Chajcar vase, the mandible on a cord around the neck of a bearded figure and the fan in his hand. Thus these glyphs apparently refer to symbols of rank. Barthel (1955*a*, pp. 9–10) regards the axe in the following glyger and the *nabte* 'spear' glyger as referring to war. While I think they may have this connotation, I would here regard them as names or titles. It may be mentioned that R. L. Roys (1940, p. 43) lists *nabte* as a Yucatec personal name.

Thus, during the past ten years, we have become able to recognize glyphs referring to people and places; some dynastic sequences have been established; there seem to be occasional references to tribute, conquests, and intermarriages; and the framework of a history which is somewhat more than a mere list of dates is beginning to emerge. There is still a great deal which is obscure to us, but we now see human beings rather than astronomical abstractions. Even religious ceremonies are seen to be associated with particular historical situations. Although the data are little more extensive than the data presented in a very different way by the Mixtec historical manuscripts, they have the tremendous advantage of being based on contemporary records and of being directly correlated with archaeological information. For the first time, we know something of the history of an American Indian group which is comparable to what we know of many Eurasian groups.

The following linguistic reconstructions, derived from Kaufman 1964, may have some relevance to the glyphs which have been considered in this section.

Reconstructions apply to the whole family unless otherwise specified. Periods are used to separate reconstructions for one meaning from reconstructions for the next.

Man's brother-in-law: *bël/bay/bax. Son-in-law: *ngi' (H.?). Daughter-in-law: *'al'ib. Elder male relative, paternal or maternal uncle: *ikan. Woman's son: *'al (H.?). Woman's sister-in-law: *xawan. Sister-in-law or brother-in-law of the other sex: *mu'. Mother: (a) *chuch; (b) *mim; (c) *me'/mi'; (d) *nan/na'. Grandfather, father: *mam. Father: *tat. Cousin, nephew: *'ikyaq'. Older brother: *tyaq'. Younger brother: *'ihtz'in. Grandson: *'i'. Young boy: *ky'aajol. Youth: *'unin. Old woman: *'ihnam/'ixnam. Old man: *'icham. Boy, male relative: *xiib. Woman: (a) *'ix, H.-Chu.-Kan.-Jac.; (b) *'ix-oq, Yuc.-Pch.-Kek.-Toj.-Chr.-Chl.-Mam-Q. Man: *'winaq. Masculine prefix: *'aj-, (H.?). Feminine prefix: *'ix- (=woman) (H.?). Ruler, lord: *ajaw. Name: (a) *bih/bi', Tzel.-Tzo.-H.-Pch.-Toj.-Mam-Q.; (b) *kw'aba', Yuc.-Kek.-Chl.-Chr. (Chu.-Kan.?). Orphan, widower, poor person: *meba'. Twin: *lot/loh.

Chapter 12
Methods
of Decipherment

The full decipherment of a Maya glyph involves recognition of the object depicted, knowledge of the phonetic value of the glyph, knowledge of its meaning or meanings, and understanding of how these are interrelated. Under certain conditions, it may be possible to achieve any of the first three results without the others, and such partial decipherments are still frequent. The preceding chapters have given practical examples of most of the methods to be considered. This chapter is designed to emphasize the common principles underlying the varied decipherments which have been made and to consider profitable avenues of future research.

The surest and most important method of decipherment is proof by context, involving either parallel passages with one varying element, corresponding to a varying element in the accompanying pictures (if in the codices), or a normal correspondence of a particular glyph to a particular action, object, or being. The correspondence is seldom invariable, because of substitution of synonyms, minor distinctions which are not important to us but were distinguished verbally by the Maya, or use of one glyph with several different meanings. This method has been especially important in the divinatory almanacs of the codices and has been the basis of the greater part of the accepted decipherments given in the previous pages. There are still discoveries to be made in the codices through a careful use of this method, although without new material, it is likely that it will gradually give way to others. Matching of glyphs from the inscriptions with data supplied by the accompanying sculptures or paintings is a form of proof from context which is just beginning to be used.

A method which promises to give very valuable results is what Barthel has called "category-bound deciphering." This involves grammatical categorization of the known glyphs according to their use as names, action glyphs, attributive or adjectival glyphs, numerical classifiers, verbal suffixes, locatives, etc. It has been implicit to some extent in the studies of all scholars who have worked with the glyphs, but as a formal method of analysis it seems to have been developed by Zimmermann and Barthel, based on Thompson's demonstration that some of the affixes correspond to known grammatical particles.

Closely related to this method is analysis to determine the general subject matter of a text, which will often furnish further clues to specific decipherments. The recognition of the lunar nature of the Supplementary Series is a good example of this procedure. The presence of even a few known glyphs or glygers may throw a considerable amount of light on what subject is under discussion. Two important hypotheses of Thompson illustrate both the advantages and the difficulties of this kind of study. In a study of various tables in the *Dresden* codex, Thompson (1950, pp. 258–261) suggested that they were multiplication tables for use with divinatory almanacs, with the principal purpose of weather divination. The grounds for this suggestion included the rain associations of the animal associated with the 780-day multiplication table, representations of rain and other indications of storm in other tables, and a degenerate table of 'the birth of Chac' (or 'the beginning of the storm') in the *Book of Chilam Balam of Chumayel*. It had previously been supposed that these were planetary tables, an interpretation rejected by Thompson. The major difficulty with Thompson's view (as he notes in a slightly different context, 1950, p. 257) is the presence of the Initial Series which introduce these tables, involving calculations over periods of more than three thousand years. Judging from Eurasian analogies, the prediction of the weather through planetary conjunctions might have been a major feature of such tables, so that the two main suggestions which have been made are not necessarily contradictory. The long figures certainly seem more relevant to astronomy than to short-term weather prediction.

The other hypothesis (Thompson 1958*a*) is that the bird passages (see Fig. 39) are divinatory almanacs for disease. As a preliminary basis for this suggestion, Thompson points out that the goddess shown in these passages is Ix Chel, who, among other characteristics, is patron of medicine and of disease. The identity of the goddess does not seem as certain to me as it does to Thompson, but he certainly could be correct on this. The most basic glyphic reading suggested is the identification of T19 as *koch,* which he paraphrases as 'divinely inflicted sickness or punishment'. He also quotes from the Motul dictionary a meaning of *koch* as 'to carry above one on one's shoulders a cross, wood, or such like things'. The birds, regarded as symbols of particular kinds of illness, would presumably come in the category of "such like things." Further definitions show that *koch* may have had a more generic meaning of 'carry'. Thompson feels that both meanings are relevant to these passages. I have accepted Knorozov's reading, *mu,* which with the following *ti* glyph gives *mut* 'bird, tidings'. While 'tidings' is not as strong support for Thompson's interpretation as *koch,* it is not contradictory to it.

Thompson goes on to identify the names of the birds (and other burdens in other passages) as various diseases, particularly skin diseases and fits. Thus he argues that *moo* 'macaw' stands for *mo tancaz* 'macaw madness', although there is no glyph for 'madness' involved; that *ch'om* 'black vulture' stands for *ch'omch'om* 'pittings of the skin', although the glyph is not reduplicated; that *maax* 'spider monkey' stands for *chac nich'maax* 'an inflammation of the gums'. The glyphs read phonetically by Knorozov as *cutz* 'turkey' are read by Thompson as *ah tzo* 'male turkey', a term which also means 'pimples', and Knorozov's reading of *tzul* 'dog' is rejected in favor of *pek* 'dog, spotty infection of the skin'. Since I regard both of the Knorozov readings as sound, I tend to feel that Thompson's readings are a good indication of how easy it may sometimes be to find what one is looking for. I would suggest that if there is any degree of validity in all this, it is in the fact that certain classes of disease tended to be associated with animals. Possibly this meant that these animals might sometimes symbolize those diseases, but I see nothing in either the glyphic text or the pictures to convince me of this. Nonetheless, I regard this type of approach, attempting to get at the meaning of a whole segment of the codices, rather than merely specific glyphs, as of great value. It is vital to know the general subject matter of whole sections of the codices and of the inscriptions. The original recognition of the Venus tables is a good example of how knowing the general subject may aid in determining specific glyphs.

The Venus tables are also an excellent example of the use of mathematical relationships to determine the subject matter. Such relationships not only enable the recognition of the general subject matter of a text (see the discussion of the 819-day cycle recognized by Thompson, Chapter 3), but also are basic to such specific readings as most of the ending glyphs, the *xoc* glyph for 'count', the anterior and posterior date indicators, the glyphs of the various numerals, and the glygers of the month deities and of the Nine Lords of the Night.

Frequently, we can recognize two or more meanings or uses of a glyph, and examination of Mayan vocabularies may show us the existence of words which are homonyms and have appropriate meanings. The correspondence between the uses of *te* and of T87 is a good example. Another is the multiple correspondence between the meanings of **pok'* and T740.

Knorozov's demonstration of the principle of synharmony makes possible a type of phonetic categorization which may be quite helpful in deciphering and will probably become more important as time goes on. Since the principle is far from absolute, we cannot say from a single example what the vowel of a CV glyph should be, but if we find a certain glyph forming words by the addition of, say, the *tzu, tu, chu,* and *cu* glyphs, we can be reasonably certain that the inherent vowel is *u,* even if we once find the same glyph forming a word with *ca.* Ultimately, as we get fuller knowledge of the glyphs in certain phonetic groups, we may even find that the only CV glyph ending in *u* for which we do not already have a reading is, say, *pu,* so that this gives us a probably complete phonetic decipherment—or we may find that there are only three possibilities and try each of them in all the combinations to see if they seem to make sense.

Whorf suggested the use of a method of "linguistic configurations." The principle is that there seem to be groups of Maya words of CVC form in which the first CV contains a common semantic element. His only published attempts to apply the principle were in connection with the *ma* group, which he said had a common basic meaning of 'pass', and the *ku* group (i.e., Yucatec *cu*), meaning 'sit, rest, be set, fixed, or quiet'. In the case of *ma*-, his results can only be described as unfortunate, and in the case of *cu*, he managed to establish that *cu* was probably the first syllable of the glyger which Seler had long since shown to be *cuch* 'burden'. Nonetheless, he did present evidence for the existence of such groups, and I think the method may be susceptible of some successful application, if cautiously used by someone knowing both the present status of glyphic studies and the present status of Mayan linguistics.

Another method, which has been used with marked success by Thompson, and which, I believe, has also often led him astray, is determination of the interchangeability of one element with another. The assumption is that if two glyphs interchange randomly in a number of different situations, they are probably equivalent in sound or meaning or both. A good example is the interchangeability of the fish with the comb, where both probably have the phonetic value *ca* (see Fig. 45), or the interchangeability of the *muluc* glyph with the *xoc* glyph, where they probably have closely related meanings. The difficulty is in knowing whether the interchange is actually random or whether it involves some slight, or even some important, distinction. If there are sufficient texts, this method will give very good results. Even when the two forms are not equivalent in either sound or meaning, the fact of interchangeability under certain conditions may be of considerable importance in decipherment, particularly if the conditions can be defined.

The latter type of interchangeability leads directly to the concept of glyphic groups, comprised of elements which seem to interchange with one another with considerable freedom under rather varied circumstances yet cannot be considered strict equivalents. Thompson (1950, pp. 273–281) discusses at some length a "water group" and an "underworld group." The validity of such groupings, corresponding somewhat to a lexical field in linguistics, depends to a considerable extent upon whether the elements involved are largely ideographic or whether important phonetic substitutions are involved. To Thompson and Barthel, with their basically ideographic view of the script as a whole, such groups constitute a major step towards establishing meanings, if not direct readings, in Maya. Despite my beliefs as to the importance of phoneticism in the script, I think that it is valuable to recognize such groupings; the meanings and readings derived from use of this method are most effective and valid when the glyphs concerned actually are used ideographically. Sometimes such a group may be a grammatical category rather than a grouping of semantically similar ideographic glyphs. (See my interpretation of Thompson's "count group," Chapter 10).

A method which may yet yield important results is that of comparing text passages in the codices or inscriptions with known mythological materials, either Mayan of later date or Mexican. Seler established important facts about the calendar, world directions, and deity sequences in this way, and the analogy of the Nine Lords of the Night in Mexican mythology was basic to Thompson's recognition of the nature of Glyph G of the Supplementary Series. While Barthel's specific comparisons of the series of heavens of the Rain God in Mexico and the places visited by God B in the *Dresden* sometimes seem dubious, the overall concept appears to be similar. This method has enabled me to point out unexpected support for Knorozov's reading of the name of one of the Venus gods as Ulum 'Turkey' and to make some suggestions as to the names of the month deities. Such readings have an importance quite aside from any interest in mythology, as the names are usually composite, and the glyphic elements frequently appear in other combinations.

The use of particular glyphs as markers for other classes of glyphs is beginning to be important in decipherment. T740 (**pok'* 'be born') and T684 (*hok* 'be inaugurated'), associated with ceremonies of the beginning of a reign, are normally followed by the names of human beings. The sequence T1.1038b is normally preceded by a glyph for some kind of offering.

In some respects, the most basic method of all is the establishment of the origin of a glyph, by comparison of the forms in which it occurs with Mayan depictions of animals, plants, gods, artifacts, etc. Recognizable pictographs were the opening wedge for perceiving the parallelism between texts and pictures in the codices, from which nearly all subsequent decipherment stems in one way or another. If we can determine what a glyph represents and can reconstruct a proto-Mayan word for the object depicted, we have almost certainly established at least an approximate phonetic reading and can probably determine the meanings in our texts by searching for homonyms in the dictionaries and comparing them with the context of the particular glyph. The method was of more importance at the beginning of Mayan studies than it is now; that it can still give useful results is shown by such things as Thompson's recognition of several shell glyphs, Knorozov's recognition of the net glyph, and Cordy's recognition of the turkey pictograph. Beyer's work in this line has still been inadequately appraised, perhaps because his interpretations of the meaning of his identifications did not lead to decipherments which other scholars were ready to accept.

A very preliminary step toward identification may be taken by classification of the shape of glyphs, when these are not the usual oval, although no one has yet attempted to do this formally.

Reasonably sophisticated matchings of frequencies of occurrence of graphemes against frequencies of morphemes in Yucatec have so far been undertaken only by Knorozov (1967, pp. 44–45). Unfortunately, he gives us only a very generalized statement of procedure and results. The potential usefulness of the method and the way he has applied it may be gathered from his statement: "Hieroglyph 069-069 can be read as *ma-m(a)* (the name of a god), since sign no. 069, as well as the syllable *ma*, belongs to the group most used in root morphemes, while this particular reading fits more exactly the meaning of the hieroglyph in a text unit of type CB (D57a) than do other syllables close to it in relative frequency (*bob, bab, kok, pap*)" (Knorozov 1967, p. 49). Unfortunately, he did not publish the tables of relative frequencies of root morphemes and of graphemes which apparently underlie many of his decipherments. The use of computers working on such principles may become a major research tool.

Structural analysis of whole texts often reveals patterned similarities and variations, not apparent from inspection alone, which suggest equivalence of use of particular glyphs. This equivalence of use may help in determining grammatical structure, in recognizing grammatical particles, in recognizing names, and in other forms of categorization which may lead directly to decipherment.

All of these methods are of value, and most of them have already produced important results. None of them gives promise of radical increase in our knowledge of the glyphs, but the slow accumulation of acceptable decipherments will continue. Methods which will continue to be of major importance are identifications of the meaning of glyphs in the codices, particularly verbs; mythological studies, especially comparisons of characteristics in order to identify deities by name rather than by the abstract designations now used; computing of frequencies of glyphs and comparisons of them with morpheme frequencies in Yucatec or other Mayan languages; examination of vocabularies for words which fit the multiple meanings of particular glyphs; and determination of the appellative glyphs in the inscriptions from structure, by glyphic markers, or in other ways.

Scholars working in the varied ways which are most congenial to them can expect to discover new patterns, whether in astronomy, mythology, phonetics, or grammar. Computers will produce valuable correlations of data which would require an inordinate amount of labor for a human scholar, but humans will still appraise the results. Thompson has made the pessimistic comment that ideographic decipherment, unlike phonetic decipherment, does not automatically lead to further decipherment. I, however, think that any addition to our knowledge of the glyphs tends to have a feedback effect, helping us to achieve additional results. Recognition of a single phonetic glyph or grammatical affix may lead to the correct matching of a deity name with its glyphic equivalent. A deity name may include graphemes used phonetically or as grammatical particles elsewhere. The **pok'* glyph sharpens our understanding of the way the Mayas recorded lunar phases, while a knowledge of astronomy may lead to the identification of glyphs which are important in still other contexts. All glyphs have some sort of relevance to the decipherment of other glyphs.

Chapter 13 Presentation of Texts and Structural Analysis

A student of Maya hieroglyphs needs access to long texts, presented in a way which shows their structure and indicates what kind of information might be given in particular glyphs or clauses. This chapter includes a brief review of research on the structural analysis of long texts and illustrates the principles involved through presentation of selected long texts, some from the codices and some from the monuments. These particular texts are chosen to emphasize patterning and problems and to give some idea of what degree of interpretation is now possible. No attempt is made to discuss or justify readings here, and substantially different interpretations are possible in many instances.

The first attempt to make a detailed structural analysis of a Maya text was Cyrus Thomas's study of the Palenque Tablets in 1882. He showed that the repetition of elements in successive passages made sense only if read in double columns, from left to right and from top to bottom. Thomas thus opened up promising avenues of structural analysis that, unfortunately, few later scholars have been willing to explore fully, although many investigators have dealt with portions of texts for purposes other than structural analysis.

Eduard Seler (1902–1923, III, 695–709) drew attention to parallel passages found in both the *Madrid* and the *Dresden* which give the same data in different ways. The similarities extend to minor details. One of these series has already been considered (the bird passages, see Chapter 5). Figures 84–87 show some additional parallels. Here the underlying calendrical similarities form a structural base on which the other similarities appear in regular order. The use of different glyphs for similar subject matter and the parallelism of the depictions may give us information one source alone could not give.

Beyer (1937) emphasized the importance of parallel clauses in different inscriptions at Chichen Itza but did not consider any inscription as a whole. Whorf (1933, pp. 6–9) showed the grammatical structure of short clauses in the codices. Thompson (1950) pointed out parallel clauses in inscriptions from several sites, but he did not analyze the entire structure of any inscription. Barthel (1955a), considering whole inscriptions from Chichen Itza, discussed the meaning of certain parallels, but he did not in any way emphasize a structural viewpoint. In a study of the parallel passages in the very lengthy inscription from the Temple of the Inscriptions at Palenque, Berlin (1963) considered a very substantial portion of a text in a way which showed the patterned form of the repetitions. As far as I know, this is the fullest

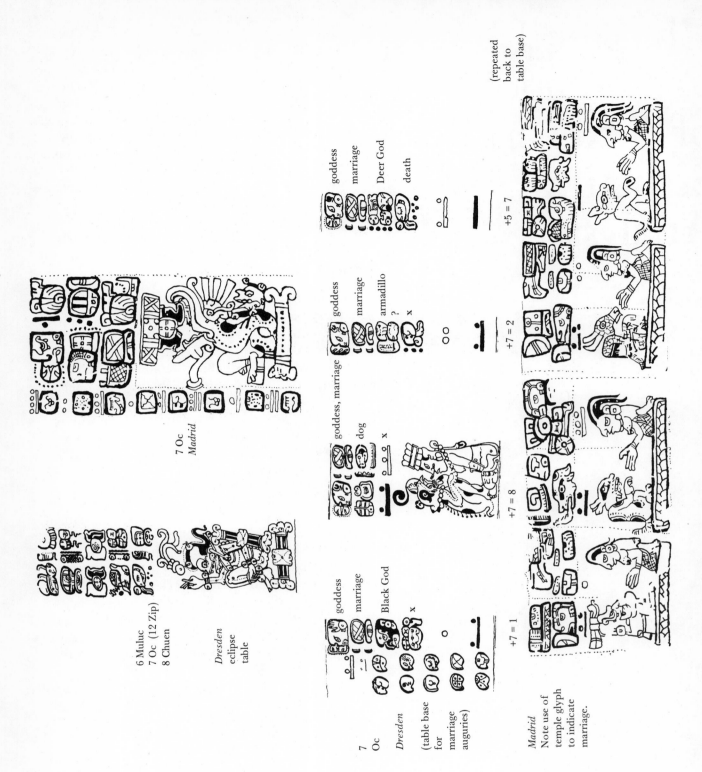

6 Muluc
7 Oc (12 Zip)
8 Chuen

Dresden
eclipse
table

7 Oc
Madrid

7
Oc
Dresden
(table base
for
marriage
auguries)

goddess

marriage

Black God

x

Madrid
Note use of
temple glyph
to indicate
marriage.

goddess, marriage

dog

x

+7 = 8

goddess

marriage

armadillo
?.
x

+7 = 2

goddess

marriage

Deer God

death

+5 = 7

(repeated
back to
table base)

+7 = 1

Figure 84. Parallel passages from *Dresden* and *Madrid*.

Madrid

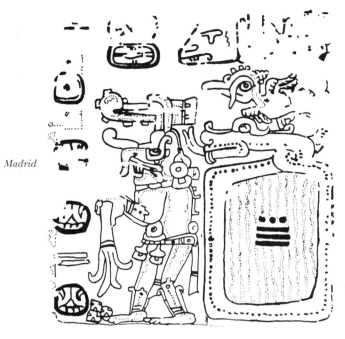

2. East   turkey sacrifice   3. North   deer sacrifice

Dresden

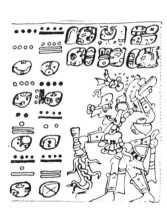

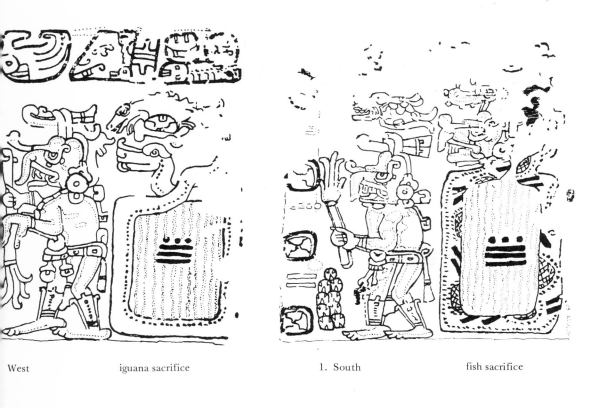

West   iguana sacrifice   1. South   fish sacrifice

    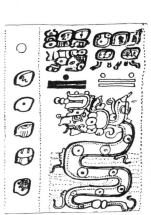

Figure 86. Parallel passages. Numbers show original order in *Madrid*.

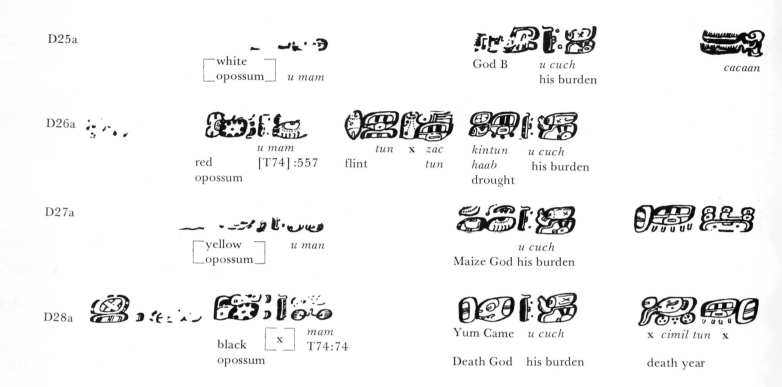

Figure 88. New-year texts from *Dresden*.

structural analysis, implicit or explicit, since Cyrus Thomas's original effort. The present attempts to consider the structure of particular texts go substantially beyond previous studies.

As a beginning, to demonstrate the necessity of such a preliminary analysis, Figure 88 shows the texts of the new-year ceremonies from the *Dresden,* rewritten in linear form. Cordan (1963*a,* pp. 16, 20, 26) read each row vertically before passing to the next row. The effect of this is to make the sequence of glyphs completely different in the different years. The numbering system of Villacorta and Villacorta (1930) presupposes reading as in the inscriptions, in double columns, from left to right and from top to bottom. The correctness of this view is indicated by the order in which the parallels appear. The parallelism is such as to allow us to fill in a number of destroyed glyphs with reasonable confidence. The initial verb is preserved only on D28a, and the following glyph block is entirely destroyed in all four years. The third and fourth glyph blocks in all cases give the names of the opossums below, associated with the colors of the particular year. The parallelism of D26a

with the other years makes it clear that T557 substituted for T74 in a glyger to be read *u mam* (probably to be paraphrased here 'lord of the year's end'). This is then followed by a deity name or phrase indicating the name of the god carried by the opossum and then *u cuch* 'his burden'. From D25a, it is clear that the next passage would have indicated the kind of offering and would have been followed by 'his offering'. This in turn is followed by four glyph blocks in the first three years and five in the fourth year which are unclear in subject matter but may refer to the fate of the crops. These are followed by a glyph of unknown meaning with a number prefixed, followed by another glyger, x-*kal-te* with a number prefixed. The presence of *te* suffixed to *kal* in the third and fourth years makes it likely that the same was intended in the second year, where it is not found. This is the last glyph block in the account of the second and fourth years, but it is followed in the third year by a glyph block containing the title of Itzamna and in the first year by two glyph blocks containing material of unknown meaning. While a general knowledge of the content of these passages goes back to Cyrus Thomas, the need for published structural studies may be seen

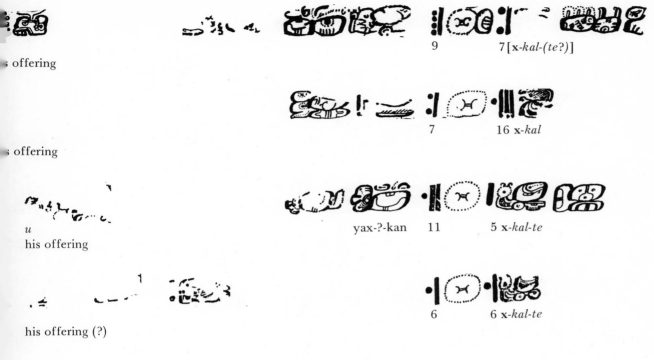

offering

9

7[x-*kal-(te?)*]

offering

7

16 x-*kal*

u

his offering

yax-?-kan   11   5 x-*kal-te*

his offering (?)

6   6 x-*kal-te*

by the fact that, as late as 1963, Cordan read these glyphs in the wrong order. In this case, the parallelism of structure throws light on specific details which could not be determined from the description of one year alone.

There is a similar parallelism of structure in the "serpent number" passages of D61 and D69. In each, an opening passage of four glyph blocks of unclear import is followed by a glyger which in other contexts means 'house' or 'temple' and here has the past-tense verbal suffix -*ah*. This is followed by the pictun glyph and a statement of '18 (tuns?)'. Then in each passage appear two net glyphs with deity heads. All four deity heads seem to me to be different gods of the God N group. These are followed in turn by the katun glyph and a notation of '8 tuns and 16 days', with an unusual prefix on the latter. Then the initial verb is repeated with a statement of '1 uinal and 19 days', followed immediately by the date 4 Ahau 8 Cumku. Throughout the passages to this point, numbers are often given in head forms, and the glyphs for 'day' and 'month' may have the agentive prefix *ah;* both texts are closely parallel in content, although variable in form. From this point on, the two diverge.

D61 gives a glyger which includes *kal* and follows this by the glyger for the deity seated on the snake. Then comes an unidentified glyph, then *ti-naab* with *tzab* (?) prefixed, and then '1 pictun' with an unidentified glyph intervening between '1' and 'pictun'. *Tzab,* Yucatec for 'rattles of a rattlesnake' and a name given to the Pleiades, does not have any obvious contextual meaning here. The identification of the glyph is certain, but the validity of a reading based solely on Yucatec and without contextual support is open to question. On D69, we find '5 *kaat*-x' in the first glyph block following 4 Ahau 8 Cumku, then *ti-naab,* without the *tzab* glyph, and then a statement of '1 pictun, 3 uinals, and 1 day', in which all three have *tzab* prefixed. Then the initial verb is repeated a third time, followed on D61 by '15 katuns, 9 tuns, 1 uinal, 3 days', and on D69 by '15 katuns, 9 tuns, 4 uinals, and 4 days'. The difference between these two statements is the same as that between the '1 pictun' statement of D61 and the '1 pictun, 3 uinals, 1 day' of D69. On D61, '19 *tzab(?)-naab*' (i.e., 19 cycles of some sort?) follows the interval and is followed by a brief phrase, which can be partly transcribed but not adequately translated, and, finally, the date 9 Kan 12

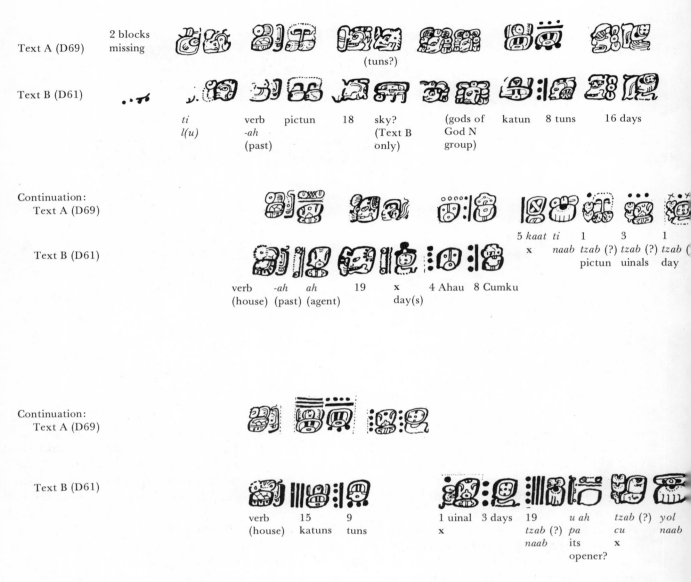

Text A (D69)   2 blocks
missing

(tuns?)

Text B (D61)

ti   verb   pictun   18   sky?   (gods of   katun   8 tuns   16 days
l(u)   *-ah*   (Text B   God N
         (past)   only)   group)

Continuation:
   Text A (D69)

                                                    5 *kaat*   *ti*   1   3   1
                                                    x   *naab*   *tzab* (?)   *tzab* (?)   *tzab* (
   Text B (D61)   pictun   uinals   day

verb   *-ah*   *ah*   19   x   4 Ahau   8 Cumku
(house)   (past)   (agent)   day(s)

Continuation:
   Text A (D69)

Text B (D61)

verb   15   9   1 uinal   3 days   19   *u ah*   *tzab* (?)   *yol*
(house)   katuns   tuns   x   *tzab* (?)   *pa*   *cu*   *naab*
                                                    naab   its   x
                                                                 opener?

T327:17   T327:17

parallel
passage
from
Madrid

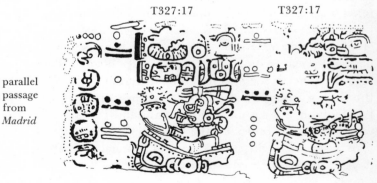

Figure 89. The serpent number passages.

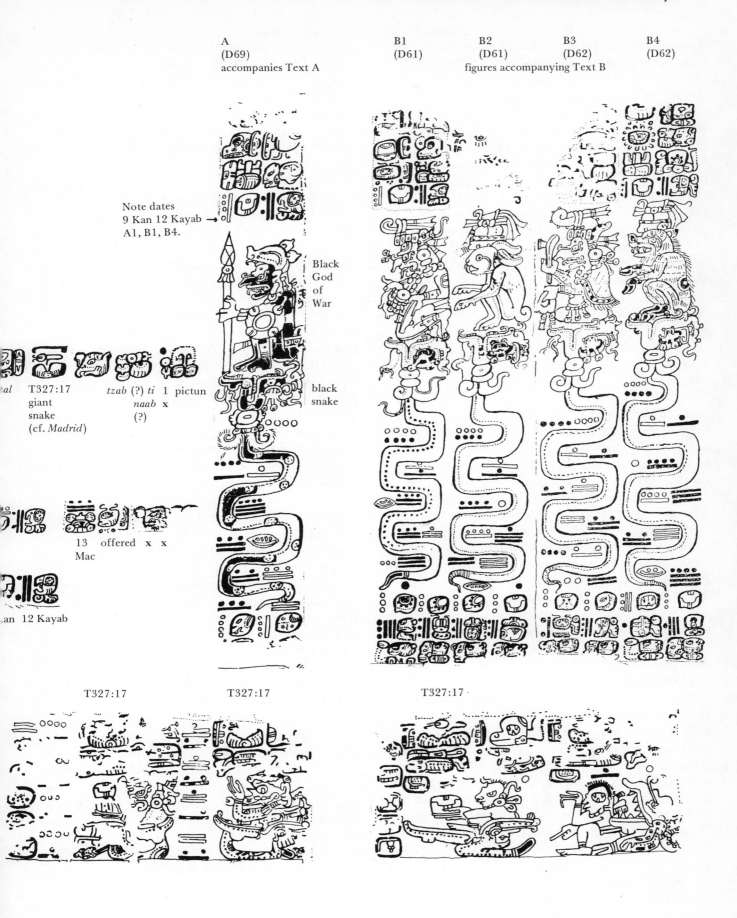

A
(D69)
accompanies Text A

B1
(D61)

B2
(D61)

B3
(D62)

B4
(D62)

figures accompanying Text B

Note dates
9 Kan 12 Kayab →
A1, B1, B4.

Black
God
of
War

black
snake

al   T327:17   *tzab* (?) *ti* 1 pictun
    giant   *naab* x
    snake   (?)
    (cf. *Madrid*)

13   offered   x   x
Mac

an 12 Kayab

T327:17   T327:17   T327:17

Kayab. On D69, the date 9 Kan 12 Kayab directly follows the interval and is followed by the date 13 Mac, then by the 'offer' verb and a couple of additional glyph blocks.

The parallels between the two passages and between parts of the passages make it clear where the breaks in subject matter come. The verbs may be recognized, and one is repeated. The grammatical subject of this repeated verb is apparently the period of time which follows it, for the period glyphs have the agentive *ah* prefixed, and there are no other glyphs which could be the subject. Even with our very limited knowledge of the subject matter of these texts, the grammatical structure emerges clearly. Valid decipherments must fit the pattern thus revealed. The glyphs should not be studied merely as isolated entities, but rather as parts of complex statements whose structure can be determined.

A passage from *Madrid* also shows deities seated on serpents with brief accompanying texts. The accompanying glyph for the serpents is also found in the *Dresden* texts, where its identity is clear from *Madrid*.

As an additional example of the way an analysis of the structure may throw light on long-studied materials, an examination of the Venus table is revealing. In the introduction to the table there are three columns of glyphs. If we attempted to read the first column from top to bottom before reading the next, we would find five consecutive occurrences of 'Venus' with no other glyph intervening. If we read across all three columns, we would find two consecutive examples of 'Venus' and an apparently meaningless and irregular association of different deity glyphs. The structure itself makes it clear that the first two columns must be read together and the last column must be read as a separate glyph sequence. Figure 90 has been retranscribed in linear form in accordance with these remarks. The fourth glyph block (the first one now legible) is the same 'dog + bundle', T765:103, which appeared as the last legible glyph on D69 with a different prefix. Passages on D62–63, D69, and D70 suggest that this combination with prefix T14 regularly follows T588:140.181, the 'offer' glyph. The second glyph block following is that of Venus; then comes 'east(ward)' and then the verb which marks the positions of Venus throughout the Venus table. The topics of the main table are identical with those of the introduction but are presented in a more extended form; the table is subdivided into three sections. The first is associated with the date 13 Mac and following dates at Venus intervals, the second with 18 Kayab, and the third with 3 Xul. The 13 Mac section is that of the first two columns of the

introduction, although they are associated with two dates 1 Ahau 18 Kayab, one shortly before the Maya Era, one at 9.9.9.16.0. The third column of the introduction corresponds to the extensive texts and accompanying pictures which make up the right-hand side of each page of the table. Since brief texts accompany both the 13 Mac section and the 18 Kayab section, and since the bottom of the tabular area gives the 3 Xul section, it is highly probable that the pictures belong to the 3 Xul section. The third column is counted forward from 4 Ahau 8 Cumku of the Maya Era, apparently by 9.9.9.16.0, which would reach 1 Ahau 18 Kayab again, but instead one finds 1 Ahau 18 Uo, a possible later base for Venus calculations. One would judge from column 3 that the 3 Xul table was in some way relevant at the inauguration of the Maya Era, a very different interpretation from that which would make it correspond to ME 11.5.2.0.0 (ME 4502) (Thompson 1950, p. 226). In any case, the consistent use of T181, a past-tense suffix, with the picture texts in the introduction and on pages 47, 48, 49, and part of page 50 with the 13 Mac section suggests that the table largely refers to past events rather than future calculations. The absence of this suffix in the last column of page 50 and in all four columns of page 46 strongly suggests that the 13 Mac section was current when the table was constructed.

Structural analysis of the inscriptions is of considerable interest for the light it throws on subject matter and on the weight given to different kinds of information. The tremendous amount of space given to dates and calculations shows the importance that time measurement had to the Mayas. Although we now know that the dates refer, in most cases, to such historical events as births, deaths, and conquests, the glyphs referring to the events usually take up much less space than the glyphs giving the dates. A good example is Stela 36 from Piedras Negras (Fig. 91). Here twenty-three glyph blocks give calendrical material and associated calculations, two glyph blocks indicate events, one glyph block gives the Piedras Negras Emblem Glyph, and six glyph blocks give the name (twice repeated) of the contemporary ruler. This inscription also shows the difference between reading the text (in a linguistic sense) and comprehending the meaning. In this case, the entire inscription is, in a broad sense, comprehensible, but only a few glyphs can be read as a Maya would have read them, and there is dispute even about these few. For all its greater permanence, such a typical inscription really conveys less to us than a page of a Mixtec codex.

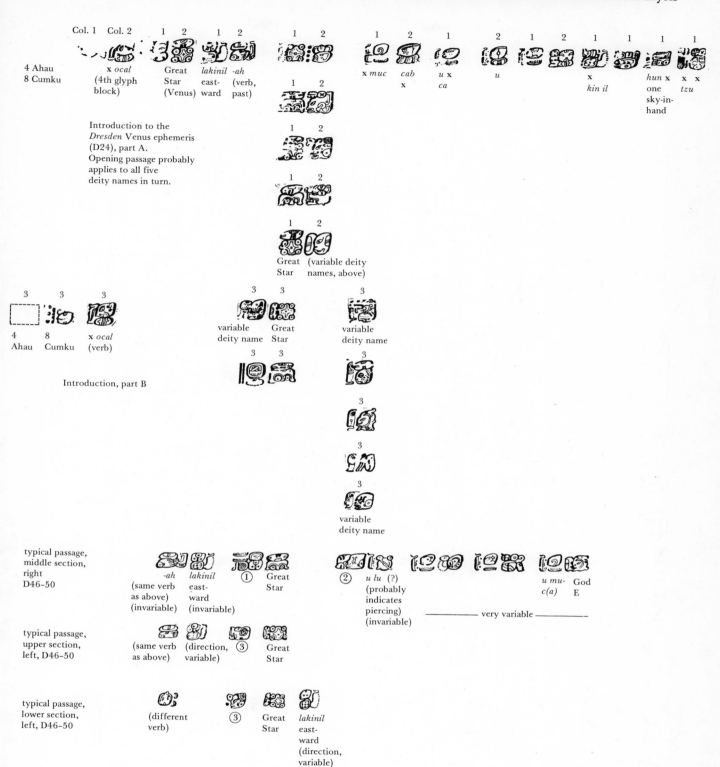

Figure 90. *Dresden* Venus-table text, retranscribed in linear form. Numbers in introduction indicate the columns of the original. Circled numbers at the bottom indicate: (1) a variable deity name including the two deities above in Introduction, part B; the name of the god shown throwing a spear; (2) a vari-able deity name, identical with the five deities above in Introduction, part B; the name of the god pierced by a spear; (3) a name from a set of twenty variable deity names, in sequence (Fig. 28); those assigned to the east correspond with those above in Introduction, part A.

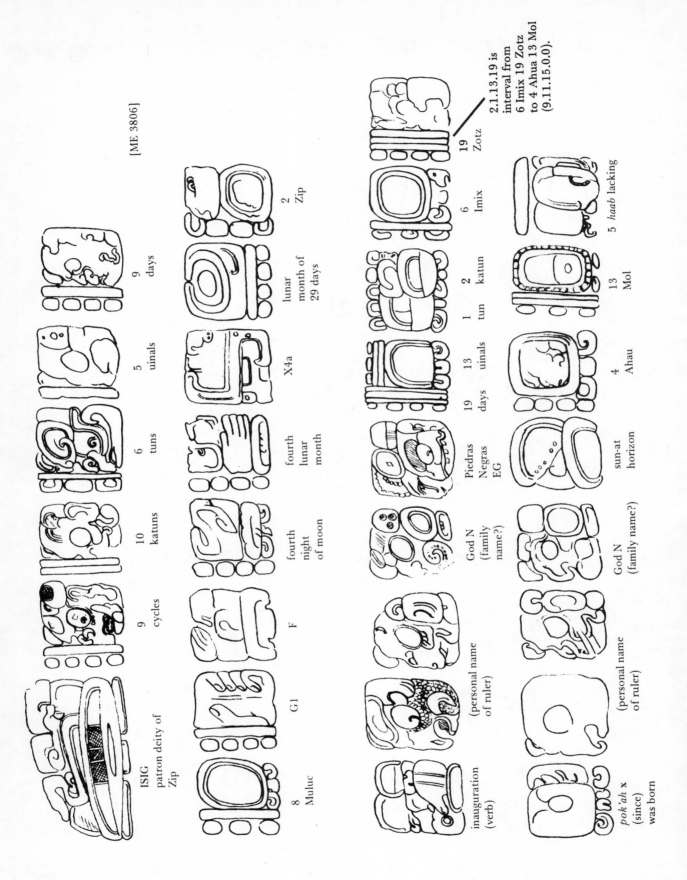

ISIG patron deity of Zip

9 cycles

10 katuns

6 tuns

5 uinals

9 days

[ME 3806]

8 Muluc

G1

F

fourth night of moon

fourth lunar month

X4a

lunar month of 29 days

2 Zip

pok'ah x (since) was born

(personal name of ruler)

inauguration (verb)

God N (family name?)

Piedras Negras EG

19 days

19 Zotz

(personal name of ruler)

God N (family name?)

sun-at horizon

13 uinals

1 tun

2 katun

6 Imix

4 Ahau

13 Mol

5 haab lacking

2.1.13.19 is interval from 6 Imix 19 Zotz to 4 Ahua 13 Mol (9.11.15.0.0).

Figure 91. Piedras Negras, Stela 36. A fairly typical inscription.

While the accumulation of knowledge which can be built up from the typical inscriptions is considerable, important new insights are more apt to come from the relatively rare long inscriptions. Here, detailed analysis of the structure is highly desirable and often throws new light on the subject matter. Unfortunately, such analysis has been extremely rare in the past and usually has been limited to a few points. Figures 92 and 93 show a major inscription from Structure 12 at Yaxchilan. This inscription was written on seven lintels, spanning seven doorways, several of which had been walled up. All the lintels have fallen, and most are broken. It is believed that Structure 12 is a late building and that the lintels were moved from an earlier building and reset. The order of lintels in Structure 12 was 34-47-48-36-35-37-49 (Morley 1937–1938, II, 365–367). L36 had a standing figure on it, whereas the others were entirely glyphic. Unfortunately, L36 is so badly eroded that it can contribute little, other than the probability that it was originally the first of the sequence. L48 is the beginning of the text, and its subject matter (the Initial Series) continues onto L47. With this much established, it seems highly likely that the badly damaged L34 (still lacking many pieces) followed L47. For the remaining three lintels, Morley has suggested the order 49-37-35. The evidence for this comes from a chronological glyph (T676:178) with numerical prefixes. Morley misinterpreted this as the day sign Oc, while Zimmermann (1933, p. 400) has suggested that it is a sign for a period of fifty-three days. On L49, it occurs probably three times but is illegible the first time, where its presence is indicated by the following glyph. Morley (1937–1938, II, 379) says that the second occurrence has a numerical prefix which is clearly 'six', despite considerable destruction, and this reading should probably be accepted, although the published photograph does not wholly exclude the possibility of a reading 'eight'. The third occurrence has the prefix 'seven'. The sign appears on L37 first with a prefix of 'eight' and second with a prefix of 'nine' and on L35 with a prefix of 'ten'. An order which preserves the sequence 7/8-9/10 certainly seems preferable to 10/8-9/x-6(?)-7, which is the only other sequence that is at all likely. I have, therefore, accepted the Morley sequence for the text in Figures 92 and 93 with only minor misgivings.

The text may easily be divided into three major sections. The first gives the Initial Series date and the normal subsidiary information in the Supplementary Series and includes L48 and the first six glyph blocks of L47. The remainder of L47 is perhaps a general explanation of the subject matter of the text. Internal structure is not clearly marked, and few glyphs have known meanings. The remainder of the text, perhaps starting with the last two glyph blocks of L47, consists, in the legible portions, of a series of short clauses of two to five glyph blocks each. These are of three classes. The first consists of the previously mentioned chronological glyphs (T676:178) with their numerical prefixes, a regular glyph consisting of two legs (T700) with the *ich-ben* prefix, a varying glyph, and a regular glyph (T169:518a, b) with a varying, sometimes absent, suffix. The varying element in connection with the number eight is the glyph of Bird Jaguar (I), a fact which strongly suggests that the other glyphs are also personal names, as they are interpreted by Proskouriakoff (1964a, pp. 183–184). The individual named in connection with the number seven seems to be the same person mentioned on Yaxchilan L21, in connection with the date 9.0.19.2.4 (ME 3619) 2 Kan 2 Yax, where his name is followed by 'seven *hel*' with unusual suffixes. The conjunction of the name and the number seven suggests that the so-called *hel* glyph (T573) is in some way comparable to T676, with which it has sometimes been confused, or perhaps to the combination of T676:178 with T700. If T573 is actually correctly deciphered as *hel,* it may here refer to succession in office in some way.

The second class of clauses opens with T78:514. In three cases, this is preceded by a hand (T220), and in each of these cases it is followed by a color glyph (*zac* 'white' in the first case, *chac* 'red' in the second case, *kan* 'yellow' in the third case). The general character of the glyphs associated with this clause, where the third clause is also found, suggests names, possibly of deities. In two cases where the third clause is not found, we have identifiable names: Bird Jaguar (I) (with an unidentified Emblem Glyph) and Net Turtle (God N), with the Piedras Negras Emblem Glyph.

The third set of clauses, where found, always follow a clause of the second class. They open with T125v.168:513:142, according to Thompson's transcription, although I doubt that the main sign is either T513 or T518. The meaning here is unknown, but if the preceding class of clauses has been correctly identified as containing nominal glyphs, I suspect that this glyph indicates a relationship, not necessarily biological. In all but two of the eight occurrences of this clause, the *ich-ben* superfix is found associated with known or probable Emblem Glyphs at the end of the clause, and the intervening glyph block seems always to be a name. We find Net Turtle (God N's name) of Piedras Negras again and an unidentified ruler of Tikal. Knotted-Eye Jaguar, whose name occurred as the variable glyph in the Class 1 clause associated with the number nine, appears, and his

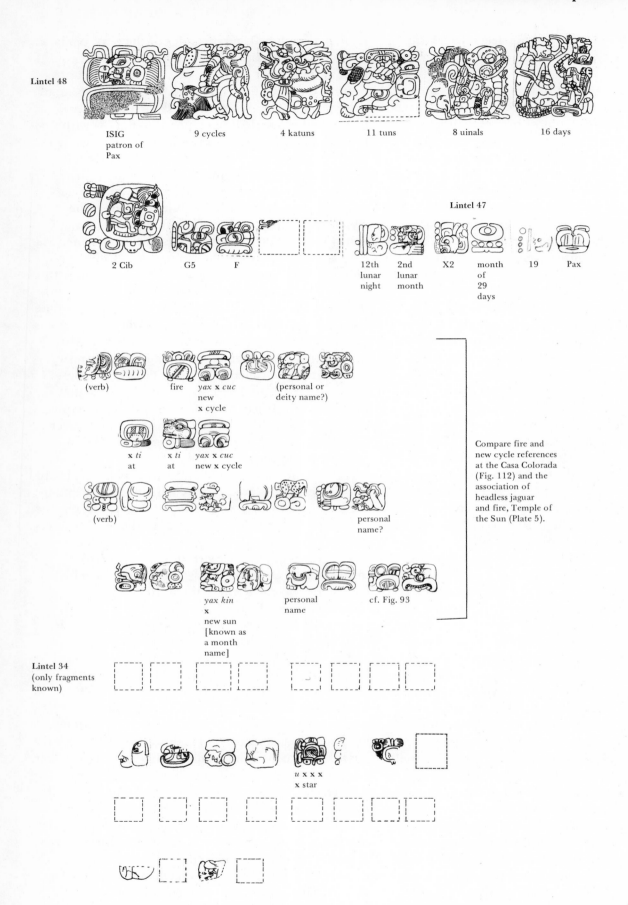

Figure 92. Yaxchilan, Structure 12, Lintels 48, 47, and 34. The opening lintel, 36, is too badly weathered to include. It contains the only nonglyphic sculpture from this building.

name is followed by a glyph (apparently an EG) which also followed the glyph of Bird Jaguar in the Class 2 clause previously mentioned. This clause follows the Class 2 clause with 'yellow'. This same EG(?) occurs in the Class 3 clause which follows the Class 2 clause with 'red' and the Class 1 clause with Knotted-Eye Jaguar. The last Emblem Glyph is a reptilian head, closely resembling that which appears with the Series II ruler from Piedras Negras. This may well be the head variant of the Piedras Negras EG, but it might also indicate an unidentified site from which that ruler came. These three classes of clauses account for all glyphs on the last three lintels except three glyph blocks at the very end of the inscription and two earlier glyph blocks. The last phrase seems somewhat similar to some of the others; the introductory element is different, but the last glyph block seems to be an unidentified Emblem Glyph, and the intervening glyph block is probably a personal name.

A considerable number of lengthy inscriptions come from Palenque. Again, structural analysis of the texts helps us to categorize parallels which would not otherwise appear and to recognize classes of meaning or information even when the details escape us. The continuous text from the three panels of the Temple of the Inscriptions (Figs. 94–98) is one of the few which have already received a substantial amount of structural analysis. Thompson (1950, pp. 43–44, Fig. 3) isolated clauses from this text, although he did not consider the text in its entirety. Finally, Berlin's work on the Palenque Triad involves an extended structural analysis of part of this inscription, associating parallel clauses. The text seems to refer to similar characteristics of a series of katuns, starting with 9.4.0.0.0 (ME 3680—a katun 13 Ahau) and running to 9.13.0.0.0 (ME 3920—a katun 8 Ahau). There is a marked patterning of the glyphs within each katun, and there are recurrent phrases. Deity names are important elements, as are apparent ritual phrases, and the Palenque EG appears frequently. On the middle panel, there appears a much fuller account of katuns 12 Ahau and 10 Ahau (Fig. 96). Along with the regular passages are three lengthy accounts in each of these katuns referring to the deities of the Palenque Triad and apparently associating them with cyclical phenomena of some sort. These are shown separately, as the other parallels stand out more clearly without them. One clause of six glyph blocks of katun 10 Ahau seems to refer to astronomical phenomena. On the third panel (Figs. 97–98) the structural relationships are quite difficult, and the only really clear-cut feature is the division between calendrical and noncalendrical glyphs. Here, true historical data appear, tied in with

calculations going over two million years into the past and over four thousand years into the future.

A clause isolated by Thompson recurs four times in a formula '9 sky—x—16 days—9 hel', in which x is an unidentified varying element (see Fig. 95). In three of its occurrences, it is followed by a brief phrase, x-pa-ti, followed respectively by 3 Ahau, 1 Ahau, and 12 Ahau. The ti is probably to be understood here as the locative prefix and 3 Ahau, 1 Ahau, and 12 Ahau as the respective katuns, named by their ending days. This seems to be a forerunner of the "short-count" system of katun naming. In two cases, the 9-16-9 phrase is preceded by a phrase containing ich-ben-tzukin. The astronomical nature of the second of these two phrases suggests that the first may likewise be astronomical. In the first of the two phrases, ich-ben-tzukin is preceded by 'one sky-in-hand', which exactly parallels the occurrence of these two glyphs together on *Dresden* page 24 (in the Venus table) and on D53a (in the eclipse table), further suggesting an astronomical meaning.

The structure of the six long parallel passages from the middle panel (Fig. 96) shows a framework of identical glyphs interspersed with variable ones. In the first three passages, there are two sets of variable glyphs. The second set consists of the three gods recognized by Berlin as the Palenque Triad. The first set includes a glyph which contains all the elements of the headdress of the rear head of the two-headed dragon and is almost certainly its name glyph. This makes it highly likely that the other glyphs in this set are also deity names, as Berlin suggested. In the second three passages, there are three sets of variable glyphs (aside from minor variations), two of which are like those of the first three passages. The third set of variable glyphs contains the prefix yax 'new' in J7 and N2 and possibly in K6. In J7, this is followed by 'fire' and an unidentified glyph. In K6, the remainder of the glyph block is unintelligible, but the next glyph block is 'sky'. The context suggests ceremonial.

The third panel (Figs. 97–98) shows much less obvious structuring. The chief factor in dividing this portion of the inscription is the long series of dates. Much of the material in this panel seems to deal with the woman born on 9.8.9.13.0 (ME 3769) 8 Ahau 13 Pop, who seems to have died on 9.12.11.4.8 (ME 3851) 6 Etz'nab 11 Yax in her eightieth year. History and myth here seem to be remarkably intertwined; recognizable deity names alternate with references to apparent human beings; extraordinary calculations go from historical dates far into the past and future. A considerable amount of the material on this panel partly parallels that from the Palace Tablet (Ruz 1) (Figs. 99, 100); the apparent historical material is

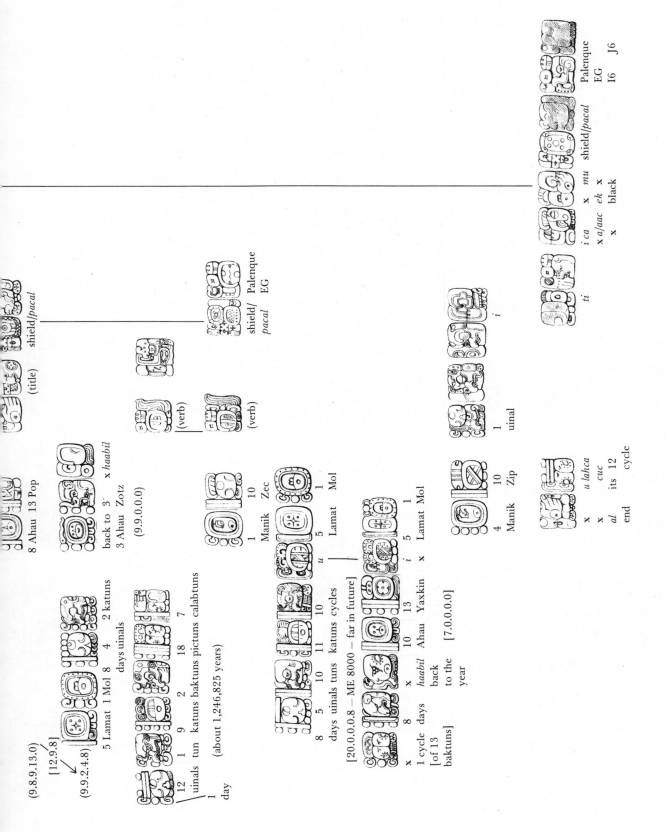

(9.8.9.13.0)

[12.9.8]

(9.9.2.4.8)

12 1   9   2   18   7
uinals tun katuns baktuns pictuns calabtuns
1
day   (about 1,246,825 years)

5 Lamat 1 Mol 8 4 2 katuns
                  days uinals

8 Ahau 13 Pop

back to 3'   x haabil
3 Ahau Zotz

(title)   shield/pacal

(9.9.0.0.0)

1   10   5   1
Manik Zec   Lamat Mol

(verb)   (verb)   shield/ Palenque
                  pacal   EG

8   5   10   11   10   13   i   5   1
days uinals tuns katuns cycles   x   Lamat Mol

u   Ahau Yaxkin

[20.0.0.0.8 – ME 8000 – far in future]

x   8   x   10   13
1 cycle days haabil back
[of 13   to the
baktuns]   year

[7.0.0.0.0]

i

1
uinal

4   10
Manik Zip

x   u lahca
x   cuc
al its 12
end   cycle

ti   i ca   x   mu   shield/pacal   Palenque
     x a/aac   ek   x   EG   J6
     x   black   I6

Figure 97. Text from the Temple of the Inscriptions, Palenque (Part 4).

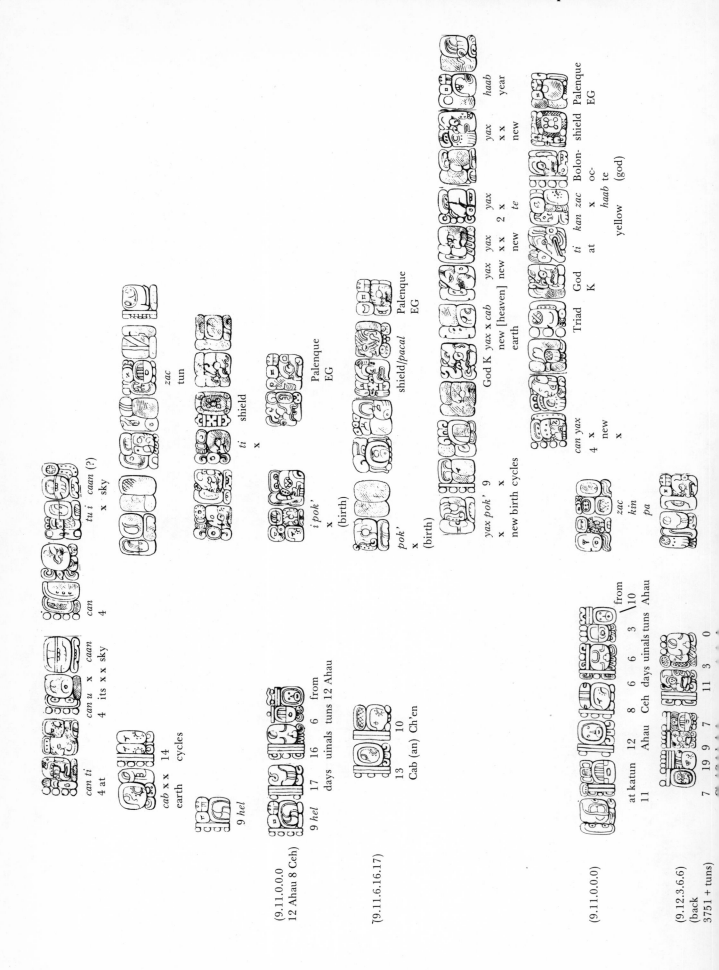

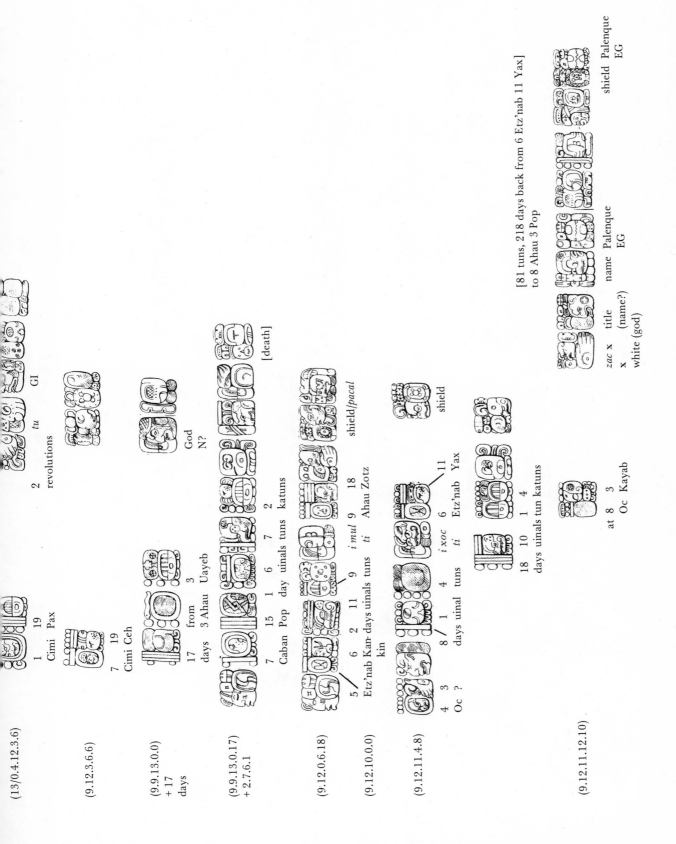

Figure 98. Text from the Temple of the Inscriptions, Palenque (Part 5).

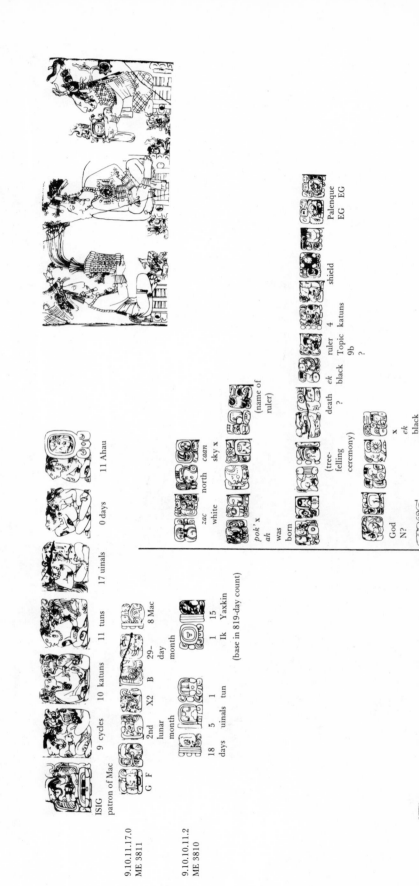

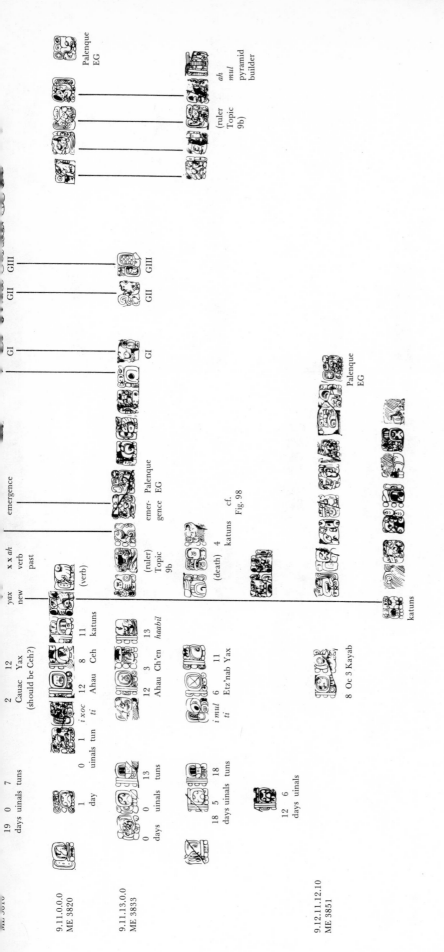

Figure 99. Ruz 1 text from Palenque. Vertical line divides calendar text on left from narrative text on right. Text is continued in Figure 100.

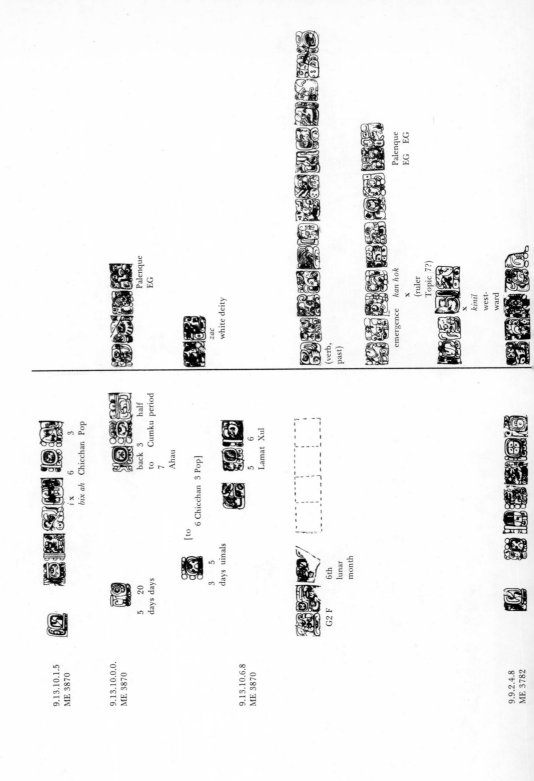

9.13.10.1.5
ME 3870

i x
bix ah Chicchan Pop
6 3

Palenque
EG

9.13.10.0.0.
ME 3870

5 20
days days

back 3 half
to Cumku period
7
Ahau

zac
white deity

[to
6 Chicchan 3 Pop]

3 5
days uinals

(verb,
past)

Palenque
EG EG

emergence *kan hok*
x
(ruler
Topic 7?)

9.13.10.6.8
ME 3870

5 6
Lamat Xul

G2 F 6th
lunar
month

x
kinil
west-
ward

9.9.2.4.8
ME 3782

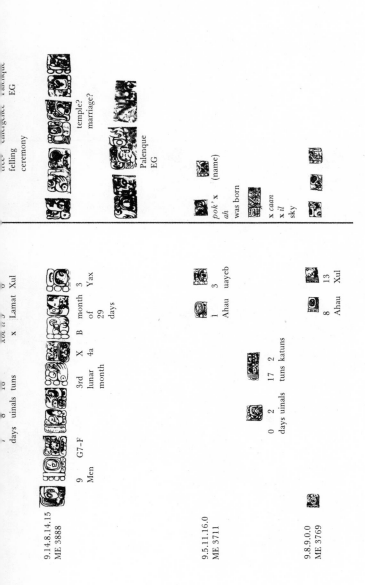

Figure 100. Ruz 1 text (continued).

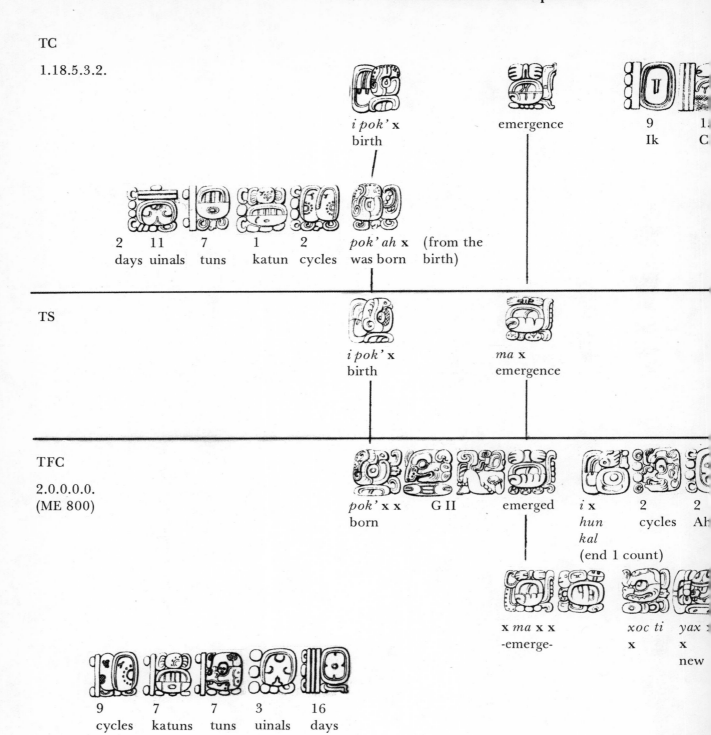

TC

1.18.5.3.2.

i pok' x
birth

emergence

9
Ik

2   11   7   1   2   *pok' ah* x   (from the
days uinals tuns katun cycles was born   birth)

TS

i pok' x
birth

ma x
emergence

TFC

2.0.0.0.0.
(ME 800)

pok' x x   G II   emerged   *i* x   2   2
born   *hun* cycles Ah
                    kal
                    (end 1 count)

x *ma* x x   *xoc ti*   *yax*
-emerge-   x   x
                        new

9   7   7   3   16
cycles katuns tuns uinals days

Figure 101. Parallel texts from the Temple of the Cross, Temple of the Sun, and Temple of the Foliated Cross, Palenque (Part 2). Text began in Plate 5 and is continued in Figures 102–108.

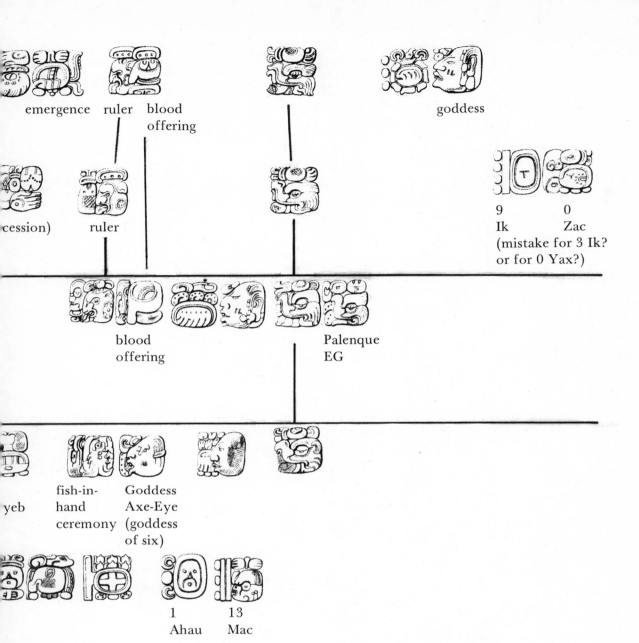

emergence   ruler   blood
                    offering

goddess

(cession)   ruler

9   0
Ik   Zac
(mistake for 3 Ik?
or for 0 Yax?)

blood   Palenque
offering   EG

yeb   fish-in-   Goddess
      hand   Axe-Eye
      ceremony   (goddess
                  of six)

1   13
Ahau   Mac

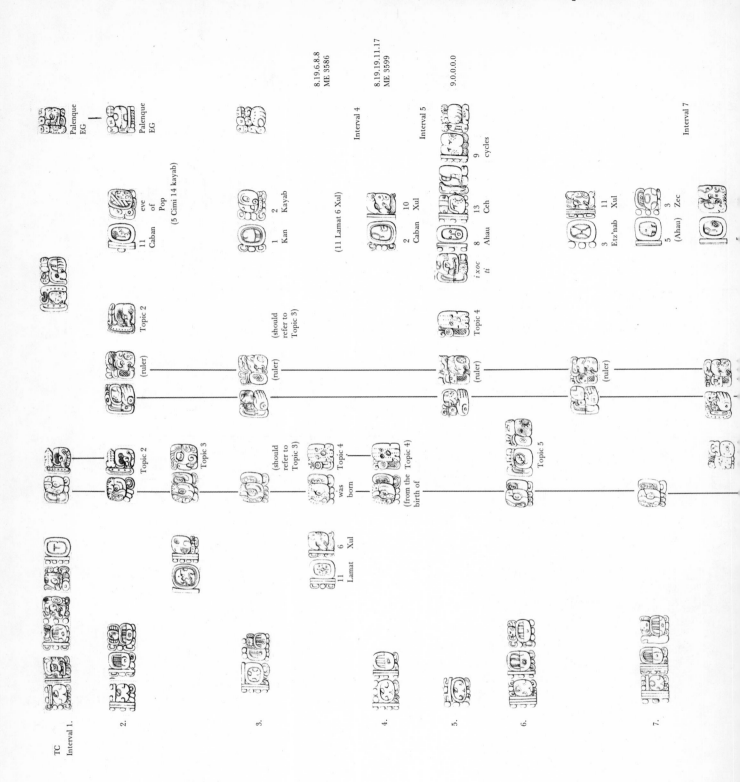

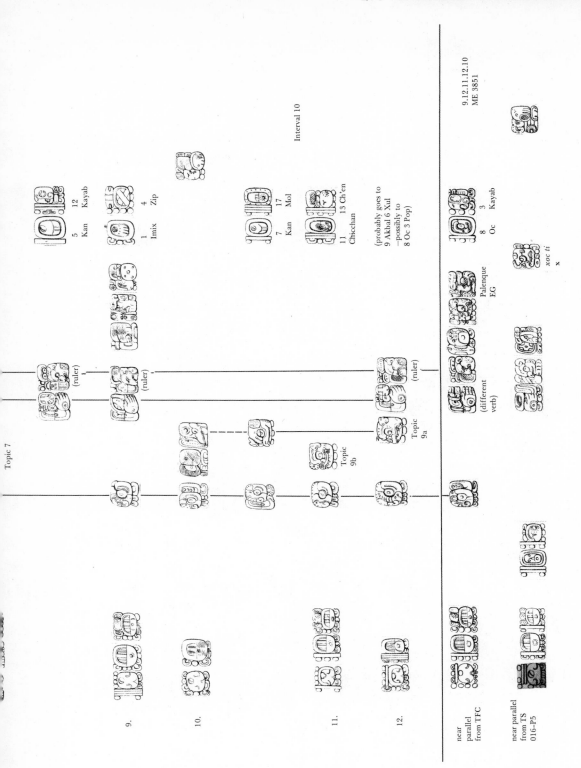

Figure 102. Parallel texts from Palenque (Part 3).

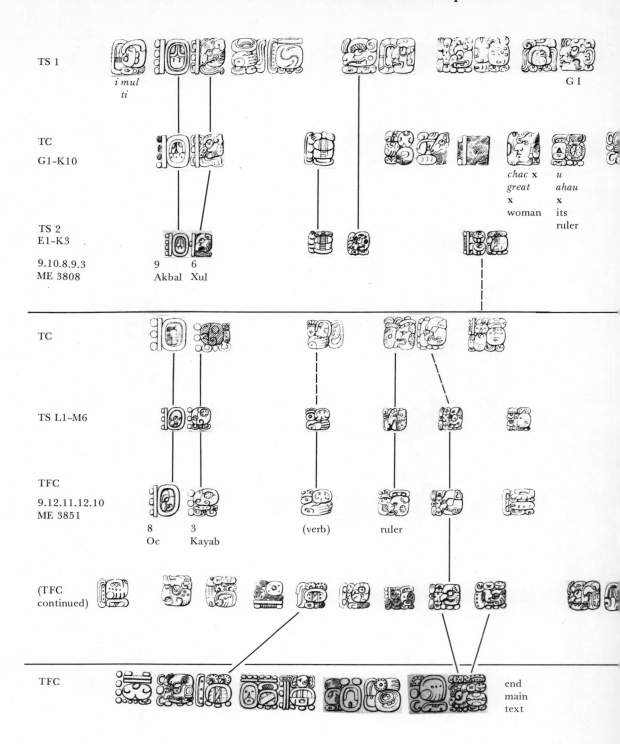

Figure 103. Parallel texts from Palenque (Part 4).

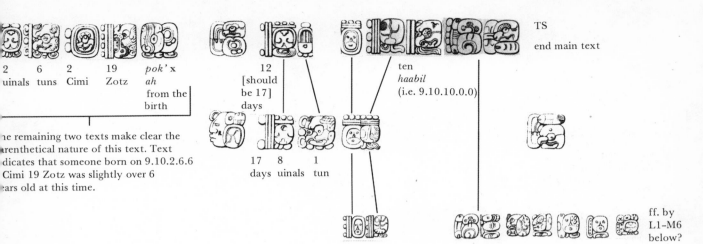

2	6	2	19	pok' x
uinals	tuns	Cimi	Zotz	ah
				from the
				birth

	12			ten
	[should			haabil
	be 17]			(i.e. 9.10.10.0.0)
	days			

TS
end main text

he remaining two texts make clear the
arenthetical nature of this text. Text
dicates that someone born on 9.10.2.6.6
Cimi 19 Zotz was slightly over 6
ears old at this time.

17	8	1
days	uinals	tun

ff. by
L1–M6
below?

ff. by
2 Cib 14 Mol

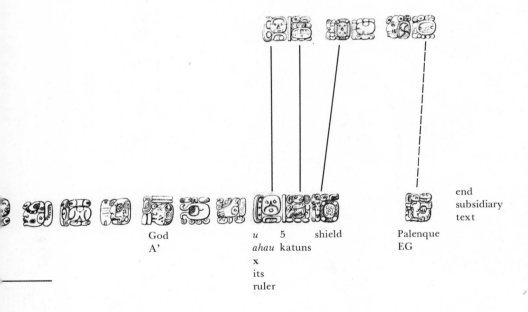

	God	u	5	shield	Palenque
	A'	ahau	katuns		EG
		x			
		its			
		ruler			

end
subsidiary
text

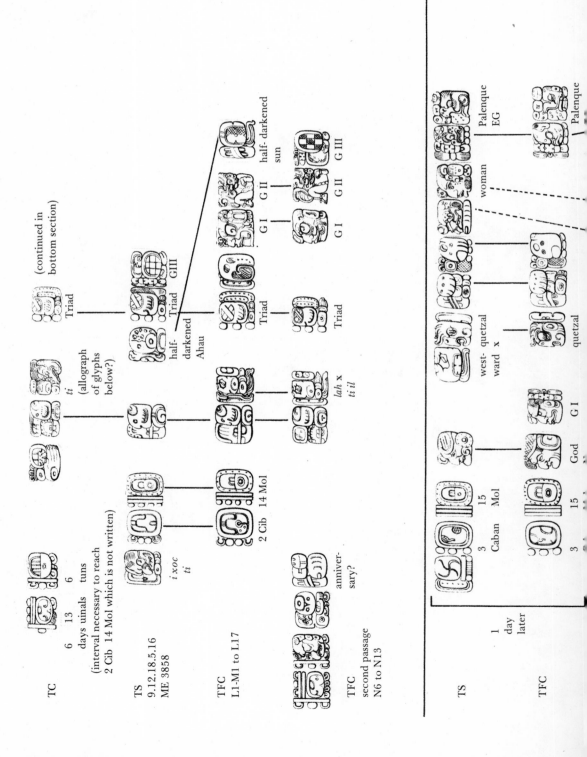

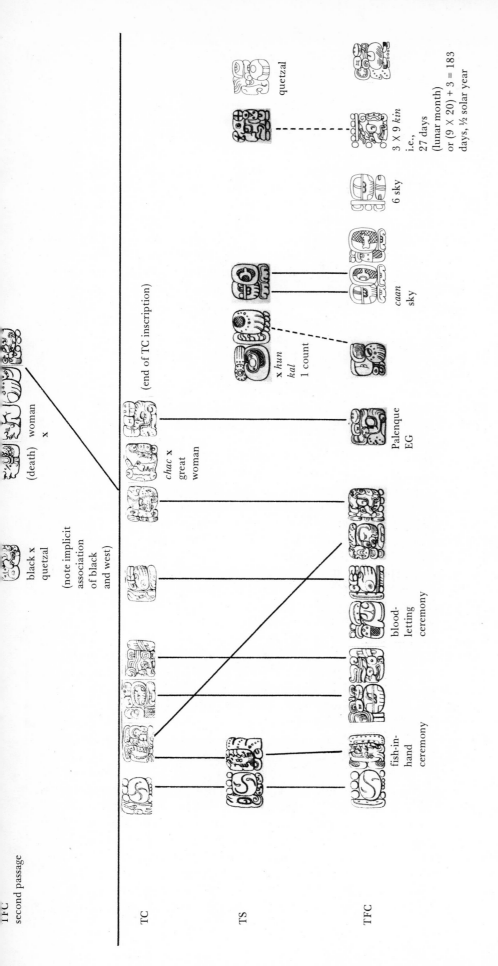

Figure 104. Parallel texts from Palenque (Part 5).

treated more fully on the Hieroglyphic Stairway of House C of the Palace.

Of the other Palenque inscriptions, that from the Palace is the least patterned. Despite the repeated occurrence of a few phrases, most of the breaks are indicated only by the dates. Many of these recur in other inscriptions at Palenque, and the variation in the accompanying glyphs in different cases helps us to recognize different ways of referring to the same events.

The famed tablets from the Temples of the Cross (TC), Foliated Cross (TFC), and Sun (TS) need to be considered as a unit because of the apparent unity of their subject matter and the detailed parallels between them (Plate 5, Figs. 101–108). I have suggested elsewhere (Kelley 1965) that they deal with the birth of the gods. All three inscriptions open with an offering passage which includes a verb 'offer', a glyph of God K, and a direction glyph (Plate 5). The following passages differ in their details, but all three contain the birth glyph. There are also references to the blood-offering ritual in the TFC and TS, and to the fish-in-hand ritual in the TC (Fig. 101). The left-hand sections of the three panels seem to deal with mythical and astronomical phenomena, and the right-hand sections seem to be largely historical. In the TS and TFC, rather lengthy parallel passages deal with a date 2 Cib 14 Mol, and in the TC a very similar passage is associated with the same implicit date, which, however, is not actually recorded there (See Fig. 104). These parallels strongly suggest that Spinden is correct in thinking that the half-darkened *kin* and the half-darkened Ahau convey similar information. The fact that the latter has the prefix *chac* ('great, red') in the TC suggests that it is some unusual phenomenon. Structural analysis therefore generally supports Berlin's attempt (1965a) to define the glyphs of the rulers of Palenque, and only two minor additional points should be noted. The date 1 Kan 2 Kayab (Fig. 102) is followed by a glyph block whose main sign is mistakenly regarded by Berlin as a reference to his Topic 3. Comparison with a similar passage following the date 8 Ahau 13 Ceh shows the recurrence of the same glyph there, and comparison with the passage referring to Topic 2 shows that there the date 11 Caban 0 Pop is followed by the Palenque EG. Since the glyph which Berlin mistook for Topic 3 may also have the *ich-ben* superfix, I believe it is a place-name glyph, probably that of the mythical place which ends the sequence of thirteen heavens (?) on D69b. The second point is that the passages assigned by Berlin to his Topic 9 are more numerous than those assigned to the others, and the glyphs seem to differ

somewhat. I believe that the reference is actually to two rulers, rather than to one, as Berlin thought, and I have distinguished them as Topics 9a and 9b.

An important early monument which lends itself well to a careful breakdown into clauses is Stela 31 from Tikal. Barthel's important study of this monument (Barthel 1966b) covers the major points of interest but does not systematically present the parallel phrases. Two relatively short phrases are found on the sides of the monument (Fig. 109), and the back is covered by a very long text (Plate 6). Interestingly and unusually, this contains two Initial Series. Unfortunately, the pattern of the repetition is much freer than that in many Mayan texts. The recurrence of particular glyphs is adequate to show that the same topics are being repeated in different contexts but not sufficient to clearly delimit classes of meaings, other than some personal names; apparently references to both historical individuals and deities are included.

Another monument of great interest is Copan Stela A (Fig. 110). A striking passage is the fourfold repetition of references to 'four(th?) sky' (='fourth heaven') with different grammatical particles between the number and 'sky' (*can te caan,* etc.). This is immediately followed by the Emblem Glyphs for Copan, Tikal, an unidentified site, and Palenque, in which the latter three have a common affix lacking on the (local) Copan EG. Despite such indications of grammatical structure, it is obvious that this type of stereotyped repetition lacks many elements normally found in the phrases of the inscriptions. The same is true of the following passage, which contains one introductory glyph (a verb?) followed by 'sky' ('heaven'), 'earth', 'east', 'west', 'south', and 'north' with differing grammatical affixes.

At Piedras Negras, the famed Lintel 3, with the ruler on his throne, is accompanied by a lengthy historical text (Fig. 111) which seems to mention junior members of the ruling family at Piedras Negras, as well as giving references to rulers of Yaxchilan and Tikal. In this text, we now have a fair idea of the identity of some of the people referred to, but our ignorance of the verbs still prevents us from understanding what is said about them in most cases. The text is in marked contrast to that from Throne 1 (which seems to be the throne represented on Lintel 3), which includes a rather extensive astronomical passage as well as some historical data.

Finally, an extensive text from the Casa Colorada at Chichen Itza seems to deal very largely with fire ceremonies, including the related fish-in-hand rite. I

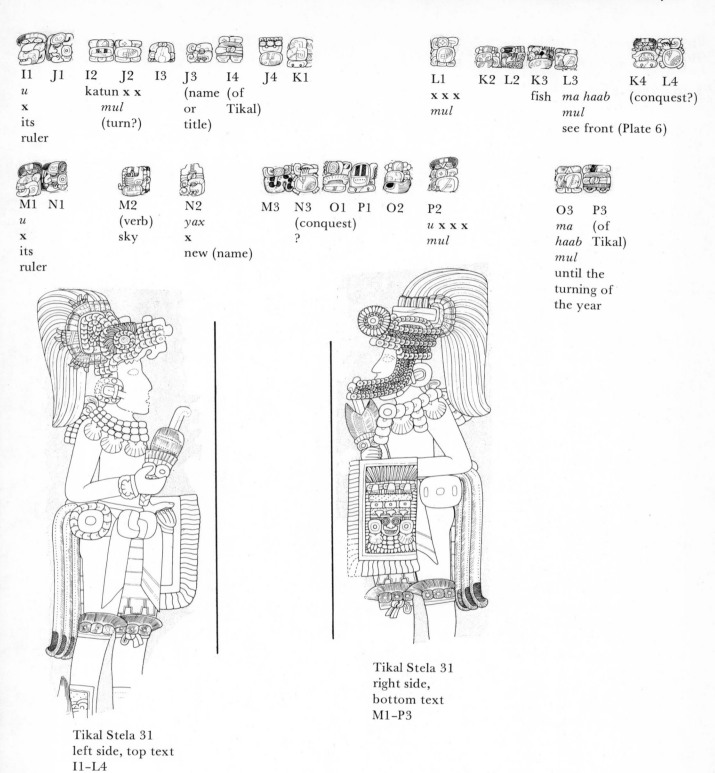

I1　J1
u
x
its
ruler

I2　J2　I3　J3　I4　J4　K1
katun **x x**
mul
(turn?)
(name　(of
or　Tikal)
title)

L1
x x x
mul

K2　L2　K3　L3
fish　*ma haab*
mul
see front (Plate 6)

K4　L4
(conquest?)

M1　N1
u
x
its
ruler

M2
(verb)
sky

N2
yax
x
new (name)

M3　N3　O1　P1　O2
(conquest)
?

P2
u **x x x**
mul

O3　P3
ma　(of
haab　Tikal)
mul
until the
turning of
the year

Tikal Stela 31
left side, top text
I1–L4

Tikal Stela 31
right side,
bottom text
M1–P3

Figure 109. Miscellaneous glyphs from Tikal Stela 31. *See also*
Plate 6.

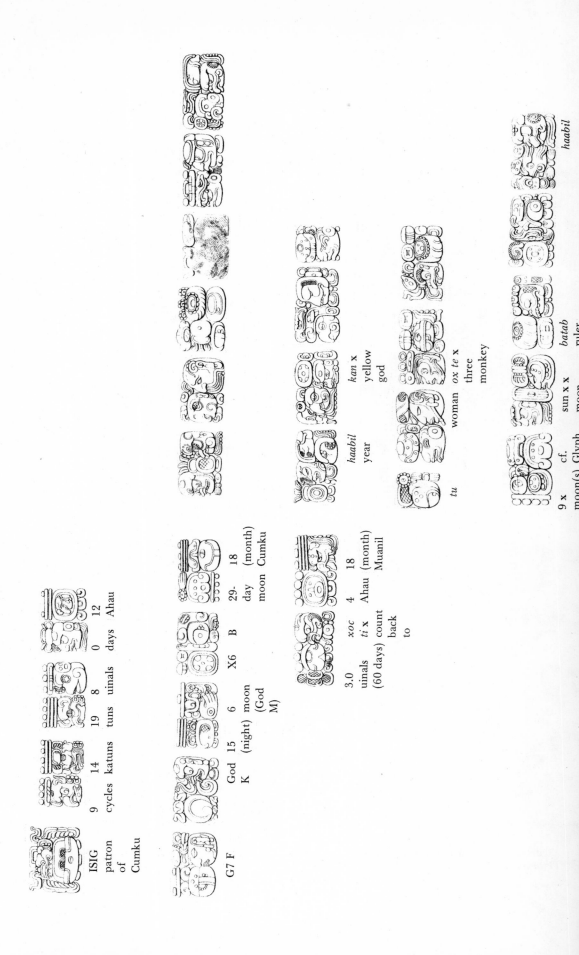

ISIG 9   14   19   8   0   12
      cycles katuns tuns uinals days Ahau
patron
of
Cumku

G7 F God 15 6   X6   B   29-   18
      K (night) moon   day (month) Cumku
                 (God   moon
                 M)

             3.0   xoc   4   18
             uinals   ti x   Ahau (month)
             (60 days) count   Muanil
                       back
                       to

             haabil   kan x
             year   yellow
                      god

             tu   woman ox te x
                             three
                             monkey

9 x   sun x x   batab
moon(s) Glyph moon   ruler
cf.

haabil

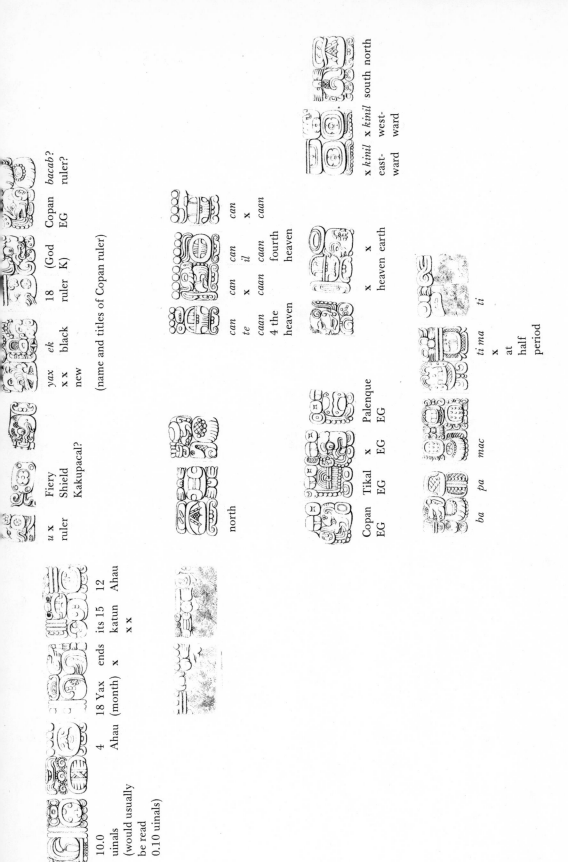

Figure 110. Structural analysis of text of Copan Stela A.

ISIG 9.15.18.3.13 5 Ben GI, not drawn

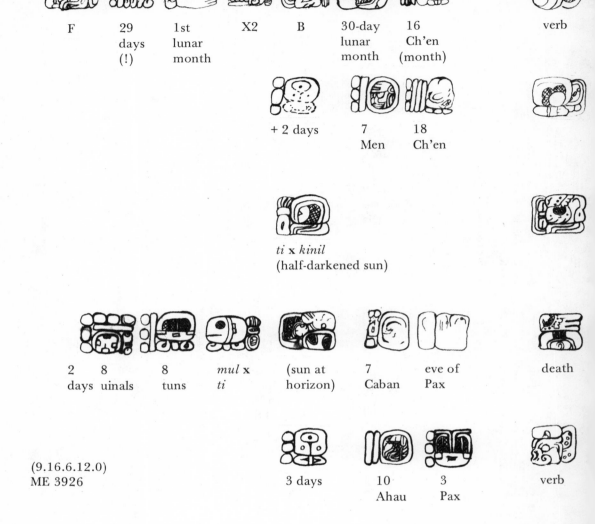

| F | 29 days (!) | 1st lunar month | X2 | B | 30-day lunar month | 16 Ch'en (month) | | verb |

| | | | | + 2 days | 7 Men | 18 Ch'en | | |

ti x *kinil*
(half-darkened sun)

| 2 days | 8 uinals | 8 tuns | *mul* x *ti* | (sun at horizon) | 7 Caban | eve of Pax | death |

(9.16.6.12.0)
ME 3926

| 3 days | 10 Ahau | 3 Pax | verb |

Figure 111. Main text, Piedras Negras Lintel 3.

ti x *le*   personal   God N   P.N.   jaguar   Yaxchilan
at the   name   (family?)   EG   EG
inaugura-
tion?

            x x Macaw   God N   P.N.
            (personal   EG
            name)

ti-ca-l(a)   Fish   God   x *ti*
            x x   N   x
            (personal
            name)

                   God   P.N.
                   N   EG

                  God N

atun   P.N.
                              EG

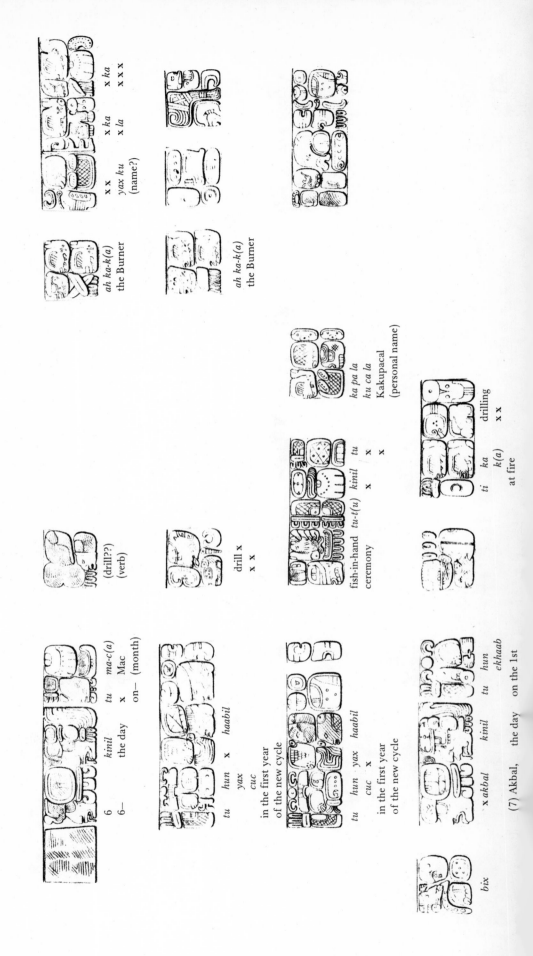

x x   x ka   x ka
            x ka   x x x

x x   x ka   x la
yax ku
(name?)

ah ka-k(a)   ah ka-k(a)
the Burner   the Burner

ka pa la
ku ca la
Kakupacal
(personal name)

(drill??)   drill x   fish-in-hand   tu-t(u)   kimil   tu   x
(verb)   x x   ceremony   x   x   x

ti   ka   drilling
     k(a)   x x
at fire

6   kinil   tu   ma-c(a)
6–   the day x   Mac
                     on— (month)

tu   hun   x   haabil
     yax
     cuc
in the first year
of the new cycle

tu   hun   yax   haabil
     yax   cuc   x
in the first year
of the new cycle

x akbal   kinil   tu   hun
          the day on the 1st   ekhaab

bix

(7) Akbal,

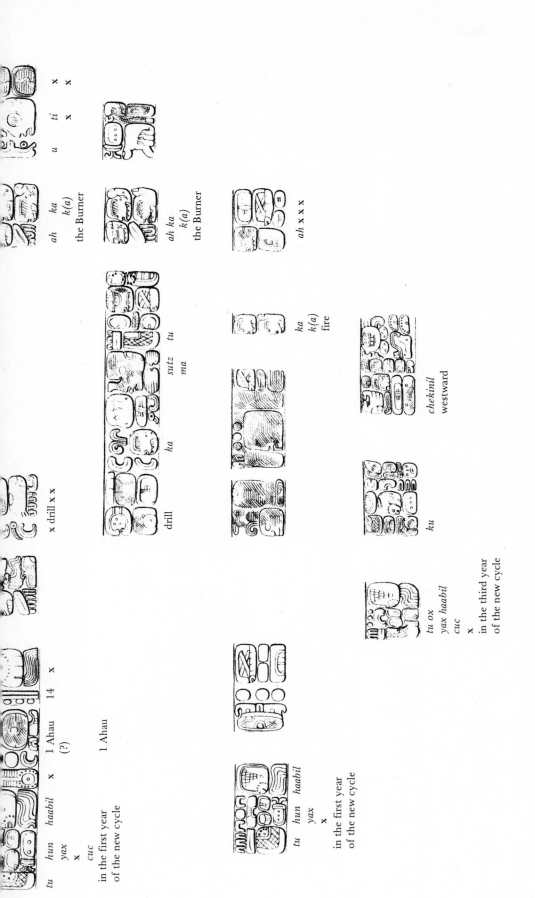

Figure 112. The Red House (Casa Colorada), Chichen Itza.

Figure 113. Olmec inscription from the Tuxtla statuette. Possibly Proto-Mayan script. Date not as clear on original as in this drawing.

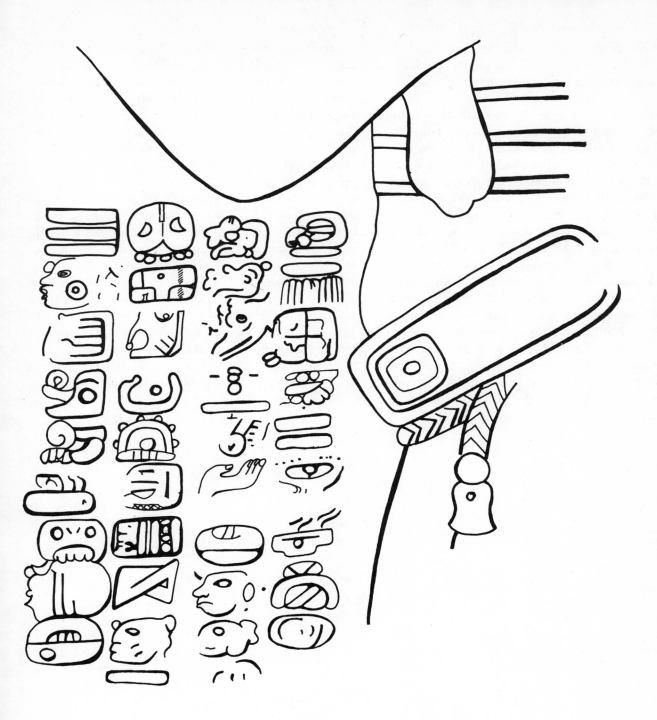

re 114. Altar text from Kaminaljuyu, Guatemala.

believe it also refers to a historical individual, Kakupacal. Not all of the breaking points are clear, but many phrases can be distinguished.

Besides the Maya texts in the strict sense, I include in Figures 113 and 114 the texts from the Tuxtla statuette and from an altar at Kaminaljuyu. Both texts are considerably earlier than any surviving texts from the Maya lowlands. The Kaminaljuyu text contains a number of glyphs which seem very similar to those in later Classic Maya inscriptions, and it seems likely that it represents ancestral Maya. No attempt is made here to analyze this text. The Tuxtla Statuette, in Olmec style, has a date which has been read as 8.6.4.2.17 and regarded as counted from the Maya Era. This would make it ME 3324. Neither the reading nor this interpretation is certain. The angular style of the glyphs is different enough from that of later Maya monuments that recognition of glyphs is difficult. The few that are identical are simple enough to discourage any assurance that this is, in fact, an early Maya monument. However, the possibility that it is Maya makes it desirable to reproduce this text.

Structural analysis allows us to recognize parallel statements within a text from which we may frequently recognize the grammatical category in which a glyph belongs. Often, it may enable us to determine a substantial part of the subject matter and to know that particular glyphs refer to ceremonies or to gods, while others refer to astronomy, to history, or to human rulers. Frequently we can recognize minor variations in glyphic depiction or in grammatical particles. Occasionally, parallels or grammatical necessity may allow us to reconstruct substantial portions of damaged texts. Even though the decipherment of complete long passages is not yet possible, structural analysis gives us certain types of information not otherwise available. It is a neglected facet of the total picture of decipherment that should receive attention and that should be kept in mind as decipherment of individual glyphs proceeds. Some new information could probably be gleaned from most texts with a systematic study of the structure. Such studies should be a normal part of the publication of new texts.

Chapter 14 Discussion of Catalogs of Maya Hieroglyphs

In 1931, William Gates published *An Outline Dictionary of Maya Glyphs,* the first attempt to catalog the various forms of glyphs in a systematic way. This rested, in part, on unpublished work of C. C. Willoughby. Gates used an elaborate and complex numbering system, in which a particular grapheme was assigned a number, and separate subordinate numbers were assigned to each glyger in which it appeared. This particular way of treating the relationship of graphemes and glygers is most unsatisfactory, and the Gates catalog numbers were hardly used in publications by other Maya scholars. Gates's catalog had extensive commentaries on many of the glyphs, some of which are still useful, but his numbers are now of no practical value. The hieroglyphs of his catalog were restricted to those appearing in the codices.

Twenty-five years later, after nearly a hundred years of Maya studies, Günter Zimmermann published the first satisfactory catalog of Maya hieroglyphs. Like Gates, Zimmermann restricted himself to the glyphs in the codices; unlike Gates, he assigned separate numbers to all recognizable graphemes, and only to graphemes. For each numbered grapheme, he listed the glygers in which it appeared and the pages on which it was to be found. Affixes were treated in much more summary fashion than main signs, with a simple reference to the numbers of the glyphs to which they were affixed. By design, commentary was restricted to a minimum. The usefulness of the neutral numbers was immediately apparent, and Zimmermann's system was adopted by a substantial number of scholars in their published work.

In 1961, the Russian scholars Evreinov, Kosarev, and Ustinov published the *Dresden* and *Madrid* codices with a Maya-Russian dictionary, a catalog of Maya glyphs, a list of accepted decipherments, a complete transcription of the codices into the catalog numbers and into Maya, and an index to all occurrences of each glyph. The transcription into Maya received the most attention, with a certain amount of favorable comment from non-Mayanists and an apparently unanimous rejection by Mayanists. If readings had been correctly assigned to glyphs to the degree claimed, then the problem would have changed from one of deciphering the glyphs to one of fairly straightforward translation. Since some of the readings seemed to be patently derived from earlier studies which had been rejected even by their authors, this seemed unlikely. An electronic computer was given the credit for the correlation of glyphs with spoken Maya phonemes and morphemes; given the results, most Mayanists felt that a more human element must have entered strongly into the programming. If not, then it must be concluded that a computer could only produce faster results and that a clerical transcription could have done the same thing much more cheaply. The central problem of correlating by machine is that a single morpheme may or may not correspond to a single grapheme, and hence one has to count frequencies without knowing whether the frequencies of colonial morphemes and phonemes are really comparable to the frequencies of graphemes in the codices or inscriptions. Another problem is that differences in subject matter will affect frequencies of many morphemes, although phoneme frequency may be similar between glyph and spoken Maya. Frequencies of grammatical particles would not be affected as much as those of other classes of words.

Because attention was centered on the claim of virtually complete transcription into (Yucatecan) Maya, the value of the transcription of the codices into the catalog numbers was not fully appreciated. This meant that whenever one found a glyph of possible interest, one had the accompanying transcription and could easily turn to the index and check all other occurrences of the glyph. Moreover, one knew immediately how the glyph had been transcribed, and errors of transcription tended to become immediately apparent. The index was similar to Zimmermann's but much more comprehensive, since it included all appearances of all affixes as well as all appearances of main signs. This means that it is invaluable for study of the grammatical particles. For this particular purpose, the Russian catalog and accompanying index are as far superior to Zimmermann's catalog as Zimmermann's is to Gates's.

A year later, in 1962, Eric Thompson's long-awaited book, *A Catalog of Maya Hieroglyphs*, finally appeared. This was the first catalog which gave glyphs from the inscriptions as well as from the codices. Thompson attempted to survey all the glyphs and to give the location of all occurrences of a particular glyph either in the inscriptions or in the codices, with some account of its glyphic context. Arduous though it would be, one could reconstruct virtually the entire corpus of Mayan inscriptions from the catalog. Thompson had originally tried to use the Zimmermann numbers, but the very substantial number of glyphs known from the inscriptions and absent in the codices led him to abandon this scheme. Thompson, like Zimmermann, treated affixes much more summarily than main signs. Although a full account is given of the occurrences of main signs, affixes are merely listed in terms of the main signs to which they are affixed. Since glyphic context is given for each main sign, it is possible to check occurrences of the affixes, but it is a much harder and more time-consuming job than checking the main signs. Thompson commented on the meaning of many of the main signs but deliberately avoided discussion of previous work. There is no commentary on the affixes except those which are, in his terms, "used as main signs." Since only Thompson's catalog adequately deals with the glyphs from the inscriptions, it must occupy a central place in any attempt to study Maya writing.

In 1963, Yurii Knorozov published a study of the Maya writing which is the most comprehensive one-volume source book on the subject now available. Knorozov included a Maya dictionary, a catalog, a commentary on the glyphs with a bibliography giving previous suggested interpretations, drawings and photographs of most of the A. P. Maudslay and Teobert Maler records of inscriptions, and all three codices. The catalog gives glyphs from both the codices and the inscriptions, but a great many of the latter are not included, and it is completely inadequate in that respect. In the cataloguing of the glyphs from the codices, finer distinctions are drawn than appear in the previous catalogs, and apparent variants which differ visually are given separate numbers. The way in which visually similar glyphs are grouped together is more consistent than that used in the Thompson catalog, and I find Knorozov's catalog easier to use from the standpoint of locating a glyph. The numbers given correspond closely to those of Evreinov, Kosarev, and Ustinov, although there is some variation. For attempting to trace the history of past attempts at decipherment of a particular glyph, the commentary on the Knorozov catalog is the most useful yet published, and the 1967 English edition makes this material much more widely available. Knorozov made no attempt to unite his catalog with any sort of index of occurrence of the glyphs.

Finally, Juan José Rendón and Amalia Spescha, of the Comisión para el Estudio de la Escritura Maya (CEEM), have recently published a "plastic" classification of the Maya hieroglyphs which creates still another catalog (1965). At present, this contains only glyphs from the codices. They have published a valuable concordance of the numbers of their catalog with those of all previous catalogs except that of Gates. The general intent of the classification is to lump together glyphs which are generally similar in appearance and thus to make it easier to find the number of a particular glyph. This catalog has been organized with the primary aim of "conversing" with the computers rather than with other humans. Its groupings should facilitate programming at different levels of distinction between the glyphs. It forms a very useful index to the existing catalogs but will not replace the Thompson catalog in the writings of Mayanists. The Rendón and Spescha catalog is likely to be used chiefly for official works of the CEEM.

Presumably, all the catalogs have the primary purposes of facilitating access to the data of the codices and inscriptions and of establishing a system which may be used for convenient reference. The central problem of such catalogs is the correct classification of nonsignificant variants under a single number and of significant variants under different numbers. It may safely be presumed that all of the catalogs err in both regards. Thus Z1339 corresponds to T528, K143, EKU153, and J12. However, these numbers correspond to two glyphs, not one. A valid distinction between two similar glyphs, recognized by Thompson in 1950, is ignored in all the catalogs, including Thompson's own (see Chapter 9 for the distinction in *Dresden* between *haab* and *cu*). Conversely, Thompson frequently gives different numbers to a glyph which appears as an affix and the same glyph when it appears as a main sign. Knorozov assigns different numbers to glyphs which differ visually and then says in his comments that they are variants of a single glyph, to be read in the same way. The complex problem of the association of head variants with their symbolic forms is not adequately treated in any of the catalogs. Ideally, such glyphs should probably be given adjacent numbers, where possible, or even subletters of a single number. A new catalog organized on such principles at this stage of our work would be frightening rather than helpful, but a certain amount of revision in one of the existing catalogs might produce a more adequate scheme. Even necessary revisions reduce the value of a catalog as a communications system, and each new system which appears makes it harder for Mayan scholars to read each other's papers.

Chapter 15
Summary

People will continue to work with those methods they find most effective, and we can expect a constantly accumulating series of reasonably certain decipherments. Of the approximately eight hundred known Maya graphemes, a substantial number can now be read in Maya. I have suggested that there are nearly sixty logographs which can be read in Mayan. In many cases, the objects represented in these glyphs can be recognized, but there are also many which cannot be. There are also about ten logographic glyphs of which we know the approximate meanings. We can expect identifications of most of these shortly. In my opinion, we also have satisfactory phonetic definitions of an additional twenty glyphs of CV pattern which were used phonetically. These make up about thirty clearly identified glygers and enable us to read a considerable number of additional glygers whose meanings are not determinable from context. Thus, I think we have good usable data on about one-tenth of the glyphs.

Besides these, we have a few miscellaneous glygers whose meanings are demonstrable from context, about thirty glygers for deities, perhaps twenty glygers for mythical places, about fifteen identified Emblem Glyphs, and a considerable number of nominal glyphs representing the names of rulers at various Mayan cities.

This estimate is a conservative one. The members of the Mérida school have attempted identifications of most of the glyphs in the codices, as have Evreinov, Kosarev, and Ustinov. Both Knorozov and Barthel have suggested a very considerable number of readings which seem to me still inadequately demonstrated, and Thompson has not been idle in proposing new readings of glyphs. General acceptance of any large proportion of these readings would substantially increase the percentage of glyphs which we can read.

Over and above this detailed level, we now know the general structure of the Maya writing. We can recognize verbs, nouns, and sometimes adjectives and grammatical particles, and we can usually recognize the general subject matter of an inscription. This is no mean accomplishment when compared with the situation as it was even twenty years ago. Progress has been rapid, and we can expect it to continue for some time to come.

Glossary

affix: a physically smaller glyph, often of irregular shape, associated with a main sign in a single glyph block.

Ahau Equation: the number of days added to a Maya long-count date to convert it to a Julian Day number.

allograph: a glyph which occurs in the same contexts as another glyph, suggesting that it is a different way of writing the same thing. The commonest variation is between a geometric form and a head or full figure of a god or animal.

anterior date indicator: a glyph which indicates that a following date refers to an earlier time.

baktun: a period of four hundred tuns of 360 days each; a pseudo-Maya term.

Borgia group: a group of related codices from southern Mexico of uncertain origin. Contents are calendrical, religious, and astronomical. Style is like the Mixtec historical codices.

calabtun: a period of 160,000 tuns; a pseudo-Maya term.

calendar round: the 52-year period which must pass before a day of the 260-day cycle will recur on the same day of the month.

Chilam Balam: a name applied to colonial Yucatec manuscripts, written in European script but in the Yucatec language, giving information on mythology, religion, calendar folk beliefs, etc.

Chumayel: one of the more important books of *Chilam Balam*.

clause: a patterned sequence of glyphs, such as a series of names and titles of an individual, or a sentence.

correlation constant: Ahau equation.

count group: a series of affixes showing substantial interchangeability with each other, believed by Thompson to be associated with counting, but probably partially interchangeable grammatical particles.

cycle: (*a*) an older term for what is now usually called a baktun; (*b*) any of the many re-entering series of Maya calendrical-religious phenomena, particularly the fifty-two–year period.

determinative: (*a*) in chronological studies, a date believed to indicate the shift in position in the tropical year of the date 4 Ahau 8 Cumku, from which the Maya Era was counted; (*b*) a glyph accompanying or infixed in another glyph in order to help read it correctly, either to choose between homonyms with different meanings or to choose between phonetically different synonyms.

Distance Number: a number giving the interval of days (and larger periods, if any) between two dates.

Distance Number Introducing Glyph: a glyph (T573) which normally precedes Distance Numbers.

Dresden: one of the three surviving Maya codices.

element: any part of a glyph smaller than a grapheme.

Emblem Glyph: a glyph which is typical for a particular place and represents some local phenomenon, perhaps a place name.

Fejervary-Mayer: a codex of the *Borgia* group.

full-figure variant: an elaborately carved representation of a god or animal which is an allograph of some much simpler glyph.

geometric variant: an allograph of simple form, often not identifiable as a depiction of a particular object, and generally contrasted with *head variant*. *Symbolic variant* is a synonym.

glyger: a sequence of two or more graphemes, found together in the same order repeatedly, apparently having a single referent or meaning.

glyph: hieroglyph.

Glyphs A, B, C, D, E, F, G, X, Y, and Z: various glyphs or series of glyphs found as part of the Secondary Series. Glyphs F and G refer to the Nine Lords of the Night, while the others form the Lunar Series.

glyph block: a physical division of an inscription, usually containing one or two main signs and one or more affixes.

grapheme: the smallest unitary symbol of the writing system.

haab: a Maya term for 'year', applied normally to the period of 365 days, but probably sometimes to the "year" of 360 days.

head variant: a glyph which shows the head of an animal or deity, probably usually an allograph of a symbolic variant.

hieroglyph: a grapheme or a series of graphemes normally found together or a substitutable series of graphemes used in similar context; equals a *glyph*.

ideograph: a grapheme or more complex hieroglyph believed to convey information irrespective of language, such as the numerals in our society and in Maya society.

inaugural date: a date marked by the "toothache glyph," now read *hok* 'install in office'.

infix: a grapheme placed within another grapheme.

initial date: a date marked by the "upended frog" glyph, now read **pok'* 'be born'.

Initial Series: the glyphs which open a Mayan inscription and give the time elapsed since the base date of the Maya Era.

Initial Series Introducing Glyph: a large compound glyph, often written across two glyph columns, containing a variable central element, which is apparently the name of the deity presiding over the month in which the Initial Series date fell.

katun: a period of twenty tuns.

kin: a day.

kinchiltun: a period of 3,200,000 years; a pseudo-Maya term.

Landa "alphabet": a series of Maya graphemes collected by Bishop Diego de Landa in the sixteenth century and assigned by him to the letters of the Spanish alphabet.

logograph: a grapheme conveying a word with all its homonyms.

long count: an interval which may be expressed in days elapsed from the base date of the Maya Era. Corresponds structurally to our year dates, such as 1969.

Lunar Series: a series of glyphs which normally follow the Initial Series and give partly deciphered astronomical and religious information, especially the age of the moon and the number of days in the current lunar month.

Madrid: one of the three surviving Maya codices.

main sign: a glyph, physically larger than an affix, usually of regular outline. In appearance it is more prominent than the affixes, but analytically it does not necessarily convey any different sort of information.

Maya Era: the count of time elapsed from a base date 4 Ahau 8 Cumku, about 3,600 years in the past, when Maya inscriptions became common. The Maya occasionally counted from other base dates, but this is by far the commonest base.

morpheme: in linguistics, the smallest unit that conveys meaning.

Nuttall: a fourteenth-century Mixtec historical-genealogical codex.

Paris: one of the three surviving Maya codices.

Pérez: another name for the *Paris* codex; also the name of one of the *Chilam Balam* manuscripts.

pictograph: any grapheme which is a recognizable depiction of an object.

pictun: a period of 8,000 tuns; a pseudo-Maya term.

postfix: an affix which is to the right of or below a main sign; often but not always equivalent to a linguistic suffix.

prefix: an affix which is to the left of or above a main sign.

Secondary Series: the series of glyphs, including the Lunar Series and the Lords of the Night, which follows the Initial Series in most Mayan inscriptions.

short count: the series of thirteen different katun endings by which the later Yucatec Maya dated events within a range of 260 tuns.

stela: a free-standing stone monument, usually sculptured.

subfix: an affix which appears below a main sign. These are always postfixes.

superfix: an affix which appears above a main sign.

Supplementary Series: a series of glyphs usually following the Initial Series.

symbolic variant: geometric variant.

synharmony: the principle that the second of a pair of CV phonetic glyphs will have the same vowel as the first of the pair; probably true in about five of six cases.

tun: Maya term for year, usually applied to the period of 360 days, but sometimes applied to the period of 365 days.

tzolkin: 260-day cycle.

uinal: the Maya "month" of twenty days.

underworld group: a series of glyphs appearing in somewhat similar contexts and believed by Thompson to refer to the underworld.

variable element: see Initial Series Introducing Glyph.

variant: an older term approximating *allograph* in use, but applied also to partially substitutable forms that may be synonyms or even antonyms; also used to indicate a slight variation in form, less than that indicated by the term *allograph*.

Vaticanus 3773: one of the *Borgia* group of codices.

Vienna: a Mixtec manuscript, probably from the twelfth or thirteenth century, containing mythical, legendary, and historical material.

water group: a series of affixes, now known to be typical of Emblem Glyphs.

Bibliography

The reader is referred to the bibliography of Thompson 1950 for additional references. The entire bibliography accompanying Knorozov 1963 has been included here, a fact which accounts for some items which are more archaeological than glyphic. I have included a considerable number of items which are mentioned in the text only in passing and a few items which I have not seen, in the hope of making the bibliography more useful.

Attention should also be drawn to Bernal 1962 as a major bibliographic resource, particularly pages 311–312 and 317–347.

Adams, Richard E. W.
> 1963 "A polychrome vessel from Altar de Sacrificios." *Archaeology* 16, no. 2:90–92.
> 1968 "Implications of a Maya elite class funeral at Altar de Sacrificios, Guatemala." Paper presented at the annual meeting of The Society for American Archaeology.

Alvarez L., María Cristina
> 1966 "Descripción estructural del maya del Chilam Balam de Chumayel." 1er Seminario Internacional para el Estudio de la Escritura Maya. Mexico City.
> 1967 "Posibilidades de estudios que presentan los radicales del maya colonial." 4 pp. Mimeographed. Mérida.
> 1969 "Descripción estructural del maya de Chilam Balam de Chumayel." Seminario de Estudios de la Escritura Maya, Cuaderno 1. Mexico City. (Revised and enlarged from Alvarez 1966.)

Anders, F.
> See *Madrid* codex; *Paris* codex.

Anders, Ferdinand
> 1963 *Das Pantheon der Maya.* Graz, Austria.

Andrade, Manuel J.
> 1955 *A grammar of modern Yucatec.* Microfilm Collection of MSS on Middle American Cultural Anthropology, no. 41. University of Chicago.

Andrews, E. Wyllys IV
> 1934 "Glyph X of the Supplementary Series of the Maya inscriptions." *American Anthropologist* (Menasha) 36:345–354.
> 1936 "Notes on Glyph G of the Maya inscriptions." *Maya Research* 3:306–308.
> 1940 "Chronology and astronomy in the Maya area." In *The Maya and their neighbors,* pp. 150–161. New York: D. Appleton–Century Co.
> 1951 "The Maya Supplementary Series." Selected Papers of the 29th International Congress of Americanists, New York (1949), vol. 1, pp. 123–141. Chicago.

Andrews, E. Wyllys IV, and George E. Stuart
> 1968 *The ruins of Ikil, Yucatan, Mexico.* Middle American Research Institute Pub. 31, Preprint, pp. 69–80. New Orleans.

Annals of the Cakchiquels
> See Recinos 1950.

Annals of Cuauhtitlan
> See Velásquez n.d.

Apenes, O.
> 1937 "Table for determination of Maya calendar round positions." *Ethnos* (Stockholm) 2, no. 4:97–101.

Araujo S., Rolando, Miguel Rodríguez D., and Hugo E. Solís C.
> 1965 *I Chol Kin.* Serie Origo. Mérida: Ediciones de la Universidad de Yucatán.

Arzápalo, Ramón
  1966 "Posibles paralelos estructurales y de significado
       entre los libros del Chilam Balam y los códices mayas."
       1er Seminario Internacional para el Estudio de la
       Escritura Maya. Mexico City.
  1968 "Algunos posibles paralelos estilísticos entre los
       códices jeroglíficos y los manuscritos coloniales."
       Estudios de Cultura Maya (Mexico City) 7:285–291.
Ayala Falcón, Maricela
  1966 "Relación entre texto y dibujos en el Códice de
       Dresde." 1er Seminario Internacional para el Estudio de
       la Escritura Maya. Mexico City.
  1967 "Relaciónes entre texto y dibujos en el Códice
       Madrid." 8 pp. Mimeographed. Mérida.
  1968 "Relaciónes entre textos y dibujos en el Códice de
       Dresde." *Estudios de Cultura Maya* (Mexico City)
       7:85–99.
Baldet, F.
  1950 "Liste générale des comètes de l'origine à 1948." In
       Annuaire du Bureau des Longitudes pour l'an 1950.
Baldet, F., and G. de Obaldia
  1952 *Catalogue général des orbites des comètes de l'an
       1466 à 1952*. Paris: Observatoire de Paris.
Barrera Vásquez, Alfredo
  1942 "El pronóstico de los 20 signos de los días del
       calendario maya, según los Libros de Chilam Balam de
       Kaua y de Mani." Proceedings of the 27th International
       Congress of Americanists, Mexico City (1939), vol. 27,
       part 2, sec. 1, pp. 470–481. Mexico City.
  1945 "Idioma quiche." In *Anales del Instituto Nacional
       de Antropología e Historia*, I, 179–190. Mexico City.
  1946 "La lengua maya de Yucatán." *Enciclopedia
       yucatanense* vol. 6. Mexico City.
  1962 "Investigación de la escritura maya con máquinas
       electrónicas: Síntesis y glosa." *Estudios de Cultura Maya*
       2:319–342.
  1965 *El libro de los cantares de Dzitbalche*. Instituto
       Nacional de Anthropología e Historia, Serie
       Investigaciones, no. 9.
Barrera Vásquez, Alfredo, and Sylvanus G. Morley
  1949 *The Maya chronicles*. Carnegie Institution of
       Washington Pub. 585, Contri. 48. Washington D.C.
Barrera Vásquez, Alfredo, and Silvia Rendón
  1948 *El Libro de los Libros de Chilam Balam*. Mexico
       City: Fondo de Cultura Económica.
Barthel, Thomas S.
  1952 "Der Morgensternkult in den Darstellungen der
       Dresdener Mayahandschrift." *Ethnos* (Stockholm)
       17:73–112.
  1953 "Regionen des Regengottes." *Ethnos* (Stockholm)
       18:86–105.
  1954 "Maya epigraphy: Some remarks on the affix 'al'."
       Proceedings of the 30th International Congress of
       Americanists, Cambridge (1952), pp. 45–49. London.
  1955a "Versuch über die Inschriften von Chich'en Itza
       Viejo." *Baessler-Archiv* (Berlin), n.s. 3:5–33.
  1955b "Maya-Palaeographic: Die Hieroglyphe Strafe."
       Ethnos (Stockholm) 20:146–151.
  1958 "Die gegenwaertige Situation in der Erforschung der
       Mayaschrift." Proceedings of the 32nd International
       Congress of Americanists, Copenhagen (1956), pp.
       476–484. Copenhagen.
  1961 "Die Inschriftenanalyse als Hilfsmittel zur
       Rekonstruktion der klassischen Mayageschichte." In

       Homage to Hermann Beyer, El México Antiguo
       9:173–181.
  1963 "Die Stele 31 von Tikal." *Tribus*, no. 12, pp.
       159–214.
  1964a "Comentarios a las inscripciones clásicas tardias de
       Chich'en-Itza." *Estudios de Cultura Maya* (Mexico City)
       4:223–244.
  1964b "Einige Ordnungsprinzipien im aztekischen
       Pantheon." *Paideuma* 10:77–101.
  1965a "Gedanken zu einer bemalten Schale aus
       Uaxactun." *Baessler-Archiv* (Berlin), n.s. 13:131–170.
  1965b "Comentarios epigráficos marginales." *Estudios de
       Cultura Maya* (Mexico City) 5:145–152.
  1965c "Das Herzopfer in Altmexiko." In *Das Herz im
       Umkreis des Glaubens*. Biberach, Germany.
  1966a "Mesoamerikanische Fledermäusdamonen." *Tribus*,
       no. 15, pp. 101–124.
  1966b "Yaxchilan Lintel 60." *Baessler-Archiv* (Berlin),
       n.s. 14:125–138.
  1966c "El complejo emblema." 1er Seminario
       Internacional para el Estudio de la Escritura Maya.
       Mexico City.
  1967a "Notes on the inscription on a carved bone from
       Yucatan." *Estudios de Cultura Maya* 6:223–241.
  1967b "Mayahieroglyphen." *Bild der Wissenschaft*
       1967:452–463.
  1967c "Intentos de lectura de los afijos." *Escritura Maya
       Boletín Informativo (Working Paper)* 1, no. 2:4–13.
  1968a "Historisches in dem klassischen Mayainschriften."
       Zeitschrift für Ethnologie (Braunschweig) 93, nos.
       1–2:119–156.
  1968b "Götter–Sterne–Pyramiden." *Paideuma*
       14:45–92.
  1968c "El complejo emblema." *Estudios de Cultura Maya*
       (Mexico City) 7:159–193.
Bastarrachea M., Juan Ramón
  1966 "Supervivencia de algunos dioses en grupos mayas
       actuales." 1er Seminario Internacional para el Estudio de
       la Escritura Maya. Mexico City.
  1968 "Bibliografía etnolinguistica mayance."
       Mimeographed.
Batres, Leopoldo
  1909 *Las ruinas de Palenque*. 21 pp. Mexico City.
Belmont, G. E.
  1935 "The Secondary Series as a lunar eclipse count."
       Maya Research 2:144–153.
Benson, Elizabeth P., ed.
  1973 *Mesoamerican writing systems*. Washington, D.C.:
       Dumbarton Oaks.
Berendt, Carl Hermann
  1869 *Analytical alphabet for the Mexican and Central
       American languages*. 16 pp. New York.
Berlin, Heinrich
  1955 "News from the Maya world." *Ethnos* (Stockholm)
       20, no. 4:201–209.
  1957 "A new inscription from the Temple of the Foliated
       Cross at Palenque." Carnegie Institution of Washington,
       Division of Historical Research, Notes on Middle
       American Archaeology and Ethnology, no. 130.
       Washington, D. C.
  1958 "El glifo 'emblema' en las inscripciones mayas."
       Journal de la Société des Américanistes (Paris), n.s.
       47:111–119.

1959   "Glifos nominales en el sarcófago de Palenque."
Humanidades 2, no. 10:1–8.

1963   "The Palenque Triad." Journal de la Société des
Américanistes (Paris), n.s. 52:91–99.

1964   "El glifo zotz invertido." Antropología e Historia de
Guatemala (Guatemala City) 16, no. 1:3–7.

1965a   "The inscription of the Temple of the Cross at
Palenque." American Antiquity 30, no. 3:330–342.

1965b   "Estudios epigráficos." Antropología e Historia de
Guatemala (Guatemala City) 17, no. 2:3–12.

1965c   "Neue Funde zu alten Zeichnungen." Ethnos
(Stockholm) 30:136–143.

1968   The tablet of the 96 glyphs at Palenque, Chiapas,
Mexico. Middle American Research Institute, Pub. 26,
Preprint, pp. 135–149.

Berlin, Heinrich, and David H. Kelley
1961   "The 819-day count and color-direction symbolism
among the Classic Maya." Middle American Research
Institute, Pub. 26, Preprint, pp. 9–20.

Bernal, Ignacio
1962   Bibliografía de arqueología y etnografía:
Mesoamérica y Norte de México 1514–1960. Memorias
del Instituto Nacional de Antropología e Historia 7.

Beyer, Hermann
1926   "Die Verdopplung in der Hieroglyphenschrift der
Maya." Anthropos (St. Gabriel Mödling bei Wien)
21:580–582.

1929   "The supposed Maya hieroglyph of the screech
owl." American Anthropologist (Menasha) 31:34–59.

1934a   "La historia de la escritura maya."
Investigación y Progreso (Madrid) 8:300–305.

1934b   "Ueber das Datum auf der Russelmaske von
Labna." El México Antiguo (Mexico City) 3, nos.
3–4:9–13.

1937   Studies on the inscriptions of Chichen Itza. Carnegie
Institution of Washington Pub. 483, Contri. 21.
Washington, D.C.

Blom, Frans
1928   "San Clemente Ruins, Guatemala." Journal de la
Société des Américanistes de Paris (Paris) 20:93–102.

1930   "Preliminary notes on two important Maya finds."
Proceedings of the 23rd International Congress of
Americanists, New York (1928), pp. 165–171. New
York.

1935   "A checklist of falsified Maya codices." Maya
Research (New Orleans) 2:251–252.

Bollaert, William
1863   Introduction to the palaeography of America.
Memoirs of the Anthropological Society of London, no.
1. London.

1866a   A Maya hieroglyphic alphabet of Yucatan. Memoirs
of the Anthropological Society of London, no. 2, pp.
46–54. London.

1866b   "Hieroglyphics, including the recently discovered
figurated writing." Archaeology (New York) 4.

Books of Chilam Balam
See Barrera Vásquez and Rendón 1948; Makemson 1951;
Roys 1933; Roys 1965.

Borgia codex
1898   Il manoscritto messicano borgiano del Museo
Etnografico della S. Congregazione di Propaganda Fide:
Riprodetto fotocromografia. Rome: Edition of the Duc
de Loubat.

Bourgeois, Julia F.
1942   The true calendar years of Aztecos and Mayas and
the true Mayan calendar system. Mexico City: Editorial
Cultura.

Bowditch, Charles P.
1901   Notes on the report of Teobert Maler. Memoirs of
the Peabody Museum of American Archaeology and
Ethnology, Harvard University, vol. 2, no. 1. Cambridge,
Mass.

1910   The numeration, calendar systems and astronomical
knowledge of the Mayas. Cambridge, Mass.

Brasseur de Bourbourg, Charles E.
1861   Popol Vuh. Paris: A. Bertrand.

1866   Palenqué et autres ruines de l'ancienne civilisation
du Mexique. Paris: A. Bertrand.

1869   Lettre à M. Léon de Rosny. Paris: Amyot.

1870   Entzifferung der yucatekischen Hieroglyphen.
Stuttgart.

1872   Dictionnaire, grammaire et chrestomathie de la
langue maya. Paris: Maisonneuve et Cie.

Breedlove, Dennis E., and Nicholas A. Hopkins
1970   "A study of Chuj (Mayan) plants, with notes on
their uses." The Wasmann Journal of Biology (San
Francisco) 28, no. 2:275–298; 29, no. 1:1–23.

Brinton, Daniel Garrison
1870   The ancient phonetic alphabet of Yucatan. 8 pp.
New York.

1884   "A grammar of the Cakchiquel language of
Guatemala." Proceedings of the American Philosophical
Society (Philadelphia) 21, no. 112:345–412.

1886   "On the ikonomatic method of phonetic writing."
Proceedings of the American Philosophical Society
(Philadelphia) 23, no. 124.

1887   "Critical remarks on the editions of Diego de
Landa's writings." Proceedings of the American
Philosophical Society (Philadelphia) 24, no. 125.

1894   "What the Maya inscriptions tell about."
Archaeologist (Waterloo) 2:11.

1895   A primer of Mayan hieroglyphics. University of
Pennsylvania Series in Philology, Literature and
Archaeology, vol. 3, no. 2. Philadelphia.

Brito Sansores, William
1966a   "Intentos historico-lingüísticos para el descifre de la
escritura maya." In Publicaciones del Instituto
Tecnológico de Mérida. Mérida.

1966b   "Algunos descifres de textos no calendáricos en el
códice de Dresde." 1er Seminario Internacional para el
Estudio de la Escritura Maya. Mexico City.

Buenaventura, Fray Gabriel de San
1684   Arte de la lengua maya. Mexico City.

Bunge, O. D. E.
1935   "Signes et noms des jours et des mois tzeltal."
Journal de la Société des Américanistes de Paris (Paris)
27:35–73.

1936   "Les pages des abeilles du Codex Tro." Journal de la
Société des Américanistes (Paris), n.s. 28:305–322.

1940   "Contribution à l'astronomie maya." Journal de la
Société des Américanistes (Paris), n.s. 32:69–92.

Burland, Cottie A.
1947   "Einige Bemerkungen über den Codex
Vindobonensis Mexic. 1." Archiv für Völkerkunder
(Vienna) 2:101–107.

1958   "The inscription on Stela I, El Castillo, region of
Santa Lucia Cotzumahualpa, Guatemala." Proceedings

of the 32nd International Congress of Americanists, Copenhagen (1956), pp. 326–330.

Cakchiquels, Annals of the
See Recinos 1950.

Calderón, Héctor M.
1962 *Clave fonética de los jeroglíficos mayas.* Mexico City: Editorial Orión.
1966 *La ciencia matemática de los mayas.* Mexico City: Editora Cuzamil.

Capitan, A.
1911 *Quelques interpretations nouvelles de figures d'un manuscrit maya (Codex Troano).* Paris.

Cardos de M., Amalia
1959 *El comercio de los mayas antiguos.* Acta Antropológica, ser. 2, vol. 2, no. 1.

Carillo y Ancona, Crescencio
1937 *Disertacion sobre la historia de la lengua maya o yucateca.* Mérida.

Carmack, Robert M.
1973 *Quichean civilization.* Berkeley and Los Angeles: University of California Press.

Caso, Alfonso
1958 *El calendario mexicano.* Memorias de la Academia Mexicana de la Historia, vol. 17, no. 1. Mexico City.
1959 "Glifos Teotihuacanos." *Revista Mexicana de Estudios Antropológicos* (Mexico City) 15:57–70.
1961 "Nombres calendáricos de los dioses." *El México Antiguo* (Mexico City) 9:77–100.
1965a "Zapotec writing and calendar." In *Archaeology of southern Mesoamerica: Part two,* edited by Gordon R. Willey, pp. 931–947. Handbook of Middle American Indians, edited by Robert Wauchope, vol. 3. Austin: University of Texas Press.
1965b "Mixtec writing and calendar." In *Archaeology of southern Mesoamerica: Part two,* edited by Gordon R. Willey, pp. 948–961. Handbook of Middle American Indians, edited by Robert Wauchope, vol. 3. Austin: University of Texas Press.

Castro, Carlo Antonio
1965 *Narraciones tzeltales de Chiapas.* Universidad Veracruzana-México, Cuadernos No. 27. Mexico City: Impr. Nuevo Mundo.

Cazés, Daniel
1966a "Codificación y preparación de los materiales utilizados por la CEEM para su proceso electrónico." 1er Seminario Internacional para el Estudio de la Escritura Maya. Mexico City.
1966b "Frecuencias de algunos elementos lingüísticos del Chilam Balam de Chumayel." 1er Seminario Internacional para el Estudio de la Escritura Maya. Mexico City.
1967 "Trabajos de descifre de la escritura maya en México, 1963–1968." 7 pp. Mimeographed. Mérida.
1968 "Frecuencias de algunos elementos lingüísticos en el Chilam Balam de Chumayel." *Estudios de Cultura Maya* (Mexico City) 7:339–351.

Cazés, Daniel, and Juan José Rendón
1968 "Concordancias de los códices de Dresde y Madrid por glifos: Primeros resultados." *Escritura Maya* 2, no. 2:3–24.

Chadwick, John
1958 *The decipherment of Linear B.* New York: Random House.

Charencey, C. F. H. G. de
1870 "Essai de déchiffrement d'un fragment d'inscription palenquéenne." *Actes de la Société Philologique* (Paris) 1, no. 3.
1875 *Essai d'analyse grammaticale d'un texte en langue maya.* Le Havre.
1879 "Le déchiffrement de plusieurs caractères mayas." Proceedings of the 3rd International Congress of Americanists, Brussels (1879), part 2, pp. 758–760. Brussels.
1896 "Mélanges sur quelques dialects de la famille maya-quichée." *Journal de la Société des Américanistes de Paris* (Paris) 1, no. 2:43–60.
1910 "Sur la langue tzotzile et sa numération." Proceedings of the 16th International Congress of Americanists (1908), pp. 597–610.
1912 "De la formation des voix verbales en Tzotzil." Proceedings of the 17th International Congress of Americanists, Buenos Aires (1910), pp. 167–175. Buenos Aires.

Chi, Gaspar Antonio
1952 *The historical recollections of Gaspar Antonio Chi: An early source-account of ancient Yucatan.* Edited and translated by M. Wells Jakeman. Provo, Utah.

Chilam Balam, Books of
See Barrera Vásquez and Rendón 1948; Makemson 1951; Roys 1933; Roys 1965.

Chumayel, Book of Chilam Balam of
See Roys 1933.

Codex Vaticanus B
1896 *Il manoscritto messicano vaticano 3773.* Rome.

Coe, Michael D.
1957 "Cycle 7 monuments in Middle America: A reconsideration." *American Anthropologist* (Menasha) 59, no. 4:597–611.
1966 *An early stone pectoral from southeastern Mexico.* Studies in Pre-Columbian Art and Archaeology, no. 1. Washington, D.C.: Dumbarton Oaks, Trustees for Harvard University.
1973 *The Maya scribe and his world.* New York: Grolier Club.

Coe, Michael D., and Elizabeth P. Benson
1966 *Three Maya relief panels at Dumbarton Oaks.* Studies in Pre-Columbian Art and Archaeology, no. 2. Washington, D.C.: Dumbarton Oaks, Trustees for Harvard University.

Coe, William R.
1965 "Tikal: Ten years of study of a Maya ruin in the lowlands of Guatemala." *Expedition* 8, no. 1:5–56.

Cordan, Wolfgang
1963a *Introducción a los glifos mayas.* Serie Origo, no. 1. Mérida: Universidad de Yucatán.
1963b *Götter und Göttertiere der Maya.* Bern-Munich: Francke Verlag.
1964 *La clave de los glifos mayas.* Serie Origo, no. 2. Mérida: Universidad de Yucatán.
1965 "Gott Tritonshorn als Gott des Jahresendes." *Baessler-Archiv* (Berlin), n.s. 13: 317–338.
1966 "La fiesta de las abejas del códice de Madrid." In *En Memoria de Wolfgang Cordan.* Mérida: Universidad de Yucatán.

Cordy, Napoleon
1931 "The meaning of the Maya day names." *The Masterkey* 5:135–143.

1946 "Examples of phonetic construction in Maya hieroglyphs." *American Antiquity* (Menasha) 12:108–117.

Cortesiano
See *Madrid* codex.

Cuauhtitlan, Annals of
See Velásquez n.d.

Culbert, T. Patrick
1965 *The ceramic history of the central highlands of Chiapas, Mexico.* New World Archaeological Foundation Papers, no. 19. Provo, Utah.

Díaz Bolio, José
1967a "El idioma de los códices." *Novedades de Yucatán* (Mérida).
1967b *La geometría de los mayas e el mayarte crotalico.* Mérida.

Dieseldorff, Erwin P.
1939 *Los secretos contenidos en el tablero del Templo de la Cruz de Palenque, la joya más valiosa de la prehistoria mundial, conservado en el Museo Nacional de México, D.F.* Pamphlet, 16 pp. Mexico City: El Sobre Azul. Copy in Rochester University Library.
1951 *Das alte und das neue Reich der Maya.* Munich.

Dittrich, A.
1936 *Die Korrelation der Maya-Chronologie.* Reprinted from *Abhandlungen der Preussischen Akademie der Wissenschaften.* Berlin.

Dresden codex
1892 *Die Maya-handschrift der Königlichen Bibliothek zu Dresden.* Edited by Ernst W. Förstemann. Dresden. Reprint: Berlin, 1962.
See also Förstemann 1880; Gates 1932; Thompson 1972b; Villacorta and Villacorta 1930.

Durbin, Marshall
1966 "Writing systems and linguistics." 1er Seminario Internacional para el Estudio de la Escritura Maya. Mexico City.
1968 "Linguistics and writing systems." *Estudios de Cultura Maya* (Mexico City) 7:49–57.
1969 *An interpretation of Bishop Diego de Landa's Maya alphabet.* Middle American Research Institute Philological and Documentary Studies, vol. 2, no. 4. New Orleans.

Dütting, Dieter
1965a "Das Knoten-Graphem bei den Maya." *Zeitschrift für Ethnologie* 90:66–103.
1965b "Algunas consideraciones sobre el trabajo de H. Berlin 'The Palenque Triad'." *Estudios de Cultura Maya* 5:135–144.
1968 "On the inscription and iconography of Kuna-Lacanha Lintel 1." Unpublished.

Edmonson, Munro S.
1964 "Historia de las tierras altas mayas, según los documentos indígenas." In *Desarrollo cultural de los mayas,* edited by Evon Z. Vogt and Alberto Ruz Lhuillier, pp. 255–278. Mexico City: Universidad Nacional Autónoma de México.
1965 *Quiche-English dictionary.* Middle American Research Institute Pub. 30. New Orleans.
1967 "Classical Quiche." In *Linguistics,* edited by Norman A. McQuown, pp. 249–267. Handbook of Middle American Indians, edited by Robert Wauchope, vol. 5. Austin: University of Texas Press.
1971 *The book of counsel: The popol vuh of the Quiche*

Maya of Guatemala. Middle American Research Institute Pub. 35. New Orleans.

Eggan, Fred
1934 "The Maya kinship system and cross-cousin marriage." *American Anthropologist* 36, no. 2:188–202.

Eichhorn, A.
1905 *Die Hieroglyphen-Bildschrift der Maya-Völker.* Berlin.

Escalante, Roberto
1966 "Método de desciframiento." 1er Seminario Internacional para el Estudio de la Escritura Maya. Mexico City.
1968 "Método de descifre." *Estudios de Cultura Maya* (Mexico City) 7:65–78.

Evreinov, E. V., Y. G. Kosarev, and V. A. Ustinov
1961a "Investigation of ancient Mayan manuscripts with the aid of an electronic computer: Methods; Investigation . . . computer: Algorithms and programs; Investigation . . . computer: Preliminary results; Foreign developments in machine translation and information processing." Mimeographed. U. S. Dept. of Commerce, Office of Technical Services, no. 40.
1961b *Primenenie elekytronnikh vichislitelnikh mashin v issledovanii pismennosti drevnikh maya.* 3 vols. Novosibirsk.

Fernández, Miguel Angel
1945 *Exploraciones arqueológicas en la Isla Cozumel, Quintana Roo. Anales del Instituto Nacional de Antropología e Historia,* no. 1. Mexico City.

Fernández, P. Jesús
1957 *Diccionario Poconchi. Anales de la Sociedad Geográfica e Historica de Guatemala,* no. 14. Guatemala City.

Fewkes, J. W.
1894 "A study of certain figures in a Maya codex." *American Anthropologist* 7:260–274.
1895 "The God D in the Codex Cortesianus." *American Anthropologist* 8:205–222.

Förstemann, Ernst W.
1880 *Die Mayahandschrift der Königlichen Öffentlichen Bibliothek zu Dresden.* Leipzig: Verlag der A. Naumann'schen Lichtdruckerei.
1904 Translations of various papers. Bureau of American Ethnology Bulletin 28, pp. 393–590. Washington, D.C.
1906 *Commentary on the Maya manuscript in the Royal Public Library of Dresden.* Papers of the Peabody Museum of American Archaeology and Ethnology, Harvard University, vol. 4, no. 2. Cambridge, Mass.
See also *Dresden* codex.

Fought, John
1965 "A phonetic and morphological interpretation of Zimmermann's affix 61 in the Maya hieroglyphic codices." *Estudios de Cultura Maya* 5:253–280.

Frias, Marta A.
1966 "Catálogo de las características de los personajes en el códice de Dresde." 1er Seminario Internacional para el Estudio de la Escritura Maya. Mexico City.
1967 *Ampliación del catálogo de personajes en los códices mayas.* Comisión para el Estudio de la Escritura Maya Pub. 2. Mexico City.
1968 "Catálogo de las características de los personajes en los Códices de Dresde y Madrid." *Estudios de Cultura Maya* (Mexico City) 7:195–239.

Friedrich, Johannes
    1955 *Kurze Grammatik der alten Quiché-Sprache im Popol Vuh.* Wiesbaden.

Friedrich, J.
    1957 *Extinct languages.* New York: Philosophical Library.

Fuente, Beatriz de la
    1965 *La escultura de Palenque.* Mexico City: Instituto de Investigaciones Estéticas, Universidad Nacional Autónoma de México.

Fuentes y Guzman, Francisco Antonio
    1933 "De los caracteres y modo de escritura que usaban estos indios en su gentilidad." *Anales de la Sociedad Geográfica e Histórica de Guatemala* (Guatemala City) 9:364–369.

Gann, T. W. F.
    1905 "The ancient monuments of northern Honduras and the adjacent parts of Yucatan and Guatemala, the former civilisation in these parts, and the chief characteristics of the races now inhabiting them." *Journal of the Royal Anthropological Institute* 35:103–112.
    1917 "The Chachac or Rain Ceremony, as practised by the Maya of southern Yucatan and northern British Honduras." Proceedings of the 19th International Congress of Americanists, Washington (1915), pp. 409–418. Washington, D.C.
    1926 *Ancient cities and modern tribes: Exploration and adventure in Maya lands.* London: Duckworth.
    1930 "Recently discovered Maya city in the southwest of British Honduras." Proceedings of the 23rd International Congress of Americanists, New York (1928), pp. 188–192. New York.

Gann, Thomas, and J. Eric S. Thompson
    1931 *The history of the Maya.* New York: Charles Scribner's Sons.

Gates, William E.
    1920 "The distribution of the several branches of the Mayance linguistic stock." Appendix 12 to *The inscriptions at Copan*, by Sylvanus G. Morley, pp. 605–615. Carnegie Institution of Washington Pub. 219. Washington, D.C.
    1931 *An outline dictionary of Maya glyphs.* Baltimore: Maya Society.
    1932 *The Dresden codex.* Baltimore: Maya Society.
    1935 *The Gomesta manuscript of Maya hieroglyphs and customs in facsimile.* Maya Society Pub. 7. Baltimore.

Genet, Jean
    1934 "Les glyphes symboliques dans l'écriture maya-quichée: Le glyphe symbolique de la guerre." *Revue des Etudes Mayas-Quichées* (Paris) 1:23–32.
    See also Landa 1928–1929.

Genet, Jean, and Pierre Chelbatz
    1927 *Histoire des peuples mayas-quichés (Mexique, Guatemala, Honduras).* Paris: Editions Genet.

Girard, Rafael
    1948 *El calendario maya-méxica.* Mexico City: Editorial Stylo.

Goetz, Delia
    See Recinos, Goetz, and Morley 1950.

Goodman, J. T.
    1897 "The archaic Maya inscriptions." Appendix to *Archaeology: Biologia Centrali-Americana*, by A. P. Maudslay. London.

Gordon, George Byron
    1902 *The Hieroglyphic Stairway, ruins of Copan: Report on explorations by the museum.* Memoirs of the Peabody Museum of American Archaeology and Ethnology, Harvard University, vol. 1, no. 6. Cambridge, Mass.
    1925 *Examples of Maya pottery in the museum and other collections.* Philadelphia: The University Museum, University of Pennsylvania.

Graham, Ian
    1961 "A newly-discovered Classic Maya site." *Illustrated London News*, April 22, 1961, pp. 665–667.
    1967 *Archaeological explorations in El Peten, Guatemala.* Middle American Research Institute Pub. 33. New Orleans.

Graham, John
    1964 "Sobre la escritura maya." In *Desarrollo cultural de los mayas*, edited by Evon Z. Vogt and Alberto Ruz Lhuillier, pp. 243–254. Mexico City: Universidad Nacional Autónoma de México.
    1966 *Ancient Mesoamerica: Selected readings.* Palo Alto.

Gruning, E. L.
    1930 "Report on the British Museum expedition to British Honduras." *Journal of the Royal Anthropological Institute* 60:477–483.

Gruyter, W. J. de
    1946 *A new approach to Maya hieroglyphs.* Amsterdam.

Haberland, Wolfgang
    1954 "The golden battle discs of Chichen Itza." *Ethnos* 19:94–104.

Hagar, Stansbury
    1915 "The Maya day sign Manik." *American Anthropologist* 17:488–491.
    1917 "The Maya zodiac at Santa Rita, British Honduras." Proceedings of the 19th International Congress of Americanists, Washington (1915), pp. 211–219. Washington, D.C.

Halpern, A. M.
    1942 *A theory of Maya tš sounds.* Carnegie Institution of Washington, Division of Historical Research, Notes on Middle American Archaeology and Ethnology, no. 13. Cambridge.

Hammond, Norman, David H. Kelley, and Peter Mathews
    In press "A Maya 'pocket stela'?" To be published by the Archaeological Research Facility of the University of California at Berkeley.

Hamp, Eric P.
    1967 "On Maya-Chipayan." *International Journal of American Linguistics* 33:74–76.

Hamy, Ernst T.
    1887 "An interpretation of one of the Copan monuments (Honduras)." *Journal of the Royal Anthropological Institute* 16:242–247.

Harber, Hubert E.
    1969 "Five Mayan eclipses in thirteen years." *Sky and Telescope* 37, no. 2:72–74.

Harris, Margaret
    1947 "Nombres clasificadores chontales." *Anales del Instituto Nacional de Antropología e Historia* (Mexico City) 2.

Hill, Archibald A.
    1952 Review of *Maya hieroglyphic writing: Introduction*, by J. Eric S. Thompson. *International Journal of American Linguistics* 18, no. 3:184–186.

Holden, Edward S.
1881 "Studies in Central American picture writing." In *First annual report of the Bureau of Ethnology 1879–1880*, I, 205–245. Washington, D.C.

Holland, William R.
1963 *Medicina maya en los altos de Chiapas.* Mexico City: Instituto Nacional Indigenista.

Hopkins, Nicholas A.
1966 "A method for the investigation of glyph syntax." 1er Seminario Internacional para el Estudio de la Escritura Maya. Mexico City.
1967a "A short sketch of Chalchihuitan Tzotzil." *Anthropological Linguistics* 9, no. 4:9–25.
1967b "A preliminary study of Chuj (Mayan) numeral classifiers." 47 pp. Mimeographed. Austin: University of Texas.
1967c "A preliminary study of Chuj (Mayan) plant names." 59 pp. Mimeographed. Austin: University of Texas.
1967d "Summary of the first seminar for the study of Maya writing." *Latin American Research Review* 2, no. 2:91–94.
1968 "A method for the investigation of glyph syntax." *Estudios de Cultura Maya* (Mexico City) 7:79–83.
1970 "Numeral classifiers in Tzeltal, Jacaltec and Chuj (Mayan)." In *Papers from the sixth regional meeting of the Chicago Linguistic Society, April 16–18, 1970*, pp. 23–35. Chicago: Chicago Linguistic Society.

Jakeman, M. Wells
1945 *The origins and history of the Mayas.* Part 1, *Introductory investigations.* Los Angeles.
See also Chi 1952.

Johnson, J.
1940 "The linguistic map of Mexico and Central America." In *The Maya and their neighbors*, pp. 88–114. New York: D. Appleton–Century Co.

Justeson, John S.
1973 "The identification of the Emblem Glyph of Yaxha, El Peten." Mimeographed. Stanford University.

Kaufman, Terrence S.
1964 "Materiales lingüísticos para el estudio de las relaciones internas y externas de la familia de idiomas mayanos." In *Desarrollo cultural de los mayas*, edited by Evon Z. Vogt and Alberto Ruz Lhuillier, pp. 81–136. Mexico City: Universidad Nacional Autónoma de México.

Keller, K. C.
1955 "The Chontal (Mayan) numeral system." *International Journal of American Linguistics* (Washington, D.C.) 21, no. 3:258–275.

Kelley, David H.
1957 "Our elder brother Coyote." Ph.D. dissertation, Harvard University.
1962a "A history of the decipherment of Maya script." *Anthropological Linguistics* (Bloomington, Ind.) 4, no. 8:1–48.
1962b "Glyphic evidence for a dynastic sequence at Quirigua, Guatemala." *American Antiquity* (Salt Lake City) 27:323–335.
1962c "Fonetismo en la escritura maya." *Estudios de Cultura Maya* (Mexico City) 2:277–317.
1965 "The Birth of the Gods at Palenque." *Estudios de Cultura Maya* (Mexico City) 5:93–134.
1966a "Mayan fire glyphs." 1er Seminario Internacional para el Estudio de la Escritura Maya. Mexico City.
1966b "Kakupacal and the Itzas." 1er Seminario Internacional para el Estudio de la Escritura Maya. Mexico City.
1968a "Mayan fire glyphs." *Estudios de Cultura Maya* (Mexico City) 7:141–157.
1968b "Kakupacal and the Itzas." *Estudios de Cultura Maya* (Mexico City) 7:255–268.
1972 "The Nine Lords of the Night." In *Contributions of the University of California Archaeological Research Facility* V, no. 16, pp. 53–68.

Kelley, David. H., and K. Ann Kerr
1973 "Mayan astronomy and astronomical glyphs." In *Mesoamerican writing systems*, edited by Elizabeth P. Benson, pp. 179–215. Washington, D.C.: Dumbarton Oaks.

Kelly, Isabel T.
1938 "Northern Paiute tales." *Journal of American Folklore* 51:364–438.

Kidder, Alfred V.
1921 "The archaeological problem of the Maya." *Art and Archaeology* 31, no. 6:291–297.

Kidder, Alfred V. II
1965 "Tikal: 1965." *Expedition* 8, no. 1:3.

Knorozov, Yurii V.
1952 ["The ancient script of Central America."] *Sovietskaya Etnografiya* (Moscow) 3:100–118. Available to me in an unauthorized Spanish translation: *La antigua escritura de los pueblos de America Central.* Mexico City: Fondo de Cultura Popular. Also available in English, with a brief editorial note, as "Knorozov's deciphering of Maya glyphs." *The Current Digest of the Soviet Press* 4, no. 50:3–9.
1955a *La escritura de los antiguos mayas (ensayo de descifrado).* Authorized Spanish translation. Moscow: Academy of Sciences.
1955b *A brief summary of the studies of the ancient Maya hieroglyphic writing in the Soviet Union.* Authorized English translation. Reports of the Soviet Delegations at the X International Congress of Historical Science in Rome. Moscow: Academy of Sciences.
1958a "New data on the Maya written language." Proceedings of the 32nd International Congress of Americanists, Copenhagen (1956), pp. 467–475. Copenhagen. Also published in the *Journal de la Société des Américanistes de Paris* 45 (1956): 209–217.
1958b "The problem of the study of the Maya hieroglyphic writing." *American Antiquity* (Salt Lake City) 23:284–291.
1959 "La lengua de los textos jeroglíficos mayas." Proceedings of the 33rd International Congress of Americanists, San José (1958), part 2, pp. 573–579. San José, Costa Rica.
1963 *Pis'mennost' indeitsev maiia* [Writing of the Maya Indians]. Moscow-Leningrad: Academy of Sciences.
1965 "Principios para descifrar los escritos mayas." *Estudios de Cultura Maya* 5:153–188. Translation by Mercedes Mimó de Pintos of pp. 222–238 of Knorozov 1963.
1967 *The writing of the Maya Indians.* Translation by Sophie Coe of Chapters 1, 6, 7, and 9 of Knorozov 1963. Collaborating editor, Tatiana Proskouriakoff. Peabody Museum of Archaeology and Ethnology, Russian Translation Series, no. 4. Cambridge, Mass.

Kroeber, Alfred L.
1939 *Cultural and natural areas of native North America.* University of California Publications in American Archaeology and Ethnology, vol. 38.

Kubler, George
1973 "The clauses of Classic Maya inscriptions." In *Mesoamerican writing systems,* edited by Elizabeth P. Benson, pp. 145–164. Washington, D.C.: Dumbarton Oaks.

Laj C'oc'lel
1957 Chol Text. Mexico City: Summer Institute of Linguistics.

Lamb, Dana, and Ginger Lamb
1951 *Quest for the lost city.* New York: Harper and Brothers.

Landa, Diego de
ca. 1566 *Relación de las cosas de Yucatán.* Has appeared in many editions. Most fully annotated is Tozzer 1941.
1928–1929 *Relation des choses de Yucatan: Texte espagnol et traduction française I–II.* Translated by Jean Genet. Paris: Editions Genet.

La Rochefoucauld, F. Aymar de
1888 *Palenqué et la civilization maya.* Paris: Ernest Leroux.

Larsen, Ramón
1955 *Vocabulario huasteco del estado de San Luis Potosí.* Mexico City: Summer Institute of Linguistics and Dirección General de Asuntos Indígenas de la Secretaría de Educación Pública.

Le Plongeon, Augustus
1885 *Ancient Maya hieratic alphabet according to mural inscription.* New York.
1886 *Sacred mysteries among the Maya and the Quiches, 11,500 years ago.* New York: R. Macoy.
1896 *Queen Móo and the Egyptian sphinx.* London: Kegan Paul and Co.

León-Portilla, Miguel
1968 *Tiempo y realidad en el pensamiento maya.* Serie de Culturas Mesoamericanas 2. Mexico City: Universidad Nacional Autónoma de México, Instituto de Investigaciones Historicas.

Lewy, Ernst
1937 "Die Sprache des Quiché (Kice) von Guatemala." *Anthropos* 32:929–958.

Lizardi Ramos, César
1941 "El glifo B y la sincronología maya-cristiana." In *Los Mayas Antiguos,* pp. 243–269. Mexico City.
1942a "Computo de fechas mayas." Proceedings of the 27th International Congress of Americanists, Mexico City (1939), part 2, sec. 1, pp. 356–359. Mexico City.
1942b "El glifo B y la sincronología maya-cristiana." Proceedings of the 27th International Congress of Americanists, Mexico City
1959 "Los jeroglíficos mayas y su descifración." In *Esplendor del México antiguo,* edited by Raúl Noriega, Carmen Cook de Leonard, and Julio Rodolfo Moctezuma, I, 243–262. Mexico City: Centro de Investigaciones Antropológicas de México.
1961 "Las Estelas 4 y 5 de Balancán-Morales, Tabasco." *Estudios de Cultura Maya* (Mexico City) 1:107–130.
1962 "El cero maya y su función." *Estudios de Cultura Maya* (Mexico City) 2:343–352.
1963 "Inscripciones de Pomoná, Tabasco." *Estudios de Cultura Maya* (Mexico City) 3:187–202.

1964 "Presuntos métodos mayas de cálculos cronológicos." *Estudios de Cultura Maya* (Mexico City) 4:267–304.

Long, Richard C. E.
1918a "The Maya and Christian eras." *Man* 18, no. 8:121–126.
1918b "The Maya and Christian eras." *Man* 18, no. 9:132–138.
1923 "Maya and Christian Chronology." *Journal of the Royal Anthropological Institute* 53:36–41.
1924a "A link between the earlier and later Maya chronologies." *Man* 24, no. 6:89–91.
1924b "The age of the Maya calendar." *Journal of the Royal Anthropological Institute* 54:353–362.
1926 "The Zouche Codex." *Journal of the Royal Anthropological Institute* 56:239–258.

Long, Richard C. E., and B. A. Long
1934 "Maya writing and its decipherment." *Maya Research* (New Orleans) 3, nos. 3–4:309–315.

Lothrop, Samuel Kirkland
1952 *Metals from the Cenote of Sacrifice, Chichen Itza, Yucatan.* Memoirs of the Peabody Museum of American Archaeology and Ethnology, Harvard University, vol. 10, no. 2. Cambridge, Mass.

Loukotka, Čestmir
1956 "Y. V. Knorozov: Sistema pisma drevnich maija." *Ceskoslovenská Ethnografie,* no. 3.

Lounsbury, Floyd G.
1973 "On the derivation and reading of the 'ben-ich' prefix." In *Mesoamerican writing systems,* edited by Elizabeth P. Benson, pp. 99–143. Washington, D.C.: Dumbarton Oaks.

Lounsbury, Floyd G., and Michael D. Coe
1966 "Linguistic and ethnographic data pertinent to the 'cage' glyph of Dresden 36c." 1er Seminario Internacional para el Estudio de la Escritura Maya. Mexico City.
1968 "Linguistic and ethnographic data pertinent to the 'cage' glyph of Dresden 36c." *Estudios de Cultura Maya* (Mexico City) 7:269–284.

Lundell, Cyrus L.
1933 "Archaeological discoveries in the Maya area." *Proceedings of the American Philosophical Society* (Philadelphia) 72:147–179.

McArthur, Harry, and Lucille McArthur
1956 "Aguacatec (Mayan) phonemes within the stress group." *International Journal of American Linguistics* 22, no. 1:72–76.

McQuown, Norman A.
1955 "The indigenous languages of Latin America." *American Anthropologist* 47:501–570. (Pages 501–511 deal with the Mayan family as a type example.)
1956 "The classification of the Mayan languages." *International Journal of American Linguistics* 22, no. 3:191–195.
1964 "Los orígenes y la diferenciación de los mayas según se infiere del estudio comparativo de las lenguas mayanas." In *Desarrollo cultural de los mayas,* edited by Evon Z. Vogt and Alberto Ruz Lhuillier, pp. 49–80. Mexico City: Universidad Nacional Autónoma de México.
1966 "La estructura tonal de las formas canónicas del maya yucateco." 1er Seminario Internacional para el Estudio de la Escritura Maya. Mexico City.
1967 "Classical Yucatec (Maya)." In *Linguistics,* edited by

idem, pp. 201–247. Handbook of Middle American Indians, edited by Robert Wauchope, vol. 5. Austin: University of Texas Press.

1968   "La estructura tonal de las sílabas del maya yucateco." *Estudios de Cultura Maya* (Mexico City) 7:293–301.

Madrid codex

1967   *Codex Tro-cortesianus (Codex Madrid): Einleitung und Summary von F. Anders.* Graz, Austria: Akademische Druck- und Verlagsanstalt. Includes two fragments originally published as separate codices, the *Cortesiano* and the *Troano.*

See also Rada y Delgado 1892*b*; Villacorta and Villacorta 1930.

Makemson, Maud Worcester

1943   *The astronomical tables of the Maya.* Carnegie Institution of Washington Pub. 546, Contri. 42. Washington, D.C.

1951   *The book of the Jaguar Priest.* A translation of the *Book of Chilam Balam of Tizimin.* New York: Schuman.

1957   *The miscellaneous dates of the Dresden codex.* Publications of the Vassar College Observatory, no. 6. Poughkeepsie, New York.

Manrique Castañeda, Leonardo

1966   "Esquema de un proyecto de cooperación internacional para el estudio de la escritura maya." 1er Seminario Internacional para el Estudio de la Escritura Maya. Mexico City.

1967   "Lingüística computacional en México." 13 pp. Mimeographed. Mérida.

1968   "El Primer Seminario Internacional para el Estudio de la Escritura Maya: Resultados y perspectivas." *Estudios de Cultura Maya* (Mexico City) 7:371–383.

Manrique Castañeda, Leonardo, and Juan José Rendón

1966   "Descripción estructural de una muestra de la escritura maya." *Anales de Antropología* 3:205–209.

Martin, Paul S.

1944   "Mayas and Aztecs were only American Indians to develop a system of writing." *Chicago Natural History Museum Bulletin* 15, nos. 7–8:3–7.

Martín del Campo, Rafael

1961   "Contribución a la etnozoología maya de Chiapas." In *Los mayas del sur y sus relaciones con los nahuas meridionales.* Sociedad Mexicana de Antropología, Mesa Redonda, vol. 8, pp. 29–39.

Martínez Hernández, J., ed.

See Motul dictionary.

Martínez Parédez, Domingo

1964   *Hunab ku.* Mexico City: Editorial Orión.

1967   *El idioma maya hablado y el escrito.* Mexico City: Editorial Orión.

Mayers, Marvin K.

1957   "Pocomchi verb structure." *International Journal of American Linguistics* 23, no. 3:165–170.

1958   *Pocomchi texts.* Summer Institute of Linguistics, Linguistic Series, Pub. 2. Norman, Oklahoma.

1960   "The linguistic unity of Pocomam-Pocomchi." *International Journal of American Linguistics* 26, no. 4:290–300.

Morley, Sylvanus G.

1909   "The inscriptions of Naranjo, Northern Guatemala." *American Anthropologist* 11:543–562.

1911*a*   "Ancient temples and cities of the New World: Uxmal, the city of the Xius." *Bulletin of the Pan American Union* (Washington, D.C.) 32:627–642.

1911*b*   "Ancient temples and cities of the New World: Copan, the mother city of Mayas." *Bulletin of the Pan American Union* (Washington, D.C.) 32:863–879.

1912   "Quirigua—an American town, 1,400 years old." *Scientific American* 107:96–97.

1913   "Excavations at Quirigua." *National Geographic Magazine* 24, no. 3:337–361.

1916   "The Supplementary Series in the Maya inscriptions." In *Holmes anniversary volume*, pp. 366–396. Washington, D.C.

1920   *The inscriptions at Copan.* Carnegie Institution of Washington Pub. 219. Washington, D.C.

1925   "The earliest Mayan dates."Proceedings of the 21st International Congress of Americanists, Göteborg (1924), part 2, pp. 655–667.

1927   "New light on the discovery of Yucatan, and the foundation of the new Maya empire." *American Journal of Archaeology* 31, no. 1:51–69.

1931   "Report of the Yaxchilan expedition." *Carnegie Institution of Washington Year Book* 30:132–139.

1937–1938   *The inscriptions of Peten.* Carnegie Institution of Washington Pub. 437. 5 vols. Washington, D.C.

1946, 1947   *The ancient Maya.* Stanford: Stanford University Press; London: Oxford University Press.

Morley, Sylvanus G., and George W. Brainerd

1956   *The ancient Maya.* 3d ed. Stanford: Stanford University Press.

Motul dictionary

1929   *Diccionario de Motul, maya-español, atribuido a Fray Antonio de Ciudad Real y Arte de lengua maya por Fray Juan Coronel.* Edited by J. Martínez Hernández. Mérida. (Original sixteenth-century manuscript missing; copy, said to be seventeenth-century, in John Carter Brown Library, Providence. This also contains Spanish-Maya sections omitted from Martínez Hernández edition.)

Mukerji, Dhirendra Nath

1936   "A correlation of the Mayan and Hindu calendars." *Indian Culture* 2, no. 4:685–692.

Noriega, Raúl, Carmen Cook de Leonard, and Julio Rodolfo Moctezuma, eds.

1959   *Esplendor del México antiguo.* 2 vols. Mexico City: Centro de Investigaciones Antropológicas de México.

Norman, B. M.

1844   *Rambles in Yucatan: Including a visit to the remarkable ruins of Chi-Chen, Kabah, Zayi, Uxmal, etc.* New York: J. and H. G. Langley.

Nuttall, Zelia

1910   "The Island of Sacrificios." *American Anthropologist*, n.s. 12:257–295.

Nuttall codex

1902   *Ancient Mexican codex belonging to Lord Zouche of Haryworth.* Introduction by Zelia Nuttall. Cambridge, Mass.: Peabody Museum of American Archaeology and Ethnology.

Olderögge, D. A.

1955   *The Maya hieroglyphic writing and its deciphering.* Voks, Bulletin No. 6 (95). Moscow.

Olson, Ronald D.

1964   "Mayan affinities with Chipaya of Bolivia I: Correspondences." *International Journal of American Linguistics* 30:313–324.

1965   "Mayan affinities with Chipaya of Bolivia II: Cognates." *International Journal of American Linguistics* 31:29–38.

Oppert, Jules
1878   "Rapport sur l'essai sur le déchiffrement de l'écriture hiératique de l'Amérique Centrale de M. Léon de Rosny." *Actes de la Société d'Ethnographie* (Paris), n.s. 2:48–51.

Owen, Michael G.
1966   "Yucatec phonology and Mayan glyph values: A case." 1er Seminario Internacional para el Estudio de la Escritura Maya. Mexico City.
1968   "Yucatec phonology and Mayan glyph values." *Estudios de Cultura Maya* (Mexico City) 7:303–310.

Pacheco Cruz, Santiago
1934   *Estudio etnográfica de los mayas del territorio de Quintana Roo*. Mérida.
1935   *En defensa del idioma maya*. Mérida: Imp. Oriente.
1939   *Lexico de la fauna yucateca*. 2d ed.
1958   *Diccionario de la fauna yucateca*. Rev. and enl. ed. of Pacheco Cruz 1939. Mérida.
1960   *Usos, costumbres, religión y supersticiones de los mayas*. Mérida.

Pacheco Cruz, Santiago, ed.
1967   *Breviario de toponimias mayas*. Mérida: Gamboa Guzman Press.

Palacios, Enrique J.
1932   "Maya-Christian synchronology or calendrical correlation." Middle American Research Series, no. 4, pp. 147–180. New Orleans.
1943   "Las sincronologías A y B, y la Nueva Tesis del Doctor Spinden." In *El norte de México*. Sociedad Mexicana de Antropología, Mesa Redonda, vol. 3, pp. 324–338. Mexico City.

Paris codex (also called *Perez* or *Peresianus*)
1969   *Codex Peresianus: Einleitung und Summary von F. Anders*. Graz, Austria: Akademische Druck- und Verlagsanstalt.
See also Rosny 1887; Solís Alcalá 1949b; Villacorta and Villacorta 1930; Willard 1933.

Parsons, Lee A.
1964   "The Middle American co-tradition." Ph.D. dissertation, Harvard University.

Pendergast, David M.
1966   "The Actun Balam vase." *Archaeology* 19, no. 3:154–162.

Pérez, Benjamín
1968   "Fonología preliminar del chontal de Tabasco." *Escritura maya* 2, no. 2:25–37.

Pérez codex
Both the *Paris* codex and the *Book of Chilam Balam of Mani* are sometimes called the *Pérez* codex. See those entries.

Peterson, Frederick
1959   *Ancient Mexico*. London: George Allen and Unwin.

Pijoan, José
1946   *Arte precolombiano mexicano y maya*, vol. 10 of *Summa artis: Historia general del arte*. Madrid.

Pike, Kenneth L.
1946   "Phonemic pitch in Maya." *International Journal of American Linguistics* 12, no. 2:82–88.

Pimentel, Francisco
1903   *Obras completas*. Mexico City.

Pío Pérez, Juan
1866–1877   *Diccionario de la lengua maya*. Mérida.

Pohorillas, Noah
1913   *Das Popol Wuh*. Leipzig: J. C. Hinrichs'sche Buchhandlung.

Pollock, Harry E. D.
1936   *Round structures of aboriginal Middle America*. Carnegie Institution of Washington, Pub. 471. Washington, D.C.
1952   "Department of archaeology." *Carnegie Institution of Washington Year Book* 51:235–243.

Pollock, Harry E.D., Ralph L. Roys, Tatiana Proskouriakoff, and A. Ledyard Smith
1962   *Mayapan, Yucatan, Mexico*. Carnegie Institution of Washington, Pub. 619. Washington, D.C.

Popol vuh
Colonial Quiche manuscript; has appeared in many editions. See Edmonson 1971 for a recent translation and full bibliography. See also Recinos, Goetz, and Morley 1950.

Pousse, A.
1884   "Nouvelles recherches pour l'interpretation des caractères hieratiques de l'Amérique Centrale: Rapport sur un mémoire de M. A. Pousse adressé à la Société Américaine de France." *Archives de la Société Américaine de France* (Paris), 2d ser. 3:118–127.

Primera cartilla lacandon
1955   Summer Institute of Linguistics.

Proskouriakoff, Tatiana
1950   *A study of Classic Maya sculpture*. Carnegie Institution of Washington, Pub. 593. Washington, D.C.
1954   "Mayapan the last stronghold of a civilization." *Archaeology* 7, no. 2:96–103.
1960   "Historical implications of a pattern of dates at Piedras Negras, Guatemala." *American Antiquity* (Salt Lake City) 25:454–475.
1961a   "The lords of the Maya realm." *Expedition* (Philadelphia) 4, no. 1:14–21.
1961b   "Portraits of women in Maya art." In *Essays in Pre-Columbian art and archaeology*, by Samuel K. Lothrop et al. Cambridge: Harvard University Press.
1963   "Historical data in the inscriptions of Yaxchilan." *Estudios de Cultura Maya* (Mexico City) 3:149–167.
1964a   "Historical data in the inscriptions of Yaxchilan (part II)." *Estudios de Cultura Maya* 4:177–202.
1964b   "El arte maya y el modelo genético de cultura." In *Desarrollo cultural de los mayas*, edited by Evon Z. Vogt and Alberto Ruz Lhuillier, pp. 179–193. Mexico City: Universidad Nacional Autónoma de México.
1968   "The jog and the jaguar signs in Maya writing." *American Antiquity* 33, no. 2:247–251.
1973   "The *hand-grasping-fish* and associated glyphs on Classic Maya monuments." In *Mesoamerican writing systems*, edited by Elizabeth P. Benson, pp. 165–178. Washington, D.C.: Dumbarton Oaks.

Putnam, F. W., and C. C. Willoughby
1896   "Symbolism in ancient American art." *Proceedings of the American Association for the Advancement of Science* (Salem) 44:302–322.

Quirarte, Jacinto
1968a   "Tikal Stela 31." Unpublished.
1968b   "Central Mexican presence in the Peten cities of Tikal and Uaxactun." Paper presented at Society for

American Archaeology meeting, May 1968, Santa Fe, New Mexico.

Rada y Delgado, Juan de Dios de la

1892a "Le Codex Troano et le Codex Cortesianus." Proceedings of the 8th International Congress of Americanists, Paris (1890), pp. 652–654.

1892b *Códice maya denominado cortesiano que se conserva en el Museo Arqueológico Nacional (Madrid).* Madrid.

Ralph, Elizabeth K.

1961 "Radiocarbon 'effective' half-life for Maya calendar correlations." *American Antiquity* 27, no. 2:229–230.

Rau, Charles

1879 *The Palenque tablet in the United States National Museum, Washington, D.C.* Smithsonian Contributions to Knowledge, vol. 22, no. 5. Washington, D.C.: Smithsonian Institution.

Rauh, James H.

1966 "A computer project for the codices together with some observations on codices Madrid and Paris." 1er Seminario Internacional para el Estudio de la Escritura Maya. Mexico City. Also in *Estudios de Cultura Maya* (Mexico City) 7 (1968):353–369.

1968 "A structural analysis of pages LXXVII–LXXVIII of *Codex Madrid.*" Paper presented at the Congress of Americanists, Stuttgart.

Raynaud, Georges

1890a *Etude sur le Codex Troano.* Paris.

1890b *Notes sur l'écriture yucatèque.* Paris.

Recinos, Adrián

1950 *Memorial de Sololá: Anales de los Cakchiqueles: Titulo de los Señores de Totonicapán.* Mexico City: Fondo de Cultura Económica.

Recinos, Adrián, Delia Goetz, and Sylvanus G. Morley

1950 *Popol vuh: The sacred book of the ancient Quiche Maya.* Norman: University of Oklahoma Press.

Redfield, Robert

1941 *The folk culture of Yucatan.* Chicago: University of Chicago Press.

Rendón M., Juan José

1966 "Descripción estructural interna y externa de un cartucho constante del Códice de Dresde." 1er Seminario Internacional para el Estudio de la Escritura Maya. Mexico City.

1967 "Utilidad de las concordancias en el descifre de la escritura maya." 11 pp. Mimeographed. Mérida.

1968 "Descripción estructural interna y externa de un cartucho constante en el Códice de Dresde." *Estudios de Cultura Maya* (Mexico City) 7:115–139.

Rendón, Juan José, and Amalia Spescha (with appendix by Daniel Cazes)

1965 "Nueva clasificación 'plastica' de los glifos mayas." *Estudios de Cultura Maya* 5:189–252.

Reyes, Ma. Eugenia

1966 "Programas de computación electrónica usados por la Comisión para el Estudio de la Escritura Maya." 1er Seminario Internacional para el Estudio de la Escritura Maya. Mexico City.

Reygadas Vértiz, José

1929 "The ruins of Labna, Yucatan." *Art and Archaeology* 28, no. 4:126–130.

Ricketson, Oliver G., Jr.

1925 "Burials in the Maya area." *American Anthropologist* 27:381–401.

1927 "Report on the Uaxactun project." *Carnegie Institution of Washington Year Book* 26:256–263.

1928a "Astronomical observatories in the Maya area." *Geographical Review* (New York) 18:215–225.

1928b "Notes on two Maya astronomical observatories." *American Anthropologist* (Menasha), n.s. 30:434–444.

1929 *Excavations at Baking Pot, British Honduras.* Contributions to American Archaeology, vol. 1, no. 1. Carnegie Institution of Washington, Pub. 403. Washington, D.C.

1930 "The Excavations at Uaxactun." Proceedings of the 23rd International Congress of Americanists, New York (1928), pp. 185–187. New York.

Ricketson, Oliver G., and E. B. Ricketson

1937 *Uaxactun, Guatemala, Group E, 1926–1931.* Carnegie Institution of Washington, Pub. 477. Washington, D.C.

Ritual of the Bacabs

See Roys 1965.

Rivard, Jean Jacques

1967 "Representations of maize in the Maya codices." *The Chesopican* 5, no. 2:27–50.

Robles U., Carlos

1966 *La Dialectología tzeltal y el diccionario compacto.* Mexico City: Instituto Nacional de Antropología e Historia.

Rochefoucauld, F. Aymar de

See La Rochefoucauld, F. Aymar de.

Romero Castillo, Moisés

1961 "Formas pronominales del maya-yucateco." *Anales del Instituto Nacional de Antropología e Historia* 14:345–348.

Rosny, Léon de

1875a *Monuments écrits de l'antiquité Américaine.* Paris.

1875b *L'interprétation des anciens textes mayas.* Paris.

1878 *De la formation des mots dans l'écriture hiératique du Yucatan.* Paris.

1883 "Vocabulaire de l'écriture hiératique yucatèque." In *Codex Cortesianus [Madrid]*, pp. I–XXX. Paris.

1887 *Manuscrit hiératique des anciens indiens de l'Amérique Centrale conservé à la Bibliothèque Nationale de Paris (Codex Paris).* Paris.

Roso de Luna, Mario

1911 *La ciencia hierática de los mayas.* Madrid: Librería de Pueyo.

Roys, Lawrence

1934 "The engineering knowledge of the Maya." In *Contributions to American Archaeology,* no. 6, pp. 27–105. Carnegie Institution of Washington, Pub. 436. Washington, D.C.

Roys, Ralph L.

1933 *The Book of Chilam Balam of Chumayel.* Carnegie Institution of Washington Pub. 438. Washington, D.C.

1940 *Personal names of the Maya of Yucatan.* Carnegie Institution of Washington Pub. 523, Contri. 31. Washington, D.C.

1949 *The prophecies for the Maya tuns or years in the Books of Chilam Balam of Tizimin and Mani.* Carnegie Institution of Washington Pub. 585, Contri. 51. Washington, D.C.

1954 *The Maya katun prophecies of the Books of Chilam Balam, Series I.* Carnegie Institution of Washington, Pub. 606, Contri. 57. Washington, D.C.

1957 *The political geography of the Yucatan Maya.* Carnegie Institution of Washington, Pub. 613. Washington, D.C.

1965 *Ritual of the Bacabs.* Norman: University of Oklahoma Press.

Ruppert, Karl

1952 *Chichen-Itza: Architectural notes and plans.* Carnegie Institution of Washington, Pub. 595. Washington, D.C.

Ruppert, Karl, J. Eric S. Thompson, and Tatiana Proskouriakoff

1951 *Bonampak, Chiapas, Mexico.* Carnegie Institution of Washington, Pub. 602. Washington, D.C.

Ruz Lhuillier, Alberto

1952a "Exploraciones arqueológicas en Palenque: 1949." *Anales del Instituto Nacional de Antropología e Historia* (Mexico City) 4:49–60.

1952b "Exploraciones en Palenque: 1950." *Anales del Instituto Nacional de Antropología e Historia* (Mexico City) 5:25–46.

1952c "Exploraciones en Palenque: 1951." *Anales del Instituto Nacional de Antropología e Historia* (Mexico City) 5:47–66.

1955a "Uxmal: Temporada de trabajos 1951–1952." *Anales del Instituto Nacional de Antropología e Historia* (Mexico City) 6:49–67.

1955b "Exploraciones en Palenque: 1952." *Anales del Instituto Nacional de Antropología e Historia* (Mexico City) 6:79–110.

1958 "Exploraciones arqueológicas en Palenque: 1953." *Anales del Instituto Nacional de Antropología e Historia* (Mexico City) 10:69–116.

1961a "Exploraciones arqueológicas en Palenque: 1957." *Anales del Instituto Nacional de Antropología e Historia* 14:35–90.

1961b "Exploraciones arqueológicas en Palenque: 1958." *Anales del Instituto Nacional de Antropología e Historia* 14:90–112.

1964 "Influencia mexicanas sobre los mayas." In *Desarrollo cultural de los mayas,* edited by Evon Z. Vogt and Alberto Ruz Lhuillier, pp. 195–227. Mexico City: Universidad Nacional Autónoma de México.

1966 "Desciframiento de la escritura maya: Historia, resultados y perspectivas." In *Summa anthropológica en homenaje a Roberto J. Weitlaner,* edited by Antonio Pompa y Pompa, pp. 173–185. Mexico City: Instituto Nacional de Antropología e Historia.

Sáenz, César A.

1964 "Las estelas de Xochicalco." Proceedings of the 35th International Congress of Americanists, Mexico City (1962), part 2, pp. 69–84. Mexico City.

Sáenz de Santa María, Carmelo

1940 *Diccionario cakchiquel-español.* Guatemala City: Tipografía Nacional.

Sahagún, Bernardino de

1948 "Relación breve de las fiestas de los dioses." *Tlalocan* (Mexico City) 2, no. 4:289–320.

San Buenaventura, Fray Gabriel de

See Buenaventura, Fray Gabriel de San.

Sánchez, George I.

1961 *Arithmetic in Maya.* Austin, Texas.

Sapper, Carl

1896 *Altertümer aus der Republik San Salvador.* International Archiv für Etnographie, no. 9. Leiden.

1907 "Vocabular in Chorti, Chol und Pocoman von Jilotepeque." Proceedings of the 15th International Congress of Americanists, Quebec (1906), pp. 440–465. Quebec.

Satterthwaite, Linton

1938 "Maya dating by hieroglyph styles." *American Anthropologist* 40, no. 3:416–428.

1942 "Hieroglyph styles at Chichen Itza." *Revista mexicana de estudios antropológicos* (Mexico City) 6:1–2.

1948 "Further implications of Thompson's readings of Maya inscriptions at Copan." Proceedings of the 28th International Congress of Americanists, Paris (1947), pp. 467–493. Paris.

1950 "Reconnaissance in British Honduras." *The University Museum, University of Pennsylvania, Bulletin* (Philadelphia) 16, no. 1:21–37.

1951 "Moon ages of the Maya inscriptions: The problem of their seven-day range of deviation from calculated mean ages." In *The civilizations of ancient America,* edited by Sol Tax, pp. 142–154. Proceedings of the 29th International Congress of Americanists, New York (1949). Chicago: University of Chicago Press.

1954 "Sculptured monuments from Caracol, British Honduras." *The University Museum, University of Pennsylvania, Bulletin* (Philadelphia) 18, nos. 1–2:1–45.

1956a "Maya dates on stelae in Tikal 'enclosures'." *The University Museum, University of Pennsylvania, Bulletin* (Philadelphia) 20, no. 4:25–40.

1956b "New radiocarbon dates and the Maya correlation problem." *American Antiquity* (Salt Lake City) 21:416–419.

1958a "The problem of abnormal stela placements at Tikal and elsewhere." The University Museum, University of Pennsylvania, Museum Monographs, *Tikal Reports,* no. 3, pp. 61–83. Philadelphia.

1958b "Five newly discovered carved monuments at Tikal and new data on four others." The University Museum, University of Pennsylvania, Museum Monographs, *Tikal Reports,* no. 4. Philadelphia.

1959 "Early 'uniformity' Maya moon numbers at Tikal and elsewhere." Proceedings of the 33rd International Congress of Americanists, San José (1958), part 2, pp. 200–210. San José, Costa Rica.

1960 "Maya 'long count' numbers." *Expedition* 2, no. 2:36–37.

1961a "Maya long count." *El México Antiguo* (Mexico City) 9:125–133.

1961b "Inscriptions and other dating controls." Appendix to *The carved wooden lintels of Tikal,* by William R. Coe and Edwin M. Shook. Tikal Report No. 6, Museum Monographs, University of Pennsylvania.

1962 "An appraisal of a new Maya-Christian calendar correlation." *Estudios de Cultura Maya* 2:251–276.

1964a "Dates in a new Maya hieroglyphic text as katun-baktun anniversaries." *Estudios de Cultura Maya* (Mexico City) 4:203–222.

1964b "Long count positions of Maya dates in the Dresden codex, with notes on lunar positions and the correlation problem." Proceedings of the 35th International Congress of Americanists, Mexico City (1962), part 2, pp. 47–67. Mexico City.

1965 "Calendrics of the Maya lowlands." In *Archaeology of southern Mesoamerica: Part two,* edited by Gordon

R. Willey, pp. 603–631. Handbook of Middle American Indians, edited by Robert Wauchope, vol. 3. Austin: University of Texas Press.

1967 "Radiocarbon and Maya long count dating of 'Structure 10' (Str. 5d-52, first story), Tikal." *Revista Mexicana de Estudios Antropológicas* 21:225–249.

1971 "The form, dating and probable use of Landa's Christian-Maya year table." *Revista Española de Antropología Americana* 6:9–44.

Satterthwaite, Linton, and Elizabeth K. Ralph
1960 "Radiocarbon dates and the Maya correlation problem." *American Antiquity* (Salt Lake City) 26:165–184.

Saville, Marshall H.
1894 "The ceremonial year of the Maya Codex Cortesianus." *American Anthropologist* 7:373–376.

1921 "A sculptured vase from Guatemala." *Art and Archaeology* (Washington, D.C.) 11, nos. 1–2:66–67.

1930 "Ancient causeways of Yucatan." *Indian Notes* (New York) 7:89–99.

1935 "The ancient Maya causeways of Yucatan." *American Antiquity* 9:67–73.

Schellhas, Paul
1897 *Die Göttergestalten der Mayahandschriften: Ein mythologisches Kulturbild aus dem alten Amerika.* Dresden: Verlag von Richard Bertling.

1904 *Representation of deities of the Maya manuscripts.* Papers of the Peabody Museum of American Archaeology and Ethnology, Harvard University, vol. 4, no. 1. Cambridge, Mass.

Schuller, Rudolph
n.d. "On comparative vocabularies of the Mayan languages." MS in Peabody Library, Harvard University.

Schultz, Wolfgang
1913 *Einleitung in das Popol Wuh.* Leipzig: Hinrichs'sche Buchhandlung.

Schultze-Jena, Leonard
1933 *Leben, Glaube und Sprache der Quiche von Guatemala.* Jena: Gustav Fischer.

1944 *Popol Vuh.* Stuttgart: Verlag von W. Kohlhammer.

Schulz Friedemann, Ramón [R. P. C. Schulz]
1942 "Apuntes sobre algunos fechas del Templo de la Cruz de Palenque y sobre astronomía y cronología de los antiguos mayas." Proceedings of the 27th International Congress of Americanists, Mexico City (1939), part 2, sec. 1, pp. 352–355. Mexico City.

1961 "Otra vez las series de números en las páginas 51a–52a y 58 del Códice Dresden." *El México Antiguo* 9:183–194.

1964 "Algunos problemas de la astronomía maya." *Estudios de Cultura Maya* 4:251–266.

Schumann, Otto
1968 "Sobre el fonetismo vocálico en Pocomam." *Escritura Maya* 2, no. 2:44.

Schwede, Rudolf
1912 *Über das Papier der Maya-Codices und einiger altmexikanischer Bilderhandschriften.* Dresden:Bertling.

Séjourné, Laurette
1960 *Burning water.* New York: Grove Press, Inc.
1962 *El universo de Quetzalcóatl.* Mexico City.

Seler, Eduard
1887a *Das Konjugationssystem der maya Sprachen.* Berlin: Druck von Gebr. Unger.

1887b "Namen der in der Dresdener Handschrift abgebildeten Maya-Götter (Vortrag)." *Zeitschrift für Ethnologie* (Berlin) 19:224–231.

1889 "Caractère des inscriptions aztèques et mayas." *Revue d'ethnographie* (Paris) 8:1–113.

1890 "Altmexikanischen Studien: Ein Kapitel aus dem in aztekischen Sprache geschriebenen, ungedruckten Materialen zu dem Geschichtswerke des Padre Sahagun." In Publications of the Museum für Volkerkunde 4, pp. 118–181.

1892a "Ein neuer Versuch zur Entzifferung der Mayaschrift." *Globus* (Brunswick) 62:59–61.

1892b "Does there really exist a phonetic key to the Maya hieroglyphic writing?" *Science* (New York) 20, no. 499:121–122.

1893 "Is the Maya hieroglyphic writing phonetic?" *Science* (New York) 21, no. 518:6–10.

1900–1901 *The Tonalamatl of the Aubin collection.* Berlin and London.

1901 *Die alten Ansiedelungen von Chaculá.* Berlin.

1901–1902 *Codex Féjérvary-Mayer.* Berlin and London.

1902–1903 *Codex Vaticanus Nr. 3773 (Cod. Vatic.B).* English translation of commentary. Berlin and London.

1902–1923 *Gesammelte Abhandlungen zur amerikanischen Sprach- und Alterthumskunde.* 5 vols. Berlin.

1904a English translations of nine of Seler's articles. In *Mexican Antiquities.* Bureau of American Ethnology Bulletin 28. Washington, D.C.

1904b "Venus period in the picture writings of the Borgian codex group." Bureau of American Ethnology Bulletin 28, pp. 353–391. Washington, D.C.

1909 "Die Tierbilder der mexicanischen und der Maya-Handschriften." *Zeitschrift für Ethnologie* 41, pp. 381–457. Also in Seler 1902–1923, vol. 4.

1911 "Die Stuckfassade von Acanceh in Yucatan." *Sitzungsberichte der Königlich preussischen Akademie der Wissenschaften* (Berlin) 47:1011–1025.

Shattuck, G. C.
1933 *The peninsula of Yucatan: Medical, biological, meteorological and sociological studies.* Carnegie Institution of Washington, Pub. 431. Washington, D.C.

Shook, Edwin M.
1940 "Exploration in the ruins of Oxkintok, Yucatan." *Revista Mexicana de Estudios Antropológicos* 4:165–171.

1957 "The Tikal project." *The University Museum, University of Pennsylvania, Bulletin* (Philadelphia) 21, no. 3:36–52.

1960 "Tikal, Stela 29." *Expedition* 2, no. 2:28–35.

Shook, Edwin M., and Alfred V. Kidder II
1961 "The painted tomb at Tikal." *Expedition* 4, no. 1:2–7.

Slocum, Marianna C.
1953 *Vocabulario tzeltal-español.* Mexico City: Instituto Lingüístico de Verano and Secretaría de Educación Pública.

Smiley, Charles H.
1960a "A new correlation of the Mayan and Christian calendars." *Nature* 188:215–216.

1960b "The antiquity and precision of Maya astronomy." *Journal of the Royal Astronomical Society of Canada* 54 no. 5:222–226.

1961a "The paths of solar eclipses." *Journal of the Royal Astronomical Society of Canada* 55, no. 5:211–217.

1961b　"Bases astronómicas para una nueva correlación entre los calendarios maya y cristiano." *Estudios de Cultura Maya* 1:237–242.

1962　*The Mayan calendar.* Astronomical Society of the Pacific, Leaflet 392.

1963　"An interpretation of two cycles in the Dresden codex." Providence: Ladd Observatory, Brown University.

1964　"Interpretación de dos ciclos en el Códice de Dresde." *Estudios de Cultura Maya* 4:257–260. Spanish version of Smiley 1963.

1967　"A possible periodicity of hurricanes." *Cycles,* November 1967, pp. 283–285.

Smiley, Charles H., and Eugenia Robinson

1969　"The sky on zero day of the Mayan calendar." Providence: Ladd Observatory, Brown University.

Smith, A. Ledyard

1950　*Uaxactun, Guatemala: Excavations of 1931–37.* Carnegie Institution of Washington, Pub. 588. Washington, D.C.

Smith, A. Ledyard, and Alfred V. Kidder

1951　*Excavations at Nebaj, Guatemala.* Carnegie Institution of Washington, Pub. 594. Washington, D.C.

Smith, G. Elliott

1924　*Elephants and ethnologists.* London.

Smith, Robert E.

1937　*A study of Structure A-1 Complex at Uaxactun, Peten, Guatemala.* Contributions to American Anthropology and History no. 19. Carnegie Institution of Washington, Pub. 456. Washington, D.C.

Solís Alcalá, Ermilo

1949a　*Diccionario español-maya.* Edited by Paulino Novelo Erosa. Mérida: Editorial Yikal Maya Than.

1949b　*Códice Pérez: Traducción libre del Maya al Castellano.* Mérida.

Sousberghe, L. de, and C. Robles Uribe

1963　*Nomenclature et structures de parenté des maya du Yucatan.* Travaux de l'Université de Bujumbura B., Faculté des Sciences Sociales, no. 2, 38 pp. Bujumbura, Burundi.

Soustelle, Jacques

1952　"Knorozov, Y. V.: L'ancienne écriture de l'Amérique Centrale." *Journal de la Société des Américanistes de Paris* (Paris) 41.

Spinden, Herbert J.

1913　*A study of Maya art: Its subject matter and historical development.* Memoirs of the Peabody Museum of American Archaeology and Ethnology, Harvard University, vol. 6. Cambridge, Mass.

1916　"The question of the zodiac in America." *American Anthropologist* (Lancaster) 18:53–80.

1917　"Recent progress in the study of Maya art." Proceedings of the 19th International Congress of Americanists, Washington (1915), pp. 165–177. Washington, D.C.

1920　"Central American calendars and the Gregorian day." *Proceedings of the National Academy of Science* (Paris) 6, no. 2:56–59. Paris.

1924　*The reduction of Mayan dates.* Papers of the Peabody Museum of American Archaeology and Ethnology, Harvard University, vol. 6, no. 4. Cambridge, Mass.

1928a　*Ancient civilizations of Mexico and Central America.* 3d ed. Handbook Series, American Museum of Natural History, no. 3, New York.

1928b　"Ancient Mayan astronomy." *Scientific American* 138, no. 1:9–12.

1928c　"Deciphering Maya mysteries." *Scientific American* 138, no. 3:232–234.

1930　*Maya dates and what they reveal.* Brooklyn Institution of Arts and Sciences, vol. 4, no. 1. Brooklyn.

1949　"Mexican calendars and the solar year." In *Smithsonian Institution Annual Report for 1948,* pp. 393–406. Washington, D.C.

Steggerda, Morris

1943　"Some ethnological data concerning one hundred Yucatan plants." Bureau of American Ethnology Bulletin 136, pp. 189–226.

Stempell, W.

1908　"Die Tierbilder der Maya-handschriften." *Zeitschrift für Ethnologie* 40:704–743.

Stoll, Otto

1885　"Supplementary remarks to the grammar of the Cakchiquel language of Guatemala." Edited by Daniel Garrison Brinton. *Proceedings of the American Philosophical Society* (Philadelphia) 22, no. 120:255–268.

1886　*Guatemala: Reisen und Schilderungen aus den Jahren 1878–1883.* Leipzig.

Strömsvik, Gustav

1947　*Guide book to the ruins of Copan.* Carnegie Institution of Washington, Pub. 577. Washington, D.C.

Strong, William D., Alfred V. Kidder, and A. J. D. Paul

1938　*Preliminary report on the Smithsonian Institution–Harvard University archaeological expedition to Northwestern Honduras, 1936.* Smithsonian Miscellaneous Collections, vol. 97, no. 1. Washington, D.C.

Swadesh, Mauricio [Morris]

1961　"Interrelaciones de las lenguas mayenses." *Anales del Instituto Nacional de Antropología e Historia* (Mexico City) 13:231–267.

1966a　"Porhé y maya." *Anales de antropología* 3:173–204.

1966b　"Algunas orientaciones generales sobre la escritura maya." 1er Seminario Internacional para el Estudio de la Escritura Maya. Mexico City.

1968　"Algunas orientaciones generales sobre la escritura maya." *Estudios de Cultura Maya* (Mexico City) 7:33–47.

Tapia Zentano, Carlos de

1767　*Noticia de la lengua huasteca.* Mexico City: Bibliotheca Mexicana.

Teeple, John E.

1930　"Factors which may lead to a correlation of Maya and Christian dates." Proceedings of the 23rd International Congress of Americanists, New York (1928), pp. 136–139. New York.

Teletor, Celso N.

1959　*Diccionario castellano-quiché y voces castellano-pocomam.* Guatemala.

Termer, Franz

1931　"Zur Archäologie von Guatemala." *Baessler-Archiv* (Berlin) 14:167–191.

1952　"Die Mayaforschung." *Nova Acta Leopoldina* (Leipzig), n.s. 15:93–164.

Thomas, Cyrus

1882　"A study of the manuscript Troano." *U.S. Department of the Interior: Contributions to North American Ethnology* (Washington, D.C.) 5:1–237.

1884 "Notes on certain Maya and Mexican manuscripts." *Third Annual Report of the Bureau of Ethnology (1881–1882),* pp. 3–65. Washington, D.C.

1888 "Aids to the study of the Maya codices." *Sixth Annual Report of the Bureau of Ethnology (1884–1885),* pp. 253–371. Washington, D.C.

1892a "Key to the Maya hieroglyphs." *Science* 20, no. 494:44–46.

1892b "Is the Maya hieroglyphic writing phonetic?" *Science* 20, no. 505:197–201.

1893 "Are the Maya hieroglyphs phonetic?" *American Anthropologist* 6:241–270.

1904 "Central American hieroglyphic writing." In *Smithsonian Institution Annual Report for 1903,* pp. 705–721. Washington, D.C.

Thompson, Edward H.

1897a *Explorations of the Cave of Loltun, Yucatan.* Memoirs of the Peabody Museum of American Archaeology and Ethnology, Harvard University, vol. 1, no. 2, pp. 1–24. Cambridge, Mass.

1897b *The Chultunes of Labna.* Memoirs of the Peabody Museum of American Archaeology and Ethnology, Harvard University, vol. 1, no. 3, pp. 1–20. Cambridge, Mass.

1898 "Ruins of Xkichmook, Yucatan." Field Columbian Museum Pub. 28, Anthropological Series, vol. 2, no. 3, pp. 209–229. Chicago.

1904 *Archaeological researches in Yucatan.* Memoirs of the Peabody Museum of American Archaeology and Ethnology, Harvard University, vol. 3, no. 1, pp. 3–20. Cambridge, Mass.

1905 "The mural painting of Yucatan." Proceedings of the 13th International Congress of Americanists, New York (1902), pp. 189–192. Easton, Pa.

Thompson, J. Eric S.

1927 "A correlation of the Mayan and European calendars." Field Museum of Natural History, Anthropological Series, vol. 17, no. 1, pp. 1–22. Chicago.

1928 "Some new dates from Pusilha." *Man* 28:6.

1929 "Maya chronology: Glyph G of the Lunar Series." *American Anthropologist* (Menasha) 31:223–231.

1930 "The causeways of the Coba District, Eastern Yucatan." Proceedings of the 23rd International Congress of Americanists, New York (1928), pp. 181–184. New York.

1931 See Gann and Thompson 1931.

1932 *The civilization of the Mayas.* Field Museum of Natural History, Anthropology Leaflet 25. Chicago.

1934 *Sky bearers, colors and directions in Maya and Mexican religion.* Carnegie Institution of Washington Pub. 436, Contri. 10. Washington, D.C.

1935 *Maya chronology: The correlation question.* Carnegie Institution of Washington Pub. 456, Contributions to American Archaeology and History, no. 14. Washington, D.C.

1939 *The Moon Goddess in Middle America with notes on related deities.* Carnegie Institution of Washington Pub. 509, Contri. 29. Washington, D.C.

1943a *Maya epigraphy: Directional glyphs in counting.* Carnegie Institution of Washington, Division of Historical Research, Notes on Middle American Archaeology and Ethnology, no. 20. Cambridge.

1943b *Maya epigraphy: A cycle of 819 days.* Carnegie Institution of Washington, Division of Historical Research, Notes on Middle American Archaeology and Ethnology, no. 22. Cambridge.

1944 *The fish as a Maya symbol for counting and further discussion of directional glyphs.* Carnegie Institution of Washington, Division of Historical Research, Theoretical Approaches to Problems, no. 2. Cambridge.

1950 *Maya hieroglyphic writing: Introduction.* Carnegie Institution of Washington, Pub. 589. Washington, D.C.

1952a "The introduction of Puuc style of dating at Yaxchilan." In Carnegie Institution of Washington, Notes on Middle American Archaeology and Ethnology, no. 110, pp. 196–202. Washington, D.C.

1952b "La inscripción jeroglífica del tablero de El Palacio, Palenque." *Anales del Instituto Nacional de Antropología e Historia* (Mexico City) 4:61–68.

1953a Review of *La antigua escritura de los pueblos de América Central,* by Y. V. Knorozov. *Yan* 2:174–178.

1953b "Maya hieroglyphic writing: a rejoinder." *International Journal of American Linguistics* 19, no. 2:153–154.

1954 *The rise and fall of Maya civilization.* Norman: University of Oklahoma Press.

1958a "Symbols, glyphs, and divinatory almanacs for diseases in the Maya Dresden and Madrid codices." *American Antiquity* (Salt Lake City) 23:297–308.

1958b "Research in Maya hieroglyphic writing." In *Middle American Anthropology,* edited by Gordon R. Willey, pp. 43–52. Pan American Union Social Science Monographs, no. 5. Washington, D.C.

1959 "Systems of hieroglyphic writing in Middle America and methods of deciphering them." *American Antiquity* (Salt Lake City) 24:349–364.

1962 *A catalog of Maya hieroglyphs.* Norman: University of Oklahoma Press.

1963a "Pictorial synonyms and homonyms in the Maya Dresden codex." *Tlalocan* 4, no. 2:148–156.

1963b "Frans Blom (1893–1963)." *Estudios de Cultura Maya* (Mexico City) 3:307–314.

1963c "Algunas consideraciones respecto al desciframiento de los jeroglíficos mayas." *Estudios de Cultura Maya* 3:119–148.

1965a *Preliminary decipherments of Maya glyphs: 1.* Pamphlet, 4 pp.

1965b "Maya hieroglyphic writing." In *Archaeology of southern Mesoamerica: Part two,* edited by Gordon R. Willey, pp. 632–658. Handbook of Middle American Indians, edited by Robert Wauchope, vol. 3. Austin: University of Texas Press.

1966a *Preliminary decipherments of Maya glyphs: 2.* Pamphlet.

1966b *Preliminary decipherments of Maya glyphs: 3.* Pamphlet, 4 pp. Saffron Walden, England.

1966c "Maya hieroglyphs of the bat as metaphorgrams." *Man* 1, no. 2:176–184.

1967 *Preliminary decipherments of Maya glyphs: 4.* Pamplet, 8 pp. Bloomfield Hills, Mich.: Cranbrook Institute of Science.

1968 "Deciphering Maya glyphs." *Cranbrook Institute of Science News Letter* (Bloomfield Hills, Mich.) 37, no. 7:82–87.

1970a *The Bacabs: Their portraits and glyphs.* Papers of the Peabody Museum of American Archaeology and Ethnology, Harvard University. Cambridge, Mass.

1970*b*   *Maya history and religion.* Norman: University of Oklahoma Press.

1972*a*   *Maya hieroglyphs without tears.* London: British Museum.

1972*b*   *A commentary on the Dresden codex.* Memoirs of the American Philosophical Society 93. Philadelphia. Includes an edition of the codex.

Thompson, Richard A.

1967   "A partial Yucatec plant taxonomy." 19 pp. Mimeographed. Austin: University of Texas.

Thurber, Floyd, and Valerie Thurber

1958   "Ideographic number-writing in Maya inscription texts: Some considerations." *Southwestern Journal of Anthropology* (Santa Fe, N.M.) 14:61–65.

1961   "A comparative analysis of Maya hieroglyphs Muluc and Mol." *Estudios de Cultura Maya* 1:221–235.

1964   "Hieroglyphs Imix and Kan as non-calendrical symbols for the Maya creator couple." *Estudios de Cultura Maya* 4:245–256.

1966   "Maya Zuyua, the archaic priesthood language of metaphorical mystification." 1er Seminario Internacional para el Estudio de la Escritura Maya. Mexico City.

Tizimin, Book of Chilam Balam of

See Makemson 1951.

Tozzer, Alfred M.

1907   *A comparative study of the Mayas and the Lacandones.* New York.

1921   *A Maya grammar with bibliography and appraisement of the works noted.* Papers of the Peabody Museum of American Archaeology and Ethnology, Harvard University, vol. 9. Cambridge, Mass.

1941   *Landa's Relación de las cosas de Yucatán.* Papers of the Peabody Museum of American Archaeology and Ethnology, Harvard University, vol. 18. Cambridge, Mass.

1957   *Chichen Itza and its Cenote of Sacrifice: A comparative study of contemporaneous Maya and Toltec.* Memoirs of the Peabody Museum of American Archaeology and Ethnology, Harvard University, vols. 11–12. Cambridge, Mass.

Tozzer, Alfred M., and G. Allen

1910   *Animal figures in the Maya codices.* Papers of the Peabody Museum of American Archaeology and Ethnology, Harvard University, vol. 4, no. 3. Cambridge, Mass.

Trik, Aubrey

1963   "The splendid tomb of Temple I at Tikal, Guatemala." *Expedition* 6, no. 1 (Fall 1963):2–18. (With captions by Linton Satterthwaite.)

Troano codex

See *Madrid* codex.

Ulving, Tor

1955   "A new decipherment of the Maya glyphs." *Ethnos* (Stockholm) 20, nos. 2–3:152–158.

Valentini, Philipp J. J.

1879   "The katunes of Maya history." *Proceedings of the American Antiquarian Society* (Worcester) 74:71–117.

Vázquez, Esther

1968   "Fonología preliminar del pocomam central." *Escritura Maya* 2, no. 2:38–43.

Vásquez de Espinosa, Antonio

1948   *Compendio y descripción de las indias occidentales . . . transcrito del manuscrito original por Charles Upson Clark.* Smithsonian Institution Miscellaneous Collections, vol. 108. Washington.

Veiga de Oliveira, E.

1954   *Casas de maia.* Porto.

Velásquez, P. F., ed. and trans.

n.d.   *Anales de Cuauhtitlán y leyenda de los soles.* Mexico City: Universidad Nacional Autónoma de México.

Vienna codex

1929   *Codex Vindobonensis Mexic. I.* Facsimile. Text by Walter Lehmann and Ottokar Smital. Vienna.

Villa Rojas, Alfonso

1964   "Patrones culturales mayas antiguos y modernos en las comunidades contemporáneas de Yucatán." In *Desarrollo cultural de los mayas,* edited by Evon Z. Vogt and Alberto Ruz Lhuillier, pp. 329–361. Mexico City: Universidad Nacional Autónoma de México.

Villacorta C., J. Antonio

1938   *Prehistoria e historia antigua de Guatemala.* Colección "Villacorta" de historia antigua de Guatemala. Guatemala City: Tipografía Nacional.

Villacorta C., J. Antonio, and N. Flavio Rodas

1927   *Manuscrito de Chich'castenango (Popol Buj): Estudios sobre las antiguas tradiciones del pueblo quiché.* Guatemala City: Tipografía Nacional.

Villacorta C., J. Antonio, and Carlos A. Villacorta R.

1930   *Códices mayas: Dresdensis, Peresianus, Tro-Cortesianus.* Reproduction and commentary. Guatemala City: Tipografía Nacional.

Villagra Caleti, A.

1949   "Bonampak, la ciudad de los muros pintados." *Anales del Instituto Nacional de Antropología e Historia* (Mexico City), suppl. to vol. 3.

Vogt, Evon Z.

1964*a*   "The genetic model and Maya cultural development." In *Desarrollo cultural de los mayas,* edited by idem and Alberto Ruz Lhuillier, pp. 9–48. Mexico City: Universidad Nacional Autónoma de México.

1964*b*   "Summary and appraisal." In *Desarrollo cultural de los mayas,* edited by idem and Alberto Ruz Lhuillier, pp. 385–403. Mexico City: Universidad Nacional Autónoma de México.

Vogt, Evon Z., and Alberto Ruz Lhuillier, eds.

1964   *Desarrollo cultural de los mayas.* Mexico City: Universidad Nacional Autónoma de México.

Vollemaere, Antoon L.

1966–1967   *Notes de travail 01 à 08 concernant l'écriture maya des codex maya.* Bujumbura, Burundi.

1973   *A Belgian contribution to the world's historical inheritance: The deciphering of Mayan hieroglyphic writing.* Memo from Belgium "Views and Surveys," no. 162. Brussels: Ministry of Foreign Affairs, External Trade and Cooperation in Development.

Von Winning, Hasso

1963   "Una vasija de alabastro con decoración en relieve." *Estudios de Cultura Maya* 3:113–118.

1967   "Una vasija-sonaja maya de doble fondo." *Estudios de Cultura Maya* 6:243–250.

Waldeck, Frédéric de

1838   *Voyage pittoresque et archéologique dans la province d'Yucatan (Amérique Centrale), pendant les années 1834 et 1836.* Paris: Bellizard Dufour et Cie.

Wauchope, Robert
1947 "An approach to the Maya correlation problem through Guatemala highland archaeology and native annals." *American Antiquity* (Menasha) 13:59–66.

Weathers, Kenneth, and Nadine Weathers
1949 *Diccionario español-tzotzil y tzotzil-español.* Mexico City: Instituto Lingüístico de Verano.

Weber, Richard
1950 "Neue Untersuchungen zum Korrelationsproblem der Mayazeitrechnung." *Zeitschrift für Ethnologie* 75:90–102.
1952 "Tafel zur Umrechnung von Maya-Daten: Tafel zur Umrechnung eines Longcount-Datums in ein Julianisches Datum für die Thompson'sche Korrelation A=584285." *Zeitschrift für Ethnologie* 77:251–253.
1955 "Uso do planetario na pesquisa dos maia." *Revista do Museu Paulista* (Sao Paulo), n.s. 9:n.p.
1961 "Investigación del cielo maya en el planetario de Hamburgo." *Estudios de Cultura Maya* 1:243–260.

Weitlaner, Roberto J.
1958 "Un calendario de los zapotecos del sur." Proceedings of the 32nd International Congress of Americanists, Copenhagen (1956), pp. 296–299.

Weitlaner, Roberto J., and Gabriel de Cicco
1961 "La jerarquía de los dioses zapotecos del sur." Proceedings of the 34th International Congress of Americanists, Vienna, pp. 695–710.

Weitzel, Robert B.
1931 "Uxmal inscriptions." *American Journal of Archaeology,* 2d ser. 35:53–56.
1945 "Maya epigraphy: Methods of interpretation." *American Antiquity* 10:388–389.

Whorf, Benjamin L.
1933 *The phonetic value of certain characters in Maya writing.* Papers of the Peabody Museum of American Archaeology and Ethnology, Harvard University, vol. 13, no. 2. Cambridge, Mass.
1942 "Decipherment of the linguistic portion of the Maya hieroglyphs." In *Smithsonian Institution Report for 1941,* pp. 479–502. Washington, D.C.
1956a *Stem series in Maya and certain Maya hieroglyphs.* Microfilm Collection of MSS on Middle American Cultural Anthropology, no. 45. University of Chicago. (Written in 1930; preliminary version of Whorf 1933.)
1956b *Recent determinations of phonetic characters in Maya writing.* Microfilm Collection of MSS on Middle American Cultural Anthropology, no. 47. University of Chicago. (Paper read in December 1933.)
1956c *First steps in the decipherment of Maya writing.* Microfilm Collection of MSS on Middle American Cultural Anthropology, no. 49. University of Chicago. (Fuller version of Whorf 1956b.)
1956d *A comparative decipherment of 41 ancient Maya written words.* Microfilm Collection of MSS on Middle American Cultural Anthropology, no. 50. University of Chicago. (Written in 1936.)

Willard, Theodore A.
1932 "The Maya hieroglyphic system of writing." *The Masterkey* (Los Angeles) 6:112–115.
1933 *The Codex Perez.* Glendale, California: Arthur H. Clark Co. Photographic reproduction of the *Paris* codex.

Willey, Gordon R.
1964 "An archaeological frame of reference for Maya culture history." In *Desarrollo cultural de los mayas,* edited by Evon Z. Vogt and Alberto Ruz Lhuillier, pp. 137–178. Mexico City: Universidad Nacional Autónoma de México.

Willey, Gordon R., William R. Bullard, and John B. Glass
1955 "The Maya community of prehistoric times." *Archaeology* 8, no. 1:18–25.

Willey, Gordon R., and A. Ledyard Smith
1963 "New discoveries at Altar de Sacrificios, Guatemala." *Archaeology* 16, no. 2:83–89.

Willson, R. W.
1924 *Astronomical notes on the Maya codices.* Papers of the Peabody Museum of American Archaeology and Ethnology, Harvard University, vol. 6, no. 3. Cambridge, Mass.

Wisdom, C.
1940 *The Chorti Indians of Guatemala.* University of Chicago Publications in Anthropology, Ethnological Series. Chicago.

Wolff, Werner
1937 "Le déchiffrement des hiéroglyphes mayas et la traduction de quelques tableaux d'hiéroglyphes." *L'Etnographie,* n.s., nos. 33–34:111–115.
1938 *Déchiffrement de l'écriture maya.* Paris: Geuthner.

Ximénez, Francisco
1857 *Las historias del origen de los indios de esta provincia de Guatemala.* Vienna: Gerold e hijo.
n.d. "El tesoro de las Cakchiquels, Quiché y Tzutuhil, en que las dichas lenguas, se traducen en nuestra español compuesto por el R. P. F. Francisco Ximénez." Manuscript in the Gates Collection, Brigham Young University.

Zimmermann, Günter
1933 "Die Bedeutung der oberen Teile der Seiten 4–10 der Dresdener Mayahandschrift." *Zeitschrift für Ethnologie* 65:399–401.
1953 *Kurze Formen- und Begriffssystematik der Hieroglyphen der Maya-Handschriften.* Beitrage zur mittelamerikanischen Völkerkunde, no. 1. Hamburg: Hamburgisches Museum für Völkerkunde und Vorgeschichte.
1953–1954 "Die Hieroglyphenschrift der Maya und der Stand ihrer Entzifferung." *Mitteilungen der anthropologischen Gesellschaft in Wien* 83, no. 1:68–69.
1955 "Das Cotoque: Die Maya-Sprache von Chicomucelo." *Zeitschrift für Ethnologie* (Berlin) 80, no. 1:59–87.
1956 *Die Hieroglyphen der Maya-Handschriften.* Hamburg: Cram, de Gruyter.

1964 "La escritura jeroglífica y el calendario como indicadores de tendencias de la historia cultural de los mayas." In *Desarrollo cultural de los mayas*, edited by Evon Z. Vogt and Alberto Ruz Lhuillier, pp. 229–242. Mexico City: Universidad Nacional Autónoma de México.

1966a "Using computers for solution of certain problems in Maya astronomy." 1er Seminario Internacional para el Estudio de la Escritura Maya. Mexico City.

1966b "Resultados preliminares de la elaboración del catálogo de glifos de los monumentos." 1er Seminario Internacional para el Estudio de la Escritura Maya. Mexico City.

Index

Index of
Glyphs by
Catalog Numbers

[*In this index section, the identifications or interpretations given are those discussed in the text; not all of them are acceptable.*]